The Damrosch Dynasty

Books by George Martin

The Opera Companion:
A Guide for the Casual Operagoer
(1961; 3rd ed., 1982)

The Battle of the Frogs and the Mice:
An Homeric Fable
(1962)

Verdi, His Music, Life and Times
(1963; 3rd ed., 1983)

The Red Shirt and the Cross of Savoy:
The Story of Italy's Risorgimento, 1748–1871
(1969)

Causes and Conflicts: The Centennial History
of the Association of the Bar of the
City of New York, 1870–1970
(1970)

Madam Secretary: Frances Perkins
(1976)

The Opera Companion
to Twentieth-Century Opera
(1979)

The Damrosch Dynasty:
America's First Family of Music
(1983)

The
DAMROSCH
DYNASTY

America's First Family
of Music

George Martin

HOUGHTON MIFFLIN COMPANY BOSTON

1983

Library of Congress Cataloging in Publication Data

Martin, George Whitney.
The Damrosch dynasty.

Bibliography: p.
Includes index.
1. Damrosch family.   2. Musicians — United States —
Biography.   I. Title.
ML385.M275   1983   780'.92'2 [B]   83-315
ISBN 0-395-34408-5

CONTENTS

PROLOGUE

Prologue, p. 1. Some values held by the family. Historical, psychological and sociological points of view. The immigrant experience.

PART I

The Patriarch

Chapter 1, p. 9. The family coming over. Leopold Damrosch in New York. The Arion Society. Background in Breslau. Beginnings in New York. Leopold's letter to a friend in Breslau.

Chapter 2, p. 19. Helene and Tante. Leopold's youth in Posen. His character. The von Heimburg and Damrosch Christmas. The hostility of Theodore Thomas.

Chapter 3, p. 29. Ole Bull, Jenny Lind and Anton Rubinstein in the United States. Founding of the Oratorio Society of New York. Messiah.

Chapter 4, p. 38. Biding time. Carl Bergmann. Bayreuth and Wagner. Leopold and the Philharmonic. Founding the New York Symphony.

Chapter 5, p. 49. Rise of the conductor. Frank leaves New York for Denver. Leopold's first great success, The Damnation of Faust. The Damrosch Festival of 1881. Equality with Theodore Thomas.

Chapter 6, p. 60. Chamber music at home. Clara. Leopold's pupils. Frank in Denver. Leopold on tour, 1883. Twenty-fifth wedding anniversary.

ILLUSTRATIONS

Illustrations

PREFACE

THIS BOOK is a history of the first three generations of an immigrant family that contributed more than any other to the development of serious music in the United States — along with other achievements. Something of the family is known. There are the countless newspaper and magazine articles that accompanied their careers, and Walter Damrosch, of the second generation, wrote a charming but partial and somewhat inaccurate autobiography in midcareer, and his brother-in-law David Mannes did the same. Later, in 1945, there was a careful biography of Frank Damrosch, based on materials in the family's possession, and in 1971 Marya Mannes published her autobiography. Nothing further has appeared, but meanwhile, in the period from 1950 through 1972, members of the family's third generation gave huge collections of papers to various libraries.

This is the first book about the family or any of its members to make use of these multiple collections as well as of several smaller ones. I also have had the use of material in several small collections still held by family members, as well as the assistance of the six surviving grandchildren (now five) of the original immigrants, Leopold and Helene Damrosch, of the surviving and divorced spouses of several of the grandchildren and of several members of the family's fourth generation. Had I not had the aid of this collective family memory, the book would be very different, like some ruined temple in which the foundation is clear but the columns and pediments lie strewn about with many of the most interesting pieces missing.

Out of it all, I think, some new facts about the country's musical history emerge and some old ones take on a different aspect. To give just three examples. Andrew Carnegie, evidently, was a more active patron of music than heretofore recorded. Typically, in a biography of him, a line or two is given to the construction of Carnegie Hall, and then the writer rushes on to talk of Carnegie's work in steel or for education or for peace. From the material in the collections, however, it appears that, Carnegie Hall aside, he was one of the great patrons of music in his generation, constantly balancing deficits here and there and underwriting projects that he found congenial, chiefly those of the Damrosch family. He was less focused in his giving than Henry L. Higginson, who created and supported the Boston Symphony Orchestra, but probably he gave as much to music and, if Carnegie Hall and its annual deficits are included, more.

Less neat, and requiring more explanation, is the adjustment upward I have attempted in Walter Damrosch's reputation. To his contemporaries, roughly from 1890 to 1930, he was a dominating figure; then with critics and historians, though not the general public, he began to fall into disfavor, fast. He was at his best conducting choral music, and by World War I choral music was losing its popularity. In the orchestral field he was good but not the equal of the great interpretive conductors, Toscanini, Stokowski and others who shaped the musical scene in New York from about 1925 onward. His role in the country's musical history has been easy to slight, partly because most of his work was done outside New York's major surviving musical organizations, the Metropolitan Opera and the New York Philharmonic, so he does not appear to any extent in their published histories. Yet by competing with them, through his Damrosch Opera Company and New York Symphony, he frequently forced them to adjust their policies, repertories and corporate structures. And, as there are no published histories of his opera company and orchestra, again his presence is not felt. That is also true of his work in radio. Like Carnegie, he is a more interesting and important figure in music than is generally granted.

And the third example. There are presently no histories available of the Juilliard School of Music, founded by Frank Damrosch as the Institute of Musical Art, and of the Mannes College of Music, founded by Clara and David Mannes and continued by their son. About Juilliard, at least, there is considerable confusion over how it came into being. The book, I hope, will make that, and much else, clear.

Many persons have helped me in my research. The book originated in a chance conversation among myself, Barry Seymour Boyd and her husband, Michael, members of the family's fourth generation. It was a fortunate beginning, for without their introduction to other members of the family, and the trust that was granted me because of it, family members, I suspect, would have been more reticent.

All those I interviewed are listed in the Bibliography, and I will mention here only two: Ruth Seymour Reed and Evelyn Sabin Mannes. Ruth

Reed did considerable research for me, digging documents, letters and photographs out of trunks and out of other relatives, and, equally important, at my request she wrote descriptions of the furnishings of rooms, the clothing relatives wore, the parties they went to and what they thought of themselves and each other. Of Evelyn Mannes' contribution, I can say that the last chapters would not have been possible without her permission and assistance. She wanted the truth told about her husband, Leopold, because she believed him a great and complicated man, and she had an artist's conviction that only the truth could reveal him. She read my first draft and corrected facts but never insisted that I change an opinion. The picture of him presented here, therefore, is mine, not hers, and I hope that I have not failed either him or her.

The librarians and their staffs in charge of the various collections were all helpful, and I regret that I can list here only those with whom I had the most contact: Library of Congress, Music Division, Wayne Shirley; New York Public Library, Music Division, Frank Campbell; Pierpont Morgan Library, Evelyn Semler; Newark Public Library, Art and Music Department, William J. Dane; Boston University Library, Ted Murphy; Juilliard School of Music, Brinton Jackson; and Mannes College of Music, Barbara Railo.

I also wish to thank those others who, although not interviewed about the family, in one way or another added something to the book: Richard C. Aspinwall, Herbert T. F. Cahoon, Joan Cannon, Frank Dunand, Glen H. Elder, Jr., Stephen Garmey, Howard Gordon, Glendower Jones, Louis H. Hollister, Joseph A. Kahl, Hortense Kooluris, Samuel M. Niefeld, Phillip Palmedo, Arthur K. Satz, George Herbert Semler, Jr., Patrick J. Smith and John P. Sweeney.

With regard to the Notes and Bibliography: because this is the first book on the Damrosch family to make use of these Damrosch and Mannes Collections, I have emphasized them in the citations; also, the contemporary newspaper and magazine articles. Conversely I have left much of what might be called general musical history unannotated. I hope the result proves useful to others.

George Martin
New York City

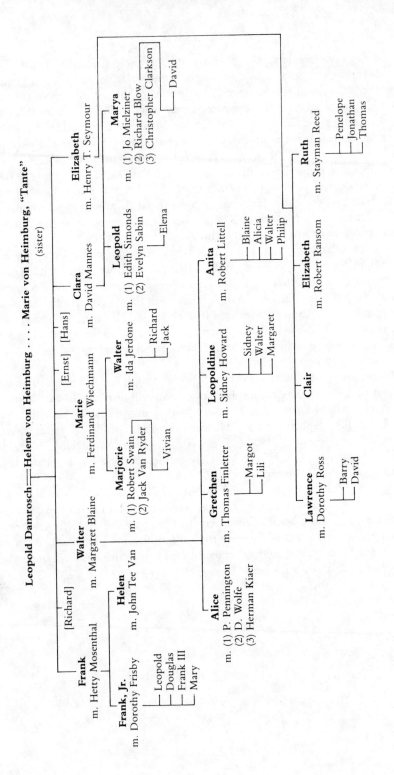

Leopold Damrosch━━**Helene von Heimburg** . . . . **Marie von Heimburg, "Tante"**
(sister)

[Richard]

Frank
m. Hetty Mosenthal

Walter
m. Margaret Blaine

Frank, Jr.
m. Dorothy Frisby

└ Leopold
└ Douglas
└ Frank III
└ Mary

Helen
m. John Tee Van

Alice
m. (1) P. Pennington
   (2) D. Wolfe
   (3) Herman Kiaer

[Ernst] [Hans]

Marie
m. Ferdinand Wiechmann

Marjorie
m. (1) Robert Swain
   (2) Jack Van Ryder

└ Vivian

Walter
m. Ida Jerdone

└ Richard
└ Jack

Gretchen
m. Thomas Finletter

└ Margot
└ Lili

Leopoldine
m. Sidney Howard

└ Sidney
└ Walter
└ Margaret

Lawrence
m. Dorothy Ross

└ Barry
└ David

Clara
m. David Mannes

Leopold
m. (1) Edith Simonds
   (2) Evelyn Sabin

└ Elena

Anita
m. Robert Littell

└ Blaine
└ Alicia
└ Walter
└ Philip

Clair

Elizabeth
m. Robert Ransom

Elizabeth
m. Henry T. Seymour

Marya
m. (1) Jo Mielziner
   (2) Richard Blow
   (3) Christopher Clarkson

└ David

Ruth
m. Stayman Reed

└ Penelope
└ Jonathan
└ Thomas

Family Table

FIRST GENERATION

Leopold Damrosch	b. 10/22/1832	d. 2/15/1885
	(Posen)	(New York)
Helene Damrosch	b. 1/16/1836	d. 11/18/1904
	(Jever)	(New York)
Marie von Heimburg, "Tante"	b. ?/?/1848?	d. 10/17/1928
	(Jever)	(New York)

SECOND GENERATION

Frank Damrosch	b. 6/22/1859	d. 10/22/1937
Walter Damrosch	b. 1/30/1862	d. 12/22/1950
Marie D. Wiechmann	b. ?/?/1864	d. 12/28/1937
Clara D. Mannes	b. 12/12/1869	d. 3/16/1948
Elizabeth D. Seymour	b. 5/17/1872	d. 11/1/1962

THIRD GENERATION

Marjorie Wiechmann Van Ryder	b. 9/29/1886	d. 1/12/1970
Frank Damrosch, Jr.	b. 11/30/1888	d. 8/31/1966
Walter G. Wiechmann	b. 11/14/1890	d. 10/12/1964
Alice Damrosch Kiaer	b. 5/18/1892	d. 4/23/1967
Helen Damrosch Tee Van	b. 5/26/1893	d. 7/29/1976
Lawrence D. Seymour	b. 4/23/1895	living
Gretchen Damrosch Finletter	b. 10/3/1895	d. 12/15/1969
Clair Seymour	b. 2/2/1896	living
Elizabeth Seymour Ransom	b. 9/28/1898	living
Leopoldine Damrosch Howard	b. 3/10/1899	d. 12/1/1964
Leopold D. Mannes	b. 12/26/1899	d. 8/11/1964
Ruth Seymour Reed	b. 3/12/1900	living
Anita Damrosch Littell	b. 11/8/1903	d. 6/17/1982
Marya Mannes	b. 11/14/1904	living

The Damrosch
Dynasty

PROLOGUE

Some values held by the family. Historical, psychological and sociological points of view. The immigrant experience.

A WORD at the start may be helpful. This is not a book about music, at least not in any technical sense. It is a book about a family of musicians, with emphasis on the family's social characteristics, the attitudes and assumptions underlying its personal relations and its extraordinary contribution to music in the United States. Indeed, no family has contributed more to the development in this country of a taste for classical music than the Damrosch-Mannes family. (Clara Damrosch married David Mannes.)

For three generations, starting with the arrival in 1871 of Leopold Damrosch, a German immigrant, through the death in 1964 of his grandson Leopold Damrosch Mannes, many members of the family pursued careers in music, most notably in the field of music education. Much of what they accomplished has passed into history, but much also remains, particularly in the institutions they founded.

But their achievements were not only in music. Leopold Damrosch Mannes, besides being a musician, was an inventor. With Leopold Godowsky, Jr., another musician, he discovered the Kodachrome process and related techniques that made color photography practical. Their work had a large part in changing the world as it has been changed only a few times in the past. Color now has a role in daily life through photography, printing, movies and television inconceivable before the development of Kodachrome in 1935.

In the family's second generation, Walter Damrosch, though in his sixties, grasped earlier than most the possibilities for music in the new medium of radio and created in his "Music Appreciation Hour," 1928–42, what many persons consider to be the best use yet made in the public interest of radio or television. Other members of the family within the three-generation span made important contributions to American life in sport, art, literature and business.

One quality that all these family members shared was a willingness to enter a new field and to improvise the techniques and institutions necessary to achieve something in it. They were pioneers, consciously so, and in the persons they married they seemed to seek, and often to discover, the same quality. For them it was part of the excitement of life.

Along with the pioneering spirit, which included a willingness to risk their own money and position, was associated a streak of idealism, a desire to be of service to others. Family members were often on crusades: to introduce Berlioz or Gershwin to classical-music lovers, to start America singing with classes for the untrained public, to aid American music students by founding conservatories or to create a U.S. Olympic ski team for women.

What they accomplished is certain and can be recounted. Why they accomplished it — of equal interest, I think — is more speculative. What values did this family hold that helped it to release so much energy and talent? I suspect that people of different temperament, on reading the record, will suggest different answers. But to the pioneering spirit and the sense of crusade six other characteristics or values clearly can be added.

Though profoundly German in background and culture, they were, by instinct, training and belief, cosmopolitan, always looking outward rather than in, always ready to move from the smaller to the larger group or purpose.

They expressed their religious feelings through music, not through church or synagogue, and this seems to have given them freedom not only to marry where they wished but to create their lives on their own terms.

Through their music they had free entry into the world both of the rich and powerful and of the poor. They had a wider range of acquaintance than most persons.

Though as artists dependent on patrons they were intensely aware of the power of money, they did little to accumulate it. Money always was traded for experience.

They had standards for their art that frequently brought them into conflict with others — social workers, patrons, society hostesses, corporate and union officials — people who wanted to use music for other than artistic purposes. But on their standards they were inflexible.

They were eager to work, to be exploited, constantly working for little or nothing. For by being exploited they could not only show what they could do, but could have a life in music.

Today some of the values by which this family lived are out of fashion, sometimes even talked of with contempt, sometimes even by members of later generations of the family. Considering the achievements, the contempt seems foolish. But the questioning of values is not. For as times change, some values prove ephemeral, facets merely of time and place, yet others seem to continue, immutable, eternal. And within the three-generation span the family had its casualties. They, too, are part of the story.

There are several points of view from which this family's three generations can be examined. Historians, sociologists and psychologists all work in the field of family history, and each brings to it a special emphasis. Thus, when young Walter Damrosch under dramatic circumstances replaces his father as conductor at the Metropolitan Opera, it is possible to stress the event's importance in Walter's career or in the institution of the Damrosch family or in Walter's psyche — for Walter, though the heir apparent, was not the eldest son. But the division has never been as real as the example implies. Good historians have always touched on all three aspects of such events, and I shall try to match them.

Here at the start, however, I think it important to declare that I have not invented facts where facts are thin. Any statement in quotation marks comes either from some document — a journal, a letter — or was made to me at least twice, after a time for reflection, by someone I interviewed. And I have not entered anyone's mind to relate what the person thought unless he or she either told me directly or left a record of it. Observance of these rules has left the account with some obvious gaps. Let them be.

Also, wherever a bit of psychology has seemed in order, I have been wary and surrounded my speculations with cautionary words: "it seems," "perhaps," "possibly" or "apparently." I did not discover, working through the family's papers, that any member of the first two generations — with the slight exception of Clara Mannes in her old age — left anything approaching a self-analysis. They did not concern themselves with inner states of mind: Am I happy? Bored? Fulfilled? A failure? They did not think of themselves in such terms. They simply reported behavior, and approved or disapproved chiefly on the basis of results. By the third generation's middle age, however, times had changed; family members, or at least some, now analyzed themselves and each other, and Marya Mannes in her published works made much of her self-analysis.

The historical and psychoanalytical points of view, I think, will take care of themselves. The sociological, though, perhaps needs an alerting word. No one will miss the importance to the family of its rituals, such as the celebration of Christmas, or in its second generation of its connecting link, the maiden aunt who kept all branches of the family informed of what each was doing. But certain other aspects may slip by unnoticed. Family life is such familiar terrain to most of us that in crossing it we all too easily assume that we know the road's direction, ignoring signs that may give pertinent information. Take, for example, a simple event like a music lesson at home, and consider what it implies.

In this family of musicians, in the 1870s, though the children took piano lessons from outsiders, they played regularly for their father. If one played badly, he or she was scolded. Sometimes a child cried. No matter. Justice to Mozart came first. No child in this family ever was told that a scale was played well when in fact it was played badly. The pull on children was always toward adult standards and interests.

Fifty years later, of course, many middle-class, professional families were becoming — in the sociological phrase — "child-oriented," as parents were told by educators that a child could develop properly only if allowed his childhood and only if his parents shared his childish interests.

Further, despite the trend of the Industrial Revolution to split work from home, in the Damrosch and Mannes families, because the work of both father and mother was in music, there was no sharp division between home and office. In both, work was done, money earned, pleasure and worry experienced. Because the father often was at home, he had a greater role than in most families in the children's lives and education, and because he often brought friends home to make music — Anton Rubinstein, Pablo Casals — the children had frequent and powerful exposures to older people. The family, at least until the third generation, when the children began to go to college, was as important as the school in education, perhaps more so.

Also, because women had an established role in music, at least as performers, the equality of opportunity for the girls was greater than in most families. Leopold Damrosch's wife, Helene, was a professional lieder singer; his sister-in-law Marie, a professional chorister. He seems to have made no distinction between his sons and daughters in the musical education offered to them; his daughter Clara became a professional pianist, and his daughter Elizabeth, an occasional singing and piano teacher, as well as lecturer. The tradition in the family was that all members of whatever sex or age worked in music, and for pay, if possible.

Then, too, the music made migration to the United States easy for this family. There was no break in cultural continuity. Bach, Beethoven and Brahms were just as acceptable in the United States as in Germany, and in most American cities in the 1870s the musical life was dominated by Germans. Damrosch, on arrival, may have had difficulty finding opportunities to exercise his skills, but immigration did not make them obsolete.

In short, the family's life in the three generations was never typical of its day or of immigrants generally. Yet behind its singularity looms always the more general immigrant experience. The Arion Society, which brought over Damrosch in 1871, was — in the jargon of ethnic history — a "culture broker" to him and his family. There were also many of the usual problems of language, with the children of the first generation speaking and writing to their parents in German but among themselves in English, and no child until the third generation completed a course in college. The First World War brought to them, as to all German immigrants, fear of the accusation of divided loyalty, and Walter defensively began his autobiography (1923): "I am an American musician."

In the end, however, it is in its singularity that the family is interesting. Its adjustments to life in the New World, while preserving its ideals, were quick and effective; its accomplishments, remarkable. Perhaps an account of it may be of some use to us, who live in such a swiftly changing world — but that judgment I leave to the readers.

PART I

The Patriarch

CHAPTER 1

*The family coming over. Leopold Damrosch in New York. The Arion Society.
Background in Breslau. Beginnings in New York. Leopold's letter to a friend in
Breslau.*

THE SAIL- AND STEAMSHIP *Hermann,* departing from Bremen for New
York on July 22, 1871, was not large, and by the time it reached mid-
Atlantic almost everyone on board was aware of the Damrosch family.
Frau Helene Damrosch, tall, stately and said by her children to be a lieder
singer, for the first week was seasick and kept to her cabin. But the three
elder children, Franz, Walter and Marie, roamed the ship and soon told
all who asked that their father, a famous musician, a friend of Liszt and
of Wagner, was already in New York and that the family was crossing
to join him.

The children were alike in family pride but already different in personality. The eldest, twelve-year-old Franz, named for his godfather, Liszt,
was quiet, and the ship's captain, favorably impressed, allowed him to
raise and lower the pennants to greet the occasional passing ship. One
day, having heard of a woman's death in steerage, Franz on his own
went to lower the ship's flag to half-mast.

Walter, three years younger, was still wholly a boy. His spirits were
quite irrepressible, and he delighted in stealing raisins from the dining
room. Marie, pretty, talkative and almost seven, played chess with
grownups and sometimes defeated them.

Clara, the family's baby, was often brought on deck by Frau Damrosch's younger sister, Marie von Heimburg, and if ever another passen-
ger offered to relieve the sociable, twenty-three-year-old Marie of her
burden, the tyrannous child would begin to wail, "Tante, Tante!" ("Aunt,
Aunt!"). Years later the still-beloved and unmarried aunt with mock dis-

content would recall, "That was the beginning of my being called 'Tante' and nothing else, the loss of my real name and identity!" [1]

Any doubt those aboard may have held about the family's musical claims was resolved one evening when Helene Damrosch sang on deck for the ship's company and passengers. The officers and cabin passengers sat before her in chairs, steerage passengers stood behind a barrier, and many of the crew climbed into the rigging. On the *Hermann*, a ship of the North German Lloyd Line, almost all of the passengers and crew were German, and many knew by heart the Schubert and Schumann lieder that Frau Damrosch chose to sing. [2]

At the recital's end it was credible that the handsome, statuesque woman had studied under Liszt, and at the Weimar opera had sung Agathe in *Der Freischütz* and Ortrud in *Lohengrin*. She had presence, and the voice was beautiful, controlled and huge. Far from being lost in the open air, it could carry the songs' nuances to the farthest person. And as she sang Schubert's *Am Meer* (*By the Sea*), to words by Heine, the song and her voice seemed to merge with the surroundings:

> *Der Nebel stieg, das Wasser schwoll,*
> *Die Möve flog hin und wieder;*
> *Aus deinen Augen liebevoll*
> *Fielen die Tränen nieder.*

> The mist rose, the water swelled,
> The seagull flew to and fro;
> While from your eyes, so filled with
> Love, the tears began to flow.

In New York, preparing for his family's arrival, Leopold Damrosch relied greatly on members of the Arion Society, which had brought him to the United States and now was bringing his family.

At that time throughout the country there were perhaps a hundred singing groups like the Arion in which German immigrants gathered for social and artistic purposes. In New York City, still limited to Manhattan Island, where the 160,000 Germans were roughly a fifth of the population, there were at least thirteen, of which probably the oldest and best established was the Liederkranz Society, founded in 1847. Though most of these groups put music first and were important in the city's cultural life, they united with the music, through balls, picnics and supper parties, much of the social and family life of the city's German-speaking community.

The Arion, for example, was born in 1854 in a tiff over food, not music. The Liederkranz had served "a particularly poor and meager supper of red cabbage," [3] and thirteen disgruntled members met in the Franz

Josef Reich Restaurant to found a new society. The offshoot flourished; and in 1870 not only did the Arion absorb the Teutonia Männerchor (Male Chorus) and buy itself a larger clubhouse at 19–21 St. Mark's Place, but it looked around for a truly distinguished musical director whose employment would proclaim its position as first among the city's choral societies. On the advice of Edward Schuberth, a music publisher with strong ties to Germany, the post was offered to Leopold Damrosch in Breslau. And to the Arion's delight, and perhaps surprise, he accepted.[4]

When in April 1871 the ship bearing him, the *Hammonia* from Hamburg, entered New York Harbor, a tender filled with music lovers, including many who were not members of the Arion, sailed out to greet him. For his arrival was recognized as a historic occasion. He was the first European musician of top rank to come to the United States to take up a permanent post.[5]

If Damrosch held any private reservations about staying, his first two appearances presumably quashed them. The first was a small concert by the Arion's Male Chorus barely a fortnight after he arrived, and he wrote of it to the family in Breslau with enthusiasm. Then on May 6 he appeared as soloist with the New York Philharmonic, playing the Beethoven Violin Concerto and using his own cadenza. His tone, though not large, was pure and consistent. A man of moderate height and spare figure, with black hair and piercing eyes, he gave an impression of dignified vigor, of nervous energy controlled by intellect. And in this more extensive test of his abilities, before a public that was not exclusively German in taste and background, he was well received.[6]

The Arion's pleasure in him grew greater, if possible, and its officers, besides paying the passage of his family to join him, found a house for him, suitable for his wife, four children and sister-in-law. It was a narrow brick building, 220 East 35th Street, three stories high, with steps from the street leading down to the kitchen and up to the parlor floor. In the back, off the dining room behind the kitchen, was a small yard only partly paved, with flowers and bushes. By the standards of the city's German community, the house was not large for a family of seven, but for immigrants it was a comfortable start. To have it ready in time, the Arion wives helped Damrosch to shop, and their taste in furniture, and presumably his, ran to heavy curly walnut with tan rep covering.[7]

Then came the morning of August 5, when the *Hermann* was due to dock in Hoboken. The day was steaming hot, and Damrosch was on the pier, as it turned out, eight hours early. Later he was joined by a committee from the Arion to greet the family and lead it to its new home. When the luggage had been found and loaded, family and welcoming committee all squeezed into carriages to drive to the ferry, and, crossing the river, the newcomers were awed by the majesty of the Hudson, so much wider than the Oder and, with its Palisades, so much more imposing. Then Manhattan, with the warehouse bustle of its riverfront, the less noisy commerce of the island's center and finally the quiet residential area bordering Murray Hill. Soon the carriages rolled east on Thirty-fifth Street and stopped before the house so eagerly imagined. Arion members helped with the luggage, said their hearty *Auf Wiedersehens* and departed, leaving Damrosch to lead his family through the house, explaining how he had allocated the rooms. Everyone exclaimed over the number of carpets, the gas lighting, the built-in closets, the real bathtub, the hot and cold running water on every floor, and the private yard. In Breslau they had not had such luxuries.[8]

The Arion's invitation, though not flattering to a musician of Damrosch's standing, had arrived in a year when he was ready to consider it, for political as well as musical and financial reasons. Though only sixteen in 1848 and too young to participate in the German revolutionary movements, he was by temperament in sympathy with their liberal and republican ideas. In Breslau, however, he was a subject of the King of Prussia, who, after Prussia defeated France in 1870, became the Emperor of Germany. Under Bismarck's leadership Prussia, between 1864 and 1870, fought with Denmark, Austria and France as steps toward unifying the diverse German states into a single, militaristic, absolutist monarchy. The Prussian historian Theodor Mommsen characterized Bismarck's leadership as "filth and fire,"[9] and Leopold Damrosch likewise saw no good in it. The streets increasingly were filled with arrogant soldiers, military rank was becoming the surest entry into society, and concern for the arts was dwindling. In the previous century Frederick the Great of Prussia had played the flute and composed; the new German Emperor, William I, had no such interests.

The political trend aggravated a problem of the musical world: in Central Europe at this time there were more good musicians than posts to sustain them. Breslau, unlike Dresden or Vienna, was not an important cultural city, and despite the artists Damrosch had lured to it, the city's leading families, with few exceptions, would not support a good chorus, orchestra or opera company. Symbolic of their attitude was the city's concert hall — still lighted by candles when most halls elsewhere had long since switched to gas. After twelve years of struggle in Breslau, Damrosch was ready to concede that no first-rate musical organization could be created there, and, as a corollary, that he could not earn enough there to maintain his family.

He could return to touring as a solo violinist, playing with orchestras and chamber groups; he had the technique and artistry to do it. But touring, which before marriage he had done with Carl Tausig and also with Hans von Bülow, would disrupt family life, to which he now was devoted.

Liszt, ever his friend and admirer, recommended him strongly to the Gesellschaft der Musikfreunde in Vienna to succeed the retiring conductor, Johann Herbeck. But the post went to Anton Rubinstein. Just at the time of this setback Schuberth arrived with the Arion's invitation to come to New York.

Once before, at the age of twenty-two, Damrosch had faced the kind of decision that was before him now. To satisfy his father he had subordinated his love of music and studied first law and then medicine at the University of Berlin, graduating in 1854 magna cum laude. A brilliant future seemed assured with a position in the eye clinic of Dr. Albrecht von Gräfe, soon to be recognized as one of the world's great ophthalmologists; but after a brief hesitation Damrosch decided for music, and from that decision never looked back.

The invitation from the United States, with its promise of financial improvement for himself and his family, offered a similar sharp choice. In Germany he was a respected member of the top rank of musicians. In New York would he be accepted? Would he find a circle of congenial musical friends? Composers of the quality of Liszt and Wagner? Pianists like Clara Schumann, Tausig and von Bülow; or a fellow violinist such as Josef Joachim? Plainly not, and he must have heard as much from everyone he consulted.

There were in the United States at the time only three permanent orchestras of any quality, the New York Philharmonic, founded in 1842, the Brooklyn Philharmonic, founded in 1857, and the Thomas Orchestra, based in New York and founded in 1862. Of these, the New York Philharmonic, a members' cooperative orchestra conducted by Carl Bergmann, had the most prestige. Besides being the oldest, it was the biggest — a hundred players — and performed in the largest hall, the Academy of Music, which had a capacity of four thousand. But it gave only five subscription concerts a year, whereas even in Breslau the orchestra had given twelve. The Thomas Orchestra, of about sixty men, played much more frequently and often better than the Philharmonic but had a more popular repertory. Wholly controlled by its creator and conductor, Theodore Thomas, it had several New York seasons in a year and subsisted between them by touring. In Brooklyn, Bergmann and Thomas alternated every year or so as conductor of a small orchestra that had an annual season of five concerts. Except for these three groups, established, professional orchestras for instrumental music were lacking. Artistically, emigration to the United States was a leap into a small pond, though one that might enlarge.[10]

Against that challenge Damrosch must have measured the needs of his family, his prospects in Breslau and the future for musicians in the new German Empire. He was thirty-eight, with six to support, and eager to use his talents to the full. He decided to go, and began at once to learn English.

For the children the adjustment to American life was easier than for the adults, though not without pain, caused in part by their father's decision about language. He was determined that all of them, even the youngest, Elizabeth (known as Ellie), born in New York in the spring, should grow up bilingual, and he decreed that within the family German should be spoken, read and written, thus depriving the children and adults of their most sheltered area for practicing English. He himself, though his rehearsals at the Arion were conducted in German, gradually achieved fluency in the new language, but he never mastered the pronunciation of *th* and *r,* and in the early years often dazzled his listeners with a vocabulary created out of imagination and Latin roots.[11]

Helene suffered less from this decree than Tante, for as mistress of the house she dealt with the outer world. She enjoyed shopping and always made of marketing an excursion, stopping to talk and joke with the tradesmen, at first in German where she could, and then, bit by bit, in English.[12] She also negotiated the daily arrangements with the family's occasional boarder and with the succession of part-time maids and cooks, most of whom were Irish. But Tante's work was mostly with the children, and she had little chance to practice. She studied English anxiously, though, in order to obtain a job in a choir, and one day she persuaded the organist of an Episcopal church to hire her, at $250 a year. Pleased with a good voice, he coached her privately in pronunciation. For Tante, fluency came through the Episcopal service.[13]

Whatever the pains caused by Damrosch's decision, in time they were justified. As adults, all five children were bilingual and familiar with both German and English-American culture. They also were fluent in French, and Walter, at fifty-eight, learned Italian. But for all of them the second language, if considered to be German, was preserved and perfected in their youth at their father's insistence.

The beginning years, however, were not easy. The house on East Thirty-fifth Street was in an Irish rather than German community, and in the streets and school the children, with almost no English at their command, were isolated and lonely. An Irishwoman, the family's first part-time maid, hearing herself surrounded by a family of singers, undertook to teach Franz his first American song: *Shoo, Fly, Don't Bother Me.* The simple tune he could grasp instantly, but not the words; and the effect, as he sang without comprehension and in a thick German accent, was too comic to be heartening.[14]

In the fall Damrosch entered Franz and Walter in the neighborhood public school, No. 40, on East Twenty-third Street between Second and Third avenues, and there the problems of language and singing multiplied. The boys were started in the lowest grades and were told they would be advanced as their English improved. For a twelve-year-old and a nine-year-old to sit among those who were six and five was mortifying, and the class work, for boys who had been studying Greek and Latin, boring. They tore into learning English and soon had it mastered. Franz — or Frank, as he was renamed in school — became a champion speller in the school's Friday afternoon spelling bees. He also, after a teacher had discovered his skill at the piano, played marches for the younger classes and accompanied the singing in the assemblies.

By German standards, let alone by Damrosch standards, the singing was appalling. When Frank was supervisor of music in the New York public schools, from 1897 to 1905, he attempted to improve it. But then, as earlier, the chief prerequisite was lacking: singing in the home.

In German families the parents, particularly the mothers, sang to their children, and it was quite usual for a child by the age of three to have twenty or thirty songs by heart. In the Damrosch family, because both the mother and aunt sang professionally, the exposure was doubly intense. Besides such ageless songs as *Kommt ein Vogel geflogen,* about a bird that sat on the singer's foot, the children grew up with Schubert and Schumann in their ears and on their lips. And with the music came the poems of Heine, Goethe and Schiller, as well as those of lesser poets such as Müller, Rellstab and Mayrhofer. The Irish and, more generally, American mothers apparently seldom sang at home, and the fathers, only when drinking. "In this country," Carl Sandburg one day would observe sadly, "when a man sings, they think he is drunk."[15] As a result, their children at school could do no more than bawl the simplest tunes with the most banal words. For all the Damrosch children the greater part of their education — with the exception of learning English — occurred outside the school.

There were other reasons. The school and many of the children were filthy, and there was much violence. The Irish in particular seemed given to brawling. The response of Frank, Walter and Marie was to spend as little time in school as possible. When their youngest sister, Ellie, entered, she was so appalled by the dirt and so terrified by the violence that she was immobilized by long fits of uncontrollable weeping and had to be taken out. For her sister Clara, tougher but extraordinarily fastidious as both girl and woman, the dirt was crucial. When she was in school, headaches plagued her; when she was out, they disappeared. So the two younger girls were sent to private schools. But like the older children, they received most of their education from the family's activities and friends.[16]

Frank did make one lifelong friend at the school, or rather, in the street outside it. One day as he was leaving, an eager voice hailed him in German. A boy a year younger introduced himself: Otto Eidlitz. He had been out of school for several months after being hit by a street car; he pulled down his stocking to exhibit the scar. As he chattered along, he mentioned his collection of lead soldiers. Would Frank care to see it? In Breslau, Frank had collected lead soldiers but had been forced when packing to leave them behind. Suddenly feelings and interests stifled for months revived.

Thereafter the two boys were constantly together. Behind the Eidlitz house was an open storage yard, into which they would disappear after school. Often Frank would stay for dinner or take Otto back to his house.[17]

The friendship had the blessing of both families. The Eidlitzes some twenty years earlier had come from Bohemia, where the family was well established: Otto's maternal grandfather was the court physician in Prague. By 1870 several branches of the family had settled in New York, and its members, as engineers, architects and contractors, would contribute greatly to the building of the city. Otto, when grown, built such New York landmarks as the Stock Exchange and J. P. Morgan & Company, St. Bartholomew's and Riverside Church, the Rockefeller Institute — and for Frank, a music school that is now the home of the Manhattan School of Music.

Moreover, like many Bohemians, the family was musical. Otto's mother was an accomplished pianist, and Otto was studying the violin. To the Eidlitzes friendship with a family of musicians seemed quite natural, and every year they invited Frank for a long visit to their summer cottage at Dobbs Ferry, on the Hudson.

To the Damrosches, particularly Helene, Otto was more than just a friend for Frank. Neither she nor Leopold was snobbish, but she, as a von Heimburg, had some social pretensions that he, as a Damrosch, did not. His family, based in Posen, was lower middle class, Jewish, with a Polish background, and, except for himself, undistinguished. Hers, with a claim to nobility in its "von," was upper middle class, Lutheran, based in Jever and Oldenburg, with members holding posts in those cities and in the Prussian army and government. In this new setting Otto was the sort of friend Helene wished for her children.

But social position was only part of it; there was artistic purpose, too. Both she and Leopold wanted to be at the center of the city's musical life, as they had been in Breslau, not merely on the margin, however sympathetic and German. Leopold through his artistry and charm soon would make friends of Gustav Schirmer and the Steinway family, in whose lives the Arion and similar societies played only a small part, and a first step toward this larger world was friendship with the Eidlitz family, already established in the city and quite outside the Arion circle.

In their attitude was also self-interest, which they made no effort to conceal. Musicians always have needed patrons, whether the church, court or a rich individual. Beethoven had an archduke; Liszt, his friends at Weimar; and Wagner, the King of Bavaria. In Breslau two families, the Eppensteins and the Kaufmanns, not only had been the chief supports of the city's musical institutions but, through gifts of food and material for clothing and through other imaginative ways, had contributed directly to the Damrosch family's livelihood. Within the family they were remembered with gratitude, and every Damrosch child grew up with a strong sense of a musician's need for a patron.[18]

But where in this unfamiliar city was a patron to be found? How was Damrosch to advance from the Arion, with its limited musical ambitions, to one of the city's established musical institutions, such as the Academy of Music, with its annual season of opera, or the New York Philharmonic, with its subscription concerts? Carl Bergmann of the Philharmonic was not going to step aside. Nor was the wild, angry, talented Theodore Thomas, whose orchestra was beginning to threaten the Philharmonic's position.

For the moment the best that Damrosch could do was to accept the occasional chance to be a soloist with an orchestra, schedule an infrequent recital of lieder with Helene — she used her first fee to buy a sewing machine — and make of the Arion as much as he could.

On May 19, 1872, after Damrosch had been in New York just a year and a month, he wrote to a friend in Breslau. Two days earlier his daughter Elizabeth had been born, and after relaying the family news, he began to write of life in New York:

> We others are well and have adapted to the life here — each according to his or her particular requirements — and don't find it too bad on the whole. I myself have made considerable progress and no longer make useless comparisons with my life and work in Breslau. I've become used to *beginning* a new life here and am grateful for every step ahead, however small. But I do not feel at home yet and perhaps I never will, in any case not until I have completely mastered the English language and have become a part of musical life in American (and not German) New York. But it would be unfair and fussy of me not to acknowledge the advantages I am already enjoying.
>
> First of all, New York with its hustle and bustle is the cosmopolitan city *par excellence,* with no room for narrowmindedness. I find the unceasing activity of the city very attractive and invigorating, something that was very much lacking in Breslau . . . Of course, the fact that one's livelihood is not only secured but, on the whole, comfortable has a lot to do with it. This is the first time since I have been married that I do not anticipate with trepidation the long — and even here not very lucrative —

summer, whereas before I was forever worried about simple survival and had to resort to all sorts of ways and means to make it to winter.

My house is comfortable, newly and well decorated, and has all that is necessary in a house, even a small garden . . . Already I need not turn every quarter before spending it. I spend a dollar more easily here than a penny over there. My living quarters and two maids cost $1400 a year, but I spend the money gladly, knowing that my house is indeed my home. Losses are not mourned for very long here. For every opportunity missed there are always ten others, and one will work out. You really can feel life moving along here: since possessions offer no security, one may as well pin one's hopes high. So here I am in the middle of a new life, and I hope not to run out of steam too soon.

Of course a lot is missing from true happiness, from complete content-edness. I shall never stop mourning the beloved lost country, the faithful, far friends. I have often the feeling now of having exchanged a rich intel-lectual and emotionally warm life for one that is dull and to all intents and purposes without content, no matter how great the likelihood that the American public's warm reception of music in general will extend to my modest efforts . . . If I were to tell you about my work and its success so far I would have to say that I have not had the opportunity to prove what I can do. I shall have to bide my time . . .[19]

CHAPTER 2

Helene and Tante. Leopold's youth in Posen. His character. The von Heimburg and Damrosch Christmas. The hostility of Theodore Thomas.

FOR THE DAMROSCH FAMILY "home" was essentially a state of mind rather than a place, a house or its furniture. No Damrosch of the second generation ever spoke with nostalgia of the sunlight slanting into the living room, of the "look" of the dining room or of a couch where "I lay alone and read all of Schiller." For them, home was always the family's activities together, and these were easily moved from house to house or even from one country to another.

In this they were not typically German. For the homesickness, or *Heimweh,* from which many German immigrants suffered, sometimes for life, included in its definition a love of place, country and community. The longing was not only for the German countryside, so much more trimly kept than in the United States, but often also for a particular town, house and furniture; the town, in memory at least, so much more compassable than the ever-expanding cities of America; the house, standing for generations, so much more secure; and the furniture, in its style and worth, a proclamation of the family's position in the community.[1]

Among the family's adults only Tante Marie, usually so talkative and forever reciting or singing Heine's poems, was afflicted with the long silences and stricken look that betokened Heimweh. And after three years in New York she and her ten-year-old niece and namesake, Marie, were the first of the family to return to Germany, for a summer's visit with relatives in Jever and friends in Breslau.

The presence of his daughter and sister-in-law in the old, familiar places evidently stirred Leopold deeply, for in a letter to them, after mentioning "the magic our homeland," he burst out uncharacteristically, "Even the best aspects of life here are meaningless compared to the one important thing — our country." Ordinarily he was too busy for such emotions to overwhelm him, and though he often spoke of retiring in old age to a German village, in fact he applied for American citizenship relatively promptly.[2]

If Helene suffered, she never revealed it. Whenever talk of the old country threatened to become sentimental, she would interject quietly some remark like, "I prefer American women to the German *Hausfrau* with her keys," or, "For me the Hudson is more beautiful than the Rhine."[3] And her letters (in German) to the two Maries were consistently cheery, filled with local news and always with a touch of self-deprecating humor:

> Last night for the first time since you left, I sang with Leopold: new *lieder* by Brahms, which are very beautiful in part. My voice is sounding fine again, and next winter I think I shall make my contribution to the public well-being. My little goose from Hoboken brought her daddy to the lesson yesterday. She sang Schubert's *Ave Maria* for him on his birthday, and he came to bring his thanks and a very beautiful, scented plant. He is very content with his daughter's progress — well, what more can one want! Another pupil pays for lessons with the work of her hands; she is a dressmaker. I have just given her a cotton dress to make for me. Very practical for me, don't you think?[4]

In later life Helene's daughter Clara would complain that her mother did not share her feelings with her children and that often it was difficult for them to know what she thought.[5] But among her descendants she had the reputation of loving the United States at first sight, and indeed, long after the others had accepted its freedoms and luxuries as commonplace, there lingered with her a wonder and appreciation of them.

The family's activities together, by which so much store was set, were both a legacy of custom, descending chiefly through the von Heimburg family, and of new rituals deliberately created by Leopold.

His childhood in Posen had not been happy, though by his own admission not for lack of love. His mother died soon after his birth, leaving him an only child, and his father later, as then was not uncommon, married the mother's sister. Among the family's children Leopold, the eldest by several years, and only a half brother, felt alone. His stepmother was loving, and he was his maternal grandmother's favorite: "Indeed I was rather petted by all her family, who loved me as the only thing left to them of my dead mother."[6] Yet he was not happy, largely because of the conflict that developed between him and his parents over his determination to be a musician.

His parents were Jewish by origin but apparently not by religion, for in Leopold's brief account of his childhood not only does he never mention a synagogue, a rabbi or the Torah, but he traces all his interest in music and culture to nonsectarian schools and individuals. And further, he states what was presumably his own and his father's attitude toward Judaism, as then practiced in Posen, by giving thanks that his father "did not allow me to grow up in the narrow atmosphere in which many of my companions lived."

His father believed that full emancipation for Prussian Jews, promised by an edict in 1812 but by 1840 still only partially implemented, soon would be achieved, and that the surest road to a richer, better life lay in the field of government service, for which the best entry was legal training. Leopold never denied the validity of the reasoning, only its relevance to him, a musician.

At five he was sent to an elementary school, where, besides learning to read and write, he was taught to sing, "the foundation of my love of music in the years to come." Three years later his maternal grandmother, impressed by his love of music, arranged for him to have violin lessons. "When I walked, I sang to myself or dreamed, and my body swayed in delicious intoxication. When I had to sit quietly my fingers could not resist the sweet fancy that they were touching an instrument. I drummed and rattled on my legs until they were so tortured that they finally carried me back to my violin."

His father, however, could see no more in music than the pastime of an idle hour and rejected Leopold's plea, supported by several interested adults, to have it put first in Leopold's studies. So, as Leopold advanced in school, he was forced to spend less and less time on music. At home he fell into a pattern of silence and sullen obedience that continued for more than a year — until his father one day discovered that he was about to run away to the conservatory at Leipzig without money, proper clothing or even a letter of introduction.

In the confrontation that followed it was the father who burst into tears, finally consenting, against all his convictions, to help his son to study in Leipzig. But then a curious reversal began. The family was poor; the recent revolutions of 1848 had made loans oppressive and the father could gather a small sum for Leopold's use only with great difficulty. Distressed by his parents' sacrifices and by their continuing grief over his plan, of which they still wholly disapproved, Leopold abandoned Leipzig and music, deciding "to leave the rest to fate." When he told his parents, "their joy was the best reward for my hard won struggle and resignation." He resumed the academic course at the Posen Gymnasium and from there in 1849 entered the University of Berlin as a law student. After a year he shifted to medicine and in 1854 graduated with honors.

But the struggle with his father, lasting for more than a decade, had divided him forever from his family. He never mentioned the first names of his parents to his children, and his son Walter in 1929 could not furnish them to an editor of the *Dictionary of American Biography*.[7] The father's business also is unknown, and when and how he died.

A half brother, Siegmund, was in Kansas City in 1883 when Leopold conducted there, and apparently for the first time in some thirty years the brothers met. Leopold, writing home to his family in New York, commented:

> It is very sad that so often members of *one* family become strangers because of different education, avocations, and individual destinies. It is a great consolation to me to know that among all of us (I mean among the immediate family) there is enough love to keep us together in joy and sorrow forever. If *my* life has been made miserable because I had no family — you all shall be better off![8]

It was often observed in the nineteenth century that the typical German father had among his characteristics the extremes of harshness and sentimentality. Leopold certainly was never cruel to his children and perhaps not even harsh, but his son Frank recalled: "Father was loved and feared by us in about equal parts [and] . . . if we had an evil conscience because of a bad report from school or naughtiness at home, his eyes seemed to us to throw lightning and thunder."[9] At such moments Leopold could deliver a stinging rebuke, a spanking or even a whipping. Children often were sent to their rooms, from which release would be arranged by Helene, but only on the child's admission of bad behavior and promise of improvement.

The father's position in the family was acknowledged in its living arrangements and habits. In every house — and in New York the family moved frequently as its fortunes rose and fell — the main room, generally the back parlor, became Leopold's study, with his desk, armchair and grand piano. When he was in it, no child entered without invitation, and silence was observed around it. When he was out, Helene or Marie might use it to give a singing lesson or a child might practice on the piano, though there was always at least one upright piano upstairs for lessons and practice. And the privacy granted the father was not allowed the children. "Walter," his father would call, "what are you doing there? You are not practicing, and play slowly!"[10]

On Sunday evenings he would have the children and their friends play for him, and he would comment; and at the end of each winter he held a contest and gave prizes for accomplishment. On one such occasion Walter, hoping to distract his competitors, made silly faces at them through a glass transom. Caught by his father, he was ordered to the piano, had a Bach fugue placed before him and was told to transpose it on sight. But the penance backfired, for Walter accomplished the task without trouble, and Leopold could not conceal his pleasure.[11]

Though his lessons and contests were fun, they had a troublesome side that only gradually emerged. All the children played and sang well, but at the piano Walter clearly was the best and had the possibility of a career, starting as an accompanist for his father at rehearsals. But then what was to be Frank's role?

Similarly, among the girls Clara had a streak of determination that kept her at the keyboard, and she soon became better than her elder sister, Marie, whose energies was less focused; and better, too, than Ellie, who was easily discouraged because, as the youngest, she felt she never could catch up. In a family of musicians a talent, though great, could be a source of pain as well as pleasure, and even for Clara there might arise someday a question of the extent to which her parents would foster a career for her if it began to compete with those of her elder brothers. But for all except Frank, such problems were still a decade in the future.

One activity with their father that all the children in succession adored was his storytelling and reading aloud. This he did apparently only while they were young and seldom to more than two at a time. But the children divided naturally into groups. Frank led off, alone; then, close in age, Walter and Marie; then the youngest, Clara and Ellie. Between Frank and Walter the gap had been caused by the death in infancy of a brother Richard, godson and namesake of Wagner; and between Marie and Clara, by the early deaths of two more boys, Ernst and Hans.

The storytelling was often of Greek or Norse mythology, and for reading Leopold favored Grimm's and Andersen's fairy tales, the Arabian Nights and sometimes parables from the New Testament. Or he made up his own stories, filling the familiar rooms of the house with goblins, fairies, beasts and knights. The children responded to the stimulation by reading voraciously on their own. In Breslau, Walter's favorite book when he was eight was an illustrated edition of the *Iliad,* and dressed as Achilles in a costume made by his mother, he dragged Marie, dressed as Hector, round and round the dining room table in a chariot made of a chair.[12]

For the three older children the reading and storytelling were associated with the apartment in Breslau; for the two youngest, with the houses in New York. After dinner Leopold would invite Clara and Ellie into his study to sit on either side of his armchair. Calling them "Bidebu" and "Badibu," he would ask about the day's work and pleasures, letting the questions and answers lead slowly into a story. According to Clara, who may have been more sentimental in memory than the facts warrant, "We meanwhile let our fingers play with his soft black curls which lay on the back of his neck under his silver white hair."[13]

The family's rituals for holidays, chiefly birthdays, Easter and Christmas, descended through the von Heimburg family, and the greatest of these, for which preparations began months in advance, was Christmas. But only in the most nominal sense was the family's festival religious.

Though Helene, like all her family, had been raised a Lutheran, as an adult she seems never to have entered a church except as a professional singer. And the good-night prayer that she taught Frank has no sectarian reference or symbol:

> *Weiss nicht woher ich bin gekommen,*
> *Weiss nicht wohin ich werd genommen,*
> *Doch eines weiss ich, ob mir ist*
> *Eine Liebe, die mich nie vergisst.*[*][14]

Leopold reportedly had been baptized in the Lutheran church,[15] perhaps as a prerequisite to marrying Helene. If so, it was a condition easily met and of no consequence. He kept a Bible on his desk, for he liked to read in the New Testament, and he talked to his children of the virtues extolled in the Ten Commandments and the Sermon on the Mount, but without attaching any dogmas to them. Clara as a young girl, on being asked her religion by a new friend, was unsure but thought she was a Lutheran, and Walter in middle age named as his favorite hymn Luther's *Ein' feste Burg*.[16] But for the children, as well as the parents, religion was the cantatas, passions, masses and oratorios of Bach, Handel, Mozart and Mendelssohn, and the faith was in the music. That was also true, in general, for the von Heimburg family, particularly for the manner in which they celebrated holidays.

The mother of Helene and Marie, Helen von Heimburg, had been passionate for singing, and in the small town of Jever she regularly had sung the solo parts in the oratorios. Whenever a great artist like Jenny Lind sang in Oldenburg, Helen, clutching her latest baby — there was always another — would make the eight-hour trip by coach, and on her return would sing to the family whatever she had heard.

Before her death, at forty-three, Helen bore fourteen children, five girls, nine boys, of which her namesake, Helene, was the eldest, and Marie, twelve years younger, the eleventh. With such a mother all the children sang, and even if some were absent, there were enough for a family choir. Birthdays typically began with a sung morning's greeting, and later, at a feast resplendent with whatever fruit and flowers were in season, there would be more song.

---

*From whence I came, I do not know,
  Nor know the way I am to go,
 But this I know, and know full well,
  O'er me an unforgetting love doth dwell.
  (translated by Hetty Damrosch)

But Christmas Eve was the great family festival, with a tree as large as the room could hold and all the family gathered in a half-circle before it to sing their favorite carols: *Stille Nacht, Ehre sei Gott in der Höhe, O du Fröhliche* and many others. Under the mother's direction the carols were sung with expression and in harmony, for all the family's singing was done in three or four parts. If one was well sung, it might be repeated so that its beauty could be savored; if badly sung, repeated so that its beauty could be enhanced. After the mother's death the family's carol-singing was continued, in Marie's words, "like a memorial."[17] Though the carols might tell of "the Virgin" and of "the Child," there probably was little of Christianity in anyone's mind. The celebration was of the human family, not the divine, and by music in the family's home, not prayer or ritual in a Lutheran church.

In the Damrosch family preparations for Christmas would begin as much as ten or twelve weeks in advance. One by one the children would be invited into Helene's bedroom, blindfolded, and materials or patterns held against them for cutting. Sometimes if the eyes were kept focused on the toes, despite the blindfold a child could see the cuttings on the floor and have a hint of the clothing's color. For the boys the move to New York changed the style of shirt. In Breslau they had worn Russian blouses, easy to make; in New York, the style was more closely fitted. But there were also socks, underclothes and trousers. Sometimes Helene would bring in a seamstress to help, but for the most part she and Marie, who was exceptionally skillful with a needle, made the children's clothes until they were sixteen or so and began to need, for outer garments at least, a professional fit.

The children, for their part, were expected to make presents for each other and to prepare some new musical or poetic offering for the festival. Of course, not all presents were homemade; there were always books, and sometimes a sketch pad or a paint or tool box, but apparently, with the exception of dolls, seldom games or toys.

Then one night, perhaps a week before Christmas, the children would be "shooed" — they had all adopted the word from the song — upstairs to bed, and the tree would be brought into the house and installed in the parlor. By von Heimburg family tradition its tip had to touch the ceiling, which sometimes required a bit of wedging, but failure in this respect was unthinkable. From then until the holiday, the parlor was closed to the children, who were kept busy, upstairs and down, making decorations for the tree. Upstairs they constructed garlands of gold and silver paper, cut out stars and paper flowers and attached strings to the ornaments that were saved from year to year, little houses, wooden birds and colored balls.

Downstairs, Helene was in charge of making cookies and gilded walnuts to hang on the tree. The cookies, though in strange shapes, were simple; the nuts, complicated. First a string had to be attached to a nut with sealing wax, then the nut dipped in white of egg and, last, the strips of gold leaf applied. Deft fingers were needed, and most of the nuts were completed by Helene despite the children's help.

Finally, at the end of the longest, busiest, slowest day of the year, came Christmas Eve. At the hour appointed all the family gathered in the hall, except Leopold, who was in the parlor lighting the candles on the tree. When he moved to the piano and struck up *O Tannenbaum,* Helene and Marie would throw open the doors, and the children would march in to gaze with awe at the tree, now lit by candles from floor to ceiling and shining in a soft glory. In the corner, always, was a pail of water and a sponge tied on a tall stick.

Then, still standing before the tree, the family sang all the verses of *Stille Nacht,* and only after the last, hushed tones had faded was each child led by a parent or Tante to a chair or table where a white cloth concealed his or her presents. These were, of course, mostly clothing or other necessities for school that each child would have received in any event, but the season attached to them a special affection.

After unwrapping the presents, everyone sat facing the tree and sang the carols, sometimes with Leopold on the violin or piano, sometimes unaccompanied and often in parts. In later life this was a part of Christmas the children always recalled with pleasure, a part that, wherever they found themselves, they were quick to reproduce.

When supper was finished, it was their turn to entertain the adults with their newly learned poems or piano pieces, which of course Helene and Marie had been hearing for weeks as the children practiced. Still, the adults feigned surprise and perhaps pleasure, for sometimes, what with the excitement of the day and the cup of Rhine wine at supper, a child would get "stuck" in the middle, forget, and burst into tears.

One time Clara, in an effort to avert disaster, accepted help from Walter. She had been practicing Bach's G Minor *Gavotte* but could not master the trill in the left hand. "Don't worry," said Walter. "I'll sit beside you, as though turning the pages, and when the trill comes, *I'll* play it." And so it was done, except that he forgot to moderate his tone to hers, and suddenly in the midst of her gentle, cautious rendition out rang his trill with devastating virtuosity, and the family wept with laughter.[18]

Though in time the Damrosch family would be judged to have done more than any other to develop a taste in the United States for classical music, the individual most responsible was Theodore Thomas. Like Damrosch, he was an immigrant from Germany, brought by his father to New York in 1845 at the age of ten. His father had been a town musician at Esens, in the Kingdom of Hanover, and gave his son a few preliminary instructions on the violin, but by the time Thomas was thirteen, he was on his own, in music and in life.

At that age, after several years of fiddling in New York at dances, weddings, in theaters and saloons, he left for the South, as much to see the country as to make music, though he supported himself by an occasional recital. He carried with him posters announcing a concert by "Master T. T."; and whenever he needed money, he would add a time and place, usually the dining room of a hotel. He would stand by the door and collect the receipts, "after which I would go to the front of the hall, unpack my violin and begin the concert."[19] The repertory was light, and a favorite was *Home Sweet Home* with variations.

After returning to New York in the summer of 1850, he discovered that the musical world there was in the midst of a fundamental change. German musicians, immigrants following the failed German revolutions of 1848, had begun to oust English and American musicians from many of the theater orchestras. Increasingly, German rather than English or American music was played during the interludes and intermissions, and German became the language of rehearsals. Then, in 1850, the New York Stadt Theatre was founded for the presentation of German plays and operas in German, and its orchestra, which gave Sunday night concerts, soon became the best of its kind in the city, contributing to the growing belief that good music was necessarily German.

Thomas, a German with more American experience than most, was well equipped to profit by the change; and he was able steadily to improve his position, as well as his knowledge and taste in classical music, until by 1858 he had become concertmaster in the orchestra recruited for the opera season at the Academy of Music. One night, when the conductor was ill, he directed the performance of Halévy's *La Juive,* a score he had never seen, and did so with such success that the sick man was retired and his post given to Thomas.

Thereafter his interest shifted to conducting and particularly to raising the level of orchestral playing and programs. Realizing that what was needed most was greater rehearsal time and continuity among the players, in 1862 he created his own orchestra, and several years later, in order to keep it together for months at a time, began to tour. The concert circuit he developed stretched from coast to coast, and thousands of people west of the Hudson heard their first classical music at a concert of the Thomas Orchestra.

That was true, also, of thousands in New York, for his missionary role in the country's musical capital was equally important. He played six Symphony Concerts each winter, but his most important work was done in the summer, particularly in the eight seasons from 1868 through 1875. In those years almost every night from May to October he played at the Central Park Garden, a semi-outdoor beer garden attached to a

restaurant at Seventh Avenue and Fifty-ninth Street, close to Central Park.
Though some of the repertory was popular, there were "symphony
nights" and "composers' nights" and always programs designed to convince the audience that classical music was enjoyable.

George Templeton Strong, the diarist, soon to be president of the
Philharmonic Society, went to a concert on July 30, 1869, and noted:

> After dinner [a large party and] I took a starlight drive in the Park and
> spent some time at Theodore Thomas' Concert Hall or Musical Lager-
> bier Garden. Crowded. Orchestra good. Programme generally rather me-
> diocre; much of it flashy, but better than any mere popular concert-music
> we have had. Of course, it will not do to be wholly "classical" till people
> are educated up to that standard. This seems a civilizing institution. It is
> in operation every night and is cheap and innocent. There are no signs of
> rowdyism — people seemed mostly drinking nothing heavier than lager,
> and I dare say Theodore Thomas has kept a good many clerks and others
> out of mischief.[20]

Progress was made, and at the end of the next year Thomas was able
to rejoice in his notebook: "At last the Summer programs show a respectable character, and we are rid of the cornet! Occasionally a whole
symphony is given."[21]

The importance of these concerts can be shown to some extent by
numbers: in its first fifty years, 1842 to 1892, the Philharmonic played
259 concerts; in the eight summers at Central Park Garden, Thomas
played 1127. And just because of the greater number, the Thomas Orchestra was the better schooled. When Damrosch first heard it, he judged
it to be the equal of the best in Germany, and by September 1873 its
reputation had begun to reach Europe.[22]

The personality that Thomas developed, however, contained the defects of his virtues. He was self-reliant, but often arrogant; self-respect-
ing, but often vain; self-educated, but in some areas ignorant and preju-
diced; eager to improve public taste, but avid for public approval; hard-
working, but at times almost to the point of brutality. He was a large
man, physically strong, and in speech and action often blunt.

But between 1865 and 1880, he was by far the most important musician and impresario in the United States, controlling through his influence and contracts access to many of the country's best players and concert halls. No musician or musical society could ignore him, for all, sooner
or later, had to do business with him. And this was especially true of a
newcomer like Damrosch, seeking ways to make use of his talents.

Yet Thomas, despite his commanding position, evidently did not feel
secure. Introduced to Damrosch one day in Schuberth's music store on
Union Square, he glared down from his greater height and roared, "I
hear, Dr. Damrosch, that you are a fine musician, but I want to tell you
one thing, whoever crosses my path, I crush."[23]

CHAPTER 3

Ole Bull, Jenny Lind and Anton Rubinstein in the United States. Founding of the Oratorio Society of New York. Messiah.

ON SEPTEMBER 10, 1872, the great Russian pianist, composer and conductor Anton Rubinstein arrived in New York aboard the steamship *Cuba* and put up at the Clarendon, at Eighteenth Street and Fourth Avenue, a hotel much favored by celebrities for its luxurious suites. Outside it two nights later a crowd of several thousand gathered as the Philharmonic Orchestra, in the first such serenade since the arrival of Jenny Lind in 1850, entertained the illustrious guest with Wagner's Overture to *Rienzi,* the Andante of Beethoven's Symphony No. 5 and Meyerbeer's *Torch Dance.* In Rubinstein's suite the society's president, George Templeton Strong, made a speech of welcome, and Rubinstein, whose English was good, expressed his thanks to the crowd from the balcony. Those who heard him were impressed by his courteous and kindly manner, his noble head and massive brow. The Rubinstein year in American music had begun.

To some extent, the development of a love for classical music in the United States, and the appreciation of the technique needed for its performance — at least for the three major instruments, the violin, voice and piano — can be attributed to the tours of three artists from Europe. The first to come, in 1843, was the Norwegian violinist Ole Bull, who had studied with Paganini and played with Liszt and Chopin. Before his death, in 1880, he would return four times. His influence lay less in what he played, mostly Scandinavian or American airs or his own compositions, than in his technique, particularly in double-stops, staccato and harmonics. He could take a simple tune and give it an unforgettable performance. Theodore Thomas recalled with admiration how in the *Arkansas Traveller* Bull "would move slowly backward on the stage as he played softer and softer, and finally only continue the movement of his bow, without touching the strings, leaving the listener to the illusions of his imagination."[1] After Bull's tour, music lovers in America distinguished between fiddling and playing the violin.

Next came the Swedish soprano Jenny Lind, who toured for two years, from 1850 to 1852. In the first year she was managed by P. T. Barnum with all the showmanship for which he became famous. Because of his advance publicity a large crowd greeted her ship, and only with difficulty could she drive from the dock to the Irving House, where twenty thousand soon gathered. That night she was serenaded by the New York Musical Fund Society, an orchestra of two hundred that was escorted to the hotel by twenty companies of firemen, all bearing torches. At her first concert, at Castle Garden, she sang under an illuminated inscription, "Welcome, Sweet Warbler," and the tickets were auctioned, with the top bid at $225. Later, in Providence, a William Ross made a bid of $650, the highest of the tour, and then achieved further immortality by not attending the concert. Nevertheless, Lind toured with her own conductor, tenor and baritone, and though she might close a concert with *The Last Rose of Summer,* followed by *Home Sweet Home,* before these numbers the audience had heard at least two overtures played far better than usual and six or seven arias or duets from Italian opera exquisitely sung, with text and translation in the program. Again a new standard was set, not only in technique, but in warmth, grandeur and tragedy.[2]

Before Rubinstein came, several famous pianists had toured the country, among them Henri Herz, Sigismond Thalberg and the American-born, Paris-educated Louis Moreau Gottschalk. But their performances typically had been presented as part of a show. A Herz concert in Philadelphia, for example, was billed as a "Great Festival in Honor of the Declaration of Independence," and he shared the stage with five orchestras, eighteen hundred singers and a lecturer whose topic was "The American People and the Rights of Women." Rubinstein, starting out twenty-five years later, was able to insist on good music, but the concept of the show continued.

He had been hired by Steinway & Sons to make a tour of two hundred concerts, each to be played on a Steinway piano, at a fee of $200 a concert, an enormous sum for those days and the foundation of Rubinstein's financial independence. But he was not allowed to tour alone. Steinway's manager surrounded him not only with an orchestra but with two vocalists and a first-class violinist, Henri Wieniawski. To present even a Rubinstein alone, or merely with an orchestra, was considered too risky. But he proved otherwise.

In part he succeeded through personality and his own kind of showmanship. With his leonine head, string tie, crumpled suit and unsuspended socks, he seemed to many to resemble Beethoven and even to play as possibly Beethoven had played. His attack at the piano was breathtaking in its bravura. In New York, making his debut in Steinway Hall in his own D minor concerto, when he raised his large hands for the piano's entry and brought them down in a thunderous chord, many in the audience rose with excitement; some, according to eyewitnesses, even involuntarily shouted. This was not the charm and fluency of Gottschalk in *The Dying Poet* or *The Last Meditation*. It was titanic, raw energy, for which Americans, with their continent to conquer and new world to make, now suddenly seemed ready.

But what was most remarkable about Rubinstein's tour — he played 215 concerts in 239 days — was that toward its end, against the advice of his managers, he began in New York and Boston to give solo recitals. And he proved that even these could be financially as well as musically profitable. "You have underestimated the power of good music," he told his manager, and ordered him to announce a farewell series in New York of seven recitals in nine days. The programs, again against all advice, were uncompromising. For the first, Bach, Handel, Scarlatti and Mozart; for the second, six Beethoven sonatas — and audiences gathered for all seven recitals. Then on May 24, 1873, having brought New York to maturity in the piano repertory, he sailed for Europe, never to return. Before going, however, he had a conversation with Leopold Damrosch, and that, too, had consequences.[3]

As soon as Rubinstein had arrived in New York, Damrosch, who often had been his host in Breslau, invited him to the house for Sunday lunch. Walter, who was ten, as a treat was allowed to eat with the adults, and after the meal Rubinstein, who enjoyed playing, gave a short recital. Perhaps with Walter in mind he closed with his show-stopping encore, *Valse-Caprice in E-flat*. As Walter later recalled:

> I stood goggle-eyed behind him, watching his hands do incredible things on the piano despite the long black hair almost completely covering his face. I remember especially his last number, his famous waltz, which ends with a constant skipping in the right hand from the middle octave to an immediate reiteration on the piano's highest notes. I was beside myself with excitement as his hand made this terrific jump over the keys, again and again hitting the high notes with the precision of a marksman hitting the target in the center with every shot.[4]

Later, in the spring, possibly over another lunch, Rubinstein and Damrosch discussed the latter's future as a musician in the United States. Rubinstein was distressed that Damrosch's talents were so little used, and Damrosch had new cause for discouragement.

The Arion Society recently had declined his suggestion that it expand its fifty-man Male Chorus into a larger Mixed Chorus with women's voices, which would have opened to both singers and conductor a more interesting repertory. The movement in nineteenth-century Germany for men's four-part singing had started in Berlin in 1808 or 1809, partly as a response to Napoleonic domination, and much of the repertory that developed was of patriotic or sentimental songs by such composers as Joseph Panny, Conradin Kreutzer and Carl Friedrich Zelter. By far the best music in this form were the *Prisoners' Chorus* from Beethoven's *Fidelio* and the hunting choruses from Weber's operas, but the Arion's chorus could not sing these at every concert. Nor, while the society's focus remained on its chorus, could its orchestra of forty be expanded to do justice to contemporary romantic works; to sound well these needed an orchestra of at least sixty-five or, better, eighty.

The Arion's decision was symptomatic of a weakness in all the German choral groups around the country. Primarily their purpose was to conserve the culture the German immigrants had known, not to enlarge it or to spread it to others. Non-Germans seldom, if ever, were invited to join the groups; the repertory generally was restricted to German works; and for the most part no effort was made to reach an audience of any but Germans.

The Arion, typically, also put on winter carnivals and summer-night festivals, at which, in addition to singing, men would recite poetry, perhaps Goethe's *Erlkönig* or Heine's *Die beiden Grenadiere,* offer comic impersonations or perhaps stage a one-act farce. Often the evening would end with dancing. At some of the more serious of these festivals Leopold used Helene as a soloist. Also occasionally a small scene from an opera would be presented, and usually in the spring and fall an operetta would be staged, such as Carl Reinecke's one-act *Ein Abenteur Händels (An Episode in the Life of Handel)* or Weber's *Abu Hassan.* Finally, as the climax, every year or so in some city there would be a *Sängerfest,* or singing competition, to which the Male Chorus would be sent. These could be enormous events — 174 societies with six thousand singers gathered in Brooklyn in 1900 — but again, they were all-German in their personnel, repertory and audience.[5]

In 1859, under Carl Bergmann's leadership, the Arion had provided the New York Stadt Theatre with both men's and women's choruses for a production of *Tannhäuser,* the first staged performance in the United States of a complete Wagner opera. And in 1870, again for Bergmann, it provided choruses for a staged production of *Der Freischütz.* But such events were considered quite exceptional, and, for the moment, unlikely to be repeated. For a conductor like Damrosch, eager to work with a large orchestra and the best music, the post at the Arion was frustrating. Yet there was no question of resigning. The salary was vital to the family.

In his conversation with Rubinstein he told him of his meeting with Thomas in Schuberth's store and of Thomas' remark, which, through gossipy repetition, had seemed to gain rather than lose antagonism. Rubinstein, after six months of touring and performing with both the Philharmonic and the Thomas Orchestra, was aware of the personalities involved and, after thinking, said: "Why don't you begin by founding an oratorio society? And that may lead to other things."[6]

It was an astute suggestion, which on examination revealed additional virtues. Choral work was the area in which Thomas was least active, and, what Rubinstein probably did not know, two of the city's choral groups for mixed voices recently had failed for want of leadership, so there was an opening for a new organization. Further, for the men's voices, Damrosch probably could call on the Arion, if he needed to, and in his wife and sister-in-law he had two professionals around whom to build the women's voices. Also, if he scheduled works that required an orchestra, the orchestral part would be relatively easy, one that a "pickup" orchestra, gathered for a single event, or even amateurs would be able to play well. Then, too, an oratorio society would build on his reputation as a choral conductor that his work at the Arion had begun to circulate.

A few weeks later Rubinstein was on his way to St. Petersburg, and Damrosch had begun to organize an oratorio society.

His first step, it seems, was to suggest the idea at a small dinner party at the house of Elkan Naumburg, who, like himself, was an immigrant from Germany. Though Naumburg was a successful banker, he was also passionate about music, played both the violin and piano — though on the latter he played everything in the key of F major — and of a Sunday afternoon he enjoyed gathering a few friends, among them Damrosch, to play string quartets. He and his wife, Bertha, were at the heart of musical life in the city, and they and their guests greeted the idea with enthusiasm. Bertha promptly proposed a name: it should be called the Oratorio Society of New York. And so it was.[7]

The initial meeting to organize the new society was held in the Damrosch house on East Thirty-fifth Street. Besides Leopold, and presumably Helene, Marie, Elkan and Bertha Naumburg, there were some thirteen others, among them Gustav Schirmer, the music dealer, and his wife, Mary; a friend and neighbor of the Damrosch family, Morris Reno, who agreed to serve as treasurer; and also, perhaps, the society's first president, Frederick A. P. Barnard, the president of Columbia College, then still on Forty-ninth Street near Fifth Avenue. Barnard, who was stone deaf and famous for his loquacity, served only a year and was a figurehead. The workhorse of the organization was Morris Reno, who remained the treasurer for twenty-one years.[8]

The first musical meetings were held in Trinity Chapel on West

Twenty-fifth Street, and among the sopranos were Helene and Tante; among the altos, young Walter. Rehearsal space at the chapel soon proved inadequate, for as word of the society spread, singers turned up asking to join. One of these was an important addition, Theodore Toedt, who in a few years would become an outstanding tenor soloist for operas in concert and oratorios. By the fall of 1873 the society, now numbering forty singers, moved its rehearsals to a room in the warehouse of Knabe piano, on lower Fifth Avenue. The room, long and narrow, unfortunately was not good for singing. Nevertheless, after weekly meetings throughout the fall, it was there that the society, on December 3, 1873, gave its first concert.

No public announcement was made and no admission charged. The concert was for the singers and their friends. To avoid the monotony of a succession of short vocal works, Damrosch inserted among them a Beethoven trio for violin, piano and cello and a pair of violin solos, but the focus was on the chorus. Among its selections were some, such as Palestrina's unaccompanied motet *Adoremus Te* and Bach's cantata *To God in Whom I Trust,* that seldom, if ever, had been sung in New York. In addition there were vocal works by Handel, Mozart and Mendelssohn.[9]

One newspaper, the *Tribune,* sent a reporter, who wrote:

> The first concert of the New York Oratorio Society was given last night at Knabe's piano rooms, in Fifth Avenue. The audience was a good one, the performance was creditable, and the Society may be said to have begun its public career under very favorable auspices. It has been but a few months in existence, and numbers, as yet, not more than fifty or sixty members, largely recruited, we should judge, from German families of the highest class — a section of the community which manifests a better taste and warmer enthusiasm for music, and much more perseverance in the drudgery that vocal societies must undergo, than any other nationality. In the person of Dr. Leopold Damrosch, the Society has secured a valuable conductor . . . Dr. Damrosch takes the *tempi* of most of the choruses with more freedom than has been customary in New York, varying the accent and expression by that means with rather striking effect; and although he must be, on that account, rather a difficult conductor to follow, the Society seems to have a perfect understanding with him.[10]

By the time of its second concert, on February 26, 1874, the society had outgrown its room at Knabe and moved to the auditorium of the Young Men's Christian Association on Twenty-third Street. This time the unusual music was by Stradella and Orlando di Lasso, but again there was no public announcement. Yet when Reno arrived to check the hall, he was greeted by the janitor with the news that already there were people at the front door waiting to buy tickets. The possibility of an unsolicited audience eager to pay had not occurred to anyone, but on the spot

Reno created a box office, put the janitor in it and by the concert's start had collected about $25.

The problem of rehearsal space was never happily resolved. Within its first eleven years the society moved eight times, making use of, besides the piano warehouse and the reading room of the YMCA, several more churches and even the hall of the German Savings Bank. But no place was satisfactory: if free of charge, the halls were acoustically poor; if rented, too expensive. And sometimes what was free turned out to have its price: at Knabe, though the room was free, the workmen who pushed the pianos aside had to be paid. To keep expenses down, for the first five years Damrosch took no salary.

For its performances, however, the society in its third concert came to rest in Steinway Hall, on Fourteenth Street. The capacity there was twenty-five hundred, more than adequate; the stage could hold a large chorus; and there was room also for an orchestra. So on May 12, inviting the public to attend, and to pay, the society presented its first full-length oratorio, Handel's *Samson,* with organ and orchestra.

The evening represented both an achievement and an attitude on Damrosch's part. For any musical group to become a factor in a city's musical culture, it must make regular contact with the general public. And it was just this final step that the German singing societies were unwilling to take. Similarly in their labor unions, often the first in the field, the Germans would not take the final step of recruiting non-Germans; and ultimately their trade unions, among them an excellent bakers' union, lost significance. Damrosch, however, always conceived of music in terms of the whole city, others as well as Germans, and one consequence of his attitude was the speed with which, aided chiefly by Reno, he turned the Oratorio Society into more than just another German choral group singing German music.

At some point in this second season, it seems, a curious and sad event took place. In the fall, a lawyer named S. V. Speyer had taken the office of secretary, but evidently in some way his behavior offended Damrosch, for one evening when Damrosch was invited to the Naumburgs' for dinner, he refused to come if Speyer was to be present. Mrs. Naumburg, according to her son, seized the opportunity to persuade her husband to write Damrosch that it was he who no longer would be invited to the Naumburg home. Presumably there had been friction between Damrosch and Mrs. Naumburg earlier, but on what account is not known. The rupture — the only one of its kind in Damrosch's career, for he was an extremely agreeable man — was complete: all visiting between the families stopped, and the Naumburgs, one of the city's more important musical families, never again supported any Damrosch enterprise.[11]

The society, however, was not affected, and its final concert in 1874 took place in Steinway Hall, with a performance on Christmas Day of Handel's *Messiah*. For the occasion Damrosch enlarged the society's chorus by joining with the Handel and Haydn Society of Brooklyn, and the result, apparently, was an exceptional performance. The *Times*, reviewing it under "Amusements" — an editorial custom that had infuriated Rubinstein — found the vocal solos "not so impressive as the choral and orchestral parts of the program" but had high praise for the conductor. One of the city's musical traditions, which recently had died, showed signs of reviving.[12]

Handel's *Messiah*, though severely cut, seems to have been performed for the first time in America in Trinity Church, New York, on January 9, 1770, and thereafter was presented, in whole or in part, with some frequency. The tradition of singing the work every Christmas season, though, probably originated with the Harmonic Society in New York, about 1850. But that group gradually lost its vitality and disbanded early in 1873.

With the Oratorio Society the tradition revived and has continued unbroken to the present, a span of 108 years, during which the society has performed the work 161 times. And for most of that time members of the Damrosch family have been active in the society's affairs. For its first thirty-nine years its musical directors were Leopold, Walter and Frank, and later, when it briefly fell into financial difficulties, Walter returned for four seasons. Today a great-great-grandson of Leopold Damrosch is a vice-president of the society.

But what in *Messiah* led musicians and audiences to grant it a special place in the musical season? Why should Damrosch, who had no allegiance to any organized religion, have put it first in the society's repertory? Besides the majesty of the music and the happy chance that the text's original language is English, the answer lies, possibly, in the work's structure, which, like the prayer Helene taught Frank, is religious without being sectarian.

Unlike the typical musical Passion, which offers a narrative of the martyrdom and ascension of Christ, *Messiah* never presents the person of Christ, and the text avoids almost all narrative detail concerning Him. The drama is abstract rather than specific. The Child who is born is not called Jesus: "His name shall be called Wonderful, Counsellor, the Mighty God, the Everlasting Father, the Prince of Peace." And the chorus that celebrates His birth focuses not on the Child, but on "Glory to God in the highest, and peace on earth, good will towards men."

Similarly, in the succeeding sections of the Passion and Resurrection, Handel preserves a contemplative distance. The story is told in a series of pictures, only loosely connected, in which Christ is perhaps as much Everyman as the Son of God. In short, with very little dogma the oratorio concerns the eternal verities of human life: hope, suffering, faith and renewal.

Also, its musical style is secular. Handel was never a church composer, as were Bach and Palestrina. His music is not liturgical or even introspective; its style is always dramatic, popular and external. He produced his oratorios in music halls, theaters and hospitals, places in which persons of different religions could meet comfortably.

This coming together of men and women for a renewal of life and spirit, but without the bond of specific doctrine, seems to have been particularly appealing to members of the middle class in the nineteenth century, particularly to artistically inclined Germans, and perhaps English, who were increasingly agnostic and socialistic. In 1824 Beethoven — in a work much performed by Damrosch — had expressed the spirit by choosing for the choral close to his Symphony No. 9 Schiller's *Ode to Joy,* through which runs like a refrain the line *"Alle Menschen werden Brüder"* ("All men will become brothers"). And at the close of the century Tolstoy wrote in the concluding chapter of *What Is Art?:* "Art is not a pleasure, a solace, or an amusement; art is a great matter. Art is an organ of human life transmitting man's reasonable perception into feeling. In our age the common religious perception of men is the consciousness of the brotherhood of man — we know that the well-being of man lies in union with his fellow-men." [13]

It was partly in that sense of union that *Messiah,* with its monumental choruses for mixed voices, offered men and women, both in the chorus and in the audience, a religious as well as a musical experience. And there was even more of religion, perhaps, in the oratorio's extraordinary quality of affirmation: in the Christian sense that after death comes resurrection; in an even older, more universal sense that after winter comes spring. When better to sing the work than at Christmas, near the date of Christ's birth and also of the winter solstice?

A century later that sense of union and renewal seemed to have weakened, and musical works expressing them have a looser grip on their audiences and performers. But for Germans and English of the mid-nineteenth century, *Messiah* was the large-scale work at which all choral groups aimed.

CHAPTER 4

Biding time. Carl Bergmann. Bayreuth and Wagner. Leopold and the Philharmonic. Founding the New York Symphony.

PARTLY BECAUSE of Damrosch's success in launching the Oratorio Society, it looked for a time in the spring of 1874 as if the Philharmonic Orchestra might elect him its conductor for the following season. Bergmann, though only fifty-three, had begun a spiritual as well as physical decline, suffering apparently from a melancholia whose only relief was drink, and the orchestra played increasingly badly. Though everyone talked of the unhappy situation, the orchestra was not yet ready to force retirement on a man who had led it for nineteen years, so, over mounting opposition, he was re-elected. But plainly retirement was close. And, inasmuch as Thomas seemed to prefer his own orchestra and competition with the Philharmonic, Bergmann's eventual successor was likely to be Damrosch.

Despite the disappointment in 1874, therefore, spirits in the Damrosch family continued high, and Helene, writing to her sister Marie — Tante — visiting in Germany, reported of the Philharmonic, "It is only postponed," and continued with family news:

> I have put up new and pretty shelfpaper in all the closets and hung up new curtains . . . The basement is looking spiffy — for the moment — and only the fat person sitting in it looks terrible. Since you are no longer taking care of my beautification, I have become a sad sight, so much so that Leopold has demanded that I make steady appointments with a hairdresser since the hairdo I give myself — the hair is pulled straight back — is not very flattering. Instead, I spend an extra five minutes in front of the mirror to fix my hair and the result is rather more pleasing. When one's husband doesn't want to look at one any longer, something must be done . . . Leopold and Mr. Reno are playing *an awful lot* of chess, turning into

bitter enemies and fighting so vociferously in the yard or with the window open that I am ashamed to face the neighbors. But they seem to thrive on it, especially Leopold . . . Even without the Philharmonic, next winter is going to be interesting and productive, and it will be worth your while, dear Marie, to return to us.[1]

That summer, to help make ends meet, Leopold increased the number of his private pupils, taught at a small conservatory in New Brunswick, New Jersey, and early in June played in a recital at Miss Porter's Young Ladies' School, in Farmington, Connecticut. The latter was an annual or sometimes more frequent event for him. The school's music director, Klaus Klauser, was an energetic, knowledgeable musician, and under his guidance the school presented in these years what may well have been the best chamber music recitals in the country. Leopold played sometimes with Helene as soloist, sometimes as part of a trio with Max Pinner, piano, and Frederick Bergner, cello, and always enjoyed the outing. It was music-making in a congenial atmosphere.[2]

One source of income, however, he refused ever to tap again, regardless of financial difficulties. Writing to Marie in Germany, he declared roundly, "I will not *under any circumstances* have a boarder in the house again." The most recent, a Mr. Bing, had reneged on three months' rent and, faced by Leopold, had argued. In the end Leopold had settled for one month's rent and Mr. Bing's departure.[3]

In summer it was customary for Germans to live very much in the open air, and sometimes when Leopold went to the conservatory in New Brunswick he would take Frank and Walter with him and leave them for the day at a friend's farm in the country. In the city the children had the yard behind the house, which Helene and Tante had turned into a garden, and the street, which, though hot and dusty, was an inexhaustible source of interest. Occasionally Mr. Reno would hitch up his horse, Flora, and take the little girls for a drive, up to High Bridge, which carries the aqueduct across the Harlem River, and with his family he took Walter for a two-week holiday to Highland Falls, New York. Frank, as always, had a long visit with Otto Eidlitz at Dobbs Ferry.[4]

In mid-July, in another letter to Marie, Helene wrote:

How happily we would share some of the new heatwave (it's been warm all the time) with you. Ellie and Clara are very hot even in their thin white dresses, and Leopold moves from room to room in search of a cool place to lay his head . . . I feel like shouting: a kingdom for a bad joke! If I can find such a grateful audience in you — but alas! — there is a great drought on the field of jokes. I don't even have a respectable thought to communicate . . . Clara and Ellie are looking marvelously. Clara in fact has never looked so healthy; unfortunately the picture didn't catch her well, she is much prettier in real life, but Ellie's picture is sweet, isn't it? You should hear her this moment in the street shouting with a loud voice, "Want strawberries!" and when the policeman talks to her, looking up innocently and saying, a little frightened, "Ellie is very good!" . . . The enclosed pictures will make up for my miserable letter. Leopold always writes all the interesting news . . .[5]

She closed with an unidiomatic English phrase, "God by all," and then came the postscript in German, *"Elli Damrosch grüsst!!!"* ("Greetings from Ellie Damrosch"), followed by Helene's *"Allein geschrieben"* ("She wrote it herself").

That summer Leopold also began to direct Walter's musical studies more personally and, as he wrote to Marie, "I practice quite often with Walter now, and he has to play for me on Sundays, not without tears, but the boy is sensible and willing."[6] The following winter he arranged for Walter to sing alto at Christ Church (Episcopal). The choir, as was often the case in churches, had twenty sopranos and no altos, so Walter was encouraged to sing lustily and was paid $3.00 a Sunday — "enough," Tante recorded, "to pay for his clothing and soda waters."[7]

In addition to his teaching, Leopold practiced the violin two hours a day, rehearsed the Arion in its summer concerts and operetta and prepared for the musical season ahead, which, even without the Philharmonic, would be busy. For besides the concerts of the Arion and the Oratorio Society, he planned to introduce two of his compositions to New York: with the Oratorio Society, his *Scriptural Idyll — Ruth and Naomi;* and with the Philharmonic, under Bergmann, his Concerto for Violin.[8] His talents as composer, conductor and soloist would be on display; his person, available for any post that came open.

One musical plum that fell to Damrosch eighteen months later because of Bergmann's illness was the New York première of Tchaikovsky's Piano Concerto No. 1, with his old friend Hans von Bülow as soloist. The occasion, on November 22, 1875, was one of several that month to celebrate the opening of Chickering Hall (with a capacity of fifteen hundred), at Fifth Avenue and Eighteenth Street. To advertise itself and its new hall, the Chickering piano firm had hired von Bülow, to whom the concerto was dedicated, to tour the country with it, playing of course on Chickering pianos. Bergmann had been scheduled to conduct the world première in Boston on October 25, but had withdrawn, and Benjamin Lang conducted in Boston and Philadelphia. Damrosch, with whom von Bülow also would give a number of chamber recitals, conducted in New York.[9]

Four months later, with Bergmann now wholly incapacitated, the Philharmonic demanded his resignation, and the season's March and April concerts were conducted by its first-desk violist, George Matzka. The forced resignation coupled with his wife's death intensified Bergmann's melancholia. He shunned his friends, became a solitary and in August died. He was buried from the German Aschenbrödel (Cinderella) Society, and the service was entirely musical: no minister officiated; no service was read. As the coffin left the house, the Arion's Male Chorus sang the *Pilgrims' Chorus* from *Tannhäuser*, Bergmann's favorite and a piece closely associated with him.

To his contemporaries his retirement from the Philharmonic seemed epochal: a giant had left the stage. In Boston in 1853 he had conducted the country's first all-Wagner concert. In New York in 1859, with *Tannhäuser*, he had staged the country's first complete performance of a Wagner opera. In the 1865–66 season he had become the first conductor of the Philharmonic to receive an annual salary rather than merely honor and a player's share of profits. And he was the first conductor to take a permanent orchestra and put his personal stamp on its style and repertory; the first conductor, in an interpretive sense, the country had known.[10]

Yet despite his achievements, his retirement from the Philharmonic would change little in the development of the country's musical taste, for his two most likely successors, Thomas and Damrosch, shared his training and background. They were all part of the German immigration to the United States that jumped sharply after the revolutions of 1848, reached its peak of 1,452,970 in the decade 1881 to 1890, then declined swiftly to the start of World War I. For almost seventy years the musicians among these newcomers overwhelmed the performance of serious music throughout the country, to such an extent that for most persons serious music became equated with music of German-Austrian composers — despite furious protests by American composers. But at the Philharmonic, for example, every conductor from 1852 through 1902 was German-Austrian born and bred. Of the orchestra's personnel the percentage of those of German background rose from 42 percent in 1842 to 79 percent in 1855 to 97 percent in 1892. Not surprisingly, until World War I about 70 percent of the orchestra's repertory each year consisted of works by German-Austrian composers, and in the next fifty years that percentage only gradually became halved.[11] In the long view, therefore, Thomas and Damrosch were far more alike than different, though of course they did not appear so to contemporaries. After Bergmann's resignation in early 1876 the city's music lovers began heatedly to argue the merits of his successor, Thomas or Damrosch.

Meanwhile the agitation within the Damrosch family caused by the pending Philharmonic election was heightened by Leopold's decision to go to Germany for August to attend the first cyclic performance of Wagner's *Der Ring der Nibelungen*. He had missed the première of *Tristan und*

Isolde at Munich in 1865 for lack of money to stay on when the soprano's illness had postponed the performance, and for a production of *Die Meistersinger* he had been unable to afford even the short journey from Breslau to Dresden. Now it seemed for a time as though distance and expense again would defeat him. He had bought a ticket in lottery with a trip to the première as the prize, but of course he had not won. Gustav Schirmer, however, saying, "Doctor, you simply must go," pressed on him $500. Then, happily, Charles A. Dana, editor of the *New York Sun,* offered him the same amount for a series of articles on his experiences at Bayreuth. So he was able both to go and to repay Schirmer.[12]

The weeks of preparation for the voyage and première became an intense musical experience for the whole family. In the evenings, while Leopold played through the scores, everyone, even the little girls, would sit around the piano listening to his explanations of the operas' meanings and of the development of their musical themes, and they were overwhelmed by the power and grandeur of the music. For all of them it was a time of joy and of pride in their father and in the family. At little Marie's christening supper in Breslau, attended by Liszt, the guest of honor had been Wagner. And when with dessert five-year-old Frank had been called in to meet the guests, he had drunk his sister's health, his first champagne, from Wagner's glass.[13] The stories were told and retold, and then, just before Leopold sailed, he received notice from the Philharmonic Society that he had been elected to conduct the orchestra in the following season. At Bayreuth he would re-enter the German musical world as a major figure, without need for apology or explanation.

His articles, written in fluent but slightly unidiomatic English, were published in the *Sun* on August 13, 18, 23 and 26 and September 3, 1876, and though other papers had reports from Bayreuth, by comparison they were scanty. Damrosch's initial piece, in which he told the stories of the four operas, was allowed an entire page of the Sunday paper, seven columns of small type, and was supported by an editorial asserting that *The Ring* "is believed to be the masterpiece of one of the most audacious, original and powerful geniuses of the century."[14]

Today, after so much has been written about Wagner and Bayreuth, the articles are interesting primarily for their journalistic asides: the geniality under pressure of the mayor of Bayreuth, the price of admission to a rehearsal, Wagner's efforts to prevent curtain calls, and — what Damrosch plainly enjoyed — "orchestra leaders [here] are as thick as blackberries, and the salutations and introductions go on, without end."

The articles are also interesting, perhaps, for some of his musical and dramatic judgments after two hearings of each of the four operas: *Das Rheingold* "was to me the most impressive of all"; the first act of *Die Walküre* "has no equal"; Wagner "formulated in his operas the principles conceived by Gluck." Added to these was his prediction, soon to be proved wrong for most audiences, that "the *Word* will come into, as yet, unexampled prominence. The singer will have to be distinct in enunciation, and the auditor no longer be allowed to leave his wits at home and give himself up to the mere satisfaction of the ear."

But even if the articles were not imperishable music criticism — they were addressed, after all, to an audience totally unfamiliar with *The Ring* — they were a good advertisement of their author, and the stimulation of the trip continued for months to reverberate throughout the family.

Soon after Leopold's return, Walter with young Gustave Schirmer made a theater, the size of a large doll's house, in which they presented *Das Rheingold* to an audience of family and friends for an admission of fifty cents, with larger contributions from adults gratefully received. Walter played the piano, though from time to time he had to leave the keyboard to help Gustave (whose name was spelled with a final *e* to distinguish him from his father) manipulate the characters onstage. As Walter later described the production, he was the more important half of the team; in the Schirmer family, the leader reputedly was Gustave. But all agree that, though the exact date of this 1876 production is forgotten, the production, staged before a paying audience, was the opera's American première.[15]

Wagner, and particularly the operas of *The Ring,* were to be important in the Damrosch family's emotional and musical life, and the reasons, though speculative, seem sure. In *The Ring* Wagner intended to display the evils of contemporary civilization and to suggest that these could be lessened, possibly banished, if love were admitted into the world as a social force. The conflict in the operas is between a universal love, rooted in sexual and family love, and political and economic power: repressive, unloving, authoritarian. Though Wagner conceived of the drama before Bismarck dominated Europe, Bismarck's politics of violence and trickery — a cause of Damrosch's leaving Germany — is symbolized by the behavior of Wotan in *Das Rheingold,* just as the evils of the Industrial Revolution are symbolized by the forced labor in the mines of the dwarfs ruled by Alberich. The first break in the loveless, power-driven world of Wotan and Alberich occurs in Act I of *Die Walküre* — which Damrosch thought "had no equal" — when Siegmund and Sieglinde discover their love for each other and the curtain falls as they are about to consummate it. From that union a child, Siegfried, is born, for love of whom Brünnhilde will develop such compassion and understanding that she can destroy the loveless world of Wotan and Alberich. Or, in Wagner's more abstract concepts: sexual love should lead to family love, which should lead to the universal compassion that the world so sorely needs.

The operas are full of crucial choices made by individuals, such as Siegmund's refusal to go to Valhalla if Sieglinde cannot accompany him, and Brünnhilde's consequent defiance of Wotan. So, too, were the lives of Leopold and Helene: he chose music over medicine, family life over a virtuoso's life of touring, the United States over Germany; she chose marriage and family over a career well started.

Further, what evidence there is suggests that they were extraordinarily happy together sexually, and that they consciously used their sexual compatibility to create a happy family life in which love for one another would give the entire family, adults and children, a greater strength with which to face the world. They were too modest to cast themselves as Siegmund and Sieglinde, but their belief in the significance of individual choice and the necessity of love to overcome the evils of the world was very deep, and their response to Wagner, particularly to the operas of *The Ring,* was correspondingly profound.

As Philharmonic audiences no doubt expected, Damrosch scheduled some of the music he had heard at Bayreuth for the coming season. At the first concert, on November 4, 1876, he presented the American première of Act 1 of *Die Walküre,* and followed it on December 9 with the American première of Siegfried's *Narrative, Death* and *Death Song* from *Götterdämmerung.* But it was not only of Wagner's works that he presented American premières. On January 13, 1877, there was Goldmark's "Rustic Wedding" Symphony, which would become a repertory piece; also, the quintet, septet and chorus from Berlioz's *Trojans at Carthage,* Berlioz's song *La Captive,* and five of the eight parts of Beethoven's music for Kotzebue's play *The Ruins of Athens;* and on February 17, Hans von Bronsart's piano concerto, much played in Europe by von Bülow, and *Serenade for Strings No. 1* by the Austrian Robert Fuchs. To close with a flourish, though it was not a première, in April he presented the orchestra and Oratorio Society in Beethoven's Symphony No. 9. For serious music lovers it was an exciting season.

Technically, in the opinion of critics, he improved the orchestra's playing. In midseason *Dwight's Journal of Music* reported, "There is more clearness and precision of attack in the violins and less of eccentricity on the part of the wind instruments." And in the same issue, January 20, 1877, another reviewer wrote: "The Philharmonic has improved greatly under the new leader, Dr. Damrosch, who is a very particular director, but who inspires his orchestra with something of his own musical fire and taste."[16]

Yet financially, the season was a disaster, the worst in fifteen years. The orchestra's ticket sales, which in Bergmann's last three seasons had declined sharply, slumped further, to about half of what they had been ten years earlier. Though much of that decline could be attributed to Bergmann's illness and part to the economic depression that followed the financial panic of 1873, it seemed also that Damrosch's programs, so interesting to a minority, had scared the general public. It had preferred the Symphony Concerts offered by the Thomas Orchestra. There was the rub, the competition.

It was no secret that for several years the Philharmonic's ticket sales had been slipping. Even before Bergmann's resignation, according to Thomas, members of the Philharmonic had talked with him of combining the two orchestras, but he had refused. After Bergmann's resignation and before electing Damrosch its conductor, the Philharmonic again had offered the post to Thomas, but on condition that he give up his competing concerts. And again Thomas had refused. Damrosch must have known all this. He had friends in the orchestra, and in a cooperative society, in which the members are paid by sharing the profits, there are no secrets. Damrosch had gambled on his skill and the new repertory to turn the financial tide, and he had lost.

Soon after the April concert, Thomas was elected conductor for the next year, and without conditions. He continued also with his own orchestra and its Symphony Concerts, but of course the competition over dates, repertory and personnel at once eased. By the end of the year the Philharmonic's ticket receipts had soared from $8291 under Damrosch to $12,499 under Thomas, and the member's annual dividend rose from $18 to $82. With justice, Thomas could savor the triumph as personal. He was not only better known to the public; he had its confidence.[17]

Damrosch's response was to form his own orchestra for 1877–78 and with a series of ten Saturday Symphony Matinees at Steinway Hall to challenge Thomas and the Philharmonic directly. As New York in these years had an estimated reservoir of two or three hundred first-class musicians, presumably he had no trouble recruiting players. But where did he find the money to hire them? And the hall? And the advertisements? He must have had backers, but who they were is not known. Some clues conceivably may be found, however, in an event the following year that originated, in part, in this Damrosch Orchestra.

The challenge to Thomas and the Philharmonic was as direct as Damrosch could make it, not only in dates — many of the Damrosch matinees preceded only by hours the Thomas evenings in the same hall — but also in the repertory. Though Damrosch believed that New York was large enough to support two major conductors, and though in the past he had been conciliatory toward Thomas, in this year he attacked head on, with the most notorious skirmish taking place over the American première of Brahms's Symphony No. 1.

Gustav Schirmer had received from Simrock, Brahms's publisher in

Leipzig, a single set of the orchestral parts, and these were promised, he told Damrosch, to Thomas. That seemed to end the matter, except that one day Damrosch mentioned his disappointment to Mrs. James Nielson, who was studying orchestration with him. She was a woman of considerable wealth whose husband .was a gentleman farmer in New Brunswick, and it was at the Nielson farm that Damrosch sometimes had left Frank and Walter for the day while he taught at the New Brunswick Conservatory.

Soon after Mrs. Nielson's lesson Damrosch received from her a package containing a conductor's score of the symphony. Her accompanying note offered no explanation of how she had obtained it, merely her compliments. That was on Thursday. Damrosch tore the score in three, and copyists were able, by working day and night, to have the individual parts ready for the orchestra's rehearsal on Monday. And at the Saturday matinee on December 15, 1877, Damrosch gave the symphony its American première.

Six days later Thomas played it in Brooklyn with the Brooklyn Philharmonic and on the following night in New York with the New York Philharmonic. He had expected the latter performance to be the symphony's second. In fact, it was the fourth, for that afternoon Damrosch had repeated it in his Steinway Hall series.

The incident sharpened the bitterness of Thomas and of both conductors' partisans. Damrosch, though delighting in his triumph, seemed to continue to feel that New York was big enough for them both. But from that time on, as the bitterness on each side festered, most of his family, and especially the usually soft-spoken Tante, became passionately anti-Thomas.

How did Mrs. Nielson obtain her copy of the conductor's score? Frank and Walter tell different stories. According to Walter, Mrs. Nielson "went quietly down to Schirmer's" and bought it from an unwary clerk. Frank's explanation is perhaps more likely in that it absolves Schirmer of sloppiness in protecting an important première: Mrs. Nielson, as a student of orchestration, had a standing order with Simrock for a copy of every new important work. She probably, therefore, received her copy in the same mail that had brought the parts to Schirmer. Thomas' supporters, however, were not inclined to believe simple explanations and hotly proclaimed impure motives, forgetting that the previous year Thomas had anticipated by a day Damrosch's scheduled New York première of Saint-Saëns's Piano Concerto No. 2.[18]

The success of the Damrosch Orchestra may have contributed to Thomas' decision the following year to abandon New York. For several years he had conducted the May Festival in Cincinnati, and now, after talks with some of that city's leading citizens, he accepted the post of director at the Cincinnati College of Music, with the expectation of founding a permanent orchestra in the city to make year-round use of the festival's new hall. His sudden departure left the Philharmonic without a conductor, and its members elected Adolf Neuendorff, primarily a theater conductor, over Damrosch, 46 to 29. It is unlikely that Damrosch was disappointed; probably he was already at work establishing the Damrosch Orchestra on a permanent basis.

In October 1878 was born the Symphony Society of New York, whose orchestra, the New York Symphony, was the former Damrosch Orchestra. In the minutes of the new society's proceedings its fortunes and function were tied directly to Thomas: "The general desire for a continuance of the Symphony Concerts in this City, an interruption of which was threatened by the departure of Mr. Theodore Thomas for the City of Cincinnati, induces several music loving gentlemen to form a preliminary organization . . ."[19] With the exceptions of Charles C. Dodge and Benjamin K. Phelps, the gentlemen were not outstanding figures in the city's musical or social life; most, like Morris Reno, elected the orchestra's corresponding secretary, had some connection with the Oratorio Society.

It was through Damrosch, however, that they had access to important support, for a week later the society's minutes noted: "To secure the patronage of the patrons of the Theodore Thomas Symphony Concerts Steinway Hall was secured for the dates previously selected by Mr. Thomas for his expected concerts. Our efforts met with great encouragement in the liberality of Mr. [Theodore] Steinway, who granted the use of the Hall free of expense to us."[20] Steinway, though a friend of Thomas', also admired Damrosch, and without question this gift — the hall for six concerts, six public rehearsals and additional rehearsal time — provided the society with the breath of life.

It seems that important music lovers in the city, like Steinway, perhaps the Schirmers and others, were angered by Thomas' competition with the Philharmonic and by his acceptance and subsequent desertion of its chief post; they decided, when the Philharmonic would not elect Damrosch its conductor, to back him in creating a new orchestra. Thomas and the Philharmonic Society would be taught a lesson: New York was going to have good music, if not with them, then without them.[21]

There were other gifts. August Wilhelmj, a violinist of the most majestic presence who also had served as concertmaster at the Bayreuth Festival in 1876, opened the season on November 9 with a Concerto in A, composed for him by Joachim Raff, and out of friendship for Damrosch remitted half his fee, or $250. Damrosch as conductor received only $100 a concert, including rehearsals, about half the current rate; presumably Dodge, a rich man, and other members of the society made gifts, though these were not recorded. And the *New York Times* contributed an editorial in April stating that Damrosch was "the most highly-qualified musician we have in this country." [22] At the season's end, after all expenses were paid, the society had a balance of $28.99 and announced that it would continue.

The Philharmonic, meanwhile, had suffered a season under Adolf Neuendorff, in which the ticket receipts sank even lower than they had two years earlier under Damrosch. The society's members, hearing that Thomas was unhappy in Cincinnati, persuaded him to commute between the cities in order to lead their concerts in the following season, 1879–80. But the time consumed in travel, as well as his commitments in Cincinnati that year, prevented him from resuming his own Symphony Concerts in New York. That gap of two years, during which Thomas conducted only twelve concerts in the city, allowed the New York Symphony to establish itself.

It continued for fifty years, during which it had only two permanent conductors, Leopold and Walter Damrosch. Its fortunes varied, but at times it eclipsed all competitors in daring and importance. And it ended its independent existence, in 1928, only by merging its society and orchestra with those of the Philharmonic to form the present Philharmonic-Symphony Society of New York, the parent organization of today's New York Philharmonic.

CHAPTER 5

Rise of the conductor. Frank leaves New York for Denver. Leopold's first great success, The Damnation of Faust. *The Damrosch Festival of 1881. Equality with Theodore Thomas.*

THE SURVIVAL of Damrosch's New York Symphony despite competition from the Philharmonic under Thomas showed that the audience in New York for serious orchestral music had grown greatly over the last twenty years — no doubt largely because of Thomas. The competition of the two orchestras and their conductors, since Thomas continued with the Philharmonic through 1890–91, also brought the conducting styles of the two men into sharp contrast. And the public controversy that arose over their merits and defects was something new in music: appraisal of the conductor as interpreter.

Probably both Damrosch and Thomas would have said — as conductors still say — that they tried merely to reproduce the composer's intent; audiences, nevertheless, recognized a real difference in their interpretations. In the past a conductor's job had been primarily to see that the notes were properly played, entrances correctly made and dynamic markings observed. Bergmann had begun to make of it something more, and it now began to include subtle variations in rhythm and dynamics. In this respect Damrosch was more varied and adventurous than Thomas, who seemed to aim at technical proficiency. A Thomas interpretation was apt to be clean in execution but somewhat rigid in tempo and shading; one by Damrosch, more intense, with many slight gradations in tempo and shading.

Sam Franko, an American-born, German-trained violinist, who played often under both men, in retrospect wrote:

> There could scarcely be a greater contrast than the personalities of Thomas and Damrosch: Damrosch, small and lively, didactic and talka-

tive, given to enthusiasms, free and daring in his conceptions — Semitic; Thomas, much taller, practical and matter of fact, taciturn, unimaginative, literal-minded — Nordic-Germanic. Dr. Damrosch was not so popular with his orchestra as Theodore Thomas was with his. He simply was not one of them. He talked over their heads. The musicians were easily disposed to criticize him, while they stood in awe of Thomas. At rehearsals Damrosch was hypercritical, making the orchestra nervous. When the time came for the actual performance, he was often the first to change his own previous instructions.[1]

Yet in performance, especially in the "modern" repertory — Berlioz, Wagner, Brahms — Damrosch, with his intensity and slight variations in rhythm and shading, seemed to excel. In the Schirmer family the tradition is that in the romantic repertory he was superior to Thomas; in the Naumburg family, that he was superior only in choral work and opera. But to some extent opinion seems to have divided by age, with a majority of the older preferring Thomas, and of the younger, Damrosch.[2]

Along with this new focus on the conductor as an interpreter there came a new kind of newspaper criticism, which often seemed inaccurate at best, and at worst, malicious. On March 17, 1880, for example, Damrosch led the Oratorio Society in a performance of Bach's *St. Matthew Passion.* Edwin T. Rice, a historian of music in the city, thought the performance "noble" and one that enhanced Damrosch's "standing as a musician." Most newspapers agreed, and the *Times* praised in particular the choral work. One, however, stated that "several numbers were entirely spoiled by confusion among the performers, and the whole work was sadly deficient in shading." In sum, a declaration of the conductor's incompetence.[3]

Others, on occasion, were still harsher, and at least one reporter allegedly sneered at Damrosch as a "Germanized Hebrew." Anti-Semitism was new to Damrosch. It was not a cause of his leaving Germany. There, in the von Heimburg family and among his musical friends, Wagner excepted, it seems not to have existed. Happily, too, there is no evidence that Thomas or his close associates shared it or had any part in such slurs.[4]

Nevertheless, the new style of newspaper criticism, increasingly personal and aggressive, shook Damrosch and his family. In particular, the usually mild Tante often was turned by an apparent injustice into an Electra exhorting Frank and Walter to avenge their father — though just how was lost in the swirl of emotion. Yet the passion of the controversy, both in public and at home, was felt deeply by the children, and in the case of the eldest, Frank, had a part in his decision to give up music.

★

Throughout the early years of the decade Frank's interest in music had quickened to a point where he had begun to discover his personality. The excitement of the Bayreuth Festival had revealed to him the strength of his German roots, buried but not severed by immigration. At the same time, though he was stirred deeply by Wagner's operas, especially by the Teutonic mythology, which Wagner had rescued from near-oblivion, he had begun to realize that opera appealed to him less than lieder and choral-singing. And among pianists, he discovered in the winter of 1875–76, he preferred von Bülow to Rubinstein.

Von Bülow was a curious mixture of showoff, pedant and serious musician. In a chamber recital that winter with Leopold Damrosch, in which they were to play Beethoven's *Kreutzer Sonata,* he suggested just before going onstage that they play it by heart.

"With pleasure," said Damrosch and laid down his music.

"No, no," said von Bülow; "take it onstage with you."

After they had taken their places, he ostentatiously rose, took Damrosch's music from the stand and with his own laid it under the piano.

Neatly done — except that, according to Walter, he lost his place in the last movement, and Damrosch had to improvise for a few bars until the thread was found. Yet despite such antics, which usually expressed contempt for the audience or some other performer, there was hardly anywhere a more serious musician.

During that season he gave many solo recitals in New York, playing much Beethoven and Brahms, and Frank apparently went to all of them, seeing through the occasional exhibitionism to the scholarly musician. Von Bülow's style was less vivid, less colorful than Rubinstein's, and according to some critics lacked verve and spontaneity. But he had an unusual understanding of structure and an extraordinary ability to project it. Those who liked his playing talked of his "passionate intellectuality"; those who did not, of his pedantry. In fact, he created the "German school" of playing Beethoven, and Frank found it congenial. Excited, he began to practice furiously, intending to become a concert pianist.[5]

The following summer he went as always to stay with the Eidlitz family, but that year, because Otto's elder brother Alfred had died, the distressed parents did not return to familiar Dobbs Ferry but took rooms at a hotel in Atlantic Highlands, on the New Jersey shore. And there one day the boys had a conversation.

Because of his brother's death Otto had decided to give up medicine and take Alfred's place in the Eidlitz construction business.

"I'm going to be a musician," Frank observed, "but you will become a millionaire."

"If I do," said Otto, "I'll give you $5000."

Frank laughed, but Otto was serious. "I'm going to put it in writing, and your mother can witness it."

Years later, when Frank was raising money for his Musical Art Society, Otto suddenly announced, "I'm going to pay off my note."

Remembering, Frank said, "But I've long since lost it."

"That makes no difference."

Frank, in telling the story, continued: "Under his jesting tone there was some of that earnestness of the small boy I had known. When we had passed our sixtieth birthdays he was, with me, as boyish as ever; as boyish and as reliable, always the same; always ready when needed." But Frank, as others often testified, could have been describing himself.[6]

His desire to become a musician soon weakened, however, for reasons that seem partly to do with himself and partly with his family. As the eldest child he was more aware of death than the others. Though he had no memory of Richard, the brother between himself and Walter, he could recall clearly the brief lives of Ernst and Hans, born between Marie and Clara.[7] Now there was Otto's brother Alfred. What if his own father died? Who would support his mother and three sisters?

The family lived well, but saved nothing and required the earnings of three musicians to support it. Tante was now a soloist at St. Patrick's Cathedral, receiving $600 a year, which she increased by private lessons; his mother earned less, but something; and his father, from all sources, perhaps $5000 a year. But occasionally he was cheated by managers, and at such times the family's meals were silent and sad. Then, as Clara recalled, "We children at the foot of the table, not really understanding the trouble, would feel ready to cry with subconscious misery." Unfortunately for Damrosch, the economics of music at the time seemed to ensure that piano manufacturers, music dealers, publishers and touring virtuosos made money. Conductors, doubling often as impresarios, did not. Even Thomas was constantly out of funds and turned to backers, principally to Steinway.[8]

In Breslau, Frank had seen his father close to despair over finances, and he could see the cost of success in New York. Leopold, slight in figure, intense in spirit, consuming nervous energy, hurried through the day from one appointment to another, dealing constantly with crises. At night he frequently came home exhausted, often only to change his clothes for a performance. His hair was turning white; he suffered at times from depression; he was unable to put any savings aside; and he soon would be fifty.

To Frank, it seemed clear that the son destined to be his father's right hand in music was Walter. It was not that Walter could play a Beethoven sonata better than Frank, though perhaps he could; it was two qualities that Walter had in abundance from birth — his showmanship and his geniality.

If Walter saw a play, he had to re-enact it for the family. After seeing the Hanlon Brothers, a troupe of acrobats, he rushed home to give an entire performance. Even the simplest story by its end would have him on his feet, declaiming with gestures. He could not help himself. He was born to be on the stage, on the podium, a public figure.

Along with his showmanship went an extraordinary geniality. Though Walter in life had many disappointments, he was never depressed for long. Any setback, however severe, soon was surmounted by returning good spirits. Tante, recalling how in Breslau she had sewn his knicker-bockers and Russian blouses, once said: "He looked especially pretty in these suits, and when we walked in the streets, he always used to dance along."[9]

Emotionally, Walter danced through life, and had the gift of setting others to dance with him. Unlike Frank and his father, he had no partic-ular friends; he was a friend to everyone. In part he could be of greater help to his father than Frank because his spirit was complementary rather than similar.

But the geniality and showmanship also could be tiresome, and part of what people later admired in Frank was that he never said so. Even when Walter had become *the* Damrosch for most of the country and Frank's solid achievements in music were partially eclipsed by Walter's more resplendent works, no one ever heard a word of rivalry or regret from Frank. Friends might debate whether he had the envious thought and smothered it, or simply never had the thought; but most, like his sister Ellie, believed it to be the latter, and counted him a most rare spirit.[10]

Perhaps, too, in a more personal area Frank felt that Walter, not he, was destiny's child. Walter gave promise of becoming flamboyantly handsome, a promise fulfilled as he matured. He displayed his mother's Saxon heritage in a tall, robust figure, regular features, fair complexion and pink cheeks, all surmounted by a magnificent mane of blond-red hair. People inevitably dubbed him "the Young Siegfried" and, charmed by a smile that would become famous, flocked to him.

Frank, by contrast, looked unimportant. He was his father's child: a slight figure, swarthy complexion, dark hair and dark eyes. In youth, the features were out of proportion: the eyes, too large and staring, the ears and nose protruding, and the neck scrawny. In old age, when the eyes, dark and compassionate, were set off by white hair and a neatly trimmed white beard, he was better-looking than Walter, whose hair thinned and stomach swelled. But at the start Walter had, as a facet of his showman-ship, the benefits of beauty.

In the fall of 1877 Frank decided not to return to City College, where he had completed his sophomore year,[11] but to take a job. He disliked the public controversy surrounding his father and Thomas, hated the tension it put into the family's life and concluded that if the New York musical world could not stretch enough to contain both his father and Thomas, it certainly never could absorb in addition Walter and himself. And Walter, he thought, was the more talented. Therefore, he would go into business and help to support the family. What his father, who believed strongly in education and in music, thought about this decision is not recorded.

Frank's first job, apprentice to a cabinetmaker, was arranged for him by Theodore Steinway with the idea that Frank someday might enter the Steinway piano firm. But the cabinetmaker's work day was ten hours, the work week six days, and the shop so far distant that Frank had to leave the house at 6:00 A.M. and did not return until seven or seven-thirty, in time only to eat his dinner alone — the family ate at six — and fall into bed, exhausted. Leopold, with growing distress, watched his son endure this regime, and after several months ordered him to quit. Such parental commands were rare with Leopold, and presumably he explained his reasons to Steinway.

Frank worked next as an office boy, at $2.50 a week, in the jobbing house of Foot & Knevals. He wrapped parcels, walked back and forth to the post office and sometimes was sent to the wharves, where ships unloaded cargoes of tea and syrup consigned to the firm. After many months, his weekly pay had risen to $4.00, and he proposed to his mother — not to his father — that he contribute to the family's support. Helene treated the proposal seriously, but her refusal, though kind, discouraged Frank. He seemed unable to accomplish anything.

Then one evening early in June 1879, a music-loving businessman, Rudolph Keppler, came to dinner. He had just made a tour of the West to scout for business opportunities, and was particularly enthusiastic about Colorado, where four years earlier silver had been discovered. A few days later at breakfast Frank announced quietly that he would go to Denver; there he should be able at least to support himself. Helene protested; Leopold, whatever his private thoughts, said only that the idea seemed sensible.[12]

Frank's birthday, of which the family invariably made a festival, was on June 22 and because of the season always was celebrated with cherries and roses. This year, because he would be leaving soon after for Denver, with his mother's permission he enlarged the family party to include, as a farewell gesture, his closest male friends. Unknown to him, however, Helene asked an equal number of girls to come in after dinner and secretly prepared her upstairs sitting room, which had a piano, for dancing, for in Germany on almost every occasion everyone danced, old and young. So, as the young men started on cigars and coffee, suddenly in trooped the young ladies, singing from *Pinafore*, "And we are his sisters and his cousins and his aunts!"

Leopold had his violin ready and, like the Pied Piper of Hamelin, led them round the table, out into the hall, up the stairs and into the sitting room. The rugs had been rolled back, the walls garlanded with roses, and a table spread with sandwiches, cakes and May wine. They danced until they could dance no more, and then Leopold led them downstairs to his study, where on the piano he improvised musical portraits for them to guess. One was of a girl, Hetty Mosenthal, whose Uncle Joseph was a well-known violinist, composer and choral conductor. Frank had met her through Otto and evidently was attracted by her brown curls and amiable manner. As Leopold at the piano improvised a gracious theme, *molto amabile,* everyone cried, "That's Hetty!" Then Walter, replacing his father, had an equal success with a student of kindergarten methods who talked incessantly about her work: he ran his fingers all over the keyboard but constantly returned to the same short, pedantic tune.[13]

But all too soon the day came for Frank's departure. He refused his father's offer of $300, intending to rely entirely on his savings of $25. Leopold, though, insisted that he take an additional $100; there was, after all, no assurance of any job in Denver. But Frank was not easily persuaded, and he could appeal to the story of his father's break with his family.

Only Leopold went with Frank to the station; the others said their good-bys at home. For all it was a sad day, though the two youngest, Clara and Ellie, were as much excited as saddened by the thought of Frank in the Wild West. For Helene there were no compensations: the family, which had been so close, was beginning to part.[14]

The following winter, in Steinway Hall, on February 12, 1880, with a production of Berlioz's concert opera *The Damnation of Faust,* Leopold Damrosch had the kind of success that vindicates all struggles. Although the performance was billed and reviewed as "the first time in America," in fact Thomas, on tour with his orchestra, had been able to sneak in the première in Boston two weeks earlier. But it was Damrosch's production of the work in New York that caught the public's fancy, and to such an extent that he was able to repeat it five times in the spring and thrice in December.

The work is huge, both in its imaginative scope and in the forces it can use. Its subject, as Faust is tempted by the devil to love Marguerite and signs away his soul, traverses the universe. In the final scenes Faust and the devil on two black mares gallop furiously to the abyss, fall in and are greeted in hell by a chorus of demons shouting gibberish; immediately afterward, Marguerite, purged of carnality, is welcomed by the seraphim to heaven. The work is filled with such contrasts — ideal for Damrosch's romantic conducting — and its scenes, often dramatically shifted on the devil's command, frequently are enacted before crowds represented by the chorus, which sings in almost every style: peasants making merry, an Easter hymn, students carousing, sylphs and will-o'-the-wisps weaving spells, soldiers on the march, angelic choirs and demonic hosts.

For his orchestra Damrosch used the New York Symphony, and to give Walter experience had him play at the last desk of the second violins. For the soloists he hired the best of the day, and for the chorus used the Oratorio Society, now four hundred voices, supplemented by the Arion's Male Chorus. Perhaps, too, the fact that he presented the work in English contributed to its appeal, but whatever the reasons, the work itself and its production were a sensational success. All New York talked favorably of Damrosch; his fame, already great among Germans throughout the country, now spread to non-Germans in other cities, and he was invited to take the production to Philadelphia.[15]

As the success of *The Damnation of Faust* burgeoned in the spring of 1880, Morris Reno suggested a May Festival for the coming year, and Damrosch began to plan one of five days and seven concerts, most with major choral works. For the hall he suggested the new Seventh Regiment Armory at Park Avenue and Sixty-sixth Street, which would seat ten thousand even after the construction of a special stage and sounding board. To fill the enormous cavern with sufficient sound he proposed to use the New York Symphony and Oratorio Society merely as nuclei and to expand the orchestra from a hundred to two hundred and fifty, and the chorus from four hundred to twelve hundred. Even allowing for the enthusiasm of his admirers in those groups, it says much about his reputation as an executive as well as musician that he was able to find backing for such an adventure — for New York, though it had seen some large festivals, especially of German choral groups, had never seen a single organization attempt such a varied repertory with such large forces, all concentrated in a single week. Nevertheless, under the leadership of a Music Festival Association, composed chiefly of directors of the Symphony and Oratorio societies, and with Reno as manager, the necessary money soon was in hand.

In several respects the festival would mark the arrival of Walter on the New York scene as a professional musician. He had made his debut as an amateur at the age of fourteen, at an Arion Summer Night Festival at Jones Wood, a park on the East River at Seventieth Street. His father had prepared Schubert's operetta *Der Hausliche Krieg,* based distantly on Aristophanes' *Lysistrata,* in which there is a *March of the Crusaders,* punctuated at its climax by a clash of cymbals. As Walter later described the event, though the rehearsals went off with clanging success, "at the performance, alas, a great nervousness fell upon me and as the march proceeded and came nearer and nearer the crucial moment, my hand seemed paralyzed, and when my father's flashing eye indicated to me that the moment had come, I simply could not seem to lift the cymbals, which suddenly weighed like a hundred tons. The march went on . . ." But without Walter, who slunk into the dark, his career as a cymbalist in ruins.[16]

Two years later, as a pianist, he began to assist his father at rehearsals of the Oratorio Society, and in the spring of 1878, still only sixteen, he had what seems to have been his first independent, fully professional engagement. The concert manager Maurice Strakosch had arranged a Southern tour for a group of artists, among whom was the violinist August Wilhelmj. Shortly before the opening concert, in Washington, Wilhelmj's accompanist fell ill, and Strakosch, with Wilhelmj's approval, asked Leopold for Walter, whose skill and maturity seemed adequate. In fact, Walter would develop into an excellent accompanist. Naturally, he was wild with delight, as much for the adventure as for the $100 a week and railway expenses, and his eagerness prevailed over his father's fears.[17] Probably his work for the May Festival earned him less, but it was far more demanding and began a full year in advance.

The principal choral works that Leopold scheduled for the festival were Handel's *Dettingen Te Deum* and *Messiah*, Rubinstein's oratorio *Tower of Babel* in its New York première, the Act III Chorale from Wagner's *Die Meistersinger*, Beethoven's Symphony No. 9, and, most important, the American première of Berlioz's *Requiem*. The last, however, presented a problem, in that no piano score existed for use in rehearsals. So Leopold assigned its creation to Walter and sent him to a summer language school housed in Amherst College; he could study French and Latin in the mornings and work every afternoon on the score.

One day in May 1880, therefore, Walter arrived in Amherst "armed with a grand piano, reams of music paper, and the orchestral score" of the *Requiem*. He rented a bedroom "from a farmer on the main street" and installed the piano in the parlor, "of which I had the entire use for four hours a day." He sent the music section by section to his father for correction, but it soon became clear that Walter had a remarkable gift for reproducing on the piano a complicated orchestral score, a gift that in the future would help to make his lecture-recitals on Beethoven and Wagner outstanding.[18]

Returning to New York in September, he was given by his father for rehearsal two of the six sections into which Leopold had divided the chorus of twelve hundred. Section A was the four-hundred-member Oratorio Society, which Leopold rehearsed himself; B, a group of two hundred in Manhattan formed for the festival and rehearsed by Walter;

C, the three-hundred-member Harmonic Society of Newark, New Jersey, rehearsed jointly by Walter and Henry Fiegl; D, a group in Brooklyn, led by August Cortada, a pupil of Damrosch and his assistant at the Oratorio Society; and E and F, groups in Jersey City and Nyack, New York, led by local leaders. To these, which were to sing in the four evening concerts, were added under still other leaders a boys' chorus of two hundred and fifty combined from church choirs and a girls' chorus of twelve hundred from Normal College (a teachers' college, later renamed Hunter College). The last two groups would sing in one of the three matinees, for which Leopold had scheduled a fifteenth-century hymn, *Alla Trinità,* the *Chorus of the Houris* from Schumann's *Das Paradies und die Peri,* and the introductory choruses from Act II of Wagner's *Rienzi.* Throughout the fall the sections rehearsed separately, with Leopold visiting each in turn. In January he began to bring them together for mass rehearsals, which he conducted at Cooper Union Hall.[19]

There was also, of course, the enlarged orchestra to rehearse, first in sections and then together. The Berlioz *Requiem* is unique in requiring sixteen kettledrums for the *Tuba Mirum* passage, which depicts the Call to Last Judgment, and when all the drums were brought together for the first time in rehearsal, in the foyer of the Academy of Music, the vibrations in the small space were so tremendous that, in Walter's description, "one by one the orchestra men arose and a murmur began which grew and grew and finally relieved itself in a loud shout of enthusiasm."[20] Edwin Rice, who sang in the performance, recalled that in the crescendo of the *Tuba Mirum,* at the entry of the chorus he suddenly had the sensation "of being suspended in an ocean of sound and precipitated into a musical Day of Judgment." In retrospect, however, he wondered "whether the musical substance was commensurate with the volume of sound," a doubt that still attaches to the work.[21]

For the Damrosch family, "the Great Music Festival," as the *New York Times* called it, was all-engrossing.[22] Helene, Tante and little Marie sang with the Oratorio Society; Clara and Ellie went to all the performances and most of the rehearsals; Walter was the festival's organist — and in the months of rehearsal and crises he and his father exhausted themselves. In the final days Walter's voice failed, causing him for two months to live mute. Only Frank, in Denver, missed it.[23]

Some critics, lamenting that music was lost in such a huge space as the armory, complained of the festival's "Hippodrome" aspects and declared forcefully that *Messiah,* for example, was not well served by such swollen forces.[24] And indeed, in another hundred years scholars and some performers would argue that, ideally, to match Handel's forces at a performance he supervised in London in 1754, the orchestra should be reduced to about thirty-eight and the voices to forty, with boys' voices replacing women's in the alto and soprano sections. But the festival's giantism was a facet of romantic fervor, suited to the taste of the time.

In most respects it was declared an astonishing success, and Damrosch was showered with approving headlines, wreaths and speeches. Some consequences were immediate. The Newark Harmonic Society, having worked with Walter, elected him its musical director, and from Philadelphia came an invitation to Leopold to bring over the New York Symphony and Oratorio Society to present the local première of Rubinstein's *Tower of Babel*. The success of *The Damnation of Faust* was confirmed.

Meanwhile Thomas and his backers, fearful of being put in the shade, announced — "with most unseemly haste and more than questionable taste," according to *Dwight's Journal*[25] — that the following year they would mount an even bigger May Festival. And for it they recruited an orchestra of three hundred and a chorus of three thousand, with groups coming from as far as Baltimore and Reading, Pennsylvania. This festival, too, was a success, and though Thomas in his autobiography wrote of it at length, he managed to omit, even in a footnote, any reference to the Damrosch Festival or to Damrosch personally. But in the real world he could not so easily obliterate his rival. The fact was: Damrosch with his Oratorio Society, New York Symphony and occasional festival performance had won the public's confidence; and now, leadership in the country's musical life, French and Italian opera aside, was divided between Thomas and Damrosch, as equals.

CHAPTER 6

Chamber music at home. Clara. Leopold's pupils. Frank in Denver. Leopold on tour, 1883. Twenty-fifth wedding anniversary.

MUSICIANS ARE UNIQUE among artists in that for their private pleasure they still pursue their public employment, gathering often in small groups in homes or studios to make music simply for the joy of it. In the Damrosch family, these occasions usually occurred on Sunday afternoons, when one or two artists would come by to play with Leopold; more was unusual, for to find four players of equal skill was not easy, and mostly what the children heard were piano-violin sonatas or piano trios, not string quartets. But then one year a quartet did gather regularly, and the experience of it apparently was crucial in the life of Clara.[1] One day before the great May Festival, the violinist Sam Franko, recently returned from Germany, called on Damrosch to deliver greetings from artists abroad, and in the course of their conversation asked whether his host often played quartets.

"Oh, if you only knew," said Damrosch, "how hard it is to assemble four musicians in New York who want to play merely for the fun of it!"

Franko offered to find a congenial violist and cellist, and before long a quartet was formed to play for pleasure: Damrosch, first violin; Franko, second; Charles Martin Loeffler, though only twenty and primarily a violinist, viola; and Emil Schenk, of the New York Symphony, cello. Throughout the winter of 1881–82 the four gathered every Sunday afternoon at the Damrosch house and played through the quartet literature. "I count these musical afternoons," Franko wrote later, "among the most enjoyable events of my New York life."[2]

Loeffler, in particular, became a friend of the family. Only a year older than Walter, he had the same birthday. And by all reports, Loeffler, who later became a successful composer, was a young man of extraordinary charm. When he left the next fall to take the position of second concert-master with the Boston Symphony Orchestra, then beginning its second season, his departure was keenly felt, and Clara, a precocious thirteen, corresponded with him.[3]

The musical afternoons made a deep impression on all the family, especially on Clara, who found in chamber works the kind of music she liked best. In later life, trying to explain her preference, she wrote, "The creative beauty and mastery of the great composers fulfilled my religious needs" — which was true of all the family. "No sermon," she continued, "can be worthier of God or realize the inner truth better than the immortal works of Bach or the exquisite purity of Mozart." She felt she could appreciate the emotional and imaginative appeal of Wagner but could "not ally his music with the innermost soul."[4] Evidently, to her ear the large, lush sound of a full, romantic orchestra lacked the purity of the smaller groups, in which the musical lines of the individual instruments were neither smothered nor blended. The ineffable, for her, was to be reached not by a shout and a great wash of sound but through still, small voices speaking with clarity and timbre.

At a more human level, starting with Loeffler, who was only nine years her senior and so charming, Clara developed a series of half-concealed romantic attachments to violinists that eventually culminated in marriage to David Mannes, with whom she formed a piano-violin duo. These afternoons of chamber music seem to have been the loom through which the threads of her life, artistic, religious and psychological, were gathered into a fabric and pattern. There, in the position of authority as first violin, was her revered, white-haired father; beside him, equal but subordinate as the violist, was the attractive young man; and binding all together was the music that satisfied her deepest needs.

For the most part Damrosch's private pupils were amateurs, who studied without thought of public performance. Among the minority, however, were two who made careers in music: Sidney Lanier, the poet, flutist and lecturer, and Geraldine Morgan, a violinist.

Lanier, a Georgian, was started toward a career in music when the Civil War began, and he entered the Confederate Army. Four months in the Federal prison at Point Lookout, Maryland, broke his health, and his hold on life thereafter constantly was threatened by consumption. In 1874 he came to New York to study the flute, and a friend made an appointment for him with Damrosch. Immediately after the audition, on October 29, Lanier wrote to his wife:

Today I played for the great Dr. Damrosch, and won him. I sang the "Wind-Song" to him. When I finished he came and shook my hand, and said it was done like an artist; that it was wonderful, in view of my education; and that he was greatly astonished and pleased with the poetry of the piece and the enthusiasm of its rendering. He then closed the door on his next pupil, and kept him waiting in the front parlor a half hour, while giving me a long talk. I had told him that I wished to pursue music. He said: "Do you know what that means? It means a great deal of work, it means a thousand sacrifices. It is very hazardous."

I replied, I knew all that; but it was not a matter of mere preference, it was a spiritual necessity, I must be a musician, I could not help it.

This seemed to please him: and he went on to speak as no other musician here could speak, of many things. He is the only poet among the craft here: and is a thoroughly cultivated man, in all particulars.[5]

The two men became friends, and throughout that winter Lanier studied flute and music theory with Damrosch. Afterward, he became the first flutist in the Peabody Orchestra in Baltimore and a lecturer on English literature at Johns Hopkins, where he developed interesting connections between music and language. Perhaps his most famous apothegm, which appears in his essay "Bacon and Beethoven," is "Let us abandon the idea that music is language and substitute the converse idea that language is music."

Geraldine Morgan started younger and studied longer with Damrosch and soon displayed a remarkable talent for the violin. On his urging her mother took her to Leipzig, and in his personal English he wrote to her there, on January 6, 1882:

> So, my dear Geraldine, you are thus well established in old Leipzig! I was very happy to receive your lovely letter and the New Year's card after-wards. I was afraid you would forget me entirely.
>
> Now you have it just as nice, as I supposed you would have it. Five lessons every week! But then, I must expect now great things from you, (and I do)! You ought to become the female Violin-Star of this generation!
>
> How do you like the Leipziger "Brödchen" and the "Blümchen Kaffee"?* After all it is nice in Germany, is it not? and much good music — of course sometimes bad one too!
>
> My own occupation here is as ever, my concerts very successful, and my spirits bright. Walter, my second son, has recently made his debut as pianist and conductor in Newark with his "Harmonic Society." He played the Choral Fantasie by Beethoven and conducted the Tower of Babel — I was proud of him.
>
> All the other members of my family are well and busy — each in his or her own way. Our Christmas tree was beautiful (I hope you had one too!) but there was no snow on earth! Since that time a little snow has appeared, but it melted soon away, and just now while I am writing this, it pours

---

*Leipziger *Brödchen* are the medium-sized hard rolls common in Saxony, and *Blümchen* *Kaffe* is a coffee so weak that one can see the little flowers (*Blümchen*) painted on the inside bottom of the cup.

down in torrents of rain! Think of that, on the 6th of January! I wish I was with you today, you surely had bright sunshine and perhaps some skating on the Pleisse!

Now, dear Geraldine, I think often of you and wish you all happiness in the world. If you are not *too* busy, let me hear once in a while, what you are doing and remember kindly

Your

always sincerely

Leopold Damrosch

My best regards to your dear Mama, who, I hope, is satisfied with her life in Leipzig.[6]

His "dear Geraldine" did not become the female Violin-Star of her generation *prima assoluta,* for she had to share that position with her class-mate at Leipzig, Maud Powell. But she had an international career and made her American debut on February 5, 1892, when she presented the New York première of Max Bruch's Concerto No. 3. The orchestra then was the New York Symphony, and the conductor, her old teacher's second son, Walter.

In Denver, meanwhile, Damrosch's eldest son, Frank, slowly was finding his way into a congenial line of work. The first year there had not been easy. He had been unable to find a job, had fallen ill, and had depleted his small hoard to $3.00 before being hired as a temporary clerk in a hat shop. His instructions, reflecting local prejudice, were simple: Chinamen's hats were kept in a special box and sold for a dollar; gamblers had unlimited credit; clergymen had to pay cash.[7]

In a letter at this time to his friend Ed Wiener he talked blithely of " 'the auld countree' (as I may call N.Y. now)," but worry revealed itself in uncharacteristic slang and bravado: at the job's end he would "run short of rocks very soon," and "Well, cheek and courage will go a great ways." Then suddenly his true self broke through: "I tell you, Ed, there is nothing like being alone in a strange place, if you want to *learn.* You are responsible for everything you do and say and have to provide your own bread and butter." From hats he shifted to a job with a wholesale liquor firm.[8]

Both the senior and junior partners were Jews: the older man, uncouth and surly; the younger, sensitive and kind. The latter took Frank to Temple Emmanuel and introduced him to the members, and they, too, were kind. But as Christmas approached, Frank felt more and more lonely.

His mother had written that a Christmas box was on the way and should arrive well in time. But on Christmas Eve, when Frank checked at the express office, the clerk showed him a roomful of parcels that would not be sorted and delivered until after the holiday. It was snowing as Frank left, and he felt utterly forlorn.

Recalling a doctor whom he knew slightly, and with the man's children in mind, he bought a tree, with candles, candy and toys to hang on it. Then he took the street car to the doctor's house and rang the bell. The wife opened the door, and as she listened to Frank's explanation, saw the tree and packages, her face grew grave. She was a rabbi's daughter, she explained; her children knew nothing of Christmas. Nonplussed, Frank suggested after a moment's thought that the children might enjoy the tree and presents without attaching to them any religious significance, and for himself the greatest joy on this first Christmas away from home would be in seeing her children's happiness. She invited him in for the evening.

Inevitably Frank's musical ability soon was discovered. At first he played the piano in the boarding house alone; then, violin sonatas with an elderly gentleman to whom he was introduced. One day in the street he passed a house where a violinist was practicing a Beethoven piano trio. "I stood at the gate listening. Finally, unable to restrain myself I rang the bell." A tall, blond man came to the door. "My name is Damrosch," Frank said, "and I merely want to meet someone who knows and plays good music." The man knew of Frank's father, invited Frank in, and "we played a Grieg sonata together immediately." [9]

Soon the Congregational church, unperturbed by Frank's close association with liquor or by his statement that he was not a "professing Christian," hired him as an organist and music director. Later he undertook to build an organ for Temple Emmanuel and afterward became the temple's organist. Then, after having shifted from liquor to real estate, which gave him more free time, in the summer of 1882 he caught typhus, and to recuperate came to New York for a month.

His parents urged him to remain, to take an organist's post until something else came along. But to Frank all the reasons for leaving in 1879 were now stronger. The founding of the Boston Symphony in 1881, by depriving Thomas of one of his most frequented and lucrative cities for touring, had concentrated his activities still more in New York, and to hinder the New York Symphony he was attempting to put under contract all the city's best instrumentalists, whether or not he could use them. By the summer of 1882 it was clear that he had crippled Damrosch's orchestra, particularly in woodwinds, and among the rare oboists he had almost cornered the market, either hiring them himself or arranging for them to be hired in Boston, Philadelphia and elsewhere. He also, by methods and for reasons now obscure, had persuaded Steinway to deny the hall to the New York Symphony, which was forced into a financial crisis by the need to rent the larger and more expensive Academy of

Music. The battle divided Damrosch and Thomas supporters ever more bitterly, and their recriminations spilled into the newspapers.[10] Frank returned to Denver.

There, in the fall of 1882, he invited all the best church singers to meet with him once a week in order to study choral music. There would be no concerts, at least not at the start; he would pay for the hall and music, and donate his services. About eighty-five singers joined him, practically all the solo quartets of Denver's churches, and Frank, in describing the group to his father, wrote: "I feel that I can be useful to you by doing something to fertilize the field of music and in that way prepare the ground for you."[11] The metaphor tickled his father, who replied with encouragement. By the end of the year Frank's group had organized itself as a club, with dues, to relieve him of expense, and thus was born the Denver Chorus Club.

Consciously or not, Frank was following his father's course in founding the Oratorio Society, and at Christmas 1883, Handel's *Messiah* would be presented by Leopold in New York, Walter in Newark, and Frank in Denver. In the next year Frank would cut his last business tie and begin to support himself entirely by work in music. For him, as for Lanier, being a musician was not a matter of preference, but a spiritual necessity, and try as he would, he could not resist it.

In November 1882, partly as an answer to the financial crisis plaguing the New York Symphony, Damrosch took the orchestra on a short tour of the Midwest, invading for the first time what until then had been private pasture for Thomas. For his boldness, he was rewarded with a report in the *New York Times* that the tour had been "a series of triumphs from first to last," with the evidence offered in copious quotations from the local newspapers of Cincinnati, Chicago, Louisville and Toledo.[12]

Spurred by this success, Damrosch and the Symphony Society planned a much longer tour for the orchestra in the spring of 1883, and to make it possible, he once again gambled on the more interesting but less secure artistic opportunity, and on April 3 resigned from the Arion.[13]

For twelve years the society, in its way, had served him well. Though its members never had been willing to extend themselves musically as far as he had wished, yet through their Male Chorus, their operettas and, above all, through their singing competitions with groups from other cities, they had given him the start of a national reputation. Now he, like Bergmann, who also once had been the society's director, inevitably was drawn into a larger musical world.

It was true, as well, of the other family members. The society had been their cocoon in which to adjust to American life. For a time they had gone to all the balls and picnics, relaxing in the German atmosphere and language. At a costume party Frank, his mother and Tante, in Grecian tunics, had frolicked as Wine, Woman and Song; and, as a child, Ellie, in peasant's dress, had come home from an Easter party agog over a large egg, suspended from the ceiling, that had burst open, showering the children with candies. But then Frank had gone to the West; Walter had toured in the South and spent a summer in New England; and Leopold's interests continually shifted further from the Arion. The attention of the women and girls followed, and the Arion dwindled in importance. The parting was amicable: Damrosch on occasion made use of the Male Chorus, and the Arion continued to take pride in him.[14]

His tour began in Cincinnati on May 7, progressed slowly out to Denver, and ended in Springfield, Illinois, on June 8. In all, twenty-eight concerts in sixteen cities in thirty-one days. Considering the difficulties then of travel, the schedule was tight. Predictably, Thomas, himself on tour, raised obstacles where he could, with critics, citizens' committees and, most important, owners of concert halls. With some of these he was able to stipulate that Damrosch could not use the hall before he did, which forced the New York Symphony into expensive rescheduling.[15]

In addition to the difficulties caused by Thomas, the tour was managed badly by a Mr. King, whose incompetence often seemed limitless. Because Helene at the time was on the high seas with Walter for a visit to Germany, Damrosch recounted his woes to Tante, who, as "the summer mother," was keeping house in New York for the three girls. Writing (in German) from Cleveland, he offered "only a *small* example" of King's bungling.

> Last night around midnight we had to leave Toronto. Management had neglected to book sleeping cars, and we all — men, women and baby [of Teresa Carreño, the piano soloist] — had to go to Hamilton, which took two hours, change cars, go to Niagara Falls, one hour, stop there for three, travel for eight more, until finally we arrived here (at two o'clock in the afternoon), utterly exhausted after traveling for fourteen hours. Only to find that management had not booked us hotel rooms! After a half-hour's wait we found some, though the town at the moment is overrun with visitors. Tonight we have to leave at 12:30, to arrive at ten tomorrow morning. And if my musicians don't play brilliantly in Chicago, I really can't hold it against them.[16]

And in Chicago, perhaps because of exhaustion, for the only time on the tour the orchestra played badly, and everyone knew it.

Of all the artists on the tour, Leopold found Carreño, the Venezuelan pianist, the most congenial. She was one of the great virtuosos of the day, but probably was chosen because, though well known, as a woman she could not command as high a fee as a man. "But at least with Carreño," Leopold wrote to Tante, "one can have a half-hour's decent conversation."[17]

For the tour, besides solo encores, Carreño had prepared Liszt's *Hungarian Fantasy* (1852) and Grieg's Concerto in A Minor (1868). In Liszt's lifetime his Hungarian rhapsodies for piano were the most popular of his works, and the *Fantasy* is an extended version for piano and orchestra of *Rhapsody No. 14.* Based on a Hungarian folk song and two Gypsy tunes, all sharply defined and easily grasped, it is a showpiece, and Leopold scheduled it for the smaller towns, where the audiences presumably were less experienced musically. In the cities, Carreño also played Grieg's Concerto, which on this cross-country tour she introduced to most audiences, with great success. In the coming years it became, under her hands, a truly popular piece.

In New York, Tante, who was busy having the house repapered and painted, saw to it that the girls wrote regularly to Leopold, and she wrote almost daily. But their letters, though numerous, could not quench his loneliness; away from home and out of touch for the moment with his wife, he was embarked on a venture that veered often toward disaster. From Milwaukee, to explain his mood, he described his typical day.

> Having dressed etc. I sit at the breakfast table, reading one or more papers, *alone.* After breakfast, let's say at eight o'clock, I go back to my room where (with minor interruptions) I remain *alone* until 1 P.M., when I have dinner, again mostly *alone* (especially in larger cities), after which I spend another 5 or 6 hours *alone* in my room — unless I go for a little walk, *if the weather is good,* or I see someone who has strayed in my direction. Supper at 7 and then the concert. After the concert, once again I have the pleasure of my own company, until I go to bed with myself. That is how it usually goes.[18]

To the sociable Tante, who, when left alone, was apt to grow despondent, his gloomy reports suggested catastrophe, and her despairing replies soon had him begging:

> Allow me once in a while to express my sombre views, without having to fear that I am giving you tearful hours . . . And after all, why weep? I never lose courage and so you should not either. By the time these lines reach you, we may have had three wonderful Spring days in Denver and three most successful concerts. And if not, what matter? The sun will always shine again! And when I come back to you I shall find four suns, and they must shine their brightest for me. And so, no tears, unless they are tears of joy on the return of your
>
>

fighting and thus *living*

Leopold[19]

For in-laws their relationship was unusually close and today might be suspect. He was fifty-one and vigorous; she, thirty-five, admiring and beautiful. But there is no evidence that their friendship was tinged by a sexual attraction. Though she never married, according to her nieces she had suitors; and according to her she preferred, in this particular family, to be a maiden aunt. It is a role that, under the suspicions started by Freud and his followers, has all but ceased to be possible, but in this earlier age Tante, the summer mother, throughout a long life found it both useful and happy.[20]

Despite the tour's difficulties, the concerts were well received, often with great enthusiasm. If Thomas had played recently in the same hall, or even in a neighboring city, then audiences and critics, of course, excitedly compared the performances. In St. Joseph, Missouri, where both orchestras played the Overture to *Tannhäuser,* the critic of the *St. Joseph Gazette* was honest enough to confess indecision: "There is nothing to choose between the orchestras, but there is a perceptible difference in conception of the tempo of the two directors. In the first part Thomas takes it considerably faster than Damrosch, but as to which is the better, or the nearer correct, the public must judge."[21]

Damrosch's program for St. Joseph was typical of those he offered to the smaller cities: no symphony, many marches and overtures, and two soloists.

Overture — *Oberon* .... Weber

Air .... Pacini
Mlle. Isidora Martinez

Melody..Grieg

Valse .... Tchaikowsky

Marche Militaire .... Schubert
(Arranged for Orchestra by Dr. Damrosch)

Hungarian Fantaisie .... Liszt
Mme. Teresa Carreño

Rhapsodie (new) ....Lalo

Air — *Mignon* .... Thomas
Mlle. Isidora Martinez

Overture — *William Tell* .... Rossini

Rakoczy March..Berlioz

Overture — *Tannhäuser* ....Wagner

At St. Joseph the least distinguished artist, Mlle. Martinez, proved the most popular, not because of the audience's bad taste or ignorance, but because the human voice is the most basic of all instruments, with the widest appeal. The fact underlies the arguments for singing to children, and for teaching them to sing before introducing them to an orchestral instrument. It explains why in a new country without music, so much of music started up with choral groups, in church or out; why even today an orchestra planning a benefit concert, with raised prices, will turn often to singers and program choral music; and why, on tour in St. Joseph, Damrosch allowed the distinguished pianist one encore and the undistinguished vocalist several.

The climax of the tour, eight concerts in Denver, was marred by the manager of the hall, who absconded with the advance subscription sales, leaving accounts $2500 in arrears. Also, the concerts seem to have been too many and too serious for the city, and audiences, though enthusiastic, were small. But Damrosch's troubles, which included a blizzard on May 29, soon were dispelled by his joy in seeing Frank.

Only a few days before his father's arrival Frank had presented his church singers in their first concert, Mendelssohn's *Elijah,* and among the city's music lovers he now was well known and admired. He was able to have a small orchestra serenade his father at the Windsor Hotel, to introduce him to the city's musical leaders and to stir up publicity for the concerts. But what rejoiced his father most was "the freshness and simplicity of his manner."[22]

As Leopold, the following week, pondered the importance of family love, he urged Tante and the girls at home: "Read [First] Corinthians, chapter 13 [on charity, or love]. But am I now beginning to preach? Well, I would almost rather be a preacher than a musician if I could not preach once in a while in the language of my art."[23]

Though the five-week tour was financially harrowing, it was artistically successful and laid the foundation for subsequent tours of the New York Symphony. The name Damrosch, associated with exciting events in the East, now had substance throughout the northern Midwest and Rocky Mountain states. But for the man who bore it, home seemed indescribably beautiful.

On October 21, 1883, Leopold and Helene celebrated their silver wedding anniversary, twenty-five years of life together. The true date was August 20, but presumably to make of the event a party, as was their way, they waited for summer's end and the return of friends to town. Except that Leopold did not tell Helene how many friends he had invited, and Tante successfully concealed from her the amount of food and beverage coming into the house.

On the morning of the day, by various artifices Helene was kept busy upstairs while on the parlor floor the guests assembled quietly and music stands were set up for an orchestra of forty. Then, as Helene was called down, the orchestra struck up a *Vorspiel* that Leopold had composed on

Johann Crüger's chorale: *I Sing to You with Heart and Mouth*. The piece was on a grand scale, opening quietly with woodwinds, horn and strings developing fragments of the chorale, followed by an orchestral version of a song that Leopold had composed for Helene during their engagement. Then the orchestra swelled with wedding bells (*glockenspiel*), trombones, trumpet, drums and organ, until at the climax a four-part chorus burst forth with *Ich Singe Dir mit Herz und Mund*. After this major work the orchestra closed with some froth, *The Members of the Family*, witty and charming characterizations; and all of this was, as Leopold stated in the silver-bordered program, "to render homage to his beloved wife Helene."[24]

Like many of Damrosch's compositions, the *Vorspiel* was heard only once again, in 1907, when Walter included it in a program with the New York Symphony.[25] Although Damrosch wrote a substantial number of works, his composing seems early to have become a casualty of the ungrateful economics of his life. Certainly his family thought so.[26] As a young man in Breslau, where life, though poor, was leisurely, he composed and published regularly. Of his more important works all but two date from these German years, before 1871: chiefly *Concertstücke in form of a Serenade, Festival Overture* and Concerto for Violin. The exceptions, both for soloists and chorus, are *Ruth and Naomi, A Scriptural Idyll* (1875) and the oratorio *Sulamith* (1882). But in middle age, in New York, he seemed to have time only for songs or perhaps a chorus for the Arion.

The songs, which Helene would sing to his accompaniment, or sometimes Helene and Tante in duet, were set not only to German poets — von Zesen, Heine, Rückert, Geibel — but in later years also to Byron, Shelley and Oliver Wendell Holmes. Ellie remembered the songs as "difficult, both for voice and piano," and most remained unpublished.[27] But his other music had some success; enough to suggest that if he had composed more, the success would have increased. As it was, none of the works, not even *Sulamith*, stayed long in the repertory, in Germany or in the United States, despite Walter's filial piety in scheduling an occasional performance.[28]

Yet strangely, the most lasting of all his works turned out to be some songs for children, perhaps partly because, in connection with their composition, he was stimulated greatly by a visit from Frank. In the spring of 1884 Frank was appointed supervisor of music in the Denver public schools, and in June he came east to consult his father about what he should attempt to do and how. The family had rented a cottage at Westhampton that summer, and there for several weeks Frank and his father studied the various school manuals Frank had collected, trying to decide which methods were best for teaching children to sing and, through musical notation, to sing at sight.

It happened that Damrosch had a commission from a publisher that same summer to make songs of some poems that had appeared in *St. Nicholas,* a magazine for children. The poems were not childish jingles but the works of such writers as Mary Mapes Dodge, Laura E. Richards, Lucy Larcom and Celia Thaxter; and besides the *St. Nicholas* poems a few others to be used were by such as Bret Harte and Theodore Winthrop.

The collection, *St. Nicholas Songs,* appeared in 1885, with 112 songs, many by the day's outstanding American composers, such as George W. Chadwick, Homer N. Bartlett and N. H. Allen. Ten of the songs were by Damrosch, and he had the opening page with *Jennie,* to words by Harte. Some of his others were *The Minuet* and *In the Wood,* both by Dodge; *A Valentine* by Richards; and *The Lord's Day,* for which he had adapted the text from an old German poem.

The collection's quality throughout was high and its success great. Until about 1925, and possibly later, most families with an interest in music kept a copy on the piano, and at least two, perhaps three, generations of children grew up on the songs. As late as 1947, in San Antonio, Texas, schoolchildren were singing them. Probably most never noticed who had composed them, but in this odd way, in his adopted country Damrosch entered its musical life as a composer.[29]

That summer was an especially happy one for the family. Frank finally had decided to make his life wholly in music and already had enough of a reputation to be offered, and to decline, a post in Milwaukee. Walter, besides directing the Newark Harmonic Society, had been hired for the fall as musical director at the Plymouth Church in Brooklyn, and was reaching financial independence. The eldest daughter, Marie, at twenty had grown into an astonishing beauty, with Saxon blond hair and blue eyes; she also was an extraordinary athlete and showed promise of the family's best voice, an alto, though as yet she lacked the self-discipline to train it. Her restlessness sometimes disturbed the others. She had disliked the prospect of teaching and had expressed her distaste for Normal College in a poem so clever that her father had allowed her to quit. According to Ellie, he spoiled Marie, but the opinion probably originated with Clara, who in these years dominated Ellie and seldom had a good word for Marie.[30]

Such problems of temperament were submerged, however, in the family's enjoyment of the summer. For the past several years, as Damrosch's financial position had improved, he had rented a cottage at Westhampton Center, later Westhampton Beach, and moved the family out of the city for the hottest months. The town was not yet the chic summer resort it later became, but a hamlet of some five hundred permanent residents, four hours by railroad from Long Island City. Its roads were sandy dirt, traveled by foot, bicycle or horse and carriage. The cottages were lighted by kerosene, and there was no telephone, electricity, bathrooms or central heating. There was swimming, sailing, baseball, and simple country parties in which everyone joined. At the Howell House, built in 1868, there were small dances and occasional musicales, sometimes directed by Walter. Frank was interested particularly in sailing; he entered the dinghy races, and in 1890 became one of the founders and first vice-commodore of the Westhampton Country Club, which, despite its name, had no golf at all.[31]

For Ellie the summers still were measured by physical triumphs: two years earlier she had learned to swim; the next year her father had taught her to row; and now, at twelve, she finally had grown and was becoming her own person, no longer so easily teased, no longer the timid "Ellie-Mouse," as Frank used to call her. Now she strode alone about the dunes or climbed the catalpa tree in the garden to daydream about the curious prerevolutionary Howell Cottage her mother had selected for the summer. With its ancient origin, small windows, low ceilings and uneven floors, it stirred imagination.[32]

Then early in August, in the midst of the family's happiness, there exploded a bombshell of joy. From Damrosch in New York there came a telegram — in later years Clara would insist that it came "from Father to *me*" — reporting that the directors of the Metropolitan Opera House Company had accepted his plan for a season of German opera, including a start on Wagner's *Ring*. He would be the manager at the house for its second season, in charge of the singers, the orchestra and the repertory, at a salary of $10,000. Since leaving Breslau thirteen years earlier he had waited and worked for just such an artistic opportunity.[33]

CHAPTER 7

Leopold at the Metropolitan Opera. The all-in-German season. Die Walküre.
His death.

THE ANNOUNCEMENT that Damrosch would manage the Metropolitan Opera's second season surprised almost everyone: though known and admired, he was not associated with opera; and as details emerged in the press, it became clear that his appointment was both a desperate remedy and a radical departure. The directors of the Metropolitan Opera House Company, rather than have a season without opera, which by midsummer had seemed likely, had agreed to a proposal by Damrosch that the house should substitute German for Italian opera, in singers as well as repertory. In the New York operatic world that was revolutionary.

Damrosch's proposal could have been accepted only in the summer in which it was made, for it required an extraordinary conjunction of forces — social, financial and artistic — to make it reasonable to the directors and stockholders of the Metropolitan Opera House Company. These were primarily the new rich of fashionable society, who, unable to jostle the old rich out of the boxes at the Academy of Music, the traditional home of opera in New York, had built the Metropolitan in order to display themselves. The opening of the new house, a glittering occasion, had taken place on the evening of October 22, 1883, a date chosen because it was also the opening night of the season at the Academy. In the social war there was no hiding place: a leader had to choose, sit in a box and be counted friend or enemy.

Each house offered an "Italian season" typical of the time. The Metropolitan opened with *Faust,* sung in Italian, not French, and featuring Christine Nilsson; the Academy of Music offered *La Sonnambula* in its original language, Italian, with Etelka Gerster. The following month the Metropolitan presented *La Sonnambula* with Marcella Sembrich, and the

Academy, *Faust,* in Italian, with Lillian Nordica. Then Adelina Patti appeared at the Academy, singing for the astronomical fee of $5000 a night and with a contract allowing her to cancel almost at whim, to wear any costume she chose and to skip all rehearsals — and in three years of opera in the United States she attended none. Newcomers to a cast often met her for the first time onstage, without even a run-through for the duets. In both houses the emphasis was on the singer; conductor, chorus, orchestra and staging were often second-rate and sometimes incompetent; and every opera, even *Lohengrin,* was sung in Italian. At both houses the impresarios in charge — essentially tenants, with a share in the profits — lost money. Henry E. Abbey, who had provided the Metropolitan with sumptuous scenery and costumes, lost so much, an estimated $600,000, that he refused the post for the next year. Nor could any other impresario, here or abroad, be induced to take it. As spring faded into summer, it began to look as though the Academy's patrons had won the social war. In the coming season the new house would be dark; and the new rich, in the darkness, invisible. And then to the Metropolitan's directors Damrosch offered his plan.

He lacked the money and financial backing to enter the Metropolitan in an impresario's traditional manner, guaranteeing performances in return for a share of the profits. Instead, he offered to serve as a manager, using funds provided by the owners of the house and not sharing in the profits or losses. Such an arrangement put the directors and stockholders of the Metropolitan Opera House Company deeper into the business of producing opera than was usual or, they felt, desirable. But they were desperate, and Damrosch evidently convinced them that he could produce a "German season," with all operas of whatever nationality sung in German, at low cost and little risk.

Though details of the conversations are lacking, it is clear from later events what they must have been. Damrosch evidently argued that the city contained some 250,000 German-speaking immigrants, many of them musically inclined but unsympathetic to Italian opera. What they wanted mostly to hear, as occasional performances demonstrated, were German composers, particularly Wagner, sung in German. Here was a large audience, about a sixth of the city's population, as yet untapped by either the Metropolitan or the Academy.

Ticket prices, however, would have to come down, and in fact where Abbey's top price at the Metropolitan had been $7.00, Damrosch's would be $4.00. But the reduction at the box office would be offset by the hiring of German singers from Central Europe, whose demands in fees and perquisites were far less than those of singers on the international Italian circuit.

Bolstering Damrosch's argument was the general feeling, beginning to be expressed in newspaper articles, that Italian opera was played out; was, in fact, in the last stage of decadence. Besides the domination by singers, often a sign of decay in opera, there were no new composers. Verdi's apparently final opera, *Aida,* had appeared in 1871, and Puccini was not yet on the horizon. The excitement was all in German opera, of which in New York *Lohengrin,* in Italian, was the sole, feeble example.[1]

Further, as Henry E. Krehbiel, critic for the *New York Tribune,* later wrote:

> There were many lovers of opera in New York . . . who believed that if America was ever to have a musical art of its own, the way could best be paved by supplanting Italian performances by German . . . We should, it is true, still have foreign artists singing foreign works in a foreign tongue, but the change in repertory would promote an appreciation and an understanding of truthful dramatic expression in a form which claimed close relationship with the drama.[2]

To all these arguments, social, financial and artistic, Damrosch was able to add three more that were powerful. Though he intended to recruit the chorus in Germany, for certain operas he could add to it members of the Oratorio Society. For the orchestra he could use the New York Symphony, a far better orchestra than Abbey's men, most of whom had been imported for the season from Venice and Naples. Finally, for the conductor there was himself, for every performance. Except for the singers, as yet unknown, in every musical respect the Metropolitan was guaranteed a better company than the previous year and a better company than the Academy's.

Whatever weight the directors may have given to the reasons, they voted to accept the proposal, and on August 13, only three months before the season's opening, Damrosch sailed for Germany to recruit the soloists and chorus. It was a late start, and in a pocket notebook he jotted his fears: under a list of singers he scratched in English, "All lost, if delay"; and in a financial calculation, "Outside expenses for me $4000 a week."[3]

He returned on October 1, and to a reporter for the *Times* he appeared "the picture of health and satisfaction." Though he confessed that he had arrived in Germany too late to sign up every singer he had hoped for, still, by appealing to national pride and to the eagerness of many to establish German opera in the United States, he had been able to assemble an extraordinary company. Every soloist was outstanding; every chorister, well trained. Herr Wilhelm Hock of Hamburg was "the best stage manager in Germany"; Herr John Lund of Bremen, the best chorusmaster.[4] Nevertheless, with the exception of Amalia Materna, the first Kundry in *Parsifal*, whom Thomas had brought over for his 1882 May Festival, to the public the names were wholly new. But that seemed only to increase everyone's anticipation.

Opening night, *Tannhäuser*, was set for November 17, though most of the singers did not arrive until the tenth. Their crossing was extremely rough, and everyone was seasick. First ashore, to be greeted by Helene and a committee, was the company's light soprano, twenty-year-old, vivacious Fräulein Hermine Bely: "Ach, Gott!" she cried. "If only there were a bridge, I would walk back rather than sail again." Behind her swelled a sympathetic chorus of "Ja, Ja."[5]

The season progressed unevenly. Both *Tannhäuser* and *Lohengrin* succeeded beyond expectation, but *Don Giovanni* and *Rigoletto* were relative failures. By New Year's, however, it was clear that Damrosch's premises were proving true. The house was filled. Although tickets were nearly halved in price, so were expenses, and box office receipts were almost double those of the previous year. Meanwhile at the Academy, despite Patti, or perhaps because of her, opera in the Italian style fared poorly, and the season closed early, on December 27. For this year, at least, the new rich had won, and their directors began to negotiate with Damrosch for the next.

At the Metropolitan, in the meantime, some artistic views were forming that still dominate thinking in the United States about opera. The German artists could make something splendid of *Tannhäuser* and *Lohengrin*, but their German diction and style of phrasing spoiled *Don Giovanni* and *Rigoletto*. Damrosch, recognizing the fact, promptly adjusted the schedule to give nine performances each of the Wagner and only two of *Don Giovanni* and one of *Rigoletto*. Critics, recalling the Italians' inability to do much with *Lohengrin* in Italian, began to argue that any opera, to be best performed, must be performed in the language in which it was written. In much of Europe the dictum is otherwise: it must be performed in the language of the audience.

But even the Germans had difficulty in projecting in the large house such smaller-scaled German operas as *Fidelio* and *Der Freischütz*, both composed in *singspiel* (sing-speak) style, with considerable spoken dialogue between numbers. Though the soprano Marianne Brandt was a sensational success in *Fidelio*, Damrosch would risk only three performances, and with *Der Freischütz*, the most popular in Germany of all German operas, only one. At performances of both operas, the non-Germans in the audience had grown too restless during the dialogue.

Partly for the same reason and also, apparently, because comedy tended to be lost in the large house, he canceled a production of Otto Nicolai's extremely popular *Die Lustigen Weiber von Windsor* (*Merry Wives of Windsor*). The distressing fact was that the new rich had built themselves a house so large that much of the best of German repertory could not be played in it. The Metropolitan, starting with this Damrosch season, became one of the greatest — perhaps *the* greatest — Wagnerian house in the world. Unfortunately, because of its physical limitations it also fostered throughout the United States the mistaken idea that Wagnerian opera was the only good German opera.[6]

Damrosch's schedule that winter was extraordinary. Though he no longer had the Arion concerts, he still had eight with the Oratorio Society, as well as rehearsals, and twelve with the New York Symphony. To these he had added fifty-seven at the Metropolitan, to be given in a three-month season and followed by a six-week tour. Yet he did not skimp. As always, *Messiah* was performed in Christmas week; and with the Symphony, on January 24, 1885, he offered two American premières, Tchaikovsky's *Serenade for Strings* and Liszt's *Jeanne d'Arc,* sung by Marianne Brandt. In addition the program included Schumann's Symphony No. 4, the Allegro from Schubert's Unfinished Symphony and the Prelude and *Liebestod* from *Tristan und Isolde,* sung by Brandt. The orchestra by then, because of its steady work in the opera house, had regained its polish, temporarily spoiled by Thomas' raids on its personnel.

Still, the artistic success, as great with Tchaikovsky as with Wagner, could not conceal from friends Damrosch's increasing fatigue. If anyone remonstrated, urging him to delegate more authority, he always replied, "Next year will be easier."[7] He was exhausted, but exhilarated, by his crusade to implant Wagner and Wagnerian ideas of opera production on American stages. He looked forward to February 21 not as the end of the season but as the start of a six-week tour in which he would take the best of the repertory, including a *Die Walküre* yet to be produced, to Chicago, Cincinnati and Boston.

In all areas of his musical life he now relied greatly on Walter, who became for the opera company the mascot he already was for the Oratorio Society. Whatever needed to be done, Walter did, and Marianne Brandt, writing in 1921 of Leopold as "the brilliant creator" of German opera in the United States, went on to mention "his faithful son and companion Walter, beside him with the score." It was a time, she recalled, of "the whole family living through one great success after another in the jolliest of moods."[8]

Every family member, except Frank in Denver, went to every performance, at least of the Wagner operas, and this year, for the first time since she had left Breslau, Helene took on no singing students. For the three girls the season was a continuous festival; it meant dressing up almost nightly, riding in a carriage to the opera house, sitting in a box, where Marie's beauty shone, listening to the glorious music while admiring their father on the podium, and then going home with the music ringing through their heads until the next performance.[9]

But the crusade to establish German opera in the United States was not without its renegades. Just before the performance of *La Muette de Portici* on January 9, 1885, twenty-three male choristers brought from Germany went on strike, the first at the Metropolitan. They wanted higher wages than those contracted for, $16, $18 and $20 weekly according to usefulness and for four performances; for additional performances they were to be paid extra. Before the overture, Damrosch addressed the audience from the podium, apologizing for the unequal balance of choristers onstage and promising that on the morrow the chorus would be back to full strength. The opera, in which the Neapolitan populace revolts against the local royalty, proceeded, but not without some comic moments, as when a single, vocal Neapolitan fisherman routed a platoon of well-armed but mute soldiers. By the next day all but a few of the strikers had signed a letter of apology and returned to work; the recalcitrants were replaced.[10]

The end of the month, January 30, brought the season's greatest triumph, *Die Walküre*, of all the productions the one for which Damrosch cared the most. The opera's American première had taken place under Adolf Neuendorff, on April 2, 1877, but was a disaster; and though excerpts often were played and sung in concerts, Damrosch's production was the first chance for most Americans to see and hear what Wagner meant by a union of the arts in lyric drama: an ensemble production, rehearsed for weeks until all the parts, vocal, orchestral, scenic and directorial, worked toward a single end, the composer's intent, not the singers'. In its scenery and staging the Damrosch production closely followed that of Bayreuth, 1876, except that in Act I draperies replaced the door into Hunding's hut so that, when they were dropped at the start of the love scene, a greater expanse of moonlight flooded the stage. The cast was good, particularly the women, with Materna as Brünnhilde, Auguste Kraus as Sieglinde, and the good-natured, earnest crusader Brandt in two minor roles: Fricka in Act II, and in Act III, Gerhilde, leader of the Walküre. The ensemble work of the Germans paid handsomely: the drama of the opera as well as the music made a tremendous impression on the audience, and the critic of the *New York Tribune* proclaimed the combined effect "the crowning achievement of Dr. Damrosch and his artists." So successful was the production that Damrosch scheduled six repeats of it for the remaining three weeks of the season and also promised it for the tour cities.[11]

This production of *Die Walküre*, which in succeeding years would be followed by others of the remaining operas in *The Ring* as well as of *Tristan und Isolde, Die Meistersinger* and ultimately *Parsifal*, started a revolution in operatic taste throughout the country. Italian opera, as practiced by Patti, was finished. Though audiences still flocked to hear her in an occasional performance or concert, they no longer would support her or her style in a season of opera. As the *Times* had prophesied in an editorial at the start of the season, the introduction of German opera in time would help even Italian opera to recover the lost values of drama.[12]

Then on February 16, six days before the season's end, Leopold Damrosch died.

PART II

The Widow
and Her Two Sons

CHAPTER 8

Family heroes. Walter takes the opera on tour. Marie's curious marriage. Walter brings Seidl to the Metropolitan. The U.S. première of Parsifal. Frank and Victor Herbert. Walter with von Bülow and Carnegie.

EVERY FAMILY needs a hero for the young to emulate, and if fortune is kind that hero, man or woman, will be mature, and the heroic actions, thoughtful and sustained. Leopold Damrosch's death, so sudden, at a moment of triumph, established him as a hero to his children, and their judgment seemed confirmed by the shock and emotion displayed in the larger, music-making cities of the country. At the public funeral in New York, conducted at the Metropolitan, the building inside and out was draped in black, and to a packed house the city's religious leaders delivered eulogies interspersed with musical selections by the Oratorio Society and the New York Symphony. Herr Hock, the stage manager, with an actor's skill delivered the final farewell, in German, directly to the casket, after which the orchestra echoed his words with Siegfried's *Funeral March* from *Götterdämmerung.* The ceremony, according to the *Herald,* though without "the customary religious element," was "among the most impressive ever witnessed in this city." For weeks after, journals recounted Damrosch's achievements, and many persons, in the manner of the day, wrote poems of lamentation, which they sent to the family.[1]

Helene did not take her children to the funeral, nor did she go herself, nor did Tante. Only Walter was in the opera house, striding gloomily through the corridors, attending to details. In the auditorium, filled to overflowing, the family's box remained empty.

In later years both Clara and Ellie complained of their mother's decision, feeling that they had been deprived of a share in an important ritual. Characteristically, Clara was severe: "I can never quite forgive this attitude";[2] whereas Ellie shaded off into sympathy: "But she was so stricken."[3] Though Tante, following Leopold's death, often talked enthusiastically of him to his children and grandchildren, Helene did not. She talked, wisely and equably, of current problems, hopes and solutions; but her life with Leopold was closed.

Of all the children, Walter in later years would reiterate the most insistently that he owed everything, everything to his father, perhaps because for him, of all the children, the death was the most traumatic. Damrosch took sick on a Tuesday. Following a rehearsal at the opera house, he returned home and lay down for a nap in a cold room without covering himself. He awoke thoroughly chilled, and after dinner went to the Oratorio Society to conduct a rehearsal of Verdi's *Requiem*. In the midst of a passage he laid down the baton, announcing, "I am too ill to go on."[4] Walter hurried him home in a carriage.

By the next day Leopold, who supposedly had only a chill, was weaker, and Walter, after going through the score with him, went to the opera house to conduct *Tannhäuser*, his debut at the Metropolitan, at age twenty-three.

There cannot have been many in the audience that night who had been there also on Monday, for what proved to be the elder Damrosch's final performance, but one such was a music student from Cincinnati, Ida May Hill, and of the Monday night with "Dr. Damrosch," she wrote:

> I see his finely chiselled face, his shapely head, his white hair, as he stood before the prompter's box as the first strains of *Lohengrin* floated over my being. He had much the same style and appearance as our present-day Toscanini. Much the same rigid and classical spirit. His son was always with him, not visible to the audience but always there . . .

Then, learning that he was ill and that the season would continue:

> I went on Wednesday night to hear *Tannhäuser* and after the orchestra had assembled, a youth with golden hair strode through the players, lifted his baton and Walter Damrosch led his first opera . . . in such a masterly manner that the audience forgot the singers and gave him their hearts' complete adulation. I remember every note of that first hearing of *Tannhäuser* and although it has been my joy to hear it many times since, not since has my soul ever been carried to so great heights of delight. The sight of that golden-headed boy lifting the baton which his father had just dropped brings today the same emotion it did that night.[5]

Doubtless her memory of the evening was colored by her subsequent knowledge of Leopold's death and Walter's success as a conductor, but all accounts agree on the evening's enormous emotional impact. And the next night Walter, after another session of instruction at his father's bedside, conducted *Die Walküre*, and two days later, when his father was known to have pneumonia, *Le Prophète*. The following afternoon, Damrosch died. Medically, he was a victim of pneumonia complicated by pleurisy, but many people felt he had worked himself to death, a victim of exhaustion.[6] While Walter officially mourned and helped to prepare the funeral service, John Lund, the chorusmaster, conducted the company's last four performances in New York, and then on February 23, only eight days after Leopold's death, the tour opened in Chicago, with Walter conducting *Tannhäuser*.

There was never any real doubt that the tour would proceed; too much money was tied up in it. Or that Walter would lead it, for the money was his father's. For purposes of the tour the Metropolitan Opera House Company had agreed only to loan the elder Damrosch the costumes and scenery; the greater financial risk of audiences and halls had been his, and now attached to his estate. He had left no money to his family, only his name and the opportunities stemming from it, chiefly the directorships of the Oratorio Society, of the New York Symphony, and of the opera touring company, which appears in the Metropolitan's Annals as the Damrosch Grand Opera Company. The first two were relatively simple organizations, and Walter, on his appointment, which came quickly, could assume the posts with confidence, though he lacked experience as a symphonic conductor. Managing an opera company, however, was something else, and to begin with a tour, on which he also would serve as principal conductor, was doubly perilous. Yet to cancel the tour was to bankrupt his father's estate, smudge his father's name and pauperize his mother and sisters. He assumed the double post and announced that all commitments would be met.[7]

Sentiment and several facts worked in his favor. The German artists rallied to him, "the faithful son," and the public did, too. It was eager to hear the German operas, and advance sales were good. And another fact, hardly less clear, was that, with the exception of Theodore Thomas, who was inconceivable as manager of a Damrosch opera company, there was no one but Walter to lead it. No other musician in the United States was as familiar with the company's repertory and artists.

The tour began with a near-disaster, averted partially by Frank, who had come to Chicago to meet Walter. The performance of *Tannhäuser* was scheduled to begin at 8:00 P.M., but at that hour, though every seat in the Columbia Theatre was filled, the company was not yet in the city. Its train from New York had been delayed by a blizzard, several broken couplings, a wreck on the line ahead and, finally, the need to abandon a car. And part of the trouble, as much of the audience knew, was that Walter, to save $200, had booked the trip on the West Shore Railroad instead of the New York Central, which had better equipment.

By curtain time the tour's shrunken, battered train was only on the outskirts of Chicago, but Frank had secured a priority for it, and it was hurried through the railroad yards into the station. There, Frank had carriages waiting for the singers and wagons for the props and costume trunks. The scenery, fortunately, had arrived earlier.

At about nine o'clock Walter and the evening's prima donna, Materna, entered the front of the theater, marched down the aisle through the cheering audience, mounted the stage and, after a bow and a curtsy, disappeared through the curtain. One miracle of the evening was the audience's good humor, which never flagged; another, the fortitude of the singers and players, who, after forty-nine hours on the train, much of the time without heat or hot food, never questioned the need to give the performance. For Frank and Walter, of course, the specter of refunding an entire house was terrifying.

At 10:00 P.M. Walter started the overture. Backstage was an obstacle course of unpacked trunks, discarded wigs, shoes, costume racks and unwanted props. Amid the chaos Tannhäuser's knightly armor could not be found, and he would appear as a huntsman. The ballet was to be cut. The overture ran its fifteen minutes. At its end, on Frank's request, Walter played it again, and the curtain finally rose at ten-thirty. The audience seemed not to care; long after midnight it demanded two repeats of Wolfram's aria Evening Star. The next day the newspapers were kind, overlooking the artistic shortcomings and stressing the company's gallantry.[8]

The Damrosch Grand Opera Company continued its tour, forty-two performances of twelve operas in three cities, without another serious incident until the final day in Boston, April 18, for which Walter had scheduled a matinee of Die Walküre and an evening performance of La Dame Blanche. That morning the orchestra struck, because Walter, again to save money, had booked the tour to return to New York by boat, not train. In the face of his threat to treat the strike as a breach of contract, to withhold the week's wages and to perform Die Walküre with two pianos, the men capitulated.[9]

Perhaps partly because of Walter's frugality, the tour ended, it seems, in the black, though no one talked of any profits. Artistically it had been well received, introducing Chicago, Cincinnati and Boston to their first concentrated dose of staged Wagner and giving Walter the start of a national reputation. The directors of the Metropolitan, meanwhile, had hired him for the next season as assistant conductor and assistant manager, and also Frank as chorusmaster. Out of the nettle, danger, Walter had plucked reputation and employment.

For Frank, the Metropolitan's offer, reported to him in Chicago by Walter, posed an unhappy dilemma. After a few hours' sleep following the wild performance of Tannhäuser, the brothers had risen to discuss the family's future. Both accepted full responsibility for their mother, aunt and sisters; that was part of their German heritage. Nevertheless, it was clear that Leopold's death was a staggering financial setback. The family would have to move at once from the house to a small apartment and to retrench in every way possible.

A few moments of figuring revealed that the sons' combined annual earnings might equal about a sixth of their father's. Neither was an instrumental virtuoso nor his father's equal as a conductor or manager. Walter might inherit the posts at the New York Symphony and Oratorio Society, but at reduced fees. At the more lucrative Metropolitan, for example, Leopold for the 1884–85 season had received, in all, $14,000. For the next year the directors offered Walter the double post of assistant conductor and assistant manager for $1500 and empowered him to offer Frank the post of chorusmaster at $1050.[10]

Walter urged Frank to take it and return to New York. His presence would strengthen the family. In addition Walter could turn over to Frank the Choral Club, which Walter had been leading for several years, perhaps also the Newark Harmonic Society and possibly one or two others.

The decision was probably the most painful of Frank's life. He had left New York six years earlier because he did not like its musical life. Now to return there, where he was all but forgotten; to leave a career well started in Denver, where he was liked and admired; to work in opera, a form of music with which he had little sympathy; to take a post at the Metropolitan subordinate to his younger brother and to accept Walter's cast-off choral clubs — all this was perhaps the greatest sacrifice asked of any member of the family. And Frank made it, so quietly that most of the family's members, absorbed in their own problems, seemed unaware of the cost. In later years Ellie remembered, but the others talked only of Walter's magnificent response to his father's death.[11]

Perhaps, too, the eldest daughter, Marie, made a sacrifice, or was sacrificed, for the family's benefit, though doubtless no one at first thought of her marriage as such. In those days, in middle-class German families, the father or his surrogate often behaved as if he owned the family financially and socially. Fathers selected husbands and wives for their children, or tried to, and woe to the child who disobeyed.

In the Schirmer family one of old Gustav's daughters, Florence, married an impecunious Roman Catholic organist, and converted. Old Gustav nearly had apoplexy. Young Gustave, Walter's friend, also married against his father's wishes and was read out of the family. He went to Boston, founded the Boston Music Company and prospered by publishing Ethelbert Nevin. His first child died soon after birth, and Gustave's mother went secretly to Boston, to a tearful reunion in a hotel room.

The second grandchild lived, the Reconciliation Baby, and amid copious tears on everyone's part all was forgiven, and Gustave returned to New York to resume his position in the Schirmer dynasty.[12] Against that social background must be measured Marie Damrosch's abrupt, curious marriage.

In Chicago, Frank and Walter had discussed her future, and on March 26, 1885, barely six weeks after her father's death and before the opera tour was completed, she married Ferdinand Wiechmann, a scientist specializing in the chemistry of sugar. Considering how punctiliously in those days long periods of mourning were observed, the marriage was very sudden, especially as no engagement had been announced publicly before her father's death. Tante in her *Story* insists that Marie and Ferdi had been engaged privately "while Dr. Damrosch was living. He approved of Dr. Wiechmann absolutely." But in view of Marie's visible unhappiness in later years, Tante may protest too much. In time a suspicion arose, entertained by some of Marie's nieces, that she had been a financial sacrifice, hurried by her two older brothers into an unsuitable marriage in order to shift the cost of her support to a husband.[13]

Wiechmann, who was six years older than Marie and had little interest in music, was in many respects an extraordinary man. By middle age he was a superb linguist, probably the outstanding sugar chemist in the United States and a scientist of international reputation; also, under the pen name Forest Monroe, the author of a novel, *Maid of Montauk,* about the Indians of Long Island. He was born in Brooklyn of German immigrant parents — there was talk of Prussian nobility in the family's background — and he grew into a handsome, bearded, cigar-smoking authoritarian, somewhat hard and egocentric in temperament, but an able, generous provider for his family. As he was eight months older than Frank, he became on marriage the oldest male with a tie to the Damrosch family and its only member with an advanced or even undergraduate degree; no one could challenge him. After his death, in 1919, Marie sometimes would say to her daughter-in-law, "I loved him — but like a father."[14]

He, for his part, adored his beautiful wife but treated her like a porcelain doll, which irritated her, for she was quite strong and active. Nevertheless, he forbade her to do almost anything, except, as she once wrote, "to sing *Trilby* well enough to please him with it every evening after tea."[15] She appeased her frustration by eating, and in about fifteen years she, who had been so beautiful, was obese, probably to the point of glandular imbalance. Ferdi seemed not to mind.

Gradually, over the years, her brothers and sisters excluded her from all but the largest family gatherings. They said that she was an explosive personality, always giving more trouble than pleasure, that she had a genius for offending everyone in a room, that she went about trailing clouds of glory from the Damrosch family, though she herself had never submitted to the disciplines that made the family great. Helene and Tante, while they lived, saw Marie regularly, but later her brothers and sisters at the mention of her name would roll their eyes in despair. Only Ellie seemed occasionally to feel sympathy for her, recalling that "in the park she pulled our sleds for us." [16]

Marie's own family, however, did not find her offensive, nor did all her nieces, nor all strangers. In her widowhood she developed a salon of poets, none great, who seemed to find her attractive and amusing. Though Ferdi may have wanted to keep a distance between his wife and her family, on his death that estrangement should have ceased. Yet in lonely widowhood, when Marie turned to her brothers and sisters — particularly to Walter, to whom she was closest in age — she was kept firmly at arm's length, particularly by Walter. That was visible even to strangers and the subject of comment. Granted that she was sometimes tactless, temperamental and self-pitying, how could the Damrosch family, which made such a public virtue of cohesion, exclude her? Besides a hero does a family need a scapegoat?

There is a mystery here, and the solution is lost in time. Yet one faint clue has come down through the years. Tante once told Marie's daughter-in-law that the Damrosch men — presumably Frank and Walter — always feared that Marie might embarrass the family. Once when she was at her most beautiful — probably before her marriage — a man had made improper advances to her, and she had come to Tante for counsel. The man — not identified — was important to Walter's career in New York, and Tante had counseled silence. That is all that is known. [17]

Was Marie a social as well as financial sacrifice? Whether or not Walter knew of the incident, was he anxious to have his beautiful but somewhat restless sister safely married before she could mar the family's image by an ill-considered action? In a German-American family of 1885 Walter as the acting head — for Frank was out of touch — would have had great power to push Marie into marriage, particularly in the family's financial circumstances. And then, because he was not insensitive, her subsequent unhappiness, expressed in obesity, might appear a perpetual reproach, so that he could hardly bear the sight of her. But that is all surmise. The mystery remains.

In May 1885, after the close of the tour and after leading several concerts in New York with the Symphony and Oratorio societies, Walter in his capacity as assistant manager of the Metropolitan sailed for Europe to engage singers and a principal conductor for the following season. The Metropolitan's directors had voted to continue the elder Damrosch's scheme of opera in German and, in a step toward becoming their own producing company, had elected a board member, Edmund C. Stanton, to serve as manager. Walter had expected to sail with Stanton, but when Stanton's daughter fell ill, Walter went alone. His position was awkward: he was to hire a conductor who would be his superior; and his age, twenty-three, was against him: to middle-aged, established European artists he seemed a brash young man from the provinces.

Nevertheless, backed by the Metropolitan's money, he was able to offer Stanton, on the latter's arrival in Germany, contracts for four outstanding Wagnerian performers who in the next six years created the first golden age of Wagner at the Metropolitan. These were the soprano Lilli Lehmann, the tenor Max Alvary, the bass Emil Fischer and the conductor Anton Seidl, who, until his death in 1898, was one of the world's greatest conductors of Wagner. His presence at the Metropolitan would greatly influence American standards of Wagnerian performance and, incidentally, cause Walter considerable anguish, because Walter, though he developed into a competent opera conductor, could never match Seidl in Wagner. The irony of that was not lost on his critics, and one, Henry T. Finck of the *New York Evening Post,* as late as 1926 cited as Walter's "supreme achievement" in forty years of music-making "the bringing to America of Anton Seidl." [18]

On Walter's return he took the New York Symphony to Louisville, Kentucky, where there was a large German community, eager for music. The work was pleasant, good training for both the orchestra and its conductor, and the engagement proved to be the first of a long annual series. [19] In later years Walter and the orchestra also played annual summer seasons at Willow Grove Park near Philadelphia, at Ravinia Park near Chicago and at the Pittsburgh Exposition. These summer stands for the orchestra, when combined with the tours it later undertook, made the New York Symphony and its conductor for almost forty years, from 1885 to 1925, the most widely heard and best known of the country's orchestras.

After Louisville, Walter joined the family for a brief vacation at Westhampton, where Helene again had rented a cottage, though one smaller and free of associations with Leopold. She had moved out of the town house, put most of her furniture and possessions in storage and for the winter had rented an apartment at 213 West 34th Street. From there, Frank and Walter could walk to the opera house.

In the autumn, when Helene moved the family into the apartment, she gave herself and Clara the two single rooms; Frank and Walter shared a room; and Tante and Ellie, a bed. As soon as everyone was settled, Helene resumed her teaching, using Ellie as an accompanist. Helene could strike chords at the piano, enough to move a singer along, but for a full accompaniment she needed a pianist. Ellie, though less technically proficient than Clara, played with good rhythm and phrasing and in this small way at the age of thirteen could contribute to the family's income.[20]

When the German artists arrived in New York, one of Anton Seidl's first acts was to attend a rehearsal of the chorus. Frank was working on *Lohengrin,* the opera for opening night, November 23, and though he had not met Seidl, he guessed from his visitor's short figure, broad forehead and large, calm face who the man must be. Without a word Seidl took a seat, listened through to the end and then declared his satisfaction. In the next seven years he paid Frank the greatest of compliments: he never attended another chorus rehearsal.[21]

Of the nine operas performed that season, five were by Wagner; the others were *Faust, Carmen, Le Prophète* and Goldmark's *Queen of Sheba* in its American première — not one Italian opera, and all the French, as the elder Damrosch had planned, sung in German. Seidl gave Walter three holdovers from the previous season, *Le Prophète, Die Walküre* and *Tannhäuser,* though reserving for himself the first night of the last. Of the Wagner he also conducted *Lohengrin, Rienzi* in its first Metropolitan performance and, as the chief work of the season, the American première of *Die Meistersinger,* with Emil Fischer as Hans Sachs, Marianne Brandt as Magdalene, and Seidl's wife, Auguste Seidl-Kraus, as Eva. At any time *Meistersinger,* the longest and largest of Wagner's operas, is a major undertaking, and for its première, when almost no one but Seidl and the soloists were familiar with the music, its preparation dominated the opera house for weeks. Frank's chorus, for example, was enlarged by sixty men from the Arion and Liederkranz societies, and in the final scene he had 142 choristers onstage.[22]

For both Walter and Frank the season was musically exciting, a chance to immerse themselves in some of the greatest music of the century. And it was pleasing that their father was not forgotten. At a benefit concert for the chorus, in which Frank as well as Walter and Seidl conducted, Marianne Brandt sang an aria from Leopold's oratorio *Sulamith.* Her gesture probably pleased many besides the family, for the elder Damrosch was still very much a presence in the city's musical life.[23]

Toward the season's end Walter did something that may not have been wise. For the matinee and evening of March 3 and 4, 1886, he rented the opera house for the Oratorio Society and with Fischer and Brandt as soloists presented in concert form the American première of *Parsifal.* In similar style it had been performed in England in 1884, but Walter's production was only the second of the complete opera outside of Bayreuth.

Walter had been in Germany in the summer of 1882, when *Parsifal* had had its première, had gone to Bayreuth to hear it and had received from

Wagner personally, as a gift to Leopold, a score for the choral finale to Act I, which Leopold promptly had performed with the Oratorio Society. But except for a few specified excerpts, Wagner, who had died the following year, had hoped to restrict the complete opera to Bayreuth, and to that end his widow, Cosima, had forbidden the publisher to rent orchestral parts for the complete opera.

Walter, however, had bought a miniature conductor's score in London in the spring of 1885 and subsequently had hired copyists to make the orchestral parts from it, just as his father had done with the Brahms Symphony No. 1. The purchase of the score gave Walter no right to perform the work, but the penalty, he had discovered, was only £50. And for the American première of the complete opera, he gladly paid.

Every music lover in New York wanted to hear it, and Walter had a success. He had no trouble over the copyright, or with Cosima Wagner, who did not learn of the performance until 1903. But it seems likely that Seidl's antipathy to Walter, which began to show itself in the following year, originated in these concert performances of *Parsifal*.[24]

Seidl was an intimate of the Wagner family. He had lived with them at Bayreuth, had helped Wagner to copy out the scores of *The Ring* and of *Parsifal* and had been one of Wagner's twelve pallbearers. Many people, among them most likely Seidl, looked on Walter's act as a kind of sacrilege, an insult to Wagner's memory and to his widow. And the affront was also to Seidl, for with some justification he could assume that if anyone was to introduce the complete *Parsifal* to the United States, that person was himself.

Walter, perhaps trying to imitate his father, had made a young man's mistake, and he would pay for it. As long as Seidl remained at the Metropolitan, to the extent that the scheduling made it possible, he would not allow Walter to conduct any Wagner.

In the summer of 1886 both Frank and Walter accompanied Stanton to Europe to sign artists for the coming season. It was Frank's first trip to Germany since leaving in 1871, and he was pleased to discover that he was fluent in the language and at home among the customs and people. In Berlin, he paid a nostalgic visit to the violinist Joachim, who frequently had stayed with the family in Breslau. He had been a favorite of the children, for he would sit on the sofa with them and cut out paper dolls, and one time, in anticipation of a visit, Frank had spelled Joachim's name with flowers on the threshold of the guest room.

In midsummer the brothers went to the small, sleepy town of Sonderhausen for a festival at which Liszt would preside, and on one of the programs Walter was to conduct the aria from their father's *Sulamith*, with Marianne Brandt as soloist. Characteristically, Frank decided at the reception that followed the performance not to introduce himself to Liszt, because he felt the occasion belonged to Walter. But Marianne Brandt insisted on it, reminding the old man that the young American she brought to him was his namesake and godson. Liszt kissed him, murmuring, "Your eyes are just like your father's." Frank treasured the benediction, for only two weeks later Liszt died.[25]

Frank's major musical accomplishment that summer, which was to have enormous effect on music in America, was quite inadvertent. One of his jobs was to find a soprano for the title role in the Metropolitan's first production of *Aida*. As the opera would be sung in German, Frank searched in Germany, not Italy, and in Stuttgart found a fine young dramatic singer, Therese Förster. She was eager to come, but was in love with the first cellist in the Stuttgart opera orchestra. Frank auditioned the man, who turned out to be Irish though entirely German-trained, and gave him, too, a contract.

The Metropolitan's first *Aida*, on November 12, was not a success. It was becoming clear that Seidl's extraordinary gifts as a conductor were limited chiefly to German composers. The rhythms and phrasing of Verdi escaped him. Also, with each season it was clearer that the German singers, with the exception of Lilli Lehmann, could not shape an Italian phrase in German, tending always to break it in parts with excessive emphasis. So *Aida* was dropped from the next season's repertory, and Therese Herbert-Förster, as she now called herself, for she had married the cellist, sang only Elsa in *Lohengrin* before disappearing from the Metropolitan's history.

The cellist, whom Frank also had brought over, remained in the orchestra for a time before moving on to found American operetta and musical comedy — for he was Victor Herbert.[26]

Early in 1887 Walter read an announcement in a German newspaper that Hans von Bülow, who was then at the height of his career as pianist and conductor, would spend the summer in Frankfurt am Main, teaching a class of advanced pianists. Relying on his father's old friendship with von Bülow, Walter wrote, asking to be taken as a student, not in piano but in aspects of conducting. In particular he suggested that von Bülow instruct him in the interpretation of the nine Beethoven symphonies and any other music that von Bülow might care to analyze.

Von Bülow's reply was a question: "In what manner do you conceive that your wish could be fulfilled?" And though he described himself as "very much without leisure," he did not close the door entirely. Noting that Walter would be in Europe in the summer, he suggested that they meet in Frankfurt in May. Through that half-opened door Walter firmly pushed, writing that he would leave New York for Frankfurt in late April.[27]

Walter had a problem in musical education. Because of his father's early death, he had arrived too soon at a major position in American musical life. He lacked not only experience in the arts of conducting and interpretation but even some basic training. He was at his best in choral music, was learning his way in opera and was least at home in symphonic music. But with his father dead, there was no person or institution in the United States to which he could turn for instruction.

As von Bülow's question suggested, what Walter sought lacked a model. Conservatories then had no courses on conducting or on interpretation for conductors. The post was still too new, having developed only with Berlioz, Wagner and such disciples as Carl Bergmann. The good conductors of the 1880s, Seidl, Thomas and von Bülow, were self-taught or had learned by assisting other conductors. Though conservatories might offer theory, composition or counterpoint, what they largely taught was singing and playing an instrument. The faculties of those in the United States, at least, included no one with even Walter's experience in conducting. And among Walter's superiors Seidl was, in Walter's phrase, "not friendly," [28] nor of course was Thomas. What Walter wanted he could find only in Europe and probably only in von Bülow — a distinguished conductor, kindly disposed, with the imagination to create a novel course of instruction.

Walter sailed on April 22 on the steamship *Fulda*. Among the passengers were the fifty-one-year-old Andrew Carnegie and his bride of just one hour, Louise Whitfield, who at twenty-eight was only three years older than Walter. Carnegie, whose marriage had been long delayed by his domineering mother, was to be extremely happy with Louise, and in this second half of his life, following the death of his mother and of his only brother, he began to turn his thoughts from steel to politics and philanthropy.

Though Walter had never met Carnegie, the two men had a tie. Carnegie had not known Leopold Damrosch personally, but he had known his work, admired it and had agreed, before Damrosch's death, to join the board of directors of the New York Symphony Society. In fact, he had been elected at the same meeting, on May 28, 1885, at which Walter had been elected the society's conductor. In addition, he was interested in the Oratorio Society, for he liked oratorio, and his bride, Louise, was a member of the chorus. So a friendly crossing was easy and natural, and by the time the Carnegies debarked in England, they had invited Walter to join them later in Scotland. [29]

At Frankfurt Walter had an extraordinary success with von Bülow, piercing the elder man's protective shell with charm and kindness. One night as Walter went to his room in the Schwan Hotel, where both were staying, he heard groans from von Bülow's room. When they did not cease, Walter knocked and, getting no response, went in. Von Bülow, dressed for bed, was on his knees, sobbing into the sheets. He was in a deep depression, convinced that he had failed in art as well as life and that his only refuge was in death. Gradually Walter managed to calm him and get him into bed; then, holding his hand, he sat with him until morning.[30]

Von Bülow, of course, was flattered by Walter's attention, but he also was excited by the idea of what Walter wanted from him, and said that it was the first time any musician had come to him for this sort of instruction. He sent Walter to the local conservatory to study counterpoint and had him attend most of the piano classes, but these were the least part of his program. During the three months that Walter stayed in Frankfurt, von Bülow went through Beethoven's nine symphonies with him, bar by bar, phrase by phrase, discussing such points as the need here or there to have certain instruments of the orchestra play louder or softer in order to realize Beethoven's intent. Some days the sessions in the hotel lasted all morning; others, the two men simply walked in the park or to a museum; one afternoon they stood for three hours on a station platform, talking of music. Walter wrote frequently to Frank, in English. His initial letter began: "I have just had my first lesson with Bülow, so to speak. I met him today at dinner; he was very nice, talkative and invited me to a cup of coffee at Bauer's Café where we sat and he talked away about music, conducting Beethoven, Brahms, Wagner etc. etc. He seems to have taken a liking to me, hates Seidl, and I think an hour with him is worth a year elsewhere."[31]

Eight weeks later his appreciation had deepened greatly: "He has given me courage to go on my own way and to do what I think is right, for I must confess that I sometimes lost faith in myself during the last years."[32] Looking back after thirty-six years, he wrote: "During these three months . . . I received so much from him . . . such a wealth of ideas regarding interpretation and the technic of the conductor's art, that it took me years to digest it properly."[33]

In those years Walter would be distinguished among American conductors for his enthusiasm for composers of English, French, Slavic and American background. He was deaf only to the Italian opera composers, with whom Seidl constantly saddled him at the Metropolitan. But his measure of worth for all music was German, and in symphonic music particularly it was the works of Beethoven, to which, as he once stated in a speech, "all others must be compared before they can have the proud joy of standing by themselves."[34]

His first opportunity to put his new learning to use came in Scotland while he was visiting the Carnegies. They had rented a large house near Perth and had some sixteen guests at the time, including Senator and

Mrs. Eugene Hale of Maine and, also of Maine, James G. Blaine, the Republican candidate for President in 1884. Blaine, who had with him his wife and two daughters, was a highly controversial figure in American politics and had lost the election to Cleveland in one of the country's most unpleasant campaigns. Walter found the Blaine family "charming," and as he wrote to Frank, the girls' stories of the slanders circulated about their father reminded him "of certain passages in Papa's life in America."[35]

Every evening, at Carnegie's request, Walter played for the guests. "Yesterday," he reported to Frank, "I gave them an explanation at the piano of [Beethoven's] V Symphony, its thematic development, etc. and scored a big hit." The success bred an idea, and he wondered aloud to Frank, in his letter, whether in the coming season he should attempt a series of lecture-recitals on works scheduled by the New York Symphony. "I flatter myself that I would draw a crowd . . . Mrs. Carnegie thinks the idea is splendid . . . and I must carve my way in some other mode than Seidl, as I will have no chance at the opera, I know."[36]

That fall in New York he began with Wednesday afternoon lecture-recitals that preceded the public rehearsal for each concert, and they were so well received that in the following year more were added in the evening. It was the start of another "mode" of educating the American public in a love of music, one in which Walter would excel, and which had its foundation, in large part, in the talks that Leopold at the piano had given his children in explanation of Wagner's *Ring*. In the coming years, no matter how large the hall, Walter by his charm could reduce it to a family circle and, by his obvious affection for people and enthusiasm for his subject, win the audience's attention.

Probably no one in these years could meet Carnegie without thinking of his wealth — his annual income at the time was about $1.8 million — and of how it might be put to personal advantage. Walter was no exception. He found Carnegie "a strange man, full of contradictions, of great and good ideas and small conceits," and simply by chattering about music, particularly music in New York, he was able to influence Carnegie's actions. Having discovered, for example, that Carnegie was thinking of sending Thomas and the New York Philharmonic to England, Walter talked so forcefully against the idea that he was able to write to Frank "I've nipped that in the bud." Referring to the New York Symphony, he added, "Carnegie will be all right if he is worked carefully by some of our directors . . . He will do a great deal for us. Wait and see." Then he added, "Last night I gave them the IX Symphony with explanations."[37] If Walter used Carnegie, Carnegie used Walter. Patron and artist. Any Damrosch was prepared to sing for his supper.[38]

Walter's success with the Carnegies promised well for the future; his success with von Bülow had its instant rewards. Toward the close of

Walter's first full season with the Symphony, the critic of the *Herald* had written that he was "not yet a master of his art, but the prospect which seemed so dreary and unpromising at the beginning of the season assumes a brighter and more hopeful view." Encouraging words, perhaps, but hardly the sort to pull in an audience.[39]

Now, eighteen months later, after the first concert of the new season and after Walter's three months with von Bülow, W. J. Henderson of the *Times* wrote that the future of the New York Symphony seemed assured. Though Walter was not yet the equal of his father as a musician, "he has shown himself industrious and ambitious . . . One of the wisest things he ever did was to spend several months abroad this year in hard study under Hans von Bülow. The result of this application was revealed yesterday in his excellent reading of Beethoven's Fifth Symphony."[40]

CHAPTER 9

Hard times. Frank marries Hetty Mosenthal. Walter with Carnegie and James G. Blaine. Helene takes Clara and Ellie to Dresden. Walter marries Margaret Blaine.

THE FAMILY adjusted easily to the small apartment; surroundings were never important to its members, and on most days everyone but Helene was out. Tante had her church services, rehearsals and students, most of whom she taught in their homes. Frank and Walter had their multitude of jobs, which often kept them out also on the weekends and evenings. And the two girls, who went to a private school conducted by a Parisienne, Mme. Mears, carried their lunches to school with them. On their return Ellie might sketch, for which she had a strong talent, or help her mother with a pupil; Clara, with the intensity of a seventeen-year-old, began to write a history of Venice, and reached the Fourth Crusade before quitting.[1]

Though Frank and Walter now made the family's financial decisions, Helene and Tante continued to preside over its events: the great ones, Christmas Eve and birthdays; the small ones, concerts, operas and Sunday dinners. But no one pretended that the death of the husband and father had not changed the family's life. In Tante's phrase, "He had been the center of the house."[2]

One result of his death, hardest perhaps on the two youngest girls, was the decline in the family's social life. No longer did the Schirmers, the Steinways and visiting artists come for meals, and it was not just because of Leopold's absence. Helene by herself, according to Ellie, "had little social sense," and her focus turned now almost exclusively on her family. Walter brought home amusing stories of the people he saw, but he was too young and unimportant to bring the persons themselves; and on the whole Ellie felt they were a bit out of life socially.[3]

Within the family, however, Helene continued to play a leading role. Ellie always enjoyed the trips with her mother to the Washington Market, at first by horse-drawn trolley, later by the "El," which Helene adored. "I want you to see her," Ellie wrote years later,

> tall and fine-looking, wearing a thick gray shawl and black bonnet tied under the chin, walking with a majestic stride, which she had learned on the stage; see her as she greets Mr. Kracke, the butter dealer, and with her beautiful hand takes a small scoop from each of the tubs, to taste which she likes best. Then to the Micolino brothers who had sausages and delicatessen; such kind pleasant men, with soft Italian eyes, full of gracious service. And on to the butcher, Mr. Beck, where she tests the breasts of chickens or turkeys — and so our basket is filled. Then to the wholesale grocer on Vesey St., Moses & Co., where round-faced Irish Mr. Glass, who had a scar over one eye which fascinated me, waits on her for Java and Mocha coffee. He always gave me his lovely crackers with pink sugar on top and always had his little joke with Mother.[4]

Even of marketing, Helene, through her personality, could make an occasion.

One of the greatest events of this period, sad yet proud, was the unveiling, on May 5, 1888, of a monument to Leopold Damrosch in Woodlawn Cemetery. A committee representing the Arion, the Oratorio Society and the New York Symphony had bought the plot and for a monument had chosen a design of Minerva sitting in a Grecian chair, which had been executed in marble. About six hundred people attended the unveiling. A group from the Oratorio Society sang, in English, Chorales No. 72 and 23 from Bach's *St. Matthew Passion,* and another from the Arion, in German, Martin Blumner's motet, *Sei Getreu.* The Oratorio Society's outgoing president, the Reverend William H. Cooke, gave the oration; and the incoming, Andrew Carnegie, though unscheduled, a brief address. At the close of the ceremony the committee's chairman presented the deed to the plot to the head of the family — Walter.[5]

Against the seeming permanency of the marble, however, another event already had occurred that would do much to obliterate any memory of Damrosch. In the previous summer, on July 16, 1887, the Metropolitan Van and Storage Company's warehouse at Broadway and Thirty-eighth Street burned. Lost in the flames was not only all of Helene's furniture, a kind of impairment of identity for a German housewife, but also a vital part of Leopold's identity: the correspondence between him and Liszt, Wagner, Sidney Lanier and a host of other German and American artists. Surviving were only a few charred, honorary batons of ivory.[6]

The pain for his family was not in the monetary value of the burned letters, though in future years that might have been great, but in the knowledge that in the musical histories and biographies to be written, Damrosch would not be cited or quoted. The warehouse fire had cost him his place in the record of his artistic world. Almost forty years later a scholar asking Walter for the Lanier correspondence would record: "Mr. Damrosch, throwing both hands into the air, said with feeling — 'All those beautiful letters went to ashes.' " For Helene, who understood instantly the fire's significance, in its flames Leopold died again.[7]

Besides Frank's work at the opera he led the Newark Harmonic Society, the Choral Club and several smaller singing groups in and about the city, and whenever the opera was in session he had no time for anything but work. Yet in the six months of spring and summer he had some leisure, and he began to spend much of it with Hetty Mosenthal. In fact, though he was slow to realize it, he was courting her. One night in the city, enjoying her company, he walked her home, two miles or more, in the rain.[8]

Her departure in the summer of 1887 for a trip to Europe with her mother and sister brought matters to a head. Whether or not Hetty, with her sister's aid, contrived it, Frank suddenly was alone with Hetty in the stateroom, and in that minute kissed her, for the first time, and stammered out a marriage proposal. Hetty did not reply, but Frank left believing he would be accepted. Being a musician, he promptly composed a song, with a repeated line, "Will she answer 'Yes' or 'No'?" — tempo, agitato, and ending softly on an uncertain chord. A man of different temperament — Walter — might have closed more confidently.[9]

After a visit to Hetty's father to lay the proposal before him, Frank wrote to Hetty:

> Such are my arguments and, while I know that a snug bank account would be worth a hundred more such in the eyes of an anxious parent, I think they are entitled to some consideration. Everything hinges upon the one word: love! With that my arguments are good ones, my chances are good and I may look confidently into the future. Without it — Vanderbilt's millions would not have the power to make me happy. Your father has given me no definite decision, of course, as he wants to hear your answer first. If that is favorable to me, I shall go in to the city and talk things over with him more in detail. It is a great source of satisfaction to me that my mother, who is a thoroughly practicable woman, agrees with my views and that fact also impressed your father, who said that he would take an opportunity to talk it over with her, in case you should write me the hoped and longed for "Yes."
> Whatever then the answer to my last letter may be . . .[10]

But he was too much in love to stop, and the letter goes on and on. They were married on January 10, 1888, in the Mosenthal home, surrounded by family and old friends. Frank had no best man — they were married by a judge in a nonsectarian service — but at his side were Walter and Otto Eidlitz.[11]

The marriage was pleasing to both families. Hetty's father, Herman Mosenthal, was a German immigrant, but in some respects atypical. Before coming to New York, in 1865, he had been a trader in the interior of South Africa, and his wife, Elise, though born in New Orleans of German parents, had lived much of her early life in London. The family was both more American and more cosmopolitan than the Damrosches. Yet they were just as musical. Mosenthal, whose business was insurance, played the piano well and sang German lieder even better, and his brother Joseph, the violinist, composer, conductor, was the musical director of the city's Mendelssohn Glee Club.

Despite this musical heritage, Hetty could not sing; she was one of the 5 percent, in Frank's later estimate, that truly could not hold a pitch. But it was her spirit for which he loved her, and with so much else in common in their backgrounds, they had little trouble adjusting to each other or to their families. When Helene suggested that after the wedding trip to Washington they occupy two rooms above the Damrosch apartment and take their meals with the Damrosch family, that seemed quite reasonable and natural, a part of the German way of life.[12]

In the spring of 1888 Walter again sailed for Europe with the Carnegies, who had planned a coaching party of eleven to drive from London to the castle they had rented in the Scottish Highlands. Walter was to serve as treasurer "with no salary but all the usual perquisites," as Carnegie put it, and the chief guest was to be Blaine, who, in late June, seemed likely to be nominated again in the fall as the Republican presidential candidate. With him, as in the previous summer, were his wife and two daughters, Margaret and Harriet.[13]

On the morning of June 8, while the coachman clucked to his horses and a large crowd cheered, the coach pulled away from the Hotel Metropole and started north. The day was bright, and most of the party was up top, the men in tall gray coaching hats and the women in veils. The pace was leisurely — in the month's drive the four horses were never changed — and except when the party stopped in a cathedral town, they ate every lunch by a brook or in a meadow and passed every night in a different country inn. Because of Blaine, the passage north was haunted by newsmen seeking his views, which he invariably refused. He had been a presidential nominee at four previous Republican conventions, but now, nearing the end of his political career, he wanted not the presidency but a return to secretary of state, a post he had held in 1881 under Garfield. So when word came that Harrison had won the nomination, Blaine was pleased, and conversation turned to the issues on which the Republicans might defeat President Cleveland.

After the first week Walter had to return briefly to London to conduct the Belgian violinist Ovide Musin in a concert at Prince's Hall. On the program was Beethoven's Symphony No. 7, Liszt's *Hungarian Rhapsody No. 1* and Leopold Damrosch's *Serenade* for violin and orchestra. "Papa's *Serenade* made a magnificent impression," Walter wrote Frank. According to the English pianist Harold Bauer, however, who was taken as a child to the concert, the chief interest was in Walter himself. "It seemed almost unbelievable that anything artistic could come out of America." Walter was perhaps the first American conductor to appear in London.[14]

After rejoining the party near Durham, Walter continued with the Carnegies to Cluny Castle, Invernesshire, where he stayed for another month. He found himself fascinated by the political and economic conversations between Blaine and Carnegie. There was so much more to the world than music. "Amid all the excitement of our professional life," he wrote to Frank, "we live too much alone."[15]

Carnegie, short of stature, round-faced, with intense dark eyes set off by a fringe of white hair, was a passionate talker. He enjoyed a discussion, often refusing to accept as true any statement unsupported by analysis or proof. Largely self-educated, he could recite most of Burns and much of Shakespeare, and at table the talk was frequently of poetry and history. He also loved Scottish folk songs and sometimes after dinner, with Walter at the piano, would sing them in a pinched, quavering tenor. But his favorite topics were education and peace, and often when he spoke on these subjects, Walter noticed, his fists would clench.

Blaine was more reserved and complicated. At this time he was both the most popular and most loathed man in America. Starting in 1872, thousands had marched and sung for "Blaine of Maine" to be the country's President. But after the summer of 1876, just as many had marched and sung against him as the "Continental liar from the State of Maine." In that year he had been charged with using his position as Speaker of the House, from 1869 to 1875, to advance his financial interests. The charge may have been false, but Blaine chose to defend himself by blocking the investigation and relying less on truth than on rhetoric and emotion. For that decision he paid a fearful price, not only in the loss of the presidency but in the vilification to which he was subjected every four years. To his disparagers he was "the Tattooed Man" of a famous cartoon, the personification of dishonesty in government, with all his sins burned into his body; to his admirers he was "the Plumed Knight," America's Henry of Navarre, the paladin of all virtues. To friend and foe alike he was one of the greatest orators of the age.

Whatever his public morality, Blaine in private life, as Walter discovered, was extremely attractive. A man of innate dignity, he had simple, gentle manners and a warm love for his family, which was returned with passionate loyalty. Like Carnegie, he was widely read, particularly in American and European history. In two summers, through von Bülow, Carnegie and Blaine, Walter, who had had no college education, had his horizons stretched.

He often went on walks with Carnegie, sometimes lying on the bank while the elder man fished. Even then, with his fly on the water, Carnegie sometimes would talk of his ideas for promoting education and peace. And Walter would talk, too. Carnegie's interest in music was limited. He liked choral singing — oratorio, not opera — and the more intricate symphonic works did not appeal to him. Nevertheless, at some point in the summer, perhaps on one of their walks, Walter persuaded Carnegie to accept the presidency of both the Symphony Society and the Oratorio Society. He did so in the fall, and the step proved of great importance to both groups. "Tell Reno," Walter wrote to Frank, "not to worry about the rent for the S.S. and O.S. We are all right, and as soon as Carnegie can afford it, we will have a hall of our own. Steel rails are rather low now, but the time will come!" Leopold Damrosch had discussed the need for a new hall with the Symphony Society's directors as early as January 1884. Now Walter pushed the discussions hard, and in only three years from the time he wrote that letter, Carnegie Hall, built primarily for the New York Symphony and the Oratorio Society, would be open.[16]

Every evening Walter made his contribution to the house party, and this year, because the Metropolitan in the winter was to present its first cyclic performance of *The Ring,* he concentrated on Wagner. Dinner ended at nine, and then for about an hour during the long Scottish twilight Walter at the piano would take an opera or an act and explain its story and musical themes. "Only Damrosch . . . needs candles to make out his operas," wrote Mrs. Blaine to a son. "So the time passed irresponsibly."[17]

These lecture-recitals on Wagner, expanded and introduced to New York in the fall, proved even more popular than those on symphonic music. In the first season Walter gave sixty; in the second, 110; and in later years, as the total soared into the thousands, he lost count. He had many imitators, including Seidl, who played beautifully but needed a partner to speak. But two have not the ease of one; nor could Seidl, or anyone else, match Walter's ability to create an informal atmosphere or to reproduce on the piano an orchestral score. These lecture-recitals, originating in Carnegie's Scottish homes, not only would provide Walter with a sure source of income, but, spanning fifty years, would be a powerful force in educating the country's musical taste.

By August, Carnegie's guests had begun to go, among them the Blaines. Walter, who had been charmed by the family and perhaps was more than a little in love with the daughter Margaret, wrote to Frank, urging him to call on them when they arrived in New York. If Frank tried, he failed.

The Blaines steamed into the harbor on the *City of New York,* which had just completed a maiden voyage with a record run. But few cared about the ship. Blaine, the most beloved figure in American politics between Clay and Bryan, was back. Excursion boats ploughed the harbor, with bands playing and crowds cheering. Private yachts sailed about, blowing horns. Publishers hastened aboard to get exclusive statements; politicians, to be recorded shaking the great man's hand. That night at an outdoor rally in Madison Square Blaine spoke to thousands. Then, starting for Maine, he quickened the Republican campaign with speech after speech on the tariff.

Walter, hobnobbing with Carnegie, had entered a world where Frank and the family would have difficulty following.

Evidently the financial pressure on the family during these years continued to be bothersome. Though Marie had left through marriage, Hetty had joined, and soon she and Frank were expecting a child. "My brothers," Ellie recalled, "decided to have me stop school." Though she and Clara were on half-scholarships with Mme. Mears, "it was expensive." [18]

The break was temporary, however. Formal education had never been first in the family's priorities. Experience always had counted for more, and Helene wanted her two youngest girls to have a year in Germany studying music. Since there was not enough money to pay for it, she set about creating a scheme whereby she could take them abroad and be self-supporting.

Among the family's friends and acquaintances she offered herself as a chaperone and artistic adviser for any young woman who wanted to study art or music for eight months in Dresden, at the time the artistic center of Germany. Not only did she have her own and Leopold's musical contacts to use, but through their old friends the Prellers, who were living in a suburb of Dresden, she could assure the availability of the best sketching and painting instructors. Soon she had a group of six young women, and in September 1888 she and her daughters sailed in advance to rent an apartment large enough to house nine women and at least three pianos.

Helene's activity on her daughters' behalf, and the family's response to it, were more unusual than at first it might appear. In the Mozart family, and even to some extent in the Mendelssohn family, the equally talented older sister had been denied the training and exposure given her brother.

And in the Damrosch family it would have been easy for Leopold, and even easier for his widow in a time of financial difficulty, to concentrate all the family's attention on the two older boys. That Helene did not allow this to happen, and that her sons supported her in her plan, was extraordinary.

Unlike Frank and Walter, Clara and Ellie had no memories of Germany and found many of the manners and customs strange. They were amazed by the lace paper in which bouquets were wrapped, inclined to mock the obsequiousness of servants and tradesmen and irritated by the way the elder generation in any gathering monopolized the sofas. And they were quite unprepared for Prussian militarism. On a sidewalk army officers often shouldered civilians into the street, and in the opera house they ogled women at close quarters and stared through opera glasses. Even Helene, after her years in the United States, chaffed at the number of *"verbotens"* and the presumption of the many minor officials. [19]

But with the artistic people, especially with the Prellers, they felt quite at home, though some of their instructors seemed rather eccentric. Clara's piano teacher, a Herr Scholz, kept a vase on the piano into which at the start of each lesson she was required to drop the fee. Then he would begin. He taught her a great deal about fingering and perhaps was important to her psychologically, for he insisted on treating her as a future professional. She had the same good luck with her instructor in theory, Johannes Schreyer, who would "almost faint" at any mistake and so held her to the highest standard. In this year, at age twenty, Clara became a pianist of professional competence. [20]

Ellie was less fortunate in her teachers. For piano she had a Fräulein Franke, a tiny, desiccated woman who displayed in her music room all her old wreaths and bouquets. She was enthralled by Ellie's ability to improvise and allowed her to play too much by ear, so little real progress was made. Perhaps as a result, Ellie's interest turned even more to art, in which her instructors worked her harder. [21]

In the spring, as the group broke up, Tante arrived. She had spent the winter keeping house for Walter, Frank and Hetty, and the baby Frank Jr.; but now she joined Helene and the two girls for a round of visits with friends and family, and also for a pilgrimage to Bayreuth. Helene estimated that the four of them could just afford it if they traveled there and back on the railroad third class, which meant sitting for many hours on hard wooden benches. In almost no time she and Tante had sewn little cushions, back and seat, for everyone, and they were off. They had rooms in town with a teacher, walked up the hill to the Festspielhaus, and there heard *Die Meistersinger* and *Parsifal*. During the first intermission one was supposed to eat, but in both operas Ellie found herself so overwhelmed by the music that she simply sat and stared. [22]

When at the end of the summer their steamer entered New York Harbor, Walter was on a tender to meet them, not, it turned out, to hear their news but to deliver some of his own. He was engaged and would be married in the spring to James G. Blaine's daughter Margaret. Only Tante had met her and only once, and the engagement had occurred too late for Walter to have written his mother in Europe. Suddenly the life to which they all thought they were returning was finished, and tears filled the girls' eyes. "Walter had always been living with us," Clara wrote. "His amazing vitality, humor and many interests" had kept "Mother's spirits from depression" and supported each of them. "To hear that this was all to be changed, and not to have ever seen or heard of his chosen one, was a real shock." Try as everyone did to be happy, the homecoming was spoiled.[23]

Margaret Blaine, who by the summer of 1889 was once again the daughter of the secretary of state, was an unusual person. In her features she was strong-boned, large-nosed, thin-lipped, masculine; an admirer once described her as resembling "an American eagle."[24] Yet, so the story goes, at a large party one time a man gazing across the room at her exclaimed to Walter, "Who *is* that extraordinarily homely woman?" And Walter, looking straight at his wife, asked, "Who? Who?" By conventional standards of feminine beauty, she was ugly; she knew it, and she surmounted the handicap with wit and sensitivity to others. To those who knew her best, she was beautiful. The spirit shone through.[25]

Walter seems to have told no one of his aspirations for her. While Helene, Tante and the girls were abroad, he passed much of the summer with Frank, Hetty and the baby in a cabin in the Catskills, remote and cheap. Seized suddenly with the idea of starting a bank account for little Frank, he announced that he would give a Wagner lecture for his nephew's benefit at a mountain hotel, and he cleared $100 after treating the parents to a champagne supper. Then, having outfitted himself with a new blue-and-white blazer, he left to visit the Carnegies in Bar Harbor, Maine.[26]

Blaine, whose book *Twenty Years of Congress* had been a financial success, had just built a large, comfortable house, Blaine Cottage, on Mount Desert Island, and Walter spent a great deal of time there. When he told Carnegie that Margaret had agreed privately to marry him, Carnegie protested. He himself had not married until fifty-one; there was no need for Walter to hurry. But his true reasons soon became clear: he was used to Walter, enjoyed his company and expected Walter to remain, in Walter's phrase, "as a kind of semi-attached musical member of his household." But Walter, who knew that Blaine would consult Carnegie, was young and in love, and though he was eager to keep Carnegie's friendship, he was not a toady, and he argued obstinately. Carnegie soon gave in and promised his approval. The engagement was announced publicly in September during the wedding festivities of Margaret's brother Emmons and Anita McCormick, a marriage that united America's leading political family with one of the country's great fortunes, for Anita's father had invented the McCormick reaper and in time she would own a large share of the International Harvester Company.[27]

After the McCormick alliance, how did the Blaines feel about the Damrosch connection? Some reservation might have seemed likely. Though Walter was the son of a distinguished father and was himself not without distinction, he was, after all, a German immigrant, half-Jew, half-Gentile, without a penny, and engaged in a most unprofitable trade. Yet the Blaines seemed to raise fewer questions about Walter than had Herman Mosenthal about Frank, and Mrs. Blaine soon was referring affectionately to "Margaret's Walter."[28]

The Blaines were themselves a mixed family in religion. Blaine's father had been a Presbyterian and his mother a Catholic, and the boys were raised Protestant and the girls Catholic. Blaine had a sister who was the head of a Catholic convent, and his daughter Margaret, though Protestant, had attended a convent school in Paris for a year. Perhaps this background contributed to her tolerance for persons of all kinds, just as the miseries of her father's political life may have contributed to her enduring spirit. By and large, except for her belief that her father and his branch of the Republican party were God's chosen instrument, she was remarkably free of prejudice or fear. Thus she had freedom to express her generosity to others.

The wedding took place on May 17, 1890, in Blaine's house on Lafayette Square, in Washington, in an Episcopal service conducted by the rector of nearby St. John's Church. For his best man Walter had a Frank Roosevelt, who, except for this singular occasion, seems to have had no part in Walter's life. Apparently all the Damrosch family went, even Ellie, who was suffering at the time with a facial paralysis. Curiously, not one of them has left an account of the wedding, which the *New York Times* reported on its front page. Probably the family members were impressed, and perhaps also a bit cowed, for among the guests were cabinet members, Supreme Court justices and the President of the United States. All in all, it was quite a jump up for an immigrant boy, and in the musical world it sowed seeds of envy that would bear bitter fruit.[29]

CHAPTER 10

Reorganization of the New York Symphony. The libelous article. Walter's festival to inaugurate Carnegie Hall. Tchaikovsky.

AFTER WALTER'S MARRIAGE, Helene, Tante and the two girls moved into a smaller apartment on West Seventy-second Street. Frank and Hetty, though they no longer joined them for all meals, were in the same building, and Walter and Margaret were only two blocks away, so there was much visiting back and forth and eating together. Helene constantly warned the others against expecting Margaret to adjust as easily as Hetty to the German atmosphere and did her best to moderate it.[1] For her part, Margaret, who was fluent in French, struggled to learn German, but without sufficient success for conversation, and her presence forced the others to speak English. In many other ways, too, her entry into the family gave it a sharp tug toward becoming American: in the clothes she wore, the presents she gave and her interest in American history, literature and politics. From now on Walter's Christmas tree, in addition to the usual German cookies and ornaments, always had garlands of cranberries strung on black thread, a New England custom.[2]

Some time after Christmas, apparently, in the winter of 1891, Walter decided to leave the Metropolitan. For six seasons Seidl faithfully had pursued Leopold Damrosch's long-term plan and followed Damrosch's *Tannhäuser, Lohengrin* and *Die Walküre* with productions of every other major Wagner opera except *Parsifal*. Besides first performances at the Metropolitan of *Rienzi* (1886) and *Der Fliegende Holländer* (1889), he had conducted the American premières of *Die Meistersinger* (1886), *Tristan und Isolde* (1886), *Siegfried* (1887), *Götterdämmerung* (1888), *Das Rheingold* (1889), the first performance in cycle of the four operas of *The Ring* (1889) and the Paris version of *Tannhäuser* (1889). But of this Wagnerian feast Walter's portion after the first season was only a few performances each of *Lohengrin* and *Rienzi,* though it was the Wagner operas that he wanted most to conduct.

He also was beginning to draw bad notices, perhaps unfairly. After the performance of *Carmen,* on February 20, in which Minnie Hauk, an American, sang the role in German, the weekly *Musical Courier,* in an unsigned review heavy with sarcasm, referred to the opera as "an entirely new creation, particularly on the part of young Mr. Damrosch."[3]

The critic for the *New York Tribune,* Henry E. Krehbiel, saw more deeply into the difficulty. Minnie Hauk had sung in the American première of *Carmen,* in Italian, in 1878, and now, thirteen years later,

> vocally [her portrayal] is not so fresh and charming as it used to be . . .
> Her freakishness of tempo . . . acted disturbingly on the general effect of
> the performance last night, but the fault was not hers nor entirely that of
> the conductor, Mr. Damrosch. The German company is elastic and spon-
> taneous in musical expression only when works characteristically German
> are performed.[4]

From the start this had proved the weakness in Leopold Damrosch's concept of the Metropolitan's becoming a German company: the popular Italian and French operas did not sing well in German. And Walter, to whom they constantly were assigned, frequently was given bad casts. In December 1888 he had to conduct a *Faust* in which the French opera was sung in German except by the tenor and soprano, who, not knowing German, sang in Italian. The result pleased no one.

In an effort to resolve the problem and to meet the public's demand for good performances of *Carmen* and *Faust,* the Metropolitan's directors decided, in January 1891, that seven seasons of opera in German were enough: they would abandon the concept of a German house and German company and substitute for it a French-Italian house and company. An opera in either French or Italian would be sung in that language; a German opera, including any of Wagner's, would be sung in Italian. The decision angered Walter, to whom it seemed a repudiation of his father. But by then he already had decided to leave the opera at the season's end and to take with him the New York Symphony. He and the orchestra had opportunities elsewhere.[5]

By far the best orchestra in the country at this time was the Boston Symphony, funded by the generosity of Henry L. Higginson. Each year he guaranteed $50,000 toward the anticipated deficit, allowing the players and conductor to be engaged by the year. The continuity in personnel and in rehearsal showed dramatically in performances and also allowed tours to be planned more intelligently. In contrast, the New York Philharmonic was still a cooperative society in which players at the last minute could send substitutes or drop out for part of a season. Thomas, disappointed in his hopes to reorganize it, was leaving at the season's end to found the Chicago Symphony, lured there by the promise of a guarantee fund modeled on Higginson's. For the Philharmonic's next season, sixteen concerts, the society had hired Seidl.

Walter hoped to establish his New York Symphony as a permanent orchestra, on Boston's model. To replace the Metropolitan season he planned two new concert series, one with a popular repertory designed to attract young people, another of celebrity concerts, such as three in the fall of 1891 to introduce Paderewski to the country; and, in addition to the usual tours and summer engagements outside the city, a two-month stand of nightly concerts at Madison Square Garden. Best of all, to ensure some permanency of personnel, at least among the more important players, he was able to announce on February 6 that a guarantee fund of $50,000 had been subscribed by eleven (eventually thirteen) men, including William K. Vanderbilt, J. Pierpont Morgan and Andrew Carnegie.

It was a solid achievement of organization, and most music lovers rejoiced at it. The *Musical Courier,* however, which was developing into Walter's most constant disparager, observed sourly: "Nobody expects that musically the permanent orchestra will be a success, for as everyone knows young Damrosch will conduct that permanent orchestra, and as everyone also knows young Mr. Damrosch is a permanently bad conductor."[6]

But in still another respect that winter Walter had a solid achievement before the public. On the corner of Fifty-seventh Street and Seventh Avenue a new Music Hall was rising, by 1894 to be known universally as Carnegie Hall. Walter had managed to interest Carnegie, who preferred to build libraries, in the housing problem of music in New York. The Oratorio Society and other large choral groups had no suitable place in which either to rehearse or to perform. Both Steinway and Chickering halls were too small, and the Metropolitan, for many choral works, too cavernous. Similarly, with the physical deterioration of the Academy of Music, both of the city's orchestras, the Symphony and the Philharmonic, lacked a good hall. For reasons of social prestige both were giving their concerts at the Metropolitan, but an orchestra playing on the stage had acoustic problems. For once Thomas and his Damrosch rival agreed: the city needed a new hall.

Its creation, for which Carnegie ultimately paid about nine tenths of the cost, was dominated by members of the Oratorio and New York Symphony societies. Carnegie was president of both, and Walter was the musical director. The building's architect, William Burnet Tuthill, was the Oratorio Society's secretary. Morris Reno, the treasurer of both societies, was president of the Music Hall Company, which Carnegie used to build and operate the hall, and Stephen M. Knevals, the Symphony Society's secretary, was the holding company's treasurer. But among these, not surprisingly, it was Carnegie and Walter, in different ways, who made the building rise.

On March 22, 1889, Walter wrote a quick note to Richard Welling, a director of the Symphony Society:

> My dear Welling,
>
> Mr. J. Seligman would like you to go with him on the following mission before the meeting. You know Carnegie is going to build us a hall, that is he has pledged himself to give the necessary funds to see it through; but with characteristic modesty he wants it to seem as if it were built by the two societies and so wants some of the Directors to subscribe to it, no matter how little this may be, and he will take the remainder upon his shoulders. Now we would like the Directors at our meeting next Saturday to show their appreciation of Carnegie's modesty, and so we think it would be wise if you and Seligman went to some of our more prominent Directors such as Auchincloss, Brown, Draper, Howland, Hyde, Keith, Stout, Poor, and asked them to be present at the meeting and to take a little of the stock. I shall subscribe myself and so will Reno, Knevals, and others. If you can, please see Isaac Seligman, Broad Street, about it tomorrow (Tuesday), and try with him at any rate to secure a good attendance at the meeting to do honor to Carnegie's unparalleled generosity.
>
> Yours,
>
> Walter Damrosch[7]

Because Walter's father at Symphony Society meetings had discussed with these men the city's need for a new hall and the kind it should be, Leopold Damrosch became, in their public statements about it, the man who had conceived of it.[8] But behind the scenes, working tirelessly to achieve it, was Walter.

Tuthill, the architect, not only sang in the Oratorio Society but was an enthusiastic amateur cellist and chamber musician, with considerable practical experience in the problems of acoustics. Perhaps the most distinctive feature of his design is the parabolic curve of the roof over the stage, which is reflected in the curve of the proscenium arch and the start of the auditorium's ceiling. He told Edwin T. Rice that the purpose of this and of a similar parabolic reflecting surface at the back of the stage was to project the sound to the audience in parallel waves. Whether or not that is the key to his success, his hall has exceptionally good acoustics.[9]

By January 1891, when the Metropolitan's directors decided to abandon opera in German, the new hall was sufficiently complete so that its creators safely could continue with plans to open it in May with a week's festival. Walter, who was in charge of programs, planned six concerts in five days, with the Oratorio Society and New York Symphony. In his capacity as program director, he invited Tchaikovsky to come and conduct several of his own works to give the festival international panache. Then without warning, on February 25, Walter, Carnegie and Blaine were attacked by the *Musical Courier* in a sensational editorial, probably written by the editor, Marc A. Blumenberg.

The editorial, "Blaine and Music," after reciting the relationship of the U.S. secretary of state to "young Walter Damrosch," recounted a conspiracy. Blaine, angry that Walter was not assigned German operas at the Metropolitan, wished "to wreck German opera at the Metropolitan and out of the wreck raise his son-in-law into greater prominence." He persuaded the secretary of the navy to give Carnegie's steel company a $3 million contract, in return for which Carnegie gave the New York Symphony $50,000, allowing it to expand its season. That, in turn, gave Walter an honorable exit from "the general wreck" at the Metropolitan. Then to prevent the *Tribune* from exposing the conspiracy, Blaine had arranged for its publisher, Whitelaw Reid, to be appointed U.S. minister to France, and the newspaper "was compelled to face about and support Damrosch, after many years of judicious criticism showing the young man's utter incapacity." And there was more, chiefly about the directors of the Metropolitan, who "were apparently readily handled by Mr. Blaine and Mr. Carnegie." [10]

Except that Reid was minister to France, the asserted facts were either distortions — Reid had been appointed in 1889, more than a year before the change of policy at the Metropolitan, and Carnegie was only one of thirteen contributors to the guarantee fund — or wholly without supporting evidence. On its face the article was ludicrous and probably libelous, but it was picked up by other papers and widely discussed. Walter, interviewed by the *New York World*, dismissed the statements as "not worth a reply." [11]

Carnegie and Blaine, of course, cared little or nothing about the opinion of the *Musical Courier*, and probably neither gave the attack, or its consequences, a second thought. One of its immediate effects, however, apparently put a caution into the journalistic world generally. When the new hall opened, the building was praised warmly, but its sponsors were treated rather coolly. The *World*, for example, observed that "no one will grudge Mr. Carnegie the credit of giving New York one of the finest concert halls in the world." [12] Yet the editorial's tone was — grudging. And the *Times*, in referring to the series of concerts Walter arranged for the opening-week festival, insisted they were "interesting and meritorious, though by no means extraordinary." [13] Yet they offered important American and New York premières and Tchaikovsky in person, the first great composer to come to the United States to conduct his own works.

In fact, for its day the festival was unique and a turning point in the country's musical history.

On the other hand, for Walter, in the musical world, the editorial in the *Musical Courier* and its consequences were serious. Blumenberg continued his attacks and in the coming years was seconded by the critic for the *Evening Post,* Henry T. Finck. Both men wrote as close to the line of libel as they dared, and often crossed it. Blumenberg in 1902 was sued for libel by Victor Herbert and lost. Finck, after involving his paper in three suits, which were settled, and being warned by the paper that in future he personally would be responsible for the costs of defense, grew more careful.[14]

Whatever quirks of character impelled these men to write such criticism, one source of it seems to have been envy — of Walter's youth, good looks, high spirits and, above all, his marriage. In 1926 Finck still was sneering at Walter, "Was ever a babe born with such a big golden — nay, platinum — spoon in his mouth?"[15] Of course Frank Damrosch shared Walter's heritage, but he never was so charged. It was Walter's marriage and the entry it gave him into the world of the rich and powerful that stirred the envy.

Ultimately Blumenberg, Finck and their occasional imitators affected Walter's reputation, for there are always some who believe everything they read and others who, while disclaiming knowledge, insist that smoke betokens fire. These critics successfully attached to Walter, at least for some part of the public, a charge of dilettantism: the young man without talent whose positions were bought for him by rich and influential friends. Fortunately for Walter his nature was unusually resilient, and he was able to survive the barrage. But for the next thirty-five years, starting in this winter of 1890–91, when he reorganized the New York Symphony and opened Carnegie Hall, he was subjected to what one historian has judged to be "some of the most vitriolic slander in the history of American criticism."[16]

On the pier to greet Tchaikovsky when he first set foot in the New World, late in the afternoon of April 26, 1891, was a group of five, rather oddly joined. Its leader was Morris Reno, president of the Music Hall company, under whose auspices the composer had been invited to participate in the festival to open Carnegie Hall. For support Reno had brought his daughter Alice, who spoke fluent French, and she in turn had brought a young man who has passed into history unidentified. Reno also personified the festival's orchestra and chorus, the New York Symphony and the Oratorio Society; and to represent the orchestra further he had invited one of the most hard-working and generous members of its board of directors, E. Francis Hyde.[17] A fourth man, Ferdinand Mayer, the New York representative of Knabe & Company of Baltimore, seems simply to have attached himself to the others in the hope eventually of winning Tchaikovsky's endorsement of the Knabe piano.

As Tchaikovsky came toward them, there was a problem of language. None but he spoke Russian, and his English was limited to broken phrases; in French and German, though, he was fluent. Reno spoke bad German but at his side had Alice and her French. Hyde had only English, so he smiled and smiled; the unidentified young man continued his self-concealment by remaining silent throughout. Mayer, who was fluent in German and in the coming days often materialized at Tchaikovsky's side, awaited his opportunity. On the drive to the Hotel Normandie, on Broadway at Thirty-eighth Street, Tchaikovsky sat next to "the pretty Miss Alice," as he described her in his diary, and carried on "an unbelievably amiable and incredibly animated conversation (as though I were pleased with all that was happening)."[18]

For Reno, the festival to open the new hall and the two weeks of association with Tchaikovsky were the climax and reward for twenty years of work to make better music in New York possible: twenty years of serving in the ungrateful post of treasurer or manager to organizations or festivals sparked by Leopold and Walter Damrosch. Now, despite his apprehension, for two weeks he would enjoy Tchaikovsky's company and through the great man's diary and letters achieve a modicum of immortality. For Tchaikovsky, too, the visit would be more pleasant than he had dared to hope, and but for his melancholia, which put a cloud into every sky, he might have acknowledged himself happy.

Typically, however, as soon as he and the others arrived at his hotel, his mood changed, and, suddenly despairing, he refused all invitations to dinner and begged to be left alone. When the others had gone, as he later wrote to his brother:

> I began to walk up and down my rooms (I have two) and shed many tears . . . After a bath, I dressed, dined against my inclination and went for a stroll down Broadway. An extraordinary street! Houses of one or two stories alternate with some nine-storied buildings. Most original. I was struck with the number of Negro faces I saw. When I got back, I began crying again, and slept like the dead, as I always do after tears. I awoke refreshed, but the tears are always in my eyes.[19]

The first to call on him the next morning was Mayer, who chatted pleasantly and helped him with a reporter. Then came Reno to take him to a rehearsal, and the two, with Mayer, walked uptown to the new hall, which Tchaikovsky declared "magnificent." Inside, Walter was working on the finale of Beethoven's Symphony No. 5, and, concluding, he made a little speech in German to introduce Tchaikovsky to the orchestra. The men responded with an ovation. Tchaikovsky's music was both popular and admired, and the previous season under Walter the men had given the American première of the Symphony No. 4. Now here he was, the first great composer to visit the United States, preparing to lead them in his *Suite No. 3.* The moment was solemn; the men played their best, and Tchaikovsky recorded, "The orchestra is excellent."

Following the rehearsal Mayer took Tchaikovsky to lunch. He "helped me to buy a hat, presented me with a hundred cigarettes, showed me the very interesting Hoffmann Bar, which is decorated with the most beautiful pictures, statues and tapestries, and finally brought me home. I lay down to rest, exhausted."

Soon, however, Reno appeared, eager to introduce him to Mrs. Reno and to Alice's two older sisters, Anna and Paula. The Renos in their way of life were very like the Damrosch family, and Tchaikovsky, who came from a large family, felt at ease with them. One night, after a small family dinner, he played duets with Alice, and "the evening passed very pleasantly."

That first night, he had dined with Walter and Margaret Damrosch — just the three of them. In future years Walter and Margaret would entertain visiting dignitaries lavishly, but for the moment Walter, with Carnegie's help,[20] still was contributing to the support of his mother and younger sisters, and Margaret's parents had heavy expenses in Washington. Tchaikovsky, like many others, assumed that because Blaine was secretary of state, his daughter was rich. But the official dinner in the composer's honor, two nights later, was given by the Renos.

After dinner Walter took Tchaikovsky to meet Carnegie, and the musician and the steel magnate, though conversing in French and seemingly so different in temperament and background, proved congenial. Tchaikovsky was struck and apparently comforted by Carnegie's resemblance to the Russian dramatist Alexander Ostrovsky, and when Carnegie began to talk enthusiastically of Moscow, which he had visited two years before, Tchaikovsky was charmed. Inevitably the talk turned to music, and Carnegie, who believed that "folk songs are the best foundation for sure progress to the heights of Beethoven and Wagner,"[21] asked Walter to play some Scottish songs on the piano. Tchaikovsky left impressed by Carnegie.

During the next week the rehearsals for the festival went badly and well. One was spoiled for Tchaikovsky by workmen in the hall "hammering, shouting, and running hither and thither"; another, when he felt Walter was monopolizing the orchestra's time. On the other hand the Oratorio Society, which would sing two of his songs, *Our Father* and *Legend,* greeted him with an ovation and "sang beautifully." And whenever he had a moment of leisure, there was Mayer, who showed him a great deal of New York, including the Knabe warehouse. Of lower Broadway Tchaikovsky recorded, "The houses downtown are simply colossal; I cannot understand how anyone can live on the thirteenth floor."

Mayer's fluent German was a great relief. Tchaikovsky instinctively liked Hyde, a corporate lawyer and banker, but

> the language in which we converse . . . [is] the queerest mixture of English, French and German. Every word which Hyde utters . . . is the result of an extraordinary intellectual effort: literally a whole minute passes before there emerges, from an indefinite murmur, some word so weird-sounding that it is impossible to tell to which of the three languages it belongs. Yet all the time Hyde and his wife have such a serious, good-natured air.

He found he liked the country and the people. "New York, American customs, American hospitality," he wrote his nephew, "all their comforts and arrangements — everything, in fact, is to my taste." And then the sudden swing in mood: "If only I were younger" — in a week he would be fifty-one — "I should very much enjoy my visit."

On the evening of Tuesday, May 5, the festival opened with a concert and speech to dedicate the hall. The audience gathered promptly, and among the boxes of the rich and fashionable two were distinguished with floral decorations, one for Andrew Carnegie and the other for Secretary of State James G. Blaine. Margaret sat with her father and mother, for the Damrosch family had no box, inasmuch as Walter was conducting and the five women of the family, Helene, Tante, Clara, Ellie and Marie Wiechmann, were onstage with the chorus. When Carnegie entered the rose-garlanded Box 33, many in the audience, as well as the Oratorio Society, already onstage, burst into applause. The chorus, numbering some four hundred, were on platforms to the back; the women, in the first five rows, dressed all in white, the men behind, in black. Before them, occupying nearly half the stage, was the New York Symphony. Promptly at eight Walter entered, raised his baton and led the orchestra, chorus and audience in the hymn *Old Hundred:* "Praise God from whom all blessings flow . . ."

To Tchaikovsky, in Reno's box, the hall "lit up and crowded with people was very fine and effective." Reno meanwhile was backstage, waiting to introduce the evening's orator, Episcopal Bishop Henry C. Potter. The chore, to Tchaikovsky's amusement, had caused Reno "much anxiety." Potter reviewed the roles of Carl Bergmann and Theodore Thomas in the country's musical history, admired the works of Leopold Damrosch, regretting that the man had not lived to see the hall he had conceived, and finally, in conventional, sonorous phrases, praised Carnegie for building it. Then followed the national anthem, not yet *The Star Spangled Banner,* but *America:* "My Country, 'Tis of Thee."

At last the musical part of the program began, with Walter leading the orchestra in Beethoven's *Leonore Overture No. 3,* "beautifully rendered," in Tchaikovsky's opinion. Next the composer went to the podium to conduct his *Marche Solennelle,* was greeted with loud applause and had a great success. Then followed the evening's chief work, Berlioz's *Te Deum* in its New York première. Tchaikovsky found it "somewhat wearisome; only toward the end I began to enjoy it"; and the public seemed to share his opinion. The evening ended as "Reno carried me off with him. An improvised supper. Slept like a log."

More important, of course, than the music of a single concert was the hall, and the next morning critics and public alike praised its acoustics. The architect, Tuthill, no doubt was relieved, and the hall's sponsors, delighted. At the Hotel Normandie, however, Tchaikovsky was in a crescendo of despair. A number of the newspapers, which he evidently had translated for him, spent more time discussing his appearance and personality than his music. Into his diary, with exclamation points of indignation, he copied from the *Herald:* "Tchaikovsky is a man of ample proportions, with rather grey hair, well built, of pleasing appearance, and about sixty years of age (!!!). He seemed rather nervous, and answered the applause with a number of stiff little bows. But as soon as he had taken up the baton, he was quite master of himself."

With commercial photography yet to be developed, newspapers then relied more than today on words to describe celebrities, and reporters frequently wrote carelessly. At the *Herald,* for example, they had known for months that Tchaikovsky was coming and would be a source of news, but no one had bothered even to determine his age. And several other papers on his arrival had announced that he was traveling with a young and pretty wife, because at the pier the reporters had seen him enter a carriage with Alice Reno. But it was the "stiff little bows" that upset him: "I cannot bear to think that my shyness is noticeable."

He was a composer not a conductor, and Walter soon saw that the rehearsals and concerts "fatigued him excessively." Yet "he knew what he wanted, and the atmosphere which emanated from him was so sympathetic and love-compelling that all executants strove with double eagerness to divine his intentions."[22] For Tchaikovsky, conducting was always an agony. Before the third concert, in which he was to lead his *Suite No. 3,* he entered in his diary: "This curious fright I suffer is very strange. How many times have I already conducted the Suite, and it goes splendidly. Why this anxiety? I suffer horribly, and it gets worse and worse. I never remember feeling so anxious before. Perhaps it is because over here they pay so much attention to my outward appearance, and consequently my shyness is more noticeable."

In the second and the sixth, or final, concert, Tchaikovsky had no part. These offered the major contributions of the Oratorio Society, Mendelssohn's *Elijah* and Handel's *Israel in Egypt*. The society also sang Leopold Damrosch's *Sulamith* and, an American première, Heinrich Schütz's seventeenth-century cantata, *The Seven Words of Our Savior*.

Tchaikovsky's major work in the festival was his Piano Concerto No. 1, played by Adele Aus-der-Ohe, which he led at the fifth concert, the Saturday matinee. He had invited her to the hotel, where "I showed her various little nuances and delicate details, which — after yesterday's rehearsal — I considered necessary, in view of her powerful, clean, brilliant but somewhat rough, style of playing." The performance apparently was ragged but exciting, and since it was Tchaikovsky's final appearance on the podium, he was recalled again and again. "But what I valued most of all was the enthusiasm of the orchestra."

That night, at the festival's last concert — *Israel in Egypt* — the hall's architect, Tuthill, received an ovation. Walter's programs, models for their day, had subjected the hall to many kinds of music — solo voices, unaccompanied singing, mass choral works, light Mozart, heavier Beethoven and the full romantic orchestra of Wagner, Berlioz and Tchaikovsky — and the hall had responded to each equally well. Tuthill had earned his applause.

For Tchaikovsky the visit began to wind down. He went the next night to the Carnegies' for dinner with just Margaret and Walter, the Renos, the Tuthills and a few others. Carnegie, declaring that Tchaikovsky was a genuine though uncrowned king of music, "got on tiptoe and stretched his hand up to indicate my greatness, and finally made the whole company laugh by imitating my conducting. This he did so solemnly, so well, and so like me, that I myself was quite delighted."

The next day he left for Niagara to see the falls, with all the arrangements made for him by Mayer of Knabe. "How should I have got on without Mayer?" he wondered. A few days later, back in New York, he went to say good-by to Damrosch, who was sailing for Europe. "He asked me to take him as a pupil. Of course I refused, but am afraid involuntarily I showed far too plainly my horror at the idea." As Walter's schedule was too crowded for a sojourn in Russia, it seems likely that an attempted compliment had been misunderstood.

Then Tchaikovsky went for a farewell dinner with the Hydes:

Hyde greeted me with these words: "Kak vasche sdorovie? sidite poschaljust." (How are you? Please sit down.) Then he laughed like a lunatic, and his wife and I joined in. He had bought a guide to Russian conversation, and learnt a few words as a surprise to me. Mrs. Hyde immediately invited me to smoke a cigarette in her drawing room — the climax of hospitality in America.

There remained Mayer, who finally had proposed that Tchaikovsky write a testimonial for Knabe pianos. He suggested that it should read:

"I consider the Knabe pianofortes without doubt the best in America."
Tchaikovsky responded, with the guile of innocence: "Now as I do *not*
think so at all, but value some other maker's [Steinway] far more highly,
I declined to have my opinion expressed in this form. I told [Mayer] that
notwithstanding my deep gratitude to him, I could not tell a lie." And
the encomium was changed to read: "[Knabe piano] combines with great
volume of tone a rare sympathetic and noble tone color and perfect
action."

   Then suddenly he was gone, leaving behind many who missed him.
"I have never met," Walter wrote later, "a great composer so gentle, so
modest — almost diffident — as he." [23] In the United States he had conducted at only six concerts, four in the festival at Carnegie Hall and one
each in Baltimore and Philadelphia, and Reno had talked to him about
returning the following year. With that in mind, Walter planned a three-
month tour for the New York Symphony during which Tchaikovsky
could conduct twenty concerts, not an arduous schedule, but he declined.
A year later, however, he gave the American première of his Symphony
No. 6 to Walter, who performed it with the New York Symphony on
March 16, 1894, in the hall to which Tchaikovsky had lent such luster.

   In the history of music in America the importance of Carnegie Hall
can hardly be overestimated, and the contribution of two members of
the Damrosch family toward its creation was very great. Without Leopold to plant the seed and nurture it among the directors of the Oratorio
Society and the New York Symphony, and without Walter to bring
together these directors, competent, honest and music-loving, with the
reluctant, doubtful but rich Carnegie, the hall would not have been built.
For in the same year in which the Damrosch-led forces succeeded so
admirably, Theodore Thomas, unable to reorganize the New York Philharmonic or to raise a guarantee fund to subsidize his own orchestra, left
for Chicago. As the *World* pointed out editorially, the city's music lovers
had cause for pride and shame. The *Times* was more directly disparaging
of Walter: the city was losing the better conductor, for Walter was not
the equal of Thomas in any musical capacity "excepting possibly that of
chorus master." [24]

   The significance of the hall lay both in the present and future. It gave
an immediate home to the Oratorio Society and New York Symphony,
and, beginning a year later, to the Philharmonic. These three, a majority
of the city's most important musical organizations, at once established
the hall, opera aside, as the musical center of New York. As such, with
its good acoustics and attractive décor, it exerted a powerful pull on visiting orchestras. Thomas brought his year-old Chicago Symphony to it
in 1892, and the Boston Symphony came in 1893.

   Nevertheless, at first bookings were slow, partially, it was discovered,
because foreign artists associated the official name, Music Hall, with an

English tradition of beer-hall entertainment. By the fall of 1894 programs and advertisements bore the title Carnegie Hall.

It did not pay for itself, much to Carnegie's distress. "He could understand," Walter wrote of him, "that a library, a school, or a hospital could not and should not be self-supporting, but I could not convince him that music should fall into the same category. He always insisted that the greatest patronage of music should come from a paying public rather than from private endowment." [25] Each year until Carnegie's death, in 1919, the Music Hall Company would lose about $25,000, which he would pay, always protesting.

The hall's greatest contribution was the stimulation it gave to musicians and their managers to make use of it. Here, in the cultural capital of the country, was a large, attractive hall (it had a capacity of twenty-eight hundred) with good acoustics, and any afternoon or evening that it was not in use was a reproach to musicians — and a lure. When empty, the hall cried out to be filled. [26]

But it offered more than just a space. A feature of its acoustics particularly appealing to performers was that what they heard of themselves onstage was about the same, in force, balance and quality, as what the audience heard in the auditorium. Among performers — and also audiences — it quickly earned a reputation as an aurally true and responsive hall.

It also began to serve as a focus for the country's attention, a place in which by general consent the country's standards of performance were set. A Carnegie recital or concert became in itself an accolade, a testament of worth. And perhaps some such focus was necessary for the further development of musical taste in the country. Some symbol was needed of the standard against which musicians would be judged.

Roughly, by 1890–91 the turbulent, starting years of classical music in the United States, when excuses were offered and allowed, were over. One sign of this was the standard of Wagnerian opera set by Leopold Damrosch and Anton Seidl at the Metropolitan from 1885 to 1891; another, the excellence in that same period of the Boston Symphony Orchestra; still others, the founding in 1891 of the Chicago Symphony under Theodore Thomas and the visit that year of Tchaikovsky to conduct his own works; and finally, not the least of these, the closing in May 1890 of old Steinway Hall on Fourteenth Street and the opening, just a year later, of the larger, better, still-excellent Carnegie Hall.

CHAPTER 11

*Frank's disappointment in Bayreuth. Walter in love. Frank founds the People's
Singing Classes. Ellie marries Harry Seymour. The first union strike against a
symphony orchestra. Frank founds the Musical Art Society.*

IN THE SUMMER OF 1891 Frank went to Berlin for three months to
study with Moritz Moszkowski, composer and pianist, then at the height
of his fame. The trip caused him considerable anguish. For lack of money
he and Hetty decided that she must remain at home with Frank Jr., almost three. It was only a summer, but the summer was Frank's only
period of leisure. Further, Hetty's Uncle Joseph, himself an outstanding
teacher of music, thought the project ridiculous: Moszkowski was not
worth a trip to Europe, and Frank did not need more musical education.

Without any formal training, Frank at thirty-two had attained a recognized position among New York musicians, not only as the chorusmaster at the Metropolitan and conductor of its occasional ballets, but
as a director of small choral groups. He felt deficient, however, in composition and musical theory, and he was inclined by birth and upbringing
to think that only in Germany, perhaps only in Berlin, where his father
had studied, could he find the specialized training he needed. His interest
in music in these years was continuing to shift from virtuoso performance, whether on piano, stage or podium, toward scholarship, education and choral singing, and it may be that unconsciously he wanted to
test himself against European standards before moving in ways yet un-
imagined in musical education in the United States. Howsoever, the
summer proved crucial.

He sailed on the *Columbia* with Walter and the Carnegies. Walter
planned only a short trip to recruit instrumentalists for the reorganized
New York Symphony, but the Carnegies once again had rented Cluny
Castle in the Scottish Highlands, and they invited the brothers to visit,

together or separately. Walter at once accepted, but Frank, until he had arrived in Berlin and learned Moszkowski's schedule, declined.

At times he could hardly bear the separation from Hetty. For Frank, marriage and family life were based on shared experience, and the impact of any event, however stimulating, was diminished if unshared. He wrote long letters home so that Hetty could see with his eye and hear with his ear, and the letters are a declaration of musical independence.[1]

His lessons with Moszkowski, who refused any pay, were entirely satisfactory: Frank learned what he wanted of canons, fugues and the sonata form. In general, however, the standard of musical performance in Germany disappointed him, particularly of Wagner's operas.

> Yesterday . . . *Tannhäuser* formed a fitting climax to the gradual demolition of all my fond recollections of Bayreuth, which had begun to crumble in *Parsifal,* to totter in *Tristan* and to fall headlong in *Tannhäuser.* Musically, our New York performances were better . . . To think that *I* should ever lose my faith in Bayreuth when hitherto I have been so full of its praise and so certain of its success as an education in art . . .[2]

Frank, though he did not think of himself as such, after six years as Seidl's chorusmaster and of professional association with singers like Materna, Brandt, Lehmann, Alvary and Fischer, was an expert in Wagnerian performance, and he judged competently. Perhaps, in disappointment, he also judged too harshly.

> The *musician's* confidence in Bayreuth is gone. There will be numbers of amateurs for some time yet who will come here because it has become the fashion, but it has ceased for the present to be the high school for the musician where he was taught what standard to set for himself in striving for perfection. It is no longer the model . . .[3]

In the future, for artistic leadership he would look to himself, not Germany. And as in art, so in politics. "I wish I were home. I am sick of Europe. It is all a delusion and a snare . . . We have a beautiful, broad productive country and free institutions and a spirit lives in our people which causes them to strive continually for greater perfection in every way. We do not need Europe."

Of all the Damrosch children Frank, the eldest, had the strongest ties to Germany, and his break with it came hard. Only five years earlier a visit to Germany had seemed to revive his roots there, but now at home he had a wife, and a child who was learning, Hetty wrote, big words like "otherwise." And Frank's passion was not only in rejecting Europe but in taking the United States to heart. Unlike his brother and sisters, who had seldom left New York, he knew something of the country as a whole. "Let the art student who can see understandingly," he wrote to

Hetty, "come here and learn both how to do and how not to do, and then go home and labor in his art inspired by *American* ideals."[4]

Unconsciously, in the midst of his summer of study in Berlin, he was describing himself and his attitude toward his art in the years to come.

A prize that Walter brought back from Germany, in the summer of 1891, was a new concertmaster for the New York Symphony, Adolph Brodsky, a Russian violinist and senior professor at the Leipzig Conservatory. Brodsky was an internationally known performer, the first to play Tchaikovsky's Violin Concerto, in Vienna, in 1881; and under his leadership the violins of the New York orchestra improved.

Walter and the Symphony Society had an advantage over the Philharmonic in their ability to better the orchestra by hiring foreign musicians. The members of the Philharmonic, a cooperative society of local musicians, were not inclined to import players more expert than themselves, and ordinarily they made a virtue of the Musical Mutual Protective Union's "six-month rule," which provided that a foreigner could not become a union member, and therefore could not accept a position, until he had resided in the United States for half a year. In Brodsky's case Walter apparently was able to persuade the union to waive its rule on the ground that the position of concertmaster required an extraordinary musician not otherwise available.

Brodsky's leadership, however, was not limited to the orchestra. To lure him to New York Walter had talked of the city's need of a good resident string quartet and had promised support in founding one. Soon after Brodsky arrived, therefore, he helped him to organize the New York Symphony String Quartet, which for three seasons, until Brodsky went to England, gave recitals in the Carnegie Chamber Music Hall; and on two occasions, when a pianist was needed, Walter played. The quartet's success was great. The cellist was a Dane, the others, all Slavs, and they played with brilliant dynamics and vivid color, in contrast to the more usual German style, which tended to be rhythmically less varied and without much vibrato. In Edwin Rice's opinion, it was "the most distinguished quartet which New York was to have between the disbanding of the [Theodore] Thomas–[William] Mason Quartet in 1868 and the arrival of the Flonzaley Quartet in 1904." And for it he gave some credit to Walter.[5]

Without the opera Walter was able to give full attention to the orchestra, and though the Philharmonic, conducted now by Seidl, still had more prestige as the country's oldest orchestra, the Symphony, which performed more often, was improving its quality steadily and in the excitement of its programs often surpassing its rival. But not all the excitement was of Walter's making. Some arose simply because Walter and the orchestra, to keep at work, were available for hire.

In the fall of 1891, for example, Steinway & Sons, to advertise their pianos, arranged a tour for the latest European sensation, a Pole named Ignace J. Paderewski. On November 17, backed by Walter and the New York Symphony, he made his American debut in Carnegie Hall, playing his own Concerto in A and Saint-Saëns's Concerto No. 4. The gross receipts were only $500, and many tickets were distributed free. But never again. With a second and third concert that week, the Paderewski phenomenon began. Girls, at first hired but later acting spontaneously, on the final note would rush down the aisles, shrieking "Paderooski!" Grown women, too, seemed to go quite mad — over his nobility, his sadness, his fantastic red hair — and Steinway expanded the tour from eighty to 107 concerts. "Not since Liszt . . ." said everyone. And later tours, which followed almost every year, became royal processions. In the countryside crowds waited at railroad crossings to see his private car pass, and in the cities people often lined the streets from his hotel to the concert hall.[6]

As always, to make ends meet and to keep the orchestra together, there was extensive touring, which Walter at this time found particularly difficult. Margaret was pregnant, and on May 18, 1892, bore a daughter, whom they named Alice, after Margaret's sister. Walter heard of the birth by telegram in Buffalo, just as he was about to start a concert, and afterward his colleagues insisted on a supper, with many toasts to the baby. Back in his room at 2:00 A.M., though exhausted, he sat down to write to his "dearest, dearest Mag."

Despite rehearsals, travel and concerts, he wrote to her almost every day, and as much about her as the baby. "I have been dreaming of my little daughter. She was a kind of miniature Margaret Blaine and I was holding her in my arms and kissing her and she seemed to grow until it was you I held, but I kept right on kissing."[7]

Later that summer when he was in New York conducting concerts nightly at the Madison Square Garden and Margaret was in Maine with her parents, he wrote her a poem of forty lines, in which he imagined himself on a train "To meet my Margaret."

> Her skin like alabaster white
> Her tresses raven as the night
> Her eyes like coals of fire glow
> Her breasts like luscious mounds of snow . . .[8]

The metaphors and conceits may be wholly unoriginal, but his mind was on her, which cannot have displeased her.

Her side of the correspondence is lost, but evidently she responded to his passion, though she was shyer in the expression of her feelings. In one letter, for example, he follows "How I shall pet you when I get home!" with "I can see the frown on your face as you read this."[9] But in his letters his sense of his body, its health, needs and attributes, is always strong and open.

He was not insensitive to other needs, however. For the Blaine family the summer of 1892 was "that dreadful summer," which climaxed a series of tragedies. In January of 1890 Blaine's eldest son, Walker, his political heir and assistant, had died, and within three weeks also his eldest daughter, Alice. Two years later, at the Republican convention at Minneapolis in June, the fifth convention in which Blaine figured as a possible presidential candidate, he was represented by his second son, Emmons, married to Anita McCormick. And immediately after the convention Emmons died of ptomaine poisoning, so suddenly that his parents' first knowledge of the fact came from a newspaper. By then Blaine, who had developed Bright's disease, had resigned his cabinet post, and the family, with the stricken Anita and her year-old child, gathered at Bar Harbor. Blaine's death, on January 27, 1893, was plainly forecast.

From New York Walter wrote:

My dearest Margaret,

Whenever you write me about your mother and Anita, and their inconsolable sorrow . . . I ponder and ponder on the mystery of it. Why we have these strong personal affections and why, after the loss of one we love, life seems to offer so little for enjoyment. To those who have the old simple faith the question is a more simple one. They can wait with calm confidence, even with joyful anticipation, for the reunion in another world to come.

But what is then left to those who cannot believe the old creed, to whom the future means nothing but a mysterious veil through which they cannot pierce . . .

It is very difficult to put into words, but I have a strong conviction that ART is destined eventually to supply the necessary softening to the sorrow of the World. I mean the search after the Beautiful, the education of our sensibilities to its perception as it exists constantly around us, whether in the marvelous workings of Nature, in earth, water, sky, or in the creations of the artists, the poets, painters and musicians. This is the divine revelation on earth . . .

That which is beautiful, perfect, can never cease to exert its power, its charm on the mind and heart of those who have once come under its influence, and to those who cannot believe the old faith Art will become the only possible substitute. Both are a protest against the hopelessness of sorrow. —

In reading the above over again I find it so clumsy and imperfect in its contentions that I am half tempted not to send it to you at all. But still I think you will understand what I mean.

Your loving,
Walter[10]

★

On August 27, 1892, while Frank was at Newport, teaching singing to a club of rich women, a workman at the Metropolitan dropped a lighted match on the stage, and the interior of the house burned. The directors canceled the coming season, and Frank, the chorusmaster, was out of a job. But —

no one was happier than I to chuck the opera. There was never time to devote study enough to anything so it could be perfected. For instance, the chorus imported from Germany knew all the standard works but each knew it in a different way, with different cuts etc. There was never time to make it a whole. It made me unhappy and I wanted to get clear of it, but I was married and even $1500 could not be given up.[11]

Frank had many small posts to sustain him and Hetty, such as the Choral Club and the Newark Harmonic Society; and to these he added others, among them the Spence School, the Bridgeport Oratorio Society and the Orpheus Club in Philadelphia. But for the next few years he and Hetty were hard pressed financially, and with the birth of a second child, named Helen, after her grandmother, and the addition to the family of a nurse-cook-companion, "Swedish Annie," who stayed with them for fifty years, they could contribute only little to the support and education of others.

Fortunately the needs of others were decreasing. Clara, after her year in Dresden, had been able to start a career as piano teacher with Walter's aid in getting pupils, and now, like Tante, was almost self-supporting. There remained only Helene, nearing sixty and no longer teaching, and Ellie, who was attending the Art Students League. Frank and Hetty, living in the same apartment house as the four women, provided emotional support; and Walter and Margaret, only slightly farther away, probably with help from Carnegie and perhaps an occasional contribution from Frank, covered any financial needs.

Freed of the opera, Frank debated his course. What he wanted to do most was to found a music school, and occasionally he talked to rich men about his ideas, but none as yet had offered to back him. So for the moment he put that idea aside and turned to another.

On Sundays he played the organ for services of Dr. Felix Adler's Society for Ethical Culture, which advocated, roughly, the ethics of the Jewish and Christian religions without their dogmas. Adler postulated that a moral law existed, that a person had a sense of duty and that each individual was of infinite worth. Everyone, therefore, had a duty to love and help a neighbor, and adherents of the Ethical Culture movement were often pioneers in establishing free kindergartens, settlement houses, visiting-nurse and legal-aid associations and educational courses for adults. The movement had its center in New York, in Adler, but extended to other cities.

The emphasis on ethics and behavior, without dogma, appealed to Frank. By nature he was a silent man, and even with Hetty he never discussed such enigmas as the meaning of injustice, the purpose of life or of death. Yet he was not unmindful of such questions, and with Adler's philosophy as a premise he gradually conceived of the idea of exposing the rewards of music, emotional and philosophical, to the poorer classes or, as they then were called, Working People. He would teach those who wished to learn how to read music and to sing.

He took his idea to a man, Charles Stover, who was administering some model tenements maintained by the Society for Ethical Culture. Stover called in a local labor leader, Edward King, who promised the support of the trade unions, provided that the singing classes were self-financing, not objects of charity. Only Frank's services, King's and those of their assistants should be donated, which was also Frank's feeling. From their meetings emerged a bulletin addressed by Frank

To the Working People of New York:

Recognizing the fact that music contributes more than any other art to brighten and beautify our lives, and that it is the art which can be practiced by the greatest number of people, since nature has furnished nearly every person with a correct ear and a singing voice, I have decided to open a course of lessons in reading music and choral singing.

It is my purpose to teach everyone who desires to learn, to read music from notes, and I hope ultimately to form from the members of these classes a grand People's Chorus that shall be able to sing the greatest works of the greatest masters.

The classes shall be practically free, the small fee of 10 cents a lesson going only towards paying for the rent of the hall and such incidental expenses as may be necessary to the proper maintenance of the classes. There will be no extra charge for music, or books of any kind. If there should be a surplus in the treasury at the end of the first season, it will be placed to the credit of a fund for the future development and enlargement of these classes. My own services and the services of all officers assisting me in the management will be given free.

All persons desiring to become members should send their names and addresses to the General Secretary, Edward King, No. 146 Forsyth Street, so that there may be no delay in preparing their membership cards.

The regular lessons will be given every Sunday afternoon in large hall, Cooper Union, at 4 o'clock, until further notice, beginning October 23, 1892.

No male applicant under eighteen years of age, and no female applicant under fifteen, will be admitted.

Frank Damrosch[12]

On the back side were some general rules, chiefly to the effect that bad behavior would not be tolerated, in artistic matters Frank's word would be law, and at the end of the year a rebate of $1.00 would be offered to every singer with an unbroken record of attendance.

The bulletin suggests Frank's position in the city. Though many persons, no doubt, knew the name only through memories of his father or knowledge of his brother, still it was the opinion of Stover and King that Frank's name alone, without title or job description, would suffice. Simply, Frank Damrosch.

At the first meeting he and Hetty went down to Cooper Union together. Outside in the street there was a crowd of a thousand or more around the front door, apparently not yet opened. In fact, the hall was filled, and the crowd was overflow. Frank had to explain his plans to several "sittings" in the hall and to promise that instead of a single class the following Sunday, there would be two, at three o'clock and at four.

The following Sunday the classes began, and the singers apparently represented every country in Europe, with the majority perhaps from Germany, and among them a number of Negroes. Most were, indeed, from the poorer, working class; most, but not all, were young, and women outnumbered men by three to two.

Frank began with single notes and their position on the musical staff, which he drew on the blackboard. Soon he had a scale, and the class, following his lead, sang it up and down, sometimes reversing direction, sometimes skipping a note. When the singers seemed almost perfect in the scale, he turned the blackboard around and on its back wrote a simple tune, with words, "Oh, how lovely is the evening." They sang it in unison, and then he divided the group into three, and, to their own amazement and mounting excitement, they sang it as a round. After the second class had concluded, an executive committee, elected by class members under the guidance of Edward King, met to administer the business affairs of what were now called the People's Singing Classes.[13]

Enrollment swelled, and before Christmas two subsidiary classes were started on the city's East Side, to the north and south of Cooper Union. From Italy, in November, Carnegie wrote to Frank:

> Your distinguished Brother had better look out or the highest laurels of the family may cover your head. Mrs. Carnegie and I rejoice at your success; am almost jealous of Cooper Institute that's doing a work which would have honored ours [Carnegie Hall], but I suppose the location determined the matter; besides our President may be so full of profitable engagements for the Hall as to render him unapproachable by poor people . . . Congratulations on your *original* idea and its popular triumph.[14]

In the spring, as his pupils' reward, Frank hired Carnegie Hall for Sunday afternoon, May 28, 1893, and presented some five hundred of the best of them to themselves and friends in a concert. The opening number, *God Save Our Native Land,* had been written for the occasion by Hetty's uncle, Joseph Mosenthal, and dedicated to the People's Singing Classes. To make up the program Frank asked several professionals to contribute their talents, among them Clara's friend the violinist Geraldine Morgan, who played a mazurka by Wieniawski. But the chief part of the program was the singers themselves in such works as Handel's *See, the Conquering Hero Comes,* Hauptmann's *Resolute Lovers,* Barnby's *Sweet and Low* and Morley's *Now Is the Month of Maying.* At the end, as a surprise, the tenor Plunket Greene came onstage to sing Irish songs with Walter Damrosch at the piano.[15] The concert was declared by everyone to be a great success. And every spring there was another, starting the next year with the New York Symphony as accompanying orchestra, so that more ambitious works could be presented; even, eventually, complete oratorios.

The number of people eager to sing continued to increase, and the next year two classes on the West Side were added to the three existing, all under assistants chosen by Frank from teachers with whom he had worked. He visited each subsidiary class at least once a month, and he himself taught an advanced class, to which all who had missed not more than a third of the lessons were admitted without examination.

Music critics and reporters, attending some of the early classes and concerts, were perplexed by what they saw and heard. Was it music, social service work or perhaps a public variation of a German singing society? What standards should be applied? By the end of the second year the questions were still unanswered, but as enrollment steadily mounted and new classes continued to form, it was clear that Frank's People's Singing Classes were indeed a popular triumph and, in their ambiguous nature, a highly original contribution to life in New York.

In the winter of 1892–93 it became evident that Ellie, who soon would be twenty-one, had fallen in love. At the Art Students League, where she studied under Kenyon Cox, she and other students had formed a sketch club that on weekends included a night student named Harry Seymour. Toward spring the club had an exhibition of members' works, and Tante noticed that Seymour bought all of Ellie's sketches, "showing which way the wind was blowing." Soon they were engaged.[16]

Seymour was a businessman, eleven years older than Ellie. As a boy he had sketched horses by the hour and dreamed of becoming an architect, but on his father's sudden death he had been forced to leave college and take a job with a hardware firm to help support his mother, sister and brother. About music he seems to have known or cared little, but his love of art continued with him for life.

Like Margaret Blaine he gave the Damrosch family another sharp tug toward American ways. He was a simpler person than Margaret, without her sophistication. He was not fluent in a foreign language, was less familiar than she with European culture and not so knowledgeable about American history and politics. On the other hand he had an adventurous spirit and in the coming years would do much to establish American business in the Orient. Though sensitive, he was less likely than Margaret to adjust easily to the customs of the Damrosch family, and Ellie, in marrying him, made a sharper break with her family than had Walter in marrying Margaret; sharper perhaps than she expected or was prepared to make.

The wedding took place on the evening of November 1 in Helene's apartment, and Frank and Hetty's, which adjoined, was also used for the reception and dancing. Ellie, like all her family, was of no religious denomination, and Harry could be described as a dormant Episcopalian. So the service was conducted by an Episcopal minister against a distinctive Damrosch touch: throughout, Walter softly played Wagner on the piano; not Lohengrin, however, but Parsifal. In other respects the wedding was more conventional. Ellie wore a simple white dress of Chinese crepe with a tulle veil, was given away by Frank and attended by Clara as maid of honor, and as her bridesmaids had her two best friends, Mary Lawrence, a cousin of the groom, and Alice Reno. Seymour's best man was his cousin Henry Lawrence. All the Damrosch family was present, including Marie and Ferdi Wiechmann, the first to marry and now the parents of a girl and boy; also all the Renos and Mosenthals. On the groom's side, because Harry's mother was in North Carolina, tending his sister Julia, who had tuberculosis, the largest clan was Lawrence.[17]

After the dancing began, the party became lively, and Walter, as always, provided much of the fun. One of his jokes, heavy-handed in a Germanic sort of way, left Clara ruffled. Almost fifty years later she recorded, "The rascal placed me on a chair, auctioning me off as a remnant that could be had cheap! I was the only unmarried member of the Damrosch family!"[18] The jibe had stung.

After the wedding Harry and Ellie started on a trip to the South while Tante and Helene prepared an apartment for them on West Eighty-first Street, unpacking all their presents, including a splendid sterling tea service from the Carnegies. The goal of the southern trip was Asheville, where Harry's mother and sister were. There, every day the honeymooners rode horseback through the mountains bright with autumn color, but it became a Damrosch family joke that despite the sights of Washington, Richmond, Norfolk, Asheville and the glories of the Carolina mountains, all that Ellie talked of in her letters was the good food.

In December 1893, Walter, as he had done earlier with the violinist Brodsky, attempted to improve the New York Symphony by importing a Scandinavian, Anton Hegner, to lead the cellos. He expected the Musical Mutual Protective Union to grant Hegner an honorary membership and thus to waive its six-month rule. Though throughout the country there were many nonunion orchestras, of which the Boston Symphony was the outstanding example, in New York City membership in the union, which had started in 1860 as a German fraternal club, was important. This time, however, Walter's plan went astray.

At the meeting in the union's clubhouse, at Third Avenue and Ninety-first Street, Walter was accused of trying to bring over "rafts of pauper musicians."[19]

He replied that his purpose was "purely artistic." Herr Hegner — though the language of the meeting apparently was English, the overtones were German — would replace Herr Hekking, who had left to tour Europe as a soloist. An exceptional cellist was needed, and Walter, calling the residence rule "obnoxious," urged the meeting not to enforce it in Hegner's case: "It prevents a foreign musician from coming here and earning his own living from the beginning as nine-tenths of the members of this union have done." And he stated, perhaps too bluntly, that much of the objection to Hegner came from "certain members of my orchestra whom I have not re-engaged for this year."

As Walter read his motion to grant Hegner honorary membership there were murmurs of opposition around the hall, followed by cries of denunciation, and one member, according to the delicate *New York Times,* cried out, "We don't give a —— for art — all we are after is dollars and cents."

"If you do not care for art," snapped Walter, "this is no place for me." He offered his resignation, and in anger walked out.

Two days later, at Carnegie Hall, as he was preparing for a concert, Walter told the orchestra, "The Advisory Committee and myself have decided that Herr Hegner is to play the cello in the New York Symphony. The rest lies with you."

The men conferred. Under union rules the penalty for playing once with a nonunion musician was $10; twice, $20; three times, expulsion. At a time when $30 a week was high pay for a musician, the fines were heavy, and in New York City expulsion meant a change of occupation.

A spokesman asked Walter whether he would pay their fines.

"No, I will not."

"Well, we will play for you anyhow."

The concert went ahead as scheduled, and the union assessed the fines. The men undoubtedly hoped that Walter and the union president, Alexander Bremer, would work out a compromise. But there seems to have been no negotiation. Bremer, who earned his living not as a musician but as an official in the city government, apparently had little sympathy for the orchestra, and Walter was either a victim of his own anger or, just possibly, hoped to win through to a nonunion orchestra, like the Boston Symphony.

On Sunday evening, December 17, came the second concert, and according to David Mannes, then a violinist in the orchestra,

> when we were seated Mr. Hegner took his place. Not a sign of disturbance appeared, but the men looked pale and worried. The opening number was the overture to *Phèdre,* by Massenet, the first bars of which are played by the brass. Mr. Damrosch's stick descended. Not a sound. The tension was frightening. The conductor pleaded with the men, begging them to help him in what he considered a rightful cause. At such a moment one forgot the audience . . . The baton again descended. Silence and absolute stillness.

The *Times,* headlining its story DAMROSCH WAVED IN VAIN, reported that "the audience became excited and Mr. Damrosch nervous. He advanced to the edge of the platform and, facing the audience, said: 'I regret to say that my men refuse to play with my imported cellist, Mr. Hegner. I am very sorry that this has happened. The audience will get back their money at the box office.' "

Walter then rushed from the stage. A member of the orchestra's strike committee tried to read to the audience a statement explaining the strikers' position, but the audience refused to listen, and there were cries of "Shame! Shame!" Meanwhile a few of the orchestra, including Mannes, hurried to Walter's dressing room, where they found him "weeping bitterly."

Two days later the Symphony Society announced the cancellation of its season, a hundred concerts in twenty-five weeks. The *Times* reported that the orchestra "which Walter Damrosch has worked so hard for the last three years to establish is a thing of the past." Walter, asked by a reporter for his plans, said, "I have no plans."

By the week's end, however, an agreement was reached. The Symphony Society would proceed with its season and pay the orchestra for the week of nonperformance. The union would reinstate Damrosch and rescind the fines of the men. Hegner could play solo performances and, after being in the country six months, could join the orchestra. On all important points the union had won.[20]

The strike was the first in a full-fledged symphony orchestra in the United States, and it exhibits in plainest fashion several themes that would turn up often in the union movement among musicians. The real issue was not working conditions or wages but job monopoly — in this case a single job lasting only a few months, for there was never any question that Hegner, after six months and a day, would be admitted to the union.

The more expert, full-time musicians did not control the union; the orchestra was quite content with Hegner. Those who objected were chiefly the less expert, part-time musicians like Bremer, a full-time municipal worker. And in the majority's objection there was, apparently, a good deal of personal animosity against the conductor for setting the standard the majority could not meet.

Some part of artistic control was transferred from the conductor or employer of the orchestra to the union, and used, whether for personal or principled reasons, to impede musical improvement. On occasion in the future this shift in power would affect the competence of an orchestra and even its repertory.[21]

In the United States one of the great arguments for unions in industry has been that they bring to the factory or mine the democracy of the country's politics. In music, however, the argument always has been less persuasive, for music seems to thrive on tyranny, whether Wagner's at Bayreuth, Higginson's over the Boston Symphony, or, in the 1930s, Toscanini's over the New York Philharmonic. The German immigrant musicians who founded in most cities the fraternal societies that developed into the local music unions seem to have felt the difficulty, and for a long time refused to associate themselves with the union movement. For some, perhaps, this was snobbery: Germans versus other nationalities, and artists versus laborers. But others saw real differences between music, a profitless trade, and industry, which generated wealth. Yet for lack of any original, imaginative alternative to industrial unionism the existing musical societies began in 1896 to affiliate with the American Federation of Labor. Perhaps the trouble was that the most original, imaginative minds in music were not in the union clubhouse but elsewhere, making music. For all of musicians, though, the penalty for not devising a more suitable tool for protecting wages and working conditions often has been strikes of great bitterness.

For Walter the arrival on the musical scene of a powerful union was a tremendous shock. It was not something with which his father had been forced to contend. In the field of classical music Walter, with justification, could claim that no musician in New York was doing as much as he to establish a full-time orchestra on a permanent basis — yet he was opposed by the union. And, of course, there was *amour propre:* that this should happen to a Damrosch. He felt hit from behind by a force that had never been there before. In the years to come, he would have many fights with the union and through them all manage to retain his good humor, even when publicly censured. This first time he not only lost his temper, but to the *Times* reporter "he certainly looked a man who was very much worried and unstrung by his troubles and as if they had preyed upon him more than he was willing to say, possibly more than he knew."[22]

In the fall of 1893, while Walter struggled with the union, Frank brought into existence a musical organization that was to make a profound contribution to the development of musical knowledge and taste in the United States. This was the Musical Art Society of New York, which for twenty-six seasons offered two concerts a year in Carnegie Hall, introducing to the country's musicians and music lovers the unaccompanied, or *a cappella,* choral masterworks of the sixteenth and seventeenth centuries. And in origin and structure the society was quite the opposite of the People's Singing Classes.

For several years in the late summer Frank had gone to Newport, Rhode Island, to teach a group of women to sing. These were rich, society women, among them Mrs. Nicholas Fish, Mrs. Robert Goelet, Miss Mary Callender and Miss Laura J. Post. The women did not pretend to be musicians, but they enjoyed their singing, and they liked Frank. As a result, when he proposed in September, having talked first with Miss Post, that the group found a society to put on professional concerts of esoteric music — works by such as Palestrina, Sweelinck, Scarlatti and di Lasso — they listened, and asked him to prepare an estimate of cost.

In New York on November 9, at a meeting at Mrs. Fish's house at 53 Irving Place, Frank laid before the women a plan for a Musical Art Society "whose objects should be the improvement of choral and concerted music; the introduction here of the works of Palestrina and other great masters, and the placing of this music within the reach of teachers, students, etc., at a nominal price." The emphasis on education was typical of Frank.[23]

He proposed a chorus of fifty professionals who would be paid $20 a concert. Soloists would have to be hired and might cost as much as $500 apiece. His own services would be donated, at least — because the women protested — until other bills were paid. Carnegie Hall was available on March 3 and April 21, and he strongly urged the second concert in order to fix the society and its purpose in the public mind. Each concert would cost about $4000. Would the women underwrite the concerts and manage the business affairs of the society?

They were not inexperienced; they knew what they were getting into: mailing lists, subscription seats, prima donnas on the stage and in the audience, crises and the constant need to raise money. Yet they agreed, electing Mrs. Fish president, Mrs. Andrew Carnegie, Mrs. Richard Irvin and Mrs. Robert Goelet vice-presidents, Miss Post secretary, and Mr. Dyneley Prince treasurer. Frank reserved the hall for the two nights and began to hire and train his chorus. Among the sopranos were Tante and Ellie, or, as they appeared in the program, Miss Marie von Heimburg and Mrs. Henry Trowbridge Seymour.[24]

Frank once had written Hetty that the American artist should study in Europe "and then go home and labor in his art inspired by American ideals."[25] The People's Singing Classes in aim and organization were very American, and so, too, in its organization, was the Musical Art Society. In Europe the usual patron of musicians was the king, the archbishop or nobleman; the usual supporting institution, the court or church; and over the centuries a powerful tradition of sponsoring music and musicians had developed. In the United States, which had no court or established church, there was no such tradition, and although Carnegie and others fitted the pattern of the rich nobleman, they were too few for a continent where institutions of all kinds needed to be created at once, from scratch. Into the vacuum moved the American woman. Some men like to mock the women's committees. These men are fools. In the United States the role of women in the support and spread of music has been vital.[26]

For the first concert the chief choral works were Bach's motet for double chorus *Sing Ye to the Lord,* Palestrina's *Stabat Mater* and, to close, a part song by the nineteenth-century Englishman Henry Leslie and a madrigal by the eighteenth-century musicologist John Stafford Smith. The soloists varied the program with a chaconne for violin solo by Bach, an opera aria by Gluck and two Italian songs by Rontani and Scarlatti. It was, for its day, a highly unusual program and set the pattern that Frank developed more fully in subsequent concerts: the first section, liturgical and usually unaccompanied; the second, instrumental and with vocal soloists; and the third, modern music that continued the spirit of the earlier sections. By the end of the society's third season, in April 1896, it had presented fifty rarely heard works, of which fifteen were American premières.[27]

With the Musical Art Society, Frank made another highly original contribution to life in New York, matching the People's Singing Classes. And the difference between the two, one so scholarly, the other popular, exhibited the range, within choral work, of his musicianship. Following his father's death, in 1885, he had returned to New York from Denver wondering whether he could accomplish any useful work in the city. Ten years later he would have appeared on any list of the city's ten outstanding musicians.

CHAPTER 12

Clara and settlement work. Early life of David Mannes. Clara and David.

IN THE YEARS immediately after Ellie's marriage, Clara, Tante noticed, was "rather lonely and unhappy." As the last unmarried child, she continued to live with her mother and aunt, but she had many piano pupils and, except that she paid no board, was self-supporting and independent. Her first savings had been spent on a trip to the Chicago World's Fair, and later, with her mother's approval, she traveled through Europe alone, shocking the conservative von Heimburgs in Jever and Oldenburg but delighting the artistic Prellers. She made no effort to save: money, on her parents' example, was to be used "to further interests that meant not only pleasure, but experience and inner growth." [1]

To do something for others, however, she worked part time one winter at a settlement house, teaching music to the children of the poor and organizing outings for them. Her efforts there failed, and she had the courage to acknowledge the reason. "I hate dirt, and when walking through those utterly neglected slum streets and at my room in the Settlement where all the very dirty smelly children clung to me, my humanitarian instincts faded." She had no love for people in the mass. "My strong, deep affections always have been limited to relatively few." Still, she tried to discipline herself, and took the children to Bedloe's Island "to give them a taste of pure air and country." The outing was not a success. The children complained that the country "smelt funny," and she, that the children were "only too glad to get back to their grimy streets and tenements." After a year she quit, "thoroughly ashamed of myself," but refusing to persist in a role for which she felt ill suited. [2]

She continued to study music and also sketching, for which she had considerable talent, but her life was without plan, undoubtedly a reason for her unhappiness. Generally speaking, for a woman instrumentalist in these years the only option for a career was either touring as a virtuoso or teaching, and Clara had no desire to travel alone as a concert pianist back and forth across the country. Unlike her brothers she did not wish to conduct, even supposing they could widen for her the very narrow church and school career then open to women as conductors. She had a nice alto voice and sang with the Oratorio Society, but her voice was not so grand as Helene's or so well trained as Tante's. Chamber music was still her great interest, and for pleasure she frequently played piano and violin sonatas with her friend Geraldine Morgan. But for a woman pianist at this time a career in chamber music was impossible: the works played were almost entirely string quartets, the players almost invariably men, and the audiences very small, existing as yet in only a few cities. For Clara the future seemed to hold only a succession of piano students with perhaps an occasional recital or concert.[3]

Then one evening on her return home from teaching she found her mother and Tante in the living room, entertaining two men. One was Orrin Parsons, a painter in her sketching class; the other, she learned, was David Mannes, a violinist in the New York Symphony. She recognized his face and recalled that Parsons had remarked that Mannes wanted to meet her. An introduction, therefore, was the purpose of the call.

Clara could see that Helene was either bored or disapproving, for her mother's manner was reserved, even cold, and if not for Tante, the conversation would have stalled altogether, for Parsons was scarcely talkative, and Mannes, almost speechless. He was tall, thin and ill placed on a three-cornered chair that thrust his long legs and arms into prominence. To Clara he seemed all wrists, knees and shanks, and looking at him, she hardly could repress a smile.

Parsons soon rose, murmured his good-bys and departed. To the women's surprise Mannes stayed, so once again Clara and Tante picked up the conversation and tried to shake it into life. Almost by chance Clara said to him, "You must come and play with me some time," but he seized on the words as a true invitation and accepted promptly, another meeting ensured. Seeming only then to notice that Parsons already had gone, he uncoiled from the wretched chair and left. When she returned from the front door, Clara burst out laughing.[4]

Whereas Clara, as a Damrosch, had a royal road to a life in music, Mannes, as a child of very poor Polish immigrants, had to create his own, though his parents helped where they could. They had come to New York in 1860, and all but the eldest of their children — David was the fifth of seven — were born in the city, in its roughest section, known as the Tenderloin. There, because of saloons on every corner and whorehouses between, rents were low, and Henry and Nathalia Mannes, Orthodox Jews, attempted to raise decent, loving children. Two of the seven died early; of the four boys who survived, one went west to become a lumberjack, one sank into a life of crime and prison, David became a musician and his nearest elder brother, Owen, joined the father in creating what in time, after several failures, became a successful store and interior decorating business, the Hampton Shops, Incorporated. Madeleine, the youngest and the only girl, apparently never married and led a quiet life.[5]

Though the parents took their children to synagogue, their religious temperament evidently had room for independent thinking, for young David was allowed, with only mild rebukes, to joke about the hypocrisy of the pious.[6] Later, articulating a family attitude, he deplored Jewish exclusiveness: "Only the limited Jews want to wall themselves up with their own kind."[7] Ultimately he did not subscribe to any religious group and with justification entitled his autobiography *Music Is My Faith*. Yet all his life he read the New Testament, accounted Jesus the supreme example to be emulated and considered music, in light of that example, "merely an instrument towards serving others."[8] From another of his heroes, also regarded as a model of service to his fellows, Abraham Lincoln, he drew much the same lesson.

When he was five, in 1871, he had an accident that influenced the course of his life. One day in the kitchen, while teaching a younger brother to walk, he stepped backward and tipped into a boiler of steaming linen that his mother had only just taken from the stove. His screams brought help, but his back, shoulders to hips, was so severely scalded that the doctor feared he might die. For months he suffered the agony of mustard plasters applied to open sores; later, in convalescence, unable to walk, he was pushed about the streets in a baby carriage by his father. For years he could sleep only on his stomach.

He was never thereafter very strong, and in the summers his parents sent him to visit his father's cousin who lived in Cobbleskill, New York. The cousin had married the daughter of a Lutheran minister who had a farm nearby, and there young David saw the cycle of birth, life and death among animals and also discovered that he was handy in fixing anything mechanical.

At home he learned Polish and German, partly because his mother, who was illiterate, never mastered English. His father spoke it, but not easily or well, and the children learned most of their English in the street and at public school. Mannes spent only four years in school, because he hated it: "The hard benches, the crowded rooms, the fetid atmosphere, the spitting boys and tired, irritable teachers — these were no incentive to learning. The filth was indescribable (there was no plumbing whatsoever), and the heat and litter of the crowded basement yard at recess-time made even that small oasis sordid." Like his future wife he was extremely fastidious, for which his brothers laughed at him, but he persevered, introducing the family to the toothbrush and nightshirt. "Heretofore, one shirt had served adequately (so they thought) for the entire twenty-four hours."[9]

One day, curious about the pitch and quality of sounds, he experimented with strings under tension and soon had made of a cigar box and other odds and ends a one-string fiddle. He was taking months, even years, to achieve the musical understanding that the Damrosch children, with Leopold and Helene for parents, were granted almost at birth. The Mannes parents, though, were impressed and sympathetic, and they bought their son a cheap violin and arranged for lessons from a man in a theater orchestra.

Here again in comparison to the Damrosch children Mannes suffered a lag. Although in half an hour with their father they could learn what top-quality playing was, it took Mannes two years and several teachers before he had a clear understanding of his goal. And even that came by chance. A man passing in the street heard him practicing, rang the doorbell and asked to be introduced.

This man, John Douglas, was a Negro, "well-dressed, short and stout, wearing a moustache and goatee à la Napoleon III."[10] When he was a young man, his mother's employers, white people, had sent him to Dresden to study under Eduard Rappoldi, and later he had studied in Paris. He spoke French and German, was a first-class violinist and was thoroughly educated in classical music. He became, for love of music, Mannes' friend and teacher and more than any other started the young boy on the way to becoming a better-than-average violinist. His own life, however, was tragic. Because of his color no symphony orchestra would hire him, and though he could support himself by playing the guitar, he eventually grew despondent and took to drink. Mannes felt his friend's fate keenly and all his life sought to improve the opportunities for Negro musicians, in part by founding in Harlem the Music School Settlement for Colored People and serving as a trustee and adviser to the music department of Fisk University.

By the time he was fifteen Mannes was playing regularly in small dance bands that would take any job offered. One, at the Coney Island roller-skating rink during the summer, was too much for him physically. Under the long hours, sweltering heat and incessant noise of the skates, he began to lose weight and had to quit. The nicer jobs were playing at parties in respectable houses; the less nice, of which at first he had to take many, were playing in public dance halls and whorehouses.

The events at the latter were often appalling. At a ball given by the Coal Shovelers Association at Walhalla Hall, on Canal Street, the lights went out and amid screams a man was stabbed. That, at least, was in the dark. In a whorehouse one night his eye was distracted by a man vigorously shaking a bottle of champagne while holding his thumb over its mouth to develop a good head of fizz. Then suddenly with his left hand the man lifted a woman's skirt from the back, bent her over double, exposing her naked bottom, and with a loud cry inserted the bottle neck-deep in her rectum.

Young David's jaw went slack, his bow slithered from his fiddle and he was recalled to his duties by the leader's insistent voice: "Play, you little son-of-a-bitch, play!" [11]

As a boy he kept such incidents to himself. Even when grown, he seldom talked of them and never romanticized them. What he had seen was man at his most brutish, and even the memory of it was upsetting.

For a time he was kept out of the musicians' union by the chairman of the examining committee, who bore his father a grudge. And this kept him out of the better jobs, in theater rather than dance orchestras. Fortunately, one day he auditioned for the leader of a theater orchestra who was eager enough to hire him to raise a row within the examining committee, which then admitted him, and his life greatly improved. The pit orchestras of the time, often no more than eight or ten men, used to play light and classical music before, after and during the intervals of the plays. If there was some music associated with the play, it would be used: Mendelssohn for *Midsummer Night's Dream,* Beethoven for *Coriolanus,* and so on. Mannes loved the theater, and it, in turn, provided him with the education he lacked: poetry, history, thought — in time he would place Shaw as a hero beside Jesus and Lincoln — and the English language. Listening night after night to the declamation of Richard Mansfield, Edwin Booth or William Faversham, he gradually replaced the grammar and accents of the Tenderloin with the most polished and expressive of the day.

Yet with each step forward he suffered hours of increasing depression, when the gap between what he could hear in his mind and what he could play on his violin seemed ever greater. The Damrosches, too, had their moments of despair and discouragement. Even Leopold had been afflicted by his "Daemon," as Helene called the brooding silence and physical inactivity that sometimes followed a real or imagined failure. [12] But none suffered so severely as Mannes, who could be reduced for hours, even days at a time, to inert existence, sitting silent, staring and unresponsive.

Throughout his years in theater orchestras Mannes' ideal musician was Leopold Damrosch, partly because he had read somewhere that Damrosch, like himself, had no immediate ancestors who were musical, but also because of "my mother's adoration of him." [13] One evening he took his mother to the balcony of the Metropolitan to hear Damrosch's *Die Walküre,* and she, perhaps more easily than those who could read and write, had given herself wholly to the music drama and made of the conductor a hero. From then on, of an evening, she had delighted in walking with her musical son past the Damrosch house merely to gaze at the great man's windows.

Six years later, despite a summer of study in Berlin and an occasional pickup job in a symphony orchestra, Mannes still was playing in theaters, although now sometimes conducting the orchestra, which he greatly enjoyed. But on the opening night of a comedy, *All the Comforts of Home,* with William Faversham, he was first violinist, and after the first act he played a solo, standing in the orchestra pit. To his surprise there was long and enthusiastic applause, and others in the orchestra told him that the applause was led by Walter Damrosch, sitting in a box with friends. Damrosch, they said, was rumored to be looking for violinists for his new, permanent symphony orchestra, which was to open Carnegie Hall in May. Mannes, who often had been disappointed, assumed that nothing would happen: "I went home feeling I had caught a glimpse of a world, a star that had gleamed for an instant but whose light was not meant for me. I told no one."

The next morning, his father in the greatest excitement called upstairs through the speaking tube from the store: a Mr. Kayser, Mr. Damrosch's orchestra manager, was here to see David. And Mannes was requested to audition for Walter at the opera house. The audition went well: "He accompanied me, sitting easily at the piano, watching me most of the time. At last he said, 'Why did you not come to me before?' I said that I thought I wasn't good enough. 'Kayser,' he called through the open door, 'make out a contract for David Mannes, as first violin at thirty-five dollars a week and for the season of forty weeks.' "

The contract made a great change in Mannes' life, not all of it joyful. Everyone in his family recognized that it would lift him at once into a world in which his brothers had no part or interest and which, because of the time and attention it would demand, necessarily would loosen his ties with his sister and parents, whom he greatly loved. Yet everyone rejoiced for him. "Mother's joy had an added flavor, the proving of her prophecies, the entire fulfillment of the dream. The son of the man she had adored had sought me out and placed me among the highest. She cared not about the salary or its conditions; her romance it was, and always continued to be."[14]

Characteristically he felt inadequately prepared, and with Walter's approval he skipped the May Festival in Carnegie Hall, going instead to Berlin to study under Carl Halir, to whom Walter gave him an introduction. He stayed abroad all summer, the longest he had ever been away from his family, and returned just a week before the orchestra's rehearsals began. He was placed among the first violins at the fifth stand, and at the opening rehearsal Walter, speaking in elegant German, welcomed the men briefly, called for attention and began with the program's principal number, Beethoven's Symphony No. 5. Mannes had never played a Beethoven symphony.

But now the musical experiences he had missed because of poverty, ill health or conflicting hours of work came in dizzying profusion. On Paderewski playing Beethoven's *Emperor* concerto: "What I had simply hoped and prayed for had come to pass. The instrument was forgotten, a great interpreter had revealed the master." On *Messiah* with the Oratorio Society: "To hear the greatest of all dramas — the New Testament I had read and read — set in perfect musical form, was to me a religious experience." And then there was simply the pleasure of associating with so many who shared his interest. On the tours, waiting in railroad stations for midnight trains, the men often would sing old German songs, and sometimes Damrosch would join in with his "piercing voice. (You know how it carries in any hall or room!)"[15]

Gradually Mannes advanced to the position of concertmaster, a post he would hold for ten years before resigning. Meanwhile, at rehearsals with the Oratorio Society he became fascinated by a woman in the alto section. Her face had regular, aristocratic features, and she sang with assurance, seldom taking her eye from the conductor. Among the others she seemed to stand out, and Mannes, inquiring who she was, was told: Clara Damrosch. Again he felt as if he had seen a star "whose light was not meant for me," and for a long time he did nothing. Then one day he asked his friend Orrin Parsons to arrange an introduction.

The formal call was just as difficult as Mannes had expected. "I shall always remember that curiously shaped three-cornered chair," he exclaimed years later.

He was overwhelmed to sit "face to face with the widow of Leopold Damrosch," and though Helene's reception of him was "rather chillingly impersonal," he was impressed by her "strong and majestic personality" and also by how much her son Walter resembled her: "the same pure, strong features, as if chiseled out of marble." Tante won him at once with "her helpful remarks about seeing me in the orchestra" and "the enthusiasm of my attitude to the conductor's beat." But it seemed forever before Miss Damrosch arrived. Finally she appeared, "with a spring of step and the joy of living in her face, as if she had been having lots of fun instead of teaching four or five hours that day, or perhaps more."

Besides taking immediate advantage of her rather vague suggestion that they play sonatas together, he arranged for his sister, Madeleine, to study piano with her, and every lesson "was an event for me also, for it meant hearing from Madeleine interesting and intriguing details about the one who occupied my thoughts persistently." Clara might think of him only rarely, or not at all, but with a quiet man's determination he began to create opportunities to be with her.[16]

CHAPTER 13

Walter and his Damrosch Opera Company.

WHEN THE DIRECTORS of the Metropolitan Opera in the season of 1891–92 substituted for the German company, originated by Leopold Damrosch and carried on by Anton Seidl, a French-Italian company under the management of a triumvirate — Henry E. Abbey, Edward Schoeffel and Maurice Grau — they disaffected a sizable part of their audience. To the German-speaking public, *Die Meistersinger* in Italian, even if conducted by Seidl, which was increasingly seldom, was not the same aesthetic experience as the opera sung in German. Public and critics alike complained.

In hindsight, in this decade a new concept of opera production was evolving. The old way was for an impresario to put together a company, almost invariably, except for soloists, of one nationality, and then, after hiring a house, to offer a season of French, Italian, German or even English opera. In essence this procedure continues today in many smaller cities, touring companies and festivals.

The new style, which might be called the division or "wing" system, reached its furthest development only in English-speaking countries and only in the large cities with houses devoted almost entirely to opera. Here the impresario, less of an entrepreneur and more the employee of the house, assembled a company of two or three rather separate divisions, usually French, Italian and German, each devoted to producing opera in its own language. Thus one company, through its different divisions, would present *Faust* in French, *Aida* in Italian and *Lohengrin* in German. Between divisions, except for an occasional soloist or conductor, there would be little crossover. In theory, every opera would be performed by specialists in its language and style.

In practice, the system is difficult to operate. The orchestra and chorus must be equally fluent in three or more styles and languages, a goal rarely attained, and many more soloists and conductors must be under contract, resulting in greater bickering over rehearsal time, roles, comparative pay and publicity. Yet in London and New York this was the system to which the managers of the leading opera house more frequently turned, partly because immigration and the lack in either city of a strong native tradition of opera allowed marked "divisions" within the audience to continue for generations. In the evolution of this new system at the Metropolitan, Walter, as well as his father, had an important role.

When Walter left the Metropolitan in the spring of 1891, he did not abandon Wagner but frequently scheduled orchestral and vocal excerpts of the operas in his New York Symphony concerts. Seidl, who under the French-Italian regime conducted less at the Metropolitan, did the same with the New York Philharmonic, which he led from 1891 to 1898. These concert excerpts were sung in German, and the contrast in quality to the opera house, where Wagner and Beethoven were sung in Italian or French, was marked. For despite excellent French and Italian opera with soloists like Francesco Tamagno, Victor Maurel and Jean and Edouard de Reszke, German opera at the Metropolitan steadily declined in quality. The nadir, perhaps, was reached on November 20, 1896, when *Tannhäuser* was presented in French, with some parts sung in Italian and the title role sung by a tenor, Jules Gogny, who shifted from one language to the other. To those who loved German opera such treatment was a scandal.

The managers at the Metropolitan, however, would do nothing. They claimed, as managers with bad productions often do, that the composer was at fault. Pointing to their unsold seats, they said: No one cares for Wagner. The argument infuriated Walter, and inevitably, he eagerly moved to prove it wrong.

On February 17, 1894, in Carnegie Hall he gave a fully staged performance of *Die Walküre,* in German. The scenery was makeshift, the staging rudimentary and the critics unkind; but the singers were Materna, Schott and Fischer, and the public flocked to hear them and to hear the operas sung in German. Excited by the response, Walter rented the Metropolitan for March 26, 28 and 31, and with the same cast repeated *Die Walküre* and followed it with two performances of *Götterdämmerung.* Because of Seidl's monopoly on Wagner at the Metropolitan from 1886 to 1891, these were Walter's first performances of more than excerpts of *Götterdämmerung,* and according to the *Times* he "acquitted himself with great credit." [1]

Walter now was thoroughly aroused, but so was Seidl. Each saw in the Metropolitan's disaffected German audience a chance to conduct his favorite composer, and each started to organize backers to support a season of Wagner in German. In such a race Walter, with his extraordinary energy and executive ability, soon had Seidl outmatched. William Steinway then tried to merge the two camps, and as a compromise Walter offered to share the conducting with Seidl on equal terms, each to lead four of the eight Wagner operas Walter tentatively had scheduled. But Seidl wanted all or none, and Steinway gave his support and a check for $2500 to Walter. The Seidl camp thereupon dispersed.[2]

Meanwhile Walter, backed by a Wagner Society organized and led by women, succeeded in winning an astonishing number of subscribers for the projected season. One reason perhaps was that he and Margaret sold their house on West Fifty-fifth Street and used the proceeds to fund the incipient Damrosch Opera Company. That act, which soon became known, doubtless stimulated others to support the Damrosch crusade for Wagner.

Just how Walter and Margaret had amassed enough money to buy a house in an expensive neighborhood is a mystery. Though her father had died in January 1893, her mother still lived, and Walter had not yet begun to earn large sums. The house may have been another instance of Carnegie's aid. If so, presumably it was sold with his approval. Though Carnegie had little interest in opera, he seems to have given the project his blessing and aided Walter with financial advice.[3]

Armed with money, an impressive list of subscribers and the New York Symphony for his orchestra, Walter approached Henry Abbey, the leader of the Metropolitan's triumvirate, suggesting that a German night be inserted into each week of the Metropolitan's regular season. Abbey refused, offering instead to rent Walter the house for eight weeks at the season's end, February 16, and on favorable terms. "My boy," he warned, "don't do it. You'll lose every cent you have in the world."[4] But Walter was filled with a kind of religious zeal. "No one," he wrote later to H. E. Krehbiel, "seemed to share my almost fatalistic belief in Wagner opera," and he described himself as being "driven into it . . . by an irresistible impulse."[5] So, assured of a season in New York and with a five-week tour planned to go as far west as Kansas City, he sailed in May to recruit his singers in Germany, to hire a German stage manager and to contract with a Viennese firm for scenery. To reintroduce Wagner in German to the United States he was repeating, in 1894, what his father had done ten years earlier.

There was a difference, however. His father had acted with the Metropolitan's full resources and prestige behind him. Walter acted on his own, and his ability to organize a company, bring it to New York, mount, rehearse and perform seven of the most difficult works in the operatic repertory struck Krehbiel "as an even more remarkable feat than that accomplished by his father."[6] Walter, though, saw it not as competition, but as vindication: "To re-enter the Metropolitan on such a

Wagnerian wave after German opera had been so ignominiously snuffed out five years before, was a great triumph and satisfaction for me, especially because my father had laid the foundation."[7]

In New York the season, which opened on February 25, 1895, and closed on March 29, offered twenty-one performances at the opera house of *Tristan* (3), *Siegfried* (4), *Lohengrin* (4), *Götterdämmerung* (2), *Tannhäuser* (3), *Walküre* (3) and *Meistersinger* (2), and two performances of *Parsifal* in concert form at Carnegie Hall. By comparison the Metropolitan in a season of fifteen weeks gave seven performances, all in Italian, of *Lohengrin* (6) and *Meistersinger* (1). Similarly, on tour the Damrosch repertory was 100 percent Wagner, in German; the Metropolitan's, about 7 percent, in Italian.

The schedule for Walter and the orchestra was staggering. The worst period was the four days, March 20 through 23, when he and his men, in addition to rehearsals, gave six performances of five operas, *Walküre, Siegfried, Meistersinger, Tristan* and *Parsifal* (2). It was the sort of schedule that had killed his father, but Walter was physically stronger and also, at thirty-three, twenty years younger. But he never again worked as hard as he did in this first year of his opera company.

Though some New York critics complained of some of the company's staging (the German stage manager had lost his life in a shipwreck on the voyage over) and of some of the choral work, the New York public bought almost every seat to every performance and the *Times* proclaimed the March 20 *Walküre* "one of the best ever given in the Metropolitan."[8] The tour went equally well, and after thirteen weeks the Damrosch Opera Company closed its books with a profit of $53,000.

Walter and the members of his Wagner Society were ecstatic, and he immediately began to plan the next season: it would be five months in all and would carry the gospel of Wagner as far west as Denver and as far south as New Orleans. Carnegie advised against it: "Many people who have come for curiosity only . . . will not come back." But Walter was not to be dissuaded.[9]

Now, however, the difference between his own and his father's enterprise became important. Leopold had worked *for* the Metropolitan, so his triumph was also its triumph. But Walter worked outside the Metropolitan, and the greater the success of the Damrosch Opera Company, the more it threatened the Metropolitan. Abbey this season refused to rent to Walter on any terms, and Walter had to take the discredited, dingy old Academy of Music, where no opera had been given since 1888.

Further, Abbey hired Seidl to conduct five Wagner operas, three in German. One of the latter, *Tristan,* was cast with Jean de Reszke and Lillian Nordica, given untold hours of rehearsal and was a great success. But the others, despite Seidl, were not well done, and the Damrosch company, with such sopranos as Johanna Gadski, Milka Ternina and Katherine Klafsky, outshone the Metropolitan. The *Times* called it "the strongest German opera company ever heard in America,"[10] and *Harper's Weekly* proclaimed, "Damrosch has found his *métier* — that of operatic recruiting-officer and major-general."[11] But in the South, where the company's season opened, except in New Orleans the audiences for Wagner were very small, and the company arrived in New York in arrears. With no house and very little money, Walter and Margaret put up with friends in order to save the cost of a hotel, but even so the season closed with a loss of $43,000.[12]

In the course of this second season Walter added three non-Wagnerian operas to his repertory: Beethoven's *Fidelio*, Weber's *Der Freischütz* and his own *The Scarlet Letter*, with English text, his first major composition. He had read Hawthorne's novel in August of 1892, almost certainly at Margaret's suggestion, and on a hot summer night he wrote her a long, enthusiastic letter:

> His genius is the natural result of New England birth and training. The race is not a strong one physically and the intellect has always been cultivated at the expense of the body and in turn the lack of stolid robustness (which characterizes the English and the German) has had its influence on the trend of the mind. In most cases the ruling passion of money-getting developed the intellect in that direction but, with it all, a critical and analytical trait which made the "inquisitive yankee," the inventor, the founder of religious sects, and, in prose which makes Hawthorne so great a master.[13]

Margaret, a daughter of Maine's first family, doubtless was amused by Walter's Germanic view of the New England character, but she also must have been pleased by the enthusiasm with which he took to American literature, and she probably was the one who introduced him to Hawthorne's son-in-law, George Parsons Lathrop, who prepared the libretto.

Though Walter had given excerpts of the opera with the Oratorio Society on January 4 and 5, 1895, its first full, staged performance was in Boston, on February 10, 1896, with the first great American operatic baritone, David Bispham, singing Roger Chillingworth, and Gadski, Hester Prynne. Helene, who had gone to Boston for it, returned to New York and wrote to Margaret (in English) what gradually became the general opinion of Walter's opera: "If he could get away from Wagner (conducting his performances, etc.) for a long time . . . and then dip his pen in the rich fountain of his own originality there would appear, I am sure, something still better than *The Scarlet Letter*."[14] Though she wrote with love and pride for "my boy," as an artist herself she would not overpraise his work.

One incident in connection with the opera caused Walter some embarrassment. At a supper party following a performance, some of those with a hand in the opera's production, after considerable ceremony and many complimentary speeches, presented him with a large scarlet letter **A,** which they placed upon his breast. The incident was passed off with laughter, and Walter stated later that the leading spirits of the caper were foreigners who did not fully understand the opera's text. But the little joke alerted gossips to their work, and beginning about now, when Walter was thirty-four, they began to link his name with first one soprano and then another.[15]

Though the season, with its Southern tour, ended with a deficit, the Damrosch company had lost considerably less on its almost all-German repertory than had the Metropolitan on its smaller German "wing," and Abbey, with a humility rare among impresarios, now approached Walter. He wanted some of Walter's German singers in order to strengthen his incipient German wing, and in return he offered Walter some Italian and French singers, notably Emma Calvé, so that Walter could present *Carmen* on his tours, for Walter was discovering that audiences, particularly in the South and West, wanted a more balanced repertory than just Wagner. So the Damrosch company and the Metropolitan each took a step toward the division or wing style of opera production. In addition, Abbey agreed again to rent the Metropolitan to Walter in March 1897 for his New York season.[16]

Though Margaret was not present at Walter's meetings with Abbey or with the financial committees of the Wagner, Oratorio or Symphony societies, he always discussed the details with her. This was the tradition in both the Damrosch and Blaine families, and Margaret had grown up ᵉexpecting to make a true partnership with her husband. Her mother always had managed Blaine's finances, freeing him to pursue political and literary work, and Margaret did the same for Walter, just as Helene had done for Leopold. Margaret, unlike Helene, had no musical judgment to bring to her partnership, and she made no pretense of it. She was full of common sense, however, and financially sophisticated. In the coming years, as she and Walter prospered, she managed their real estate and investments, calling the broker almost every day, correcting the bank on its occasional errors and giving an account of the family's financial position at any time it was needed. When Walter, writing later of the Damrosch Opera Company, stated, "After a long consultation with my wife we both decided . . . that we could well risk another season," he was being not gallant, but factual.[17]

For the next two seasons, 1896–97 and 1897–98, the company showed small profits, aided in part by the fact that the Metropolitan company in 1897–98 did not perform, while Maurice Grau, following the death of Abbey in October 1896, reorganized it. Damrosch, meanwhile, for the

1897–98 season formed a partnership with Charles A. Ellis, who managed the soprano Nellie Melba. With her in his company Walter was able to announce, and continued to advertise, a "Season of Grand Opera in French, German and Italian." Melba sang *La Traviata, Aida* and *Il Barbiere di Siviglia* in Italian, and *Faust* and *Roméo et Juliette* in French. The conductor for the Italian operas was Oreste Bimboni; he and Walter shared the French, and Walter led all the German. The wing system of producing opera had come into its own.

In addition to the more usual Wagner operas, Walter this year added a production of *Der Fliegende Holländer,* which had been performed last at the Metropolitan in 1892 in Italian. According to Bispham, who sang the Dutchman, it proved to be the surprise success of the season, and he gave as the chief cause "that Damrosch took up the work with enthusiasm, whereas my previous performances in London had been conducted in a perfunctory manner by those who did not really care for the music."[18]

On tour, after performing in Boston, Chicago and Cincinnati, the company divided, with the German wing under Damrosch going to Cleveland, Buffalo and Detroit while Melba and the Italian-French wing went to the Pacific Coast. With the Metropolitan inactive, the Damrosch-Ellis Company was the country's undisputed leader in opera. As long as Walter, who was perhaps the most competent musical entrepreneur of his generation, stayed in command, its future seemed secure. Yet on April 8, 1898, he announced that he would not manage it another season, though he would conduct some performances of German operas for Charles Ellis, who would continue with a greatly reduced company.

There were many reasons, and one seems to have been exhaustion, for at the same time that he resigned his "duties as an opera impresario," he resigned his posts with the New York Symphony and the Oratorio Society.[19] For four years, while he carried on his other work, he had sustained a major opera company that had no home base, and even the seasons in New York had been given under all the pressures of touring. Though he had managed to lighten the scheduling somewhat, it was still too crowded, and on one occasion in his final New York season he and the orchestra had to follow an afternoon concert in Carnegie Hall, in which Beethoven's Symphony No. 3 was the chief work, with a performance at the opera house of *Götterdämmerung.*

With his extraordinary resilience, however, he might have found a way to ease his own and the orchestra's schedule still further — if he had wished. But after four years he was tired, in particular, of dealing with singers. Many impresarios have written of the difficulties of working with singers, but none has described the personality of the typical singer — of course there are exceptions — with greater sweetness or truth.

I found that many singers were like children with no clear conception of right or wrong. Their constant life in close proximity to each other at rehearsals and performances often begets an exaggerated conception of themselves and their importance to the world. They think that as their contact with the public is only over the footlights, where they receive enthusiastic acclaim for their artistic representations, the public literally exists only for the purpose of hearing them sing, and they willingly ignore the fact that the public may have other interests, such as family, finance, politics, or religion, to claim its attention. As it is important for a manager not only to maintain a balance in his ledger but to seek the best results that a disciplined ensemble may attain, he cannot always be in harmony with all the individual desires and demands of his artists. He must often cast his opera in opposition to their personal pride, and I have letters to-day from several of the greatest artists of my company insisting that they must leave or break their contracts because I had wounded their deepest sensibilities in putting so and so in the role which they claimed for their very own.[20]

He goes on to describe a tenor's effort to increase a fee by blackmail, threatening to be sick at the scheduled performance, and he treats that act as comic in comparison to others, which were "really wicked." After four years of managing such children he preferred "to confine myself absolutely to purely musical work."[21]

In retrospect the importance of his venture into opera management is clear. Not only did he introduce thousands of the public to Wagner, on the stage, sung in German, and reintroduce thousands more, but he demonstrated to the unbelieving directors and managers of the Metropolitan the size of the audience they were ignoring. Further, in about equal parts he forced and led the Metropolitan to a new solution of the chief operatic problem of the late nineteenth century: how to admit the ten masterworks of Wagner into the established repertory. In 1884–85 Leopold Damrosch had offered one solution: make the company an all-German enterprise and sing all operas in German. In 1891–92 Abbey, Schoeffel and Grau offered another: revert to the traditional French-Italian company and sing Wagner in French or Italian. Walter, spurred to balance his ledger, moved from an all-German company and repertory to the wing system, and Grau at the Metropolitan, to meet the competition from Walter, imitated him. Today it is the system operating in the big opera houses of most large English-speaking cities.

CHAPTER 14

Frank and the struggle over the People's Singing Classes. Helene and the grand-children. Tante. Clara marries David Mannes.

THE PEOPLE'S SINGING CLASSES, which Frank with Edward King, a labor leader, and Charles Stover, a social worker, had founded in October 1892, steadily expanded, but with success came disagreement among the three over fundamental purpose. The struggle that ensued was muted, for like Frank the other two were mild-tempered. But by the end of the second year, when they were ready to turn administrative control of the classes over to the people themselves, the issues were clear and symptomatic of any artistic enterprise in which some of the leaders want to use the art for purposes other than its own ends.

By the spring of 1894 the original two classes had grown into four elementary and one advanced, with as many as perhaps three thousand singers involved. The best among them — chiefly the advanced class of 650, augmented by almost as many from the elementary classes — had given two concerts at Carnegie Hall; and throughout the year Frank had arranged for four hundred seats at all New York Symphony and Musical Art Society concerts to be available to class members at half price, or on some occasions at even less, or even free. In addition to these musical events the class members enjoyed a considerable social life, which often included families and friends. In June 1894, for example, the classes ended their second year with a reception and dance at Männerchor Hall, at which Frank and Hetty were guests of honor. By then, the management of the classes, collecting dues, scheduling rehearsals, concerts and social events, had grown into a demanding job.

In the autumn of 1894, therefore, the founders, in another bulletin over Frank's name, called on members of the advanced class to form a People's Choral Union, of approximately five hundred members, that would elect officers and committees to manage the financial and administrative affairs of all the classes. And one of the first acts of the PCU, as it soon was called, was to found a monthly journal, *Harmony*, which, distributed free to all singers, might bind them together with news of common interest.[1]

In the second issue, February 1895, in an article entitled "Influences of Choral Singing," Frank expressed the extramusical purposes of the classes:

> But aside from the great musical value of choral singing, it has another at least as great . . . its influence upon character . . . It teaches discipline, obedience, subordination, self-reliance, attention, concentration, precision . . . the larger lessons of unselfishness and cooperation, and points the way to the broader view of human life by its example of fellowship and brotherhood.[2]

These were the ends that King and Stover wanted to put first, before those of music. They considered the elementary classes, for example, more important than the advanced one, and wanted Frank to teach them, or some of them, and to leave the advanced to an assistant. To Frank, this was backward. He more quickly could instruct assistants how to teach an elementary class than how to conduct a concert in Carnegie Hall. And the concert, as the goal of the musical year, was important.

King and Stover also wanted, in effect, a means test for class members: only working people who earned less than a certain wage could join. Frank saw no reason why a bank teller should be excluded from learning how to sing, and believed, further, that the banking skills might be useful in managing the classes' finances.[3]

Similarly, though the pressure in this instance may not have originated with King and Stover, Frank was asked to teach the classes some popular songs, apparently on the theory that ordinary people prefer ordinary music. Without announcing what he was doing, he tried a popular song and was pleased to receive notes from several singers entreating him to teach them "only the beautiful music." He had had the same experience in Denver, and its repetition confirmed his belief that from the start he should aim for the best: Handel, Bach, Mendelssohn.[4]

Finally, King and Stover wanted each class to have its own governing body so that more people would have the experience of leadership. To Frank, the problems of management were too complicated to be entrusted to elementary classes, where the turnover was apt to be greater and the skills fewer.

In short, King and Stover wanted to use the classes primarily as a way of keeping young adults off the streets, of giving many older adults some management experience and of creating a stabilizing influence in poor neighborhoods. All worthy aims, and most of them realized in the music school settlement movement that in another ten years would begin to flower under the leadership of David Mannes. But none was Frank's primary aim, which was to teach thousands of people how to sing to the best of their abilities.

In this disagreement Frank quickly bested King and Stover, and the People's Choral Union was formed as Frank wished, as the top of a hierarchy, into which members of future advanced classes would move as positions came open, just as members of the elementary classes would move into the advanced. Also, Frank was to work with the Choral Union and the advanced class, and assistants with the elementary classes, though he would visit each of the latter at least once a month. The pull, always, would be toward the best music.

Still, evidence of the basic disagreement kept surfacing. At a meeting of the Choral Union, in July 1895, King, speaking as a spectator, urged that the members should always remember the founders' aim to go down deep into the mass of the people and uplift the lowly. There was a danger, he warned, that as Choral Union members advanced in culture and refinement through the beneficial influence of music, they would forget those left behind.[5]

Frank's reply appeared the following month as a letter to the editor of *Harmony* and included the statement "I do not believe, as some do, that our work is a failure unless our membership is recruited entirely from the poorest of the poor."[6] And again the following summer, as the PCU planned the fall's organization of classes, King raised his point and Frank replied through a letter to *Harmony*.[7]

In this struggle Frank inevitably was the winner, less because the original idea was his than because he was the teacher. He had the loyalty of his assistants and, in every class, of the most enthusiastic and attentive singers. Also, the three tiers, elementary, advanced and Choral Union, worked musically. As singers improved, they moved ahead; in cases where they showed an inclination to remain in a lower class, perhaps through affection for its teacher or convenience of its location, Frank would hold an audition and push them ahead. By 1897 the Choral Union and the best of those in advanced classes — by now there were several — were ready for their first full oratorio, *Messiah,* and the performance at Carnegie Hall on May 3 was sold out and well received. The next year, again at Carnegie Hall, Frank presented all three tiers in a three-day festival. On May 23, six hundred of the best of the elementary classes, led by Frank, sang, as part of a concert of solos and choruses, *See, the Conquering Hero Comes* from Handel's *Joshua,*[8] the *Coronation March* from Meyerbeer's *Le Prophète, America, The Star Spangled Banner* and the Lutheran hymn *Ein' feste Burg.* The next day, under Frank and two assistants, one advanced class of three hundred sang Mendelssohn's *95th Psalm;*

another of two hundred, Schumann's *Gipsy Life* and Bruch's *Jubilate-Amen;* and then they joined for Gounod's *Gallia.* The third day, the Choral Union, under Frank, sang Bruch's *The Lay of the Bell.* The festival, with its different levels of competence, fascinated the critics, but not the public, which stayed away, causing *Harmony* in an editorial to echo King's thought: "While the critics have been won, the public has been lost . . . Does it justify the inference that as the movement advances in the *musical* sense, it necessarily declines in a *popular* one?"[9]

To Frank, the critics' praise and the public's absence were both somewhat irrelevant. What counted more was that thousands of persons who otherwise might have remained passive had become active in music to the point of being able to perform songs and cantatas creditably.

Because of the public's lack of interest the festival had a deficit of $2000, but the Choral Union was prepared, and the Singing Classes were able to continue without break and without looking beyond their members for dues or contributions. Unquestionably under Frank's leadership the classes enrolled as many lower-middle- as lower-class workers. But without that leavening of skills and stability, it seems unlikely that they could have been self-sustaining for a life of twenty-five years or accomplished as much musically.

Though Frank and his assistants gave their services to the classes, one important paid post came to him directly as a result of his work. In the spring of 1897 the city's Board of Education created a position, supervisor of music for the public schools, at an annual salary of $4000, and from the moment the post was announced the Choral Union lobbied for Frank's appointment and stirred other organizations also to petition for him.[10] Frank held the post from 1897 to 1905, and though he got little enjoyment from it, the salary and its certainty were vital to many of his other projects.

Among Frank's singers his position as teacher brought him a great deal of affection. The younger women in particular had an insatiable appetite to know all about him and his family, of which in the early years he often made use. For the first spring concert, on May 28, 1893, he had opened the program with *God Save Our Native Land,* composed for the People's Singing Classes by Joseph Mosenthal, who was, the women quickly reported, "Mrs. Damrosch's uncle"; he had closed with Plunket Greene singing Irish songs accompanied by Walter, "Mr. Damrosch's brother"; and they had known that "Mrs. Damrosch," Hetty, could not attend because she was just delivered of a baby girl, on which they had complimented the father. Sometimes as a treat for a class that had done well he would produce "Miss Damrosch," Clara, to play the piano, and frequently with the Choral Union he used as an accompanist "Mrs. Damrosch's father," cheery, cherubic Herman Mosenthal, who was living proof to the singers that a man could work all week at insurance and still on Sunday be a pretty good musician.[11]

When in the spring of 1897 Frank and Hetty sailed for a summer in Germany, four hundred singers turned up on the pier to see them off and — it was supposed to be a surprise — to sing. But as *Harmony* reported: "A couple of our most zealous lady members allowed their enthusiasm to supersede their judgment by insisting upon greeting Mr. Damrosch with handshakes while at the same time their familiar music sheets were kept painfully in evidence, thus in the words of one of our estimable officials, 'giving the snap dead away.' " Nevertheless, they sang beautifully: Berlioz's *Absence* and, Frank's favorite, *Lo, How a Rose E'er Blooming.*[12]

The sense of sharing something fine evidently was passed along even to many who did not come to the classes. In the summer of 1896 the Choral Union, six hundred strong, sang at a concert in the Mall in Central Park, and to everyone's astonishment about sixty thousand people turned up, apparently drawn chiefly by what they had heard of Frank Damrosch and his People's Singing Classes.[13] By 1909, in Manhattan, in addition to the Choral Union there were six elementary classes and one advanced class; in the Bronx, two elementary classes and one advanced; in Brooklyn and Hoboken, one elementary class each; and in Jersey City, two elementary classes — in all, perhaps, eight thousand working people actively singing, with their interest spreading to thousands more through families and friends.

In the fall of 1912, after twenty years, Frank relinquished the leadership to Harry Barnhart, and the classes continued adding and dropping numbers and locations until World War I began to break up their organization. Their twenty-fifth season, 1916–17, seems to have been their last.[14] By then Yale University, in 1904, had conferred an honorary degree on Frank, and to his pupils, singers and journalists generally he had become Dr. Damrosch, or Dr. Frank Damrosch, to distinguish him from Walter. From 1892 to 1917, though Walter may have been better known outside the city and in purely musical circles, to the average New Yorker Frank, because of his work in the schools and through the singing classes, was *the* Damrosch.

Despite the swirl of the family's activities there was always repose at its center, in Helene's apartment. Though she shared it with Tante and Clara, in everyone's eyes they lived with her; she was the head of the family. And increasingly, as grandchildren reached the age of speech, she was referred to by all as O'mama, a child's contraction of Grossmama.

The first grandchild, born only a year after Leopold's death, was Marie and Ferdi Wiechmann's daughter, Margaret Helen, who as a young girl successfully insisted that she be called Marjorie, a name she had picked from a book.[15] By 1898, when she was twelve, she showed promise of her mother's beauty, which in her mother was beginning now to fade into fat. She also showed talent for painting and music, but again like her mother seemed to lack the self-discipline to develop it. Already within the family she was notorious for her tantrums.

In all, by 1898 O'mama had eight grandchildren. Besides Marjorie, the Wiechmanns had a son Walter and another, Harold, who died very early. Frank and Hetty had Frank Jr. and Helen, and in these two families the complement was set. In the Walter Damrosch family there were two girls (in time there would be four), Alice and Margaret Blaine. The latter was known always by the German diminutive, Gretchen, or sometimes among family and friends as Gay. The Seymours had a son, Lawrence Damrosch Seymour — there would be jokes in later years over the number of first and second cousins who had Damrosch as a middle name — and a daughter, Clara, who later changed her name to Clair. In this third generation the family names evidently oppressed some grand-daughters, for ultimately three of the ten changed them.*

For the children, a visit to O'mama's apartment always was interesting, because it contained adornments not found at home. One of these, standing on a pedestal, was a two-and-a-half-foot reproduction of the Louvre's *Winged Victory,* and the children were fascinated by the lady's lack of any head or arms. There was also a *Venus de Milo* and a large sepia-tinted reproduction of Raphael's Sistine *Madonna,* the original of which, their elders constantly explained, all the family had seen many times in the gallery in Dresden.

The room was entered through a dark velvet curtain hanging from big wooden rings on a bar, and except for the curious three-cornered chair, the furniture was typical of the German-American style of the day: simple, somewhat heavy wooden and wicker chairs with thick cushions and pillows tied across the back. The upholstery was in soft greens, olive or sage; the draperies, dark red with lace undercurtains; and the glass and china lamps were lace-fringed. On the mantel were a striking clock and two small sculptures, and in the windows, among several spider plants, were two large tea plants in huge pots. In the corner was a Steinway grand piano.

Standing at the room's end and casting into it a slight sense of awe, for the children at least, was an easel bearing a portrait in oils of their grandfather Leopold. It had been painted many years earlier by the father of one of Leopold's pupils and given to Helene on Leopold's death. It showed the head and shoulders, with the head partly turned. Painted in dark colors, the portrait presented him as a youngish man, dark-haired,

---

*To avoid confusion, after the first, explanatory reference I will use the names by which they were known as adults.

handsome, with large dark eyes. Helene kept twined around the frame smilax or some other vine with small green leaves, and whenever these faded, she substituted a fresh cut. Though she seldom talked of Leopold, still, as David Mannes observed, it was in Leopold's artistic legacy that "his family now spiritually lived and had its being."[16]

In widowhood Helene dressed in black with an occasional touch of white lace. Her skirt, which always touched the floor, often had sharp ruffles about the hem, and on her silver-white hair she wore a cap of black velvet, trimmed sometimes with lace. When at home, she wore little black slippers with straps.

The children liked her. The reserve in her manner, of which her daughter Clara sometimes complained, allowed her to seem always the same: loving, kind, not too attentive and, above all, calm. When they came, she always had some food on hand, German cookies or chocolates, and as they played on the floor, overhead the conversation between the grownups would flow swiftly in German, broken by occasional laughter. Often as O'mama talked, she sewed, doing so with complete repose.

Among her own children in these years her attention focused on Walter. She was intensely ambitious for him. It was not that she loved the others less — none ever complained of that — but that Walter was repeating so closely what his father had done. She enjoyed singing under him in the Oratorio Society and going to Carnegie Hall for the New York Symphony concerts, sitting in the Damrosch family box and watching him conduct. She knew that in the audience people looked up and recognized in her the founder's widow and the conductor's mother. She liked that, and, persuaded probably by Margaret and Walter, who had preceded her, she enrolled in the New York Social Register. By 1896, so had Frank and Hetty and the Seymours.[17]

Though Walter's career, continuing his father's organizations and concepts, was of greater interest to her than Frank's more original work, of the two sons it was Frank, not Walter, who honored her publicly for her help in music. In speech after speech Walter ascribed all his early training, all his stimulation to his father alone. But Frank, at a dinner in his honor, said: "I owe to my mother my musical heritage, as well as to my father, for my mother was a beautiful singer and my first acquaintance with music was when mother sang Schubert's songs to me." And when in the course of his school work he met with groups of mothers, he constantly urged them to sing at home.[18]

Clara, on the other hand, did not until late in life think that her mother had been extraordinary. Then one day, as Clara recalled the family's early years in New York, her year in Dresden arranged by her mother and her mother's backing for her to take a trip alone to Europe, the thought came like a thunderclap: "She was an amazing, progressive woman, be-

by practicing on his piano. To her astonishment, instead of two grand pianos in the room there was only an upright with a scarf over it. Opening the lid, she found the keys dusty.

Perplexed, yet feeling more than ever in need of a nervous release, she seated herself on the stool and began to play. Her finger exercises brought the housekeeper into the room in a state of wild excitement, imploring her *not* to play. Herr Busoni even at that moment was in court, on a complaint from the "Herr General" upstairs, to sign an agreement that the piano in this room would *not* be played. The Herr General thought music was a nuisance. After leading Clara through hallways to the back of the apartment, she brought her to a library, where two grand pianos stood back to back.[24]

That summer, when Clara was twenty-six, was the last in which she did any sketching. She had a strong talent for it, and at Schandau, where she was often with the Prellers, she did much of it. But probably because of Busoni, whose lessons she found "inspiring," she decided for music and against art, even as a pastime. In later years she made a point of her belief that talented persons are apt to have several talents, and they must choose between them while still young. To her many students she constantly stressed the need for concentration on a single talent; and within the family she would imply that Ellie was an example of one who had left the choice until too late, and so could not have a full life in music. Mixed with the truth of her observation there came to be a touch of self-satisfaction that sometimes offended people, especially relatives.[25]

It was a summer of decisions for Clara. Though she saw Mannes regularly in Berlin, at Schandau she received a steady stream of letters from him, and then one day he arrived for a two-week visit, staying at the same inn and eating all his meals with her. Every morning each would work alone on music; in the afternoon they would go for a walk, and he would carry her paint box and sketching pad. Back at the inn, one afternoon, he proposed marriage, after four years of courting, and was accepted. That night he could not sleep, began to feel unworthy and feared a terrible mistake for her. But the next morning, when Clara came down to breakfast in the garden, "the mist of doubt passed away."

A few days later Clara asked, "Why do you want to marry me?"

"Because," he replied, "I am searching for the truth." Her expression revealed that she did not understand him, but he felt, then and later, that he knew what he meant.[26]

At the end of the summer they joined Tante at Stade on the North Sea, where Clara's Uncle Paul, Major von Heimburg, was stationed, and when he heard of the engagement he gave Clara and David an officers' dinner to celebrate the event. Uncle Paul was a congenial soul, and the party went well, but as happened to Clara so often in Germany, she was slightly put off by the spirit of militarism. One officer said to David in a gay, assured voice, "First we go to England, and when we have conquered there, we come to you!" Between two other officers there was tension over the wife of one, which Clara learned later led to a duel. And the general, who had no voice at all, insisted on singing, with Clara at the piano, a transposition of Siegmund's *Spring Song* from the first act of *Die Walküre*. To Clara, the injury to Wagner was bad enough, but worse still was the loud, obsequious applause of the officers and their wives.[27]

Tante, of course, was not surprised to hear of the engagement; in her warm manner she already had taken David to heart. But both Clara and David worried about the more austere Helene, and they asked Tante to write their news for them. In the eyes of the world and in his own eyes David was not much of a catch. "What was I but a young orchestra violinist of no particular distinction, with no particular promise of a brilliant future, of a family of the average small-business outlook, modest and honest good people of very little cultural background." But evidently Tante's letter was a good one, for on the pier to meet them in New York was Helene with an approving smile, and the others in the family soon followed her lead.[28]

They were married the following spring, on June 4, 1898, in Harry and Ellie's house in Middle Granville, New York, a village north of Troy near the Vermont border. The Seymours had lived there through the winter while Harry managed a small factory nearby, and the idea of a rustic wedding appealed greatly to Clara and David. They had become engaged, after all, at a country inn outside Dresden, with tea and breakfast in a garden and walks into the surrounding hills. The Seymours' house, with its porch, lawn, lilacs and hydrangea, seemed the right setting.

Clara went up several days in advance and took to bed with a cold. The morning of the wedding she was greeted by her three-year-old nephew Larry Seymour, who, fearful that the great event might be canceled, burst into her room, counseling, "Sheer up, Tante Clara, sheer up."

A few hours later, from neighbors' houses, where they had spent the night, the guests began to gather: all the Damrosch family, David's parents and his sister and a few of his and Clara's best friends. Before the ceremony Walter found his mother weeping on the front porch. Nonplussed for once, all he could think to say was the commonplace "Mother, you're not losing Clara."

"It's the lobster," Helene sobbed. It was to have been her chief contribution to the wedding breakfast, but despite the ice pack, on the long, hot train ride and during the night it had spoiled.

For a wedding prelude and procession David's sister and two of

Clara's friends played one of her favorite pieces, the Adagio from Beethoven's *Trio No. 4*, Opus 11, and David, in his dreamy fashion, became so engrossed in turning pages for the players that he forgot to take his place before the minister. Then he answered the minister's question "Do you take this woman . . ." with a confused "I am," and later, as he and Clara drove away in an open carriage, he forgot his violin; so they had to go back for it, and the surprised guests had a second chance to throw their rice.[29]

But as everyone said, it was a most satisfactory wedding, and with Clara now married, the next would be a grandchild's.

CHAPTER 15

Walter's festival for the Oratorio Society's twenty-fifth anniversary. His year of composition. His return to the Metropolitan and year with the Philharmonic. Failure all around.

WALTER'S year of retirement to compose, though seriously undertaken, was only partially realized. He had commitments to fulfill, primarily with the New York Symphony, meetings of boards and committees to attend and an eagerness to participate in the city's musical life that could not be wholly quenched. Margaret also was more attuned to the hurly-burly of the city than to the country's quiet, so they went not to Vermont, or even to Connecticut, but to Hartsdale, in Westchester County, just across the city line and close to the railroad. And of course, Walter, being Walter, could not begin the year by slipping quietly away but had to start with an event.

This was a four-day festival, on April 12, 13, 15 and 16, 1898, to commemorate the Oratorio Society's first twenty-five years. Leopold had led it for twelve, from its founding until his death, in 1885; Walter for thirteen, through the festival, after which the new artistic director and conductor would be Frank. So Damrosch leadership would continue unbroken into the society's second quarter-century, just as still among its members, singing in the concerts, were Helene, Tante, Marie Wiechmann and Clara. Of the family, only Ellie was not involved in some way, and only because she and Harry recently had moved to South Orange, New Jersey.

In its twenty-fifth year the society continued to have remarkable financial and artistic health. Though Morris Reno, after serving as treasurer for twenty-two years, had retired, Carnegie still was president, and Tuthill, the architect of Carnegie Hall, was secretary. The membership had risen to 442, of which about a sixth lived outside the city. Not everyone, of course, sang in every concert; only those who had attended enough of the Thursday night rehearsals. Each year, because of death or another reason, some seventy members would drop out, but thus far another seventy always had been ready to pay the dues and fill the places. Beyond question the society had become the city's chief choral group.

In its twenty-five years it had given 227 concerts, of which sixty-eight had been in conjunction with other organizations. It had sung fifty-six works, presenting twenty-one for the first time in the United States, among them Brahms's *A German Requiem,* Liszt's *Christus,* Saint-Saëns's *Samson and Delilah* and Wagner's *Parsifal.* The most frequently performed were *Messiah* (53), *Elijah* (16), *The Damnation of Faust* (15), Beethoven's Symphony No. 9 (13), *St. Matthew Passion* (12) and *The Creation* (11).[1]

The first of the festival concerts was a tribute to the society's founder. The program opened with Leopold's *Festival Overture,* followed by a brief eulogy by the Reverend Henry Van Dyke, and continued with four choral works Leopold had selected for the original concert in Knabe's warehouse. Then came the main work, Leopold's oratorio *Sulamith,* with Johanna Gadski as soloist. This was not the resurrection of a dead work. In addition to the many times that Marianne Brandt and others had sung selections from it, the society had sung it complete on three occasions, and W. J. Henderson of the *Times,* in reviewing the festival performance, declared, "Wagnerisms and all, the oratorio is a work of genius and is fully entitled to a place among the choral classics."[2]

For Helene, singing in the chorus, the evening must have been profoundly moving. The oratorio recounts the struggle between Solomon and a shepherd for the love of a country girl. It makes no effort toward dramatic characterization but simply celebrates romantic love, Leopold's love for Helene. The words of the final chorus, taken from the Song of Solomon, 8:6–7, are: "Love is strong as death; many waters cannot quench love, neither can the floods drown it. Love is strong as death."[3]

The following night, with another work that had historic overtones for the Damrosch, the society presented *The Damnation of Faust;* then two days later, an American première, Horatio Parker's *The Legend of St. Christopher;* and, finally, *Elijah.* In reviewing *The Damnation of Faust,* Henderson of the *Times* wrote that the orchestra "has arrived at a proficiency which makes the prospect of its disbandment distinctly a pity."[4] Walter already had ended its subscription concerts in New York, and, except for some annual summer engagements, notably at Louisville and Willow Grove Park, near Philadelphia, the orchestra would cease to exist.

That summer of 1898 the country was excited by events of the Spanish-American War. On Febrary 15 the battleship *Maine* had blown up in Havana Harbor, with the loss of 260 lives, and when a naval court of inquiry fixed as the cause an underwater mine, "Remember the Maine!" became a cry for war with Spain, declared by Congress on April 20. Eleven days later, on May 1, Admiral Dewey with the Pacific Squadron steamed into Manila Bay and, without losing a man, destroyed the Spanish navy. By the end of July the war was over, though not the excitement, for there were victorious troops to return and parade through the cities, Teddy Roosevelt to rush his horseless *Rough Riders* into print and campaign for governor of New York and, in time, the return to the country of Admiral George Dewey.

To celebrate the victory Walter, at Hartsdale, composed a *Manila Te Deum* for soloists, chorus and orchestra, which Frank and the Oratorio Society presented at Carnegie Hall on December 3, 1898. The evening was turned into a military gala — the auditorium draped with flags, and officers of the army and navy invited to come in dress uniform. The work they heard used several familiar bugle calls as themes on which Walter based the fugal developments of the chorus, and throughout the finale, *O Lord, in Thee Have I Trusted,* he entwined *The Star Spangled Banner.*

It was entirely an occasional piece. A month later he conducted it in Philadelphia, then at a Dewey celebration in Chicago and, on February 6, 1900, again in Carnegie Hall, with Dewey and Roosevelt present. Henderson admired the counterpoint and chord progressions, which were "of the most unexpected and eloquent sort," but noted that there were "not many tunes." He concluded: "It is well made, shows a masterful command of the forces employed, and has one or two spontaneous pages. But much of it shows the result of earnest and ambitious effort rather than of inspiration."[5]

On the other hand, the *Musical Courier,* always Walter's enemy, after rating Frank's conducting and the society's singing as "absolutely amateurish," reported the work to be "fearfully heavy, dreary, perfectly unsingable and unplayable and musically illogical . . . a hodge-podge of undesirable effects . . . written by one who, if he ever knew anything about the limitations of voices and instruments, wantonly chose to disregard that knowledge . . . We condemn it less severely than it deserves."[6]

Four months later, on April 21, 1899, at a morning recital in the Waldorf-Astoria ballroom, Walter formally emerged from retirement to present to the public some results of his year of composition. The chief work, first on the program, was a violin sonata, which he played with David Mannes; then two motets for unaccompanied double chorus; a dramatic scene, *Mary Magdalen,* for soprano; and six songs, most of them for baritone, sung by David Bispham. The texts reflected Walter's wide reading: Elizabeth Barrett Browning, Dante Gabriel Rossetti, Rudyard

Kipling, Robert Louis Stevenson, Edmund Clarence Stedman and the Negro poet Paul Laurence Dunbar.

The most successful of the works, in fact composed the previous year, was Walter's setting of Kipling's *Danny Deever*. It was more of a dramatic scene for baritone than a song in the usual sense, and Bispham, who loved it and to whom it was dedicated, sang it frequently and with stunning effect. Ultimately it proved the most durable of Walter's compositions, continuing for fifty years in the recital repertory of American operatic baritones and often sung as the final number.[7]

Predictably, the *Musical Courier* concluded that "Mr. Damrosch, known here principally as a son of his father and as a third-rate conductor . . . has nothing to say, not only nothing new, but literally nothing . . . 'Danny Deever' is vulgar." To the contrary, Henderson thought the violin sonata had "some genuine charm," though overall, like the *Te Deum*, it showed "studious effort rather than spontaneity." Then he pinpointed a feature of Walter's style: "[He] composes songs with strict regard for every detail of the text and thus his work comes to have an intellectual seriousness which is not found in much of the music of our native composers. But the method is antagonistic to the development of symmetrical melodies and a good deal of Mr. Damrosch's song writing runs into declamatory recitative."[8]

At times, as in *Danny Deever,* this could be very successful, and the *Musical Courier* notwithstanding, Walter had something to say and the start of a personal style for saying it. If he had been a young man, not yet in the spotlight, Henderson's praise might have seemed warm and encouraging; but to a thirty-seven-year-old, who for a decade had been one of the country's most publicized musicians, it no doubt seemed tepid. Still, if he had been a born composer, the warmth or its lack would have been irrelevant. But when Maurice Grau invited him to conduct at the Metropolitan for the 1900–01 season, offering him nine Wagner operas and *Fidelio,* all with top casts who would sing in German, Walter could not resist. Abandoning Hartsdale, he and Margaret, with the children, hastened back to the city, to rooms rented in the Cambridge Hotel, at Fifth Avenue and Thirty-fourth Street. Composition, it seemed, came second to conducting.

It was not a question of money. Rather, Walter loved a performance: the planning, the preparation, the glamour of the event, the response of the audience. On his return to the Metropolitan he revived his Wagner lecture-recitals, and with such success that he became a kind of matinee idol. To discover what all the excitement was about, the *New York Sun* sent a reporter to the lecture-recital on *Tristan,* which Walter delivered four days before the opera's first performance that season at the Metropolitan.

On Thursday afternoon at Sherry's Walter Damrosch gave a lecture and
musical recital upon the theme of Wagner's *Tristan und Isolde*. Incidentally
he gave an exposition of the gentle art of fascinating young women. On
the whole Mr. Damrosch and the women were more entertaining than
Wagner . . . Nine-tenths of the audience were young and uninspiring but
appreciative. There were four men in the crowd; but they were manifestly
bored and escaped as early as possible . . . [Damrosch], the clerical-look-
ing young gentleman at the piano, was intoning a portion of the Episcopal
Church service in the most approved High Church fashion. There was a
soothing cadence about the rhythmic rise and fall of his voice and the
chromatic harmonies he evoked. The uninitiated wondered vaguely why
he did it, but the admiring young women said that the poetic dreaminess
of his accent was too perfectly lovely . . . His running explanation of the
Wagnerian motives is in the form of a chant, harmonized to the accompanying rendering of those motives on the piano. There are times when
it is effective.[9]

It was easy to underrate the musical substance in the lecture-recitals,
particularly perhaps for musicians. Gustave Schirmer, who loved Debussy's *Pelléas et Mélisande* and had heard it often in Paris, went to one of
Walter's lectures on it, fearing the worst. But he came away deeply impressed. Walter had not allowed his showmanship to distort the piece
but had used it effectively to project the opera's fragile essence to a large,
spellbound audience. And this was true pioneer work, for the opera's
American première was still in the future.[10]

Grau of the Metropolitan again hired Walter, for the 1901–02 season,
to conduct the German wing, to which was added Mozart's *The Magic
Flute,* sung in Italian; Paderewski's *Manru,* in its American première; and
concert performances of *Messiah* and of Verdi's *Requiem.* In these two
years, despite his out-of-town spring and summer engagements with the
New York Symphony, Walter's chief occupation again became opera;
for what with tours before and after the New York stand, the Metropolitan's season was six months, November through April, and included
cities in the South and Midwest and on the Pacific Coast. But now Grau,
not Walter, was the impresario who had to deal with the singers, and
when the tour arrived in Memphis and Sybil Sanderson attempted to
sing Manon while drunk, Walter wrote of the "uproar" to Margaret with
all the delight of one not involved.[11]

These two years, described by Walter's daughter Gretchen in the opening chapters of *From the Top of the Stairs,* were extremely happy for the
family. Though Margaret at times may have fretted over life in a hotel,
her two elder daughters, Alice and Gretchen, loved it, and the baby,
Polly, born in the year at Hartsdale, was still too young to notice or
care. Polly, perhaps reflecting her father's disappointment that he still
lacked a son, had been burdened at baptism with the name Leopoldine,

but no one used it. And then in the midst of this happy life in opera, the Philharmonic Society, much to Walter's surprise, invited him to conduct its 1902–03 season.

After Theodore Thomas left New York in the spring of 1891 to found the Chicago Symphony, the Philharmonic had been able to meet the challenge of Walter's improved New York Symphony by electing as its conductor Anton Seidl. For several years the two orchestras competed, both doing moderately well. The Philharmonic had the more subtle conductor; the New York Symphony, the more adventurous programs. But when Walter began to use the Symphony primarily for the Damrosch Opera Company, the Philharmonic's ticket sales began to soar. Seidl, though he had lost to Walter in opera, won in orchestral music, and under him the Philharmonic solidified its position as the city's finest orchestra for symphonic music. Then, quite unexpectedly, on March 28, 1898, Seidl died.

He was only forty-seven, and apparently the immediate cause of death was an ill-preserved fish whose poison aggravated a cirrhosis of the liver. The suddenness greatly increased the shock of his death, and, like Leopold Damrosch thirteen years earlier, he was given a huge and dramatic funeral in the opera house.

The bereft Philharmonic tried first to engage the Belgian violin virtuoso and conductor Eugène Ysaÿe and, on his refusal, succeeded in luring from the Boston Symphony Emil Paur. Then followed one of those curious failures that sometimes occur in music. Paur was a good conductor, but he seemed unable to make any impression in New York, and under him the orchestra's ticket sales steadily declined. At the end of his fourth year, in the spring of 1902, though he wished to continue, the Philharmonic's members voted 46 to 13 to offer the post to Walter.[12]

Undoubtedly one reason was that Andrew Carnegie the year before had accepted the presidency of the Philharmonic Society, and the members hoped the election of Walter might unlock Carnegie's millions to their benefit. Also, in both opera and symphonic music Walter had proved himself a competent conductor and an outstanding impresario. He could attract an audience.

For Walter the invitation was flattering and came at a time when he was ready to give up the German wing at the Metropolitan. Not counting rehearsals, in the two seasons he had conducted 131 performances of Wagner, forty-four of them of *Lohengrin;* and before the Metropolitan there had been four years of Wagner with the Damrosch Opera Company. He wanted greater variety, and though the Philharmonic had been "ever since my father's day, the rival orchestra," he accepted.[13]

Almost at once he discovered that he had blundered. The orchestra's situation was worse than he had imagined, largely because of its cooperative structure. In theory the members of the Philharmonic Society, with the exception of several acting as administrators, were the members of the orchestra. Thirty years earlier, in 1872–73, that was almost true: the society then had 104 members, and in concerts requiring a hundred players, on average ninety-two would be society members. But by 1902–03 the society's membership had shrunk to seventy-three, of which an average of only fifty-nine turned up for concerts requiring a hundred players. At no time now could the society by itself field a full orchestra, and on occasion the substitutes and extras that had to be hired almost outnumbered the society's members. In fact, the cooperative orchestra had become a myth; it could be described better as a large clique of instrumentalists who acted as their own concert management and hired an orchestra for each concert, reserving certain places in it for themselves. This was expensive, disruptive and, in a time of increasing competition, ineffective. And further, chiefly because of age, the abilities of many in the clique had begun to decline. Yet how could these men, who were the management, be replaced? And how could rich men like Carnegie be persuaded to underwrite such a system?

Characteristically, with great energy Walter set about creating a plan of reorganization that would put the orchestra on a permanent basis, just as he had done with the New York Symphony in 1891 and just as Theodore Thomas in the same year had tried to do, and failed, with the Philharmonic. At first the society's members responded with enthusiasm, but when they realized that Walter's plan for a "permanent orchestra fund" was conditional on a reorganization of the society itself, they drew back. They were not ready to pass artistic and financial control to a board composed largely of nonplayers, particularly as it became clear that Walter thought several of the older playing members, including the concertmaster, should be retired at the season's end. By February, tempers all around were short.

To make matters worse, Walter's season with the Philharmonic promised to be almost as bad financially as his father's in 1876–77. The parallel, in fact, was quite extraordinary, as Walter, for the first time in his career, seemed unable to attract an audience. The decline in ticket sales that had started under Paur continued, and without even the excuse of a competing resident orchestra. The public, for both men, simply stayed away.

Meanwhile at the Metropolitan, because the impresario Maurice Grau was retiring in the spring, the directors of the Metropolitan Opera and Real Estate Company solicited proposals from potential successors of the terms on which each would lease the house and organize a company. Perhaps because Walter sensed disaster at the Philharmonic, he applied, despite his protestations five years earlier that he never again wanted to manage a company of singers. Also applying were Heinrich Conried, the manager of the Irving Place Theater in New York, and George H. Wilson of Pittsburgh.

To most people, Walter, because of his greater experience, was the obvious choice. But the *Musical Courier,* of course, was against him, and now it was joined by Henry T. Finck of the *New York Evening Post:* "I hadn't the slightest doubt," Finck summarized later, "that Mr. Damrosch would make an excellent manager; he had the requisite knowledge, experience and business ability; he spoke several languages and was a 'good mixer.' But — he was a composer and a conductor! The idea that he might produce a new work of his own most every season and personally conduct all the most important performances, did not fill my soul with unmitigated joy. So I came out for Conried." And he did so in his usual style, so derisive of Walter that his article produced letters of protest to his editor.[14]

In early February, at a time when Walter's relations with the Philharmonic had begun to sour, the Metropolitan directors, by a vote of 7 to 6, awarded a five-year lease on the house to Conried. The decision turned apparently on financial considerations: Conried had succeeded in establishing a richer group of backers than Walter had and was prepared to post $150,000 as a guarantee to the directors against loss. There may also be truth in the contention that Otto Kahn, who fast was becoming the dominant director in Metropolitan affairs, preferred a man who had no existing constituency among Metropolitan employees and supporters. Whatever the reason, the vote, so close, disappointed Walter, and to have suffered the journalistic abuse, all to no end, can only have increased his frustration.[15]

Two weeks later the *Times*, in an article discussing the reforms needed at the Philharmonic, made public Walter's difficulties with the orchestra.[16] By now the player-members opposed him and his plan with anger, and it seemed clear that they would not again elect him conductor. Anticipating defeat, Walter on April 7 wrote the concertmaster, who was also vice-president of the society, asking that his name not be submitted for the post, and he sent a copy of the letter to the *Times*. Politely, softly, he reiterated the problems:

> . . . You know that the Philharmonic orchestra of today is incomplete and that about thirty strings and one-half the necessary wood-wind players . . . have to be engaged from whatever material may be available in New York at the time. And as the Philharmonic gives only night concerts [about twenty-two] during the season, some of the best players are often drawn away by other organizations which offer greater pecuniary inducements . . . To be compelled, as some of your members are, to play at the dances in October and the balls in January is no proper preparation for

a symphony concert, and I had hoped that the orchestral fund, judicially used, would enable us, in a comparatively short time, to place the orchestra in a position where its members would no longer be compelled to earn their living in this manner.[17]

In another six years the orchestra would have forced on it a reorganization much like the one Walter had suggested. But the player-members would never forgive him for having been right.

Walter's father and brother each had suffered a crisis in his choice of career and had been forced to think hard about what he wanted to do with his life and how to go about it. Helene, too, had faced a crisis in choosing to give up her career in opera and lieder to marry an impecunious violinist in Liszt's orchestra. Walter, like every performer, had suffered moments of doubt and terror, but he never had suffered the spiritual anguish of giving up a part of himself, a talent, in order to hew more closely to what was most important to him. His sister Clara, who believed strongly in focusing on one talent, might have asked: Are you a composer? Then give up the celebrity of conducting. Are you a conductor? Then don't reorganize the New York Symphony only to abandon it in order to compose. And any observer might have said: You cannot in the same year, in the same month, bid for control of the Metropolitan Opera and the New York Philharmonic. The jobs are too big. You only will confuse and divide your supporters and, by your arrogance, increase your enemies.

Walter had reached forty without any major setback in his career, and he behaved like one who thought there were no limits to his talents. Then suddenly every project blew up in his face, and half the musical world was angry with him. The experience was salutary, for it made him think hard about what he wanted to do most. But it was painful, and the events wrung from him a rare cry of pain. His letter to Carnegie is lost, but Carnegie replied:

> It is all too sad. I cannot quite understand it but don't be too deeply discouraged. Skies will not always lower.
> There is no question of your ability to succeed in more than one field —
> These great artists have always suffered in Material things — and even for Conductors how very narrow is the demand.
> I thot [sic] your Lectures a grand Success. Cannot that field be Widened — a Course in each of the big cities for instance.
> Mrs. C & I are rejoicing at dear little Gretchen's recovery . . .[18]

Carnegie, good friend that he was, no doubt meant to be kind to Walter, but how that suggestion of lecturing must have hurt.

CHAPTER 16

Helene at Seeley Farm. Frank's Concerts for Young People. Birth of Leopold Damrosch Mannes. Ysaÿe calls him "the reincarnation of Mozart." Helene dies.

ELLIE'S MARRIAGE to Harry Seymour was happy but also, for her in some respects, traumatic. There were four children in five years — Lawrence, Clair, Bess and Ruth — and though Harry could support the family, often including a Fräulein who helped the children with German, at first there was not much money. After a year in Middle Granville, where Ellie, a city girl, had to cope with heavy snow and shopping by sleigh, he returned to New York and invested $25,000 in the New York Export & Import Company, becoming its vice-president and director. To make ends meet, he settled in South Orange, New Jersey, an hour from the city. Life there was easier than in Middle Granville, and the family began to prosper.

Always Helene was helpful. Among her children and their spouses she never showed preference. Though Harry and Ellie lived the farthest away, every month without fail Helene, taking the train alone, with her black overnight bag and a box of chocolates or marshmallows for the children, would arrive for a visit of a night or two. Sometimes she would listen to the children's songs or go for walks with them, and in the evenings she would talk with Harry about his business or his drawings, which she admired. But most of any visit would be spent in the sewing room, helping Ellie to catch up on the family needlework and, most important, listening to Ellie talk. By telephone Ellie heard most of the family's news from Clara, who called almost every day, and whenever a call came through from Tante Clara, the children would ask, "What's happened now?" But with O'mama there was peace in the house and affection.[1]

In the summer of 1904 Harry, through his friend Mary Webster, the wife of an architect, arranged for the family to spend two months at a farm near Washington, Connecticut, owned by Mary's friends the Seeleys. Harry himself, working a half-day on Saturday, had only Sundays and his two-week vacation at the farm, but he hoped that from two months with the animals the children would learn something of life. And they did, within the comprehension of each. Larry that summer was nine; Clair, eight; Bess, almost six; and Ruth, four; and while they were at the farm, a calf was born, cows were milked regularly, chickens and ducks laid eggs and sometimes were slaughtered, and there were also pigs, horses and guinea hens.

Besides Ellie, the family that summer included a Fräulein, and for several weeks the daughter of Frank and Hetty, eleven-year-old Helen. In addition, there were four Seeley boys, two full grown, one of eleven and one of nine. Also that summer Mary Webster came up for a visit with her three children, and she, too, in a way provided some education.

Both Harry and Ellie, perhaps because of their art studies, had brought up their children to accept a certain amount of nakedness as natural, even among adults, and without a thought the Seymours, like the Seeley boys, plunged naked into the swimming hole. So, too, did Mary Webster, and considerably more openly than the other adults. Larry noticed that his Uncle Frank, who had brought Helen to the farm, could not keep his eyes off Mary Webster.

But for the children the most important visitor that summer was O'mama, who came up for a week. They showed her everything — the calf, the chickens, the swimming hole, the brook, the blueberry patch and the picnic places. She, in turn, did something she had never done before. For several afternoons she gathered them all, including the Seeley children, on the verandah, where they were out of the afternoon sun, and there, without a stumble or hesitation, she told them the stories of the Wagner operas, half-humming, half-singing the arias as she went along. To Larry, in memory, "it was impressive." [2]

Like Walter, Frank had his failures, less spectacular but nonetheless disappointing and in public, and one of them came about because of his success with the People's Singing Classes and also, in part, because of his work in the city's public schools.

As supervisor of music, from 1897 to 1905, he, together with his twenty-six assistants, had to contend with seven thousand teachers and 300,000 pupils, most of whom, starting with the superintendent of schools, cared nothing about singing. At Frank's first meeting with school principals, the superintendent introduced him by announcing that the New York schools had always had the finest music in the United States and the new supervisor of music would not revolutionize anything. Frank responded by saying that from personal experience he knew the music in the schools to be execrable and that he intended to revolutionize everything. Later he stated that his goal was to have each child at the age of six start in a singing class and, by the time he or she was fourteen, be able to sing three-part songs at sight.[3]

The general problem was that the children tended to shout rather than sing, reflecting, in Frank's opinion, the lack of singing in the homes. More particularly, the Jewish children beginning to arrive in the city from Poland and Russia had a rasping nasal twang to their voices that proved almost impossible to eradicate. Culturally, these children and their parents were more attuned to stringed instruments than singing, and as they replaced Germans and Italians on the city's lower East Side the People's Choral Union discovered that it could no longer recruit a singing class there. On the other hand the neighborhood's Music School Settlement, in which David Mannes had begun to teach, soon had tripled its violin class.

Aside from the problems of tone production and lack of interest, however, there was the greater problem of lack of knowledge. Almost none of the children and very few of the teachers had any idea at all of what serious music was or could be. To combat this ignorance, at least for the older and more enthusiastic students as well as for their teachers, Frank started in October 1898 a series of Symphony Concerts for Young People, six performances a season in Carnegie Hall on Saturday afternoons. He recruited the orchestra of sixty chiefly from the New York Symphony; priced tickets for students and teachers at ten or twenty-five cents — and for others, considerably higher; gave the administration to a committee of women led by Laura J. Post, secretary of his Musical Art Society; and persuaded Carnegie to pay the hall's rental fee for the first year, $1500. As the concerts came closer to self-support, Carnegie covered a smaller deficit.[4]

Educational concerts for young people are now so common that it is hard to imagine a time when no one had thought of them, and the difficulty is compounded by the inability of historians to fix on who thought of them first: Theodore Thomas, Walter or Frank Damrosch. Thomas, in 1885–86, using his own orchestra, gave a series in New York of twenty-four Young People's Matinees, and in 1891 Walter, with the reorganized New York Symphony, held an afternoon series of six Young People's Concerts. Thomas and Walter each offered his series for only one year, and though it is possible, even probable, that each at some point spoke directly to the audience about the music, that was merely by the way rather than the series' purpose. The title "Young People" apparently meant only that light music, mostly overtures, marches and waltzes, would be played.

In contrast, Frank's concerts, which by succession and merger continue today, were from the first primarily educational and encompassed complete symphonies. He preceded each work with an explanation of its form, sometimes having the orchestra demonstrate a point or repeat a movement, and the programs were arranged roughly in chronological order to demonstrate the musical developments about which he talked. Thus Frank, rather than Walter or Theodore Thomas, seems to have created the educational concert for young people.[5]

But if Frank created them, Walter, when he took them over in 1912, gave them a highly personal stamp. His greeting to the Saturday afternoon audience in Carnegie Hall became famous, "Good AH-H'fterNOO-OON, my young freh-ends." And with his smiling personality he seemed to bestow the good afternoon, not merely wish it. As one member of that audience later recalled, "He was a nice man. He made you like him, so you were willing to listen to what he had to say. So you were willing to listen to the music." Two who listened were adults, Sir Robert and Lady Mayer, who took the concept back to England, where, in 1923, they started their Children's Concerts, and so the Damrosch idea spread.[6]

Nevertheless the concerts were Frank's creation and annual project for fourteen years, and their initial success stimulated him to pursue an idea that had occurred to him two years earlier, in connection with the People's Singing Classes. This was to build an auditorium with a large enough capacity to allow the various people's musical groups more easily to become self-supporting. He estimated that if ticket prices were to range from ten to fifty cents, the auditorium would have to seat eight thousand. Possibly he had in mind as a model the Royal Albert Hall in London, which had opened in 1871 and seated six thousand, with room for a thousand standing. Its oval shape, with two foci, produced a disconcerting echo, but it was at its best acoustically for large choral groups. An auditorium for eight thousand, however, was only part of what Frank envisaged. The People's Singing Classes, and other groups, needed a library to store and circulate music, as well as several rehearsal halls of various sizes, which could also be used for concerts and recitals; and there was also a need for a museum to display old music and instruments. He estimated that this complex of purposes, a prototype of a modern music center, could be housed in one building, a Temple of Music, and erected for $2 million.

He discussed the idea with a number of men and women, and in the spring of 1900 New York State granted a corporate charter to the American Institute of Music, whose chief purpose was to build the music center. Among the petitioners for the charter, besides Frank, Andrew Carnegie and several representatives of the People's Choral Union, were the city's mayor, Abram Hewitt; its leading contractor, Otto Eidlitz; the amateur cellist and investment banker James Loeb, of Kuhn, Loeb & Company; also Jacob Schiff, of the same firm; and Rudolph Schirmer, president of the music publishing house.[7]

The project was launched in April with considerable publicity, and on April 6 both the *Tribune* and the *World* had articles endorsing it, but cautiously. Frank wrote to the *Tribune*, which published his letter, attempting to answer some of the questions raised:

> As to the objection to monster concerts, I realize fully its validity, viewed from the standpoint of purely artistic considerations. At the same time there is something so inspiring in the co-operation of the masses, either as performers or auditors, or both, that this would compensate to a great extent for a lack of the highest artistic finish, especially in the case of a popular audience.[8]

To which Marc Blumenberg of the *Musical Courier* snapped editorially, "This merely means that the back of Mr. Damrosch will be 'inspiring.' It is Damrosch first with Art a good second!"[9]

Two weeks later, in another editorial the *Courier* condemned Frank's work as supervisor of music, called for an investigation of it and dismissed him personally as "formerly a sheet music dealer in Denver, Colorado."[10]

On the other hand, the People's Choral Union, through *Harmony*, alerted all the members of the People's Singing Classes to the project and raised money for the building fund through benefit concerts and the sale of ticket books. Many music lovers in the city contributed to the fund. But after three years of effort on everyone's part it was clear that the $2 million would never be raised. The money that had been gathered was returned.

Clearly one cause of the scheme's failure was its inability — or Frank's inability on its behalf — to arouse interest among the rich. Carnegie had given one hall and was not going to give another, and his colleagues could see that his earlier gift had become a continuing burden. The new hall, which would be almost two and a half times as large, might end by being just that much more burdensome. They may also have feared that a hall seating eight thousand would not, could not, have good acoustics for music. The Metropolitan, after all, seating only about thirty-six hundred, had proved bad for all but opera, and the Royal Albert Hall was good only for the most exceptional artists or choral groups.

Then, too, there was a question of purpose. Frank, characteristically, was mixing musical and social ends, and many persons other than Blumenberg doubted the wisdom of it for music, just as many in the mid-twentieth century would question whether music benefited by being harnessed to urban renewal.

There was also a question of scale, of the amount of interest in the city for music. The Greeks could build their huge outdoor theaters because those were truly community projects. When the drama festivals began, everyone in town went. That was not true of music in New York. The city by 1900 had a population of three and a half million, and Frank himself estimated that among them there were at most only fifty thousand music lovers. At concerts, recitals or operas the same faces constantly appeared. An auditorium with a capacity of eight thousand might well prove impossible to fill, even at low prices. Or perhaps the concept was ahead of its time. Whatever the mixture of reasons, Frank's idea of a people's music center, despite its prestigious backers, could not win support enough to be realized even partially. The failure was complete.

After their marriage and a summer of visiting friends, Clara and David Mannes returned to New York to the building at 327 Amsterdam Avenue that housed not only Helene and Tante, but Frank, Hetty and their two children, Hetty's parents, the Mosenthals, and her sister, Therese. Helene and Tante had prepared an apartment for Clara and David simply by dividing their own in two. The apartments were connected through a door, but each had its own entrance and kitchen. Directly overhead were Frank and Hetty, connected by a circular, "secret" staircase that led now into the Mannes quarters and was the delight of visiting children.

David adjusted to the Damrosch way of life with ease. In his own family and environment, though never lacking parental support, he always had been the odd member, and now, without any strong ideas of his own about how to live, he moved into a large family that shared his chief interest. The break with his past, consequently, was sharp. Until marriage, for example, he had given all his earnings to his mother, and except for carfare carried no money on his person, having developed an abhorrence of it. He continued the habit with Clara, who now managed all his affairs and periodically paid off his debts. Those who knew of his idiosyncrasy — doormen, shopkeepers, secretaries of schools where he taught — kept accounts, and there was never any trouble.

With an apartment of her own Clara taught most of her students at home, saving herself the time and expense of going from house to house, and David, for his pupils, sublet Walter's studio in Carnegie Hall three afternoons a week. By 1900 he was an important member of the New York Symphony, by then primarily a touring orchestra, and he sometimes served as concertmaster, playing an occasional solo, and even once or twice replaced Walter as conductor. In addition, in New York he conducted a small, private children's orchestra that gathered regularly at the home of Dr. Clarence Rice, and many of the children were among his pupils.[11]

One day an older sister of one of the violinists suggested that he accompany her to Rivington Street on the lower East Side, where an interesting experiment in music had been started among the Jewish immigrants most recently arrived from Poland and Russia. "There I met Miss Wagner, a young woman who had started teaching the children in this most sordid and filthy neighborhood. Some of these children paid ten cents for their lessons on either the piano or violin. This work started in the basement of a church and no rental was asked as it was considered a charitable venture."

Emilie Wagner had opened her school in 1894 in a Bowery mission. By 1900, when Mannes was introduced to her, the school had become the Music School of the University and College Settlements, two settlement houses on the lower East Side, and had its own small schoolhouse at 31 Rivington Street. Various committees raised money for it.

David saw in it the opportunity to realize a dream he long had held: to teach music to the poor, not to encourage mediocre professionalism but as a means for providing spiritual enlightenment, as a substitution for religion. He promptly volunteered to take a small class of violin players and was not disappointed to find "most of them without musical experience, and very few of them showing any particular talent." They were enthusiastic and worked hard, even though they often had to share one violin among three. Soon, with the help of the committees, he found more instruments for them and formed them into a small string orchestra, with one viola and one cello.[12]

Clara admired David's work at the school and developed a theory that perhaps their married life was happy "because 'chemically' and in life experiences, David and I are opposites. He had to fulfill his desires and destiny in the hard way, which means a much more interesting personality. He loves humanity as a whole and can give himself generously to anyone's needs and confidences."

Clara had discovered, in attempting to do settlement work, that she did not love humanity as a whole and was put off by the dirt and filth of the poor. Some of the reasons, she felt, were physical, even musical. David had the gift of repose: "He could sit for hours, doing nothing, is never bored." Whereas "for me, sleep is not natural. I am continuously active in both brain and temperament . . . David can quietly listen to music while I, when I am listening, am practically performing the music inwardly and can hardly refrain from singing it aloud."[13]

Clara always was a better performer than teacher, and the less talented the pupil, the worse she became as a teacher. Bad playing was a physical discomfort for her; it wasn't for David. He would smile, talk gently and concentrate on some small point that could be improved. But Clara inwardly grew frantic at the mistakes, and in her self-repression her eyes flashed, her lips pursed and her voice became harsh. She sometimes even knocked the pupil's hand from the keyboard. Often her less-talented pupils burst into tears, and they complained privately of her German perfectionism.[14] She could not do what David did, so she contributed to his work by organizing his life so that he could do it easily and efficiently.

On the day after Christmas 1899, their first child, a son, was born. The delivery, at home, was difficult; a specialist had to be called, and for several weeks a trained nurse lived in the apartment and cared for the baby, whose large, staring brown eyes only rarely closed in sleep. In Clara's mind, it seems, there was never any question: he would be named for her father: Leopold Damrosch Mannes.

To her intense pleasure he very soon began to show a marked precocity in music, far greater than any other of O'mama's grandchildren. According to his mother and to his Uncle Frank, when Leopold was only one and a half he could sing twenty of the St. Nicholas Songs, which he had heard his mother singing around the apartment, and he could name the song when she tapped only the rhythm on the windowpane. Almost as soon as he could stand, he reached for the piano, and though his parents made no effort to make a prodigy of him, in this particular family his musical development inevitably was rapid.[15]

When Leopold was three and a half, in April 1903, his parents went to Brussels for six months, taking him and his Negro nurse, Nana, with them. David wanted to study with Eugène Ysaÿe, and though apparently he and Clara had told no one, they seem to have begun to think of touring as a piano and violin duo. When they had become engaged, they had sworn to each other never to perform together in public.[16] But they had discovered that they greatly enjoyed playing chamber music together, and seemed to do it well. From time to time Frank had asked them to play for the People's Singing Classes, and they'd done it, thinking that their vow still held, since a performance for charity was not for a paying public. They also had played from time to time in private homes, with success. There was not at that time any piano–violin duo regularly performing in the United States, and they could be the first. Their marriage made them an attractive team and also made it possible for them to tour without attracting gossip. In fact, it opened for Clara a kind of career that otherwise would not have been possible. In the six months abroad, while David studied with Ysaÿe, she could perfect her half of the repertory.

The trip, even in prospect, greatly stimulated Leopold. When he heard them speak of Europe, he was puzzled. He knew of French and German, but, he asked, "Can one speak Europe?"[17]

Once in Brussels, he began to pick up French rapidly, and as soon as the rented piano arrived in the apartment, he toddled to it and played

My Country, 'Tis of Thee with both hands. The harmonies were not always correct, but for a child his age, the feat was remarkable. Later, when his father was studying the César Franck sonata with Ysaÿe and his mother was practicing her part at home, and after he had heard the parts often separately and together, he tried to reproduce them both at the piano, prattling to his parents as he went along about which part he was emphasizing, and why.

One day Ysaÿe, astonished by Leopold's abilities, suggested to Clara that the boy must be "the reincarnation of Mozart."[18] It was an unfortunate remark to make to a parent already proud.

On November 18, 1904, Helene in her sixty-ninth year died suddenly of heart failure. Only four days earlier Clara's second child had been born, a girl, named Marie after Tante, but later in life always known as Marya. She was the last of Helene's fourteen grandchildren, and one of Helene's final pleasures, in Tante's phrase, was to give the baby "a kiss of welcome."[19]

The funeral was held in the cemetery at Woodlawn, a stop on the suburban railroad, and, as was often done in those days, the railroad reserved a car for the family on the afternoon train while several hundred friends and members of the Oratorio Society rode before them in the public cars. At the graveside the society's members sang Bach's chorale *Come, Sweet Death* and the opening chorus of the *St. Matthew Passion,* and after a few words by a minister, the Reverend John D. Elliott, Helene was buried beside Leopold.[20]

It happened by chance that at the Oratorio Society's next concert, only two weeks later, the chief work, conducted by Frank, was Brahms's *A German Requiem,* which Leopold had introduced to the United States on March 15, 1877. Its repetition now, its fifth performance in New York in twenty-seven years, must have seemed to the family not only a requiem for Helene but a vindication of hers and Leopold's life in music. For at its première neither audience nor critics had understood the work, and the critic for the *Times* had stated, "Its length and monotonousness are such that it is scarcely likely to impress any but students." Now, performed to a large audience, it was "a monumental work . . . of so lofty and supreme beauty as to place it irrevocably among the great masterpieces of its kind."[21] Leopold and Helene had sung Brahms's songs together, and the nurturing of a taste for his music was a development in which all the family could rejoice and feel it had a part.

The Damrosches did not believe in the resurrection of the body or of an individual spirit. In all their correspondence, journals and published works, there is no indication of it. The newborn baby, years later, would state their feelings best, in a novel in which a dead woman talks from beyond the grave to her descendants:

> Do not demand that the dead retain their contours and their names. That is for your comfort, not for ours . . . [After] the final transmutation had taken place . . . I would now exist, not as myself, but as a single atom in the imperishable dust of creation. There was no end . . . It was only Self that died . . . Remember your moments of greatest happiness; and you will remember when you lost yourselves. You will then understand the splendor of this anonymity and this participation; and be content to call it heaven . . .[22]

Of course, those left among the living continue with their earthly feelings, and of all the obituary notices that Frank and Hetty must have read they chose to save one that began: "Mrs. Leopold Damrosch, born von Heimburg, will long be remembered as an aristocrat in our own little musical world, the Queen Mother of New York's most musical family . . ."[23]

PART III

Pre–World War I: Second Generation at Flood Tide

CHAPTER 17

Walter, Flagler and the revived New York Symphony. Margaret's part in Walter's career. Their marriage.

IN THE SPRING OF 1903, when Walter lost both his bid to become the impresario of the Metropolitan Opera and his conductor's post at the New York Philharmonic, all he had left was the remains of the New York Symphony — whose importance he had been decreasing steadily for the past five years. Reduced to fifty players, it now was suitable only for touring; had no New York season, no subscribers, no guarantors; and existed only for short spring and fall tours, including the annual stand at Louisville and another at Willow Grove Park. For the following winter, it seemed, Walter for the first time in nineteen years would have no post in New York — total eclipse in the country's cultural capital. The prospect was the darkest hour of his career.

With Margaret, immediately after his final concert with the Philharmonic, he sailed for Europe, probably only to exit gracefully from a disastrous and unpleasant scene. As he well knew, there were many who rejoiced in his multiple defeat. While abroad, and no doubt in close consultation with Margaret, he evidently thought hard about what he wanted to do most and how to go about it, for on his return in May he began to act consistently on lines from which, for the rest of his life, he never departed. He would be a conductor primarily of symphony, not of opera or even of choral groups; his orchestra perforce, because plainly now the Philharmonic never would be his, would be the New York Symphony, which he would revive and reorganize completely; and his composing, if done at all, would be subordinate to his conducting.

Along with these decisions went several others, as premises or conclusions more slowly reached. Regardless of any difficulties, his base would

be New York, and for the family to live there — Margaret was expecting their fourth child in the fall — they would buy a house; no more
hotels or apartments. By late 1905 they had found what they wanted and
moved into a wide, five-story brownstone at 146 East 61st Street. The
house was convenient, within walking distance of Carnegie Hall and relatively cheap, because it was too far east to be fashionable. Here they
lived for twenty-five years, creating not only a happy home but a center
of New York's musical and social life.

To this, as a summer alternative, in time was added Blaine Cottage,
in Bar Harbor, Maine. Margaret's mother, after ten years a widow, died
in midsummer 1903, and for a number of years thereafter the three surviving children and heirs of the three who had predeceased the parents
held jointly the family houses in Bar Harbor and in Augusta, Maine's
capital. Eventually Margaret, who of the survivors had the most children, took the rambling summer house, and her younger sister Harriet,
the one in Augusta. After World War I Harriet gave hers to the State of
Maine, and it is today the Governor's Mansion. The parents' burial plot
close by, with a memorial erected by the state, became a small park. For
the family their connection with Maine and descent from James G. Blaine
continued a vibrant heritage, and during the next forty years Margaret,
Walter, their children, nieces, nephews and grandchildren would pass
long periods of the summer at Bar Harbor.

In two respects, at least, the disasters of the winter ultimately may
have worked to Walter's benefit. Though he had proved himself an excellent operatic impresario, the need to deal with childish singers always
had chaffed him; this and the relatively narrow repertory of works performed were the reasons he later gave for his decision against opera. But
he may have been lucky in that the new operatic composer of the coming
quarter-century was no longer Wagner or any other German, but Puccini; and in place of Alvary and de Reszke, the new tenor was Caruso,
followed by Gigli and Martinelli. Walter was deaf to Italian opera, unable
to develop any ear for it. Conried, who had defeated him for the Metropolitan post, was not a musician and could follow the lead of the box
office. Walter would have had artistic ideas, almost certainly counter to
the trend, and after a time might have been ousted, whereas in symphonic music his appreciation of Berlioz and Saint-Saëns led him easily
into a liking for Debussy and Ravel, and here he was not only abreast of
the trend but able to lead it.

In a different fashion his failure at the Philharmonic and the subsequent
need to devote all his time to rebuilding the New York Symphony may
have helped by preventing him from composing. The problem here was
temperament. Though Walter longed all his life to win a composer's
laurels, he loved too much the day-to-day excitement of a great city's

musical life ever to turn from it for long. He simply could not put composing first. So the need to compete with the Philharmonic may have forced him to develop a greater skill further than he otherwise might have done.

In his time of trouble Walter, of course, was not without friends. Though Carnegie's position as president of the Philharmonic Society, from 1901 through 1909, was largely honorary, because of it he could do little publicly; and E. Francis Hyde, who twenty years before had done so much for the New York Symphony, was now wholly a Philharmonic supporter and extremely effective on its behalf. But there was another rich man, eight years younger than Walter, who had entered the Philharmonic's affairs only in December 1902 and who had been impressed both by Walter personally and by his plan of reorganization. This was Harry Harkness Flagler, son of Henry M. Flagler, who, after John D. Rockefeller, was the chief stockholder of the Standard Oil Trust and also the major developer of Florida real estate. Young Flagler accompanied Walter out of the Philharmonic into the New York Symphony, which became his chief interest in life. Beginning in 1914, following his father's death and on the example of Higginson of Boston, he annually guaranteed the orchestra's deficit. Though contributions from others were still received, from 1914 through 1928 he came close to supporting the orchestra single-handed. Ironically the Philharmonic in its competition with the Symphony, though it gained Hyde and neutralized Carnegie, lost Flagler. But in 1903 no one, certainly not Walter, fully grasped how rich the new oil barons were.[1]

The corporate structure of the Symphony Society was still intact; it needed only the breath of life, and at a series of meetings in the spring and summer of 1903 new directors were elected and Walter's friend Daniel Frohman, the theatrical producer, made president for the coming year. Frohman, through his contacts on Broadway, was useful in finding outside work for the orchestra's members to eke out their salaries. He was succeeded by Samuel S. Sanford, dean of Yale's Music School, whose father had made a fortune as president of the Adams Express Company. Sanford quickly became one of the largest guarantors of the permanent orchestra fund, collected each year to assure the principal players, at least, of sufficient pay to obviate the need for outside work. Others besides Sanford and Flagler who supported the fund were Walter's old friend Mary R. Callender, Rudolph Schirmer and sometimes as many as five of the Seligman family, investment bankers, who since the days of Leopold Damrosch steadily had supported the orchestra.[2]

Though Carnegie, still president of the Philharmonic, was not among these generous supporters of the Symphony's fund, it seems likely that it was in this period that he began to give Walter on his birthday each year a present of $5000. Carnegie, who died in 1919, continued this custom through his will for Walter's life, so when Walter died in 1950 he had received personally from Carnegie almost a quarter of a million dollars. This annual gift, which was to continue to Margaret after Walter's death, when combined with income from a trust fund set up for Margaret by her sister-in-law Anita McCormick Blaine, gave Walter and Margaret a financial security that no other Damrosch or Blaine child achieved, assuring for them the position of head in both families, and, of course, giving Walter in the world of music an unusual and enviable financial independence.[3]

With the Symphony Society's rejuvenation well begun, its directors announced, in August 1903, that the New York Symphony during the coming season not only would resume its playing for the Oratorio Society and for Frank Damrosch's Symphony Concerts for Young People, but would give a subscription series of five concerts on Sunday afternoons.[4] The number of subscription concerts was not extraordinary, but the time of performance was novel, even daring, because it was in violation of a municipal ordinance prohibiting "Entertainments of the Stage" on Sunday. But as Walter surmised, the unusual time attracted attention and proved popular; indeed, the percentage of men attending was higher than at most concerts.

For his second season Walter expanded the Sunday series to six, though without making any concessions to popular taste in the works played. At the opening concert, for example, he offered Elgar's *In the South,* which would have been an American première, except that Thomas with the Chicago orchestra beat him to it by two weeks, and Mahler's Symphony No. 4, which was not only an American première but, according to the critic for the *Times,* the first performance in the country of any work by Mahler.[5]

By the fall of 1907 the society was scheduling twenty Sunday afternoon concerts, and a judge had ruled them violations of the ordinance. A new ordinance, or an amendment to relax the judicial interpretation, seemed the best hope, and Walter, among others, argued at a hearing in City Hall that the concerts were educational, not frivolous, and were put on at a loss by philanthropists for the public's benefit. What happened next is obscure. The new ordinance apparently passed, for the concerts continued, but in June 1911, Richard Welling, the society's secretary, wrote in alarm to Walter: "The Corporation Counsel [the city's lawyer] tells me you get a license for Sunday concerts every year. Is this true?" To which Walter replied: "No, my dear Dick! We never get a Sunday license! We always 'let sleeping dogs lie.' " And there the matter apparently was allowed to rest. Times had changed, the old entertainment laws increasingly were ignored and throughout the country orchestra managers were beginning to follow Walter's lead by scheduling concerts on Sunday afternoons.[6]

In reorganizing the orchestra's personnel Walter's goal was to have roughly a hundred men who would remain constant, rehearsing together almost every day and putting the orchestra's engagements first in their commitments. He started in 1903 with a nucleus of fifty, the touring orchestra, to which he added others as needed for the New York concerts and those in the big cities. In Chicago, for example, if he had only fifty men, he would schedule Haydn but not Wagner. By the fall of 1907, however, thanks to the growth of the orchestra fund, he was able to guarantee salaries to ninety-five men for a seven-month season in and around New York. Tours were in addition, and aside from the overnight stands he was able to add to Louisville and Willow Grove stops of three to seven weeks at Pittsburgh and at Ravinia Park, near Chicago. By the spring of 1916, when he started a ten-week transcontinental tour with Josef Hofmann as soloist, he was able to travel with an orchestra of eighty-five.[7]

It was slow work: finding the right man, enough money, and bringing the two together in a contract, because a frequent problem was the player who treated the contract as a mere declaration of intent, not as a binding agreement. In 1906, for example, Caesar Addimando, an oboist, suddenly threatened to leave if not paid double, and Walter wrote to him: "Do not act hastily. If you deliberately break your contract, you will find it impossible to accept any other engagements, as both the laws of the State of New York and the laws of the American Federation of Musicians would prevent that, and do not forget that I want to remain your friend as long as you deal honorably with us. Come some morning this week and talk it over."[8]

An agreement was worked out, but not for long: Addimando was restless. But against such behavior Walter's ability to stand firm, with good humor and even kindness, constantly benefited the orchestra.

In his concertmaster he was lucky, for he had David Mannes, whose loyalty was incorruptible and whose solo work in these years, particularly in Bach's *Brandenburg Concerto No. 1* and Wagner's *Good Friday Music* from *Parsifal,* became renowned. The string section on the whole was good, the brasses slightly less so, and the woodwinds, compared with those of the Boston Symphony, weak.[9] The Boston orchestra, which Walter used as the standard of excellence, continued to have an advantage over both New York orchestras in that it was nonunion, and its sponsor, H. L. Higginson, could hire the best, regardless of a player's geographical origin. But in New York the union decreed that impresarios must hire first from the local union's roster; then, if no available player was satisfactory, from rosters of other local unions; but on no account could a foreigner play with a union orchestra, except as a soloist, until he had been elected to the union — after six months' residence in the country.

To Walter, and to many others, the French and Belgian woodwind players were the world's best. Though the modern flute, for example, essentially fifteen holes and twenty-three keys and levers, had been invented in 1847 by a Bavarian, Theobald Böhm, thereafter the French schools, particularly the Paris Conservatoire, produced the best players, whose tone was sweeter, purer and more precise. Boston had several Paris-trained woodwind players, but in New York, where the local union's roster was almost entirely German, none was available. Walter, as he had done in the past when importing Adolph Brodsky and Anton Hegner, decided to ignore the union's residence rule, went to Paris early in 1905 and returned with contracts for five outstanding players, of which the greatest, ultimately, was Georges Barrère, a flutist. He played with the New York Symphony until 1928, when it merged with the Philharmonic, and by his example and pupils set the standard for flutists in the United States for the next forty years.

In 1891, Walter had succeeded in persuading the union to waive its rule and to admit the violinist Brodsky at once. Two years later with Hegner, the cellist, he had failed and suffered a strike. Now once again he counted on public opinion and reason, as he saw it, to carry the day. How else could he build an orchestra to compete with Boston's? But the union balked, threatening a strike if Barrère and the others played except as soloists.

In ten years, however, the situation had changed slightly, for the New York union meantime had joined the American Federation of Musicians and was now only a "local." Walter therefore had a forum to which to appeal, and he was fortunate, or farsighted, in the timing of his confrontation. Barrère landed in New York on May 1, and in that month the federation was meeting in a national convention in Detroit. Walter hastened out to lay his case before its executive board, and was opposed by the delegates from New York, one of whom, a German by birth, stated bluntly, according to Walter, "Ve don't vant to have our pisness spoiled by those foreigners." [10]

A compromise of sorts was reached. Barrère and the other four players were to be admitted to the union at once, but Walter was to pay the federation a fine of $1000 for not advertising his vacancies sufficiently. Under protest Walter paid, on May 31, having lost only a month of his players' services. He felt he had won, or, at least, that the penalty was not too severe. But once again the fundamental conflict of artistic standard versus job monopoly was not faced and no procedure created for resolving it. The wrangle would continue. [11]

Problems of a different kind were raised by the need to increase the orchestra's opportunities to play. One way to keep the men together between New York performances was to send the orchestra out on small tours, such as one in January 1905, when in a fortnight it played fourteen concerts in ten cities. Such concerts usually were funded by a guarantee of a local impresario or committee, but often the local people were reluctant to risk their money.

In 1907, for example, the orchestra's manager, Henry N. Morse, concluded that Poughkeepsie, with Vassar College close by, should be able to support a concert, and he wrote to Charles H. Hickok, who owned the city's music store. Hickok replied: "Your favor of May 22nd to hand. I have firmly decided *not* to take on the concert. I know what it all means, and I dread to go through it. I have the one big event in October I spoke to you about, and that is all I can do. So do not come out to talk 'it over' — and it is uncertain as to my being at the store at the time you mention in your letter."

Morse was not so easily put off. Patiently he explained the orchestra's need to find twenty-five cities in which to give single concerts, cities near New York, so that the orchestra could go out and back without losing too much time from rehearsing. "Poughkeepsie," he wrote, "is a logical place," and he estimated that ticket sales at a concert in the Collingwood Opera House would bring in $1500, at least: "Guarantee us a minimum of $900, you take the next $200 for local expenses, and the profits we'll divide thus: 40% for us, 60% for you . . . I don't want you to lose money or even 'to come out even.' I want you to make money. I want you not to dread it, but to look forward with pleasure, as all good Americans do, to the chance of making money."

Hickok still was reluctant, but Morse, who went out to see him, was persuasive, and a concert in the opera house was scheduled for March 27, 1908.

Then in midwinter disaster loomed, and Hickok wrote posthaste:

> When you were here last summer, we looked up the dates that would be favorable to us at Vassar. And we thought we had it *right*. But some one blundered, and it proved to be all *wrong*. As I informed you some time ago the spring vacation at Vassar begins March 27th. The young ladies return Wednesday April 8th. The time just before or after these two dates is not favorable . . . It would be hard to interest the young ladies just before their departure as they would be full of "the going home" and no money to spare from their R. R. tickets, etc. The young ladies at Vassar are not spending as much money as formerly, the financial squeeze making itself felt there as elsewhere . . . but I am getting older now, so unless you can carry this date over into the later part of April, or any time in May (May much preferred), I must ask you to release me from the concert March 27th.

But the best Morse could do was advance the concert two days, to the twenty-fifth, and sales in the cheaper seats, which the young ladies should have filled, were very poor. In all, 614 seats were sold, and the total proceeds, instead of $1500, were only $917. Hickok stood to lose several hundred dollars, a large sum for a Poughkeepsie music store proprietor. So Morse, with the society's approval, released him from the contract: "Send me your check for $625, and we'll call it quits."

"Your letter is very welcome," replied Hickok. "The concert made a splendid impression. There will be concerts in the future when I hope to be able to reward you for your kindly treatment this time." [12]

Events, however, did not always end so happily. From Hartford, John Gallup of the local music store wrote bluntly, "The last concert which I took with your orchestra was very disastrous to me financially," and refused to try again. On the other hand, in Montclair, New Jersey, after an agitating beginning, in which the local sponsor may have been more alarmed than pleased at being called "the Andrew Carnegie of Montclair," the orchestra started an annual concert series that continued for years. But behind each success was much hard work. [13]

Walter, at the center of the maelstrom of personnel, scheduling, repertory and money-raising, soon decided he needed a personal secretary, someone to keep his correspondence straight and through whom he could do business while on tour. Frank was aided by Hetty, who was fluent in three languages and had learned to type in order to help him. But they had fewer children than Walter and Margaret, were less often separated and had a different relationship. Frank and Hetty, it seemed, made the most of life because they thought as one; Walter and Margaret, because they thought as two. So Walter began to ask around, and soon a young man, George Engles, applied for the job.

Engles, who was seventeen, had a part-time job as secretary–office boy at Proctor's Theatre, and a friend told him that Walter Damrosch was looking for a secretary. Engles was doubtful: he had no musical background, had never set foot in either the Metropolitan or Carnegie Hall and assumed that all serious musicians dressed in frock coats and wore their hair shaggy. "But," said the friend, "what can you lose?" So Engles phoned and was asked to come to the house on Sixty-first Street on Sunday morning.

He was shown into a room, and in a moment Walter appeared. "I saw a gentleman in a business suit come into his library, and after placing a log on the fire, turn to greet me cordially." Engles succumbed to Walter's smile. "I immediately felt that I wanted the position." But the questions were disheartening. "No, I spoke no languages. No, I had no college training. No, I knew nothing of classical music. I knew shorthand and typing."

Asked his age, he replied that he was twenty-three. "It was the only untruth; but I excused myself for it because youth had been a handicap several times previous."

Walter looked at him — later he would claim to have spotted the lie at once — and said, "We can try each other out." But he suggested that Engles for the time being continue also with the part-time job at the theater. Soon he asked him to give it up.

Like the house and the orchestra, Engles became part of Walter's life. For a few years he worked for Walter personally, but gradually he worked more for the orchestra than for Walter, though the two were hardly distinguishable, and by 1917 he had become the orchestra's business manager, a post he held until 1925, when he became director of the National Broadcasting Corporation's Artists Service, a management bureau. But that was just at the time that Walter's interest in radio burgeoned, and he was laying the groundwork for his NBC "Music Appreciation Hour." Through radio, millions of children would come to call him "Uncle Walter" or perhaps "Dr. Damrosch," but to Engles he was always "My Boss."[14]

Walter's work on the orchestra, the money spent on it, showed. With the constant playing together the men developed a consistency and richness of sound that was striking. The orchestra had played in Chicago in 1905 under Felix Weingartner and not been much admired. Chicago, after all, was used to an orchestra schooled by Theodore Thomas, who had died only the year before. But when the New York Symphony returned in 1906 under Walter, the critic for the *Chicago Examiner* exclaimed that it "surpassed the orchestras of Pittsburgh and Cincinnati . . . [and] fairly challenges comparison with the two greatest orchestras of the country — our own and that of Boston."[15]

The New York Philharmonic was not among the orchestras mentioned partly because its first tour — New Haven, Springfield, Providence and Boston — did not take place until the season of 1909–10, the first year of its reorganization along the lines of Boston and the New York Symphony. In the years immediately preceding, it was quite overshadowed by its New York rival. In 1908–09, its last season as a cooperative society, it offered only eighteen concerts, led by Vasily Safonov, its first permanent conductor of non-Germanic background and training since 1851. The New York Symphony, in contrast, offered thirty-four concerts in New York, including a repeat of its extraordinarily successful Beethoven cycle, with the symphonies and other works played in historical order; a Tchaikovsky festival, with the American première in concert of *Eugene Onegin;* a Mendelssohn retrospective; and three concerts conducted by Mahler, who that year was at the Metropolitan. A reporter for the *Times,* in a forecast of the Symphony's season, excitedly concluded: "Here is an attempt, certainly novel, and certainly daring, to create a demand for orchestral music in New York of such an extent as it has never had before, and then supply it."[16]

Perhaps the most interesting programs to audiences in these two years were Walter's two Beethoven cycles. In the first, March and April 1908, the opening program presented Symphony No. 1, continued with some smaller Beethoven works and closed with Symphony No. 2. The sixth and final concert closed with Symphony No. 9. Finck of the *Evening Post* and the *Musical Courier,* which quoted him, reported that "a more lifeless, wooden, mechanical, inartistic performance of a great masterwork has seldom been reeled off in this city." But the *Times* was ecstatic, and the audience gave Walter an ovation.[17]

For the next year's cycle, in February and March 1909, Walter changed the programs slightly. For the final concert, on March 16, he played Symphony No. 9 twice, an idea he took from von Bülow. In addition, he varied the performance from the previous year: this time he gave the solo parts to a small chorus of three sopranos, three contraltos, four tenors and three basses. Also, within the double performance he varied: the first time, he separated the slow movement and the finale by a pause, as he once had heard Weingartner do; and the second, he proceeded without break, which emphasized the jarring opening chords of the finale. The critics on the whole were interested but not entirely convinced, and though a number of the audience left in the intermission, the majority stayed. In those days, before recordings brought orchestras into the home, most persons knew the symphonies chiefly through four- or eight-hand piano reductions, and a chance to hear all nine, with orchestra, was rare.[18]

Against the number and excitement of the New York Symphony's programs, the Philharmonic in these years showed poorly. As the reporter for the *Times* observed hopefully, "The Philharmonic Society after long years of conservatism in the old ways promises reform." For its supporters the problem was one not of staying abreast but of catching up.[19]

A guarantors' committee, led by Mrs. George Sheldon, an able executive and banker's wife, brought about the change gradually during the close of the 1908–09 season. The cooperative structure after sixty-seven years was ended and a subsidized orchestra under the committee's management substituted. Mahler was hired as conductor, the season extended from eighteen to forty-six concerts, the first tour scheduled and more than $118,000 raised to pay for the increased activity. The reorganization, however, did not go easily. Mahler was a difficult personality, and by the spring of his second season, he was dying. Mrs. Sheldon was not always diplomatic, and some critics, notably Krehbiel of the *Tribune,* who was also author of the Philharmonic's program notes, disapproved of Mahler's musicianship. At the Symphony Society, Walter, Flagler and their staff were a happier team. Nevertheless, by 1911–12, when Josef Stransky became conductor, the Philharmonic was on the road to becoming one of the country's better orchestras, more than merely a tradition or, in its cooperative structure, a curiosity.[20]

It had far to go, though, to pull up to the New York Symphony, which had played together longer under a single conductor, had more interesting programs and, in its far more extensive touring, a much larger audience. Even in Boston, citadel of perfection, it finally was acknowledged to be the equal of the best. Henry Taylor Parker of the *Boston Evening Transcript,* perhaps the city's most perceptive critic, wrote of it, following a concert on November 16, 1915:

> What Mr. Higginson with his endowed orchestra has accomplished for Boston, Mr. Flagler now bids fair to do with his for New York . . . Mr. Damrosch has now gathered and practices a notable orchestra of musicians . . . The string choir is rich, warm, precise, transparent and euphonious of tone, in persuasive balance between the darker and the brighter voices . . . The whole band plays with a largely resonant, full-bodied, warmly colored and sufficiently sensitive tone . . . It has unity and it has individuality and Mr. Damrosch can seemingly work his full will with it. As it stood yesterday, the New York Symphony Society may take its just place beside those of Boston and Chicago.[21]

At Walter's side in the development of the orchestra, helping where she could, was Margaret. Though she was always ready to make light of her effectiveness — she wrote once to a daughter, "I am altogether in that muddled state in which so much of my conduct seems to lose itself" — she was, in fact, extremely efficient and created a happy home for Walter and the children, one from which they departed each morning for work, whether school or orchestra, in good health, free of worry and eager to meet whatever the day might bring. That was part of her Blaine heritage: to go out into the world and work.[22]

She herself often served on public committees, usually those concerned with education or citizenship. But like her father, she also had an introspective streak and read a great deal, not only on current issues — she was a passionate supporter of any action for women's rights — but on general subjects. Richard Welling, a lawyer, political reformer and for thirty-five years the secretary of the Symphony Society, stated flatly that she was "the most intelligent woman in all my acquaintance." But in the musical world what most people saw was her ability as a hostess.[23]

She and Walter entertained constantly, chiefly artists, journalists and the rich who gave or might give money to the orchestra. But their guest list was always broader. "They were very social," said one frequent guest, "but not snobs. You might meet anyone at their house." The only criterion, apparently, was a willingness to speak up and be an individual.[24]

Because of the artists there was sometimes light music in the evening, but music or not, the evening usually ended with Walter at the piano and everyone singing the Damrosches' singular equivalent of *Good Night, Ladies:*

The frogs, the frogs they are a happy pair,
They do not need a comb and brush
Because they have no hair! [25]

But behind the scenes in orchestra affairs Margaret sometimes also played an executive role, though it is often hard to uncover. In the spring of 1909, Carnegie, finishing his tenure as president of the Philharmonic, was asked by one of its women's committees for help in renting Carnegie Hall for some Sunday afternoons. The next season was to be Mahler's first at the Philharmonic, and he and the women proposed to start a series of educational concerts with a popular repertory on those days.

The proposal was aimed directly at Walter and the New York Symphony, who for six years had been building their highly successful Sunday afternoon series in the hall. The weakness in Walter's position was that he did not rent the hall for every Sunday afternoon, and even on those he rented he sometimes gave the concert in the New Theatre. Evidently Carnegie directed the hall's manager for the coming season to refuse the rent for the afternoons the Symphony orchestra would play elsewhere and lease to the Philharmonic.

The issue came to a head in April, while Walter was in the South on tour, and he, who had little liking for the manager, a man named Barry, was furious at what he considered highhanded treatment. In Norfolk he drafted a letter to Carnegie that he sent first to Margaret, suggesting that she discuss it with the Flaglers before delivering it. "I think I know A.C. better than they [the Flaglers] do and that my brutal frankness will be better than any cowardly 'caving in' on my part. Any how it's the only kind of letter I can write to him . . . What's the use! The old gentleman will never be friendly again, and my letter will at least put the issue and my position squarely before him." [26]

But Margaret, who had been to see Carnegie, thought otherwise, held back the letter and evidently urged Walter to write in a different vein, which he did:

Dear Mr. Carnegie,
I return to you herewith and in accordance with your wish Barry's letter unopened. As soon as I learned that you personally wished me to give up my lease for the Carnegie Hall Sundays I knew I could do nothing else, and if I had been in New York and known how keenly you felt about it one personal interview would have been sufficient to arrange the whole matter . . .
I had no obligations or sentiment towards the management of the Hall and certainly none towards the women pushing the new Philharmonic scheme — only an immense debt of gratitude towards you who twenty years ago helped me to bear the burden of supporting my father's family and in the years after proved so true a friend in so many ways. There is

the whole situation in a nut shell, and there is my one great and sufficient reason for giving up what I consider to be my rights, although by so doing I admit an unfair competitor into a field that I have hitherto developed and occupied alone. You will readily perceive that as a business proposition the release of my Sundays to the Philharmonic is detrimental to my interests. The Sunday concert public for serious music is not yet sufficiently large to be divided among two organizations . . .

Thanks for your telegram about Margaret, she is not only wise but so good and staunch that I thank my stars every day for my good fortune. You remember our conversation when I told you that I was engaged and you were afraid and thought I should have waited.[27]

And to Margaret, from Spartanburg, South Carolina, he wrote:

Dearest, dearest darling,

I am so tired that my eyelids are drooping . . . Do you know, I don't care a hang about the Hall matter now.

Every letter I get from you makes me feel again and again that in you I have such a treasure not only of "wisdom" as the sage A.C. observes, but of love which makes all these things seem petty and unimportant . . .[28]

So she saved him from a foolish mistake, and he loved her for it.

When in 1896 some members of Walter's opera company, following a performance of his opera *The Scarlet Letter,* had presented him as a compliment with a large scarlet **A,** they may have intended a joke, but, in fact, about then Walter began what seems to have been a ten-year period of occasional adultery.

The obvious reasons seem sufficient explanation. He was away from home and wife for long periods when he was still young, charming, handsome, full of energy that normally would find some release in bed and was associating closely with others in the same condition. Throughout his life gossip would link his name with various artists, primarily Isadora Duncan and the actress Margaret Anglin. Both of these, however, entered his life after he seems to have returned to fidelity to his wife. And without further evidence it is not possible now to fix the time or women with whom he had affairs. About such matters he believed in silence, and so did Margaret.

But there is no doubt that he had *"affaires de coeur,"* as they were called in the family. He admitted them years later to his niece Marya Mannes in a confrontation over events in her life. His sister Ellie with admiration told her daughter Bess how Margaret took them: in stride, with lightness, and able to tease him to see "the funny side."[29] And there exists a letter that he wrote Margaret on April 30, 1909, from Birmingham, Alabama, where he was on tour with the New York Symphony. The Dick and Cecil he talks of are the journalist Richard Harding Davis and his wife.

> Dearest One,
>   I certainly enclosed Cecil's letter (or thought I did).
>   I want you to see her evident chagrin that Dick should prefer another and her determination not to "stand in his way." Now I suppose they have patched it up. I certainly do not want her·confidences and have not invited them. I have written her a "nice letter" which will I think prevent any further confidences on such a subject.
>   You know my views about keeping one's domestic affairs quiet and to one's self, and yet I've had the misfortune through no fault of mine to receive revelations from many of your sex on the causes of their marital unhappiness. However don't think that I mean to be flippant about it. You and I had to stumble about a bit before we understood what marriage really meant. I should like to forget it but I suppose that in remembering it, it makes my real love for you now all the greater.
>   But please be discreet and don't tell any one what you know about the Davis menage and what I have told you. Not even Cecil.
>   My tour now is fixed as follows . . .[30]

The letter suggests that some time before 1909 Walter's period of infidelity was over. Thereafter he continued to be charming, handsome, full of energy and to have almost as many opportunities for affairs as before, but he now declined them. Of course, he did not discuss the reasons, which are buried too deep in the mystery of his personality to be fully recovered, but there seems to have been more than merely the decline of the heyday in the blood.

Walter's parents had raised him by precept and example to believe that marriage could be the most profound of all human relationships. No doubt his vision of it was tinged by Teutonic idealism, particularly as expressed in Wagner's *Ring;* but that was less important than the reality of his parents' marriage, their courage together, their loyalty and their open and complete communication with each other. Walter was a man of taste; he wanted the best.

By 1907, in his letters to Margaret he seems to be reaching for a deeper relationship with her, and gradually between them there seems to develop a very strong sense of loyalty and mutual respect, born of their life together. To no one else could either talk so freely, so fully, with so many connotations shared, and with such enjoyment, so for him affairs may have ceased to have much appeal. Yet he wrote, "You and I had to stumble about . . ." Did Margaret, too, have affairs?

There is an earlier letter to her from Walter unlike any other that has survived. Again he was on tour, at Altoona, Pennsylvania, and at the time of writing the last of their four children, all girls, had been born.

Dec. 20/1907
10 A.M.

Dearest One!

The orchestra departed on an early train but I've allowed myself the luxury of a later breakfast and a later train as it is only an hour to Johnstown. I am thinking of you a lot and with much love mixed up with my thoughts.

Tonight you will go to the theatre with a young man, then to a supper and then — you will take him home with you!

Horrible thought but I am noble and magnanimous!

I shall sit at the Crystal Hotel in Johnstown Pa. alone and solitary and shall solemnly empty a pint of champagne to "you and the children." I have an idea that you and I have weathered our last storms, financial and otherwise and that we are sailing into the fair harbor of middle age and gradually — along a gentle river of many turnings — into the last harbor of all.

Always Yours with love
Walter[31]

Was it a joke and the young man merely a nephew? It seems unlikely. The letter is somber; does not name the person he talks of, though Walter loved names; and does not soar, in his usual style, from the serious into the witty. And in his other letters of this time, he repeatedly assures her that they are, indeed, reaching a deeper relationship. For example, with his emphases: "We are so complete in each other if we only realize it and remember it *always* and for *all time*."[32] Or, "I have my piano, stationery, etc, and all I need is you to quarrel with for you *have* become a perpetual need."[33] Or, in the midst of a hastily scratched note about train schedules, "Please come to Philadelphia, go to the Bellevue-Stratford and get a nice room for us; then await the coming of your lord, master, lover and slave — all in one. We go to Atlantic City next morning at 9:40. I shall be oh so happy to kiss your hands again and to rest my weary head on your sweet breast."[34]

Years later their niece Marya would say what many believed: that the sexual attraction between Walter and Margaret must have ended early, because she was so homely. But perhaps not. In any event, their daughter Gretchen saw more deeply into the relationship.

It has been said that in happy marriages husbands and wives often grow to look like each other and eventually evolve a common character. This has not been the case with my father and mother. Over the years their personalities have met, head on, and I have never seen that either one made the slightest dent on the other's character. But what surprised their daughters was that the differences which we recognized in them . . . always astonished my mother and father.

As children we knew that my mother hated surprises and that my father liked them; that my mother loved picnics and being lost in the woods in the rain and that such things disturbed my father; that he liked certain kinds of European food which my mother would not touch. And yet year after year my father hopefully surprised my mother, my mother tramped my father over mountains with only a sandwich and no path map, and he continued to urge on her food that she would not eat.

Neither ever gave up in trying to change the other and they were continuously thunderstruck at their differences. But perhaps the deeper truth, which we were too young to understand, lay in the fact that neither one enjoyed anything very much unless the other shared it; and if my father wanted to read something aloud, and in the middle of it my mother decided to mow the lawn, my father still found her his best and favorite audience.[35]

In later years they became known as an exceptional couple. But if they succeeded in marriage after stumbling about a bit, it was because they worked at it. He wrote the letters. She replied and sometimes, at least, went to Philadelphia.

CHAPTER 18

The Clara and David Mannes duo. His work at the Music School Settlement. Tante's decision. Young Leopold at the Seymours'. David and the Music School Settlement for Colored People. Its failure. His depression.

WHEN CLARA AND DAVID MANNES returned from their six months of study abroad with Ysaÿe, they were ready to present themselves to the public as a piano-violin duo, but uncertain where to start. Their opportunity came through the Music School Settlement, where David steadily was increasing his volunteer work, teaching violin and directing the students' orchestra. The school needed to raise money, and its president, Mrs. Howard Mansfield, suggested a recital by David and Clara. This became a series of six programs during the winter 1903–04, played in the large music room of a private house on Park Avenue. The programs were arranged chronologically from the early Italians down through Brahms and César Franck, and they not only raised money for the school and created an interest in the music, which was little known, but won for David and Clara a professional agent, who began to schedule recitals for them. By the fall of 1904 the Mannes duo was in business.[1]

Apparently, it was the first such duo in the country's history to have a continuous life; it existed from 1904 through 1917. In years past, of course, violin and piano players occasionally had performed together, usually Beethoven's *Kreutzer Sonata* or Tartini's *Devil's Trill,* but these were mostly one-time or one-tour affairs, without much impact on the country's musical taste or knowledge. David and Clara, however, soon had increased their recitals to forty or fifty a year, and besides performing in the big cities, they played frequently in schools, colleges and universities, to which they were apt to be invited back to give two or three recitals in place of one, often in programs historically ordered. With justice they considered themselves pioneers in revealing to the country the violin-piano repertory. They were the first, it seems, to give an entire program to Beethoven or Brahms, or to play the sonatas of Enesco, Lekeu and Carpenter. And the Franck sonata, now so common, which Franck had written for Ysaÿe, became almost their signature piece. By 1917, when they stopped touring, they had played in England, Canada and some thirty of the forty-eight states.

Their playing together was not without tension, a sign of which was Clara's asthma, always worse on tour. Neither of them was, as Clara put it, "a respectful, modest follower. We each had our own definite ideas about tempi, phrasing and sound adjustments," and sometimes the taxi ride to the recital hall was a trip of utter misery, with both silent, angry and worried. "Especially maddening would it be when in public performance I would expect David to take the tempo he had insisted on, and then he turned to mine, and a quick readjustment had to be made." But such difficulties may have been the spice that precluded blandness. In the audiences, apparently, no one sensed the conflicts, and reviewers, like one in *Musical America,* often remarked on the "rare artistic sympathy between them that gives their playing an exceptional degree of smoothness, balance and finish."[2]

Many of the nonmusical aspects of the recitals pleased Clara. She delighted in projecting the image, with David, of the remarkably talented, handsome couple. For performances she favored a Fortuny dress that hung freely from the shoulders in graceful folds, with a large pattern and loose sleeves stopping at the elbows. The style suited her. Somewhat short and inclined to plumpness, she was never beautiful, but she had a finely modeled face, brilliant blue-green eyes and a radiant smile, and onstage she moved and sat with an attractive dignity. David, for recitals, generally wore a stiff collar, ascot tie, cutaway coat and impeccably pressed striped trousers. Tall, thin, with intense burning eyes and his remarkable profile thrown into relief by the violin, he was a ravishing figure, and sometimes after a performance he would receive mash notes from women. Indeed, after several years of playing at Westover, a school for girls, they had to stop because the girls' letters to David became too personal.[3]

For Clara this sexual excitement apparently was subsumed in their marriage. She was very conscious that she and David, who played her father's Maggini violin, were repeating the example of love, marriage and music set for her by her parents, and the even more famous example set by Robert and Clara Schumann. Though she never mentioned a word of sexual matters to her children, and even on a beach was extremely modest about displaying any part of her person, she was quite aware of the force of sexual attraction even in such supposedly dry-as-dust pursuits as chamber music. And she always noticed what a man wore.

In March 1904 she played Beethoven's *Sonata in A Major* with Pablo Casals, and he forgot his formal coat and had to go onstage in a short brown velvet smoking jacket, "which, to tell the truth, made a lovely color combination with his 'cello!" Onstage and off she had excellent taste in clothes, and she enjoyed grooming her good-looking husband to cut a swath among women.[4]

Occasionally, however, incidents and persons in his background still took her by surprise. They had agreed, because it was the sort of idea that always appealed to David, to play for the men at Sing Sing prison, in Ossining, on the Hudson. As they walked down an aisle of the auditorium to mount the stage, a voice called loudly, "Hey, Dave!"

They stopped, and David located a man waving. "Well, hello, Leonard," he replied. "How are you?"

"Just fine, Dave. Just fine."

They went on, with Clara clutching her husband's sleeve. "I didn't know your brother was still here."

"Evidently," David replied.

They played their Bach and Brahms to applause extravagantly led by a certain part of the auditorium, and afterward had a visit with Leonard. David returned to see him several times.

Later he used to tell the story with amused delight, and Clara would say with a sigh, "Must you tell that every time we go out?"[5]

But this loyalty to his origins, not so much to a particular brother with whom he had never had much in common as to the immigrants and their children on the lower East Side, was part of what many found attractive in David. In these same years when he was having such a personal success he expanded his work at the Music School Settlement, taking on in addition to his volunteer work the paid post of instructor to student teachers one afternoon a week, and then, in October 1910, he accepted the school's top position, musical director.

His goal for the school, which he expressed in various ways, was to assist others to find in music some of the values he felt it had given to him. Chief among these he might have listed gentleness, respect for others, self-respect and a sense of the beautiful. Once, after he had attempted to articulate his ideas to a meeting of parents, he led the student orchestra in several numbers to allow the music to speak for itself. Evidently it was eloquent, for an old Jewish woman rose. "I know what Mr. Mannes wants," she cried. "He wants this to be a temple — a place of worship."[6]

Some time later, still struggling to find the precise words, he restated his idea: "I have realized for a long time that, especially for the Jews in this neighborhood, something had to be substituted for religion. Saturday is no longer the Sabbath to many of them; it is a business day like any other. And I dreamed that if I could put music into their souls, they would have an ideal." He was the artistic counterpart of Morris Hillquit and Eugene Debs, who in these same years offered to the more politically minded of the neighborhood, as a kind of secularized Judaism, Socialism and the Socialist party.[7]

Like Frank Damrosch, David Mannes believed that music could be a civilizing force, leading people, through the practice of cooperation and self-discipline, to become better citizens. He also thought of it as a liberating force: "The right teaching is to help the child to find and to express his own ideals."[8] Music might not be the way for everyone; it had not served his brothers. And individuals, of course, would travel different distances along the way. Coming on an older woman one day, a woman without talent who was struggling at the piano to master a five-finger exercise, he asked her what she wanted of music. "To play *Nearer My God to Thee.*" He put the exercise aside and taught her to play the tune first with one finger, then with the right hand and lastly with a few, simple chords. It was all she ever learned of music, but she went away ecstatic, with a prized possession. His ideal was not to create mediocre or even good professionals, but to enrich lives.[9]

Under the pressure of his work at the school, the recitals with Clara and the concerts with the New York Symphony, his health began to fail, and in the spring of 1912 he told Walter that he would resign his position as concertmaster of the orchestra. Probably the decision was a step backward financially, but he wanted more time for the school. By the end of 1911, at the close of his first full year as director with Mrs. Mansfield as president, the school occupied three buildings, debt free, on East Third Street (today it is called the Third Street Music School Settlement), had a hundred teachers and social workers, and a thousand music students, with a waiting list. Forty thousand lessons were given during the year; there were four student orchestras, several sight-singing classes, a chorus of eighty and uncounted numbers of lectures and recitals.

Toward the cost the children paid small fees: the largest, twenty-five cents for an individual half-hour lesson; the smallest, five cents for a group sight-singing class. Though there were scholarships for those who could pay nothing at all, the school, and David, believed that if the children paid something toward the cost, they would appreciate the music more. And in 1911 the children, from their jobs or as gifts from their impecunious parents, paid fees totaling $10,000.[10]

The school's program, which also called for social workers to visit the sick at home, arrange country holidays for the children and help to organize the huge street concerts, had a strong impact on its neighborhood, and beginning about 1910 requests for information on the various programs began to flow in from settlement houses in other cities. At David's suggestion representatives of eleven of these, most of them in part modeled on the Third Street School, met there on May 21, 1911, to found the National Association of Music School Societies, with the aim of promoting and standardizing their work. For this purpose David was a good spokesman, though he did not enjoy public speaking. But he was by far the best-known professional musician connected with the music school movement, and wherever he went on his tours, with either the New York Symphony or Clara, he almost invariably was invited by some group to speak. And after years of listening from the orchestra pit to professional actors, he spoke well. By May 1915 there were scattered about the country some thirty or forty music school settlements imitating the structure and programs of the Third Street Music School.

Of all the family the one most shaken by Helene's death was Tante. From her sixteenth year, in 1864, she had made her life with Leopold and Helene, and of their children only Frank could remember a time when she had not been with them. But at fifty-six, with all the children married and with families of their own, she began to think she should return to Germany to rejoin those who were left of her brothers and sisters. In her grief and uncertainty she became ill herself and was told by her doctor to give up her teaching, the German classes at the Spence School and her own singing classes. But then what would she do?

It happened that Hetty's only sister, Therese, had died a few months before Helene, and as she had been unmarried and lived at home, her death had upset the Mosenthals deeply. Among Hetty, Frank and the other Damrosch children a plan evolved: Tante should accompany the Mosenthals on a trip to California; and to make it possible the nieces and nephews would pay her expenses. Then, after a change of scene and a new experience, she could decide about Germany and the future.

For Tante, California, with its soft air, flowering shrubs and orange groves, was a sanitarium "for my shattered nerves."

> From day to day the old strength returned, but the real peace came over me when we had reached the climax of our trip, the Grand Canyon of Arizona, the greatest of all wonders, overwhelming and yet so quieting at the same time. Gazing at these gigantic temples and fortresses carved in stone by nature through thousands and thousands of years, I felt small enough to think back upon the interesting geography lessons in the little school in Jever, where dreams of travel filled the whole heart of a certain girl who never dared hope that any of her wild dreams ever could come true.[11]

Though she returned to New York still talking of "my beloved Germany," she was not yet ready to end her life's adventure in the United States.

She lived most of the time with David and Clara, finding in their frequent absences opportunity once again to be "the summer mother." But she herself often was away. She took up Helene's pattern of visiting Ellie and the others, each in turn, darning and sewing, and sometimes preparing German cookies and marmalades so that they would not forget. She called regularly on her namesake, Marie Wiechmann, refusing to isolate this one family member, as the others seemed inclined to do, and in her journeys from niece to nephew she became the vine through which the various branches of the family communicated their news: schools, sickness, plans for summer. But she did it quite in her own fashion.

Helene in her last decade, as O'mama, had been the family's Great Matriarch, quiet, calm, fair, always in black and a bit austere. Tante to everyone, in all generations, was a gay, chattering companion, a passionate partisan. Though she mourned Helene, she did not wear black for long, and she began soon to do things she had never done before. She allowed a former student to carry her off to Italy for three months; she went frequently to Germany and brought back news of the nieces and nephews over there; and when cigarettes became popular, she smoked: Puff! Puff! Everyone laughed, including herself. Though she never had much money and relied more and more on the generosity of Walter and perhaps of Frank and of Clara, she could repay all debts in her own, special coin. In every family group, she was wanted.

With each visit to Jever and Oldenburg, however, she had to rethink her role in life, weighing Germany against the United States. Finally she put her decision in writing:

> With three generations to love . . . I could never consent to end the rest of my life in Germany as my brothers over there suggested . . . They don't understand how the strong arms of the first generation, the loving sympathetic ties of the second and the darling little baby hands of the third generation hold me here tight and that I would fade away for homesickness if I left them for good, for I hope to see all my lovely nieces and grand-nieces happily married and the young striving geniuses famous —
> So hier bleibe ich; ich kann nicht anders. Gott helfe Euch!!*
> Amen[12]

For the winter of 1909–10 the ten-year-old "reincarnation of Mozart," Leopold Damrosch Mannes, was sent to live with his Tante Ellie in South Orange. In the past year he suddenly had begun to grow, and a doctor, finding him wan, had suggested a winter in South Orange with the Seymours to toughen him. Since he was ahead in school, he could take a year off, do some tutoring in languages and drill once a week with the

* So here I stand; I cannot do other. God help me!! Amen. (Martin Luther, Speech at the Diet of Worms)

Essex County Cadet Corps. Meanwhile his weight could catch up with his height.[13]

Clara, a careful mother, taking her six-year-old daughter, Marya, with her, went out for a day in late September to look the house over and concluded that the large attic room that Ellie offered would be satisfactory, provided that a knotted rope, in case of fire, was bolted to the floor near the window. The weather that day was cool but not cold, and the three Seymour girls, Clair, Bess and Ruth, barelegged and barearmed, gazed with pity and astonishment at Marya, encased in leggings and mittens.

Finally Leopold came, with his own suitcase — much admired — and a large ball of twine. Though the doctor may have thought him anemic, he was not without energy. "I will teach you all the Morse code," he said, and within a day had connected all the bedrooms by string and was instructing the girls how to send SOS signals to the attic. "Just don't trip the cook," warned Tante Ellie, "and dinner is ready."

The differences in mode of living among the various branches of the family were real, and the children were aware of them. Frank and Hetty's household, whether in New York or their large cottage in Seal Harbor, Maine, called nostalgically Die Heimburg, was the most Germanic in its paternalism. At table Frank would carve, and no one would begin until all were served and he had said, "One, two, three, EAT!" Though the manner was kindly, and the command a game, the sense of order behind it was firm. Conversation at meals was light and pleasant, usually about the family's activities, but no child ever challenged one of Frank's opinions. Similarly, out of doors, in Maine, sailing in the harbor they observed the boundaries he had set, for they knew that from the porch his eye was on them. When he was absent, Hetty exercised his power but always in a way to make his presence felt. The regime was strict, but Hetty had the ability to make anyone, child or adult, feel welcome. In New York when she began to be "at home" once a month on a Friday afternoon, people came, because they liked her. On such occasions, to occupy the little children she kept a covey of mechanical birds that could be wound to skitter about the floor. Children felt secure with Uncle Frank and Tante Hetty: the rules were clear, little more than observance of them was demanded and the adults' love for each other was very plain. Even children noticed.[14]

At Uncle Walter's and Aunt Margaret's house the mode was more complicated and at times alarming. At table they frequently disagreed. In the realm of music, of course, he was never contradicted, nor she, as the daughter of James G. Blaine, in politics; but in all else — religion, food, education, relatives — the opinion of either was open to dispute, and participation in the general conversation was encouraged.

If Margaret saw a child sitting silent, she might stop the others to ask the inarticulate family member or guest, "Now what do *you* think?" Or if conversation lagged, she might go round the table asking the names of the cabinet officers: treasury? agriculture? state? She had a good mind, well stocked, and children could learn from her, but for the shy child or stranger it could be unnerving. "Start a topic," Aunt Margaret might say, and all eyes would turn to the victim. Certain subjects were forbidden: crime, and the physical or spiritual defects of anyone at the table. But almost anything else would do.

One time her youngest daughter, Anita, trapped her. The conversation had shifted to certain unattractive qualities of a Dr. Colton, and Margaret ordered, "Everyone around the table must say something nice about Dr. Colton."

There was a pause, and then Anita said, "Dr. Colton had a bath last Tuesday."

"I forbid you to say that," cried Margaret.

"Dr. Colton did not have a bath last Tuesday," said Anita — and her father laughed.[15] The remarks, the laughter and the kind of relationships they implied could not have occurred at Uncle Frank's table.

But Margaret's efforts, which owed much to her political background, proved successful. Her four girls grew up to be articulate, amusing and able to talk with almost anyone on any subject. The methods, however, often scared nieces and nephews unused to them, and little Marya, for one, always responded by pursing her lips and saying nothing, no matter how prodded.

The Mannes household, even with Tante present, was more Bohemian than the others, though entirely within a family setting. Mealtime was more apt to vary, and the conversation to be more clamorous and imprecise. David at his end of the table usually sat with his legs to one side or, as Clara said, "on the bias," and he frequently lapsed into daydreams, during which he often transferred from the serving dish to his own plate all the food. Recalled to the conversation, he would re-enter it by remarking wistfully, "I never get a chance to say a word in this family."[16]

Naturally, with two musicians at the head of the family, the conversation turned chiefly to music, though with many detours into theater, travel and literature. But of politics, business or religion there was none. Whereas Walter and Margaret entertained all kinds of people, partly out of liking and partly out of the need to find backers for the New York Symphony, David and Clara entertained almost only musicians. Pablo Casals, Artur Schnabel and others would come of an evening, and there would be chamber music in the home. But Carnegie, Flagler or anyone merely social seldom was included. Clara was proud of the concentration on music, and it may have been good for her musical son, but in the end it cut her off from anyone nonmusical — friends, nieces and nephews and even her daughter, who rebelled against it.

At the Seymours', among whom little Leopold was to live for the winter, life was very different, because Uncle Harry was a businessman and commuter. He would eat breakfast with his gold watch on the table beside him and the morning paper propped before him. Tante Ellie might talk to the children or tell of her dreams, but no one disturbed Papa. When he had finished his coffee and eggs, he lit his cigar and decided whether to hurry for the 8:01 or take the 8:18. Then, putting his watch in his pocket, he would hand the paper to his wife and go.

In the winter, at the end of the day, the children waited to hear his step on the verandah. "He had a very clear footfall," Ruth remembered, "as if he put his shoe exactly where he meant to put it — always black shoes with rounded toe, dark trousers, a heavy black coat with velvet collar, pink cheeks and blue eyes twinkling. Once you saw his eyes you didn't look anywhere else. Sometimes he took off his derby and put it on a child's head. On kissing, his face was cold and prickly."

The family's life in South Orange was somewhat isolated, particularly for the girls and mostly because Ellie refused to take any interest in her neighbors: "They simply play bridge and gossip." She did not play bridge, nor did she gossip, but she listened to her hairdresser, thin, angular, energetic Annie Walstead, who came every third week to give a shampoo and marcel wave. Annie would whisk the curling irons in and out of the gas flame, testing them near her cheek and, if too hot, spinning them round in the air to cool. And all the time her tongue never stopped about the neighbors.

The kind of social sense that came to Hetty naturally, and that Margaret tried to instill in her girls, Ellie lacked. She told her daughter Clair one day not to play with the neighboring Stevenson children, because "they talk through their noses." As a result of her expressing such feelings, perhaps too freely, her daughters sometimes were omitted from the local parties. She could be similarly ungracious to Harry's business partners and clients. She thought them boring, and was civil, just. He was proud of her musical background, but she never would play the piano for his guests, and her rejection of requests was often abrupt. To many she must have seemed a snob.

Yet wherever she went, she always drew, like a magnet, individuals who enjoyed her music, courage and style. In South Orange and the neighboring communities there were many who admired her. After the birth of her last child, in March 1900, her interest in art had dwindled, and she turned more to music. For pay, she created and conducted a women's chorus, lectured to women's clubs on Wagner's operas and gave individual piano and singing lessons. She gave free singing lessons at a settlement house in Orange, and one Christmas trained the children to go through the streets singing carols, as she had seen children do in Munich. She enjoyed the work, and one day over the clothesline to her daughter Ruth she remarked angrily, "Men are lucky. They get out into the world. We women get an overdose of domesticity." But the women who came to the house to sing or play were not interested in the children, and the typical mothers of the town looked with suspicion on a household whose wife and mother was "different."

For the girls the slight isolation in the community, which affected their brother hardly at all, was repeated to some degree in the family's habits. Ellie did not like to be interrupted when practicing the piano, and the girls could either stay in their bedrooms or get out of the house. Their father's interests were painting and reading, both silent occupations, and on a weekend he might disappear outside to sketch or settle into his Morris chair to read. On the table by his chair there was always the *National Geographic* and a biography borrowed from the Mercantile Library.

Into this busy but quiet family, somewhat solitary and introspective, there entered a potential extrovert, Leopold, five years younger than Larry and the same age as Ruth. At first he was very timid, needing reassurance from Tante Ellie about the attic, the darkness, the possibility of fire and the Essex County Cadet Corps. He disliked the idea of soldiering but was enticed into it by the thought of traveling alone to and from the weekly drill on a train. Larry, disapproving of his cousin's limp wrist, called him "Lilypad" and tried to teach him the manly art of self-defense. Leopold learned nothing except how to stop a bloody nose. But he seemed not to mind, nor to care that he was no good at games of catch. Gradually, as he gained confidence, he began to show what he could do. He could sing and play all their favorites from the *St. Nicholas Songs;* he could play the piano without looking, even with his back toward it; he could make a slot machine, which to everyone's amazement, worked; and to get coins for it he organized a shoe-shine business, with his Uncle Harry as best client. To avoid carrying a rifle at the County Cadets, he joined its band and soon became its solo bugler, and for Clair's birthday he composed a long and splendid funeral march.

Best of all were the nights that he and Larry played the piano together. Larry recently had decided against Chopin as "sissy" and substituted Irving Berlin, especially *Alexander's Ragtime Band.* He could play it well, but Leopold at the top! Such wild fantasies! Thrilling variations! Tremendous crescendos! Beyond anyone's imagination.

As the boys went over and over it — youth loves repetition — Ruth couldn't sit still. She went hopping and skipping about the room until her mother, hurrying in from the kitchen, shrieked, "The lamp!"

Turning to the piano players, Ellie said, "Leopold, your mother would be horrified if she could hear you now."

"But Tante Ellie," said Leopold with a twinkle, "she isn't here."

The Seymours never forgot that winter. Leopold stirred them all up.

★

Of all the music school settlements imitating the Third Street School, the one most interesting to David Mannes was one he himself started in Harlem, the Music School Settlement for Colored People. He always had longed to honor the Negro violinist John Douglas, who "helped to shape my life,"[17] and in the spring of 1911 he found his chance. A group of dedicated and competent philanthropists, including Dr. Felix Adler and George Foster Peabody, wanted to found a settlement house in Harlem to aid the Negroes who for the past decade had moved into the neighborhood by the thousands. At a meeting of the group David urged its members to make the settlement a music school. "Music," he said, "is the racial talent of the Negro, and through music which is a universal language, the Negro and the white man can be brought to have a mutual understanding."[18]

He was persuasive. A board of trustees was chosen to which an equal number of prominent Negroes soon were added, and he was given the job of engaging a Negro director and faculty, not an easy job, as few Negroes then were trained to teach violin, voice or piano, or had the time and money to work for little or nothing. But soon a house in Harlem was leased, pianos were installed and the school was open for business, on the lines of the Third Street School: small fees, a few scholarships, a few paid and many volunteer positions and a board active in raising money to cover the deficit.

Month by month the school prospered and expanded, and in the spring of 1912 a Negro bandleader, James Reese Europe, suggested to David that he and his 125-man band, the Clef Club, give a benefit for the school. The idea appealed to David and his board of trustees. The school's students as yet were too inexperienced to give any kind of public performance, but Europe's band or orchestra — for besides brass, drums, guitars, bandolas, pianos and saxophones, it included flutes, violins, cellos, basses and even an oboe — was the outstanding Negro orchestra in the country, and Europe was a successful composer of popular songs. Further, aside from any money the concert might raise, it would advance the school's aims by presenting for the first time in prestigious Carnegie Hall Negro musicians in a concert of serious music. The date was set for May 2, 1912.

The first problem to be faced was that Europe wanted fourteen upright pianos onstage, but on the school's board was Elbridge L. Adams, an official of the American Piano Company, and he guaranteed to produce them. Next, Europe needed the hall reserved for several all-day rehearsals, because, as he explained, until the night of the performance the players never would be all together; holding other jobs, they could rehearse only in their free hours. During the day they would drop in and out, and he would coach them individually and in groups. David had moments when he feared the result would be chaos, but watching Europe work, he was impressed by him as a conductor and impresario. Europe could make happen what he said would happen.

Lastly there was the sale of tickets. The school's benefit committee worked hard and managed to sell about a third of the house, but on the morning of May 1 nearly two thousand seats remained unsold. That afternoon the *New York Evening Journal* published an editorial, in large type, double-columned and conspicuously placed, in which it stated:

> Mr. David Mannes and others interested in music . . . have organized a concert, exclusively of negro music, to be given at Carnegie Hall tomorrow night at 8:15 . . .
>
> Of all the races in this country, the negro alone has developed an actual school of American music. All that we have except negro melody, is imitation.
>
> The negroes have given us the only music of our own that is American — national, original and real.
>
> And this concert which is organized for tomorrow night at Carnegie Hall will be from beginning to end a concert of negro music by negro musicians.
>
> Seats for the concert range in price from fifty cents to one dollar and a half — boxes at higher prices — and may be bought now at the box office . . . The proceeds will be devoted to the Music School Settlement for Colored People . . .
>
> There are in New York more than 90,000 colored men and women. Very little is done for them, and very little for their children.
>
> In all directions they are denied, repressed and kept back.
>
> Everyone should gladly help them to find expression for their great musical talent, and to find happiness in that expression.
>
> The men and women acting as directors of the Music School Settlement for Colored People are earnest and capable . . . The *Evening Journal* hopes that many of its readers will attend the concert, enjoy it, and perhaps find prejudice based on ignorance give place to sympathy and good will . . .
>
> Those who cannot attend the concert, but would contribute to the support of the Music School Settlement for Colored People, may send contributions to . . .[19]

Just who was responsible for the editorial is not known, but it reads very much like the kind of statement the school's board constantly published about its aims. In any event it seems to have proved crucial, for by late afternoon a run began on the box office and by the next evening every ticket was sold, with many persons turned away. To an integrated audience, Europe and the school presented a concert that included orchestral numbers, plantation songs and an aria from Saint-Saëns's *Samson and Delilah*. The opera aria generally was felt to be beyond the singer, but the plantation songs, in arrangements by Will Marion Cook, a Negro composer who had studied under Joachim, were much admired, and the evening's high point was Europe's own *Clef Club March,* in which, for the final chorus, he brought in the fourteen jazz pianists and a hundred other instrumentalists, all going full-out.[20]

"The receipts of this concert," Mannes noted soberly, "netted close to five thousand dollars, a great help to the school." Then he added what was equally or more important. "Besides which, a wedge in opening the public halls and theatres to colored performers had been made."[21]

The high point for David and Clara in their piano and violin work came in June and July 1913, when they went to London to present a series of three afternoon recitals, each a week apart. Though 1913 is well within the twentieth century, they made the short tour in what today would seem the manner of another millennium.

They arrived early and stayed, in all, seven weeks. After settling Tante, a nurse and the two children in a hotel in Seaford, on the Channel, they went up to London, where they had rented the studio of May Mukle, possibly the first virtuoso woman cellist. They were taken at once into the heart of the city's musical circles. They were invited by Paul Draper to impromptu musicales, where they heard Arthur Rubinstein and Casals play, and Edward Elgar gave a soirée in their honor at which they played the Franck sonata. And eventually came the day of the first recital.

Their agent had booked them into Bechstein (now Wigmore) Hall, built and operated by the Bechstein piano company and designed for chamber music. (It had a capacity of 550.) Clara was to use a Bechstein grand. Though she had rehearsed on it and been pleased with it, she discovered on the afternoon of the recital that a large sign reading BECH-STEIN had been fastened to the side facing the audience. Backed by David, she refused to play on the piano. The hall's staff, Bechstein employees, seemed unable to imagine any solution to the problem, so "we finally found a sort of scarf and draped it over the sign." Then they tried to make beautiful music.

Evidently they succeeded, for the reviews were good. At the first recital the hall was half-empty, which was expected; at the last, almost sold out, which was not. For the next year their agent began to plan a tour of England and the Continent. But the threat of war prevented it, and by 1919, when they could have picked up their start of an international career, their interests had shifted.[22]

In April 1915 David resigned as director at the Third Street School. He had been thinking of doing so for more than a year. Mrs. Howard Mansfield, with whom he had built up the school, two years earlier had moved from president to chairman of the board, a less active post, and Mrs.

Frank Rowell now was president. Under the latter's leadership David privately felt that progress had "finally come to a halt, and where progress was impossible it seemed immoral for me to stay."[23]

Though he never publicly discussed his reasons for resigning, it seems likely that he was distressed by the school's turn to programs that were more social than musical. The conflict was in the name, Music School Settlement, and it was the same conflict that Frank had faced in starting the People's Singing Classes and that always arises when an art is used for social purposes: Will artistic standards or social purposes prevail? For Frank, the issue had arisen at the start of a project of which he was founder and director; for David, after fifteen years in a project that, ultimately, others controlled. To reporters, of course, he said nothing against the school's new leadership and stressed that he wanted to give more time to the Music Settlement School for Colored People. In fact, there he was being pushed out.

From the first, apparently, James Europe, for whom David developed a great admiration, had warned him that to foster the pride of the Negro people it was absolutely necessary that Negroes assume control of the school as quickly as possible. The question was: How soon was financially feasible? Europe, who ran several bands and an employment agency for Negro musicians, had a business experience and skill very rare at the time among Negroes. He understood the problems of raising money to sustain a school; most other Negro musicians did not.[24]

There was also an artistic problem that plagued the school and that was reflected in its annual benefit concerts and in the reviews of them. Should the school teach its Negro pupils only Negro music, serious or jazz, or concentrate on the classical tradition of Haydn through Brahms? On this point David had no doubt. His Negro teacher, John Douglas, had been a master of classical music; Negroes, aside from plantation songs, spirituals or "blues," should sing Brahms and Schumann.

But at the third Carnegie Hall concert, on March 11, 1914, at which David spoke for the school, he plainly was not in full control of the program. In the opinion of *Musical America,* the concert, "though more creditable than the two previous, fell short once more of the serious purpose to which these talents might be directed." It praised the Negro baritone Henry T. Burleigh for his arrangements and singing of Negro spirituals but scolded him for adding a popular song, *Why Adam Sinned.* It also reprimanded the school's director, J. Rosamond Johnson, a man with a sound classical training, for singing his Broadway song, *Under the Bamboo Tree,* and recommended that the orchestra, led again by Europe, "give its attention during the coming year to a movement or two of a Haydn Symphony."[25]

By the fourth concert, on April 12, 1915, in which for the first time

David seems to have had no part, Johnson had resolved the artistic question by deciding to present only Negro music — the single exception was Foster's *My Old Kentucky Home* — but only music classically oriented. The concert was notable for providing the first appearance in New York of Roland Hayes, the Negro tenor who went on to have an international career in lieder as well as spirituals. And the improvement in the orchestra, according to *Musical America,* showed clearly Johnson's "earnest intent, hard work and real interest in music."[26]

By then, however, David and the white members of the school's board of trustees all had been ousted, and the school was in financial trouble. Six months later it closed.

The chief reason, apparently, was the war, which greatly diminished contributions to the school. Another, perhaps, was the school's lack of a wide base among Negroes, most of whom were more interested in blues and jazz than in classical music. Unfortunately, too, the wise and experienced Europe was continually away, touring with the dancers Irene and Vernon Castle and helping to start throughout the country a craze for the fox trot and a new kind of social dancing. And there are hints that the ousting of the white philanthropists was done hastily and arrogantly. David in his brief account is unusually tight-lipped, and says only, "Our school came into life at least twenty years too soon." Undoubtedly its failure was the greatest disappointment of his life.

In the summer of 1915, while the Mannes family was in a rented cottage at Chatham, on Cape Cod, David suffered the worst of his occasional depressions. These had grown steadily more severe as he progressed in his career, and no doctor seemed able to help him, except one who simply by talking sometimes could stir a response. Mannes' daughter, Marya, thought the attacks were "the result of overpowering modesty," caused perhaps by the enormous distance he had traveled from poor beginnings to an extremely rich cultural life as violinist, conductor, founder of a music school and friend to some of the world's greatest musicians. He was always aware that he was only a good, not a great violinist, and fearful that in some way his late start and intermittent training would undermine his work. Yet with the single exception of this experience in the summer of 1915, the depressions could be contained, and if they were the price of his sensitivity, then with his love for music he paid it gladly.[27]

There is no evidence to tie the Chatham depression to any particular cause, but its timing suggests that the major reason may have been the closing of the Negro school, with which he was so emotionally involved. Less important but contributing, perhaps, was a sense of loss in leaving the Third Street School. Also, the horrors of the war were mounting steadily.

David's depressions, in which he would conceive of himself an utter failure and sit or lie inert, not responding to any stimulus, typically lasted no more than two days or, at most, three. And often he could be hastened out of them by Marya's doing some silly dances or Leopold's making musical jokes at the piano. Sometimes Clara could rouse him by insisting that he meet an obligation. But this time, according to Marya, every effort failed, and by the fifth or sixth day they all, including Clara, were frightened.

Clara insisted at first that the family's regime should continue and the children go out and play with friends. But the children soon discovered the play had no fun. Their father's condition drew them home. So, in order to keep some structure and anticipation to the day, Clara began to read Dickens' novels aloud to them, in David's presence.

A week passed. Ten days. A fortnight. Clara, having finished several of the shorter novels, started on *Little Dorrit,* the account of a girl, born in debtors' prison, whose small stature is compensated for by the greatness of her heart. Clara was a good reader but was always moved to tears by any sentimental scene, and her easy weeping was a family joke. Now, as David entered a fourth week of depression and as the sentimental scenes of *Little Dorrit* came in ever-greater frequency, Clara, no doubt herself near breaking, began to snivel continually.

Finally, in the midst of the death scene, David spoke. "Oh, do stop crying."

"I'm not crying."

"Yes" — sigh — "you are."

Thereafter whenever he suffered a depression, the family feared a repetition of Chatham. But none occurred, and as he grew older, even the shorter depressions became less frequent.[28]

CHAPTER 19

Clair Seymour, Walter and Isadora Duncan. Frank founds the Institute of Musical Art. Frank Jr. elopes. Frank's work with the Musical Art Society.

IN THE WINTER OF 1905–06 Ellie took the four Seymour children to Munich for eight months. Harry at the time was in Asia for his export-import company, trying to sell, among other products, Ford cars, and Ellie proposed meanwhile to give the children an experience of living in Germany such as Helene had arranged for her and Clara. Ellie liked to repeat patterns of living, but in this case the differences were greater than she may have estimated, and also she was not as efficient as her mother. The family arrived in Munich to discover that the pension had no rooms for them.

Actually, the chief reason for the trip was that Ellie wanted to study singing, and the children were to fit in where they could. But where Clara and Ellie had been older, specialized students meeting with tutors, the three elder Seymour children, eleven, ten and eight, entered large classes, where, ignored for the most part by the teachers and students, they were lonely; six-year-old Ruth, in the confusion, never reached school at all. In the spring, the eldest, Larry, caught a cold that turned into pneumonia, and the better to nurse him Ellie moved the family to Switzerland, where there was a Fräulein who had lived with the family in South Orange. Before then, however, Ellie had taken her eldest daughter, Clair, to a theater to see Isadora Duncan in a recital that included children dancing. That afternoon was crucial in Clair's life and, through her, important to her Uncle Walter and even to Duncan.

Clair and her two sisters in varying degrees felt that their brother was preferred by their parents, particularly by their mother, which they ascribed to her German background. Clair, born only ten months after Larry, felt it strongly. "The children came too fast," she said later.

"Mother was overwhelmed. I often felt just not wanted." She grew up a solitary child. Her nearest sister, Bess, was "always neat, clean and organized," and by comparison Clair felt awkward and inarticulate, "a loner."

As a girl at South Orange one misty morning, she had had a strange experience. When she was preparing to wave good-by to her father, who had started for the train, she suddenly saw directly behind him, quite plain, two beautiful deer. She prayed that her father would not move, "for I knew then the deer would vanish, which is what happened." Later that day she built herself a nest in the field and felt deeply at home.

That afternoon in the theater at Munich, watching Duncan and the children, accompanied by a piano, dancing selections from Schubert waltzes and Beethoven écossaises, she had a somewhat similar experience: her mind seemed larger, her eyes more open, her ears more acute, herself more alive than ever before and, in some inexplicable way, more at home. That night and the next morning she begged her mother to find out about the Duncan school, which recently had been founded outside Berlin, and Ellie, impressed, went to see Duncan. But when she heard that Clair would have to stay at the school until she was sixteen, Ellie declined the opportunity. How could she leave Clair alone in Germany for six years?

Nevertheless, dancing became Clair's life, though she started too late to make a name for herself. In 1920 in Switzerland she studied with Elizabeth Duncan, Isadora's elder sister and head of the Berlin school. "We danced on a tennis court until a Catholic priest complained, and we had to move. This was an old story to the Duncan girls but quite upsetting to me." Later she studied with Martha Graham at Bennington, and with Hanya Holm, "learning how to relate to space." After returning from Switzerland, like Tante she taught private classes and occasionally in schools, and again like Tante, she remained unmarried and, as she grew older, she sometimes lived with members of the family as a companion or summer mother.[1]

Among the Damrosch blood-relatives, with the exception of her Uncle Walter and his daughter Gretchen, no one considered dance to be Art, not real Art, so Clair and her interest were rather ignored. Perhaps that was for the best, for within a dominating family it left her free with her modest talent and training to create a life for herself. When the family came home in the spring of 1906, Ellie talked of Duncan and of the impression made upon Clair, and evidently Walter listened.

Though Duncan had danced in the United States in the last years of the century, she had not met with success and, discouraged, had gone to Europe. Finally, in Budapest in 1903, and Berlin in 1904, she was discovered and acclaimed. Her style, in which much of modern dance originates, was an attempt to unite dancing and music as she imagined the fusion to have been in classical Greece, taking as her models the poses and movements shown on Greek vases. She considered classical ballet, with its shoes, tights and tutus, quite artificial and inexpressive; she danced barefoot, without tights and generally in a Greek tunic. No one had done it before, and there were, of course, many who mocked.

At a performance a typical stage setting would be merely some green or blue curtains falling in folds at the back and sides of the stage and leaving a semicircular floor in the center. The lighting would be dim, rose-colored and varied by shadows. She danced only to the best music — that, too, was quite revolutionary — and in Bach's *Suite No. 3,* for example, after the orchestra had played the Overture and begun the Air, the slow movement, which violinists play on the G string, she would appear backstage, stand poised for a time in the shadows and then advance, beginning to move her arms and slowly shift the positions of her body. In the two Gavottes, which followed, she would move about freely in vivid imitation of her Greek models. The Bourée she left to the orchestra, but she danced the Gigue, and the orchestra alone closed the performance with the Polacca from the *Brandenburg Concerto No. 1.* [2]

Though her musical training was almost nil, her intuitive sense was extraordinary. One day, rehearsing Chopin's *Etude,* Opus 25, No. 1, with Harold Bauer, she said, "You are playing that wrong. The crescendo must continue until the very end of the phrase, and you can soften it later."

Bauer pointed to the music. "I can't help that," she said. "The music must go that way, otherwise there would be nothing to do with my arms."

After a battle, he gave in, and later discovered that Chopin's manuscript bore the precise dynamic curve that she had sensed and that in printing had been altered. [3]

In 1908 Duncan, for the first time in almost a decade, returned to the United States, danced a few performances in New York with a pickup orchestra and again was a failure. But Walter, alerted by Ellie's report of her and of her effect on Clair, had gone to the Criterion Theatre, seen Duncan dance Beethoven's Symphony No. 7 and, despite the bad orchestra, had been impressed. He went to her loft in the Beaux Arts Building and, after watching her dance some Schubert waltzes, offered an engagement with himself and the New York Symphony. As she later wrote, "I joyfully assented," and he, probably then and there, wrote out in longhand their initial agreement. [4]

The risk for him was as great as the benefit for her. Great orchestras even now seldom play for dancers, and then, never. A failure would bring out in force all his enemies, and even a success would mean controversy, for starting with his sister Clara there were many musicians and music lovers who abhorred the idea of using Schubert or Beethoven to accompany dance. For Duncan, the opportunity Walter offered, coming after her recent stumble, was like a sudden benediction: the chance to return home — she was born in San Francisco — under the aegis of one of the country's best-known conductors and orchestras. Even in Germany she had been forced to dance with theater bands, and the one in Munich had been execrable. Now when she danced in the Elysian Fields of Gluck's *Orfeo,* she would have Georges Barrère as flute soloist.

Her good fortune in Walter personally was very great. In business affairs she was a booby, and he was expert and honest. And he did not stint: even some of her publicity releases are written out in his hand. Artistically, she would later write, "I felt such sympathy with Walter Damrosch that it seemed to me when I stood in the centre of the stage to dance, I was connected by every nerve in my body with the orchestra and with the great conductor." [5]

Needless to say, Walter's gamble vindicated both, and in a series of concerts with the orchestra in 1908, 1909 and 1911, both in New York and on tour, Duncan established her art throughout the country. The composer Otto Luening has described how a Duncan-Damrosch concert struck an eight-year-old boy in Madison, Wisconsin:

> It was the first time I had seen or heard a full symphony orchestra. The beautiful shapes of the string instruments, varnished with shades of brown and sometimes yellow; the wood-wind instruments, in those days made of wood with a beautiful array of silver keys, mysterious and complicated; the shiny brass instruments and forbidding timpani and bass drum made me want to have something to do with an orchestra. And the artists in full dress with white ties looked magnificent. Walter Damrosch had the airs and manners of the ambassador to the Court of St. James's. When he conducted he projected the dignity of Metternich presiding at the Congress of Vienna. His conducting was restrained but the program was dashing. Isadora Duncan danced Beethoven's Seventh Symphony. She pranced about on the stage trailing a pink veil, sometimes winding herself up in it and sometimes daringly showing some bare shoulder. Her impression on me was that of a woman with great vitality, athletic and fun to watch as she created gestures supposedly to make Beethoven's symphony more palatable. Mother thought she was pretty risqué trotting around in public in bare feet. [6]

An older child, Walter's thirteen-year-old daughter Gretchen, recalled that on seeing Duncan dance to Gluck, "I cried — my first tears shed at the startling quality of beauty." She imagined that Duncan was Daphne, soon to be transformed by Apollo into a tree. "But now she wanted only to dance alone to the music of Gluck, a wild and happy creature — for she was free." After the performance Gretchen bought yards of cheese-cloth and, when her sisters were out, danced about the top of the house, having moments when she, too, felt free. Years later, among the children of friends in New York, she arranged a series of private classes for her cousin Clair to teach. Among those who saw vitality, freedom and joy in Duncan's dancing there was a bond.[7]

To the others Walter tried to be helpful, sometimes with remarks before the performances, sometimes in letters. To one who had written, he replied:

> Your argument that Beethoven would have designated it [Symphony No. 7] as *dance* music if he had so intended it, is in my judgement not good. Dancing in Beethoven's time was if anything more stiff and stilted than in ours. He knew no other . . . His Scherzos and Allegrettos are *idealized* dances . . . I have never felt the real "joy of Life" in an almost primitive innocence and glory as in her dance of the Scherzo. The *Finale* is a "Bacchanale" of such tremendous intensity that one little dancing figure on a large stage is not sufficient. The stage should be filled with twenty Duncans, but alas, so far our age has produced only one.
>
> Mrs. Damrosch who, as you know, is not a professional musician, feels the beauty of it perhaps even more keenly than I do.
>
> How far the arts should be combined is a question which even Wagner has not solved. The union of scenery (stage scenery) and music seems to me to dwarf the power of the music. I feel that strongly in the Wagner Musicdramas. In fact, I am beginning to think that *rhythmic pantomime* is the only art which seems to unite legitimately with music.[8]

But many remained unconvinced. It seems clear, backed to some extent by Walter's experience, that Duncan's most powerful appeal was to those who had the fewest preconceptions about the music, children and nonprofessional music lovers, like Margaret. Walter's tour managers, for example, recommended more performances in the South and West, but not in the East. There, apparently, for every Harold Bauer or Walter Damrosch who was willing to allow Duncan "a try," there were ten who thought the music should not be subjected to the attempt. When she performed the *Dance of the Apprentices* from *Meistersinger,* the *New York Times* critic Carl Van Vechten approved; when she danced the *Liebestod* from *Tristan,* he asked, "Why?"[9]

Several times during these seasons Duncan came in the afternoon to call on Walter, and Gretchen, her young adorer, always rushed downstairs to join the group. Duncan "would appear in a velvet cloak and Victorian bonnet, the costume she affected during the daytime, and my mother . . . would praise her latest performance to the skies. Isadora would thank my mother graciously and then ask if a lamp or two could be turned out because she could express herself better in a dim light."

Then at length she would expound on her theories about liberation and self-fulfillment while in the semidarkness Walter and Margaret slowly turned frantic. Gradually Gretchen realized that, though Duncan "as an artist had genius, as a person she was a goose."[10]

But the moment she danced, the genius returned. One night after dinner she announced to Walter and the guests that she would dance if he would play, so the room was cleared, the lights lowered and the guests sat on the floor. "There followed," according to David Mannes, "for about fifteen minutes, one of the most extraordinary and beautiful impressions of artistic intention among my recollections." Then she asked David to play for her, and while he stood in the center of the room playing several movements from Bach solo violin sonatas, she danced around him. So effective was the combination that she asked him to join her onstage for her recital at the Metropolitan the following evening, but he refused. "I did not think these rare moments could be recreated."[11]

Clara presumably was less impressed, for gradually among Duncan disciples in New York she became known as the Damrosch who disapproved. No specific remarks have come down through the years, but the tradition holds that she viewed Walter's interest in Duncan's art, in rhythmic pantomime, as "a distraction" from the serious pursuit of music.[12] And the point of view suits her character as it seems to have developed in these years.

Clara alone of Helene's five children had followed her parents' example and married a musician, and after Helene's death it was she who took the portrait of their father and continued the custom of keeping it on an easel in the living room and trimming its frame with smilax. Even if she rented a cottage for the summer, the portrait went with her. Bit by bit, no doubt unconsciously, she became the self-appointed priestess of the family's musical tradition. Nothing Frank did was wrong; nothing Marie Wiechmann did was right. Marie, apparently, was never to be forgiven for dissipating her musical talents and failing to add to the family's glory (and perhaps, too, for being, supposedly, her father's favorite among the girls). Walter's taste was variable and needed watching, and Ellie also was unreliable. Whenever Ellie with a Seymour child came in from South Orange for a New York Symphony concert, Clara would greet her in the family box by saying, "Good, Ellie, I was afraid you would be late!" And Ellie would respond, "Nonsense, Clara, I told you that the 1:07 would get us here in plenty of time."[13]

Imagine, then, what Clara must have thought when in 1933, five years after Duncan's death, Walter staged in Madison Square Garden a "Pageant for Peace" in Duncan's style, laying hands on Beethoven's Symphony No. 9. He had a full orchestra, a chorus of hundreds, the Irma Duncan dance corps of fifty, and six hundred members of the Folk Festival Council as supernumeraries. In all, 1866 artists created a spectacle for an audience of about 15,000.

Duncan had never danced the symphony but always had longed to, and according to Irma, her disciple and adopted daughter, Walter worked out a scenario "exactly as Isadora had dreamed it."

Walter's staging, played before a magnificent background of pillars and curtains created by Joseph Urban to suggest a temple before which stood a great altar, began with a war-weary multitude pleading despondently in pantomime for peace in the world. Then faintly, as if in the distance, the orchestra introduced "the Hymn of the brotherhood of man." As the volume increased, the people seemed to awake, and dancers began to decorate the temple and altar with garlands. When the chorus started on Schiller's *Ode to Joy,* representatives of the nations of the world in native costumes poured down the aisles toward the temple. After them, "youths" and "half-naked athletes" bearing banners and more garlands marched through the audience to the stage. The dancers among them began a dance of joy, and on the words "Be embraced O Ye Millions, this kiss to the whole world!" they all embraced and symbolically wafted the kiss of brotherhood to the audience and the world beyond.

Then came the climax of the poem and music, with the words mimed by the multitude: "Brothers! over yonder starry tent a loving Father must be dwelling! O ye millions, ye fall down, feel ye not the Creator? Search Him above the starry tent, far above the stars he must dwell." Afterward, as the tempo quickened, soldiers deposited their arms around the altar, on which "a flame of eternal Peace" was lighted, and the symphony ended with movements and expressions of universal joy.[14]

The performance gathered reviews reflecting the controversy over the use of symphonic music for dance. The *Musical Courier* strongly disapproved: "There were red lights, flags, dances, evolutions, and the like. It cannot be said that the spectacle was in place at a serious concert." But *Musical America,* almost regretfully, concluded that "the whole thing was, in any inclusive sense of the term, a decided success."[15]

One of Frank's dreams was to found a music school. Pedagogues by nature seem to disapprove of their fellows' aims and methods, and Frank, with his long experience in the public schools and with singing groups, felt that he had exceptional skills to offer.

There were at the turn of the century several good music schools in New York. One, the National Conservatory of Music, founded in 1885, charged no tuition (until 1915), had a distinguished faculty, and from 1892 to 1895 had been led by Dvořák and from 1899 to 1902 by Emil Paur. But it was frequently in financial difficulty. Another, founded in 1876, was the New York College of Music, which continued as the city's oldest independent music school until 1968, when it was absorbed by New York University. One of its students in 1902 was Jerome Kern.

Frank believed that a different kind of school was needed. He felt that almost all schools, in Europe as well as in the United States, concentrated too much on producing concert performers — always a good advertisement for a school — and too little on general musical education. As a corollary, almost no attention was given to preparing music teachers to work in the community, where, if effective, they might raise the level of music appreciation. Indeed, if the reports of the time are true, many of the teachers then were charlatans who made big promises, charged high fees and produced, at best, technique unquickened by any real musical understanding.

Frank's theories of musical education, remarkably uncluttered by jargon, originated in his Damrosch childhood and the German tradition behind it. All musical education, he felt, should begin at home, with song. Let the child learn from its mother songs for every occasion, and it will begin to sense key structure, major and minor modes, the relationships of pitch, legato and staccato and other elements of phrasing long before it needs to know the terms. So his mother had taught him.

More pedantically put, training the ear is the first step and should continue for several years before a child approaches any instrument. Ear and voice, not lip or finger agility, are the basic tools.

Even with an older child Frank still would teach as far as possible through singing. At a piano, for example, in discussing the relationship of pitch in a chord or phrase the teacher should have the child sing the notes rather than play them, for singing will fix their relationship in the mind, whereas playing tends to fix it only in the mechanical position of the notes on the keyboard.

Of course for grown pupils, for whom Frank imagined his school, most of this would be in the past, underlying the present effort to interpret a musical work. Here, "it must be the teacher's duty to strip the pupil's mind and soul of artificiality, insincerity and affectation." For "great art must spring from noble impulses and must be given expression in a noble form, that is, with sincerity, beauty and spirituality."

If anyone suggested that some great artists exhibited lamentable weaknesses, Frank had an answer ready: "Their best work sprang not from the weak but from the strong elements of their character."[16] This was, at the time, the usual way of divorcing Wagner's many unattractive deeds and qualities from his music, and it seemed to have the blessing of Beethoven, who said once to his publisher, "Everything I do apart from music is badly done and stupid."

Frank, who saw art and morality as obverse sides of a single coin, expected the faculty he would gather not only to teach the scale but also to inspire the students to think of music as a step to a better, fuller life. To that end he would require all students to take courses in the history and theory of music, quite apart from instruction in their particular instruments. He wanted them to have the same general education in music he had received from his father in years of daily explanation and example. Perhaps then, as the students themselves became teachers — for in Frank's view all musicians by definition were teachers — the quality of music teaching throughout the country would begin to rise.[17]

But by 1900 he had not been able to persuade any rich man to back him, and temporarily he was distracted from the idea by his efforts to create a Temple of Music, efforts that failed. By the summer of 1901, however, Carnegie had completed his home in Scotland, Skibo Castle, and he invited Frank and Hetty over for a visit. To Frank it seemed the chance to approach Carnegie about the school, and he went over alone for the month of July.

At first he was hopeful, though Carnegie, he wrote to Hetty, "dreads going into anything alone as that would imply a responsibility which he wants to avoid." When, for example, the directors of Carnegie's Music Hall Company had changed their building's name to Carnegie Hall, which they did while he was in Scotland, they had fixed the financial burden of it on him for life. Still, he had called Frank "the best man in America to organize and direct a large educational musical institution."[18]

Frank played golf with him and tramped through the woods and fields of the castle's park, but Carnegie would not commit himself. To Hetty, Frank lamented, "I am, as you know, a poor hand at pushing anything in which I am personally interested and besides am a poor conversationalist." At the month's end he left, without the support he had sought.[19]

In December, perhaps to soften Frank's disappointment, Carnegie underwrote a special performance by the Oratorio Society of *Elijah,* to which as the guests of himself and Mrs. Carnegie he invited all the members of the People's Choral Union and the music teachers in the public schools. For the occasion the Choral Union was seated in a bloc on the orchestra floor near the stage; the teachers and friends of the Oratorio Society were in the boxes and galleries above; and everyone present was given a handsome commemorative booklet. Just before the final chorus was begun, Frank suggested to the audience that at its conclusion they all join in a hymn of thanks to their hosts. And then it became clear why the Choral Union had been seated downstairs near the stage, for on Frank's signal, instead of *America,* which would have been usual, suddenly twelve hundred voices broke out in Handel's *Hallelujah Chorus,* one of Carnegie's favorites. In his box, to the thunderous applause that followed, he would only bow, his eyes beaming, his lips pressed. He would not follow the great thrill of sound with mere words.[20]

About six months later, apparently without Frank's knowledge, Hetty on his behalf approached Carnegie directly — a risky move. Hetty's touch in such affairs was not as sure as Margaret's, and she sometimes was put down as "pushy." Carnegie wrote his reply on a train.

> I hasten to assure you that instead of losing confidence in Frank it increases constantly — I think he is doing greater work spreading the love of music among the people, hundreds, yes thousands of them than he can ever do Establishing an expensive School for the few Capable of becoming professionals . . . There can be Music so finished as to rob it of feeling — Boston Orchestra often recalls this to me . . . This Superfine stuff only tickles the fancy. A violin Concerto is often — I might say always — a travesty of Music — The Great Musician intense & wrought up in his calling is very apt to miss what is really uplifting in Music — There must be such characters but it is not such I wish to help . . . I cannot help hoping that he will fail . . . I must not be asked to serve as Director, or have anything to do with his venture because I doubt very much its success, and granted its success I don't consider it the best work he can do for the spread of Music in this Country.
>
> Now you understand my position.
>
> Yours Ever & his
> Andrew Carnegie

> Frank called the Messiah — & Elijah "pot-boilers" at one meeting & to me these are the highest and purest musical treats altho I don't believe many words of the text — He does not see in Music what I feel — "Music sacred tongue of God I hear thee calling and I come." It is purely a thetre [sic] to him and to Walter also — It is more to me — *My organ says all my prayers.*[21]

His postscript reflects a shift that was taking place in musical taste. Among musicians and the public, interest in large choral works, particularly oratorios, was beginning to wane, replaced in part by the growing interest in orchestral works and the virtuoso conductors. Members of the older generation, like Carnegie, sensed the change and regretted it. Something in music, a religious component, the brotherhood of man, was being lost. Younger men, like Frank and Walter, kept a foot in both camps, but among Leopold Damrosch's grandchildren none ever expressed much interest in the musical form that had inspired their grandfather to compose *Sulamith,* his most popular work. That was another era.

In June 1903, while on a Sandy Hook steamer from Atlantic City to New York, Frank found the man to back his school: James Loeb, recently retired from the family banking firm, Kuhn, Loeb & Company, and a fine amateur cellist. While the small steamer chugged north along the New Jersey coast, Loeb consulted Frank about creating a memorial to his mother, Betty Loeb, who for many years had been a figure in

New York's musical life. He proposed to endow a fellowship in music at Columbia University. What did Frank think?

It happened that Frank, only weeks before, had been consulted by the university's president, Nicholas Murray Butler, about deflecting another such proposal and knew that Columbia at the moment was unlikely to accept such a gift. Frank, no doubt, was scrupulously fair in relating the university's position, and only afterward suggested that Loeb might consider a music school in his mother's memory. But by the time the steamer docked, Loeb was interested.

A few weeks passed, during which Frank and Loeb had lunch one day with Rudolph Schirmer, who either then or soon after promised to give the school the Schirmer Circulating Library of Music, a large collection. Meanwhile Frank was to find nine other subscribers besides Loeb to guarantee $50,000 each to found the school. But in July and August people were out of town, and Frank could do little. Then early in October 1903, Loeb called him: Frank should go ahead with his plans; Loeb would provide an initial endowment of $500,000 to found the school.[22]

James Loeb, born in 1867, was an extraordinary man from an unusual family, and his life contained a tragedy that may explain to some extent the intensity with which he supported the three projects that he helped to found, Frank's Institute of Musical Art, Harvard's Loeb Classical Library and, late in life, a neurological and psychiatric research center in Munich under Dr. Ludwig Binswanger. Loeb's father, Solomon Loeb, was an immigrant, a child of Orthodox Jews but himself an agnostic, and an extremely successful banker. He wanted a son to succeed him at Kuhn, Loeb, but the pressure he put on his elder son, Morris, caused the boy to become too eccentric for business, and Morris finally was allowed to be a chemist. His other son, James, or Jim, as he was usually known, hoped to become a classicist or Egyptologist. On graduating from Harvard, in 1888, he was offered a chance to study Egyptology in Paris and London, with a curatorship at the Boston Museum of Fine Arts and a teaching post at Harvard to follow. Instead, his father forced him into Kuhn, Loeb, where it soon was evident that, although Jim was competent, the company's future lay with Solomon's son-in-law Jacob Schiff. Then Jim fell in love and planned to marry. Even the girl's name, according to Stephen Birmingham, the historian of the city's German-Jewish banking families, "has been written out of family records, but it is known that she was beautiful, loved him very much, and was a gentile." Though Solomon was not a practicing Jew, because of the girl's religion he forbade the marriage and marshaled support against it from his wife, Betty, and, most powerfully, from Schiff. Jim stood firm, and then, according to Birmingham, quoting the family, "extreme pressures" were applied.

Under these, whatever they were, Jim broke, the marriage was called off and he soon went abroad to consult a neurologist, Dr. Sigmund Freud, in whose house for a time he lived. In New York Jacob Schiff rewrote his will to disinherit any child who married a Gentile.

A less intelligent, perceptive man than James Loeb might have come to hate his parents, and even he sustained a deep injury. He withdrew from Kuhn, Loeb two years before his father's death, and increasingly began to live abroad. He bought a house in the deep woods at Murnau, near Munich. Over the years, watching his good works from afar, he became a recluse. Toward the end of his life he married his nurse and companion, who shared his bibliographical interests, and in 1933 he died.[23]

In the beginning years of Frank's school, however, Loeb followed it with interest and not only made important additional gifts but persuaded his brother and sisters also to contribute to it, in their mother's memory. Though the family was not as rich as Carnegie, its members gave in all more than $1.5 million, permitting the school to expand, to increase its scholarships and to maintain an exceptional faculty. Though many others also supported it, in its early years it was the financial creation primarily of the Loeb family.[24]

It opened on October 31, 1905, in a renovated building, Lenox House, on Fifth Avenue at Twelfth Street, calling itself the Institute of Musical Art. Its students often referred to it simply as "the IMA" or "the Damrosch school." Even before its first student entered, it had pre-eminence among the country's music schools because of the faculty Frank had lured to it. This was not entirely the result of the salaries offered. In Europe as well as in the United States Frank's work was known and admired, and he himself was liked. The country's greatest string quartet of the day, the Kneisel Quartet, consisted of Franz Kneisel, Julius Theodorwicz, Louis Svenčenski and Alwin Schroeder. All were friends of Frank, and all, though previously based in Boston, came to New York to head the school's string departments. The piano faculty was led by Sigismund Stojowski; voice by Etelka Gerster and Georg Henschel; orchestral instruments by Georges Barrère; theory by Percy Goetschius; and organ by Gaston Déthier. Enrollment at the end of the first year, expected to be between twenty-five and 150, was 467, at an average tuition of about $165, higher than most schools; and the students came from twenty-eight states. Each year more applied, and in 1910 the school moved to a new building at 120 Claremont Avenue, built by Otto Eidlitz and intended for six hundred students. Soon an annex just as large was added, and enrollment mounted to a thousand.[25]

The school's tone was authoritarian and paternal. Frank and his faculty told the students which courses they must take. In most schools at the time all courses were elective. Frank was strict about behavior and dress, and made recommendations about the use of free time and outside reading. Standards, regardless of student disappointments, were maintained.[26]

One day Frank called into his office a young soprano who already had performed professionally.

> His manner was kindness itself. He asked me to tell him with utter honesty what kind of singer I hoped to become. "One of the great ones, singing the great roles."
>
> "No other kind of singing career would do?"
>
> "No. Just to be a struggling second-rate singer would be too heartbreaking."
>
> Gently he asked me to face a hard fact. "You've tried to make a child's throat do the work of a trained artist. It is a sick voice. With endless patience and years of work you could sing artistically. Freely, spontaneously? I doubt it. But you have a dramatic instinct. It shows in your singing. Why not turn to a career where you would not be starting with a definite handicap? Why not go on the stage?"
>
> "I don't want to be an actress," was all I managed to reply.

Her disappointment was bitter. "I found myself living in a vacuum. The orderly routine of study had ceased." But the need to earn a living was pressing, so she tried the theater — where she had a great success as Blanche Yurka.[27]

For many, of course, there was no happy ending, and some who fell afoul of Frank's authoritarian ways disliked him and the school. But, then, they could go elsewhere.

As the school expanded and took more of Frank's time, he sloughed off his other jobs, resigning as supervisor of music in the public schools in 1905, as director of the People's Choral Union and Singing Classes in 1909 and of the Oratorio Society in 1912, ending his tenure there with a Brahms Festival shared with Walter and the New York Symphony. The next year, for the first time in forty years, the society's director was not a Damrosch. Thereafter, except for the Musical Art Society, with which he continued to give two concerts a year, he gave all his time to the Institute of Musical Art.

Frank now was an older man, fifty-three, and two events, in 1911 and 1912, brought home his age to him sharply. His son, Frank Jr., had started Yale in the fall of 1906 but before graduating had left to enter theological school to prepare for ordination in the Episcopal Church. Both Frank and Hetty believed in a life of service, but they had never attached themselves to any particular creed, not even to Dr. Felix Adler's Society for Ethical Culture, in which they had a loose but continuing interest.

Whatever they may have thought initially about their son's decision — and tradition holds that they were somewhat dismayed — it soon was made more complicated for them by the role in it of a young woman. At New Haven, Frank Jr. had been influenced by an Episcopal minister, Father Fred Burgess of Christ Church, who had introduced him to the Frisby family, the widow, son and four daughters of Augustus Frisby, an insurance salesman, who had been an active Episcopalian. The family, whose ties with Burgess had remained close, was extremely hospitable; students frequently were invited to the house, often for church events, and three of the four girls eventually married Episcopal ministers. Frank Jr. found the family and parish life appealing and soon was in love with the youngest girl, Dorothy, a very religious person. Undoubtedly his conversion, which probably started with Father Burgess, was assisted by Dorothy, and few doubt that she urged him to become a minister; some even have wondered whether she did not make it a condition of marriage. In any event, while he was still in theological school and she at Vassar, they proposed to marry.

Frank and Hetty, apparently, told Frank Jr. that while they had no objection to Dorothy personally, he must wait until he had finished school and been ordained. He did not. In the spring of 1911 he and Dorothy eloped.

In a German household such filial disobedience usually signaled a complete rupture. In the Schirmer family in the previous generation old Gustav had disinherited his son for marrying without approval, even though young Gustave at the time was working and was financially independent. But here were Frank Jr. and Dorothy both still in school, and he not to be ordained for another year.

What Frank and Hetty thought is not recorded, and in later years no one talked of the event. What they did was to have the young couple to meals just as often as possible. Night after night was not too often in their effort to reintegrate the family, and gradually the tension eased. Ultimately for Frank, at least, the pain that the young people had caused so carelessly was erased by an equal affection for both. But for Hetty, perhaps overly possessive as a mother and denied the usual period of adjustment to a daughter-in-law, a touch of discord with Dorothy remained.[28]

The following year, 1912, the couple's first child was born, Leopold Damrosch, and Frank was a grandfather, a position his own father had not lived to attain.

With the Musical Art Society, Frank's group of about sixty professional singers, he specialized in the unaccompanied, polyphonic music of the sixteenth and seventeenth centuries. He was the first in the country to revive this music on any large scale. Doubtless on occasion a work was sung by some German choral group, such as the Arion Society, but it cannot have been often, for at the time most of such music — works by Aichinger, Allegri, Anerio and Arcadelt, to take only composers from the start of the alphabet — was not available. Making it available was a purpose of the Musical Art Society.

Much of the music existed only in old, manuscript copies, written with obsolete clefs, without phrasing or dynamic markings and for the most part incomprehensible to all but scholars. In Paris a musicologist, Charles Bordes, had begun to transpose some of the works into a modern style and publish them, and Frank acknowledged a debt to him. But Bordes died in 1909, and much of Frank's work was done afterward. In the opinion of Randall Thompson, a composer of the next generation who distinguished himself in choral music, "Dr. Damrosch's editing . . . was and remains beautifully scholarly and exceptionally appropriate from the point of view of choral style and expression — tempos, dynamics and all."[29] Many of these works as edited by Frank were published by Schirmer's and for the first time became available to choirs and singing groups in modern editions, at low prices. Some of these editions continue in use.

The music was not to everyone's taste, if only because it was so different from the contemporary style of Brahms, Tchaikovsky or Elgar. For example, Gertrude Schirmer Fay, the daughter of Gustave Schirmer, confessed that at times her attention wandered.

> We went to every concert because Father was determined to support Frank. He thought him a truly noble man, particularly for his lack of envy or irritation over Walter's achievements. Father hated what he called "social music," glittering occasions and society patrons. That was the world of Walter and of Uncle Rudolph. The Musical Art Society Concerts were more like going to church or school. Father probably enjoyed every note, but I suspect that most of us went out of a sense of duty. The music often was very beautiful, yet sometimes I was slightly bored.[30]

The concerts were held in Carnegie Hall, and without Frank's personality to pull in well-wishers, it probably would have proved too large. Yet for connoisseurs of choral music the chance to hear long-dead works brought back to life was thrilling, and the singing, ravishing. In assessing Frank as a choral conductor Thompson wrote:

> His singers were perfectly devoted to him; and by the gentlest means he exercised control over them. This is the greatest single attribute of a choral conductor. Combined with his profound knowledge of music, his adoration of it, and his mastery of choral technique, his effortless hold over his singers enabled him to perform miracles in the realm of *a cappella* literature, sacred and secular.[31]

CHAPTER 20

Christmas at Uncle Walter's.

FOR THE SEYMOUR CHILDREN, in South Orange, Christmas was near when Ellie announced that the time had come to put away their father's reading chair, lamp and table to make room for the tree. Every year Harry would point out that there was room for the tree in the hall, but Ellie would insist on the living room: that was the Damrosch way. After a protest Harry would rub his forehead gently with his fingers and say, "I give up."

Ellie, however, had to concede on stockings by the chimney. That was a Seymour custom, and for years she resisted. But when the children reached school age, heard of their classmates' stockings and then discovered at home that they had their father's support, their clamor rose and Ellie had to give in, though she never did as well with the stockings as she did with the tree.

Once the tree was in the house and set up, with its base covered by a soft golden drapery that Harry had brought back from India, Ellie would produce from some far closet a canvas to throw over the dining room table, and then all the decorations for the tree were brought down from the attic, spread out and checked. There were long necklaces of colored balls, red and silver, and some that were shorter, multicolored. To hold the candles there were clips of pressed metal, some shaped like butterflies, with red or white smooth-sided candles to be well waxed in. There was a box of special ornaments: a tiny Santa, birds, an orchestra of wooden angels, sprigs of cherries, sugar plums and, best of all, a tiny nest with eggs watched by a red-breasted bird; to weigh down the lower branches, there were a few glass icicles. Each year, new, there would be "angel hair," or lamella, which Ellie would buy in the city at F. A. O. Schwarz, a German store that imported only the best German tinsel. It had to be put on with care, only one or two strands to a branch at the tip end. Finally were added, each on its own string, cookies, candies, marzipan, tiny sacks of nuts and, for the lower branches, lady apples. During the fortnight after Christmas, when the children brought in their classmates, their friends would gasp: no one else in town had such a tree.

Very early in the afternoon of Christmas Eve — for they had many family parties ahead — the Seymours would celebrate their own Christmas. When all the candles were lit, Ellie at the piano would strike up *O Tannenbaum,* the double doors would be slid back into the walls and the family would enter. Standing before the tree, led by Ellie, they would sing five or six carols, everyone but Harry singing in German, and always they ended with Franz Gruber's *Stille Nacht.* Then they would have their stockings and presents, which were not under the tree but, in Damrosch family custom, placed in chairs, one to a child or parent, and covered by a napkin until after the carols. Ellie, with her eye on the clock, would hurry them along so that they could catch the five-thirty train to New York, and while Harry helped the children with their coats, she counted and recounted the shopping bags with presents for the cousins, aunts and uncles.

From the train, though outside it was almost dark, they still could see the telephone wires skim by in waves. The conductor punched the family's commutation ticket, and the children watched for the huge new electric sign in Newark: PRUDENTIAL, THE ROCK OF GIBRALTAR. They knew in advance by the smell of coal dust when they were approaching the tunnel, but once inside there were compensations as the smoke and odd light made strange reflections in the windows; and then they were in the railroad yards, with the engine hissing slowly and leading them into the Hoboken Station. Ellie hurried them down the platform to see whether a ferry was in or if they had just missed it; and now the railroad sounds and smells, screechy wheels, steam and coal, began to mix with the ferry's brackish water, wet ropes and clanging metal walkways that dropped onto the upper deck. Once they were aboard, the smells changed to linoleum, machine oil, varnish and, because the cold forced them inside, stinking cigar smoke and butts. At Twenty-third Street they took the elevated up to Uncle David and Tante Clara's apartment, where they had a supper with the Mannes family and Tante. Then it was upstairs to Uncle Frank and Tante Hetty's, where there were more loud greetings, exchanges of presents and sometimes a carol or two. Christmas, as Ruth said, was "smile, smile, smile, all the way!"

The next day, after a night in which the visitors were distributed between the Mannes and Damrosch apartments, all three branches of the family, led by Tante, would start about twelve-thirty for Uncle Walter and Aunt Margaret's house on East Sixty-first Street. Here the children

would meet Tante Marie, now grossly fat, and the rest of the Wiechmann family — Uncle Ferdi, Marjorie, their oldest cousin, who was very
beautiful but quite unpredictable, and her younger brother, Walter, who
always seemed rather silent and cold.

Besides the relatives, numbering nearly thirty, Margaret and Walter
always asked an equal number of friends, some of whom returned year
after year: David Bispham, Harold and Marie Bauer, Louise Homer and
her daughter Louise, Olive Fremstad and Marcella Sembrich. In addition, there was Margaret's younger sister, Harriet, and her only child,
Walker Blaine Beale. Harriet, whom all the children called "Aunt H,"
had been divorced soon after marriage, and Walter and Margaret always
included her and their nephew in any family gathering. Walker was like
a son to them and a brother to their four girls. He was an exceptional
young man, smart, attractive, and already had more than a touch of James
G. Blaine's charisma. By the time he was midway through Harvard,
even people not related to him were beginning to talk of Walker as a
potential leader of the Republican party and even, someday, its presidential candidate. Like Leopold Damrosch Mannes, two years younger,
Walker Blaine Beale seemed certain to leave a mark on the world.

The tree at Uncle Walter's, where the room was bigger and the ceiling
higher than in the other homes, was the grandest of all, for here, too,
family tradition was observed, and the tree's top scraped the ceiling. The
highest candles were far beyond the reach of a child or even an adult,
and the pail of water, mop and sponge were all on hand, plainly visible.
The other decorations were not so different from the Seymours', except
that here, as a concession to Aunt Margaret's New England background,
there were garlands of popcorn and cranberries strung on thin, almost
invisible thread. These last could not be made too far in advance lest the
cranberries dry out and crinkle, which would be noted with sympathy
but counted a failure for those decorating the tree.

The festivities began, as the guests gathered, with sherry in the living
room for the adults, and during this first half-hour the children often
visited upstairs. Then Uncle Walter would summon them with a few
loud chords on the piano, Uncle David would tune his violin and on
signal everyone would burst into a joyous O Tannenbaum, in the language of his or her choice. More carols followed, with everyone standing
in two large circles round the tree, and the final carol always, very hushed,
was Stille Nacht.

After the singing the four Damrosch daughters, Alice, Gretchen, Polly
and Anita, would distribute the presents piled beneath the tree. These
were simple but individual, and miraculously there was always one for
the latecomer, even for the old friend who might have come unan-
nounced. The girls, with a pile of presents on a tray, would search out

the person for whom the tag proclaimed the gift, while everyone stood chatting until the last present and person were matched. Aunt Margaret's hand was everywhere in the smoothly run party, but nowhere more personally than in these simple gifts with which she welcomed everyone to her house.

Buffet lunch followed, in the dining room, which faced the garden in the backyard. The more elderly sat at small tables and the younger on pillows or on the floor. The main dish usually was a chicken-and-oyster pie, said to be a specialty of New York, and dessert was always accompanied by champagne, with which Uncle Walter greeted every occasion.

After lunch, upstairs again and beside the tree, the Damrosch daughters, led by Alice, would divide the group in two for charades, and the sides would compete to see which team by the superior acting of a few of its members could guess most quickly the definitions or phrases assigned. These generally were literary quotations or the political slogans of the day. Often before the acting began, while the girls were gathering props and costumes or the actors working out their skits, the guests would entertain each other with musical numbers. One, repeated almost every year, was a rendition by David Bispham of Walter's setting of *Danny Deever*. Clair loved this, and when a child, she would, if she could, sit under or near the piano, where the resonance of Bispham's voice and Walter's playing would seem to shake the walls.

Sometimes artists displayed talents quite outside their chosen field. Bauer, a concert pianist, rolled up his trousers, bowed out his legs and, with Walter at the piano, gave a perfect imitation of Harry Lauder singing *Roamin' in the Gloamin'*. Another time, in a charade, he came running into the room in a bear's costume and in a few seconds of caricature created an animal, terrified, ferocious and looking for a handout from a tourist in Yellowstone Park.

No one who attended a Christmas party at Walter and Margaret's was likely to forget it, but many had mixed feelings about it. The pressure to perform, to be talented or at least attractive was great. Ellie loved it; Harry did not; and always after lunch, after he had told his one story to Margaret, he would retreat upstairs to the library to start the biography she just had given him. Some of the cousins disliked being bossed about by Alice and thought the four Damrosch girls were rather too conscious of themselves as attractive. The season, and this party in particular, seemed to force them all into roles — the sick child, the troublesome child, the child in college or not in college — in which they did not always feel comfortable. But it was one of Aunt Margaret's virtues as a hostess at these large Damrosch parties to recognize that not everyone enjoyed them equally. The shy child, her brother-in-law and guests, if they wished, were allowed to slip away.

At the party's end, the Seymours were among the first to leave. Whereas on the trip into the city they had been eager and talkative, they were now tired and silent. Always, or so it seemed, they just missed the Christopher Street ferry, arriving as the gates clanged shut and then having to sit for the next quarter-hour in the chilly, smelly waiting room. The ferry would bang and bump its way into the slip with much creaking of the wooden piles. The crowd in the waiting room would rise too soon, surge forward, be forced to wait, and only finally be allowed to board. As night by then had come, the river looked black, with perhaps an occasional floe of ice reflecting ghostly white. Then the train to South Orange in the clackety car, the walk from the station to their house — lungs full of fresh air — under bare branches and stars. At last in their own home, they would gather up their family presents, look once again at their own tree and disperse, each to his or her room, exhausted but with a mind full of memories.[1]

CHAPTER 21

The Mannes School founded. Seymours at York Harbor. Tante's citizenship. Larry Seymour and Jascha Heifetz. Effects of World War I on orchestras and the repertory.

THE WAR YEARS were not the most favorable for founding a music school, but David and Clara Mannes, besides being eager, were almost forced into it by events in their careers. The war had prevented their recital tour of England and the Continent at the same time that David's voluntary and forced retirements from the Third Street and Negro Music School settlements, early in 1915, left him with little to do. Meanwhile Clara, who for several years had watched his increasing unhappiness over the direction each school was taking, had been urging him to found one of his own, in which he would set the policy. They had discussed it often, so regardless of the war they went ahead.

From the first, though they would name the school the David Mannes School of Music, Clara was an equal partner. (Today, it is the Mannes College of Music.) They knew, from their discussions, exactly what they wished to create and how it would differ from Frank's Institute of Musical Art. Frank aimed at training potential professionals, who, on graduation, would become virtuosos, enter an orchestra or choral group or teach. He also wanted these professionals to have a full education in music, tested by examinations and proclaimed by a diploma.

Clara and David wanted to do as much, and more, though in a different fashion. Their school, as David put it, would embrace "under the same roof not only the intense development of the potential professional, but the efforts of those who wanted merely to enrich themselves through a better understanding or playing of music without the responsibilities of a career." In short, along with the professionals they proposed to educate amateurs — dread word.[1]

To David, relying on his experience with such a program in the settlement schools, there was not only no problem in such joint education; there was an advantage: "A school directed solely towards education for a career runs the danger of becoming institutional, while a purely cultural school for the amateur runs the opposite risk of becoming lax in standards, bereft of the stimulus that only serious artistic qualities can give."[2] To mix the two and avoid a dispiriting sense of competition, the school would educate without examinations or diplomas, offering each student "a constant, helpful supervision at all times."[3]

In the coming years the Mannes School, like any other, would have its admirers and disparagers, and often the disagreement between these would focus on the role in the school's program of education for amateurs. The admirers typically would rejoice that Mannes offered more than "mere arid professionalism"; the disparagers would deplore its "dilettantism."

The concept of educating both amateurs and professionals came naturally to Clara and David from their chamber music background, which in turn had roots in the Central European tradition of Hausmusik, music played in the home by family and friends. That tradition, which Austrian, German and Czech immigrants had brought to the United States, had political and social overtones. It was not the aristocratic world of Esterházy employing a private orchestra under the leadership of Haydn, or even of H. L. Higginson and the Boston Symphony, but the more bourgeois world of Schubert and the Schumanns, men and women making music together for their own pleasure and instruction. And by its continuation or decline, the tradition had a role to play in the future of music in the United States. Like Carnegie, Clara and David perhaps felt in the world of music the beginnings of a shift that they instinctively disliked and wished to counter.

Chamber musicians and to some extent lieder and choir singers are apt to have a rather different view of the musically educated amateur than does the instrumental virtuoso, opera singer or conductor. They know, for example, that much of their music, such as the trios of Mozart and Haydn, was written for amateurs, played by amateurs and the final judgment of its worth made by these amateurs. Publishers in the eighteenth and nineteenth centuries at times refused to publish music that they felt was unappealing to amateurs — so important was the market. And today, as then, professionals and amateurs frequently play together, though often the amateurs pay the professionals to lead the group.

There is no such intermingling for, say, the virtuoso pianist. Tchaikovsky wrote his Piano Concerto for a professional to project from a stage. No group gathers to play it at home; no publisher issues the score with amateurs in mind. The public still has a voice in judging the worth

Leopold Damrosch, from a drawing by Friedrich Preller, Weimar, October 7, 1857
(*Courtesy Marya Mannes*)

Family tea party in Breslau,
1867: Frank, Tante, Helene,
Marie, Leopold, Walter

Frank and Walter, June 1871,
just before sailing for America

Walter and his father, circa 1880, when Walter was eighteen and Leopold forty-eight

Tante and Helene in New York, circa 1875 (*Photograph by Rockwood; courtesy Douglas S. Damrosch*)

Hetty Damrosch, circa 1897

Frank in 1897, when he was
thirty-eight

Walter in middle age (*Photograph by Mishkin; courtesy Douglas S. Damrosch*)

Margaret Blaine Damrosch (*Courtesy Sidney Howard Urquhart*)

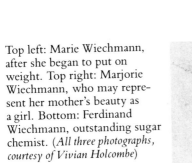

Top left: Marie Wiechmann, after she began to put on weight. Top right: Marjorie Wiechmann, who may represent her mother's beauty as a girl. Bottom: Ferdinand Wiechmann, outstanding sugar chemist. (*All three photographs, courtesy of Vivian Holcombe*)

Ellie (*Courtesy Barry Seymour Boyd*)

Ellie in middle age (*Courtesy Elizabeth Seymour Ransom*)

Harry Seymour, circa 1935
(*Courtesy Elizabeth Seymour Ransom*)

David Mannes

Clara Mannes

Tante and the Mannes family,
circa 1910 (*Courtesy Evelyn S.
Mannes*)

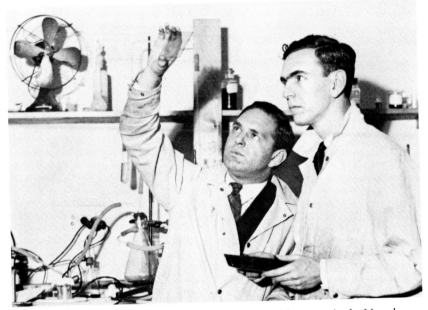

Leopold Godowsky, Jr., and Leopold Mannes in their laboratory in the Nevada Hotel (*Courtesy Evelyn S. Mannes*)

David, Clara and Leopold Mannes at the school, circa 1946 (*Photograph by Larry Gordon; courtesy Evelyn S. Mannes*)

Evelyn on her wedding day (*Courtesy Evelyn S. Mannes*)

Evelyn dancing Gershwin's Prelude No. 2 (*Photograph by Leopold D. Mannes; courtesy Evelyn S. Mannes*)

Marya Mannes, circa 1927,
from a drawing by Leo Mielziner (*Courtesy Marya Mannes*)

Marya Mannes in middle age
(*Courtesy David J. Blow*)

John Tee Van holding a panda
at Tagaytay in the Philippines
(*Courtesy Evelyn S. Mannes*)

Helen and John Tee Van
(*Courtesy Evelyn S. Mannes*)

Frank as he appeared to his
students in his last years
(*Photograph by Mishkin;
courtesy Douglas S. Damrosch*)

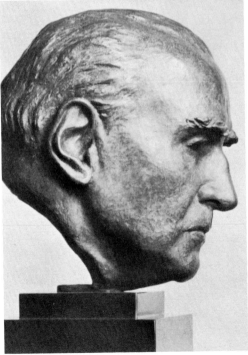

Walter, sculpted by his niece
Marya (*Courtesy Marya Mannes*)

The Institute of Musical Art. The building later housed the Juilliard School and today is the Manhattan School of Music. *(Photograph by Frank Dunand)*

The Mannes College of Music *(Photograph by Frank Dunand)*

Damrosch Park in Lincoln Center, with the family name misspelled (since corrected), as it not infrequently is (*Photograph by Frank Dunand*)

of such music, but the gap between the amateur in the audience and the professional onstage is greater; and it seems, unfortunately, to breed in many professionals an arrogance about any amateur's taste, knowledge and, of course, proficiency.[4] Then, as orchestras enlarged and music became more complicated, the gap widened. A Beethoven or Mendelssohn symphony reduced very nicely for home playing to four or eight hands at the piano; Prokofiev or even Richard Strauss did less well, but it was still possible to learn the music by re-creating it at home. Today with the still greater range of complication, including electronic effects, the gap has become even wider, and perhaps because of it the audiences for such new music grows steadily smaller.

The educated amateur, it seems, has a vital role in music: to form the core of an audience, to serve on boards and committees and to guide patronage. Higginson and Flagler of the Boston and New York symphonies were both trained amateur musicians; so was James Loeb; and even Carnegie could articulate exactly what he would support and why. But in the coming years, as such men were replaced more and more by foundations, their informed, personal judgments were lost. The foundation executives, for the most part, modestly announced that they knew nothing of music and — to make the example extreme — typically appointed an advisory committee, often made up of composers, conductors, or publishers, who gave the foundation's money to their friends — other composers, conductors or publishers — with the result that the judgment of an audience of educated amateurs never came into operation. Music frequently was commissioned, performed, published and recorded simply because a foundation paid for it, though no audience of any size would listen to it.

Clara and David were not clairvoyant about the predicament of music fifty years in the future. But looking back over two hundred years they could see that part of the strength of the German tradition, particularly in chamber music, was the role in it of educated amateurs. And so with a clear view of the past and perhaps a dim foreboding of the future they made educating amateurs a part of their purpose.

Announcing that the school would open in October 1916, they rented a building at 154 East 70th Street. Later the fact that they had located the school in "the fashionable upper East Side" was used by disparagers to reinforce the charge of dilettantism. But there was a financial reason for the choice. Neither Clara nor David had a backer like Carnegie, Flagler or even Loeb. They did not know such persons, or not well enough, and with only modest contributions from friends and well-wishers they had to put the school in a neighborhood convenient to the rich, who could pay a high tuition fee.

Their financial projection for the first three years exists, a memorandum typed on a single page, and the figures, compared with Frank's $500,000 opening gift from Loeb, seem almost childlike in their simplicity.

MEMORANDUM

In order to assist Mr. and Mrs. David Mannes in establishing a music school in New York City, a number of their friends have expressed their willingness to underwrite the estimated total cost of the work for the first year and a decreasing proportion of the cost for a second and third year. This underwriting is based upon the following estimates of cost per annum, which has been prepared by Mr. and Mrs. Mannes:

Rental — — — — — — — — — — — — — — —	$7,000.
Upkeep, including heat, light and cleaning — —	2,000.
Advertising — — — — — — — — — — — — —	2,000.
Secretary and office help— — — — — — — — —	1,500.
Incidentals— — — — — — — — — — — — — —	1,500.
Salary for Mr. and Mrs. Mannes to supplement	
their receipts from concert work — — — — —	8,000.
Total.	$22,000.

Against which there are the following sources of income:

100 pupils averaging $150 each — $15,000.		
Less salaries of teachers, say —	10,000.	5,000.
Net income from Mr. Mannes' present pupils —	3,000.	
		$8,000.

It is expected that the number of pupils will be considerably more than 100 and that the amount realized from their tuition fees applicable to the underwritten budget will be considerably more than $50 each.

It has been thought prudent to secure the underwriting of the total estimated cost for the first year, namely $22,000; for the second year $17,000; and for the third year $12,000. It is hoped that after the third year the enterprise will be self supporting.

Since a number of the friends of the school have expressed their desire to contribute outright the full amount of their underwriting, it is understood that their pledges will be paid in full each year and that whatever amount thereof is not required to meet the underwriting requirements will be set aside by the treasurer, to be used for such needs of the school as may from time to time arise.[5]

In fact, in each of the three years the school enrolled more than a hundred students and was able to save about half of the year's underwriting. The success lay in the reputations of Clara and David and of their faculty, chiefly Angela Diller, who taught theory; Elizabeth Quaile, piano; and Howard Brockway, advanced composition and instrumentation. David taught advanced violin students and a course on teaching methods, and also conducted the senior orchestra. Clara, besides doing most of the administrative work, taught advanced students in chamber music combinations and supervised the ensemble department.

To cap their first year's success two not unrelated events took place. Casals arrived in New York and as always came to the Mannes apartment with his cello for an evening of chamber music. This time, hearing of the new school, he suggested quietly that he give a program there of the two Brahms sextets for strings. Of course, his offer was accepted, and of course Clara and David had no difficulty signing five of the city's best string players to play with him. And one of the winter's distinguished evenings of chamber music took place at the new Mannes School of Music.[6]

The second event concerned their son, Leopold, who recently had turned sixteen. His parents had not hurried his musical training; neither wanted a child prodigy. They wished for Leopold a full, adult life in music. But for a number of years his interest in it seemed to have weakened. In its place, he had developed a strong interest in photography, particularly in experiments with color, and a passion for mountain climbing. He still played the piano, with skill but superficially.

In the Mannes household, where there was so often music in the home, David and Clara usually made little of it. But a Casals evening was different. For Casals, David would urge Leopold and Marya to change any plans, invite the friend in if necessary, but stay. This particular evening Leopold seemed stirred, and later he attended all the rehearsals — there were at least six — as well as the performance of the two Brahms sextets. Two weeks after the recital Clara and David were astonished to hear him at the piano, reproducing many sections of the sextets with harmonic accuracy and perfect phrasing. As there was no piano score for the pieces, he was exhibiting not only a prodigious memory but an extraordinary ability to transpose complicated string works onto the piano. In a short time he had the sextets perfect and complete. David rejoiced. "We knew then, against our fears, that Leopold's musical enthusiasm had not waned: on the contrary, it had retired within and grown stronger."[7]

For the summer of 1916 Harry and Ellie rented a house at York Harbor, Maine. The vacation was in a way a celebration, though perhaps the children, because of their father's quietly humorous manner, were not fully aware of the gravity behind it. Several years earlier the president of Harry's export agency had misappropriated $50,000 of the firm's capital, and Harry, to save the company, had merged it with another. The combination survived and in 1916 reorganized itself as Dodge & Seymour. (The firm exists today as L. D. Seymour & Company.) Since its business was chiefly in Asia, it was unaffected by the war in Europe and became profitable. But for several years the family's finances had been meager, and the previous summer Margaret and Walter had given Ellie and the children a vacation on Lake Champlain.[8]

Ellie went up to York Harbor in May and returned ecstatic. She had found a small house large enough for the entire family and Tante. Larry, who was graduating in June from Princeton and was secretary of his class, could have friends up over Labor Day, when Tante would be visiting Frank and Hetty at Seal Harbor. There was a golf course just across the road and a summer orchestra that the girls could join, so they must take their violins and cello. The lilacs were gorgeous, the beach lovely, and Walter could give them introductions to the interesting people. And indeed, when Ellie and the girls arrived in June — Larry had managed to avoid the confusion of the move — the large house seemed cosy, the sun shone and the beach sparkled.

Then almost at once came the first interesting person. Ellie was upstairs lying down after lunch, and sixteen-year-old Ruth, supposing the doorbell announced a friend, hurtled down the stairs and flung open the door. A man and two women faced her. He introduced himself, Mr. William Dean Howells, and handed her his card. Ruth, feeling confused, read it carefully: Mr. William Dean Howells. He must be one of Uncle Walter's friends, she was thinking, when she heard him ask, "May we wait to see if your mother will receive us?"

"Oh, yes." As she turned to dash upstairs to get her mother, he spoke again. "May we come in to wait?"

"Oh, yes."

She led them into the hall, and he, not unkindly, took control. "Perhaps we can wait in there?"

"Oh, yes," she said again, and leading them in, waved at chairs for them to sit on. As she was leaving the room, she realized she had put Mr. Howells on the piano stool.

When she returned — for Ellie had insisted that she go down to entertain the visitors — he was dutifully where she had put him, clutching his knee and smiling.

For several minutes he led the conversation. Did she play golf? Did she think she would like to learn? Did she play a musical instrument? The cello! Then Ellie entered, murmuring as she saw Mr. Howells on the stool, "Oh, dear! That is not the place for you."

Ruth fled, near to tears and angry with her mother. Why hadn't she told her what to expect, how to behave? How was a girl to know if her mother never told her?

A day or two later a Mrs. Ryan called. "How lovely to have another musical family come to our little colony. The young people have a small orchestra and will welcome additions to the strings. Especially the cellos," she added, smiling at Ruth.

The conversation turned to the war, and Mrs. Ryan told of rumors of a German submarine refueling at night in one of the Maine harbors. Ellie was shocked and agreed that the United States should declare war. After the sinking of the *Lusitania,* what was the government waiting for? Privately she expressed her feelings in a poem lamenting Germany's "dark obsession" with power and urging a return to the belief that "Love is Might."

Then Tante arrived, with her silver hair, long skirts and knitting bag. As a present for the household she brought a set of linen table mats of her own design and weaving. Sitting on the beach the next day with Ellie, she talked of the family in Germany. Her brother Paul was in charge of a prison camp on the Rhine; all her nephews were in the army or navy; her nieces, doing war work. She was agitated, spoke intensely, in German, and Ellie replied in German, trying to reassure her. Suddenly Clair and Ruth noticed that no one any longer was sitting near them. The others on the beach were watching them, talking about them. The atmosphere was hostile.

Thereafter, without discussing it, the two girls contrived to keep Tante at the house much of the time. They encouraged her to sit out on the lawn and dictate her life's story to Bess, who had been studying shorthand and typing. Somehow, reminiscing about her youth in Jever and life in Breslau with Leopold and Helene seemed to ease Tante's spirit. Bess would put the day's work in order and then read it back to her. If Ellie suggested that they all go to the beach, Ruth would say, "It's too cold"; or Clair, "It's too late." But when the young people's orchestra started to rehearse, the girls were not asked to join.[9]

There can be many reasons why a person starts a diary or a journal: egoism, religious ecstasy or merely the desire to record political or family events. The timing of *Tante's Story,* however, suggests that it was partially an effort at self-identification, brought on by the pressures of the war. In telling of Leopold's decision that his children speak German in the home, she added, "How sad that there should have come a time when the Americans should hate the sound of his dearly-beloved mother tongue." She did not go on to criticize the Americans, of whom she now counted herself one, but implicit in the story is her love of German culture, which she would not deny or denigrate. In part her story is the stand of a private, courageous woman against the anti-German fanaticism sweeping the country.[10]

But the war grew steadily more disturbing for Tante, her agitation culminating in May 1918, when she discovered that she was not a United States citizen. Leopold, on application, had been granted a citizenship on May 13, 1880, and the grant had included his wife and minor children, as all the children then were, but not his sister-in-law. Margaret wrote to her daughter Alice, "Poor Tante! I think she may have to register as an enemy alien. When she first came to this country, before suffrage or anything like suffrage was agitated, the idea of women getting out citizenship papers was never thought of, so she never took hers out." There seemed a possibility that she would be forbidden to live near a seacoast or might even be interned.[11]

Fortunately, she had Walter and Frank, with their connections, to work on her behalf, and by midwinter she was a citizen. Walter and Margaret gave a family party to celebrate, in the midst of which the phone supposedly rang. Margaret loudly sent Walter to answer, and he came back, radiant, saying in an excited, amazed voice that the President wanted personally to congratulate Tante and welcome her as a citizen. For a long moment she believed Walter and became very excited, then joined in the laughter. But the prior distress had been real.[12]

For the winter of 1916–17 Larry Seymour with two friends joined the Princeton-in-Peking program and went to the University of Peking, where he taught the English language and a course on American literature. While he was there, on Good Friday, April 6, the United States formally declared war on Germany, and Larry, like many others in Asia, hurried to find a berth on a ship for home. He and his friends managed to book passage on the *Siberia Maru,* a Japanese liner of 11,814 tons, sailing out of Shanghai. Aboard was a mixture of Russians, Chinese, Japanese and Americans, and among the last, a considerable number of sons of missionaries and businessmen.

The weather was hot, the small ship hotter still, so when the ship's crew erected a canvas swimming pool on the deck, it became a center of the passengers' daily life. Around it there was always a great deal of horseplay by the boys and younger men. After a day or two Larry noticed that the fooling had changed in character and that the butt of it was a silent, very thin Russian of about sixteen, who not only was unable to speak English fluently but seemed unable to cope with his fellows in any of the usual boyish ways.

Finally one day Larry told the chief persecutors, missionaries' sons, to stop it, and announced that he would back his edict with his fists and those of his two friends. The Russian, from then on, was let alone.

The next day the boy's father sought out Larry in the smoking salon and introduced himself, Ruvim Heifetz, father of Jascha. After expressing his thanks he said emotionally, "This boy is not usual. In his hands he has God's gift for the violin. He has already played before many of the best audiences in Europe." And he went on to talk of Heifetz's coming debut in America, a recital in New York at Carnegie Hall on October 27, 1917, followed by performances with the New York Symphony and Walter Damrosch.

"My uncle," said Larry.

Every day young Heifetz practiced for two hours in his stateroom while his father, a professional violinist and his first teacher, stood outside listening, smiling or sometimes looking grave. Besides the father and son, the family aboard included a mother and two daughters.

On arriving home, Larry told his mother of the extraordinary young violinist about to blaze across the musical sky, and Ellie bought tickets for them to Heifetz's second solo recital on December 1, 1917, in Carnegie Hall. By then besides his recital debut he had played Bruch's Concerto in D Minor twice with Walter and the New York Symphony, and his artistry was proclaimed. Every seat was sold, including those placed on the stage. Using a Tononi violin (he had not yet acquired the Guarnerius del Gesù, of which he later became so fond), he played a program of Handel's *Sonata in D Major, No. 4,* Saint-Saëns's Concerto No. 3 (an oddity, played without orchestra), Bach's *Chaconne* and Wieniawski's *Polonaise.*

After the endless encores Larry and Ellie went back to the green room, where hundreds were waiting to greet the new idol. After a time the elder Heifetz saw Larry in line and with a joyful smile of recognition came to take him and his mother directly to Jascha. A representative of a recording company was talking about a contract, but when he was through, the Seymours stepped up, chattered their congratulations, and Larry in closing said, "Not like the *Siberia Maru,* Jascha!" To which the violinist, with a shy, sad smile, murmured, "No." [13]

Even while the United States was still neutral, many of the war's effects were felt among the country's serious musicians, most of whom were Germans or of German heritage and whose sympathies often lay with the German and Austro-Hungarian empires. In the New York Symphony, besides the preponderant Germans, Walter had men of twelve other nationalities, with all the warring states represented; and in the autumn of 1914 he gave his men a talk, suggesting that the tours in particular, where they were forced into close companionship, might be difficult, but as artists gaining their living in the United States their duties were to their art, to the orchestra and to their families, whom they were supporting in honorable fashion. For the good of all, he urged, they must keep their political differences in check.

The men tried to live by this rule, and with regard to the music there was never any trouble. Frenchmen played Beethoven or Wagner with the same care and enthusiasm they brought to Berlioz or Saint-Saëns, and the same, in reverse, was true of the Germans. Personal relations, however, were more difficult, veering sometimes from banter to abuse. The leader of the second violins was a Prussian-born United States citizen who combed the tips of his blond mustache upward. After a concert in Toronto his colleagues accused him of turning the ends down for the Canadian audience. He at first denied it absolutely. Then, though confessing that he had turned down the tip on the audience's side, he insisted that he had kept the inner one defiantly upward. But there was no good humor in Omaha when a double-bass player, on hearing that the *Lusitania* had been torpedoed, announced, "We Germans are going to celebrate tonight."[14]

Walter, aided by Margaret, who continually sent him books and articles, tried to ferret truth out of the claims of the opposing sides. Early in 1916, in the midst of reading Friedrich von Bernhardi's *Germany and the Next War* (1912), a book widely publicized by the Allies as an example of German ambition and amorality, he wrote to Margaret that, though Bernhardi did not believe in any power of justice more potent than the armed power of the state, such a power "must come because based on justice and not on force, and no cynical estimate of the general depravity of human nations can prevent us from working for such an ideal."[15]

Writing again to Margaret, still on Bernhardi, he concluded, "Of course his conception of the state is to an American mind monstrous and menacing, and if comes to a fight it may be over that radical difference between us." Meanwhile, to avoid becoming "infected with the *War Mania*," he wanted the United States to have universal military training, armed neutrality and no restrictions on future actions.[16]

But as the war continued, touring became more difficult. Canada forbade entry to any musician who was still a German citizen, and Walter had to plead with the authorities and offer personal guarantees for several of his men whose applications to the United States had not yet been granted. Other orchestras were less fortunate or their leaders less persistent, for the New York Symphony was the only American orchestra to play in Toronto and Montreal during the war.[17]

With impromptu speeches to audiences and careful statements to the press, Walter worked hard to maintain his own and his orchestra's favorable image with the public. At a concert in Carnegie Hall, in February 1917, after leading the *Star Spangled Banner*, he assured the audience that "our national anthem symbolizes to us the country we love, the United States of America. Some of us were born in the nations now at war, but whether we were born here or thousands of miles away, this is the country of our choice."[18]

But within the orchestra, as the months passed, the men's tempers frayed. That same month, in Cleveland, with the United States' declaration of war still two months in the future, Walter again lectured his men — on gum-chewing at rehearsal, grumbling because rehearsals were called and "on their patriotic duties towards the country in which they made their living." The Germans in the orchestra had objected to being made to play *America* so often, "as if we were an American orchestra." Walter told them, "That is just what we are." [19]

Then in April 1917 the United States entered the war, and the German musicians who were not citizens became enemy aliens. The problems this posed for the country's orchestras, opera companies and choral societies might have been solved in some sensible fashion, if the war hysteria that Walter and others feared had not swept across the country like a fire storm. Overnight, self-proclaimed patriots began to suspect a spy in any German and treason in any citizen with a German background, name or accent. In Chicago Anita McCormick Blaine, though she loved her sister-in-law's German-born husband, as early as August 1915 had refused to hire a gardener in part because he was of German origin, and after war was declared, she felt it her "stern duty" to advise President Wilson that two of the McCormick family friends might be spies. [20]

Unfortunately, many of the country's leaders, instead of cooling such passions, fanned them. Chief among these was former President Theodore Roosevelt. In speech after speech throughout the German-American centers of the Midwest he excoriated divided allegiance, which he defined to include almost any sympathy for anything German. He wanted the abolition of the German courses in public schools; loyalty oaths for teachers, with dismissal of any who refused them; and a requirement that German-language newspapers be compelled gradually to publish in English. He approved the indictment of the Milwaukee Socialist and pro-German Victor Berger, and regretted that several others were not given the same treatment. When race riots against German-Americans broke out in East St. Louis in the summer of 1917, he denounced the rioters, and when in the spring of 1918 a German alien was lynched in Collinsville, Illinois, he denounced the lynchers. But hardly a man did more than he to create the climate that nurtured such events. [21]

Another like him was Elihu Root, who had been secretary of war under McKinley and Roosevelt (1899–1904), secretary of state under Roosevelt (1905–09), U.S. senator from New York (1909–15), and a recipient of the Nobel Peace Prize (1913). He believed every word of Britain's dishonest reports on German atrocities, and in a speech at Carnegie Hall proclaimed, "It is a war between Odin and Christ." Like Roosevelt, he urged that every effort be made "to discourage the common use of German by any part of our population." To say "Tante" instead of "Aunt" was to give aid and comfort to the enemy. His constant theme was "The Boche are as cunning and tricky as they are gross and brutal." A week after the Armistice he announced, from the pulpit of the Cathedral of St. John the Divine, "God Himself was on our side." [22]

With such examples in high places, many in the country misconstrued patriotism, and the pressure they put on the leaders of the musical world — conductors, trustees, committee members — was often more than these could withstand. At the Metropolitan Opera the board of directors, after a series of statements that they would continue to produce Wagner, suddenly announced, a week before the season's opening on November 12, 1917, that German operas would be dropped "lest Germany should make capital of their continued appearance." Another reason given was pressure from subscribers. At least five soloists were dismissed because they were enemy aliens, and also several members of the chorus, two of whom attempted to forestall dismissal by americanizing their names.[23]

Fritz Kreisler, a violinist and a former officer in the Austrian army, found his concerts and recitals frequently picketed or boycotted or suddenly canceled. In the first two months of the war he had fought on the Russian front, been wounded and discharged, and returned to the United States, his wife's country, in November 1914. Soon after the protests began he announced that he would not play for personal gain, only for charity; but in 1918, slandered, libeled, threatened with violence, he announced that until the war's end he would withdraw from all public performance. Walter publicly approved of the decision.

Among the orchestras, because the numbers involved were greater and the tours more easily disrupted, the furor created still greater havoc. In Chicago, though the symphony's organist was fired because he refused to stop speaking German, the situation was handled relatively sensibly. In August 1918, the conductor Frederick Stock, not yet a citizen, though his application had been started in 1916, was allowed to resign, stay in the city and watch over the orchestra. The following winter, after the war's end and after he became a citizen, he was rehired, and the orchestra's continuity was not broken. But elsewhere the patriots were less easily satisfied. They seemed to seek confrontations, as if hoping to humiliate every German in the country, to goad each into some statement or action that could be construed as disloyal. At Pittsburgh the orchestra's association, which controlled the hall, suddenly banned all German music, and the visiting Cincinnati Symphony had to cancel a concert. The Philadelphia Orchestra, with more time to rehearse, substituted Tchaikovsky for Beethoven. At the New York Philharmonic its president, Oswald Garrison Villard, though native-born, was forced to resign because he was a pacifist; and a member of the society's executive committee, Mrs. William Jay, started a campaign to ban all German music. At Cincinnati the orchestra's conductor of five years, Ernst Kunwald, an Austrian, was accused of engaging in enemy propaganda, was arrested, interned and ultimately deported.

At Boston, Karl Muck, technically a Swiss citizen but thoroughly pro-

German, was accused of spying and, in an incident turned by reporters and patriots into a sensation, of disrespect to the national anthem. Muck had arrived in Providence to conduct a concert and suddenly had been presented by the local sponsors with the demand that he lead the orchestra in the *Star Spangled Banner*. Though the orchestra had played the anthem regularly at its "Pop" concerts, these were not conducted by Muck, and he had not rehearsed the piece. He refused, and issued a statement that "it would be a gross mistake, a violation of artistic taste and principles for such an organization as ours to play patriotic airs. Does the public think that the Symphony Orchestra is a military band or ballroom orchestra?" [24]

A reporter from the *New York Herald*, knowing the statement was about to appear in rival papers, inveigled Walter into issuing a counterstatement, published the same day. Walter called Muck "cowardly" because he was hiding behind art, rather than stating honestly that, as "a loyal citizen of Germany," he would rather not conduct the anthem. The following day the critic for the *Times*, Richard Aldrich, observed: "We think that Mr. Walter Damrosch is nearer right in saying that he did not wish to hear Dr. Muck conduct our national anthem, feeling as he does and must necessarily feel about the war, than Col. [Theodore] Roosevelt, who declared that Dr. Muck should be locked up if he refused to." [25]

Meanwhile Muck had begun to conduct the anthem at all his concerts, but the patriots, stirred up by the newspapers, refused to accept any conciliatory gestures or explanations of what had happened in Providence. Now Muck's tempos with the anthem were judged disrespectful, or the arrangement used, or the fact that at its conclusion he did not turn to the audience and smile.

Walter, for his part, would have been wiser not to have responded to the reporter's blandishment, for he now was cast as the "good" German against the "bad," and his correspondence on the issue increased. And doubtless there were some who thought his patriotism, which grew more shrill as he had to defend himself and his position, was partly the desire to injure a competitor. That was not so, but it was a fact that Walter, the New York Symphony and other conductors and orchestras all would gain by the destruction of Muck and the Boston Symphony.

Soon the patriots had succeeded in building a roster of eight tour cities — Brooklyn; Cleveland; Baltimore; Springfield, Massachusetts; Detroit; Washington; Pittsburgh; Providence — that by ordinance or threat of violence refused to allow Muck to conduct. In the spring of 1918 he was arrested, though on grounds never made public, interned and, after the war, deported. Some thirty members of the orchestra, because they were German, were discharged, and Higginson, now eighty-three, weary and perplexed, saw his life's work wrecked. The Boston Symphony Orchestra, which had always had been led by German or Austrian conductors, had been from 1898 to 1917, under Wilhelm Gericke, Artur Nikisch and Muck, possibly the greatest German orchestra in the world.

Among some musicians, at least, behind the patriotism lay self-interest, and in *Musical America* the editor deplored the "almost delirious exultation on the part of the English, French, Italian, Russian musicians here, many of whom seem to feel they will get a fair show now that the stranglehold which they claim the Germans have always had on our musical life has been lessened, if not removed." [26]

Walter and the New York Symphony came through better than most. He was, among the leading conductors, the closest to native-born. He could speak English fluently and with great charm, and at concert after concert he spoke. He was married to James G. Blaine's daughter, so Margaret's political and social contacts helped to protect him, and he was insulated from financial pressures by the generosity of Flagler, who now was prepared to cover any of the orchestra's deficits. Yet even Walter was not without his troubles. [27]

Though *Musical America* in December 1917 appraised his behavior favorably, the judgment was phrased rather ambiguously, and in November 1918 *The Chronicle* scolded him for scheduling too much German music. But his worst experience came in the summer of 1918. [28]

Sent abroad in June to organize an orchestra of elderly, unemployed French musicians to play at American army camps, a way of combining aid to the musicians with entertainment for the soldiers, he was required as a civilian to be under the auspices of some welfare organization. To that end he enlisted in the entertainment division of the Young Men's Christian Association, and obtained as an endorsement an enthusiastic letter of recommendation from Theodore Roosevelt.

All details had been worked out with the French government, the U.S. Army and the musicians, and Walter was in Paris, ready to lead the orchestra's opening concert, when the YMCA balked. It would not issue a permit to travel in France to anyone born in Germany, regardless of United States citizenship. The impasse eventually was broken, but not before Walter's German birth — his less than full Americanism — had been thrown in his face again and again by YMCA officials, even to the point of their finding him unworthy to wear their uniform or insignia. In his autobiography Walter sputters for pages in his indignation, and even ten years later, in a "Profile" in *The New Yorker,* his feelings had no cooled. His loyalty had been impugned. [29]

But Walter and Tante were not the only family members to have trouble during the war. Walter's daughter Alice, stationed at Brest with the YMCA, seemed likely for a time to have her passport lifted and withheld. Evidently in her fashion, which was forthright, she had said something that others construed as pro-German, and a report went to the Department of State. Her remarks are not known, but there was an investigation, and she was cleared. Apparently, too, complaints were made to the government about Frank's loyalty.[30] He was on record as describing the *Star Spangled Banner* as "a bad poem squeezed into a drinking song," and he firmly opposed Mrs. Jay's efforts to ban all German music, even that of dead composers. To the editor of *The Chronicle,* who had published her plea and asked his view of it, Frank replied, "I refuse to believe that the American people are so unintelligent as to be unable to distinguish between the German militaristic government and Beethoven's music . . . Nor will [Germany] be defeated by the persecution of harmless German artists." Fortunately for the Damrosches, they were too well established to be forced from their posts, but their children remember the war as an unhappy time in which their elders' loyalty to the country constantly was questioned.[31]

In the history of serious music in the United States the war and the Russian Revolution, which accompanied it, are important divides. Under their pressures many changes that might have come more slowly were forced. In 1912, when Leopold Stokowski took over the Philadelphia Orchestra, all rehearsals were conducted in German. Though he thought the custom "ridiculous," he continued it. Some time during the war, the Philadelphia, the New York Symphony and probably most of the other leading orchestras shifted to English. In 1918 the New York Philharmonic changed the title of the first violinist from concertmeister to concertmaster.[32]

The pressure to drop all German music at times was very great. Walter's policy, which the Philharmonic shared, despite the efforts of Mrs. Jay, was to play the works of dead composers, who could not receive royalties. Thus, Beethoven, but not Richard Strauss. As he explained to a minister who had written to him, "Bach, Beethoven, Mozart, Mendelssohn, Brahms . . . belong to the world at large and [their works] were created at a time when Germany had not become brutalized and Prussianized by the lust for material gain and power." About Wagner, he was less staunch. He argued that Wagner "has been wrongly put up as an exponent of modern Germany just because, unfortunately, the German High Command used characters from his operas in naming their line of defense, such as Wotan line, Siegfried line . . . Actually, the philosophy of Wagner's Nibelung Trilogy is a complete condemnation of the reign of force and the lust for gold. Both are destroyed in the final drama of the *Twilight of the Gods* and give way to a new religion of self-sacrifice through love." Nevertheless, he restricted himself to instrumental excerpts from the operas and would perform other German vocal works only in translation. Ultimately, at the Metropolitan Opera, Wagner re-entered the repertory first in English, with *Parsifal,* in 1920, and then with *Tristan,* in German, in 1921–22.[33]

The ban against living German and Austrian composers accompanied a sharp drop in the percentage of the repertory held by all German–Austrian composers from 65 percent to 40 percent. Though after the war the percentage rose again, it soon settled at about 50 percent. This change in repertory probably was inevitable, just as the preponderance of German players in time would have decreased, but the war hastened both and injected into the musical world an animosity against Germans and German art that lingered. Walter defensively began his autobiography, published in 1923, "I am an American musician," and wrote in it, with a notable lack of humor, compassion or even, on some points, accuracy, another attack on Muck. And the following year the New York Symphony still thought it wise to state in a publicity release that of its hundred men, forty were American-born; seventy-two, full citizens; twenty-eight had completed their "first papers"; and all the Symphony's rehearsals were conducted in English.[34]

Years later some of Walter's admirers, including several of his nieces, said that during the war period and thereafter Walter's Americanism had been applied consciously and rather too stridently. He himself, on his seventieth birthday, in 1932, tried to confess in an interview with the *Times* that "this psychosis of war got me as it did millions of my fellow citizens. Of some of it I am today heartily ashamed." But he did not specify just where he felt he had fallen short of his ideal, and for whatever reason the newspaper cut the paragraph.[35]

Part of the new repertory that came into favor was Russian, reflecting the great exodus of Russian musicians who emigrated after the Revolution. Heifetz, though not a refugee, decided not to return home and was one of the first of the many Russians who settled here and had a continuing role in the music of the country: men such as Nathan Milstein, Sergei Rachmaninoff, Serge Koussevitzky and Leopold Auer. Though the Russians contributed little to the country's vocal tradition, they helped to create new standards of instrumental technique and to break down the old prejudice that the only good music, even the only good musician, was German. Those of German heritage, however, though they shifted to make room for others, did not go away and in the schools especially, where the Damrosches were well established, they continued to have a strong hand in the history of serious music in the United States. Nevertheless, an era had come to an end, an era beginning in the 1850s with the immigration to the country of many German musicians and lasting until 1917. For Germans and those of German background, despite personal animosities, it had been a cosy world in which they all had shared the same premises. The new musical world would be more eclectic and in many ways for practicing musicians increasingly difficult.

PART IV

Postwar Difficulties and Adjustments

CHAPTER 22

The war ends the Musical Art Society and the People's Choral Union. Changes in the family. Rise of anti-Semitism. Walter takes the New York Symphony on the first tour to Europe of an American orchestra.

WITHIN THE FAMILY and its projects some of the changes caused by the war were direct and obvious; others, more mysterious. One of the latter, reflecting a change of taste in the new decade, was the demise of Frank's Musical Art Society. After its founding, in November 1893, it had flourished steadily for twenty-five years, giving two concerts each winter in Carnegie Hall and presenting primarily the unaccompanied choral works of the sixteenth and seventeenth centuries. Then, in the spring of 1918, because Frank was giving considerable time to the U.S. Army's Bandmasters' School, he postponed the twenty-sixth season. When held, in 1919–20, it was as artistically successful as ever, but the year's gap and the changed times evidently had weakened the society's hold on its public. The audiences were sparser, their financial contributions smaller, and in the midst of the society's fund drive its enthusiastic president, Eugene Delano, died. As Frank later explained to Randall Thompson, "Something got hold of the people. They did not seem to be the same kind of people. They did not like the same sort of thing. We felt that the time had come when we couldn't carry on with the same high quality as before, so it was dropped." [1]

Twenty-six seasons, however, were not without influence on a generation and a half of musicians. Frank had been the first in the country to revive *a cappella* music on a large scale, and never again in the United States would it be as unknown and unsung as in the years before he brought the Musical Art Society into being. In a sense, his work was done.

Another disappointment, though perhaps less severe because he no longer was involved directly, was the failure of the People's Choral Union and its Singing Classes to survive the disruptions of the war. The Choral Union's last concert, with 350 members singing and the New York Symphony playing, took place on February 22, 1917, in the Great Hall of City College. The occasion marked the organization's twenty-fifth anniversary, and for it Frank returned to conduct several of the shorter pieces. Then came the U.S. declaration of war against Germany, the Selective Service Act and the consequent breakup of the mixed choruses. After the war's end the citywide organization, built on volunteers, did not revive.[2]

But twenty-five years is a long time for any musical organization to survive as a voluntary association. In music, generally, for any organization to outlast the enthusiasm of its founders, usually no more than ten or fifteen years, it must encase itself in some kind of corporate structure, even though by so doing it introduces into its daily life struggles for corporate power that often are antagonistic to its musical aims. The People's Choral Union and Singing Classes had remained remarkably true to their original structure of voluntary self-help and were an outstanding expression of one generation's idealism; to the next, probably, the concepts seemed quaint, and the energies of the young and middle-aged went elsewhere.

Frank, on his first birthday in the new decade, June 22, 1920, was sixty-one, and with his hair, mustache and neatly trimmed beard now fully white, he was the image of the kindly, stern grandfather who with quiet voice and quiet manner sets the standards for life and art. In his remaining years, until retirement, he would give all his attention to his third great project, his school, the Institute of Musical Art. His work there would continue to keep his name before musicians and students, but his performing career as conductor and musical director was over; he would be less in the public eye. Slowly, in the way of the world, people outside his chosen field would begin to forget him, but he cared not at all. He never had sought celebrity; only good work to do, and to do it well.[3]

Like Frank, Clara and David Mannes after the war focused their attention on their school, which in November 1919 moved into its present building, at 157 East 74th Street. The painters were slow in finishing, and classes for a time were held in studios around the city, but on February 7, 1920, the new building, which was three brownstone houses remodeled into a single, faintly Classical façade, at last was dedicated. Walter Damrosch and Lyman Abbott, editor of *The Outlook,* spoke; Yvette Guilbert sang some French songs; and Clara and David played an adagio from a Beethoven violin sonata.[4]

The final year in which they had toured as a piano-violin duo was 1916–17, the first year of the school; and probably by the mid-1920s to perceptive ears their skill was beginning to fail, particularly David's. Unlike Fritz Kreisler, whose technique was so natural that he could perform publicly with almost no rehearsal or daily practice, David's technique had been a triumph of will over late and faulty training, and as he ceased daily practice for recitals, his tone became thin and wandered slightly from pitch. For Clara the fall-off in technique was both slower and less severe, but her touch became heavier, and with Chopin, for example, runs up the scale began to end a little too definitely, preventing imagination from carrying them farther. Those who heard Clara and David for the first time in the 1920s may have wondered at reports of others who had heard them twenty years before and had wept over the beauty of their playing.[5]

For Clara the school became totally absorbing. She was a good administrator, excellent at dealing with committees, trustees and potential patrons, and because of her the school, though always poor, survived. She was less good with students, but there David was strong; and together, through their wide acquaintance and charm, they successfully brought to their faculty, year after year, outstanding men and women. Possibly the greatest teacher of composition in the country between the wars was Rosario Scalero, brought from Rome by David and Clara; and he taught at the Mannes School for nine years before being lured by a fourfold increase in salary to the Curtis Institute of Music, in Philadelphia. That pattern often recurred.[6]

For David, however, the school was not all of his musical life, for along with it he developed a small but important career as a conductor. In 1906 he had led a concert of the New York Symphony at a private reception at the Metropolitan Museum of Art, and from time to time he conducted other concerts at the museum for its members and guests, generally with a small pickup orchestra of fifty-four. Then in February 1918, Edward S. Harkness, a trustee of the museum, underwrote two public concerts in the huge entrance hall, admission free. These were intended as a patriotic gesture, dedicated to the country's soldiers and sailors and, though little advertised, drew an audience of 2707. Some were servicemen; some, young couples; but more were elderly women, apparently poor Polish and Russian Jews, the city's newest immigrants.

David, of course, was delighted with the audience and eager to expand the two Saturday evenings into an annual series. More important, John D. Rockefeller, Jr., and several other trustees were equally enthusiastic, and for the following year a series of eight concerts was announced. The audience totaled 39,071, again many of them elderly and poor, and so began what for the next twenty-eight years, through 1947, would be one of the city's most beloved musical institutions — the Museum Concerts under David Mannes.[7]

Besides being free, the concerts in their format were quite unusual but very much to David's design. The orchestra, which never numbered more than sixty-five, was seated in the north gallery of the entrance hall, invisible to the audience, who sat downstairs, on the stairs, in the side and south galleries and sometimes even in connecting galleries, where they heard the music over loudspeakers. David, standing, was partly visible to a few, but from the first the emphasis was on the music, disembodied, and without any intruding personality, of conductor, orchestra or soloist. In the thirty years that David led the concerts he never scheduled a soloist, though several offered their skills without fee. For the audience the experience apparently was rather like today's listening to music at home. Many of the women brought knitting or sewing; some brought children; and men and women coming straight from work often slept.

David's aim to reach an audience that could not afford the glamour of Carnegie Hall was aided further by the fact that he was not a great interpretive conductor. He made up interesting programs and presented them well, but without individual flair. Indeed, with age — he was fifty-four in 1920 — he seems to have grown more matter of fact about music. At one concert, after a woman had gushed, "I feel as though God had spoken to me," David later complained to the man beside him, "Was it not enough that she felt it was very great and beautiful music? Why must people try to relate music to some act or scene?" But if the concerts did not establish him as the interpretive rival of Stokowski or Toscanini, they did much to confirm the credentials of his school. For despite the end of the Mannes duo, of his individual career as a violinist and of his work with settlement houses, within the city his name retained a strong resonance.[8]

Among the younger generation the war's disruptions were often more abrupt. Walter Wiechmann, Larry Seymour and Walker Blaine Beale, Margaret's nephew who had grown up with her four daughters, all entered the army, received commissions and were sent to France. Walter's tour of duty was uneventful, but Larry's was almost fatal. In February 1918 he was put off the troopship *Agamemnon* at Brest with a case of pneumonia and left to lie on the open dock until transferred to the army hospital. Fortunately, his first cousin Alice, his Uncle Walter's eldest daughter, was stationed at Brest with the YMCA and, alerted by one of Larry's fellow officers, succeeded in having him transferred from the army to the navy hospital, which was far better staffed and equipped. There he slowly recovered, considering ever after that his life had been "saved" by Alice.

To cause an army officer to be transferred from an army to a navy hospital for treatment and convalescence was a remarkable feat, but Alice, who was now twenty-six, had grown into a remarkable woman, a forceful personality whom some admired and others did not. She had been the boss of her sisters and also the best athlete at an age when athletics seemed important. She was used to having her way and causing others to fall in with it. In September 1914, in a country wedding at her family's cottage on Lake Champlain, she had married a mild-mannered architect, Pleasants Pennington, and as the couple, in a canoe, left the cheering wedding guests, Pleasants sat in the center motionless while, in the stern, Alice paddled.

By 1917, though appearances were kept up, the marriage had foundered. Both Alice and Pleasants went to France, but to different stations, and she had begun to take lovers. At the time Larry arrived in Brest she was sleeping with the admiral in command of all its naval forces, and that was how Larry was saved.[9]

Of course all his relatives rejoiced at his good fortune and chattered approvingly of Alice's executive ability: so like her to take charge and do the right thing. Yet her ill-concealed extramarital affairs were disturbing to those who learned of them. They were something quite new among the women of the family. Even if understood to be the product of the loose sexual mores that war always has fostered, they seemed bound to lead to divorce, and that, too, would be something new to the Damrosches.

The family's third army officer, Walker Blaine Beale, was killed by a shell at St.-Mihiel, only two months before the Armistice. He had been James G. Blaine's youngest grandson and the rising political star in the family. To the surviving Blaines, their family sometimes seemed cursed. In the 1890s Blaine had lost in quick succession his daughter Alice and his two political heirs, his sons Walker and Emmons, and now among his grandsons the family lost the two most promising, for only a month after Walker's death, Anita McCormick Blaine's only child, Emmons, died of flu caught when he was working in a shipyard near Philadelphia. For Margaret the double deaths were traumatic, and to her daughter overseas she wrote an extended, perhaps therapeutic account of how she had gone to Philadelphia to help Anita with Emmons, arrived too late and, going to the top of the stairs on the second floor, sat down, "just miserably crying." The following week there was a memorial service in Washington for Walker.[10]

Because Walker had been so closely associated with his Aunt Margaret and Uncle Walter's Christmas parties, helping to organize the charades, acting as the son and brother of the family, they decided never again to give a Christmas party in quite the same way. In the years after the war there was always a party in the Christmas season, with the tree in place, candles lit and perhaps a carol or two, but now it was often after the New Year. Though all the family continued to be invited, its members no longer dominated the event. There were fewer children, many more musical and theatrical people and a more sophisticated atmosphere. One year, for example, the party began on the front step. As the guest rang the bell, the door cracked open, a hand poked out with a glass of liqueur and a mysterious voice ordered, "Drink this." Later there was a gargantuan lunch, served informally by various daughters and other female relatives, all dressed as waitresses. And this always was followed by a partially planned and rehearsed vaudeville at which Walter, who could be endlessly witty on his feet, acted as master of revels.[11]

It was all good fun, but not to everyone's taste. Bess Seymour brought her new husband, Robert Ransom, to several of the parties. He was a quiet-spoken man, an electrical engineer, and according to his wife, "he came, he watched, he talked to a few of the in-laws, and that was it." Marya Mannes, too, had doubts:

> My uncle was always center-stage: charming host and perfect showman, setting the party mood with rousing pianistic flourishes or calls to action. I loved him even when I could not help knowing the diminutions my father suffered from the brighter musical spotlight cast on his brother-in-law, or comparing the dominant values of success that prevailed in this convivial home with the serious questioning of them in our own as standards of worth.[12]

One branch of the family, the Wiechmanns, gradually disappeared from these parties. Ferdi had died on April 24, 1919, but even before then Margaret and Walter often had not included him and Marie in smaller parties in order that these might not be spoiled, in Margaret's words, by "uncongenial elements." Still, for the larger events Marie, her children and their spouses were always included, and also the grandchildren when they became old enough.[13]

Walter Wiechmann had married a Southerner, Ida Jerdone, and except for Tante, whom they saw regularly until her death, in 1928, they and their two sons drifted slowly out of the family. Walter, a lawyer, was bright enough to hold a job for forty years in a good firm, Sullivan & Cromwell, but not forceful enough to amass clients or become a partner. Similarly, in the Damrosch family, perhaps by choice, he left little personal impression.[14]

His sister, Marjorie, was quite different. Not only did she have a unique position as the eldest grandchild of Leopold and Helene and therefore a longer memory than any of her cousins of their grandmother, but she was beautiful. In addition she had a charming daughter, Vivian, and a husband, Robert T. Swaine, whom all the family liked and who was on the way to becoming one of the country's outstanding lawyers and creators of the great law firm Cravath, Swaine & Moore.

Yet Marjorie even more than her mother seemed to lack in her personality some inner discipline, some brake on temperament. As a child she had been known for her tantrums; so, too, as an adult. Only now the fits of ill temper were longer, the shrieks louder, the tears more copious and the effect on others more dismaying. Further, she had developed a prejudice, perhaps adopted from her father, whom she adored, of violent anti-Semitism. It cannot have endeared her to her mother's family.

Before the decade was ended, she and Swaine had divorced and she had married, immediately, an Arizona cowboy, Jack Van Ryder, who became a successful, self-taught artist, working mostly in oils and etchings. He encouraged her to pursue her amateur's interest in sculpting, and after studying under Gutzon Borglum and Edward C. Potter, she began to cast small animal bronzes, which, signed M. Van Ryder, she sold through Gorham's. But before heading west and leaving the Damrosch family forever, she put her mark on New York. Potter, while she was studying with him, had been working on the two lions that sit before the New York Public Library, and she did most of the work on their tails.[15]

Marjorie's anti-Semitism was symptomatic of the decade. In any society in which Jew and Gentile mix, anti-Semitism, and the no less real Jewish prejudice against Gentiles, are always present, however inert. For on either side there are always some persons who will use the expression of distaste, even hatred, of those on the other as a way to define themselves to their own satisfaction. In the years 1900 to 1930, however, there was a continuous rise in the country of a more serious kind of anti-Semitism, and for reasons that are clear.

The first Jews, twenty-three in number, arrived in the country in 1654, and by 1830 they still totaled only six thousand in a population of about thirteen million. In the next fifty years the figures rose to 250,000 in fifty million, or roughly half of 1 percent. Most of these Jews came from German-speaking countries and in their customs, manners and speech were similar to German Protestants. Like German immigrants generally, they spread themselves across the country so that, like New York, Chicago, Cincinnati and San Francisco became major Jewish centers. Their religion they practiced in the new Reform style, with brief, quiet services, often in English and accompanied by choirs and organs, and in 1875 their leaders opened Hebrew Union College in Cincinnati, the first Jewish seminary in the United States. Thus far, anti-Semitism, where it appeared, was an aberration of individuals, not a trend of society.

But in the next forty years, 1880 to 1920, some 2.3 million Jews from Eastern Europe, known collectively as Russian Jews, entered the country, and by the end of the period Jews of all origins in the United States numbered four million in a total population of 106 million, or about 4 percent. Of these, five out of six were Russian Jews, and unlike those from the German countries, their customs, manners and speech were strange to most Americans. For the most part they did not speak German, Polish or even Russian, but Yiddish; they worshiped their God not in the Reform but in the Orthodox style, which, by comparison, seemed foreign and ritualistic; and they did not distribute themselves across the country but settled almost entirely in the Eastern seaports where they landed and in Chicago. In New York City, by 1920, every fourth person was a Jew, often instantly recognizable through manner, dress or accent.

The impact of such a great migration on the few cities where the majority of Jews settled was overwhelming. Not only were large geographical areas taken over, becoming to former residents as alien as foreign countries, but also many institutions. In higher education in New York, for example, City College in the late nineteenth century had enrolled a diverse student body chiefly from those of English, Dutch, German and French descent; by 1920, 85 percent of the students by descent were Russian Jews. The same was true of Hunter College, and at Columbia University the figure was 40 percent. At the lowest end of the cultural scale many of the notorious criminals of the day were Russian Jews. Needless to say, many people in the city, including Jews who had been there for generations, found the problems of such an immigration deeply disturbing, even terrifying.[16]

Further, the Russian Jews brought with them two secular ideologies, Socialism and Zionism, of which the former was the first to reach importance. In 1914 the Socialist party in New York elected a congressman, and in 1917 it gathered 22 percent of the mayoralty vote and elected ten state assemblymen and seven city aldermen. Two years later, though divided by a prolonged public debate on the use of violence to force a change on government, those advocating only nonviolence still managed to elect five assemblymen. But by then the Russian Revolution, in which Eastern European Jews were prominent, had installed a Communist government in Russia, and in the United States a period of fear and hysteria known as "the Red Scare" had begun. At Albany the State Assembly denied the five Socialists their seats and then joined the Senate in a bill outlawing the Socialist party. Anti-Semitism throughout the country increased, and in the Congress pressure mounted to limit immigration from Southern and Eastern Europe. Meanwhile, along the relatively short seaboard from Baltimore to Boston, where some 60 percent of the country's four million Jews were settled, colleges began to impose quotas on Jewish applicants; resorts, hotels and clubs increasingly closed their doors to Jews; and among Gentiles the snide remark, knowing wink and gentlemen's agreement aimed at Jews multiplied.

The situation was particularly hard on the country's Jews of German origin, for they were torn between denying or asserting a kinship with the Russian Jews, with whom in many ways they were unsympathetic. Most of them ultimately acknowledged a special relation to the newcomers and worked hard and with great generosity to aid them. But the decision was not easily reached or permanently resolved, for at bottom were fundamental questions, to be raised in the future by Zionism, about the character of Jewish group identity and the nature of American society.

Until the 1920s such questions had not arisen in the Damrosch family. Though the name was Hebrew in origin, meaning "redheaded," and though the original immigrant, Leopold, was Jewish by blood, his religion had been music and his culture wholly German. He thought of himself as German, and, equally important, so did others. Helene, his wife, was Aryan by blood, German in culture and had professed music as her faith.[17]

Yet the increase of anti-Semitism outside the family eventually caused questions to rise within it. One day at dinner, before guests, one of Walter's daughters asked, "Well, how Jewish are we?" And the family's blood lines and religious practices, or lack of them, were explained. But in the 1920s such a question, asked in a lighthearted manner before strangers, declared how the daughters felt. For them, as for the family generally, anti-Semitism was an academic issue. Whether they considered themselves wholly Gentile or part Jewish, they felt socially secure. Music was too cosmopolitan a field to nourish anti-Semitism, and in the Gentile social world the family was too well established, too much admired, for any discrimination to arise.[18]

Only David Mannes at times would feel the need to reply to pressures put on him because his parents had been Jewish by blood and religion. Ironically, these pressures often came from Jews who charged him with denying his Jewish heritage. How should one judge, if at all, that his son, Leopold, reached the age of twelve before learning of his Jewish descent? Or a comment by Gerald Warburg that David and Clara had been careful always "to keep the Jew from the door"?[19]

To all such remarks, many of which in effect began, "You, as a fellow Jew, ought . . ." David would reply, "I am not a Pole or a German, a Jew or a Gentile; I am an American." And he would be emphatic in saying it, for he intended not to evade an issue but to declare a dominant loyalty. It was not in his nature to remind others that he had volunteered many, many hours of his life to Russian Jews at the Third Street School, but neither would he allow others to define him or to assess his duties. In that respect he was rather like the family into which he had married, and by setting a strong example for his children, he helped them to keep a firm footing in a world in which anti-Semitism now lurked more frequently than before.[20]

In the spring of 1919 Walter received a letter from the Ministre des Beaux Arts in Paris, thanking him and the New York Symphony for their services to French music and inviting them to make a tour of France the following year. Though no direct subsidy was offered, in every other respect the government promised its assistance. In New York, among the Symphony Society's directors the invitation caused a stir, and Henry H. Flagler, who was now the orchestra's chief support, said at once that it must be accepted, for it was the first such invitation from a European country to an American orchestra.

While it probably is a fact that Walter and the Symphony had played more French music than had other American orchestras, and probably had played it better — for besides Walter's sympathy for it, many men in the orchestra were of French origin, including the concertmaster — it is unlikely that the French government by itself would have noted the fact or acted on it. More lay behind the invitation than Walter's repertory.

Throughout the war he had been president of a group, the American Friends of Musicians in France, that had raised money to help French musicians and their families. One of its projects, the one that brought Walter and the YMCA into conflict, had been to organize and underwrite an orchestra of fifty-five French musicians to play, with Walter as conductor, at U.S. Army posts in France. Though the project ultimately had been abandoned because of the difficulties of wartime transport, Walter had led the orchestra in several concerts in Paris, and at one, on July 14, 1918, his soloists had been Nadia Boulanger, organ, Henri Casadesus, viola d'amore, and Alfred Cortot, piano. Among musicians in the audience was Charles Marie Widor, the French organist and composer. Through his war work Walter had landed in the midst of the French musical world, and on both sides respect and liking flourished.[21]

When taking the orchestra on tour had proved impossible, Walter immediately was enlisted by General John J. Pershing, commander of the American forces in France, to improve the army's bands, and Walter had set about founding a Bandmasters' School at Chaumont. He convinced Pershing, however, that the school should teach more than just the notes of American Patrol or Stars and Stripes; what was needed was a solid musical foundation, even if built on a greatly accelerated program. For help in recruiting a faculty of French artists he turned to Henri Casadesus's brother Francis — a single generation in this family produced seven professional musicians — who also became the school's director. So successful was the school that it continued for many months after the war's end, by which time both Francis and Walter were thinking about how it might be transformed into a kind of finishing school at which young American musicians could study with French artists trained in the classrooms of the Paris Conservatoire. Out of their deliberations emerged, on June 25, 1921, the American School of Music at Fontainebleau, which would have an extraordinary influence on the history of American music. Meanwhile, the invitation to the New York Symphony came from the Ministre des Beaux Arts because Walter for the past two years had been in almost daily contact with a host of influential French musicians who had found him to their liking.[22]

By January 1920, when the orchestra's manager, George Engles, left for Europe to make the final arrangements, the tour had expanded to seven weeks, from May 6 to June 20, and to twenty-eight concerts in six countries, France, Monaco, Italy, Belgium, Holland and England. But as the projected costs mounted — the exchange rates were unfavorable, the railroads were still disrupted, strikes threatened — Walter suggested to Flagler that they postpone it a year. Flagler brushed the fears aside. "Now is the psychological moment," he said, and on April 22 the orchestra sailed on the S.S. *Rochambeau* for France.[23]

Walter and Flagler had agreed that they should present to Europe the best in American music, not only in the orchestra but in its soloists and music, and for soloists Walter had selected Albert Spalding, a violinist born in Chicago, and John Powell, a composer and pianist born in Richmond; both, before the war, had toured in Europe. For the music he scheduled a performance in every country of Powell's *Negro Rhapsody for Piano and Orchestra* and often works by Charles Martin Loeffler, who, though not born in the United States, had lived all his adult life there. Ten years later, when Toscanini led the merged Philharmonic-Symphony orchestra abroad, he took no American conductor or soloist and played not one American work.[24]

In addition, whenever possible Walter scheduled works by living composers of the host country. Thus in the three concerts in Paris, besides presenting works by Berlioz, Lalo and Franck, he played d'Indy's *Istar, Variations Symphonique,* Ravel's *Daphnis et Chloe Suite No. 2,* Saint-Saëns's Violin Concerto No. 3 in B Minor, a selection from Fauré's *Pélleas et Mélisande* and another from Ravel's *Ma Mère l'Oye.*[25]

In Brussels, where the people revered the memory of the talented composer Guillaume Lekeu, who had died in 1894, at age twenty-four, he scheduled Lekeu's *Adagio for Strings,* a work of tender melancholy, and the performance evidently touched the audience deeply, for it would not cease its applause. Finally, Walter took the score from the conductor's stand and raised it high to suggest that the applause was homage to the composer, in which he and the orchestra joined. After the concert, as he was preparing to leave the theater, two ladies brought forward an elderly gentleman and introduced him as Lekeu's father, but when the old man tried to express his thanks, he burst into tears.[26]

All tours in their triumphs are much alike: the standing ovations, the dignitaries at the receptions, the practical jokes of pranksters in the orchestra and, later, the scrapbooks of favorable reviews. More interesting, when they can be found, are the moments of puzzlement, the moments in which the orchestra and conductor failed to carry the audience with them, either at first or ultimately.

In Paris, curiously, it was not Walter's way with French music that astonished people, except that he and the orchestra were so good at it, but his conducting of Beethoven. At the opening concert in the *Eroica,* Symphony No. 3, he evidently used more shading of tempo than the French were used to, and there were some in the audience who did not like it. Later, Vincent d'Indy, in a public letter of welcome to the orchestra, specifically approved it:

> Whether it is classical, romantic or modern music, Damrosch first of all endeavors to set off and illustrate what we call the "melos," the element of expression, the voice that must rise above all other voices of the orchestra. He knows how to distribute the agogic action, the dynamic power, and he is not afraid — even in Beethoven's works and in spite of the surprise this caused to our public — to accelerate or slacken the movement when the necessities of expression demand it. And so it is that Walter Damrosch and his orchestra give us true emotions of art.[27]

Others, in Amsterdam and London, made the same point. Evidently in Europe at the time most conductors of Beethoven varied the tempos less.

There was the same hesitation to accept the orchestra's unanimity of bowing, an attitude that had surprised Walter when he conducted a concert in London in 1888. Though everyone admired the precision of the orchestra's strings, several critics, speaking presumably for at least a part of the audience, wondered if such precision had not cost a certain spontaneity that came from individual bowing. Walter, while acknowledging that "a good conductor must guard himself from the temptation to make a god out of technic," felt that "proper phrasing can only be secured if the sixteen first violins, for instance, who have to play a phrase in unison, play as one." But on the whole the precision gained was admired more than any loss, real or imagined, was regretted; and today most conductors require uniform bowing.[28]

Then there were the jokes, or what Walter took as jokes. Though most reviewers found the orchestra's sonority full, rich and mellow, one in Bordeaux complained that it played "with that dryness characteristic of all North Americans." Walter, noting the town's position in the wine industry, took the remark as disapproval of the U.S. Constitution's recent Prohibition Amendment.[29]

In London, he and the orchestra had a remarkable failure, though with only one man. That man, however, was Ernest Newman, critic for the *Sunday Times* and fast becoming England's leading critic. He wrote:

> Mr. Damrosch's *Eroica* I found for the most part simply irritating, in spite of the superb work of the orchestra . . . Mr. Damrosch's arbitrary hastening of this theme and drawing out of that became a terrifying obsession long before the first movement was over . . . This sort of thing is not genuine rubato, the giving an air of greater naturalness to the melody by a subtle holding back here and pushing forward there: it is merely an unnatural distortion of the plain features of the melody.[30]

At a later concert, Newman reviewed Walter's playing of Elgar's Symphony No. 1. Exclusive of French music, Elgar's works probably were Walter's favorite among those of living composers, and Walter had conducted the U.S. première of both the Symphony No. 1, on January 3, 1909, and the *Falstaff, Symphonic Study,* on December 12, 1913. Frank Damrosch with the Oratorio Society had led the U.S. premières of Elgar's cantatas *The Dream of Gerontius* and *The Apostles.* Elgar himself later came to New York to lead the society in *The Apostles* and *The Kingdom,* and his music, including several shorter works, had won an admiring audience. Relations between the composer and the family were friendly, and Walter had heard Elgar conducting his own works.[31]

After he and the orchestra, in an afternoon concert at Queen's Hall, finished the symphony, there was, as in Brussels, tremendous and unceasing applause; so Walter, as he later that night happily wrote to Elgar, had held up the score and pointed to it "to show to whom the real tribute was due."[32]

But the next day in the *Sunday Times,* Newman wrote as a news item, in addition to reports in his regular column:

> For one thing, at any rate, I am grateful [to the visitors] . . . I had always wondered why Elgar was disliked and despised in New York. Now I know, and knowing, I wish to apologize to the Americans. I had thought them amazingly lacking in taste; now I see that it was the excellence of their taste that made them reject such an Elgar as Mr. Damrosch and his orchestra has [*sic*] presumably been giving them.
>
> If Elgar really were the pompous dullard he was made to appear yesterday afternoon we should be of the same opinion as the New Yorkers with regard to him. But the thing, so far as I heard it (I fled at the end of the third movement, unable to endure any more), was the merest burlesque of Elgar — none the less a burlesque because Mr. Damrosch's intentions were evidently of the best. The trouble is simply that he has no imagination, no insight into Elgar.

I would not have missed this experience for anything. If any one had told me that a work I know virtually by heart could be played in such a way that at times (I do not exaggerate) I could not recognise it, I should have smiled in his face. Yet yesterday the miracle was performed. The tempi were wrong, the rubati were senseless, there was hardly a trace of imaginative insight into the world of beautiful and vital thought in which the symphony lives: it was all noise and false emphasis, and of a dullness that made it impossible for some of us to sit it out.

The playing of the orchestra was coarse and unimaginative; it sounded throughout like a second-rate organisation. Mr. Damrosch's methods, indeed, are calculated to destroy the spontaneity of any orchestra. He draws each melodic contour for it in such rigid lines, and with such abrupt angularity, that it is not to be wondered at that the men play stiffly. The whole thing was the orchestral equivalent of a pianola badly played.[33]

No other critic seems to have agreed with him, and the next day the reviewer for the *Daily Telegraph* answered him point for point. And plainly the audience in Queen's Hall had enjoyed what it heard. What happened to Newman?

The most likely explanation seems to be that an extremely passionate man — he had been born William Roberts but wrote criticism as Ernest Newman, because about music he was "a new man in earnest" — who had written a book on Elgar and probably thought he knew more about the music than anyone else, came up against a genuinely different interpretation of it, and he took offense, personal offense, and lost his balance. This perhaps was easier to do then than now, though critical self-esteem is no less strong today; but then, before radio, tapes and recordings carried musical interpretations back and forth across the Atlantic, it was possible for American and English traditions of playing a composer, even Beethoven, to develop quite differently. Then the revelation and assertion of a different point of view doubtless was a shock. Today, however, interpretive traditions around the world are more similar; and foreign tours for orchestras, less risky critically, and for audiences, less exciting.

Newman's review may have had sad consequences. Walter, presumably, preferred to forget it and does not mention it in his autobiography, though of course his old enemy Finck of the *Evening Post* picked it up and rebroadcast it. But its venom apparently hurt Walter deeply, deeply enough to have cost him his confidence, for the fact is that he, who up to now had been one of Elgar's champions, though continuing to praise Elgar as one of the greatest of early twentieth-century composers and continuing to schedule Elgar's works for guest conductors with the New York Symphony, himself never again conducted an Elgar work.[34]

Performers, it seems, not critics, are the ones who advance music, whether new or old. For it is the performer, like Frank with his Musical Art Society, who makes the real commitment: learns the music, hires the hall and runs the critical and financial risks. Harold Bauer the pianist once wrote: "I have never been able to see in what way music critics have contributed to cultural progress; although on the other hand, there is no denying that their writings have frequently delayed it." Newman's piece, if it did lead Walter to give up conducting Elgar, by injuring Elgar can serve as example of Bauer's dictum.[35]

But Walter was never one to brood on real or fancied injuries, and in any event the tour plainly had been a great success. Beyond the official honors heaped on the orchestra, soloists and conductor, their chief aims had been achieved: European music lovers in the thousands had been alerted to the excellence of an American orchestra, and some interest had been stirred in American composers. In a more parochial sense, the tour strengthened the orchestra's morale and enhanced its reputation throughout the United States as one of the country's best; some would say, with the Boston orchestra temporarily in disarray, the best.

For Walter, it also cemented his good relations with French artists at a time when French music was increasingly to the fore. In the next few years Saint-Saëns would write two songs for him to include in a songbook for American schoolchildren, d'Indy would come to New York to conduct the Symphony, and Boulanger would become one of the outstanding teachers at the American School at Fontainebleau — all pleasant associations in the world of music.

During the war Walter had discovered that he loved Paris, and when there he always stayed in the Hôtel France et Choiseul in the Rue St. Honoré. So when in 1920 his second daughter, Gretchen, wished to marry a Philadelphia lawyer, Thomas Finletter, Walter suggested that they marry in Paris, at the end of the tour, and he would give the reception at the hotel.

All his musical friends came — Boulanger, Cortot, the Casadesuses and even the portly, genial but sometimes crusty Saint-Saëns, who at eighty-five was the reigning patriarch of French music.

Arriving at the buffet, Saint-Saëns said, "I am thirsty."

"Here is some champange," said Henri Casadesus.

"No, that is too cold."

"Well, here is some chocolate."

"Too hot."

Whereupon Saint-Saëns poured one into the other and drank the mixture with relish.

Walter loved every moment of it.[36]

CHAPTER 23

Rise of the third generation. Leopold Mannes at Riverdale and Harvard. Leopold Godowsky, Jr., and Randall Thompson. Color photography. Helen and John Tee Van. Marya Mannes, London and marriage with Jo Mielziner.

IN THE SPRING OF 1920 Leopold Damrosch Mannes graduated from Harvard College, having finished the four-year course in three[1] and having set firmly in progress the two great interests of his life, photography and music. He had also formed friendships with two men that would last his life: Leopold Godowsky, Jr., with whom he later would discover the Kodachrome process, the key to practical color photography; and Randall Thompson, the composer, with whom for many years he shared his hopes and fears as a musician.

It is remarkable that in this third generation of the Damrosch family all the boys went to college and completed the course for a degree, which none of their fathers or uncles, with the exception of Ferdi Wiechmann, had done. The gap in formal education, for the men at least, that had opened because of the grandfather Damrosch's decision to abandon medicine for music, and his subsequent poverty and immigration, was closed quickly. Evidently the family's image of itself included — perhaps a bourgeois trait — the expectation of a formal education.

Before going to Harvard, Leopold for five years had attended the Riverdale Country School, just across the Harlem River, in the northwest corner of the Bronx. Every school morning he would ride the Seventh Avenue subway to the end of the line, and then either walk the last mile to school, saving the fare for chocolate, or take the trolley on Upper Broadway, bordering Van Cortlandt Park.

Riverdale, founded in 1907 by Frank Hackett, a headmaster aflame with idealism, was a good school academically, with an enrollment in Leopold's time of about seventy-five boys, most of them day students. Many were sons of actors, artists, diplomats or professional people, and to a greater extent than in most schools it was normal to be different, and talent in any line was respected. Leopold, whom his schoolmates called "Dammy," from Damrosch, steadfastly refused to play soccer and in the spring idled his way through baseball, but he regularly played the hymns in the school chapel and composed the music for the school's hymn, *It Is the Spirit,* which still is sung.

In his last year, a boarding boy, Leopold Godowsky, Jr., entered the class below him, and the two quickly became friends. Leo, as Godowsky always was known, was the son of one of the great pianists of the day and a brother of Dagmar Godowsky, who in the next decade became one of the famous vamps of silent films. Though their father, originally Polish, had become a United States citizen in 1891, he gave concerts all over the world, frequently taking his family with him, and until the war had lived mostly in Berlin and Vienna. Leo was an excellent violinist — like Leopold he had chosen a different instrument from his father — was fluent in several languages, but was without experience of team sports, notably soccer. At his first exposure he joined Leopold on the sidelines, watching with disbelief and distaste as their fellow students, in pursuit of a ball, ran about a field, yelling and bumping into each other.

Fortunately the headmaster, Hackett, instead of trying to force the misfits into the mold, allowed their talents to burgeon in other ways.

Excused from soccer, they at first were required to take walks during the athletic period, and one of these followed a class in physics in which the teacher had discussed the practical difficulties of color photography, ending with the remark that someday someone should undertake to solve them. The boys discovered that they both had ideas on the subject, and as they began to talk, Leopold said eagerly, "Don't tell me yours. Let's each write down our own and then compare." The next day, finding their ideas about lenses were much the same, they decided to work them out together, and the partnership was born.[2]

At the school they received permission to use the physics laboratory, and for a "home" laboratory they had the Mannes apartment at 181 West 75th Street, where Clara and David at the time had two adjoining apartments. In the smaller, in which Tante and the two children had their bedrooms, Leopold's was the former dining room, and he and Leo promptly set up the unused kitchen to be their weekend laboratory. Looking around for a darkroom, they persuaded the selfless Tante to give up her clothes closet. The odors from the kitchen laboratory frequently were nauseating, and Clara was aghast at what the chemicals did to her towels. Nevertheless, the boys' enthusiasm was infectious, and so ignorant was everyone about the problems of practical color photography that they all believed the next batch of pictures surely would achieve true color, perfect texture and precise definition.[3]

The school shared in the excitement when Hackett arranged for the boys to give a color show, perhaps the world's first evening of *son et lumière*, for to allow the projector's lights to cool, they alternated the pictures with a piano-violin recital. The photographs, made by the autochrome method and cast on a white wall, required powerful, theater lighting, and the pictures often were "grainy." But the colors were true and exciting to the audience, because, except in the *National Geographic*, most of the students and faculty had never seen a colored photograph, and yet here before them were pictures of local scenes and people, even of themselves. At the best pictures the audience often burst into cheers.[4]

In the spring the boys went to a movie, *Our Navy*, billed as a "color" film and made by a process called bichrome. The colors were poor, orangey-reds and bluish-greens, not even as good as the boys were producing at the school, and their enthusiasm and determination increased. Though at the end of the school year they had not solved any of the larger problems of color photography, they were not in the least discouraged. Leo went with his family to California, and Leopold with his to Maine. There he succeeded with a specially constructed camera in taking a fine color picture of Josef Hofmann, who was himself an inventor and interested in the boys' project. With the Hofmann picture Clara was sure "the millennium had rolled in," but the boys knew better. Over the next few years Leopold at Harvard and Leo at the University of California continued to experiment, reporting regularly to each other, and one summer Leopold joined Leo in Los Angeles. But whether apart or together, their interest and friendship held firm.[5]

At Harvard Leopold for the first time was beyond the support or ken of relatives, and his anxious mother provided him with a daily stamped postcard on which to report his health. He dutifully mailed these but seems not to have had a moment of homesickness, responding at once to the new friends and intellectual stimulus surrounding him. In his three years at the college he worked hard, concentrating in physics while at the same time taking all the advanced courses in music and continuing the photographic experiments. Twice, in Feburary 1918 and 1919, he received permission from the college's administrative board to go to New York "to file patent applications," after assuring the board that the trip would be "for business and nothing else." But despite this strong, extra-curricular interest, he was able to graduate in three years, partly by amassing credits on admission for languages — Latin, French and German — and by passing an oral German requirement in the first six months; thereafter he was free to do extra work in physics and music. But characteristically, it was among the musicians that he found his friends.[6]

There was at the time among the students a music club, and its leaders, on learning of a possible addition in the freshman class, sent down one of their sophomore members, Randall Thompson, to examine the candidate's musical knowledge and skills, including sight-reading at the piano. Sixty years later Thompson still blushed at the memory: "It was a little as if I had asked Heifetz to play the violin." But out of that meeting flowered a friendship, and the two, with another member of the club, William Thayer (Billy) Richards, formed a triumvirate that sat together in classrooms, went to Boston together to the theater and after graduation sometimes studied and traveled together in Italy.

Thompson, the son of a schoolmaster and a mother who was an accomplished pianist, had grown up in music and already was demonstrating a talent for composing, choral music in particular. He would become, in time, one of the country's outstanding choral composers, with success also in instrumental music. Richards, the son of a Nobel Prize winner in chemistry, was himself a chemist and also an excellent cellist. Like Leopold, he seemed destined to combine brilliance in science with music, but somewhere in the years ahead life turned sour for him, and despite every appearance of success he eventually took his life by slitting his wrists. Yet at college and in the years immediately following he was the man of inexhaustible humor who kept others in a state of merriment.

One evening in the spring of 1918 Leopold and Randall went in to Boston to hear an army band on the Common drum up recruits and patriotic spirit. The final piece was a ragtime number, *Indianola,* with a simple theme, often repeated. As the piece, a show-stopper, was encored several times, the young men returned to Cambridge with it ringing in their ears and soon decided to write variations on it for two pianos.

These in their simplest form, the theme and seven variations, were completed in June, but their first public performance, by which time they probably were embellished further, was at a meeting of the music club — doughnuts and cider — on December 18 in Paine Hall. The success was stupendous. And word of it soon reached a professor, Edward Burlingame Hill, himself a composer, who, after listening to a run-through, invited the young men to play their *Indianola Variations* before the Harvard Musical Association at a meeting in Boston.

The evening came. The music charmed. The young men were invited to remain for dinner, were wined and dined liberally, and the event passed into oblivion — except that for Leopold it was his first public appearance, for pay of a sort, as a pianist and (joint) composer. Thompson was more experienced.[7]

By June 1920, when Leopold left Harvard, he had grown into a manhood that startled people. With his languages, music and science he seemed to have passed beyond the need for specialization and become a Renaissance prince of the twentieth century. In addition, he was fun to be with, loving words, puns and humor of all kinds. At large parties he could hold others in thrall with his antics and piano-playing; at small dinners, with the range of this thought and its clear articulation. Each year, too, he grew more handsome — tall, dark-haired, fine-boned, with an easy elegance. He had only to enter a room and start to speak for everyone to sense that he was not ordinary. Yet all these attributes were dominated by modesty. No one was more aware than he of the gap between potential and achievement, and he claimed no accomplishment.

After graduation he continued to combine his work in music and photography. To perfect his piano-playing he went to Paris to study with Alfred Cortot, and the choice of a French rather than German master reflected the shift in taste in the United States following the war. In New York at his parents' school he studied composition with Rosario Scalero and at Uncle Frank's school with Percy Goetschius. The two were quite different in their methods, and for Leopold, Scalero was the more important.

Goetschius tended to ignore early music, with its choral style, and to make a dogma of the instrumental practices of the late eighteenth and nineteenth centuries. Scalero, on the other hand, taught composition chronologically, starting with plainsong, advancing through the sixteenth-century's choral style, which he considered the most important road to perfection, up to modern times. Leopold, by 1923, was deep in the sixteenth-century style, and his compositions in these years were mostly choral preludes, motets and madrigals.[8]

He also, on October 29, 1922, made his performing debut with the New York Symphony at Aeolian Hall as one of the two pianists — the other was his Uncle Walter — in the New York première of Saint-Saëns's Carnival of the Animals. This work, scored for two pianos, flute, clarinet, harmonica, xylophone, celesta and strings, has a unique history, for Saint-Saëns composed it in 1886 for piano students and after a few private performances interned it for the balance of his life — except that in 1905 he allowed the choreographer Michel Fokine to expand slightly one of its fourteen parts, Le Cygne, and make a small solo of it for the ballerina Anna Pavlova, who took it round the world as The Dying Swan. As such, this part became possibly the best-known cello solo in musical history, even as the rest of the work remained in manuscript and unperformed. But Saint-Saëns, on his death in 1921, by his will expressly approved publication, and immediately afterward the entire work began to be heard in concert halls, where for many years, particularly in children's concerts, it was a favorite.

Richard Aldrich of the New York Times thought Saint-Saëns's reluctance to release the work was "easily understandable," and did not review it further or mention Leopold's share in its performance.[9] It is unlikely that Leopold cared; he seems never to have wanted a career as a virtuoso pianist. Clara had not forgotten Ysaÿe's comparison of him to Mozart, and of these years she wrote, "Much was expected of him in creative work." [10] For Leopold, too, it was not performing that came first but composing — though not always before photography.

For the partners, 1922 was a year of crisis and advance. Leo Godowsky, after several years in California, during which he supported himself by playing violin in the San Francisco Symphony and, later, in the Los Angeles Philharmonic, had returned to the East Coast, and he and Leopold had quickened the pace of their experiments. Abandoning their efforts to achieve good color through methods that were essentially optical — specially constructed cameras that by filters could take pictures in three primary colors on three films simultaneously and project them in superimposition — they worked instead to achieve a single picture on a single film on one exposure with the three primary colors, or their complements, in three different layers of emulsion on the film itself.

This posed a chemical rather than an optical solution to the problem, and they worked at first to perfect a film with two layers of emulsion, the top to produce a picture in blue-green, one half of the spectrum; the bottom in orange-red, the other half. The color was to be introduced into the images on the two layers after these first had been developed in black and white; a different color into each layer. Apparently some time in the first six months of 1922 they achieved this, then perfected their process, and on February 20, 1923, filed an application for a patent. [11]

At once they ran into trouble, for the patent examiner said that no claim covering an integral two-layer or three-layer film would be allowed unless it was accompanied by a workable method of developing the film. He based his stand on the fact that integral bipacks and tripacks, as they were called, had been proposed since 1905, but without a practical way of processing the film (developing being one step in processing). Leo thereupon arranged a demonstration in the patent office at which he showed the examiner a method of "controlled diffusion," or "differential depth bleach," by which the two layers could be separately colored without any need for physical separation. This was something scientists had been trying to achieve for a quarter of a century. [12]

The method, of immediate interest to others, was reported within two years to the world in a book, *The History of Three-Color Photography,* that was read by many photographers and scientists. Its summary of the process gives some idea of the complication of what Mannes and Godowsky were accomplishing in their home laboratories.

[They] patented the direct superposition of two emulsions, the front one being slow and sensitized for green and bluish-green, with a yellow dye incorporated. The lower emulsion was to be much faster and sensitive for red. This could be used for negative and positive work. The developed image was to be bleached with ferricyanide, washed, dried and then the upper image only developed, preferably with amidol and after washing the film was to be treated with ferrous chloride, which would form the usual cyantope blue on the lower stratum, but not affect the metallic silver. The upper metallic silver image was then to be toned with copper, uranium or vanadium ferricyanides, thus forming a mordant for basic dyes.[13]

Some time before filing the patent application, the partners, through friends, had been introduced to George Eastman, founder of the Eastman Kodak Company, but had been unable to interest him in their work. Possibly he simply did not believe that two musicians, working in homemade laboratories, could control such complicated experiments. And indeed, in 1922 lack of money and equipment hindered them. The chemicals, film backing, patent applications and lawyers all cost more than they could earn as musicians, giving lessons, teaching courses or playing occasional engagements. And their parents, who over the years had lent them $800, were beginning to lose patience, even Clara, and refused to advance any more. To them, the young men's interest in science was beginning to block careers in music.[14]

The final straw was added one night when Leo's father, going into his bathroom to wash his hands, stepped into a pan of developing fluid. That did it. Ultimatums were pronounced; deaf ears turned to pleas; time limits set for dismantling laboratories; and throughout the four parents preserved a united front. The sons, of course, could pursue their experiments elsewhere, but by the year's end no longer at home, and no longer at their parents' expense. In the midst of the uproar, in June 1922, Leo left with his father on a violin-piano tour of South America.[15]

On his return, fortune smiled. Leopold, while coming by boat from study in Paris, had met an employee of Kuhn, Loeb & Company, Everett Somers, to whom he had described the experiments. Somers, in turn, talked to Lewis L. Strauss, an associate of the firm (and later chairman of the United States Atomic Energy Commission). Strauss, who as a boy had been interested in photography, knew enough about the difficulties of color to see that if, indeed, Mannes and Godowsky had devised a method of taking a color picture with an ordinary camera on one exposure of a single film, then color photography was about to become available to amateurs in their millions. There would be money in it, and he agreed to come to the Mannes apartment for a demonstration.[16]

Leopold had asked his sister, Marya, a gawky girl in her last year of school, to stand by to entertain Mr. Strauss while he and Leo developed the film in Tante's closet. Strauss arrived and, after being shown the kitchen laboratory, was given a Brownie box with which he photographed some strips of colored crepe paper fastened to the wall with thumbtacks. The partners then disappeared into the closet with the film, and Marya led Strauss to the living room to converse. She was not yet the extraordinary beauty she was to become, but there were signs of it, and she already was highly articulate. She talked and talked. The developing usually took about thirty minutes, but forty passed, and then fifty. First Leopold, then Leo appeared; finally, to keep Strauss amused they played a Beethoven violin-piano sonata. The apartment, it seemed, was cold, and the processing liquids were taking unusually long to work. But in the end they brought in a developed film and, in Strauss's words, "There, to my astonishment and admiration, the primary colors, though muddy, unquestionably had been produced." [17]

He arranged for Mannes and Godowsky to have a credit at Kuhn, Loeb of $20,000, for which, in return, they would pay back any money drawn down and also pay the firm a third of any royalties they might earn on their patents. For the musicians the infusion of money came just in time, and they rented a dentist's office. From another source came further aid. Leopold one summer had met Robert W. Wood, then head of the experimental physics department and later president of Johns Hopkins University and himself a dabbler in methods of color photography. Wood now wrote to Dr. Kenneth Mees, director of research at the Kodak company, who met with the two Leopolds at the Chemists Club in New York. The result was the promise of some specially coated two-layer plates or films, made at Kodak's expense, in return for regular reports of progress. [18] The better laboratory and equipment committed the two musicians even more to their experiments. For now, on this new, more professional basis, besides what they already owed their parents, they felt a moral obligation to others to succeed. [19]

Among Leopold's first cousins there was one, Helen Damrosch, who, even more closely than he, would combine art with science — painting with zoology. Like her elder brother, Frank Jr., who liked to sing and was a member of the Episcopal Church's Joint Hymnal Commission during the preparation and adoption of the hymnals of 1916 and 1940, she enjoyed music and, when she could, made it part of her life. Helen's instrument was the piano, and though her work often kept her from it, in old age she still could play effectively some Mozart and the slow movements of the Beethoven sonatas.

Fortunately for Helen and her brother, their father had not urged either to become a musician. Frank's habit, with his children, grandchildren and students, was to discourage all except the absolutely first-rate from a career in music: the life was too difficult. He had hoped that Helen would inherit his mother's voice, for music was, as he would say softly, "the best-loved art"; but when Helen began to show a greater talent for drawing and color he encouraged her in it, even allowing her to quit school before graduation to pursue her studies in art more intently. She was a serious girl, and on first meeting, at least, not very attractive, with masculine features, a throaty voice and, when tired, a slight limp, probably the result of a mild, undiagnosed case of infantile paralysis.[20]

She studied painting under George de Forest Brush and Jonas Lie, took a course on anatomy at the Columbia University medical school and gradually, in the tradition of Audubon, became expert at drawing portraits of birds and animals that were correct in their color and anatomy. Her skill in time brought her to the attention of William Beebe, the director of the tropical research department of the New York Zoological Society, which maintains the Bronx Zoo and the New York Aquarium; and he hired her in 1921 to accompany an expedition the following winter to British Guiana, where he hoped to discover and classify new species of insects as well as adding information on many already known. Helen's job was to draw the insects, in water colors, before their bright hues, on death or exposure to strong light, faded. Eventually, of course, the discovery of a practical method of color photography by her first cousin Leopold (and Leo) would deprive Helen, and artists like her, of the job.

The expedition spent the first six months of 1922 in the tropical forest of British Guiana. In the clearing there was one small building with a big verandah on which everyone ate and worked; tents, pitched under the bamboo trees, were used for sleeping. The work came in batches. When a group of insects was brought in, everyone would fall to, for however long was needed until the job was done. Helen would be given an insect on a slide and, while she peered at it through her microscope, would sketch it in color on her pad. Then the insect and sketch would pass on to someone else for classification. Perhaps what was even more difficult artistically, she also recorded the swiftly changing colors of live frogs.[21]

In the evening when there was nothing to do, they would all loll about the verandah while Beebe read aloud, usually poetry, or would play word games. One of these was a contest to see who could make up the longest sentence using only two-letter words, and the winner was Beebe's assistant, John Tee Van: "If it is to be, it is up to me to do it."

The sentence, amazingly, was an almost perfect self-description, because as everyone joked: "Who was the best man for a field trip? Tee Van! For he would do all the work."[22] Yet there in British Guiana he and Helen found the time to fall in love and plan to marry.

He was twenty-five that year, four years younger than she, a tall, thin, mild man with dark curly hair, glasses and a long nose. He was largely self-educated. His family came from Brittany, by way of Ireland, and had settled in Brooklyn, where his father was a construction worker. His mother had died when he was four, and he had been raised by his mother's schoolmates. In 1911, at fourteen, he had dropped out of school and taken a full-time job at the Bronx Zoo, cleaning the muck out of the birdcages. In the course of it, being of an inquiring mind, he learned a great deal about exotic birds; but he also decided, for a better future, to go to night school to obtain a high school diploma. This was the only degree he held until he was given an honorary doctor of science degree in 1955 by Rensselaer Polytechnic Institute.

One day in 1916, when he still was cleaning birdcages, Dr. Beebe, who was then curator of birds, asked what he did in the evenings, and Tee Van replied that he was studying architectural drafting. Beebe thereupon gave him a bird bone to draw, and so expertly did Tee Van reproduce it that Beebe pulled him out of the birdhouse and made him his assistant in the newly formed department of tropical research.

The following year Tee Van went on his first expedition to British Guiana, doing whatever he was asked, always with a cheerful eagerness, and gradually learning and knowing more than anyone except Beebe. Ultimately he would go on thirty-two expeditions, have a termite, two flys, a crustacean, two mollusks and two fish named after him, publish thirty-four articles and become the general director, from 1956 to 1962, of the New York Zoological Park (the Bronx Zoo) and Aquarium, one of the top zoological posts in the country. But in the year in which he became engaged to Helen he was merely Beebe's assistant and the author of only three articles. With his still limited education and background he must have seemed to Frank and Hetty, for all his shy charm, a surprising choice.[23]

The wedding was at their cottage at Seal Harbor, Maine, on July 17, 1923, and the service, conducted by Frank Jr., was held on the wide porch overlooking the granite ledges, trees and ocean. The Kneisel Quartet played, and after the reception Frank and his eldest grandson, Leopold Damrosch, sailed the couple over to Great Cranberry Island, where they were to spend their honeymoon.[24]

Later that fall, in New York, Frank and Hetty, following the lead of Clara and David Mannes, moved to an apartment house on the East Side, 120 East 75th Street, just a block from the Mannes School. At the same time they arranged for Helen and John to have an apartment in the same building so that the four of them could take their meals together, in the old pattern.

John, who had known little of family life, accepted graciously the parents, aunts, uncles and myriad cousins that marriage to Helen had brought to him, and soon, like David Mannes in the previous generation, he was a favorite of those who married into the family and of its younger members, many of whom felt in him silent sympathy and support against family pressures. Some of the younger generation thought him the most interesting of any who joined the family in this, its third generation; certainly of all the additions he was the most original.

Clara and David had delayed their move to the East Side until Marya graduated from the Veltin School, which was only a block from their West Side apartment. By then Marya, who was approaching nineteen, had grown into a tall, dark-haired girl about to become beautiful. In addition, she was interesting, her mind stuffed with odds and ends of German, French and English-American culture, which she could produce in conversation often with wit and perception and sometimes with an original sardonic humor. She was also willful.

She had been so from birth. Clara and David had called her "the 'No' baby," for "she did not easily obey and always knew what *she* wanted." In this she was quite different from Leopold, who as a child had been inclined to listen and learn from adults. Nevertheless, according to Clara, Marya "always had the most beguiling ways and everyone loved her." [25]

When she was three, she went on a hunger strike and began to spit out her food. Clara and David tried every ruse they could think of to distract her, "almost standing on our heads," but finally they consulted Dr. Emmett L. Holt, a distinguished pediatrician. After examining Marya, he advised, "Let her starve. Don't give her any food. Don't force a thing on her." It was a fearful prescription for the anxious parents, but with Dr. Holt's backing they followed it, and after one day of hunger and greatly lessened attention Marya began to eat. This was the last contest of will with her parents that she lost. It was not that they spoiled her, but they simply had no idea of how to handle such a child. [26]

Some time later Clara seated Marya at the piano and was beginning to explain the keyboard when Marya vomited on the keys. After this had happened three or four times, Clara gave up. Unquestionably the dose of music in the Mannes household was very strong. Even Leopold staggered under it, and Clara and David might have been wiser to moderate their zeal for their best-loved art. In Clara's youth, after all, there had been five children to divide their parents' enthusiasm and no uncles distinguished in music to increase its force. [27]

Marya later took piano lessons, though not from her mother, but she steadfastly refused to apply herself and grew up loving music but rejecting any real knowledge of it. In later life, in her writing and public speaking, she occasionally made mistakes about it that startled her audience, such as writing of "Puccini's *Traviata*" — but, then, no Damrosch or Mannes ever displayed any feeling for Italian opera — and to a graduating class at the Mannes College of Music she explained that she had not been able to play the piano because of the smallness of her hand. In the audience the piano students, gazing at the average-sized hand she held up, knew that Josef Hofmann's hand had been smaller.[28]

Undoubtedly in part she rejected music because Leopold was so good at it. As the only son in a family of German background he probably would have received more attention than the younger girl in any event, but the tendency was reinforced by the excitement over his musical and scientific abilities. As Marya often would say, "He was a hard act to follow." Any resentment she felt, however, was not directed at him. Though five years apart in age, they grew up very close in spirit, so close that some friends thought their relationship unhealthy, incest in all but act. Even as adults they could talk in a private language spontaneously created out of foreign words, sounds and gestures. "It *is* disorienting," Clair Seymour once remarked, "to come on two persons at a family party conversing furiously in a language no one else in the room can understand."[29]

When Marya was eight, her parents entered her in a school twelve blocks from their apartment on West Seventy-fifth Street. Marya, on the first day, after being introduced to the teacher and assigned a seat in class, excused herself and ran home. Clara opened the door, and the child, in tears, leaped into her arms. "It's like a church, and I hate the faces! And it's so *far!*"

Clara, relying on charm and the cultural prestige of the Damrosch-Mannes name, applied at once to the more expensive Veltin School, one block away, and succeeded in persuading its principal to accept Marya on scholarship; and there Marya stayed until graduation. Clara was ever resourceful.[30]

The incident was characteristic of Marya in combining inconsistencies. She was eager to be free of the family, but wanted its support; she delighted in shocking it, but wanted its approval. When she was fifteen or sixteen her Uncle Frank and Aunt Hetty, living in the same building, gave her a birthday party, and Marya, who knew better, put on lipstick and perhaps powder. At the party's end she offered her face to her Uncle Frank to kiss, and he refused until she washed it. She burst into tears and ever after disliked her Uncle Frank. He was "Imperial, Prussian and inclined to be a Puritan." More than sixty years later she was still pleading for approval: "I was only trying to make myself attractive."[31]

She succeeded; some thought, too well. By nineteen she was a sexual tease. She allowed a discreet, older man , a friend of the family, to stroke her thighs and buttocks — "I thoroughly liked it" — but when she looked suggestively at a younger man who responded hot and heavy, she ran for home. Against everyone's urging she refused to go to college, insisting that she be allowed to go to London to study sculpture. What she wanted was "release from a society which I knew would try to force me into a woman's mold I did not want — marriage, children, domestic absorption." Or, as she also put it, she wanted "freedom," and "it consisted of nothing more and nothing less than not being observed by those who knew me too well."[32]

She knew that her aunts and uncles watched her with disapproval, and she was clever at turning their warnings to Clara into efforts to interfere. Clara always bristled at any suggestion of interference by her brothers or their wives, and against their advice she arranged for Marya to have nine months in London, where she would live as a paying guest with an art dealer and his wife while studying sculpture. Her parents, disappointed that she would not go to college, still could say: It is your life; you must live it.

She worked hard for a while, but gradually party-going took over, and she dropped sculpture in favor of writing. The art dealer meanwhile had run off to Paris with a mistress, and in New York Marya's aunts urged Clara to rescue her from an illicit atmosphere. David, as always, left the difficult decision to Clara, who, once again sensing interference, allowed her daughter to stay, in Marya's words, "in the belief that I was strong enough to weather reality, however unpleasant." A few weeks later she began her first love affair, with a married Scotsman, Colin MacKenzie, to whom her supposed chaperone had introduced her.[33]

Meanwhile, in her new-found identity and freedom she changed her name from Marie to its Polish-Russian equivalent, Marya. It was not a great change, and no one opposed it. Within the family she had always been called Ma Mie, a contraction in French of "my friend," and her relatives and intimate friends continued to use the endearment. But to the world she presented herself as Marya.[34]

At the year's end, back in New York, she had to return to living at home; her parents could not afford a separate apartment for her, and she, with no skills and not much education, could not find a job, certainly not the kind she fancied. So she poured her energies into writing. "I continued dreaming, endlessly typing, and planning for greatness. I could not endure the thought of obscurity." In that, she was quite different from Leopold, who had no wish for celebrity; for him the excitement was always in the work itself, never in the public acclaim that he might derive from it.[35]

Much of her social life in the next two years originated in the parties given by her Uncle Walter and Aunt Margaret. At their house she met persons of all ages in the worlds of theater and music: "Fifteen to seventy, it made no difference if you had something to give; and diversions like charades or word games or skits brought us — often hilariously — together." And there were, apparently, many private evenings with men.[36]

Most of what she wrote in these years was plays, which she read to her family, often reducing them to tears of laughter. She consoled herself that she was ahead of her time, surely too advanced for her parents or brother. But finally, in 1925, one play, *Foul Is Fair,* a three-act modernization of *Macbeth,* was produced at the summer stock theater in Woodstock, New York, apparently with moderate success.

Meanwhile, presumably through her assaults on the theater, she had met a young man, "barely older than me, who had all the qualities most of the contemporaries I met seemed to lack: talent, intelligence, wit, and kindness." He was an artist planning to become a scene designer, Jo Mielziner.[37]

They were married on March 31, 1926, in the main hall of the Mannes School of Music. An Episcopal minister performed the ceremony, and before and after it a string orchestra and organ played. Marya, who was now very beautiful, wore a dress designed by Jo, ivory satin in Empire style with a high-standing collar of old family point lace and, in place of a veil, an Empress Josephine wreath of leaves and flowers.[38]

To her Damrosch-Mannes relatives her choice of husband seemed ideal. Like her, Jo had a cosmopolitan background of mixed heritage. His paternal grandfather, Rabbi Moses Mielziner, had come to the United States in 1865 and fourteen years later became a professor of Talmudic studies and rabbinical literature at the Hebrew Union College in Cincinnati. Jo's father, Leo, was an artist, who had lived much abroad, and his mother, Ellen, a Gentile, a member of an old Connecticut family. Jo and his brother, who acted under the name Kenneth MacKenna, were talented and attractive, and Jo, whose career was just beginning, was destined to become one of the leading stage designers of his generation. The Damrosch elders, including Clara and David, no doubt privately sighed with relief that Marya's life, which had begun to seem so ill directed, was now back on course. Like John Tee Van, Jo Mielziner was a splendid addition to the family.

CHAPTER 24

Walter and American music. George Gershwin. Leopold as a composer. His marriage to Edith Simonds.

W HEN W ALTER, on the New York Symphony's European tour, scheduled in every country at least one performance of work by a living American composer, there was nothing sudden or hypocritical in the gesture. He had, among such composers generally, the reputation of being the conductor most interested in their work and most likely to perform it. In the opinion of Deems Taylor, a composer and critic, writing in 1927, "He has played more new music during the past quarter century, probably, than all his New York contemporaries put together; and as a rule has played it better."[1]

His interest in American music, which as a conductor he considered he had "a solemn duty . . . to recognize and encourage," often originated in his sociability: he would meet the composer somewhere, invite him or her to a party, become interested in the person's work and want to help. Such was Taylor, whom he seems to have met not long before presenting the world première, on March 11, 1923, of Taylor's suite *Through the Looking Glass.* The piece had a genuine success, was taken up by other orchestras, and Walter promptly persuaded the New York Symphony Society to commission from Taylor a symphonic poem, *Jurgen,* which he presented on November 19, 1925. In the next six years Taylor's chief works were two operas, both presented at the Metropolitan: *The King's Henchman* in 1927, with a libretto by Edna St. Vincent Millay, and in 1931 *Peter Ibbetson,* based on Du Maurier's novel. The latter, which he dedicated to Walter, had sixteen performances, still, in 1981, the Metropolitan's record for an American opera.[2]

A much older friend whose works Walter played regularly was Charles Martin Loeffler, who as a young man in 1881 had come to the Damrosch house on Sunday afternoons to play chamber music with Walter's father. Beginning in 1906 with *La Mort de Tintagiles,* Walter scheduled most of Loeffler's major works, *A Pagan Poem, La Villanelle du Diable* and *Memories of My Childhood,* and sometimes repeated them, for Loeffler, until about 1935, had a small but secure place in the repertory, popular with both audiences and critics.

But of course along with the successful relationships, including those with George Chadwick, Daniel Gregory Mason and John Alden Carpenter, there were the failures, one of which generated a considerable literature in which Walter is always the devil. In 1910 a friend of Charles Ives persuaded him to ask Walter to try parts of his Symphony No. 1 at a Saturday morning rehearsal of the orchestra. Walter agreed, and Ives later wrote:

> He started with the second movement (adagio), an English horn tune over chords in the strings. When he heard the pretty little theme and nice chords he called out "charming!" When the second themes got going together, and the music got a little more involved (but not very involved), he acted somewhat put out, got mad, and said it couldn't be played without a great deal of rehearsing.[3]

Also, reportedly, Walter frequently stopped to correct what he assumed were wrong notes, and at one point where the rhythm became complex, using the device of two against three, which many classic composers had used, Walter supposedly turned to Ives and snapped, "You'll just have to make up your mind, young man! Which do you want, a rhythm of two or a rhythm of three?"[4]

Later, Walter on his own, apparently, requested to see Ives's Symphony No. 2 and received a manuscript copy of the score, which he neither played nor returned. Ives, for his part, seems never to have called for it, preferring to nurse a grudge. Years later, when Ives was becoming better known, one of his admirers, the composer Bernard Herrmann, thought to ask Walter for the score, and, "sure enough, Damrosch had it, and we got it back. It was in the same cupboard that he had put it in forty years before."[5]

But alas for Walter's care. When in 1951, after his death, the symphony was finally to have its première, the manuscript he had conserved was no longer available, for whatever reason, and the score had to be reconstructed from Ives's notes. According to the scholar Vivian Perlis, "There is now no knowledge of the whereabouts of the 'Damrosch' score."[6]

Walter made no secret of his dislike of much of modern music. In writing to Lawrence Gilman, the critic for the *Herald Tribune,* he reported a conversation with Stravinsky, in Paris about 1930, in which

Stravinsky had "insisted that he was no longer interested in human emotions and aspirations — that had been done to excess by the 'romantics' . . . [and] nerve excitement was his substitute." Walter had been appalled; to him, music should express "the longings of the human heart," and he asked Gilman, "Was I wrong, or has something died in the heart of the composer of *Petrouchka* and *The Firebird* for which he is trying in vain to find a substitute?"[7]

He was equally ill at ease with atonal music. In a birthday statement for the *Times,* in 1932, he declared Berg's *Wozzeck* the best of such works, but added, "I have dwelt too long and too happily in the house of music of which Bach, Mozart, Beethoven and Wagner are the great supporting pillars, to be willing to exchange it for a new abode of strange and unfriendly design."[8]

Yet he believed it his duty to present audiences with samples of the new music, and in addition to pieces scheduled throughout the year, in both 1925 and 1926 he presented a concert, Modern Music — Pleasant and Unpleasant, at which, playing illustrations at the piano, he traced the evolution of music from diatonic techniques through chromaticism to polytonality and atonality.[9] Then he led the works, which at the concert on December 5, 1926 were:

Prelude, Act II, *Phaedre* (1926) (First time in America)	Arthur Honegger
"Fuji in Sunset Glow" (1925) (First time anywhere)	Bernard Rogers
"La Rumba" (Cuban Dance) (1925)	Quinto Maganini
Ballade for Piano and Orchestra (1920) (First time in America — Composer at the Piano)	Darius Milhaud
Suite — *Music for the Theatre* (1925) (Composer at the Piano)	Aaron Copland
"Emperor Waltz" (1889) (Not first time in America)	Johann Strauss

With those who liked the new music he disgraced himself in these concerts by closing with a Strauss waltz, which on at least one occasion he prefaced by remarking, "And you will see why I don't like modern music."[10] But he did play the music and discuss it intelligently. Even such a prickly composer as Arnold Schoenberg felt he had been fairly treated in a speech by Walter, and wrote to him in broken English: "I am very honored by your manner of consideration: my case is not one of individual taste, but one of the development of music, of the art we love both: you and I. And I am very content of your point of view for I see that you regard just so as I only the advantages of our art."[11]

One method for discovering new music Walter thoroughly disliked: the contest. He constantly was asked to serve as a judge and out of a sense of duty often did, but each experience left him, as he once observed, with "a bad taste in the mouth." [12]

One of these, in 1905, was the second Paderewski competition for an orchestral work by a native-born American: prize, $500. Besides Walter the judges were Benjamin J. Lang, Franz Kneisel, John Knowles Paine and Henry E. Krehbiel. In the course of examining the entries, which were anonymous to the judges, they discovered that one from New Jersey, *The Palisades,* was Berlioz's overture *The Corsair,* and on investigation the competitor was revealed to be a clerk at the *Musical Courier,* Walter's continual disparager. The editor, Marc A. Blumenberg, proclaimed the entry a practical joke and asked editorially, "Is it wrong for any citizen in an open competition to make an effort to ascertain through a test whether the judges are competent?" Fortunately for the judges, Walter had conducted the piece and recognized it at once, and unfortunately for the competition's winner, Arthur Shepherd, the uproar over the joke completely eclipsed him and his work, *Overture Joyeuse.* [13]

Four years later, with Loeffler, George Chadwick and Alfred Hertz, Walter served as a judge in the Metropolitan Opera's competition for an opera by an American-born composer. The prize was $10,000; there were twenty-five entries, anonymous to the judges, and the winner, *Mona,* turned out to have been composed by Horatio Parker, head of Yale's music department, to a libretto by the dramatist Brian Hooker. On March 14, 1912, it became the first full-length opera by a native-born American produced at the Metropolitan. It lasted, however, only four performances, for as Walter had predicted privately to one of the company's directors, "I cannot imagine . . . that it will make a real success . . . to write a really successful opera means a practiced hand, and native-born American composers who have acquired the technique necessary may be counted on the fingers of one hand." Probably he overestimated, for among the country's serious composers none had sufficient experience in the theater. [14]

Possibly the opera contest, ending in the sight and sound of *Mona* onstage, excited Walter to return to an opera of his own, *Cyrano de Bergerac,* which he had started in 1900. The twelve years of gestation suggest how faithfully he had kept to his decision to put conducting before composing, though he had completed a few shorter works. In 1909 he had written some incidental music for an outdoor pageant, *The Canterbury Pilgrims,* which, with a cast of two thousand, fireworks between the acts and a salvo from warships in the harbor, on August 4 had celebrated the anniversary of the settlement of Gloucester, Massachusetts. [15] Three years later he composed the music for an antiwar satire, *Dove of Peace,* by

Wallace Irwin, a well-known humorist of the day. The work was aimed at Broadway, and the tryout in Philadelphia went well; *Variety* predicted success and judged the music "of high calibre." But in New York, where Walter conducted on opening night, November 4, 1912, the show lasted only sixteen performances. The *Musical Courier* was jubilant and stated, "[The] amazing music does not bear even a remote resemblance to comic opera style." The *Herald* thought the book "uninteresting" and the music too ambitious for "the tired businessman"; and the *Times,* that the opera lacked "good comedy and tunes."[16]

Nevertheless Walter now spent every spare moment on *Cyrano,* for which W. J. Henderson had adapted a libretto from the Rostand play. On February 27, 1913, the Metropolitan produced it, and although critics generally thought it the best of the four operas by Americans, whether immigrant or native, yet produced at the Metropolitan, it had only five performances, again because the composer's hand was not practiced. Despite some attractive music, the opera ran too long, nearly four hours after cutting; and was theatrically unsure, the play's famous balcony scene being one of the opera's least effective. And finally there was the disability affecting all American composers at the time: there was very little of anything American in the style. As Loeffler put it in a letter to Walter: "There must be Opera in English — but at present there cannot be, as nobody knows how to sing it." Not even, as yet, the composers.[17]

Walter had theories about the development of music, in Europe and in America. Like many musicians, be believed that music in Europe began in the songs and dances of the people, which, over centuries, were improved and refined to become lieder, opera, orchestral and chamber music. Aside from its youth, America lacked the indigenous people, and so had no natural source for its music. It had, instead, many different immigrant groups and one of native Indians, each of which had its own heritage and style, and until these could be subsumed into something new, no truly American style could emerge. Until then the best that composers could do was imitate and learn from the best of the European tradition, which for Walter, of course, was predominantly German.[18]

In his feelings about jazz, which in the 1920s included in its definition not only improvisation in jam sessions but any popular tune with syncopated rhythms, he underwent a change. Early in the 1920s, though he knew some persons were hailing it as the start of an American style in music, he considered it a "very low form of art," merely "nervous excitement." But by 1941 he was ready to concede not only that it had some good in it but that it was "the only real national music our country has produced so far."[19]

Unquestionably this shift in attitude originated in his family, just as had his interest in Isadora Duncan. Most of his daughters, nieces and nephews were tired of Wagner and enjoyed saying so to their elders.

What they liked and sang about the house, or chose for dancing, were the songs of Jerome Kern, Irving Berlin and a newcomer, George Gershwin. Walter inevitably was interested: he always was susceptible to another's enthusiasm.

According to family tradition his daughter Alice took the lead in fostering his acquaintance with jazz, particularly with the works of Gershwin. She was now in her early thirties, still married to Pleasants Pennington, though more in name than fact, and behind appearances leading an independent life. They lived on the same street as Walter and Margaret, at No. 244, only a block away, and when she was not at work as president of the Junior League, she was much in her parents' house, helping to organize their parties. Probably she met Gershwin at some theatrical event, for like all the family she went constantly to the theater, and soon Gershwin was a frequent guest at the Damrosch house, where, at the slightest urging, he would play the piano until the party broke up. Though he was a brilliant pianist, he often provided more jazz than some of the other guests wanted, and one night Edwin Rice, stealing away, asked Ossip Gabrilowitsch, the conductor of the Detroit Symphony, who also was leaving, "What do you get out of jazz?" To which the answer came instantly, "I get out of it as soon as I can." [20]

Walter, however, was more and more impressed and attended both the final rehearsal of Gershwin's *Rhapsody in Blue* in a night club and its première at Aeolian Hall on the afternoon of February 12, 1924. The concert was billed by its impresario, Paul Whiteman, the bandleader, as an "Experiment in Modern Music," and it often has been described, incorrectly, as the concert that introduced jazz to serious musicians and to symphonic music halls. James Reese Europe's Clef Club Concert, however, put on as a benefit at Carnegie Hall on May 2, 1912, for David Mannes' Music School Settlement for Colored People, has a better claim to the distinction.

Unlike the two subsequent performances of the *Rhapsody* that soon followed, at the première Gershwin played the piano part — a necessity, for the solo passages were still in his head. He had conceived the work only eight weeks earlier on the way to Boston for a tryout of a show, *Sweet Little Devil,* and to complete it in time he had to turn the orchestration over to Whiteman's arranger, Ferde Grofé. The idea of it had come to him "on the train, with its steely rhythms, its rattle-ty-bang . . . I suddenly heard — and even saw on paper — the complete construction of the *Rhapsody* from beginning to end. I heard it as a sort of musical kaleidoscope of America — of our vast melting pot, of our unduplicated national pep, of our blues, our metropolitan madness. By the time I reached Boston I had a definite plot of the piece, as distinguished from its actual substance." [21]

Gershwin, like any American, was one in the melting pot. His mother and father, Rose and Morris Gershwin, both Russian Jews, had emigrated separately from Russia before their marriage in 1895, and the family name had been simplified progressively from Gershovitz to Gershvin to Gershwin. The family included three sons, Ira, George, Arthur, and a daughter, Frances, who in 1930 would marry Leo Godowsky. Until George was ten, when the family bought a piano, there was little music in the house, but as a six-year-old he had been rooted to the pavement by the sound of someone playing Anton Rubinstein's *Melody in F,* and later was enthralled by hearing a violinist play Dvořák's *Humoresque.* What Walter heard in the *Rhapsody,* despite its spurts of syncopation, crossed rhythms and flatted thirds, fifths and sevenths, the so-called blue notes, was this strong affinity for music of a Slavic background, particularly the style and sound of Rubinstein and Tchaikovsky.

About a year after the première of the *Rhapsody,* Walter, in a burst of confidence in his own judgment, like that which had led him to Duncan's studio, arranged for the Symphony Society to commission a piano concerto from Gershwin, called in the contract the "New York Concerto." As Gershwin later wrote, "This showed great confidence on his part, as I had never written anything for symphony before," adding that he had to buy "four or five books on musical structure to find out what the concerto form actually was!" [22]

The result, after four months of work, was the Concerto in F, Gershwin's most imposing and successful orchestral work, the counterpart of his songful *Porgy and Bess,* composed ten years later. For the première, on December 3, 1925, Walter wrote the program note, a model of brief, clear description, and took care to surround the new work with music that would complement or illuminate it without overwhelming it. There was, for example, no work of Beethoven, Brahms or Tchaikovsky that in its familiarity would be certain to please the audience and invite unfair comparison, but, instead, a *Suite Anglaise* by Rabaud, and Glazunov's Symphony No. 5. The latter, which came first on the program, had a purpose that only one reviewer, young Lawrence Abbott of *The Outlook,* bothered to mention, or perhaps noticed: "Its *finale* burst forth with the identical 'Charleston' rhythm which features so strongly in the Gershwin concerto." When Abbott asked Walter if the purpose of playing the symphony was to establish the concerto's Russian heritage, Walter replied, beaming, "Clever boy!" [23]

The reviews were mixed and, with the exception of Abbott's, unenlightening. Critics, without much analysis, took strong positions, lamenting the work's defects of form and use of the orchestra or admiring its rhythmic drive and contemporary American spirit. Lawrence Gilman of the *Herald Tribune* dismissed it as "conventional, trite, at its worst a little dull." That season, however, Walter and Gershwin played it six times, three in New York and once each in Washington, Philadelphia and Baltimore. By December of the following year, when they played it again in New York, they had won the public and established the concerto in the country's orchestral repertory, where it continues, cited often as the most authentically American composition in serious music.[24]

Just what gives the work its American spirit is hard to define. In all three movements Gershwin based melodies, as he often did in his songs, on a constantly repeated note. This quirk, played fast or slow, imbues the melodies with an assertiveness that many persons find typically American. Also, the melodies, regardless of flatted blue notes, tend to be bright and cheerful, suggesting American optimism. Even the slow movement with its muted trumpet solo, despite its blues atmosphere, is more poetic and nocturnal than low-down or despairing. The orchestral sound is often original — Gershwin's blend of symphonic and jazz timbres — and the tempo throughout generally is fast, especially when set by the composer. Gershwin felt that the American style of popular song and dance, the basis for most of his serious music, was not legato but staccato, "almost a stencilled style. The rhythms of American popular music are more or less brittle; they should be made to snap, and at times to crackle. The more sharply the music is played, the more effective it sounds," and he warned piano players against too much pedal or "the romantic touch."[25]

Walter's relations with Gershwin continued cordial, and when he heard that Gershwin had gone to Paris to complete another symphonic work, ultimately *An American in Paris,* he promptly wrote, "I would love to arrange with you to do your new work." Leopold Stokowski at the Philadelphia Orchestra also hoped to have the première, and there was a rumor that Ziegfeld had commissioned the work as a ballet for one of his musicals. But in the end Gershwin gave the première to Walter, who presented the work with the merged Philharmonic and Symphony orchestras at Carnegie Hall on December 13, 1928. Almost immediately afterward, it was put into Ziegfeld's *Show Girl* as a ballet to open the second act, where, despite its explicit program of an American man walking down the Champs-Elysées, it was danced by Harriet Hoctor in toe shoes and the sixteen Albertina Rasch girls in sandals, all in blond wigs, spangles and curious cutaway dresses. Those who disapproved of Walter's presenting Gershwin, and they were many, felt confirmed in their belief that "jazz" was essentially a trivial, debased form of music.[26]

Walter, whom *Musical America* had called "a kind of symphonic godfather to Mr. Gershwin,"[27] continued to play the works and to defend them as an important step in the development of a genuine American music. Without concession he held to his point of view stated to a reporter in February 1926:

To my mind it [the Concerto in F] is epoch-making, in that he has succeeded in elevating the much discussed, much loved and much hated music, which commonly goes under the name of jazz, into the higher realms
of art . . . After all, we are only following in the footsteps of Europe,
whose greatest masters have founded their art on the folk songs and dances
of their country. If the gifted Gershwin can carry his mastery of the
American dance to a higher plane, and imbue it with the finer emotions
and aspirations of humanity, all I can say is, "More power to his el-
bow."[28]

Two years after Leopold's photographic experiments had moved onto a
more professional footing through his and Godowsky's joint agreement
with Kuhn, Loeb & Company, his composing, too, began to attract support, and in April 1925, on the basis of an orchestral suite, he won a
Pulitzer scholarship ($1500) for composition, and also in that year had
his first work published, *Petite Suite pour deux pianos,* consisting of a Prelude, Capriccio and Sarabande. As the title suggests, the work was issued
in Paris, probably because of the influence of Alfred Cortot, to whom it
is dedicated and with whom, the previous year, Leopold had studied.
Nevertheless, it and the Pulitzer award marked the end of Leopold's years
as a student. By 1925 he was considered by others and himself to be a
professional musician, a pianist and composer.[29]

These years in the mid-twenties — Leopold, born on December 26,
1899, liked to say "I am as old as the year" — were among the happiest
in his life, and in later decades he talked of them always with pleasure.
During the winters, when he lived at 120 East 75th Street, in an apartment adjoining his parents' but with a separate entrance, he spent most
of the day, as student or teacher, at either the Mannes School of Music
or the Institute of Musical Art; in the evenings and on weekends he
worked with Godowsky in their dentist-office laboratory. In the summers, when he was not in Europe, he spent much of his time in the
Hamptons, where Clara and David always rented a cottage large enough
to include Leopold, Marya and Tante, who, though now white-haired
and frail, was as lively as ever.

The cottage usually changed, one year to the next, but all shared a
peculiarity. Clara and David, though neither could cook, in their fastidious way liked modern kitchens that could be kept spotless, and Clara
frequently preferred to rent a new cottage, however graceless, than an
old, however charming. Yet with Tante's aid she would transform the
modern living room into a replica of her town apartment, hiring a grand
piano, carrying down familiar cushions, objects and throws, and, always, setting up the portrait of her father on its easel and trimming it
with fresh greens.

Even in summer the family's routine generally set aside a long morning for work, and Leopold with his double enthusiasm often extended the period into the afternoons and evenings. Yet he led a full social life, for he was beginning to display Tante's extraordinary gift for socializing. Everyone liked him, wanted him at their parties, and he was constantly invited out. He was seldom in the Hamptons for long, however, for he spent much of three summers in Italy, where he did most of his composing.[30]

He was drawn to Italy, especially to Rome, because of the introductions his composition teacher, Scalero, could give to him in the city, and also because his friend Randall Thompson in 1922 had been awarded the first Walter Damrosch Fellowship at the American Academy in Rome. This fellowship, which had been set up in Walter's honor by his friends and admirers, ran for three years with an annual allowance of $2000, free residence at the academy, and the expectation that the Fellow would spend at least six months in Rome and the balance at the various music centers of Europe. By 1924, therefore, Randall knew the city well and was able to lead Leopold directly into its life.[31]

They had fun together, met many young people and composed without stopping. There exists in manuscript an *Etude in 4 Notes,* which Leopold dedicated to Thompson, who had suggested the theme. It is dated October 29, 1924, and Leopold noted on it carefully that he had composed it in three hours and twenty-eight minutes. They were always hurrying themselves to compose, and the next day over supper they decided that each would write a seven-part piano suite in seven days, one part each day, all to be based on a three-note motif, and they tossed a coin to see who would suggest the first and third notes, and who the second. Leopold won, and picked a falling third, A and F, into which Randall inserted a G sharp.

Leopold finished only four parts, and these have disappeared, but Randall completed the exercise on schedule, though he later revised the finale of the last movement. A year later Leopold gave Randall's *Suite* its American première at a recital he played at the Mannes School on November 16, 1925.[32]

That autumn of 1924, however, Leopold also composed the orchestral suite that won him the Pulitzer award for composition, and the next summer he began a string quartet that eventually would be published, performed and win him a Guggenheim fellowship. That second summer the friends were in Venice, where for a month with Billy Richards and a fourth Harvard man, Joseph Coletti, a sculptor, they rented the floor above the *piano nobile* in the Palazzo Papadopoli on the Grand Canal. Every morning and afternoon they worked at composing and sculpting, and every late afternoon they went to the Lido and swam. In Thompson's memory, it was "a magic month."[33]

In addition to Leopold's two larger works, the *Orchestral Suite,* which was published in a revised version in 1926, and the *String Quartet in C Minor,* in 1927, in these years he composed many songs, chiefly for soprano voice. Yet despite the steady flow of songs, he never again attempted any work as large as the string quartet, and it seems that even before the decade was out, his will to compose had begun to weaken. No one noticed the fact at the time, and he still talked of composing with the greatest enthusiasm; and, of course, his work on photography was always a handy reason to explain any delay or opportunity missed in composition. But the reasons may have been more personal than the pressures of his photographic work.

Thompson, looking back after fifty years at some of these early works, remarked of the *Etude in 4 Notes,* "The freedom Leopold exhibits . . . shows great intensity, even passion, but in a way it is all tied up in knots." And he thought Leopold's inability to finish the seven-part piano suite on schedule was another example of knots. Composing did not come easily to Leopold, partly because he had the imagination and knowledge to be a perfectionist and perhaps partly, too, because of his sense of competition with his family: anything he composed had to be good. Typically, in the seven-part suite he had attempted too much, composing for a fugue, a *double* fugue.

Thompson wondered, too, whether the great number of songs, many of them slightly antique in their style, wasn't a sign of bondage to Scalero, who in his teaching stressed so strongly the vocal style of the sixteenth century. "I am a great believer in that style," said Thompson, "but I always had the impression that Scalero was too hard on his students. Barber and Menotti, his most celebrated disciples, kicked over the traces at an early date: Leopold either did not want to, or was not allowed to."[34]

Thompson here touched on a point similar to one that many people in later years would make about Leopold as a pianist. He was often superb in a small hall or informal surroundings, but if the hall was large, he frequently seemed unable to project from the stage the same ideas and nuances that had been so ravishing in the small hall. A kind of inhibition seemed to set in, springing, perhaps, from his innate modesty. It requires, after all, considerable self-satisfaction to present oneself as a soloist to twenty-eight hundred persons. Call it showmanship: his Uncle Walter had it; Leopold did not. And the lack of it, as well as his knowledge of that lack, may have contributed to his gradual failure to progress as a composer. But for the moment that failure was concealed from him, and the future seemed bright with promise about to be realized.[35]

Meanwhile, in East Hampton, he had fallen in love with Edith Vernon Simonds, a tall, brown-haired young woman with classic English features, and had proposed marriage and been accepted. Her family was descended from William Henry Onderdonck of Great Neck, Long Island, and proud of it. For the wedding, Edie, as she was known, insisted on the family crest on the invitations, and she herself addressed all the envelopes so that they would be in her own hand. Years later, when social customs had changed greatly, she laughed at herself: "I was such a snob then."

But she was not a typical girl of her class. After being introduced to society in 1919 she had studied painting at the Art Students League and also in Paris; she had exhibited her work and sold it, and kept a studio in New York. Like Leopold, she was a professional, and her art was important to her all her life. Despite the patrician background no one in her family questioned whether she, an upper-class Gentile, should marry a middle-class musician of mixed heritage. The Damrosch family, including the Mannes branch, was too well established, and Leopold, a Harvard graduate, too interesting and attractive. "It would have been quite different," she recalled, "if I had proposed to marry an Irish Catholic."[36]

Her connection to the Damrosch family was strengthened further by a friendship with Ruth Seymour, Ellie's youngest daughter, who was also a professional artist. Ruth, a tall girl with mannish features, had started Cornell with the idea of becoming an architect but had quit to pursue painting. She did both water colors and oils and was on the threshold of a career as a muralist, not only for private houses but for a restaurant and for the panels over the elevator doors in McCutcheon's new department store at Fifth Avenue and Forty-ninth Street.

Together these two artists in August 1925 organized and mounted in Clinton Academy what seems to have been the first artists' show at East Hampton, one that, by its success and imitators, contributed directly to the construction of Guild Hall, where the annual summer show now is held. They exhibited works by Maude Sherwood Jewett, Edward King, William L'Engle, Marguerite Zorach, Alexander Calder, Lauren Ford and Louis Bouché. For themselves, Ruth hung three water colors of southern French seaports, and Vernon Simonds, as she signed her work, three drawings and a decorative screen. The *East Hampton Star* in its review had kind words for everyone.[37]

The following spring Edie and Leopold were married, on May 13, 1926, in the Episcopal church at Great Neck. Leopold had his father for best man, and almost the entire Damrosch family was present. The bridal party marched in to Wagner and out to Mendelssohn, played by Randall on "an undistinguished village organ." Later, Leopold said that he could remember nothing of the ceremony because Randall hit a wrong note. The reception was held at the house of the bride's brother, because her parents were divorced and preferring either seemed impossible; and a few days later the couple left for Rome, where, thanks to the Guggenheim fellowship, they planned to remain for eighteen months.[38]

CHAPTER 25

Frank and the merger of the Institute of Musical Art with the Juilliard Graduate School to form the Juilliard School of Music.

ON JANUARY 16, 1926, as the Institute of Musical Art passed the midpoint of its twenty-first year, its friends and trustees gave a dinner for its founder and director, Frank Damrosch. The date was the birthday of Betty Loeb, whose four children, led by her son James, were the school's greatest benefactors, and each year the occasion was marked by a chamber recital in her memory. It was also the birthday of the founder's mother, Helene Damrosch, to whom he was apt to ascribe his first interest in music; and so for this double reason the date had become, as much as any, the school's anniversary.

By its twenty-first year the institute had developed into one of the largest and best conservatories in the country, with a faculty of 118 and an enrollment of a thousand, not including a preparatory division with several sections located about the city. Except for the limitations of space and money — constant frustrations to Frank — the enrollment easily could have been doubled, for as former students went out into all parts of the country to play in orchestras, teach in schools or work for music in community groups, they sent back from all parts of the country a stream of talented students. Though many musicians would continue to go to Europe for study, for all but aspiring opera singers the necessity of doing so had been broken, in significant part because of the institute.

In addition, thanks chiefly to the generosity of the Loeb, Warburg, Schiff and Seligman families, the school owned its land and building at 120 Claremont Avenue, near Columbia University, and, though not rich, was financially sound and well administered. With justification, those who had worked hard to create it, most of them of German background, could pause to congratulate themselves on what they had achieved.[1]

The dinner, which was held at the school following the traditional chamber recital, in hindsight seems the final gathering of that cosy German world that, continually renewed by immigrants, had dominated music in the United States since 1850. Its last stronghold in New York inevitably was at the school, for in the nature of the art the performer retires to teach; and symbolic of the passing of that older world was the death of Franz Kneisel, on whom Frank had founded his violin department in 1905. Kneisel, who had studied in Vienna and played in Berlin, was invited to the United States in 1885 to become the concertmaster of the Boston Symphony, from which in 1903 he had retired to devote himself to his string quartet, the best of his generation, and to teaching, in which for twenty-one years he also ranked first. Then, less than two months after the dinner, he died, and his successor, Leopold Auer, was not another German immigrant but a refugee from the Russian Revolution, who in St. Petersburg had taught Jascha Heifetz. With Kneisel's death in March the German leadership of the institute's string department was ended.

The dinner guests, though by no means all German, included Kneisel and many other German artists on the faculty, as well as representatives of many of the city's great German families: Schirmer, Lewisohn, Warburg, Schiff, Seligman, Loeb and, of course, Damrosch. Though many of these by heritage were Jewish as well as German, there was as yet, before the rise of Hitler, no conflict between the two, and in their musical lives they felt at home in an ambiance predominantly German.

Of the Damrosch family, besides Frank, Hetty, Frank Jr. and his wife, Dorothy, there were present Miss Marie von Heimburg — Tante; Walter, Margaret and their daughter Polly; Clara, David and Marya Mannes; and Ellie, Harry and Clair Seymour. Of the second generation only Marie Wiechmann was absent, either unable to come or perhaps not invited. The evening was entirely Frank's. The toastmaster, Paul Cravath, announced, "I shall not even call upon Walter Damrosch," adding that probably it was "the first time in his life" that Walter had been present at a dinner and *not* been asked to speak. Hetty stood when requested but, despite an ovation, refused to say a word, leaving the floor to Frank, who reminisced about his days in Colorado when he had first dreamed of a school, about James Loeb, who had brought that dream to reality, and about the faculty, "those people who could make the stones speak and the woods sing — they are the ones to whom all credit is due." Characteristically, toward the end he touched on the importance of song in the home: "for my mother was a beautiful singer and my first acquaintance with music was when mother sang Schubert's songs to me, and on that foundation you can build high."[2]

Though the dinner was a lighthearted occasion, the school's future, as many saw, was not unclouded. The previous summer, after a strenuous overnight ride into the Grand Canyon, Frank had suffered a heart attack, and though his recovery apparently had been complete, he never had been robust and was now sixty-six. Further, the school at twenty-one clearly was at a change of generations, becoming, as in the violin department, steadily less German and more eclectic in its personnel and pedagogical methods. The previous year the head of the composition department, Percy Goetschius, had retired and been succeeded by Rubin Goldmark, his junior by nineteen years. In March, Kneisel would die, and already Louis Svečenski, a member of the Kneisel Quartet and head of the viola department since 1905, was fatally ill. In most departments, and Frank's post, a question of succession loomed.

In addition, three new schools recently had been founded, all with far more money behind them than the institute could muster. One of these, which had opened in 1921, was the Eastman School of Music, in Rochester, endowed initially by George Eastman of the Kodak Company with $4.5 million. Another, opened in 1924, was the Curtis Institute of Music, in Philadelphia, endowed by Mary Louise Curtis Bok, of the Curtis Publishing Company family, with $12.5 million. Partly because it took many fewer students than the Institute of Musical Art, in 1928, under Josef Hofmann as director, Curtis would abolish tuition fees altogether, an act that the institute, though it offered scholarships, could not begin to match. In 1905 when Frank had founded the institute, he had assembled an outstanding faculty and student body largely by his personal prestige; by 1926, the competition for good students and faculty was keener.

But more immediately threatening to the institute was the prospect of a new school in New York underwritten by the Juilliard Musical Foundation, which had assets of about $20 million. A New York textile merchant, Augustus D. Juilliard, who died in 1919, had left the money to aid the development of music in the United States and, more specifically, to aid students to a musical education, "either at appropriate institutions now in existence or hereafter created." The following year the trustees under his will set up the foundation, incorporated it and appointed as its secretary-manager Dr. Eugene A. Noble, a retired Methodist minister who had served as president of Goucher College, in Baltimore, and later of Dickinson College, in Carlisle, Pennsylvania. He was a man of many interests and had the money to indulge them. He had a fine kennel of Northumberland terriers and also collected Rolls-Royces, rugs and pictures. But of music he had no special knowledge.[3]

In his will Juilliard had suggested that a proper use of his money might be to aid the Metropolitan Opera, "providing that suitable arrangements can be made with such company so that such gifts shall in no way inure to its monetary profit." And Noble proposed to the company's general manager, Giulio Gatti-Casazza, some ways in which that could be done. But the proposal, whose terms are not known, was refused, and writers later sometimes cited the fact as an example of the stupidity of the Metropolitan's manager and board of directors.

In the years 1910 through 1930, however, the company was not only extending its season and repertory, but — on its books, at least — was steadily in the black, and the offer of aid presumably was not without conditions. In the next decade, for example, when the Metropolitan, because of the economic depression, appealed to the foundation for help, the foundation, before acting, demanded four seats on the board of directors, a budget that would have "every promise of operating without a deficit," a substantial increase in subscription sales and an expanded opportunity for young American singers, particularly through the device of a spring season at low prices. The conditions, to which the Metropolitan agreed, may sound innocuous, but the last impinged directly on artistic control of casting, repertory, planning and pricing of a season, and no company or director of spirit would have agreed to it — nor would do so now — unless forced.[4]

Apparently at some point in 1922–23, while the foundation was talking to the Metropolitan, it also offered aid to the institute, on conditions. The foundation's directors probably saw the reasonableness of helping the institute to expand its work rather than setting up a school or programs to compete with it; so one day Noble called on Frank with a proposal.

Again the terms are not known, but it seems likely that they included a demand for positions on the institute's board and a strong hand in policy. A small sticking point may have been that under Juilliard's will the foundation could aid only American citizens. In the country, however, and especially in New York, many young music students were not citizens because their parents were not yet citizens. Frank and Walter as boys, for example, would not have qualified for aid. In any event, whatever the terms, they were sufficiently unattractive to Frank and his trustees that, despite the money offered, they declined the proposal.

The foundation thereupon decided to open its own school, under Noble, and in late 1923 he began to create an organization called the Juilliard Graduate School, which would not charge tuition. As he developed it, the name, his own invention, proved misleading: "graduate school" implied that its students had completed a college course, and with some distinction, but the school required only a high school degree or its equivalent, and few of its students were college graduates. Even the term "school" was not used in its usual sense of an institution with some general standards applicable to all and a core curriculum that all must master. Instead, the school offered fellowships, on which students studied their specialty and little else and at the end of three years were declared "graduated" — but with a degree that had no place in the country's general educational system. What the school offered was a kind of tutorial system in which instruction was individual and both admission and progress were judged by standards that were largely individual.

Noble's faculty was very distinguished — he could afford to pay — but to a later colleague, John Erskine, he seemed to collect famous musicians much as he did his dogs or Rolls-Royces, "without much consideration of their fitness for their immediate purpose." The piano department, for example, for several years had too many teachers for the number of pupils, and the schoolhouse that Noble chose, a former Vanderbilt mansion at 49 East 52nd Street, was not well suited to its purpose: the magnificent foyer and staircase were wasted space, the acoustics in most rooms were poor and the teaching rooms were too small and not soundproof. Ernest Hutcheson of the piano department, for one, regularly scheduled classes in his home, greatly increasing the sense of tutorial instruction.[5]

By the spring of 1925 the school had about a hundred students and clearly was doing some good work; indeed, for some students it was ideal. But equally clearly, considering its resources, it was not doing enough, and its chief defect seemed to lie in Noble's failure to integrate it in any way into the country's general educational system. "The essence of education," Erskine later wrote, "the building up of a school to respond to the larger interests of society, was a secret which Heaven had concealed from him." At this point, some time in the autumn of 1925, the Institute of Musical Art, Frank and his trustees, asked the Juilliard Foundation to renew its proposal.[6]

Their reasons seem clear. Frank's heart attack the previous summer had focused concern on the school's future. Goldmark, Goetschius' successor, was already a member of the graduate school's faculty, as was Carl Friedberg of the piano department and as would be Leopold Auer, succeeding Kneisel. The emerging overlap in faculty and courses in the two schools was now plain, and also the competition it implied. The institute only could suffer if the foundation with its millions sought to replace it with the graduate school as the city's, perhaps the country's, chief music school.[7]

The foundation for its part was in trouble. The recently appointed head of the graduate school, Kenneth M. Bradley, was in constant disagreement with Noble over its development, and there was beginning to be public criticism of the foundation for its failure to apply its funds to greater advantage. In view of the free tuition the graduate school offered, an enrollment after two years of 175 students seemed shameful; the institute, which had to charge tuition, in its first year had reached 467. The foundation's trustees, therefore, were anxious to reorganize and start again.[8]

Nine days after Frank's testimonial dinner a tentative plan of merger was announced, and by the following November details had been worked out.[9] The foundation would form the Juilliard School of Music with a board of nine directors: three each from the foundation, the institute and the general musical public. But as the foundation would elect all nine members, it had control. The school would consist at first of two divisions, the institute and the graduate school, which would be fused into one as soon as possible. Everyone recognized, however, that because of commitments to students, faculty, pensions, legal restrictions and so on, this would take time. The new Juilliard School would have a president (eventually John Erskine), and under him would be Frank, as dean of the institute, and someone other than Bradley or Noble (eventually Ernest Hutcheson), as dean of the graduate school. Several years later an annex was built to the institute on Claremont Avenue, and the graduate school moved into it.

Great wealth breeds great resentment, however, and on the morning when Frank was to announce the plan to the students at the institute, he asked his secretary if she thought some would take it hard. She replied that many would grieve over it. "Then we must act," he said cheerfully, "as if we were all very happy about it."[10]

But others, comparing the size and effectiveness of the two schools to be combined, sneered that the foundation, unable to found a good school, had bought one — and probably would wreck it. Many wondered why Frank, the outstanding music educator in the country, was not appointed president of the combined school; and as the months passed, with the foundation unable to persuade its first two nominees to take the post, the question gained rather than lost bitterness. When finally, in March 1928, the appointment went to John Erskine, a novelist, literary critic, professor of English at Columbia University and highly competent amateur pianist, to many persons the meanness of the foundation's trustees seemed confirmed: Erskine was not Frank's equal as either a musician or an educator. But the foundation's trustees evidently were determined that, as it was their money, their man would control it.

The situation cannot have been easy for any of those close to it, including Erskine. Hetty and her daughter, Helen, displayed their anger privately; Frank tried always to conceal his feelings behind statements of what the combined schools now could accomplish. But in his history of the institute, written in retirement in the mid-1930s, his bitterness shows through: he regrets, to the point of sounding ungrateful to the Loeb family, that he had not been given such millions to work with, and he barely can bring himself to name Erskine.[11]

The two were men of quite different character, and Erskine, who made every effort to be tactful, unfortunately was the sort of man whom Frank instinctively disliked. Erskine's love of literature and music was genuine and he soon proved himself a competent administrator, but he was also pretentious, self-advertising and very naïve in his belief that the attention paid to him was owing to personal achievements rather than to the money he controlled.

In fact, he was the first of a new breed in the world of music, the foundation executive. Carnegie, Higginson, Flagler, and even the Schirmer, Steinway and Loeb families, had exercised the power of their money personally. Juilliard, who was dead, exercised it through an agent, on a salary that was, for an employee in the world of music, enormous — $20,000 a year — when the average member of the Philharmonic, a practicing artist, earned only $3000.

Envy over money, though, was the least part of Frank's or his students' dislike of Erskine. Despite his skill at the piano, he was not a musician, not like Josef Hofmann at the Curtis Institute, Howard Hanson at the Eastman School, or Clara and David or Frank. Remarkably, within an eight-year period, from 1943 to 1951, he would publish five autobiographies and in one, *My Life in Music,* would state: "Though I don't call myself inconstant, these were the years [twenty-five] when I thought I had said good-by to music." For him music was not the spiritual necessity it was for Frank or even for many of the institute's students, and they viewed him as an outsider to the art.[12]

Frank clung to the idea that the merger of the institute and the foundation's millions would make possible a single, great, national music school. And because Erskine, too, had that ideal, it gradually came about. But the fusion between the graduate school and the institute took place very slowly, in fact and in spirit. Though it may seem incredible, not until November 1931, five years after the merger was announced, did the institute's magazine, *The Baton,* publish an article on Augustus D. Juilliard, and the same issue contained the first articles by and about Erskine, three years after his appointment. The occasion, which hardly could be ignored, was the opening of the new annex to the institute, into which the graduate school was moving. But after the dedication ceremonies, featuring a concert led by Stokowski, the institute continued to lead a remarkably independent existence, in part perhaps because of the complications of merging endowments and pension funds. There were also, however, some advantages in keeping the graduate school a true graduate school that could take students from the institute, increasingly the undergraduate college, and give them advanced training; and through the spring of 1946, when the institute completed its forty-first year, it continued to grant diplomas and certificates in its own name. Only then, nine years after Frank's death, did the two schools, with a combined enrollment of twenty-one hundred, finally disappear into a single Juilliard School of Music.[13]

This corporate history of what has become one of the great music schools of the world has left writers and editors of reference works in a quandary. Is it accurate to say that Frank Damrosch founded the Juilliard School of Music, of which he never was president? And if so, when? In 1905, fifteen years before the Juilliard Foundation came into existence? It seems anachronistic, and writers often have confused their statements with hedging words. But the school today counts its years from 1905–06, and the most prestigious of reference works, *The New Grove Dictionary of Music and Musicians* (1980), states: "The Juilliard School, a conservatory of international reputation, was begun by Frank Damrosch in 1905 as the Institute of Musical Art."[14]

It seems just to say so.

CHAPTER 26

Walter and the merger of the New York Symphony and Philharmonic to form the New York Philharmonic-Symphony.

ON DECEMBER 14, 1926, at Walter's home on Sixty-first Street, he held a party for the press, mostly the city's music critics. As usual Margaret acted as hostess, aided by two daughters, Polly and Alice, the Symphony Society's executive secretary. Also present was George Engles, the orchestra's manager for the past seventeen years. Plainly Walter had something of importance to announce, but he withheld the revelation until everyone had drunk and eaten and was bursting with curiosity. Finally he spoke. For forty-two years, he said, he had been the musical director and conductor of the New York Symphony, and now he soon would retire. He had submitted his resignation, and it had been accepted, effective the end of the season.

He had invited them to his house, he explained, because a cold statement mailed out would not express his feelings, which he would prefer to convey face to face with those who had worked with him for the cause of music. He had not always agreed with their opinions, but differences were essential for the art to grow, and he hoped the time would never come when all would think alike about music and its interpretation.

He saw in his retirement no occasion for regret. Conductors, like prima donnas, should quit the stage before they are forced, and he, for one, wanted to leave while he was still able to swing his arms. The increased cost of orchestras made it necessary to play at least four concerts a week, which, over a long season — approaching thirty weeks — he found too great a strain; and sharing the post with another would not work well for the orchestra, which needed a single musical director. He still would make occasional appearances as a guest conductor and would continue to direct the Children's and Young People's Concerts.

He did not announce his successor.

In the talk that followed he touched lightly on future plans. He and the orchestra, as everyone knew, were in the midst of a series of Saturday night radio programs, the "Balkite Hour," and two years earlier, as part of a Beethoven cycle, he had broadcast three lecture-recitals and, with the orchestra, three concerts. He was intrigued by the power of radio to reach the public and hoped to use it to make the United States the most musical country in the world, by educating not only its children, through an extension of the existing Children's Concerts, but also those adults who had never set foot in a concert hall or seen or heard a symphony orchestra. If more reason for retirement was needed, he would soon be sixty-five and wanted more time to think and to enjoy his work.[1]

In the following days, as his resignation was announced and discussed in the newspapers, he received hundreds of letters from admirers who wished him well. Meanwhile the *Times* on its front page extolled "the end of a musical era"; the *Herald Tribune* published a tribute from Edwin Franko Goldman on Walter's services to American music; and the *American,* in an interview, quoted a jovial Walter as saying, "I am immensely pleased at the charming obituaries I am receiving." But as often happens on sentimental occasions, the hard questions were not asked, nor their answers volunteered.[2]

It was true that Walter, unlike most musicians of the day, saw a future for music in radio. But he apparently had raised the possibility of retiring as early as 1921, the year after the European tour with the orchestra and two years before his first appearance on radio. It seems likely that if radio had not yet been invented, he still would have resigned his post. He was tired of it, and there were problems facing the orchestra for which he had no sure solutions.[3]

One was personal, and yet symptomatic of a malaise beginning to afflict music generally. As Walter would admit to the *Times* in 1932, his urge to resign "was intensified by the fact that there was no great composer for whom I could pioneer work as I had done in the past for Wagner, Brahms and Berlioz." Or, he might have added, Tchaikovsky, Ravel or even Elgar. He did not find their counterparts in the generation of Stravinsky, Hindemith, Honegger, Schoenberg, Respighi, Vaughan Williams or Aaron Copland. And neither did most audiences.[4]

After World War I resistance to the new music steadily mounted. In the last quarter of the nineteenth century conductors had competed to present the premières of the leading contemporary composers — Leopold Damrosch, Theodore Thomas and their partisans had come almost to blows over Brahms's Symphony No. 1 — but by 1923 such competition was rare. That year in New York was founded the League of Composers, whose purpose was to promote performances of contemporary works and, later, to commission them. It did much good work with its concerts, radio programs and magazine, *Modern Music,* and in one form or another in the world of music there often had been such supporting organizations. Wagner had had one. But in Wagner's case, his music eventually swept the world; whereas of the league's composers, considering their works composed after 1923, none did, not even Stravinsky. By 1926 contemporary music clearly was losing its grip on audiences, and, as Walter wrote in an article, "This is not as it should be. We cannot live entirely in the past." But neither did he look forward to conducting numerous concerts of music in which he did not believe.[5]

A corollary of the audience's decline of interest in new music was its increased interest in a conductor's interpretation of the old. As Walter put it, "Hearing the standard works played several times a season, year after year, the music public naturally asks to have its interest whetted, and the method many of our symphonic organizations use to satisfy this desire, is to put new personalities on the conductor's stand." The conductor was becoming more important than the composer; the interpretation, more important than the music.[6]

In this area Walter could not match the new stars rising in New York — Mengelberg, Toscanini and, on frequent visits from Philadelphia, Stokowski. He was not their equal as an interpretive conductor, and he had no theatrical grace on the podium. A violinist, Winthrop Sargeant, later music critic of *The New Yorker,* who played under all four conductors, stated that "in the peculiar art of conveying musical ideas by means of gesture . . . [Walter] was without any trace of talent whatsoever." His beat was "automatic and mechanical" and delivered with a "curious rigidity of gesture." On the other hand, though Walter was not a great conductor, "among the great ones, I have never met one who had a more penetrating knowledge of the technical side of music." He also, with his clear beat, was splendid in any disaster and, above all, had "an uncanny ability to handle audiences."[7]

Like the Philharmonic, Walter and the New York Symphony did not begin a policy of having guest conductors until after World War I, when the resistance to new music and the expansion of the season in New York made it seem necessary. In the thirteen-year period from 1907–08 through 1919–20, when the Symphony, exclusive of its children's programs, averaged twenty-eight concerts a season in New York, Walter conducted every one, 366 in all, without a break — a sample of his extraordinary health. But in the next eight years, when the Symphony's average rose to forty-two, he reduced his share to twenty. There was not only the physical and spiritual exertion; there was the risk, obvious to everyone, of overexposure.

Walter's chief guest conductors in this later period were Albert Coates (1920–23), Bruno Walter (1922–25), Vladimir Golschmann (1923–25), Eugene Goossens (1925–26), Otto Klemperer (1925–27) and Fritz Busch (1926–28). All except Goossens, because of Walter's skill as an impresario, made their American debuts with the orchestra.

Plainly Walter and Flagler hoped to find among them a successor for the post of musical director, and for a time it seemed as if the man was Bruno Walter. He was liked and admired by the orchestra, by Flagler and the board of directors and by his sponsor, Damrosch. But Flagler, in the spring of 1925, in reporting to his board of directors on the orchestra's increasing financial difficulties, lamented:

> Another contributing cause to the situation has been the lack of drawing power of our principal guest conductor, Bruno Walter, who while possessing the highest talent and musicianship did not loom large in the eye of a public seeking for sensational or striking methods. Modest, self-effacing, appreciated and liked by musicians, he failed to make the large appeal which his qualities merited. We shall hope sometime to have him with us again, but meanwhile it is plain that other qualities are demanded by the public at large.[8]

An alternative solution to the orchestra's problems at this time was merger with the Philharmonic. As the expenses of both mounted relentlessly, the possibility was much on the minds of those controlling the two orchestras. In just one item of the budget, for example, Flagler estimated that union demands were adding about $25,000 a year to orchestral salaries; and in May 1925, citing the pressure of an income tax that had not afflicted Carnegie or Higginson, he asked his fellow directors, for the first time since assuming the deficit in 1914, to cover what might be needed beyond his annual guarantee of $100,000.[9]

Financially as well as artistically in these years the Philharmonic pulled ahead of the Symphony Society. Whereas in 1920, the year of the European tour, the Symphony had been the better orchestra with the more important conductor, by 1926 the situation had reversed, largely as a result of a merger between the Philharmonic and the new National Symphony Orchestra, which had given its first concert in 1919. It had been founded in New York by Edgard Varèse, a conductor and composer, to promote his own and other modern music. But the programs had proved so unpopular with audiences that he had been forced to cancel four of his six concerts.

Two extremely rich men, however, backed the orchestra and enjoyed the power and prestige of doing so: Clarence Mackay, president of the Postal Telegraph Company, and Adolph Lewisohn, the copper magnate. They replaced Varèse with Artur Bodanzky of the Metropolitan Opera, who offered more traditional programs, and the orchestra prospered. The next year they brought from Holland Willem Mengelberg, one of the great interpretive conductors of the period, and paid for any new players or additional rehearsals he requested; and audiences flocked to the concerts. By this time both the Philharmonic and Symphony societies had proposed a merger with the National Symphony.[10]

The Philharmonic won out, and in the fall of 1921 the two societies merged, with Mackay and Lewisohn joining the Philharmonic's board of directors, Mackay as its chairman. For the Philharmonic the infusion of wealth was vital, for along with Mackay and Lewisohn came several others only slightly less rich; and there were also strong artistic repercussions. Mengelberg shared the conductor's post with Josef Stransky, who had led the Philharmonic since 1911, but Mengelberg, though he came for only half the season, with Mackay's backing quickly established dominance and in his first year replaced more than fifty of the orchestra's players and several more each year thereafter. By 1926 the Philharmonic was a new orchestra, backed by a society with new social and financial resources, and led by a conductor of the new school, very strong on individual interpretation and, like Stokowski in Philadelphia, with a flair for publicity. Mengelberg, for example, employed a claque to cheer him at concerts. Walter, definitely of the old school in such matters, was outraged. Mengelberg, however, built an excellent orchestra.[11]

Even before Walter announced his resignation as the Symphony's musical director, he and Flagler had met privately with Mackay and perhaps one or two others from the Philharmonic, though not Mengelberg, and had drawn up a tentative plan of merger. It bluntly stated the situation facing the two societies:

> The two orchestras are giving more concerts than the music loving public of New York will adequately support except, perhaps, when attendance is stimulated by visiting conductors of great distinction. The aggregate receipts from concerts of the two orchestras are approximately $400,000 a year less than their expenses . . . One consolidated orchestra could supply New York with all the concerts it requires in addition to those given by visiting orchestras like those of Philadelphia, Boston and other cities.[12]

The problem was how "to bring about a consolidation of the two orchestras on such a basis that the financial support, goodwill, subscribers and audiences of the two existing orchestras will be preserved for the consolidated organization."[13]

What eventually was agreed on and jointly announced by Mackay and Flagler, on March 16, 1928, was a merger in which the new organizations would be called the Philharmonic-Symphony Society of New York, and the Philharmonic-Symphony Orchestra of New York, still today their legal names. Except that the Philharmonic Society would have lost its $500,000 Pulitzer endowment fund if it ceased to exist, simpler names, such as the New York Orchestra Society and New York Orchestra, might have been adopted. One purpose of the merger, after all, was to consolidate in this one orchestra the loyalties of all music-loving New Yorkers, as was the case in Boston, Philadelphia and Chicago.[14]

In the consolidation of the corporate structure Mackay became chairman of the board and Flagler, president, with other positions allotted equally between representatives from the two societies. The surprise was that the chief conductor, who would have the right to choose the players — and by the agreement at least twenty had to be chosen from the Symphony — was not Mengelberg, who had done so much to build the Philharmonic's orchestra, but Toscanini, who had served only briefly in the previous two seasons as a guest conductor. But he had been Mackay's first choice even in 1926, and for Mengelberg, who was to continue as co-conductor with Toscanini, the handwriting of dismissal was on the wall. For the conductor who hires and fires is the true leader of the orchestra.

From the agreement Walter received just what he wanted, the title of guest conductor and four weeks of conducting the orchestra as well as the continuation with it of his Children's and Young People's Concerts, eleven in all. Ernest Schelling, who in imitation had developed a series of Children's Concerts for the Philharmonic, would continue with it, but as his series was only five concerts, in this field Walter would be the dominant figure. Significantly the *Herald Tribune* topped its extended account of the merger with pictures of Flagler, Mackay, Damrosch and Toscanini.[15]

The plan for merger, though worked out in detail as early as midsummer 1926, was a secret well kept until its announcement on March 16, 1928, and by then Walter had been the center of a gala concert celebrating his final appearance as musical director of the New York Symphony, after forty-three years, and another celebrating the fiftieth anniversary of the orchestra.

The first, held at the Metropolitan Opera House on March 15, 1927, was a joint concert of the Philharmonic and Symphony orchestras, two hundred men, with the program divided between Walter, Furtwängler and Fritz Busch. Though the occasion was a benefit for the National Music League, the program was built around Walter "on the eve of his retirement," and according to the *Times,* when he appeared to conduct the Prelude to *Lohengrin,* the first of his four pieces, "there was long sustained applause, resumed after each of his performances — tribute to the man and the musician, and his long and honorable service."[16]

For the Damrosch family it was an emotional evening. As Ellie wrote later to Walter, the *Lohengrin* made her think "of father and his first beginning of Wagner at that Opera house," and she thought, too, of his battles with the Philharmonic and the founding of the Symphony. It was thrilling to see Walter "leading those two orchestras — to think of Philharmonic and Symphony — the 'lion and the lamb' — '200 feeding as one' under a Damrosch baton!" Walter agreed: "I, too, thought of father and how we owe everything to him."[17]

The second concert, his first appearance with the Symphony as guest conductor, took place in Carnegie Hall the following year, on February 10, 1928, and celebrated both the orchestra's fiftieth anniversary and the memory of its founder, Leopold Damrosch. In fact, the true anniversary of the first concert would not be reached until November 9, 1928, but by then, as still only a very few knew, the orchestra would be consolidated with the Philharmonic.

For the celebration Nahan Franko, one of the orchestra's original violinists, returned to play, and in the audience were five of the original subscribers — one of them, eighty-year-old Tante. Walter devoted the first half of the program to his father's works: the *Festival Overture;* the aria from *Sulamith,* so often sung by Marianne Brandt and now by Dusolina Giannini; and two orchestral transcriptions of Bach and one of Schubert. He closed with Beethoven's Symphony No. 5, which in 1878 had opened the orchestra's first concert in Steinway Hall, on Fourteenth Street.[18]

Shortly afterward members of the orchestra began to suspect that something was afoot when Engles, the manager, delayed issuing contracts for the next season. Then came the announcement of the consolidation, and Walter's musicians, or many of them, turned on him with a deep sense of betrayal.

Their relationship to Walter, as Sargeant observed, was essentially feudal.

> [They had] banded together to follow him. Damrosch had assumed the place originally occupied in their cosmos by Kaiser Wilhelm, the Emperor Franz Josef, Czar Nicholas . . . They would have been lost without their leader. He provided jobs. He provided a certain sense of artistic dignity, and a traditional social mechanism in which the humblest cymbal player had a valued place of his own. They treated him with respect, servility, self-depreciating clownishness and occasional truculence characteristic of the peasant serving his great lord.[19]

Over this fief Walter ruled with deliberate, quiet gestures, cultivated English and a fatherly manner, to which many responded strongly. Jack Danziger, a young first violinist of Polish heritage, was so impressed by Walter's use of English that he took a Funk and Wagnall's course in order to improve his own; later, stimulated by Walter's general level of culture, he enrolled in several liberal arts courses; and when Walter sometimes referred to him as "son," which he supposed sprang from Walter's secret disappointment at having only daughters, he was moved. For him, as for many in the orchestra and audiences, Walter was an inspiring example of what a man could be: in his culture, his family life, his skill in business and finance, his capacity to meet and mix with any sort of person and, above all, in his ability to control his temper and, in trying circumstances, to behave with dignity. As Sargeant put it, "Damrosch was the only fully adult conductor I have ever met." [20]

> But like all one-man dictatorships, however benevolent, our little feudal society was doomed to collapse. What held it together was the power and prestige of our leader . . . That Damrosch was an old man, due to retire soon in any event, that he could hardly be expected to stand forever between us and the realities of the outside world, were things that never occurred to us in the moment of catastrophe. [21]

During the orchestra's last week it began to respond sluggishly, "like an organism that is losing its powers of coordination." At the final concert, on April 1, led by the Spanish conductor E. F. Arbos, when Walter appeared to lead the program's closing work, the Adagio from Beethoven's Symphony No. 9, the men took revenge. [22]

Some of them, at least, purposely played badly, hoping to spoil what he had planned to be a dignified, commemorative rite. There were sour notes, squeaks, rasps and sloppy rhythms; Walter himself seemed affected and conducted lethargically, "like a man struggling to walk waist deep in mud." Yet at the last note applause engulfed them all. The saboteurs saw with amazement and rage that many in the audience were in tears. "As the deafening uproar of applause clattered on and on," according to Sargeant, Walter "turned to the orchestra and smiled benignly. We had been powerless, as usual, to wreck his moment of triumph. He had been able to produce a furor in spite of us." [23]

Walter's role in the consolidated orchestra was fixed for the following year by the terms of the agreement. The individual fates of his musicians were not, and even before the final concert Walter had written to Toscanini, at the Hotel Astor, offering to discuss with him which players "could, with artistic profit, be made a part of the orchestra of the new society." Toscanini replied that there must be some misunderstanding. "I cannot imagine how else you could have gained the impression that I wanted to speak to you regarding the orchestra." [24]

Meanwhile Arthur Judson, the manager of the old Philharmonic as well as of the new orchestra, and his assistant, Maurice Van Praag, had visited Walter at his house to ask for help. Toscanini was "up in the air" and they could not deal with him; he seemed unwilling to take any initiative in the selection of players. As Walter began to create on paper an ideal ensemble from the rosters of the two orchestras, Judson and Van Praag had to confess that they already had re-engaged most of the Philharmonic's first-desk players.[25]

Their action was not in accord with the agreement as Walter and Flagler understood it and, indeed, seems contrary to the plain meaning of the text. Who ordered it and why is not known, but apparently it was done in the belief that Walter and Flagler would discover it too late to make an effective protest, as happened. The result was to discourage five or six of the Symphony's best players from auditioning for the new orchestra. Barrère was not going to play second flute to anyone, and he now gave up orchestral playing to develop his "Little Symphony Orchestra." Walter, writing to Flagler, was distressed by "the premature engagement" of the Philharmonic players but in the event could recommend only that Van Praag be trusted to work out "a very delicate situation."[26]

For the rank and file of the Symphony Orchestra there were the auditions with Toscanini to be faced, and his reputation was formidable, not only as one of the greatest conductors in the world but also as one of the most terrible-tempered. In 1915, when he had stormed out of the Metropolitan Opera, *Musical America* had reported "that his great talent and mastery . . . were offset by his frightful irritability and his habit of perpetually abusing the artists," and in 1919, in a rehearsal at La Scala, he had assaulted a violinist and broken the man's bow. Though journalists probably made more of his temper than was warranted, still the prospect of an audition with him was daunting, and for the players more hung in the balance than prestige; their livelihood was at risk.[27]

String players had their auditions in a small room in Carnegie Hall in the first week in April, and Sargeant was one of those who tried for a post.

> The little white-haired man with the mustache and the piercing eyes sat beside a music stand on which were ranged orchestra parts from Richard Strauss' *Don Juan,* Beethoven's Ninth Symphony, Elgar's *Enigma Variations.* The [players] . . . filed in one by one, received a curt nod, and tried their luck . . . A day or so later we knew who was chosen and who was not . . . The world didn't need as many musicians as it had needed in the past; only a few at the top would survive. The rest, sooner or later, would have to disappear. As musicians they were finished.[28]

Sargeant was among the chosen, and in all, despite the departure of Barrère and several other of the Symphony's outstanding instrumentalists, including Danziger, twenty-three posts in the new orchestra went to former Symphony players.

To each member of the orchestra Flagler had given a pair of gold cuff links, starting up jokes about "the day we got the cuff links and lost our shirts." But for "the retiring members," those who did not receive contracts from the new orchestra, he also created a fund from which they could draw payments based on length of service.[29]

On the whole, musical historians have considered the merger to be wise. Because of it, in the view of one historian, "the Philharmonic-Symphony Society became for all practical purposes the official orchestra of the city of New York and the focus of the city's orchestral activity — acquiring thereby the stability of organization that enabled it to survive the worst days of the Depression of the 1930s." In the long run, this was perhaps the greatest gain.

The artistic results were mixed. Under Toscanini the new orchestra became one of the world's best — no small achievement — but the city also lost "the number and the variety of the concerts that had formerly been contributed by the rival orchestras." Unfortunately, too, many of their educational programs, especially the playing of works by American composers, "ground to a halt while 'the cult of personality' was fostered." Toscanini in his eleven years with the orchestra — he came, usually, for only ten weeks of the season — devoted 40 percent of his programs to three composers, Beethoven, Brahms and Wagner, and played only five American works. And when in 1930 he took the orchestra on tour to Europe, unlike Walter in the previous decade he took no American soloist and did not schedule one American work. Needless to say, there were some who questioned how much he helped the cause of music in the United States.[30]

Walter himself was not without troubles with the new organization. He had understood that as guest conductor he would be offered four weeks in midseason, when the orchestra was "tuned." Instead, Arthur Judson offered him the opening four weeks, when the players still would be individuals rather than a team. Walter protested and forced a compromise: Mengelberg would open on October 4; then Walter would have October 15 to 28 and December 10 to 23. In the second period he led Gershwin's Concerto in F, with Gershwin as soloist at the Pension Fund Benefit Concert, and then in the succeeding days the world premières of Ernest Bloch's epic rhapsody, *America,* and of Gershwin's *An American in Paris,* both of which he had brought to the orchestra.[31]

But early in March a distressed Flagler told him that the Philharmonic management — apparently Mackay acting alone — had decided not to rehire him as a guest conductor. Walter, who felt he had brought a great deal to the orchestra, not only in a repertory untouched by Mengelberg or Toscanini but also in an audience, good will and financial endowment, was astonished. He assumed that he at least would be offered his Young People's and Children's Concerts, but at the month's end he wrote to Flagler, "So far I have heard nothing from 'the gentleman in charge'

[Judson], so that I may not even be given the opportunity to refuse a half-hearted offer." Fearing the worst, he was determined to be philosophical and to believe that "all these perturbations of spirit and bruised vanities on my part will seem very foolish to me in a very short time." [32]

Margaret, however, was angry, and without Walter's knowledge she called one of the vice-presidents, Paul Cravath, who had worked hard with Walter to bring about the merger. Like Flagler, Cravath, who was in Santa Barbara, was amazed to hear that Walter was not to be rehired as guest conductor. By then it seemed clear that Judson was delaying on the orders of Mackay, who was confident, if the issue was forced, that among the society's directors a majority, however small, would support him. Finally, in mid-April, Walter received from Judson an offer to conduct the Children's and Young People's Concerts, but there was no mention of concerts in the regular season. He did not reply at once but instead wrote to Cravath:

> If I am not entitled and welcome as a conductor of distinction to direct at least one regular symphony concert of each series, in other words, two weeks, I would prefer not to conduct the Children's Concerts next season . . . If this suggestion is not agreeable to Mr. Mackay, I will write him a nice note expressing my regret at not being able to officiate as conductor for the coming season owing to my commitments in other directions. [33]

Mackay refused the compromise, and he and Walter exchanged polite notes. The public read, and believed, that Walter's increasing commitment to his work in radio caused the parting.

Walter continued philosophic and perhaps even was relieved to be free of an unpleasant situation. Margaret was furious. Walter had done as much as any man to bring about the consolidation and perhaps more than any to make it go smoothly. Now, not only was the orchestra that he and his father had built over fifty years taken from him, but also its audience, its subscription lists, endowment funds and even its Children's Concerts. To her daughter Alice she wrote bitterly,

> I am so outraged with them I can hardly bear to keep my Thursday afternoon box. I think the children are giving up their evening boxes . . . Schelling has your father's Young People & Children's — I wish with all my heart we had never tried the combination. The only thing is — of course we *couldn't* have known. [34]

Somehow, no Damrosch ever succeeded with the Philharmonic.

CHAPTER 27

Leopold as a composer. Anti-Semitism in the Hamptons; pro- and anti-Semitism in musical circles. Some good and bad in family life.

IN MARCH 1927, Marya, having heard a performance of Leopold's *String Quartet in C Minor,* wrote to him and Edie in Rome:

> The last movement is so good it hurts, and the whole thing lifts me to a positively embarrassing ecstasy. Damn your nobility, Leopold! If it weren't for a constant vision of your grinning face I should almost believe you sincere; exalted and suffering with Weltschmerz, Erdgeist, "Seid um-schlungen Millionen!" and Das Philosophie des Als Op. The whole damn thing just strains with the agony of man, the fluttering of blind moths, toward the light of love. Screams of transcendental pain and purity. O Gawd! You ought to be crowned. I still believe the first two movements too alike in mood and too ceaselessly progressive. If I had the score I could point out to you a distinct break in each — a psychological break where the excitement, strained already to the utmost, can no longer be sustained and drops gradually. Like in *Beyond the Horizon,** where, after consumption, death, disease and desertion, the woman whispers hoarsely, "There is no wood — in the grate." It's too much. I'm always tempted to let out a raucous laugh at that point. However, all this criticism is very minor and merely to remind you of my blood relationship![1]

Three months later Leopold and Edie returned from Rome, where they had lived for a year on his Guggenheim fellowship, and though he had composed many new madrigals and songs, he had done nothing on the scale of the string quartet.

Edie, reflecting much later on their year in Rome, concluded that during it she gradually had ceased to think of him as primarily a composer

---

Beyond the Horizon was Eugene O'Neill's first great success and won the Pulitzer Prize for drama in 1920. There was a revival in 1927.

His interest in photography, which he had kept alive by reading, corre-spondence with Leo and occasional home experiments, meant that he was some kind of inventor or scientist. He was also, because of his ex-traordinary skill, a pianist, as well as an academic musician who would return to New York to teach theory at both the Mannes School and the Institute of Musical Art. But only incidentally was he a composer.

> He was too easily distracted by people. He could not cut off anyone or deny anyone a minute of his time. He used to dream and talk of the ideal life — an apartment in the Ansonia Hotel, where all the meals would be sent up, where responsibilities to possessions and people would be reduced to a minimum, where he finally would be free to compose. But by and in himself he could not create the atmosphere of solitude in which to do it.[2]

The madrigals and songs, however, were well done, and Randall, who now was married and teaching music at Wellesley, asked Leopold for something for a women's chorus. Leopold sent a three-part madrigal, for first and second sopranos and altos, with a text by Shelley, *To the Moon.* In the exchange of letters following the performance, which Leopold had heard, Randall wrote, "I only reproduced as faithfully as I could what you had written. But if it is going to boil itself down to an impasse where each says the other was responsible for the atmosphere, the ten-sion and the fifteen seconds absolute silence that filled the hall after your piece was sung, the only way out is for us both to admit that perhaps, after all, P. B. Shelley may have been the man that did it."[3]

Leopold's songs, too, were attractive, and five were included in a chil-dren's song book, *New Songs for New Voices,* in which he and his parents had an editorial hand. The collection also presented five of Randall's songs, one of which, *Velvet Shoes,* to a poem by Elinor Wylie, became an art song and sometimes was included in lieder recitals. There was also a song by Frank Damrosch and three, taken from the old *St. Nicholas Songs,* by Leopold Damrosch.

Though the new collection failed to match the long success of the old, the reason probably lay less in its quality than in the new competition of radio and movies. Music-making in the home, even for children, was declining, and after the start of the economic depression the book's pub-lisher decided not to reissue it. Nevertheless, it was an unusually good book of its kind, and just as the elder Leopold's songs had been set to the works of the best contemporary poets, so, too, were the younger Leopold's, with texts by Hilaire Belloc and A. A. Milne, and with the music often displaying Leopold's own touch of humor. Though Edie might doubt that his future lay in composing, to others he seemed, with his quartet, madrigals and songs, to be following swiftly in his grand-father's steps.[4]

★

While Leopold and Edie, just back from Rome, were settling into an apartment at 111 East 81st Street, close to but not within the family's center at 120 East 75th Street, they went often for weekends to East Hampton, where Clara and David had rented a house and where Edie's mother, Mrs. Vernon Simonds, was living. She was a member of the Maidstone Club, in these years not yet on the beach and still a relatively simple social center, with a few tennis courts, rocking chairs on a porch and tea served in the afternoon, and she suggested to Clara and David that she propose them for membership. The idea was appealing. Walter and Margaret had belonged for several summers, starting about 1902, when they had rented a house in East Hampton to be near Margaret's mother, and Clara and David knew many of the members. It would be a place to take Tante.

But soon Mrs. Simonds was told by a member of the club's admissions committee that the application was not welcome because of the Mannes family's Jewish blood. Left with the task of relaying this bit of anti-Semitism to Clara and David, she chose a sunny morning when they were on the beach with Leopold and Edie. After joining the group, she explained without falsification what had happened, and announced that she would resign from the club.

There was a moment of startled silence, of confused thought. Later they and others pondered the mysteries of belonging and not belonging to a community. This stretch of Long Island, the Hamptons, was where Leopold and Helene, forty-five years earlier, had brought their children and been welcomed; where their son Frank had been a founder of one of the first yacht clubs; where Walter frequently had arranged musicales, and with Margaret had been a member of the very club of which Mrs. Simonds was now told that her daughter's husband was not welcome. Then Clara burst into tears.[5]

Marya, on Cape Cod with Jo, informed of what had happened, wrote,

> So give the poor darling gentile aristocrats of Long Island a pitying smile and turn your head kindly away from their descent into hell . . . Personally, I think you're well out of it. And your attitude of refined retirement is perfect. I can't wait to come down and vaunt my refined retirement too. We can all sing parts from the Talmud together and beat our breasts. Or I can go to the beach dressed like Christ with a placard pinned to my back "They kicked me from the Maidstone Club."[6]

The warm, noisy sympathy was typical of Marya; also that her form of help should be an imagined scene in which she had the starring role.

About twelve years later she tried to buy a house in Wainscott, a section of East Hampton where at the turn of the century her aunt and uncle, Marie and Ferdi Wiechmann, had built a large house and raised their children in the summers. But at the last moment the seller, discovering Marya's Jewish blood, and apparently under pressure from his neighbors, withdrew the property.[7]

Marya put the two incidents, merged and transformed, into her first novel, *Message from a Stranger,* published in 1948, along with her thinking on anti-Semitism in the United States. Quoting an imaginary Gentile mother warning her half-Jewish children against possible discrimination, she wrote: "Even if they do think of you as a race apart, never allow yourself that particular luxury. You're not a race apart; you're Americans." And she added, expressing her own experience in that of the imaginary children, "But the schools they went to and the people they met at home were on the whole singularly free of bias."[8]

The Maidstone episode receded without leaving scars on anyone except possibly Mrs. Simonds, who resigned from the club, and Clara, who perhaps was not so sturdy and tough as she appeared. Marya and Leopold, however, had been fortified over the years by their father's constantly telling them, "You can be anything you want. Never set any limitations on yourself." Besides the obvious command to self-fulfillment, he seems also to have meant not "wishing will make it so," but the more profound "if a donkey kicks me, who's the ass?" An individual may not be able to control events — to become, say, the world's greatest violinist — but he can control his response to his success or failure, and thereby define the kind of person he is. For David and his family, the only branch of the Damrosches to suffer directly from anti-Semitism, rejection by the Maidstone Club did not affect their love for each other, their devotion to their work or the affection of their relatives and friends; it therefore was of little, even of no importance.[9]

Unfortunately not everyone thought as they did, and in the musical world in the next half-century the question of a musician's blood, Jew, Gentile or mixed, increasingly was raised, often allowing mistake, speculation or prejudice to be presented as fact. Through the growing thicket of half-truths the Damrosch family walked with straightforward honesty, though not without scratches. Because they were the country's most prominent musical family, they constantly were mentioned as examples of this or that, and about them some myths began to form. One, which both Jews and Gentiles still occasionally recite, often with vehemence, is that the family denied its Jewish blood in order to advance in a predominantly Gentile society.

This misconception may have started in 1927 with the publication of a book with an imprecise title: *Famous Musicians of a Wandering Race: Biographical Sketches of Outstanding Figures of Jewish Origin in the Musical World.* The author was Gdal Saleski, a cellist in the New York Symphony and an admirer of the Damrosch family. He was also an enthusiast of Jewish identity, and in his preface he stated that by "Jewish" he meant not religion or culture but blood, a shift in the word's meaning that began in the last quarter of the nineteenth century. With his musicians he was "not concerned with their religion, past or present, but solely with their racial roots, as in the case of the Damrosch family. Dr. Leopold Damrosch, father of Frank and Walter, was born of Jewish parents but later was baptized in the Christian faith."

He nowhere, however, stated that the boys' mother was a Gentile and that Frank and Walter therefore might just as appropriately — more appropriately, if one follows Hebrew religious law, by which the mother is the determining parent — appear in a book of famous Gentile musicians. Nor is there any mention of Helene's musical heritage, the tradition of singing in the von Heimburg family. Though Saleski may not have intended to misrepresent, most readers would gather from the book's title and preface that Frank and Walter were wholly Jewish, and Jews and Gentiles with prejudice in their hearts often accused the family of concealing the supposed fact.

But there was no concealment: Frank and Walter, as well as David Mannes, contributed facts and photographs to the book, and its publication was reported in both the Symphony Society's *Bulletin* and the Institute of Musical Art's *The Baton.*[10]

In his preface, however, Saleski had gone still further. Noting the development among European Russian Jews of a new consciousness that immigrants had brought to the United States, he said: "That consciousness led to the establishment of certain aims, the principal one of which was that the composer-musician of Jewish origin could achieve much greater results in his work if he were to identify himself more clearly with the genius of his race."[11]

The theory lets loose a swarm of troublesome questions, enough so that by comparison Pandora's Box seems a shallow tray indeed. Again, however, there was an implicit reproof of the Damrosches, Walter especially, and though the issue seems never to have been urged against him publicly, in private conversation it was.[12]

On the Gentile side, a recent example of the kind of half-truth in which the Damrosches could become embroiled, even after death, occurred in a 1980 issue of *Partisan Review,* in an interview by Diana Trilling with the composer and critic Virgil Thomson. Speaking of the early 1920s, Thomson said: "The music world in New York was still governed by German and German-educated musicians. I won't say they were not in many cases Jewish, like the Damrosch family, but it was their German-ness which was the source of their solidarity." Then he went on to say that in 1924 the Germans, offering Frank as an example, "by dirty cracks and underground dealings" helped to oust Pierre Monteux as conductor of the Boston Symphony, chiefly because he was French. And that they approved of his successor, Serge Koussevitzky, partly because he was Jewish. "By the time World War II was over," Thomson concluded, "we had a new German establishment. But this was a German-Jewish establishment, conscious of being Jewish, not so conscious of being German — it takes German for granted — but very anti-French."

Whether any of that argument has merit is questionable, but with regard to the Damrosches, at least, it is quite misleading. Not only does Thomson not offer any evidence of Frank's alleged machinations, but Walter in certain aspects of his career was notably pro-French, such as his repertory, his choice of woodwind players and his role in founding and supporting the American School at Fontainebleau. Also, Clara and David counted as their musical godfather the Belgian violinist Ysaÿe, and as the chief glory of their faculty, for many years, Rosario Scalero. To suggest that the family, led by Frank, set out with German Jews to create, in Thomson's words, "a kind of Jewish Mafia that passed the jobs around among themselves" is to take history, twist it, and fantasize a prejudice.[13]

In Marya's novel the Gentile mother tells her half-Jewish daughter, "It's that extremely difficult road you have to tread: the middle one. And don't let extremists on either side push you off it."[14]

But the extremists, lurking often in social, religious and ethnic groups, now and then tried.

In their family life the Damrosches, including the Mannes and Seymour branches, deeply impressed those who knew them or even merely read of them. What was the secret of so much talent, individuality, affection and cohesion? They were a kind of sociological phenomenon.

One day when Walter was in Philadelphia to conduct, Margaret, seeing the temperature drop and knowing that he had only a light topcoat, sent Alice by train with one heavier. Alice, discovering at his hotel that he had left word at the desk not to be called until an hour before concert time, put the coat with a note on a chair outside his door, and returned to New York. "She thought it was nothing," said Gertrude Schirmer Fay. "Just something for 'Parp.'"[15]

A possible reason for the strength of the family bond — though it may be as much result as cause — was the evident disinclination of its members to join fully in any group's activities that did not directly advance their work. Leopold and Helene, for example, on arriving in New York in 1871 might have made their social and cultural life in the Arion Society, a usual course for German immigrants. But from the first, Leopold sought opportunities of greater musical scope than the ethnic group would allow, and in founding the Oratorio Society in 1873 he moved quickly toward a larger, more cosmopolitan world. And the full support he received from Helene and Tante suggests a shared temperament: artists tend to chafe at the loyalties demanded by groups because these inevitably are limiting.

And their attitude toward religious groups was somewhat similar. For the Damrosches of the first two generations God was in music, not in doctrine or parish work, and neither Leopold, Helene, Tante, nor any of the five children or the children's spouses, ever became an active member of a church or synagogue. The three Seymour girls, for example, all were baptized at one time in the Episcopal church in South Orange. They had come home from school one day in tears, because they had been called horrid names by classmates who taunted them by saying that without baptism they had no proper names and therefore could be called anything. So — baptism; and as Ellie was wont to say, "That's that." [16]

Life was the family and work; and except for the family, life followed work. Unquestionably this was stimulating. At any family gathering everyone usually was so eager to report what he or she had been doing that it sometimes was hard to gather an audience. On more public occasions they might attempt to restrain themselves, but often others were offended by the ill-disguised self-interest. Nevertheless, to most who knew or read of the family, it radiated an exciting vitality.

To its members, however, that vitality at times also could be exhausting. Marya once wrote to her brother:

> The reason, Leopold, that you and I seem so healthy and placid these days is partially, though undeniably due to the absence of a mother positively devastating in her energy! The more I see of her the more I realize what a terrific dynamo she is, and wonder at Father's calm. Particularly this year [1927], with more time and a little less responsibility, she knocks you over with dominant breeziness; and always, *always* sits on the edge of a chair, even if it's upholstered; and is righter and righter about things day by day; and her "Ha!"'s make you feel either like murder or like crawling out into the night and dying in some hidden corner. I begin to understand the source of several of my neuroses. [17]

Walter had the same extraordinary energy, and as he and Margaret approached seventy, his continued, whereas hers declined. The fact influenced their relationship. After he was pushed from the Philharmonic-Symphony and began to expand his radio concerts and lecture-recitals as well as guest appearances with other orchestras, she played an ever-smaller role in his career. She still entertained for him in New York, though on a reduced scale after they moved in 1930 from the house on Sixty-first Street to an apartment on the fourteenth floor at 133 East 80th Street; and when occasion demanded, she appeared with him proudly, and was fierce in his defense if she felt him attacked or even unappreciated. But she less often organized committees in his support, attended rehearsals or even performances.

There was nothing defeatist in her attitude or behavior. She continued to manage the family's finances, calling the broker regularly, writing the children advice about investments and running huge Blaine Cottage at Bar Harbor like a summer hotel in which Walter endlessly entertained relatives, friends and artists. A grandchild, Margot Finletter, used to come down early to breakfast, and always alone at the table set for eighteen or twenty was Margaret. Gradually the little girl realized that her grandmother relished these moments of solitude.[18]

In the summer of 1929 Margaret announced she would go to Europe, alone. And off she went for five weeks, leaving her daughter Gretchen in charge of Walter and Blaine Cottage. There was no diminution of affection between herself and Walter; only that, as they aged, he continued the same, whereas she changed, becoming more detached and ironically humorous about the family into which she had married.[19]

The relationship between Frank and Hetty seemed never to change, nor between Clara and David, but in the fashion of Walter and Margaret, Harry and Ellie altered slightly in theirs. With increased prosperity in his business and the children grown, he and Ellie moved to a New York apartment while keeping for weekends and the summers a small farm at Towners, near Pawling, New York. Harry, with his painter's eye for landscape, loved the fields and trees and the quiet of the country, but life for Ellie was in the city.

She enrolled again at the Art Students League and regularly attended art exhibits, but, stimulated by the activities of her brothers and sister, she continued with music as her chief activity. She resumed serious piano practice, took organ lessons at the Institute of Musical Art and directed the Sunday school Nativity celebration in the Madison Avenue Presbyterian Church. On occasion she invited string players to the apartment for duets or trios, and she announced formally with a small brochure that she was available again to "give her Musical Lectures at the piano on the Wagner Music Dramas." Schools and small groups sometimes hired her.

She loved the music festivals of Europe, and if Harry could not take her to Salzburg, she sometimes went alone. Gradually, however, they began to do more together. He had been warned by a doctor that his heart was enlarged and that he must take life easier, so, leaving much of the business to Larry, he joined Ellie on her trips to Europe. To others in the family these weeks abroad seemed always to bring them closer. They would come back, both talking enthusiastically of their experiences, and then slowly resume a pattern in which, particularly to their grandchildren, he seemed quiet and even bland while she was sharp and effervescent. Perhaps it was symbolic that in New York she never could remember that he was supposed to walk slowly.

She still took no interest in his business or business associates, and so missed an important side of him. A man whose firm was introducing the Ford car, Pond's cream and the Parker pen to Asia met some interesting people and had some amusing stories to tell, but she did not see that he was as much a pioneer as her father had been in introducing Wagner at the Metropolitan, or her brother Walter in bringing Gershwin to the Symphony. In later years, after Harry's death, in 1938, she often amused her grandchildren by announcing in the midst of an account of some new acquaintance met in a hotel or on a train: "And then I told him who I was!" And she always was Walter Damrosch's sister, not Harry Seymour's widow.

Yet once when she was old and sick, she startled her daughter Ruth by her passion in saying, "I would give anything to see your father walk in the door!" Though in middle age their interests and temperaments had diverged slightly, their loyalty remained constant.[20]

Ellie never resolved happily a conflict that distressed many of the Damrosch women: by family tradition they were encouraged equally to be creative in the arts and to marry and bear children. In the first generation Helene had resolved the potential conflict one way, and Tante, another; but despite the reverence in which Tante was held, Helene's solution was the one approved. Ellie's daughter Clair, the Duncan dancer, was the only one of Helene's ten granddaughters not to marry, and for a long time her elderly relatives watched her with suspicion. When, once or twice, at the request of friends, she posed for life drawing classes, the elderly were shocked. In Wagner, brother might sleep with sister, but no one undressed.

Clara and David, of course, were admired as the perfect solution to the problem, but no one else seemed able to achieve it. For Ellie's youngest daughter, Ruth, the conflict proved particularly distressing. Ruth's career as an artist, specializing in murals, was well started in New York when, in 1925, she went on a trip to Asia with her brother, Larry, who was traveling for Dodge & Seymour. In Singapore she met and fell in love with Stayman Reed, the head of the American Express office, but told him she would not marry him if he stayed in the Far East. Fifteen months later, by accepting a demotion, he had himself transferred to Naples, but still she delayed. She had a commission from Dutton to illustrate a children's book, and she was working on a set of murals for the screens of a sun porch. For the latter she intended to use airplane cloth to temper the glare and needed a paint that would allow light to pass through; the technical problems fascinated her.

Then word came that Stayman in Naples was seeing a great deal of an

American girl. Whether the story was true or merely invented to jolt her, Ruth never knew. But after changing her mind several times she cabled, SHOULD I COME SOON? And received the reply SOON CANNOT BE TOO SOON. So she left by ship for Le Havre, and through a friend in New York he had two dozen roses in her cabin.

But the cost to her was very great. There followed three children, and there was never time to resume the steady year-after-year work that builds a career, and the fact put a tension in her life not unlike that in her mother's. Just as Ellie never was able quite to stifle her envy of Clara's career, Ruth always would be a touch edgy about the art work of her first cousin Helen Tee Van, and as Ellie's and Ruth's lives developed, both were relatively poor mothers, intriguing spouses and superb widows. It would have seemed a pattern over three generations, except that Helene, in the first, had escaped it — perhaps because by marrying a fellow musician she had been able to release her own artistic drive through his, or perhaps because in her personality she had the ability to make a decision and never, never look back with regret.[21]

The family's attitude toward extramarital affairs, often a clue to a family's point of view in other of life's vagaries, was two-faced: image and reality. The ideal, in which the two truly merged, was the marriage of Leopold and Helene, and for their children and even for their grandchildren it was a stirring example that never lost its potency. Yet equally at the center of the family was another image and reality: Walter's *affaires de coeur* in his younger days and Margaret's response. Theirs, too, if chiefly because of Margaret, was a splendid marriage, and for many in the third generation, growing up in an era of greater sexual freedom, it set the standard by which to live.

The accepted premise was that the sexual urge was strong and natural, perhaps particularly among artists, who cultivate strong emotions for their work, and satisfying that urge outside marriage was not a sin. The danger lay in the possible injury to oneself or to some other person, and this could be contained by moderation and discretion. A few wild oats, if quietly sown, need not choke a marriage. But within the family, of course, there were as many variations in points of view as there were individuals, including one produced by Walter's daughter Polly that took everyone by surprise.

Polly was the most musical of the four Damrosch sisters and by universal report the prettiest and sweetest. Her friends felt in her at times an intensity which suggested to them that she would fall in love only once and then forever, and they wished for her in particular a happy marriage. But unfortunately she fell in love with a married man, Sidney Howard, whose play *They Knew What They Wanted* had won the Pulitzer Prize in 1925, and whose wife, the actress Clare Eames, was not in a hurry to give him a divorce.

Polly waited, and though she may have heard counsel to the contrary, decided not to sleep with Sidney. In March 1930, he was granted by a California court an interlocutory divorce on the ground of desertion and awarded custody of his five-year-old daughter. Still Polly waited. Then, early in November, Clare Eames died. Sidney was abroad, overseeing the production of his plays in Europe, but now, on the urging of her sister Alice, Polly, who was thirty-one, went to Paris and lived with him for several weeks. The wedding date was set for January 10, 1931, when he would be in New York, and meanwhile he pressed her to come to Vienna with him. Alice urged her to go, and Walter and Margaret, who happened to be in Paris, indicated they would not question her decision. Yet at lunch with a friend one day she revealed deep distress over the plan: the visit to Paris was one thing; traipsing about Europe, another. Finally the friend advised against it: "It's not your style." And she returned to New York.

There, true to her personal vision of what was honest, she announced that she would not wear white at the wedding. The family was shocked: Why raise the issue? But she was not dissuaded, and as the newspaper photographs informed the world, she was married — eyes shining with love — in a dark suit topped by a fur piece of snapping foxes. Her sisters disapproved: such honesty was excessive. A little hypocrisy in such matters made the world go round more smoothly.[22]

One quality of the family universally acknowledged was the integrity of its work, whether in music, art, business or science. No engagement, however simple, was undertaken without its full due in preparation. Edie, before marrying Leopold, had never known a professional family, and she admired its discipline. Though Clara and David played fewer recitals than in the years before founding their school, to earn money they still played for special occasions, in colleges and universities, and often in private homes; and if ever more rehearsal was necessary, a vacation would be cut short or a weekend canceled.

Edie was less pleased, even put off, by the social machinations that frequently accompanied these Mannes programs. There was often talk about people with money and how to approach them for future engagements, for gifts to the school or merely for introductions to other rich persons. On the other hand, if David and Clara played in someone's house, no matter how great the pressure, the program was theirs, not the hostess's.[23]

In the financial rewards of life Walter and Margaret not unexpectedly had proved the most successful. Carnegie, in 1919, had left by his will to Walter, and then to Margaret if she survived him, an annual stipend of $5000; in addition, Flagler soon began to give Walter an annual gift of $15,000, and Margaret had a trust fund, set up for her benefit by her sister-in-law Anita McCormick Blaine, that produced, perhaps, $10,000 a year. These various incomes, when added to Walter's healthy earnings as a lecturer and conductor, made them by far the richest of the family.[24]

The others conformed more closely to the general rule of life among musicians: live well, talk poor and die penniless — the example set for them by Leopold and Helene. Frank and Hetty had his salary and future pension, now guaranteed by the Juilliard Foundation, so the comfort of their old age was well secured; but beyond Frank's salary their accumulated assets were modest. Clara and David, as well as Harry and Ellie, earned enough regularly to make life agreeable, but there seldom was more, and what more there was David put into the school and Harry into his export company. Except for the sale value of the school and of the company, neither couple had any substantial reserves.

Inevitably, in the years 1925 to 1945, Walter's and Margaret's wealth confirmed their position as head of the family. Not only did they pick up a larger share of Tante's expenses, until these were ended by her quiet death in 1928 at the age of eighty, but they had the will and imagination to do more.

One day Walter, when talking with Frank, learned that Frank Jr., the Episcopal minister, was planning to send his eldest son, Leopold, to a small church college, St. Stephen's, at Annandale-on-Hudson, where the boy, as a minister's son, could qualify for a scholarship and be assured of a job with which to earn the balance of his expenses. The choice was necessitated by the fact that Frank Jr., who officiated at most of the family's weddings, had grown into a very amiable man who, according to his Christian precepts, loved everyone. As a result he could not distinguish enemy from friend, got nowhere in church politics and in the fall of 1929 was serving in a parish in Newark, where he earned almost nothing at all.

Both Walter and the elder Frank were distressed by the choice of St. Stephen's, which seemed a narrow, provincial school, and Walter offered to put up $800 a year to send young Leopold to Yale, where the contacts with students and faculty would be broader and the standards higher. Walter personally had little sympathy with organized religion and regretted what seemed to him an effort by Frank Jr. to guide his son into the Episcopal ministry. "Oh, the pity of it," he wrote to Margaret.[25]

More gently he wrote to Frank Jr., who had accepted the offer:

> How much longer the old rituals and beliefs will outlast modern conceptions of the universe and of the presiding Deity, no one can tell. So much has already crumbled into dust; but the idealist will always continue to exist and to search for the truth and thereby contribute his share to humanity. I am sure from what I have seen of your boy that the great grandson of my father will contribute something in this direction. Whether it be in the ministry or out of it is itself not so important.[26]

Later he and Margaret helped Frank Jr.'s second son, Douglas, with college and medical school. Each fall Douglas would be asked to tea, and after a few minutes of chitchat Margaret would say, "Now talk, Douglas, talk," and that was the signal for him to lay out the tuition, the living expenses and the money he could bring to them, while Walter, sometimes sitting, sometimes striding about the room, interjected comments, asides and conclusions. Douglas recalled, "I never felt any sense of embarrassment; there was such an air of kindness, of immense kindness in Uncle Walter. I enjoyed the show he put on, just for one, just for me, at teatime. I enjoyed every minute of it."[27]

And where Walter's kindness and imagination did not reach, Margaret's did. When Douglas married and he and his wife, Nell, were living on next to nothing while he was in medical school, Margaret secretly sent a monthly check of $25 to Nell "to help you get your hair done or to buy a hat."[28]

What a student of family life might pick out as most extraordinary about the Damrosch family in these years was the amount of communication that went on between husbands and wives, brothers and sisters, parents and children, and even across three generations. Perhaps because these family members talked to each other so much, they remained fond of each other; and the talk, being often about work — music, art, theater, science and religion — was more than gossip and provided those not still in school with a form of continuing education. Of course, there was backbiting sometimes and irritation frequently. Friends used to laugh at how swift one Damrosch was to criticize another. But only in private conversation; to the world they presented an image of affection and solidarity.

Perhaps because they were primarily artists, they found the expression of affection natural and easy, and the communication of it took many forms. There was Frank's and Hetty's infrequently articulated mutual understanding; the open discussion of Walter and Margaret and the magnificent letters both wrote to their children; the almost daily telephone conversations between Ellie and Clara; and until Tante's death her almost daily visit to at least one member of the family. And between Clara and David, a form developed only in middle age, ballroom dancing.

With characteristic intensity they began with a season's course at Arthur Murray's studio and also hired a Mexican teacher to work with them at home. David, tall and slender, made an elegant figure, and though Clara was a bit too short and square for perfection, he deferred to her with such grace that he bestowed an elegance on her. She used to complain that he sometimes did not follow the steps, but they must have been exceptionally good together, for when they danced at a hotel or on a steamer and returned to their room at the evening's close, they sometimes found flowers with cards thanking them for the pleasure of their dancing. The cards frequently were unsigned, and they seldom met the senders. Clara believed "it was only because we were not young and so thoroughly enjoyed dancing ourselves." But their silent communication with each other was so strong and attractive that it had stirred strangers.[29]

PART V

Third Generation: Family Pressures and Achievements

CHAPTER 28

Three divorces: Alice Damrosch Pennington, Marya Mielziner and Leopold Mannes. Color photography. Leopold and Mary Bancroft.

IN THE EARLY 1930S, to the distress of the family's elders, three marriages in the younger generation ended in divorce — those of Alice Pennington, Marya Mielziner and Leopold Mannes. The total was four, if Marjorie Wiechmann's earlier divorce from Swaine was counted; four out of fourteen of Leopold and Helene's grandchildren, and in each case, it was privately conceded, the chief fault lay with the Damrosch. What was wrong?

The easiest for everyone to understand, and therefore the one arousing the most sympathy, was Alice's divorce from Pleasants Pennington. Infidelities aside — though for Alice, at least, these had begun early — the problem was one of energy and ambition. Alice had inherited Walter's extraordinary vitality as well as his and Margaret's executive ability, and without children to occupy her she had held a series of jobs, president of the Junior League from 1923 to 1926, executive secretary of the New York Symphony Society from 1926 to 1928, and briefly, until her father's ejection, a post with the Philharmonic-Symphony. But the jobs, failing to exhaust her energy, had not proved satisfying, and the energy's excess frequently had been turned against her husband. As a friend of both remarked, "When Pleasants remarried, to a woman who built him up instead of tearing him down, he did fine." [1]

Alice herself in these years was often obviously unhappy. One day when she and a partner were playing mixed-doubles tennis with Walter and Helen Lippmann, the two women began to argue and soon were accusing each other of cheating. Alice was loud and angry, but Helen even more so, and to the great amusement of the spectators, Alice burst into tears. [2]

By 1929, when the divorce was imminent, she had a sense of failure. She had friends, but she knew that many people disliked her for being domineering; and despite the jobs, at thirty-seven she had no career and soon no marriage. To a family friend who took her to the theater one night she endeared herself for the only time by talking of the need to get away, to live in Europe, because every activity, every emotion seemed to start and end at her parents' house on Sixty-first Street.[3]

In August, at Blaine Cottage, she had a long talk with her father, and as Walter wrote to Margaret, who was in Europe, "The gist of it was that I assured her that I was very sympathetic to anything that she felt she wanted to do, but that I wanted her to keep an open mind regarding her future plans for a month or two."[4]

Eventually Alice decided to make her base in Europe, and for many years she kept an apartment in the Haus Angelika in St. Anton am Arlberg in the Austrian Tyrol. She had always been a mountain climber, and in the late 1920s, with the guide Otto Furrer, she had scaled the Matterhorn.[5] Now she took up stag-hunting, and in a letter to her mother she described a kill:

> For about an hour I struggled back and forth across the snowfield. Then one shot rang out. A second later, one more. There was a halloo up the gully. I struggled up. There was Oscar, and Spiess, and a long track down the side of the gully and something that looked like bare crooked sticks standing up in the snow. It was the horns of the stag. I'm ashamed to say I was not at all horrified or disgusted. He had been killed by one clean shot in the neck. The second shot was only a "gnadenschuss" in case he still lived. Somehow having plowed the tracks and everything, it seemed simply thrilling to get him. I expected to be horrified. Maybe if I had seen him alive, I would have been.[6]

In time she would become an excellent hunter, well known and admired in the Tyrol.

Alice always, apparently, had found in physical danger and exertion an exhilaration close to a mystical experience. She was not alone in the family in this. Her Aunt Marie Wiechmann reportedly had known it; and her first cousin Bess Seymour, married to Robert Ransom, in a few years would become known as the "champion woman skate-sailor" of the United States. At speeds of sixty, even seventy, miles an hour Bess would speed around the lakes of Hartford, Connecticut, while manipulating a sail on her back. For Alice as a girl and young woman the sports had been swimming and diving, and in a poem, *Swimming by Night,* she had written:

> . . . I will swim till I can swim no longer,
> I will spurn the shore that blots the starlight

From my vision, I will shake it from me . . .
I will seek the source of the creation,
Swim with mighty strokes to the horizon,
Where the drowned stars and the stars in heaven
Meet and mingle in new constellations;
I will reach them, dare to touch them even,
Cleansed and purified by many waters
Even I may breathe upon their splendor.
It is written that the night must vanish,
But this hour is mine, I will not yield it,
I defy the dawn to take it from me . . .
Oh, to live and battle thus forever![7]

Soon she wrote to her family in the United States that she had taken up skiing seriously, and in 1932, when almost forty, she became the first United States woman to win the Parsenn Derby at Davos, Switzerland, and the Golden K award of the Kandahar Ski Club. By chance she had arrived in the Alps at the very moment that women were beginning to compete in skiing, and she was to have a major role in bringing American women to the important meets, thereby contributing greatly to the sport's development in the United States.

Marya's divorce from Jo Mielziner was much more upsetting to the family. Where Alice seemed to try to make a failing marriage succeed, Marya seemed to wreck a successful marriage deliberately, out of willfulness and bad judgment, and in a manner that many of her friends and relatives found offensive.

Marya, all her life, made a point of candor, at least as she interpreted it and on the occasions she chose. Not long before her marriage to Jo she had been one of a weekend house party given by Mrs. Simonds for Edie at East Hampton, and Marya in her thank-you note wrote that she had not liked Mrs. Simonds and had not enjoyed herself. Mrs. Simonds showed the letter to Edie, and together they wondered why it had been necessary. What had Marya gained?[8]

In 1927, after fifteen months of marriage, Marya wrote from Cape Cod to her father at East Hampton:

I'm really dying to be with both of you again and blowing my rebellious mouth out once more . . . And all I demand of you and Mama is leisure in the bathroom and complete liberty of action everywhere else. Even to spending the night God knows where and with God knows whom, although it probably won't come to that. Anyway I warn you that I may seem flighty. I spend such a large part of my life in heavy, balanced, moderate rumination that I sometimes need a fling.[9]

Marya's letters to her parents that summer are full of remarks about the bathroom, and it is unlikely that Clara and David, both notably fastidious, were enchanted by the theme or by the threats of an extramarital fling. But they and everyone else seem to have ascribed such talk to a "rebellious mouth."[10]

Soon, however, Marya bagan an intense, passionate affair that for a long time she kept concealed from everyone but her brother. The lover was a man she refers to in her autobiography merely as "a brilliant Catalan, a biologist at the Rockefeller Institute," and in her correspondence as "F." In the summer of 1929, on some pretext, she followed him to Europe, only to discover that he was in a hospital near Barcelona with tuberculosis and could not see her. Uncertain about what to do, she joined her unsuspecting parents for two weeks in Switzerland. To Leopold she wrote:

> God knows what will happen, and when I'll get back . . .
> In the meantime every letter from Jo gives me an awful pang of remorse and pity — and every letter from F. binds me to him more and more . . .
> M[other] and F[ather] in fine shape, though M. drives me nuts with constant references to darling Jo. (He is darling, but this isn't a time I want to hear it!)
> Thanks for writing me. Do it again.
> And *don't* tell *any* of this to Jo. I haven't had the heart to tell him the situation yet. I want to wait until things are more decided. Poor devil — I'm not losing my head, but I may if things get any thicker.
> You can see, can't you, how this illness of F.'s precipitates — and also delays — everything?
> Well, what the hell. I'll come through somehow.[11]

Within two years, in 1931, she had divorced Jo. In her autobiography, published forty years later, she wrote, "I had at least the minimal decency to refuse alimony from a man whom I had deeply, if unwillingly, hurt."[12]

Her parents, friends, and relatives were dismayed. She and Jo had seemed so well suited; he still loved her and, despite F., had been eager to keep the marriage going. Soon, everyone predicted, F. would depart from the scene. What had she gained?

In her autobiography she gives as the gain "freedom to roam, both inwardly and outwardly, to explore, to risk, and ultimately to know a variety of loves with men."[13]

Asked once to be more specific about why she had divorced Jo, with whom she had been happy, she replied that, although in most respects he was the affectionate, warm, gay person he seemed outwardly, in the bedroom he was "too quick, too unadventurous, too self-centered" to give a partner satisfaction. Fortunately or unfortunately she had learned from others that there was much more, after which life with Jo became impossible.[14]

But others saw in the divorce some reasons less romantic than "freedom to roam." Jo wanted a family, and she did not, as she confessed to her Seymour first cousins. Not because children would impinge on her solitude for writing — there were relatives and nursemaids enough to help with children — but because childbirth might spoil her figure and lessen her attractiveness to men.[15]

Randall Thompson, who in these years knew both Jo and Marya well, thought there was still another reason: ego. Marya's playwrighting had not produced a single success. Apparently the best out of nine or ten attempts was *Café*, a play about rootless expatriates in Paris, which reached Broadway in August 1930, received harsh reviews and closed after four performances. Meanwhile, according to Thompson,

> as Jo's career in stage design began to develop, people began to pay more attention to him than to her. When they went to the theater together she was always enormously striking with her hats and gowns, but this was fashion, mere fashion, whereas his work was more creative and ultimately more exciting.[16]

She could not bear second position, Mrs. Mielziner. Marya Mannes must be first, and over the years some of her friends came to see this as a psychological reason for her many affairs: with each new lover she was again selected to be first in someone's attention. It was comforting.[17]

Marya, however, in her books and articles portrayed the divorce as a blow struck for women's freedom, and moved with her desk, typewriter, upright piano and a few other familiar pieces into a small apartment at 225 East 54th Street. Because the occasional sale of a book review or poem did not bring in enough to make ends meet, she accepted an allowance from her parents, who by now were frantic over her chosen way of life. Soon F., as predicted, disappeared, but there was always another man, generally older and single. "One at a time, to be sure. For one night, or ten, or two years . . . What was wrong with giving and receiving warmth, pleasure, affection, and release even if these could not qualify as love?"[18]

Her Uncle Frank probably thought she was a slut: every large family, sooner or later, will have one. She insisted she was creating a new way of life, better for her than the model of her parents and grandparents. She did not ask her lovers for marriage or even for help with the rent. That was provided by her parents. The lovers no doubt rejoiced. As the expression then was, Why buy a cow when milk's so cheap?

Finally one day Uncle Walter, having telephoned first, stopped by for tea. As that was not usual for him, a sense of occasion hovered over the initial pleasantries, and indeed after ten minutes or so he put down his cup: "Now, Marya — "

She remained silent, seeing no need to aid him, and he hesitated slightly as he continued. "I confess that I have a reason for this visit, a personal reason."

For a second she thought perhaps he wanted her help with some radio program, but the next words erased that hope.

"Your Aunt Margaret, and I, too," he added emphatically, "are a bit worried about you."

She looked at him.

"About the direction your life is taking."

"And what direction is that?"

"Well, your Aunt Margaret and I fear that your social life in the evenings is rather too taken up with single, older men. In fact, in this direction we fear the trend is in danger of becoming" — he pronounced the word in French — *"excessif."*

"I prefer older men," she said positively. "I find them more interesting."

"I shan't be heard to speak against them," he said, his eyes twinkling.

"And after a day alone at my desk, writing, I am eager to get out, to the theater, a concert or pleasant dinner."

"Yes, I'm sure, I'm sure, but still, Marya — "

"Still, what?"

"Still, as the Greeks carved on the temple at Delphi, 'Nothing in excess.' "

"Well, then, let's talk about numbers. How many men are 'all right'? And how many 'excessive'?"

"Oh . . ." He flapped his hand helplessly.

"I assure you," she said heatedly, "I never have more than one at a time."

"Of course not," he murmured.

"And anyway, Uncle Walter, as a young man if you slept with even a third of the sopranos with whom your name was linked — it was a scandal."

He smiled.

"And if not wrong for you, then why for me?"

"Because such scandals are more damaging to women than to men."

"But why?"

He shook his head. "It's the way of the world."

"Well, the world is changing."

When he started to protest, she interrupted: "Look. I was born curious. I come up to a corner, and I want to see what's around it. So do you, Uncle Walter."

"Yes," he said with finality. "I do." And he went on to talk of other matters.[19]

In later years she would say that she could barely have a conversation with Uncle Frank, but with Uncle Walter she could talk about anything, anything. But it was quite untrue, part of her self-serving self-deception. For, in fact, she had cut him off. He might have gone on to give her some profound advice about how to build happiness in life, but she did not want advice; she wanted approval. And she had succeeded through a mixture of clever talk and threatened anger in silencing him. It was a technique that seemed to come naturally to her, one that she would use constantly in life, with the result that she seldom heard advice, and most of what happened to her seemed unique, something happening for the first time.

After Uncle Walter had gone, she worked herself into a rage and sought parental support. She told her mother of the visit, but in such a way that Clara's fury was directed at Aunt Margaret for usurping a mother's role, for interfering. And thereafter no member of the family, with the rare exception of Leopold, attempted to advise Marya about her behavior. Among her Seymour cousins the incident was known, with sly Wagnerian reference, as "Aunt Margaret's Warning to Marya Against Too Much Lipstick."[20]

Leopold's divorce, in the summer of 1933, was the last of the three, and though Clara and David were deeply upset by it, to the rest of the family it was a distant, mysterious event, for by then Leopold and Edie had been living in Rochester for two years while Leopold and Leo Godowsky worked at Eastman Kodak's research laboratory on their photographic experiments. The distance and mystery suited Leopold, for by temperament, unlike Marya, he had no desire to make a parade or a philosophy of his problems. And again unlike Marya, though his marriage failed, in a general way he believed in marriage and family life. When Marya would rail against the "bourgeois" attitudes and institutions of their parents' generation, he would say, sometimes wearily, sometimes angrily, "Marya doesn't understand anything."[21]

The move to Rochester was the result of increasing success in his and Leo's experiments. Soon after Leopold's return from Rome, in 1927, he and Leo again had rented a small dentist's office, this time in the Hotel Alamac at Broadway and Seventy-first Street, and resumed their double lives of music by day and science on the weekends and occasional evenings. Before Leopold left for Rome they had developed and patented a method of controlled diffusion, in which, roughly speaking, color was imposed on the film after the picture was taken. Then in 1925 they had read in E. J. Wall's *The History of Three-Color Photography,* which had reported their own patent, of a system of dye-forming couplers — compounds within the emulsion layers on a film that would react with the developing agent (already modified — oxidized — by the process of silver development) in such a way as to produce color within the film itself. As Godowsky explained it later:

> Of course, we read the book from the first to the last page, and what made a deep impression on us was the mention of Rudolf Fischer's couplers. To our way of thinking, it was the greatest contribution toward color photography; it made color photography what it is today. We felt when we got hold of the Fischer coupler that we had a very excellent chance of making a multilayer film processible because we had a great deal of experience in the early '20s with our dye-mordants and metal toners. We got the separation of the layers by learning how to control our diffusion to any degree we wanted to, and it was that system of controlled diffusion that gave us courage. We realized that we could use controlled diffusion on couplers to make a worthwhile workable process.[22]

In the spring of 1930, when Dr. C. E. Kenneth Mees, the director of the Kodak research laboratory, came to New York, as usual he met with the two men to check the progress of their work, and this time, impressed by their new method of chromogenic development and controlled diffusion, he invited them to Rochester to continue their experiments in the Kodak laboratory, where they would have the support of professional chemists and photographic experts.

For neither musician was it an easy decision, but it was harder, perhaps, for Leopold, because he had aspirations to be a composer, which Leo did not, and full-time work on photography would preclude music except as an evening's pastime. Nevertheless, there was the excitement of thirteen years of research about to come to fruition, possibly in only two or three years, and on October 31, 1930, they signed a contract with the Kodak Company under which they became its employees to work on their own ideas. The annual salary for each was to be $7500, and they would retain the rights to all patents filed before the contract date and to all royalties arising from them. Only those patents filed after October 31 would be the company's property. They also received jointly $30,000, of which they used $20,000 to repay their loans from Kuhn, Loeb & Company, which still would receive a third of any royalties they might earn.[23]

The two men had musical commitments in the city that could not be broken — Leopold, for example, was teaching theory at both the Juilliard's Institute of Musical Art and at the Mannes School of Music —and though they tried to hasten the pace of their photographic work, it was not until mid-July 1931 that they were able to move to Rochester and begin work in the company's splendid new laboratory. It was against this public background of success that Leopold's marriage with Edie began to unravel.

Before the marriage Leopold evidently had sown a wild oat or two, but had kept his occasional nights abroad concealed, for apparently only Marya, Leo and Randall knew of them. Probably he intended to stop these when he married, but he soon discovered he could not. The marriage bed, though happy, was not enough. The first crisis arose in July 1927, with the engagement of Edie's sister to Randall's brother, and Leopold wrote anxiously to Randall that the latter, a friend now about to become a member of the family, must not reprove or try to reform him. Randall replied: "You retain full freedom of action in these affairs; your marriage to Edie in no way binds you to me. Perverse as this seems on the surface." Nevertheless, Randall began to worry. Leopold seemed unable to settle down, and his nocturnal prowling, so easy with the double life of photography and music, threatened not only his marriage but his composing, for which there was already too little time.[24]

Then, in the spring of 1928, Edie became pregnant, and that summer she and Leopold, instead of going to East Hampton, went to Menemsha, on Martha's Vineyard. Unfortunately, in her sixth month Edie lost the child, a boy, and both she and Leopold were deeply distressed, and shortly after that the marriage bond seems to have begun to loosen.

The following summer they went again to Menemsha, this time urging Randall and his wife, Margaret, to join them. But Randall, who always sought solitude for composing, took his family instead to Francestown, New Hampshire, whence he wrote to Leopold: "Menemsha sounds like Newport in comparison . . . 'Land trouble,' yachting people, guests. We have to think hard what any of these items are." At the summer's end Leopold had no new work completed; Randall had four. But Leopold, of course, had his photographic work, which was progressing.[25]

Either that summer or early that fall he met a married woman, Mary Bancroft, and the two fell in love. To Mary, Leopold's physical attraction was "overpowering . . . something beyond analysis."[26] She compared him to Edwin Arlington Robinson's *Richard Cory,*

> He was a gentleman from sole to crown,
>   Clean favored, and imperially slim.
> And he was always quietly arrayed,
>   And he was always human when he talked;
> But still he fluttered pulses when he said,
>   "Good-morning," and he glittered when he walked.

She was not alone in her physical response to Leopold. Many women shared it, and a reason that his casual infidelities could be so numerous was that women frequently offered themselves to him. In Mary's case, however, the attraction was mutual, and by the late fall of 1930 they were conducting, in her words, "a flaming romance," meeting, whenever they could, in hotel rooms.[27]

Mary was a strong, vital woman, interested in art, politics and men, and of the last in her lifetime she collected in differing relationships four who became well known. Of these, Leopold was the first. Later she studied with Jung; during World War II she became a mistress in all respects of Allen Dulles; and after the war she had a long, platonic friendship with Henry R. Luce, to whom she became an intellectual gadfly, challenging his opinions, the honesty of his publications, the integrity of his life. With Leopold, however, though she knew of his philandering, she wanted marriage, and she blew into his life like a whirlwind.[28]

Though she was at the time the mother of two and married to Sherwin Badger, who worked for the *Wall Street Journal,* she was ready to divorce her husband at once if Leopold would divorce Edie and marry her. But Leopold delayed, perhaps because his marriage meant more to him than he had realized, perhaps because he was a bit afraid of Mary's vitality, perhaps because Edie did not want the divorce. Leopold, unlike Marya, despite his constant infidelities seems to have had recurring second thoughts about pulling apart a marriage. Typically, in planning for a weekend with Mary at the Hotel Traymore, in Atlantic City, he was courageous, but once there he became cowardly, skulking around in fear that they would be challenged or recognized.[29]

By this time he and Edie had moved to Rochester, and the marriage bond loosened further. Both of them in the first year found living in Rochester extremely difficult; they yearned for New York and its stimulation, and they came down to it as often as they could, together or separately.

The life in Rochester, however, was easier for Leopold than for Edie. He had his science and at least some music, for there was a symphony orchestra, the Eastman School of Music and nights of chamber music at Godowsky's house, who by then was married to Frances Gershwin. But of art for Edie there was none. The scientists liked to call Rochester "the Cambridge of the North," referring to Harvard, but for Edie it was Siberia, and as the months Leopold seemed likely to remain stretched into years, she grew increasingly frantic. Years later Randall wondered whether, if the research laboratory had been in New York, London or Paris, the marriage, with more children, might not have lasted.[30]

Meanwhile Leopold continued his casual infidelities as well as his affair with Mary Bancroft. Then one day in New York, without Leopold's knowledge, Clara sent David to call on Mary. There were some situations in which David was superb. One time, for example, returning from Utica by train to New York after Larry Seymour's marriage to Dorothy Ross, he stopped at the couple's roomette to say good-by and discovered them both near tears of exhaustion from the wedding and about to have a fight. Sitting between them, he talked charmingly about nothing for an hour, until they were happy again. But faced with an elemental force like Mary Bancroft, David could do nothing; he melted before her fire and departed without even leaving behind a clear message.

When Mary told Leopold of his father's retreat, Leopold laughed.[31]

But then Clara summoned Mary to tea. Sitting on the edge of her chair, she stated precisely that she would not oppose a divorce between Leopold and Edie or even a continuation of Leopold's "close relationship" with Mary, but she would oppose forever their marriage. Leopold had too much to do in his music and color photography to take on a new wife with two small children. In any event he and Mary were unsuited. "I consider you too much for Leopold," she said. Mary was both hurt and astonished. Leopold, she had always felt, had far more energy and vitality than she. But the message was clear, and thereafter she considered Clara the major obstacle to her marriage.

Mary, though, was in love and persevered, and finally Edie agreed to a divorce, provided Leopold obtained it, which meant, because of his commitments, that it would have to be granted in New York, where the only grounds were adultery. At the time the usual method of achieving a record of adultery was for the man to hire a woman to be caught with him in a hotel room with their clothes mostly off, the bed mussed, and with corroborating testimony from a waiter that he had seen them in this condition in the room, misbehaving. Mary, who by now had obtained a divorce from Badger in Nevada, where the grounds were easier, refused to have Leopold share a room under these conditions with anyone but herself, so together one afternoon in the spring of 1933 they checked into the Prince George Hotel on Twenty-eighth Street, just east of Fifth Avenue.

As directed by the divorce attorney, they mussed the bed, took off some clothes and ordered tea. The attorney's idea was that tea was better for the purpose than supper, as it was more distinctive and the waiter who brought it would remember more clearly the couple who had ordered it and the condition of their clothing and of the room. Though what Mary and Leopold were required to do was rather less than what they often had done, the special circumstances made them nervous, and for Mary the nervousness took the form of chatting garrulously with the waiter, and for Leopold, of overtipping. As a result the waiter the next day insisted to the attorney that he had seen only a middle-class couple, well dressed, with the bed undisturbed, having a cup of tea.

So they tried again, at the Hotel Alamac, where Leopold and Leo had once had their laboratory. Mary moderated her conversation, and Leopold, his tipping. But the waiter told the attorney the next day that Leopold, whom he had recognized from the laboratory days, was a fine man, and he would not assist an obviously scheming woman to trap him. By this time Edie was ready to take the initiative, and she went to Reno, stayed the required six weeks to establish residence and procured a divorce on the grounds of cruelty.

Now Leopold began to shuffle. Mary was ready to marry, but he would never set the date. He was eager, he said, to finish his work in Rochester first. She felt she could understand that. She knew that he rose at six-thirty every morning, worked all day and sometimes into the evenings. She knew, too, that Leo and Frances Godowsky, and perhaps others in Rochester, viewed her as a home-wrecker and were not eager to welcome her. Perhaps to wait out the winter would be better. After all, as Leopold assured her, there would be frequent weekends in New York or Rochester, and between the weekends there would be letters and phone calls.[32]

> But letters, particularly daily letters such as we started writing each other, had a curious effect. Perhaps the fact that I was a writer and Leopold was not had something to do with it. But in any case, our personalities as projected in our letters were apparently not the same personalities we each knew in real life. This led to misunderstandings that resulted in phone calls that did little to clear up the misunderstandings, yet turned out to be so long and expensive that they became in themselves an added irritant. Then when Leopold did come down from Rochester, his family expected him to spend considerable time with them, which had the effect of making me feel he would *rather* spend his time with them than with me, and I would either sulk or we would quarrel, and he'd have to return to Rochester before anything had been resolved, and the letters and phone calls would start again until we both became exhausted from them.[33]

Meanwhile her family inquired periodically when she planned to marry, and each time she was unable to report a date their eyebrows went higher. The situation seemed intolerable, and she suggested to Leopold that they marry, and he could continue to live alone in Rochester, and she, with her children, in New York. Then at least when he came down he would stay with her, and her family would be off her back.

> In my eyes, the situation was beginning to resolve itself into a tussle over him with his family, specifically with his mother. And this idea became an obsession when a friend of Marya's delighted in reporting to me arguments he had overheard between Leopold and his mother on the subject of marrying me. I became convinced that I would never be able to win out against his mother. And I finally told Leopold this. Of course he denied it. I told him I didn't believe him and I wanted to break off completely with him. He said he couldn't stop me if this was what I wanted to do, although he couldn't understand why I didn't trust him and why I wouldn't believe he loved me when he did.[34]

So, though she loved him, in the spring of 1934 she broke off the relationship, and the next year went to live in Switzerland.

After the war she saw something of him again and, by then having studied with Jung, she was apt to assess persons in psychiatric terms. Asked for her view of Leopold's personality, she concluded that in his emotional life he had never matured fully, never completely grown up. She put this down to his parents: they were repressed sexually and were dominating emotionally. And she wondered, too, if the same reasons did not underlie Marya's sexual revolt.[35]

But to most of Leopold's friends and relatives, what was visible in his life in 1934 was the verge of success in developing with Godowsky a practical method of color photography. It would be a stunning achievement.

CHAPTER 29

The Tee Vans, scientific expeditions and the bathysphere. Alice and the U.S. Women's Olympic Ski Team. Leopold and the Kodachrome process.

EVEN AS LEOPOLD AND LEO came closer and closer to discovering some practical method of color photography, Leopold's cousin Helen Tee Van became more swift and expert in her water-color sketches of insects, fish and other animals, and her husband, John, set a photographic record of a kind in filming the growth of an eel's embryo. The family had more fun from the Tee Vans' work than from the two Leopolds', for Clara, attempting to report what the men in Rochester were doing —"Now they are working on the red emulsion . . ." — succeeded only in spreading the confusion in her own mind. But John and Helen could make their work comprehensible.

Even children could grasp some of John's problems in photographing life inside an egg. He had taken a deep-sea eel's egg, whose shell is transparent, and propped it up in the end of a medicine dropper placed on a table by his bed. Then, keeping himself awake by a red light that flashed once a minute, he recorded the embryo's growth in 10,000 frames of continuous motion picture over a period of four days and nights; roughly a picture every thirty seconds. By the fourth night, John, weren't you pretty tired? Well, yes, I was.[1]

Helen's stories were no less startling. After painting insects for William Beebe and the New York Zoological Society in British Guiana, she later joined him and John aboard the *Arcturus,* a three-hundred-foot wooden freighter converted into a floating laboratory. In the Atlantic, off Cuba, using nets, trawls and dredges that could descend a mile or more, Beebe had hauled up to the deck whatever deep-sea life he could catch.

Whenever a haul came over the side, the zoologists and artists were ready with pans, dishes and bowls filled with sea water to rescue any strange fish or animal showing signs of life and rush it quickly to the laboratory or artists' darkroom, where its features could be recorded. "Maybe," Helen wrote, "it will be an illuminated fish, with rows of light organs that must be portrayed before they become dull and color-less . . . or a scarlet shrimp from the 'red zone' a mile or so down, where practically all of the animal life is a vivid scarlet."[2]

This method, however, soon seemed unsatisfactory, and Helen's next step, taken in the early 1930s on expeditions based at Nonesuch Island in the Bermudas, was to put on a diving helmet and paint underwater, chiefly the fish and animal life on the coral reefs. She used oil paints on a zinc plate, and this proved practical, except that on her first descent she forgot to tether her brushes, so they floated upward, out of reach.[3]

Beebe, meanwhile, dissatisfied with the glimpse of the depths obtained by his nets, had constructed the bathysphere, a diving bell that so captured the imagination of the public that accounts of it and what Beebe saw from it were reported regularly in popular as well as scientific journals. The bathysphere was a steel ball with an inside diameter of fifty-four inches and with four windows made of three-inch-thick quartz. As underwater equipment then was, a diving helmet such as Helen used could descend about sixty feet beneath the surface; a diving suit, 306; a submarine, 383; an armored suit, 525; and the bathysphere, which was equipped with a searchlight for the darkness of the deep, 3028, or more than half a mile. Once one was inside it, with the hatch closed and screwed tight by those on the tender, there was no way out, no matter what the emergency, until the ball was brought back to the tender. Still, the rewards of a descent were great. "Nothing that our nets had picked up," John later wrote, "had prepared me for as much life as I had seen."[4]

To the younger members of the family, particularly to the young in-laws, John's accomplishments were quite extraordinary, and at tea one day when Ellie and Clara treated one of his stories as of no account, Dorothy Seymour, Larry's wife, said to John sympathetically, "Those of us who married into this family ought to have a Protective Association." Up spoke their Aunt Margaret: "I will be president, because I have had it the hardest the longest."[5]

On October 27, 1934, in Geneva, Alice Damrosch Pennington married Dudley F. Wolfe, a rich sportsman from Boston who shared her interest in skiing and mountain-climbing, and though he seemed to many of her friends as much inclined as her first husband to be dominated by her, their shared interest, backed by his money, seemed grounds for a lasting relationship.

By this time Alice was afire with the idea of creating a team of American women to compete in the international ski races of Europe, and immediately after her marriage she returned to New York with her husband to introduce him to her family and also to recruit women who could come to St. Anton to train for the winter races, of which the two most important were the FIS (Fédération Internationale de Ski), which annually determined world championships, and the AK (Arlberg-Kandahar), the most important of the downhill and slalom races. The FIS shifted locale each year, and the AK alternated between St. Anton am Arlberg in the Austrian Tyrol and the Kandahar ski club slopes at Mürren, Switzerland. Beyond 1935, Alice looked to the 1936 Winter Olympics at Garmisch, in Bavaria, and to repeats of the FIS and AK, which to skiers of the day were more important.

Women's racing in those days was still quite new and by no means universal. Women had skied and even raced in the early 1920s, but only incidentally, not with the determination and training that the men put into it. But in 1928, with the first AK race for women, that began to change, and the following year a group of English women who had trained at the Kandahar Club at Mürren astonished the ski world at the FIS races at Zakopane, Poland, and the AK at St. Anton.

These women were more than the first of their sex to train in the slalom; they were the first to wear well-cut ski clothes, displaying long straight legs encased in even longer, beautifully tailored blue trousers, and topped by trim jackets or close-fitting sweaters. Such clothes at the time were a revelation on the mountain slopes, for until then women had skied in baggy khaki trousers, with cold cream smeared across their noses and with rucksacks on their backs.[6]

In the example of the English women, however, Alice saw more than smart clothes or extraordinary courage; she saw what even a little training could accomplish. "Ten years ago," she wrote in 1937, "most women skiers were such cowards that, speaking generally, the brave girl won." By 1937, however, a woman to win needed also physical endurance developed by months of training and ski technique taught by a professional. Racing had become a very different sport from holiday skiing, and for American women Alice was the primary cause of the change.[7]

Having returned to New York immediately after her marriage, she conferred with Roland Palmedo, president of the Amateur Ski Club of New York, who not only knew who were the outstanding women skiers in the country but also was able to raise some money to send a squad of seven to the 1935 FIS at Mürren. Several of the best were already in Europe; the others Alice selected by going around the country explaining, watching and finally making her choice. Soon she had seven in training at St. Anton under Otto Furrer, three times an AK winner.

That winter the team skied in the FIS and took, in Alice's blunt words, "quite a licking." But she, Palmedo and the skiers understood that they would have to compete for several years before they could match the Europeans, and no one was discouraged. Indeed, there was reason for hope. The English expert Arnold Lunn, in writing of the straight race for the *British Ski Year Book,* noted, "I was particularly impressed by the cool courage and judgement on these slopes of a lady who is a newcomer to international racing, Miss [Elizabeth D.] Woolsey of the U.S.A."[8]

The next year Alice expanded her squad to twelve, of whom three were girls of nineteen, so that as well as training, selecting and entering teams for the year's various races, she often acted also as parent and banker. The squad's base was St. Anton, where Alice made all the living and training arrangements, and although the girls in theory paid all their own expenses, Alice by lavish entertaining often reduced these. She remained herself, however. Probably Woolsey spoke for most of the women in saying that, while she had enormous respect and admiration for Alice, she had not much affection. She felt always that Alice had little or no interest in any of them except as skiers. A bruised ankle would excite instant, expert attention; a bruised feeling would not be noticed. An acquaintance observed of Alice, "She was not cruel, just uncaring. She was always very absorbed in herself and what she was doing, but if you fell outside that focus, she had no time for you."[9]

The 1936 Winter Olympics, the first in which U.S. women skiers competed, took place in February at Garmisch and preceded the FIS championships, held that year at Innsbruck. The six-woman squad that Alice had selected wore matching red stockings, marched in the parade and refused to give the officials and Hitler the Nazi salute, and the four who raced did moderately well. In the downhill, Elizabeth Woolsey placed fourteenth. Since Alice always said that it required three years of training to make a racer, again no one was discouraged. And after the political tension in Bavaria, heightened by the journalistic silliness that always seems to surround the Olympics, the quiet of St. Anton for further training seemed doubly welcome.[10]

Alice now, with the help of Hannes Schneider, who was president of the Arlberg Ski Club and one of the world's best ski instructors, arranged for downhill and slalom tryouts, on the results of which she selected a team of six for the FIS at Innsbruck. Once again Woolsey placed first on the team.

Then came the day of the downhill race. Unfortunately, the warm weather of several days, which had melted most of the snow, exposing bare soil and tree trunks at the edge of course, suddenly turned cold the night before the race. In the morning the course, from top to bottom, was a steep, narrow strip of ice.

The officials several times postponed the start of the men's race, hoping for a thaw that never came. Finally shoulders were shrugged, and word was sent from the finish line to the top to begin. A racer races to win and wins by taking chances, but on ice the risks are doubled. The first man came in sight of the finish, slid into a bump and landed in the spectators with a broken collarbone. Racers 2, 3 and 4 did not appear at all, and 5 was carried off on a stretcher with a broken leg. As Alice remembered the race, not a single one of the six Hungarians who started came within sight of the finish; all had broken their skies or sustained injuries higher on the course.

> I clambered over the ropes and past the soldiers protecting the timekeepers and race officials, and asked if the *Damen* were going to start. A worried official told me they had to race the same course as the men because it was too late to change the electric timing. A vision of all the American mothers and fathers who had let their daughters come abroad to race rose before my eyes. "Please telephone up to the top and tell the U.S.A. *Damenmannschaft* that they are forbidden to start," I said in as loud a voice as I could muster . . . The long and short of it was, the course was shortened 400 metres and we trudged up the icy pine forest to the higher finish where the track was broader, and not so steep and no tree stumps . . . Only one girl was hurt in the entire race and that not badly. Betty Woolsey again distinguished herself by being 10th . . . Evelyn Pinching [English] won . . .[11]

The occupation of Austria by German troops in March 1938 put an end to ski-racing, at least for Alice and the Americans, for in St. Anton the Austrian Nazis dismissed the *Bürgermeister* and most of his staff, and put men of low caliber in their places. Apparently merely out of envy, they confiscated the ski school of Hannes Schneider, whom they put in jail. This created a new cause for Alice: to get Schneider, his wife and two children out of Austria. She began with perhaps more courage than wisdom by trying to face down Nazi officials, appealing to law, morality and what influence she had in Vienna, but without success. After returning to the United States, she went to see Harvey Gibson, president of the Manufacturers Trust Company, who was also an amateur skier, born and bred in North Conway, New Hampshire. The German government had loans outstanding at the bank, and Gibson, knowing the time was inconvenient for the Germans, threatened to call these unless Schneider and his family were allowed to emigrate. Schneider was released and in February 1939 came to the United States and settled in North Conway, where, after the war, when a skiing craze swept the country, he had a large part in teaching proper technique and training.[12]

Alice meanwhile divorced Wolfe and married Herman S. Kiaer, president of a shipping company and, like her, a hunter and skier. During the war, to the extent she could, she kept a small group of women training and racing in the United States, and in 1948 she managed the women's team that went to the Winter Olympics at St. Moritz, where for the first time an American woman, Gretchen Fraser, won a gold medal. Four years later, though no longer the manager, she accompanied the team to the Olympics in Norway, where the team, led by Andrea Meade Lawrence, won more gold. By then the National Ski Association had become the dominant group in the United States, and through a palace revolution control of racing in the United States passed from the East Coast to the West, and Alice's position in the sport became honorary. But for almost twenty-five years she had been, in a personal way that no one could repeat, the organizing force in the United States of women's international ski-racing.[13]

For her work she received great rewards in an astonishing variety of ways. There were not only the accolades she received in ski journals; there was the friendship of men like Otto Furrer and Hannes Schneider, of skiers like Elizabeth Woolsey, and of Herbert von Karajan, whom she met on the slopes at St. Anton and later entertained in New York; and, perhaps best of all, a quite special relationship to the town of St. Anton.[14]

During the war she had managed on a regular basis to smuggle into it from Switzerland parcels of food and medicine, so on her return after the war she was greeted by all the children as their "Tante from America," and for several years she gave them an annual Christmas party in the railroad station. As soon as it was feasible, she organized a ski meet at St. Anton to help the town recover, and she and Kiaer, who, as much as she, enjoyed hunting stag and chamois, returned regularly every year. In 1965, on the twenty-fifth anniversary of their marriage, St. Anton made her an honorary citizen, the first woman of any nationality to be so honored.

With age, achievement and a happy marriage, she began to mellow, sometimes startling old friends with her new grace and sympathy. And on her tombstone, following her death in 1967, her husband put crossed rifles and skis.[15]

The Eastman Kodak research laboratory in which Leopold and Leo started work in July 1931 had been founded by George Eastman in 1912 and still was led by its creator and first director, Dr. C. E. Kenneth Mees, an English chemist. In the early years of business Eastman's custom had been to buy up whatever patents he needed, but after the Sherman Antitrust Act became law, in 1890, and as his business prospered, this became increasingly impractical. So, on a trip to England in 1912, he offered the post of director of research to Mees, thirty years old and already an outstanding scientist and administrator. Mees, believing Eastman to be the greatest man in photography, was intrigued, but as general manager and part owner of Wratten & Wainright, a small photographic company, he saw no honorable way to accept the offer. He suggested to Eastman, however, that he buy the company. Then he went to the Continent to lecture on photography. Soon came a telegram from Eastman: OBSTACLE REMOVED. HAVE JUST BOUGHT WRATTEN & WAINRIGHT. So Mees came to Rochester, where he created one of the great corporate research laboratories of this century.[16]

As Mees set it up, the laboratory was a competitive arena in which the men, and a few women, were judged by the quality of their work. But the atmosphere, deliberately, was open. Anyone could consult anyone else; small groups met constantly over lunch or dinner to exchange ideas; and Mees regularly published reports of scientific achievement so that those responsible received recognition. The community, though, was academically oriented. The majority of the scientists held advanced degrees, most of them in chemistry or physics, and into the midst of this hierarchic community, into a privileged position, Mees set the two Leopolds, who between them held only a single undergraduate degree, Leopold's from Harvard. Inevitably, there was resentment, and the nickname soon attached to them — Man and God — was sometimes said with derision.

In addition, their use of music in the laboratory raised eyebrows. They whistled in the darkroom — classical music, often the same piece over and over. It did not occur to them to explain that they were using music to measure time. Much of their experimenting had to be empirical — such as determining how long a photographic plate with a particular emulsion must be submerged in a particular developing fluid for the image to set — and such work had to be done in total darkness. The other scientists used Kodak timers, faceless clocks that ticked and chimed, or even an assistant outside the door with a stopwatch. But the "homotheic couple," as Mees once called them, frequently whistled; for short periods of time Schubert's *Marche Militaire* or part of Tchaikovsky's Symphony No. 6; for longer, the final movement of Brahms's Symphony No. 1. With the latter, so precise was their beat, they could measure almost to the second up to fifteen minutes.[17]

Gradually the resentments disappeared. The two men were friendly and worked hard, and as the significance of some of their early patents became understood these were credentials enough.

Soon the day came when they had something to show to Mees. As Leopold later described it, we had "stopped doing little detailed experiments in glass jars and finally put a length of film into a camera, took pictures on it, processed it ourselves, loaded the film into a projector and threw a bit of 16-millimeter color onto a screen."[18]

They were excited by the pictures, their first for Kodak, and called Mees at once, who hurried to their department and sat down expectantly. The film lasted less than five minutes, and at its end they switched on the light and looked at Mees. "After an interminable moment of silence, he said in a very loud voice, 'perfectly ghastly,' and stalked from the room."[19]

The sense of pressure under which they worked grew greater as the country's economic depression worsened. They knew that everywhere corporations were cutting back research programs and that in Eastman Kodak's board room Mees constantly was challenged to show results; in particular, results from the "two wandering musicians," as a visiting Austrian scientist had called them. By late 1932 they feared they soon might be fired — at a time when musicians by the thousands could not find work.[20]

So one night they sat down together and made a list of what they wanted to do and another of what they knew they could do. Their aim was to produce a three-layer, three-color film that could be used in any camera and in any projector, with all the ease of black-and-white film, and that could produce moving pictures in color as well as individual prints for family albums or hanging on the wall.

What they were closest to being able to do was make a two-layer, two-color film, orange-red and blue-green, which could be used easily in any camera or projector. The third layer and color were still troublesome, as was the making of individual positive prints. Transparencies, in which the picture was thrown on the wall or a screen, were easier. This technique was suitable for movies, but the magic-lantern show of single pictures had gone out of style with their grandparents, and the market for single transparencies seemed likely to be too small to be of any interest to Kodak. So, for the time being, they abandoned work on the third color and positive prints in order to produce something practical, something salable in two colors for amateur movie cameras.

Though Leopold usually acted as spokesman for Leo and himself, their colleagues at Eastman Kodak never discerned any division between the two in their work. Neither one seemed more conceptual than the other, or more practical or the better chemist or physicist or even more hardworking. Their partnership was total, and their affection for each other, attractive. Outside the laboratory, however, different personalities soon emerged.

Leo's life was settled. As an old man he once observed with moving simplicity, "I have been very happy in my wife," and in his years in Rochester, though his marriage was still new, that happiness filled his home. He and Frances created what seemed to Mary Bancroft "a very homey home." It also was filled with music. Leo, because of his excellence as a violinist, had no trouble assembling groups for chamber music, and one time when his father, the great pianist, came for a visit, Leo greeted him with a small chamber orchestra. When Frances' brother George came, there was an evening of wonderful piano. There was music enough for Leo. He was content.[21]

But Leopold, after his divorce from Edie, lived in a bachelor's apartment, went out more often in the evenings and, though outwardly happy, seemed to some persons more restless. He was always trying to fit in another hour of practice at the piano to preserve his touch, and he talked often of music in New York. He did not love science less or music more than Leo did, but the twenty-four-hour day was too short for both as he wished to pursue them. Unlike Leo, he seemed unable to arrive at a balance with which he could be content.

Socially, Leo struck some people as almost too well settled, almost stodgy, whereas Leopold in his single restlessness seemed more alive and brilliant. To men he seemed to have everything: languages, science, music, elegance, style. Women, or a few, saw something else. They sensed, on meeting him, that despite all the success, all the talent, he was not a man absolutely sure of himself. There was room for another to praise him, to reassure him. Leo once said of Leopold, "He was always a troubador. He turned everything into a romance. It was a kind of immaturity he never outgrew." To many women that was not a weakness but part of his charm.[22]

Then, too, there was the restlessness of his secret philandering, which grew steadily. After his divorce from Edie, any restraints the marriage may have imposed were removed, and in addition to Mary Bancroft there were many, many others. Medically in these years Leopold perhaps could be said to suffer from satyriasis; more poetically, he suffered from Don Giovanni's disease. He pursued women of all classes, and many offered themselves to him, making assignations in advance or merely telephoning at night. Unlike Marya, he tried hard to conceal his affairs, but inevitably a widening circle knew of them, or at least of some part of them. He seems not to have wondered at the cause of his behavior or worried about the effect of it on his life and work. But Leo worried; Randall worried.

By 1933 the two Leopolds had another film ready to show Mees, a two-color film for home movies. The color was reasonably good, and the film would be easier for amateurs to use than any available, for it did not require specially equipped cameras or projectors. This time after the showing, when they switched on the lights and looked at Mees, he announced jubilantly, "This film will go on the market."[23]

They protested; they were on the verge of solving the problems of three colors and positive prints. They had meant the demonstration to be merely a report on the way to a film infinitely better. They pled for a postponement, but Mees was adamant. "This film is going into production. Whenever you have the third color, we'll change over to a three-layer color film." And off he went to talk to the heads of the departments that would manufacture the new film. Leopold and Leo looked at each other in dismay.[24]

Now they worked frantically to beat themselves and the company, to present Mees with the three-color film before the company concentrated all its energies on a product they knew they soon could improve.

Their greatest stumbling block in creating a three-color film lay in the couplers, those compounds within the three emulsion layers that should react with the oxidized special developing agent to produce within each layer a different color image. They could not yet control fully these color-formers while they were embedded in the three layers of the film. The couplers wandered slightly among the layers, spoiling the colors and the clarity of the image. So they decided for the moment to leave that problem aside and put the couplers into the developing fluids rather than into the film and to control them by the method of diffusion they had developed in the 1920s. This vastly complicated the processing of the film, so much so that all the films would have to be developed in Rochester; but as home movies had always been returned to the company for processing, amateur photographers presumably would not balk at it.

They offered this three-color method to Mees, who substituted it for the two-color, not yet in production; and on April 15, 1935, after exciting hints had begun to appear in newspapers, Eastman Kodak officially offered the world a new 16-millimeter color film suitable for amateur movie cameras. It required no special equipment in cameras or projectors, was as easy to use as black-and-white film, would be processed in Rochester and marketed under the trade name Kodachrome.[25]

The great excitement of the new film, of course, lay in its color, which quite transformed the hitherto disappointing photography of landscapes while adding enormous flair to something as different as fashion photography. But the excitement was not only in the color. The sharpness of the image's definition was extremely good, better than the usual result in black and white. The speed of its registration on the film was high, giving the photographer leeway to cope with poor lighting conditions and to take pictures in slow motion. And even artificial light offered no difficulty, except that a compensating filter was needed to reduce the high proportion of red in most artificial light. Kodachrome was a major advance in many areas of photography.[26]

The film itself was a miracle of complexity compressed into $5/1000$ of an inch, its total width. By far the largest part of this, starting from the back, was a coating of jet-black to prevent halation (the spreading of light beyond its proper boundaries), and then a thick layer of gelatin to support what followed: the three layers of emulsion separated by two strips of gelatin, each of the five about $1/10,000$ of an inch thick. Each of the emulsion layers was sensitive to a different primary color — red, green and blue — and the two gelatins served a double purpose: they helped to isolate the chemical reactions that took place in the emulsion layers and also to restrict the light received by any emulsion layer below to the color appropriate to it, because of the inclusion of a suitable dye in the gelatin layer immediately above.

Processing the film, converting the latent images formed in the three emulsion layers into dye images in colors complementary to the colors to which the layers were sensitive, was equally complicated and required twenty-eight separate operations. The company's engineers built a processing line of specialized machines, and the film was passed from one to another in a series of baths and dryings, in each of which a single operation took place. As Leopold's friend Robert W. Wood, the president of Johns Hopkins University, wrote to him:

> It is almost unbelievable, the soaking of the dye through all three layers, the washing it out of the upper two: the dying of the upper two only and the washing it out of the upper one, and the removal of the silver on which the dyes are absorbed. If anyone had come to me with this complete *plan,* I should have said *very* ingenious but you are *mad* to think it can be worked.[27]

Yet the two Leopolds had taken the complete plan to Mees, who, with others at Eastman Kodak, notably Clyde Carlton for coating and Ronald Scott for processing, had made it work. As Leopold constantly stressed in later years, "So complex has our technological world become . . . it would have been literally impossible to work out the Kodachrome process to a point where it was commercially useful without the industrial know-how of the Eastman Kodak company." Still, the two musicians put a personal stamp on it. To celebrate the production of Kodachrome they gave a party for friends and co-workers at which they alternated a violin-piano recital with color movies — just as they had done with their first color pictures at Riverdale.[28]

Following the breakthrough of Kodachrome, improvements in the film followed regularly. The next year it was offered in 35-mm rolls for still cameras. Processing for these, too, was done in Rochester, and in place of positive prints on inexpensive paper, still not available, the company offered a positive transparency that had to be projected onto a screen or at very least held up to a strong source of light. As a marketing device, however, the company returned each transparency to the photographer in a two-by-two-inch cardboard frame that could be inserted into a slide projector, which threw the image onto a screen. To the surprise of most persons, the public, far from resisting this return to the nineteenth-century slide show, embraced it and rushed to buy not only color film but screens and projectors.

Meanwhile in the research laboratory the two Leopolds and others laid the groundwork for further dramatic advances in film and processing. In 1938 the company announced a "selective re-exposure process"; in 1941, a series of improvements, among them positive color prints in various sizes, including enlargements for commercial use; and finally, in 1942, Kodacolor, in which the color couplers were incorporated into the emulsions, simplifying the processing of the film to a point where any amateur with a well-equipped darkroom could process the film at home.[29]

But in the race to include the couplers directly in the emulsions, Eastman Kodak was beaten by the German company Agfa, which introduced its film, Agfacolor Neue, just before World War II. Pride of place, however, for the discovery of a practical method of color photography is always given to Eastman Kodak for Kodachrome, and at Eastman chiefly to Mannes and Godowsky, not only for the work done in the laboratory at Rochester but also for their principle of controlled diffusion, which they had worked out in their own laboratories in the 1920s.

In the coming years photographers and journalists often would say that Mannes and Godowsky had "discovered" the Kodachrome process. The word always raised a muted protest from Leopold: it did not express well what had happened, suggesting that the process, like some mineral in the soil, was there all the time, waiting to be found. Similarly, "invention," with its suggestion of a sudden putting together of parts to create a new whole, was misleading. Trying one day in a speech to account for "the labyrinth of trial and error" through which he and Leo had worked for twenty years, he started with the maxim "Necessity is the mother of invention" and talked of what it truly meant.

There is very seldom such a thing, strictly speaking, as "an invention." Rather, it is almost always a conglomerate of ideas, each one "thought up" to avoid some difficulty. One starts working on a so-called invention with some sort of definite goal in mind. Often as not, even the goal itself may undergo a significant change during the long period of work in achieving it. In any case, as soon as one sets up such a problem for solution, it immediately breaks itself down into a series of separate problems, each one of which has to be solved to achieve the whole result. Usually, the solving of each individual problem unmasks a whole lot of hidden subsidiary problems, each requiring its own little battle for solution. Most exasperating of all, most "solutions" for the little problems create new problems which were never there before. For example, one may search for a long time for just the right dye-stuff to use in a certain stage of the manufacture or processing of a product. After painstaking experimentation, one may congratulate oneself on finding at last the dye which does the job, only to discover that this particular dye has some nasty habit which was not even part of the original problem, and which has to be tackled separately. So you see, the whole process of invention is just one attempt after another to wriggle out of one embarrassing difficulty after another. Every time you get in trouble, you must somehow get out of it and proceed into the next trouble. And there you have the real necessity which to me is the real mother of invention — the necessity which is just an endless series of necessities.[30]

Consequently, among their colleagues at Eastman Kodak, Leopold and Leo were not considered primarily inventors or discoverers, or even chemists or scientists, but technologists: men who applied known knowledge to create a workable process. And their stroke of genius was "controlled diffusion" or "differential depth bleach," which they had patented in 1923, before going to Rochester. Curiously, perhaps significantly, almost all the great pioneering developments in color photography have been made by men in their twenties, an example perhaps of the dictum that the mind then may know less but is more open to possibilities.

It is hard to exaggerate the impact on daily life as color photography became practical, available and cheap. As amateurs by the millions turned to it, taking more and better pictures, thousands of jobs were created not only at Eastman Kodak, Agfa and other film and camera companies, but also in the subsidiary firms that provided them with chemicals, plastics and parts. In addition should be counted the jobs in the thousands of retail camera shops that sprang up across the country and around the world. What had been a small, specialized business became an international industry. The only group to suffer directly, to lose work, were artists, like Helen Tee Van.

In a sense, though it was never Leopold or Leo's primary aim, their Kodachrome process and the company's success in selling it "democratized" what had been a specialist's pursuit, and perhaps it was inevitable that this revolution should have been led by two Americans and an American company: it so neatly matched American ideals.

There is also in what happened a striking parallel to the conscious efforts of Leopold's uncles Frank and Walter, and even his grandfather Leopold, to "democratize" music by such programs as German opera at the Metropolitan at reduced prices, the People's Choral Union and Walter's "Music Appreciation Hour" on radio in the 1930s. Significantly, in none of these projects was money an end. Whatever the field — music, science, art, sport — family members sought first excellence, and then to spread the joy and learning of their achievement to others. That was the tradition.

Finally, with Kodachrome began an overwhelming dispersal of color into almost every aspect of daily life. Though family movies and snapshots, enlargements on the wall and art books, had a part in this, it was accomplished primarily through advertising. It seems incredible, but once upon a time advertising along a road, for example, was accomplished by hand-painted signs or even by four-line jingles, delivered one written line every hundred yards. Contrast that with today's billboards, color advertisements in magazines, travel brochures, even simple placards in store windows, for which the basis of almost every one is a color photograph. Subtract all these mentally from daily life and imagine the black, white and gray that remain. As this color revolution swept the world, friends of the two who started it sometimes remarked, "What hath Man and God wrought!"

CHAPTER 30

Walter, radio and the NBC "Music Appreciation Hour."

DESPITE the many accomplishments of family members in a variety of fields, for the general public Walter's name and achievements continued to overshadow all other Damrosches and their work. For as Walter steadily expanded his position in the new, uncharted world of radio, he won for himself an affection in the hearts of his countrymen that few musicians have matched and perhaps none who was not a composer. Considering that his first broadcast was made when he was sixty-three and that most of his work in radio was done after seventy, it was an extraordinary late harvest.

Radio, like jazz, had its roots in the late nineteenth century but did not begin to impinge on the public's daily life until the early 1920s. Before then the "wireless" for most persons was a mystery for scientists or perhaps a toy for hobbyists, a subject to be read and written of with disbelief and, often, amusement.

The first broadcast direct from the stage of the Metropolitan Opera, for example, took place on January 13, 1910. Caruso sang in *I Pagliacci* and Destinn in *Cavalleria Rusticana,* and both operas were broadcast complete. According to radio historian Erik Barnouw, "Two microphones were used, one on stage, the other in the wings. A 500-watt transmitter was installed in a room at the top of the Opera House. The antenna, suspended from two bamboo fishpoles, led to an attic room off the ballet rehearsal room." [1]

The broadcast was heard by groups of listeners, passing earphones around, at points in New York City and Newark and also by ship operators and amateurs. The *Times* reported that "the warblings of Caruso and Mme. Destinn . . . borne by wireless Hertziann waves over the turbulent waters of the sea to transcontinental [*sic*] and coastwise ships, and over the mountainous peaks and undulating valleys of the country," were often not clearly audible. Yet one fan told the reporter that he could "sometimes catch the ecstasy." [2]

Two years later, no one was inclined to laugh, least of all newspaper reporters, as first word of the *Titanic* disaster was picked up by a radio operator, twenty-year-old David Sarnoff, at Wanamaker's store in New York. On the afternoon of April 14, 1912, he heard weak signals: S.S. TITANIC RAN INTO ICEBERG. SINKING FAST. He alerted the press, stayed at his post and succeeded in making contact with the *Olympic,* fourteen hundred miles at sea, which reported that the *Carpathia* was picking up survivors. He tried to reach it, and to aid him President Taft ordered all other radio stations in the United States off the air. Soon, despite the constant static, Sarnoff was in touch with the *Carpathia,* and names of survivors began to come through. Crowds surged round Wanamaker's, police were called out, and in the store, relatives of passengers were allowed in the wireless room to check Sarnoff's lists. For seventy-two hours he was the country's sole link to the disaster, and he stayed at his transmitter and receiver until all the *Titanic* passengers were accounted for, alive or missing. When he finally departed for bed, his name was known throughout the country, and the potential of radio, far better understood.

Many advances in use and technique were made during World War I, and with peace radio stations sprang up all over the United States. Most at first were run by amateurs, though several soon developed ties to large companies, and none broadcast more than a few hours each day. Then one sensational event followed another. On November 2, 1920, a station in Pittsburgh backed by Westinghouse, KDKA, stirred tremendous excitement by broadcasting the returns of the election in which Harding defeated Cox for the presidency.

The following year a station in Newark, WJZ, catapulted to fame on October 5 with a broadcast of a World Series ball game between the Giants and the Yankees at the New York Polo Grounds. Later an actress, Olga Petrova, brought the station more fame. She was known for her work for birth control, but she had promised the staff a program of Mother Goose rhymes. She began,

> There was an old woman who lived in a shoe,
> She had so many children because she didn't know what to do.

A switch was thrown, an engineer started a phonograph record and Petrova became perhaps the first person to be cut off the air.

Westinghouse, meanwhile, in order to stimulate sales of its receivers (not yet called radios) backed a station in Chicago, KYW, that began broadcasting on November 11, 1921. As there were not yet packaged programs available, or perhaps by preference, it chose to broadcast the

Chicago Opera, then led by Mary Garden. According to Barnouw, it broadcast the entire season, November 14 through January 21 — all the performances, afternoon and evening, six days a week — and nothing else.[3]

The effect on radio sales was astonishing:

> At the beginning of the season there were thought to be 1300 receivers in the Chicago area. No sets were yet in the stores, but people began clamoring for them. The assembly of sets by amateurs and ex-amateurs became a round-the-clock occupation. It was a popular high school activity. By the end of the opera season 20,000 sets were reported in operation in Chicago.[4]

Many of the sets, of course, were assembled by Westinghouse, and the profit to be made out of radio was plain. By 1930 there would be almost thirteen million radios in American homes, and by 1940, almost fifty-two million. Still, if the potential connection between radio and commerce was becoming clearer, so too was the potential tie between radio and music. Indeed, for the old art the new medium seemed remarkably suited, or so it seemed to Walter. Many other musicians were not so sure, and some, including Clara, were quite opposed to the broadcast of serious music.

The problem at the start was twofold: the fidelity of the sound, and fears about employment and audiences. Though vocal and instrumental solos arrived at the receiver with good sound, the fidelity to timbre disappeared as the volume was increased to an enjoyable level. The overtones that make a voice individual or distinguish a flute from a clarinet did not project. In addition, in any concerted number there was an almost complete lack of bass. Drums lost all resonance and sounded like the tappings of a small hammer. The lower strings and woodwinds failed; also the deeper voices of a chorus. To a musician like Clara, who cared very much for the individual timbres of instruments and their exact balance, radio in its infancy was a great disappointment, and she had little hope for it. Walter's interest in it, she thought, was another aberration, like his interest in Isadora Duncan; a distraction from pure music.[5]

The fears about employment and audiences were of the unknown. At first, when radio was still run by enthusiasts rather than businessmen, actors and musicians often appeared on it without pay, for the novelty of it, or to help out a friend, or perhaps for publicity. Then as it became clearer, roughly in the years 1922 to 1926, that commercial interests were going to "own" radio time and sell it at a profit, gradually a pay scale emerged, but it took six or seven years to establish itself. Meanwhile many, like Walter's old enemy Henry T. Finck, saw only the bad: "The radio is making terrible havoc in the activities and earnings of professional musicians."[6]

Walter saw some good, though as he later admitted, "When I first went into radio work, all my colleagues — Rachmaninoff, Paderewski, Kreisler — condemned me. They thought I had debased myself; they felt people would not come to hear them if they could get good music over the radio." Walter, to the contrary, felt sure that radio would build a larger audience for public concerts.[7]

His own radio work began on October 19, 1923, as part of a Beethoven cycle with the New York Symphony. He broadcast from Carnegie Hall three lecture-recitals and three concerts, of which the last, a performance with the orchestra of Symphony No. 9, brought a response from Helen Keller that must have confirmed Walter in his belief in music's future in radio.[8]

I have the joy of being able to tell you that, though deaf and blind, I spent a glorious hour last night listening over the radio to Beethoven's "Ninth Symphony." I do not know whether I can make you understand how it was possible for me to derive pleasure from the symphony. It was a great surprise to myself. I had been reading in my magazine for the blind of the happiness that the radio was bringing to the sightless everywhere. I was delighted to know that the blind had gained a new source of enjoyment; but I did not dream that I could have any part in their joy. Last night, when the family was listening to your wonderful rendering of the immortal symphony, some one suggested that I put my hand on the receiver, and see if I could get any of the vibrations. He unscrewed the cap, and I lightly touched the sensitive diaphragm. What was my amazement to discover that I could feel, not only the vibrations, but also the impassioned rhythm, the throb and the surge of the music! The intertwined and intermingling vibrations from different instruments enchanted me. I could actually distinguish the cornets, the roll of the drums, deep-toned violas and violins singing in exquisite unison. How the lovely speech of the violins flowed and flowed over the deepest tones of the other instruments! When the human voices leaped up trilling from the surge of harmony, I recognized them instantly as voices. I felt the chorus grow more exultant, more ecstatic, upcurving swift and flame-like, until my heart almost stood still. The women's voices seemed an embodiment of all the angelic voices rushing in a harmonious flood of beautiful and inspiring sound. The great chorus throbbed against my fingers with poignant pause and flow. Then all the instruments and voices together burst forth — an ocean of heavenly vibration — and died away like winds when the atom is spent, ending in a delicate shower of sweet notes.

Of course, this was not "hearing" but I do know that the tones and harmonies conveyed to me moods of great beauty and majesty. I also sensed, or thought I did, the tender sounds of nature that sing into my hand — swaying reeds and winds and the murmur of streams. I have never been so enraptured before by a multitude of tone-vibrations.

As I listened, with darkness and melody, shadow and sound filling all the room, I could not help remembering that the great composer who poured forth such a flood of sweetness into the world was deaf like myself. I marvelled at the power of his quenchless spirit by which out of his pain he wrought such joy for others — and there I sat, feeling with my hand the magnificent symphony which broke like a sea upon the silent shores of his soul and mine.

Let me thank you warmly for all the delights which your beautiful music has brought to my household and to me. I want also to thank Station WEAF for the joy they are broadcasting in the world.[9]

It was more than a year, however, before a radio station invited Walter and the New York Symphony to give a full season's program, a year in which four large corporations — Westinghouse, Radio Corporation of America, General Electric and American Telephone & Telegraph — began to consolidate their control of the new industry and to bring to it enough money to hire a symphony orchestra for a season.

The invitation came, apparently, because of Walter's extraordinary success with a program, on January 24, 1926, to initiate International Radio Week. The plan was for Europe and the United States each to listen to the other's music-making for an hour: first the European transmitters would be silent, from 10:00 P.M. to 11:00 P.M., to allow listeners there to pick up transmitters in the United States, and then in the following hour, the reverse. Walter appeared with the New York Symphony and, as was his style, made explanatory remarks before each work as well as speaking briefly in German, French and Italian. The next day many newspapers commented on the attractiveness of his voice and the clarity of his diction, and one even said, "We will except no radio announcer in the world, not even the world's premier, Graham McNamee, in our statement that announcers could learn a great deal from Dr. Damrosch's manner of addressing an audience."[10]

Not long afterward, American Telephone & Telegraph, which owned WEAF, hired Walter and the New York Symphony for a series of thirteen programs, to consist of six lecture-recitals and seven concerts. The orchestra was to be small, only fifty-three, and also the fee, $20,000, though for that year in radio it was relatively high. Before the series' end, however, it had been extended to twenty-two programs, still alternating lecture-recitals and concerts, and was presented over the newly formed National Broadcasting Company's "red" network. Walter and the orchestra, billed as the "Balkite Hour," and sponsored by Fansteel Products Company, the makers of Balkite radios, were offered to network stations across the country and taken by most of them. He played to an enormous audience, of which thirty thousand put pen to paper to write to him.[11]

The first work played on the opening program was the Overture to *Tannhäuser,* which Walter introduced by explaining the meaning of "overture," playing its musical themes at the piano and demonstrating how at its close the *Pilgrims' Chorus* "is proclaimed with the evident victory of the great power of Christianity to forgive." The next week he gave an hour's lecture-recital on *Das Rheingold,* with the promise for later weeks of the rest of the Nibelung cycle. "Now, ladies and gentlemen," he warned, "do not be frightened at the many themes which I play for you. You will forget half of them, remembering a few; but subconsciously, as we go on with this work, and you begin to see into the intricacies of these dramas, you will recognize these themes more and more, and that will aid you very much in the understanding of the whole work."[12]

No one seemed to think that he was asking too much of the public, and one night he read a few sentences from a letter he had received from a man in Saskatchewan:

> It is just to wish you a Merry Xmas and Happy New Year, that you may be as happy as you have made me in your radio lectures and orchestra.
>
> I am a sheep herder right in the middle of nowhere — no companion save my dog and radio set, & believe me its sure fine tramping about all day in the snow and biting sub-zero weather to sit down of a Saturday evening and here [*sic*] you on *Siegfried!* I have had my set 3 years and am used to hear [*sic*] good programs but yours is head and shoulders above anything I ever heard before, so please accept this small tribute and wish.
>
> My ink having frozen up am forced to use this pencil. Please excuse.
>
> D. Thompson[13]

That Saturday evening, New Year's Day 1927, the sheep herder and others were offered, with preceding explanatory comments, Victor Herbert's *American Fantasy,* Rubin Goldmark's *Call of the Plains,* Deems Taylor's *Jabberwock* from *The Looking Glass Suite,* Walter Damrosch's Prelude to Act II of *Cyrano de Bergerac,* David Griffith's *White Peacock* and Gershwin's *Rhapsody in Blue* with Gershwin playing.

The next year the program became the "RCA Hour" and then, from 1929 through the spring of 1931, the "General Electric Hour." Meanwhile, in February 1927, Walter had accepted an appointment to the Advisory Council of the National Broadcasting Company, a committee of distinguished men and women, mostly in business, that met periodically to consider the high purposes of radio. It seems to have had little power, but it did give Walter access to Owen D. Young, chairman of the board of General Electric, and when a fight flared over GE's aggressive advertising on its music hour, Walter was able to deal directly with the company's president and win a more moderate policy.[14]

He also, in May 1927, accepted the post of musical counsel to NBC, in which position he was to advise the network on all matters relating to the higher musical activities and possibilities of radio. In these years NBC, which was owned by RCA (50 percent), GE (30 percent) and Westinghouse (20 percent), and had a tight contractual agreement with AT&T, was the giant of broadcasting, and though, like the Advisory Council, the post of musical counsel had little power, it did offer a pulpit from which to preach. And Walter, already the best-known conductor on radio, began at once.[15]

In a press conference at his home on May 12, with Merlin H. Aylesworth, NBC president, at his side, Walter presented to reporters the outline of a plan for a series of concerts with talks that, through radio, could reach most of the twenty-five million students in American schools and colleges. Essentially, the format would be that of his Children's and Young People's Concerts, with the addition of considerable preliminary work to be done with the teachers.

He proposed to give twenty-four concerts, with comments, divided into three series of eight each, one for elementary schools, another for high schools and the third for colleges.

> Previous to each concert I would send to every school that desires it a questionnaire on the music to be performed and on my explanatory comments, together with the proper answers. These answers would, of course, be intended only for the eyes of the music teachers. After each concert the pupils could be examined by them and rated accordingly. If the parents are interested as well, the questionnaires could be distributed to them also, either through the school authorities or the local newspapers. The papers could print the answers a few days later.[16]

Though Walter over the years would change the format slightly, basic to it always was his concept that learning about music, however enjoyable, was also work, with questions, answers and ratings. Music was not pap for idlers.

The plan originated, he told reporters, in some of the letters he had received in praise of the "Balkite Hour." In this he was stretching the truth, as probably everyone realized, but "a call from the people" made good copy, and part of the fascination in the history of what ultimately became the NBC "Music Appreciation Hour" is the skill with which Walter developed the plan, strengthened its friends, weakened its enemies and sustained it through the country's worst economic depression.

In February, for example, three months before the press conference in New York and well before most of the thirty thousand letters on the "Balkite Hour" had been received, Walter went to St. Louis to a convention of the National Association of Secondary School Principals. He spoke to two thousand principals on "Music, the Universal Language," describing his Children's and Young People's Concerts and suggesting how they could be adapted into weekly radio broadcasts aimed at children in the schools. How each school would obtain a radio was perhaps a problem, but surely not insurmountable: "generous souls" might even donate one.[17]

His proposal received considerable favorable publicity. When a Philadelphia reporter asked Stokowski's opinion of it, Stokowski replied that its "influence will be tremendous . . . it is a fine piece of work." And whenever a school or its principal wrote to Walter, he relayed the enthusiasm at once to Aylesworth. Not a drop of favorable response was wasted.[18]

The real question, of course, was: Who will pay for the educational concerts, at an estimated cost of $100,000 a year? Walter, a good impresario, never forgot the financial underpinnings of art, and he outlined for Aylesworth three possibilities: (1) the schools might subscribe "a small proportionate amount towards the necessary funds"; (2) "a great commercial house with a proper perception of the enormous advertising possibilities of such a plan, combined with its great philanthropic value," might finance it; and (3) "some great educational foundation would underwrite it."[19]

At the press conference Aylesworth allowed Walter to say that NBC "is ready to stand back of my dream financially and make it a reality," but almost immediately afterward NBC reneged and insisted that the program be paid for by a sponsor. During the summer it seemed as if one had been found, but in September Walter wrote to Margaret that the powers at NBC "had virtually hooked our series of children's concerts to the Colgate Soap Company, but soap is slippery and seems to have fallen out of their hands again." Ultimately no sponsor was found, and the concerts were canceled.[20]

A man with less stamina might have flagged, but Walter merely shifted ground. He was still on the air every Saturday night with his adult "RCA Hour," and he now persuaded Aylesworth and David Sarnoff, vice-president and general manager of RCA, to use the January 21, 1928, broadcast as a "sample" concert to which the Schoolmasters Association of New York and Vicinity would be invited and asked to remain after the broadcast for a discussion. The sample concert would be heard via the NBC network all over the country and, further, would be followed on two Friday mornings in February by two sample educational concerts, also to be broadcast over the network and aimed specifically at the schools. Needless to say, the New York and Vicinity teachers were delighted to hold their January meeting in the NBC studio building, the wonderland of radio, and three hundred accepted the invitation. Meanwhile across the country thousands more, alerted by NBC's publicity and their professional colleagues in New York, prepared to tune in.

Before the program went on the air Aylesworth welcomed his guests at the studio to what "will go down in history as a very great experiment in radio education." Then, at the stroke of 8:00 P.M., the announcer, Milton Cross, began: "The Radio Corporation of America at this hour presents . . ." and ending, "RCA Loud Speakers, RCA Radiotrons and RCA Radiolas make it possible for millions of American families to enjoy the true richness of this and the other wonderful programs on the air." Then Walter began.[21]

One of his remarkable talents was the ability to talk on radio without a script. The programs, of course, were blocked out in advance, the timer in the control booth knowing exactly when each piece of music should begin. But Walter's intervening comments were left to him, and with only a few notes in hand and his eye on the timer he simply would add or subtract talk as needed. The result was a performance that was extraordinarily vivid.[22]

This night, to his audience seen and unseen, he talked in his usual direct, friendly style. Schoolchildren should have the opportunity to learn something of music, "this universal language of emotions." Tonight he and the orchestra would play a few selections "with such explanations as I have been accustomed to give for the last thirty-four years at my Children's Concerts." As the first piece to be played tonight would be the Allegretto from Beethoven's Symphony No. 8, for the children he might begin by explaining the words used to indicate different tempos:

Take a phrase, "How do you do today." If it is *adagio* tempo, we would be saying, "How do you do today." [Indicating.] If it is *andante,* we would say, "How do you do today." [Indicating.] If *allegretto,* "How do you do today." [Indicating.] If *allegro,* "How do you do today." [Indicating.] If *presto,* "How do you do today." [Indicating.]

Before he had finished, the repetition and his slight variations had become comic and unforgettable.

Then, after more talk — "Of course I wouldn't talk as much to the children as I am talking to you now" — he and the orchestra played the Allegretto, in which, all of a sudden, the main theme is unmistakably in the tempo, allegretto, of "How do you do today."

After the program's end he discussed with the teachers how the proposed series could be fitted into a school's curriculum. "You have heard, Dr. Damrosch," said Frank Hackett of Riverdale, "of one of the most ferocious animals ever known, called the Schedule," and he suggested the concerts be held on Saturday mornings, "outside of the regular schedule."

Walter firmly rebutted the idea. Children would resent being forced to give up otherwise free time, and music should not be treated as an "interruption but merely a continuation of what is considered a necessity of a young American's education . . . If you will just admit me sufficiently to put my foot in the crack of the door, I will see to it that gradually I shall wriggle through and be considered not an intruder or an extra but, if you permit me to say so, one of you."

The teachers were not immune to charm; they burst into applause.[23]

With the teaching profession and its allied organizations ever more solidly behind him, the two Friday morning test broadcasts proved extremely successful. In Indiana every school that requested a radio was furnished one as a joint project of the Indiana Federation of Music Clubs and the Parent-Teachers Association. In St. Louis, radio firms and RCA representatives provided speakers and receivers for the city's school auditoriums; in Peoria, businessmen donated them; in Minneapolis, the Northwest Radio Trade Association installed them for the day in every high and junior high school; and everywhere schools rearranged schedules to allow the students to listen. Thousands of enthusiastic letters poured in on Walter, RCA, NBC and the newspapers of the country. In just twelve months Walter had succeeded in creating a national demand to which the radio industry had to accede.[24]

The next year, 1928–29, the program began, sponsored by RCA and known as the RCA "Educational Hour." The year after, RCA dropped out in order to focus its energies on three subsidiaries just purchased, but NBC continued the hour as "a sustaining program" — that is, without sponsor[25] — and for the balance of its life, thirteen years, it was known as the NBC "Music Appreciation Hour." It became, probably, the most famous and influential educational program ever to be broadcast in the United States on radio or television.

Though entirely dependent on Walter, the program at its start had the aid of a number of talented persons. There was an advisory council of educators whose suggestions Walter frequently took. There was for the first year, which was crucial in creating liaisons with teacher and parent groups, a former supervisor of music appreciation in the Cleveland public schools, Alice Keith, who quickly established contact with almost every state superintendent of schools in the country as well as city and county superintendents, college presidents, principals of private or parochial schools and state presidents of the Federated Music Clubs. Not only did she keep them abreast of every development, including, of course, the dates and hours of the broadcasts in their localities, but by her articles and appearances at teachers' conventions and on radio, she successfully turned the program from just another radio hour, however special, into an educational movement.[26]

On the musical side of the program one of Walter's first jobs was to recruit an orchestra for the programs. At the time NBC had a small house orchestra, but it was not large enough for symphonic works, nor were some of its players expert enough for Walter to use them to demonstrate the qualities of their instruments, certainly not at the level of perfection that men like Barrère had done. Walter's first thought was to use men from the newly merged Philharmonic-Symphony, but because of conflicts in scheduling, this was not possible. His second was to create a wholly new radio orchestra of top quality, and he explained to NBC officials what such an orchestra could accomplish for music and for NBC. The officials caught his enthusiasm: "It would be a great feather in the cap of the National Broadcasting Company if we can form this orchestra and have you as its first conductor. It will be monumental in radio if we build the first Symphony Orchestra for radio broadcasting exclusively, and it would soon become history that Walter Damrosch was the pioneer and first conductor."[27]

The idea became a reality only in November 1937, with the creation, chiefly for Toscanini, of the ninety-five-man NBC Symphony Orchestra. Walter in 1928 had to settle for something less, called the National Orchestra, which never developed any strong identity. Essentially it was the NBC house orchestra enlarged to sixty and strengthened with the addition of expert players from the New York Symphony. For its two major purposes, Walter's evening adult hour and the educational concerts, it was adequate.[28]

To assist him in creating the substance of the programs and supporting material Walter picked as his chief assistant a former violinist of the New York Symphony, Ernest La Prade, and it was a brilliant choice. La Prade, born in Memphis and trained in Cincinnati and Brussels, was a good musician, interested in radio, and with a talent for music education almost Walter's equal, though expressed in a much more modest style. Unfortunately, perhaps inevitably, his contribution to the programs never received adequate recognition. The publicity always was on Walter.[29]

More unhappy still, after eight years La Prade and Walter had a falling-out, and in 1936 La Prade was succeeded by Lawrence Abbott, the former music critic for *The Outlook*. By then, however, the program's format was set.[30]

Each school year the NBC "Music Appreciation Hour" offered four programs, Series A, B, C and D, aimed at different levels of experience. Roughly, A for grades 3 and 4; B, for 5 and 6; C, for 7 through 9; and D, for high schools and colleges. But teachers were encouraged from the start to have their students, regardless of grade or age, listen to whatever series seemed most suitable.

Typically each series, A, B, C or D, consisted of twelve half-hour programs, broadcast sequentially every other week; that is, Walter and the orchestra broadcast on twenty-four Fridays in the school year, each time presenting two half-hour series. After the first year, and until the last, the combinations were A and B one week, C and D the next. This allowed schools wishing to give a class a full hour of music to combine series close to the same level of experience. Until 1936 the hour began at 11:00 A.M. Eastern Standard Time; thereafter, at 2:00 P.M. EST. Thus Walter's radio trademark, his greeting in his unique accent to his youngest listeners, shifted from "Good MAW-ning," to "Good AH-H'fterNOO-OON, my deah chul-dren!"

In Series A, Walter focused almost exclusively on the instruments, describing them and illustrating their special qualities with short pieces. He hoped, of course, that the teacher would have pictures or the instruments themselves in the classroom or auditorium, and the advance literature to teachers gave them the background on the instruments and on the works to be played. Series B was devoted to emotions in music; Series C, to structure and form; and Series D, to particular composers. In each series the final program, called the "Students' Achievement Program," was a review and test.[31]

In all series the emphasis fell always on nineteenth-century German composers. In Series D for 1934–35, for example, the composers presented were early polyphonic, Bach, Haydn, Mozart, Beethoven, Schubert, Schumann, Liszt, Wagner, Debussy and modern American. Beethoven was the composer most performed; the work most frequently played, however, in whole or part, was Saint-Saëns's *Carnival of the Animals,* for it neatly illustrated in solo roles so many instruments.[32]

Knowledgeable music lovers and critics sometimes complained that Walter scheduled no modern music, no Stravinsky, Schoenberg or Berg, and in Philadelphia in 1932 Stokowski proposed a plan to broadcast "modernistic" music to schoolchildren "in order to develop a liking for it by them." Walter rushed into print with an intemperate reply.

> I deeply deplore . . . Children should not be confused by experiments. Only that which has been proven worthy should be used to build the foundation of their knowledge . . . I will wager that 75% of the ultramodern works . . . were born dead because they did not spring from an inner urge but from a pathetic desire to do something different, to be "original" . . . Because our great Bach often proclaimed not the individual emotions of man but those of a cosmic deity they [the modern composers] impudently wrapped his magnificent toga around their own meagre hairy bodies, thinking to hide their ugly nakedness thereby.
>
> Art develops not by revolution but by evolution and until our young people have been well grounded by hearing the great composers from Bach to Wagner, why confuse their musical minds by the intrusion of experiments most of which have not and never will be proven.[33]

The controversy touched deep issues in music and music education still not resolved today, but typically Walter was not entirely satisfactory to the traditionalists either. In a Series B program as an illustration of an American dance, the fox trot, he played Gershwin's *I Got Rhythm,* and was condemned by some for introducing jazz. To a newspaper editor in Dallas Walter wrote,

> As you know, all my efforts over the radio have been to educate the masses into a consciousness that the great masters of music contribute something deeper and finer than the prevailing jazz tunes and croonings. But there is a little something in the best of jazz which has made its mark, and will leave some impression on the real music which will develop in our country and will reflect our racial aspirations. This little dance of Gershwin's is very good of its kind. It is ingratiating, it has spontaneity of rhythm, and overflows with life and cheerfulness.[34]

In short, Walter in the "Music Appreciation Hour" was just as he always had been in the concert hall.

The aspect of his teaching most often attacked by critics and musicians — though not at all by the general public — was his frequent imposition of a program on nonprogramatic music and of words, as a memory device, on wordless themes.

In a Series D, for example, aimed at high school and college students, he presented over two programs Beethoven's Symphony No. 5, and in the course of it stated that the fourth and final movement expressed "triumphant joy at victory over the adverse forces of Destiny." Beethoven, however, nowhere says as much. Yet Walter, undaunted, went further and described Beethoven's interpolation of a fragment of the third movement into the fourth as "a reminder, in the hour of triumph, of the pains and travail through which victory has been achieved."[35]

These terms, at least, were abstract, but in describing the second movement he was quite specific: "a walk in a lovely garden, in which one finds a statue erected to the memory of some national hero." And worse still to his critics, in presenting this second movement to a Series C audience, roughly grades 7 through 9, he gave words to the second theme, supposedly representing the national hero, and asked the students to sing:

> For the Hero has come,
> Sound the trumpet and drum.
> He has fought
> The good fight;
> He has won![36]

The words were not immutable; the jingle varied slightly as he improvised it anew on other programs. But the hero and his triumph were constant, for that was the mood of the theme, and also the trumpet and drum, which were dominant in its orchestration. Whatever the form, his critics nearly choked with distaste. "Goodness knows," wrote Harold Schonberg, "how many potential music lovers were permanently maimed by this idiotic procedure." [37]

The trouble is, the words once learned are hard to forget, and they nag the mind: "This is the symphon-ee that Schubert wrote and never fin-ished." Yet despite the technique, so irritating to the learned, no neophytes seem to have been injured, and through the words many were brought quickly to some understanding of the music. The abstract terms provided a structure for the symphony or movement, the jingles, a method for identifying themes. No teacher in a half-hour, even one as good as Walter, could have achieved as much with the Beethoven symphony by talking of the fourth movement as Statement, Fantasia Section, Interlude (with motives from the Scherzo), Restatement and Coda. The critics, perhaps to their credit, wished each child to have the equivalent of a Juilliard education; Walter, to his, worked for something less but also more. [38]

The "less" was an undeniable sentimentalizing of the music, making it at times too cute, too pictorial; [39] the "more," its democratization. As he constantly stressed, with only slight exaggeration, "the so-called musical population until now has numbered about one percent in the cities, and much less than that among those living in the country." Through radio, musicians now could reach that 99 percent. [40]

Today when almost every child and adult has the choice of listening to serious music, it is hard to grasp the impact of the "Music Appreciation Hour" on the persons for whom there had been no choice. For them good music had not existed as a possibility, and their response to some instruction in it was extraordinary. An NBC report on the hour's second year, 1929–30, estimated the student audience at somewhere between four and five million. [41] A report for the 1933–34 season listed seventeen thousand copies of the teachers' manual sold and 105,000 of the students' notebook, and through surveys on the number of teachers and students using each copy it seemed likely that the students listening then numbered about six million. [42] In 1938 NBC published a brochure in which, citing an "independent" survey, it reported that the broadcasts were part of the curriculum in seventy thousand schools, the number of students listening was estimated at seven million, and of adults, between three and four million. [43]

The adults were always a sizable part of the audience, and Walter at one time dreamed of creating a separate program for them, but in the depression years there was no money for it. Nevertheless an appreciable part of the impact of the hour was on adults, particularly on the teachers, who, through the material in their manuals, received the equivalent of a college course in music appreciation. The influence they in turn exerted on their students is incalculable, but traces of Walter's methods still are visible in books and classrooms.[44]

The "Music Appreciation Hour," though it proved its worth in educational value and audience size, never succeeded in attracting a sponsor or foundation. In 1932, in order to keep it alive, Walter agreed to a 25 percent cut in salary, reducing his annual fee for broadcasts at NBC, which included others than the "Music Appreciation Hour," from $42,000 to $32,000. Similarly with his adult "Symphony Hour." In 1929 and again in 1932 when it was without a sponsor, he agreed to a reduction in salary in order to keep it going. Undoubtedly his willingness to consider costs and how to reduce them was an important reason that the "Appreciation Hour" was able to survive the economic depression.[45]

Looking ahead, in the winter of 1933, with Aylesworth's blessing he set about to raise a fund of $500,000 to ensure the program's existence for another three years. For the fund drive he enlisted such men as John W. Davis, Paul Cravath and Harry H. Flagler, but just as the national campaign for contributions was ready to start, NBC announced that it would continue to sustain the program. Apparently for reasons of public relations it did not want to appear to abandon the educational hour.[46]

In the short run NBC's generosity was a blessing; in the long, it proved fatal, for it left the program entirely dependent on NBC's support, and in 1941–42 this evaporated. Forced by the federal government to divide its holdings, NBC kept the more profitable "red" network and let go the "blue," reputed to have the better-quality programs, including the "Music Appreciation Hour"; and on February 1, 1942, a new entity, the Blue Network (today ABC), began broadcasting. Its managers, however, were anxious to increase profits, and for the 1942–43 season, arguing that frequent and unprofitable war bulletins were a patriotic duty, they offered Walter only a half-hour, though the full program already was prepared. Rather than cut it, Walter resigned. Persons close to the scene felt the war was a pretext and the resignation forced. The issue was profit.[47]

There was also the problem of Walter's age. He was now eighty, and although vigorous, he could not continue forever. Yet there was no plan for a successor. Lawrence Abbott, his assistant in these years, later commented that no successor was possible: the program was Walter, in substance and style. So an end was inevitable; and fourteen years, perhaps enough. But educators regretted the decision and wrote to Walter and the network about reviving the program after the war.[48]

There was no revival, and the program passed into history. In the opinion of many persons, looking back on fifty years of radio and television in the United States, it is still the best use made of either medium for an educational purpose. The "best" is a large claim, but those supporting it are apt to stress the program's life of fourteen years, which gave teachers time to learn how to use it; the quality of the material presented; the quality of the man presenting it; the skill of the pedagogy, particularly in the variety and repetition of the material presented; and, finally, the work constantly required of students and teachers, which kept the program for both an active experience.

For Walter the program was an extraordinary benediction at the end of a long life. He had always been famous for his smile, half-turning on the podium when a lovely theme reappeared, as if eager to share his enjoyment with the audience, and in his music-making on radio that eagerness to share endeared him to millions. He became a national figure.

In 1932 the critic W. J. Henderson, in writing a summation of Walter's career for the *Musical Quarterly,* concluded:

> What impressed this writer most . . . is the outstanding fact that Walter Damrosch has acquired fame without gaining celebrity in any one department of his art. That he is a distinguished conductor is undeniable. That the musical public has ever ranked him with the wizards of the baton, setting him beside Nikisch or Toscanini or Weingartner, would not be asserted by his best friends. During all the years in which he was conducting the Symphony Society his activities were treated with routine consideration by the newspapers, while every star imported from Europe became the subject of speculation and analysis and even rhapsody occupying many columns.
>
> At one time Damrosch got some glory as an accompanist. But any accompanist who had to cross the Atlantic to reach Carnegie Hall got more. Of his compositions we have said enough. But one thing remains to be said, to wit, that most of them were better than dozens of imported scores which were hymned in strophic strains because they had been made in Europe.
>
> Yet here we find Damrosch today firmly placed as one of the prominent musical figures of the world. Thrown rudely into the arena in boyhood by the death of his father, he soon stamped himself upon the community in which he lived. Unqualified and incessant damnation was heaped upon him as an incompetent or a mediocrity, but his rise was unbroken. And when it seemed as if his activities must come to an end, he emerged as a national figure, the conductor and expounder of good music through the radio. Now no man can be a national figure without acquiring something of international distinction, and Damrosch in this golden afternoon of his remarkable life is known and respected throughout the entire musical world.
>
> It is not necessary to point a moral. But one cannot help thinking that a sound musician, who is also a man of energy, generous impulses and broad outlook, can get well up toward the mountain-tops without blowing his alp-horn every moment. And above all else there seems to me to be some irresistible power in that kindly, benign Damrosch smile that

even makes its way to us on the view-less wave-lengths of the radio. Many conductors are admired; Damrosch is loved.[49]

That love showed itself in the hundreds of letters he received every month. Some were stiff and formal, some jazzy, but each tried in a personal way to express gratitude for pleasure given and, most often, for a door opened into a new world. A twelve-year-old boy in the Bronx, who had faith in capitals but not in spelling or punctuation, expressed it this way.

DEAR MISTER DAMROSH MY MA SAYS YOU ARE O.K. AND ON THE RITE PAD AND ON THE SQUAIRE WITH THEM POOR TEACHER AND MA TEACHES ME PIANO AND SING FOLK SONGS AND SOULEFETSHIOS AND MIKE IS MY HIGHSCHOOL COSSEN AND WAS PROMOTED AND PLAYS VIOLIN BUT MA SAYS HE IS NOT YET IN TUNE. HAVE YOU CHILDREN. I LOVE YOUR VOICE AND YOUR SHOKES MAKE US ALL LAFE. YOU MOST BE A VERY GOOD DADDY TOO. WE MISS NO RADIO CONCERT AND MA SHOT OFF ALL JAZZ AND SAYS IS NO GOOD. I THINK SO TOO WHEN I LISSEN TO YOU.

TONI A. HECKER [50]

One time when Walter was in Florida visiting Flagler, a principal of a large public school asked him to speak to the students, suggesting that she not introduce Walter by name. Walter agreed, and in the assembly hall the principal merely said that she had an old friend who would like to say a few words. The students waited quietly while the elderly gentleman came to the front of the stage. Walter looked at them, smiled, and began, "Good MAW-ning, my deah chul-dren!"

There was a moment of shocked silence; then pandemonium. "We know you! We know you!" they shrieked. "You're Dr. Damrosch."

Walter, staggered by the noise and their excitement, stammered, "But you don't know me."

"We do! We do! You're Dr. Damrosch!"

And Walter smiled back happily.[51]

CHAPTER 31

Marya's failure in the theater, Vogue *and her second marriage. Deaths in the family. Leopold, Evelyn Sabin and the Martha Graham Trio.*

M A R Y A ' S A B I L I T Y and desire to alarm her parents seemed to decline as it became clear to everyone that she was not going to succeed as a playwright. In the early 1930s American theater was at a peak. Among the playwrights were Eugene O'Neill, Sidney Howard, Robert Sherwood, Maxwell Anderson, Elmer Rice and George Kaufman; among the stage designers, Norman Bel Geddes, Robert Edmond Jones, Lee Simonson and the young Jo Mielziner; among the actors, the three Barrymores, Lunt and Fontanne, Katharine Cornell and Helen Hayes. The theater district crackled with excitement as a large, intelligent audience went to every new show to appraise, discuss, condemn or enjoy, and the city was filled with aspiring writers eager to make a name.

Among them, in the Damrosch family, besides Marya there was her cousin Gretchen, Walter and Margaret's second daughter, and though she, too, was doomed to fail in this branch of literature, by comparison to Marya she had some success. Gretchen had three plays produced on Broadway, with one running for seventeen performances and another, which Burns Mantle called an "interesting failure," for sixteen. She also had skits used in a *Garrick Gaieties* and a play produced in Chicago. Against this, Marya, despite ten or eleven plays completed, had only one summer stock production and one on Broadway that closed after harsh reviews and four performances to empty houses.[1]

Failure for a writer, particularly a playwright, is very public, much more so than for a lawyer, doctor or housewife. For Marya, after seven or eight years of work and even more plays that no one would produce, it was a searing experience. For the first time in her life she had not been able to wheedle or to bully her way with words to her goal. Finally, to her family, to herself, she had to admit the possibility that most of the world did not care to hear what she had to say. In her autobiography she later wrote: "Geniuses may be able to produce best by self-motivation, but most writers function best on demand. And the worst that can happen to a writer (or man, or woman) is not to be wanted." She knew; she had experienced it.[2]

The family in another respect compared Marya unfavorably with Gretchen, as Marya well knew. Gretchen's husband, Tom Finletter, was a successful bankruptcy lawyer. He was active in the Democratic party and in the future would serve President Roosevelt as a consultant to the ·U.S. delegation to the United Nations conference in San Francisco and President Truman as secretary of the air force during the Korean War. His career enlarged Gretchen's experience. He also was interested in her writing and backed her in it, emotionally and financially. Marriage had given Gretchen the freedom to write; divorce had taken that freedom from Marya. By the summer of 1932 it was clear that she could not support herself by writing, even with the allowance she took from her parents. She retreated to a cheaper apartment, one in her parents' building, adjoining theirs but with its own entrance, and looked for a job.

After two failures she found one at *Vogue,* as a copy writer at $55 a week, a large sum, but not many copy writers started with her qualifications: book reviews published, two plays produced, and three poems and a "Profile" of Theresa Helburn in *The New Yorker.* Her first work, however, was writing captions for picture spreads of corsets and handbags.

After a week or two she wrote to Leopold in Rochester:

> If you think I enjoy all this imposing heading business and people's slaps on the back and getting up at eight and straphanging and sitting on my tail in a green plush room and working with a lot of women and not knowing just what the damn job is and getting home at six — well, if you remember the beginning of the sentence, the answer is No. Not yet. I am, in fact, extremely depressed . . . . I hate work. Men are brutes. Hurry up and make money so that you can support me. Otherwise I suppose I'm all right. Probably in a week things will be hotsy.[3]

At *Vogue* she advanced rapidly, but not through reporting on fashion. She was by nature and family heritage out of place in the world of fashion, so ephemeral, so material, so little of the spirit, so much of the body; fashion, in the end, was merely money on parade, an activity she and her family scorned.

Instead she became the editor's right hand for incorporating into *Vogue* some of the features of the dying *Vanity Fair,* a chatty arts magazine also published by Condé Nast, and she soon was writing a column, "Vogue's Spotlight," on theater, opera, dance — anything that caught her interest.

She also began to initiate and edit articles by leading figures in the arts, so she met and knew many of them. Her salary rose, and she enjoyed the money and the prestige of her position. As she observed later, "Wherever an editor of *Vogue* might be, the glamour implicit in her title was bequeathed to her person. Those contemptuous of such assets have not had them."[4]

Yet despite the steady work well done, the kind of life of which her parents approved still had no appeal for her. She wrote to Leopold:

> The Damrosch family is fecund as ever. Alice looks more like Uncle Frank than ever, and has got herself a very husky, quiet and rather dull husband [Dudley Wolfe] with scads of money. How do they do it? Polly is pupping again, and glassy-eyed. They're all glassy. Ruth Reed is pupping, Dorothy Seymour also, and it's all vaguely depressing. Just a lot more hearty little voices and vague talents. What I dislike most is the gleam of triumph in the eyes of the older generation. Mother will have a big blanket-winter, I foresee. I wish she'd get over the idea that there's something holy about propagating. She speaks of it in the same way that she speaks of "Gawd." Oh well.[5]

She closed by sending love to Leopold from her current lover, Kurt.

But in another year or two her own way of life began to seem equally unsatisfactory. "There had been too many mornings of self-rebuke: the smell of drink, the mouth all blurred with kissing, the rumpled sheets stale with smoke, the taste of waste." The thought began to nag her: If she slept with every man, would she somehow lose the ability to form a lasting relationship with one?[6]

In addition, she had become bored with *Vogue*. The world of fashion for most persons, she saw, was merely a rush to be first at the latest triviality. Even her own work was growing tiresome, one column after another, and by the spring of 1936 she was ready to quit and marry Colin MacKenzie, her first lover in London in 1923. They had seen each other since, and he seemed in every way compatible. Her parents approved, and to her employers Marya gave as a reason for her resignation "a possible marriage in two months or so." But then a new man appeared, who, as Marya confided to Leopold, has "upset my calculations a bit by adding a good body to an excellent brain (plus money and serious talent as a painter)."[7]

With the skill and pleasure of a practiced flirt she pitted the men against each other. "This is the acid test for Colin, who I hope will be victor in the end. But it's strong competition in several ways — upsetting me and driving mother into a perfectly useless state of worry. But what can I do?" Just as when a child, she was trying to combine inconsistencies: the liberated, independent woman was now the helpless, submissive female.[8]

She sailed for Naples still undecided and enjoying every shiver of indecision. Colin boarded the ship at Gibraltar to sail with her to Naples, where she was met on the pier by the painter, Richard Blow. In a letter surely calculated to drive her mother frantic, she wrote: "Imagine what a living hell that was, switching from a trembling man on the boat to a trembling man on the dock. I almost fainted on the gangplank from sheer tension." Then Blow "bore me off to Sicily where a hired car awaited us and off we drove . . ." In her descriptions of him she frequently mentioned his money and his ability to make comfortable arrangements. "I am not, however, facing any bridges for a month, just to leave all loopholes open. If there is to be a tragedy in the life of one man, however fine, I can't help it. I come first in this crisis." [9]

She married Blow, and until August 1939, when because of the imminent war and the new racial laws in Italy a return to the United States seemed wise, she lived with him in a luxurious villa in the hills south of Florence. But except for their son, who would be her chief emotional support in her later years, the marriage was perhaps the greatest mistake of her life. Despite the premarital bedding, she did not know the man she had married. As a boy he had kept two pet raccoons, and when his brother Fred teased them, he had locked Fred in their cage at feeding time. By the time others rescued Fred, his wounds required thirty-two stitches. And on the honeymoon with Marya, a cruise down the Adriatic, Blow brought along another friend, a woman. Marya had married a man more selfish than she, and at least some of the time, it seems, she was scared. [10]

He was angered by her talent as an artist. He painted, and she returned to her sculpture, in which she soon began to produce remarkable works. Though she always put her writing first, her bronze portrait heads of men — her Uncle Walter, Rachmaninoff, Raoul de Roussy de Sales — are splendid, and clearly she could have had a career as a sculptor. People understandably exclaimed over her work, in a way they did not over Blow's, and he was envious.

When their son was born, she discovered that the baby, too, made him jealous. She was quite prepared to abandon care of the child to nurses; she also abandoned him emotionally. "Another woman faced with another reality might, in reaction, have become more fiercely maternal. Out of fear — the fear of a palpable male jealousy — I did not. It was a cowardice that has never stopped haunting me; an evasion of clear responsibility for which I find no excuse." [11]

By the time she arrived back in New York, in the first week of September 1939, the marriage was unhappy, and in another year, as both sought escape in the war, plainly was failing. But even then, her relatives saw, she took no interest in the child. The famous "haunting," of which she made so much, was not serious. As her second divorce loomed, her family rallied to her support, but by then many of its members were more than a little tired of Marya and her problems.

In the 1930s the arrival of a new generation in the family, which Marya, though contributing to it, had found "vaguely depressing," was accompanied by a departure of the old.

The first to die was Frank, on October 22, 1937, just halfway through his seventy-ninth year. He always had said that twenty-two was the Damrosch lucky number, because both he and his father had been born on the twenty-second of a month, Leopold had sailed for the United States on a twenty-second, and Frank and the family, following, had arrived on a twenty-second. And now it happened that Frank died on the hundred and fifth anniversary of his father's birth.

Frank's last years were marred by ill health. In 1929, he not only had problems with his heart, but apparently because of a slight stroke he lost the use of his right eye. He continued at Juilliard's Institute of Musical Art, however, through the spring of 1933, after which he retired and, at Erskine's suggestion, wrote a history of the institute, recording his initial talks with James Loeb, the latter's generosity, Otto Eidlitz's building of the school and its merger into the Juilliard School of Music. The evening the typescript was ready to go to the publisher, Walter appeared on Frank's doorstep with a magnum of champagne.[12]

As Frank became more ill, he and Hetty had given up Seal Harbor, where he could no longer sail his boat, and instead passed the summers at Stockbridge, in the Berkshires, where they were neighbors to Polly and Sidney Howard in Tyringham and to Polly's youngest sister, Anita, who had given up a brief career as an actress to marry Robert Littell. Over several summers Frank and Sidney formed a remarkable friendship. Of an afternoon they would sit for hours on the verandah or lawn talking quietly, and Sidney used to say that he never left Uncle Frank without wanting to write a story about him. In Frank's last summer, his family noticed, he spoke often of his mother.

On his death the newspapers told many stories of him and the People's Singing Classes and Choral Union, the Musical Art Society, and the still vigorous Institute of Musical Art. Hetty in her initial grief gave way momentarily to bitterness and said, "The world will forget him, because it is not a world that remembers." Perhaps she was thinking of how "the Damrosch School" had been transformed into "Juilliard," or of the acclaim Walter was gaining from radio. Among the brothers' admirers the supposed competition between them would never quite die.[13]

But as the days passed, Hetty was filled more with Frank's spirit. Of the many eulogies the one that she apparently liked best was an editorial by John Finley that appeared in the *Times,* "A Breslau Boy in America," perhaps because it seemed to stress Frank's desire to be of service. "To me who knew him best," she added to "Grandfather's Story," which he had written for his grandchildren, "there was something almost Christ-like in his longing to be of use to his fellow beings." [14]

She was somewhat distressed by "Grandfather's Story," however, because typically, though Frank gave an outline of his career, "of his own self he says so little!" And she tried to correct the lack with some paragraphs of her own, including:

> To come into his room and find him sitting in his big armchair reading his book, to feel his handclasp and to see the look of welcome in his beautiful dark eyes, was like a benediction —
> The peace that passeth all understanding was his. [15]

Only two months later, three days after Christmas 1937, Marie Wiechmann died, ending a life not altogether happy. Clara the day before the funeral wrote to Leopold in Rochester. She just had returned from a champagne party given by Marya and Richard Blow in their New York *pied à terre*. She enclosed a letter addressed to Leopold — "from Colin I imagine!" — and reported that the Blows' apartment "looked lovelier than ever, and everyone was full of admiration."

At the bottom she added, "Tomorrow at 2 a little private service for Tante Marie W — nothing but father playing the *Abendlied* & Bach *Air*. All will be over in five minutes. No other news." [16]

The loss of a brother and sister affected Ellie more than Clara. If not more family-minded, she was more person-minded, and though Frank was her elder by thirteen years and they had never been close, she missed him. Or perhaps she missed the idea of him, the eldest brother, who in spirit and physique was the closest of them all to their father. In recalling Marie, who was five years nearer in age, she had twinges of remorse. Had the family treated this sister fairly? Couldn't they, or at least she, have been a little kinder to Marie, a little more attentive? Sometimes, thinking of it, she grew depressed. Not seriously so, but enough so that others noticed.

Her son, Larry, that winter was in Asia for Dodge & Seymour, but his wife, Dorothy, was in New York and planning a visit in March to friends on St. Thomas, in the Caribbean. She suggested that Ellie come, too. Harry urged her to go. A change of scene would be good, and the younger Seymours' cook could look after him while she was gone. There would be no problem. So she went, and while she was gone, Harry died.

He had had a small cold when she left, but he was seventy-seven, eleven years older than Ellie, and the cold, growing worse, put a strain on his enlarged heart; the combination proved fatal. Though everyone told her that she was not responsible, she could not stifle a sense of guilt: she should not have left him.

In the coming months she received a remarkable number of letters about Harry, many of them from strangers, those business associates whom she had never been willing to meet. They wrote to say that Harry had been an unusual man of much broader sympathy and vision than most businessmen, a pioneer in commerce and yet one who also drew pastels. They wrote of him with vibrant affection; he had been a "lovable" man. Ellie, of course, was pleased; she was also, perhaps, a little surprised.

There was an immediate problem of money. In Hetty's case Frank's pension from the Juilliard Foundation would continue for Hetty's life. In Ellie's, there was nothing comparable. What wealth Harry had amassed, aside from his annual share during life in the profits of Dodge & Seymour, was the firm's capital and could not be withdrawn easily. When Larry got back to New York, Ellie was living in the Great Northern Hotel, in itself a depressing place.

For a time Ellie tried living with Ruth in South Orange, but in good health and with no one to look after, she missed the stimulation of New York. Then briefly she and Clair shared an apartment in the city, but as Clair said, "Neither had what the other needed." Finally her daughter-in-law, Dorothy, found an apartment at 130 East 67th Street large enough for herself, Larry, the two children, and for Ellie to have a private bedroom, bath and sitting room with a separate entrance.

There she stayed for fifteen years, living with her son and his family and taking many meals with them. It was a typically German arrangement, and it succeeded because Dorothy, though not a German, was determined that it should. One day Ellie told Dorothy that she should make her son David pick up his pajamas. Dorothy replied in a voice neither soft nor hard, just matter of fact, "For twenty-five years I have been picking up your son's pajamas."

"I know," Ellie said with a sigh. "I spoiled him terribly." That, too, was German, and a reason why, as everyone recognized, she would be happiest living with Larry. The girls would never measure up. In a German family the son was everything, and in many respects Ellie was more German than perhaps she knew. As a widow she was a strong figure and made a deep impression on her grandchildren, who called her O'mama.[17]

One day Sidney Howard remarked to a friend, M. R. Werner, that he was thinking of working in Hollywood, as he needed the money and it would move Polly out of the overwhelming family atmosphere into which she was drawn. There was no dislike of the family in the observation. Sidney had become a friend not only to Frank but equally to Walter, his father-in-law. Nevertheless, as Walter's celebrity accelerated in the 1930s, his activities became a kind of suction into which everyone's attention was drawn.[18]

Not only were there the constant articles on him as Dean of American Conductors to be discussed, but also the occasional attack to be deplored; and then there were the special events, which kept proliferating. In 1933 he organized and led for the benefit of unemployed musicians a series of mammoth concerts in Madison Square Garden, one of which concluded with the finale of Beethoven's Symphony No. 9 danced in the Duncan style to Walter's scenario. At the Metropolitan Opera, on April 12, 1935, to honor his fiftieth year as a conductor, there was a Golden Jubilee Performance of excerpts, of which the most interesting were those in English of *The Mastersingers of Nuremberg*. Walter, who conducted, was now on a crusade for opera in English, and controversy over the idea and its realization continued for weeks. That same year Scribner's reissued his autobiography with an added chapter on radio, and the following year he had another opera, probably his best, *A Man Without a Country,* premièred at the Metropolitan. Later he once again became involved in an argument with the musicians' union, in the course of which he was tried, convicted and censured by the union. He testified to the Senate in Washington against the Pepper bill, whose purpose was to establish a Federal Bureau of Fine Arts. He conducted in the Hollywood Bowl and, probably thanks to Sidney, appeared in two movies. He was given an honorary degree by Brown University and another by the University of Maine, and to open the New York City World's Fair in 1939 he conducted the Philharmonic-Symphony in a performance of Beethoven's Symphony No. 9.[19]

In addition to these great events there were the small, for now throughout the city people of all classes recognized him. One day, when he was traveling by subway to a funeral far uptown, a young man offered him a seat. When Walter protested, the young man said, "But Mr. Damrosch, I want to give you my seat." Later, as Walter peered out the window, another stranger addressing him by name offered to alert him to his station. And as he left the funeral, two old ladies called from a car, "Mr. Damrosch, can't we take you home?" All these events took place in a single morning, and because Walter always was ready to chat with a stranger, each gave rise to a pleasant story to recount. His life in this decade was so full that in its arrangements, discussions and impact it tended to drain any independence of life out of those nearest to him.[20]

Polly, because she was the most musical of his four daughters, was perhaps closer to her father than the others, but even Alice, who considered Mozart "tinkly," had moved to Europe to break the pull of her father's activities. Sidney and Polly had developed a prize herd of milk cattle at their farm in Tyringham, and they were often there. Yet even so he could see a need for her sake to make a break and move farther from New York and her father.

Then one August afternoon in 1939, Sidney, who had worked the morning on a new play, *Benjamin Franklin,* sought relaxation in an afternoon of physical activity. Sawing wood was a frequent occupation, but this afternoon he planned to harrow a twenty-eight-acre field by tractor.

He went to the shed where the tractor was nosed in, turned on its ignition and, going to its front — there was less than three feet between the hood and the wall — turned over the engine by cranking. The two-and-a-half-ton tractor, which an employee had left in gear, leaped forward and smashed him against the wall with such force that the wall bulged ten inches. Pinned in an upright position as the tractor stalled, he died of suffocation, his chest crushed.[21]

He was found not long after. A neighbor, summoned to the house to help with phone calls, the children and notifying relatives, remembered most clearly Polly, sitting on the stairway in the hall, silent, dry-eyed, unresponsive, staring, hour after hour.[22]

That intensity of spirit which had caused friends to suspect that she never would love but one man now turned inward. She harbored her grief, and time did not heal the wound. Alone, with three children to raise, she turned still more to her family, particularly to her sister Anita Littell and to her parents, especially to her father. When Walter died in 1950, peacefully, after a long decline, Polly wept uncontrollably, causing some to wonder whether she was not weeping in part for herself, or for Sidney.

One afternoon in June 1964, while the children, now grown, were off swimming, she started for the cellar, presumably to fetch a bottle of wine. Apparently she tripped on the top step, for the children, on their return, found her at the foot of the stairs, unconscious. They rushed her to a hospital, where a surgeon removed a blood clot from her brain, and she lived until December in a coma. No one ever discovered exactly what had happened.[23]

In Rochester during these years Leopold fell in love, more profoundly than ever before. The woman, whom he met at a musical evening at the Godowskys' house and whom in time he would marry, was a professional dancer, Evelyn Sabin, who had grown up in Rochester, had been one of the original members of Martha Graham's first group, the Trio, and presently was associated with the Eastman School of Music. Her career, for those years, was unusual; but, then, so was she and so was her family.

Her father, Stewart Sabin, a first-class organist who played in many

Rochester churches, was music critic for the *Rochester Democrat-Chronicle* as well as publicity director for the Eastman School of Music, a not always easy combination of jobs. But according to the composer Otto Luening, who joined the music school's faculty in 1925, Sabin had the respect of the musicians: as a reviewer he was "perceptive, always there, and never made a mistake."[24]

Evelyn's mother, for whom she was named, was a professional singer who taught both singing and piano, in which she was expert, so Evelyn and her brother, Robert, four years younger, as children were surrounded by music of all kinds. Robert, who became a dance and music critic, after graduating from the University of Rochester studied music at Eastman and the University of Leipzig, and dance for three years with Martha Graham; he would know what he was writing about. In 1936 he joined the staff of *Musical America,* serving as its editor in chief from 1960 to 1962, was also an editor of *Dance Observer* from 1938 to 1964, and wrote for many magazines, including the *Musical Quarterly.* In addition he edited the ninth edition of *The International Cyclopedia of Music and Musicians,* published in 1964. But even by the year of his death, 1969, of Leopold's family only Clair Seymour, the dancer, had any appreciation of Robert's career. And the same was true of Evelyn. Leopold's Damrosch-Mannes relatives, particularly Marya, never could comprehend that Evelyn's background in music was not entirely unworthy of the musician she married.

Evelyn began studying dance as a young girl with a teacher in Rochester who had studied with Enrico Cecchetti. This was classical ballet, on point. Then in the autumn of 1925, when Evelyn was seventeen, Martha Graham, in an effort to break out of supporting herself by dancing in musical revues, came to Eastman to teach. She was not yet famous, still under the influence of Ted Shawn and Ruth St. Denis, and only just beginning to develop her own style. Her pupils, however, danced barefoot rather than in toe shoes, stressed as the seat of emotion the torso, which classical ballet tended to ignore, and sought in all movement expression rather than display. Three girls in the class proved outstanding — Evelyn Sabin, Thelma Biracree and Betty MacDonald — and that spring they formed the original Graham Trio. In a program with Graham of eighteen dances, at the 48th Street Theater in New York on April 18, 1926, the Trio inaugurated the Graham style of modern dance.

An earlier theatrical venture in which the three appeared, though not under Graham's direction, was a play produced in January by the School of Dance and Dramatic Action, *Sister Beatrice,* by Maeterlinck. But it was not *Sister Beatrice* as Maeterlinck conceived it. The director, Rouben Mamoulian, presented it as a "rhythmic drama to music," in a new translation by Paul Horgan and with an organ score by Otto Luening. Evelyn's part consisted chiefly of a five-minute wordless interlude in which she improvised the astonishment, wonder and response of a young peasant girl, on entering a convent church, to an appearance of the Virgin as a full, living figure.

Five minutes is a long stretch without words, and Luening remembers it as exceptionally well done. Evelyn in those years, he recalled, "was very beautiful." Offstage, however, neither then nor later did she dress or make up to exploit her beauty. It was simply there — if one cared to notice. Like many dancers, she was small in stature, perfectly proportioned and, of course, co-ordinated. Luening remembered Evelyn and Betty MacDonald as "constantly in the school, always together, always in a role, moving this way and that, like two little zombies under Martha's spell." In her seventies Evelyn confessed, "I still do everything to music, walk down the street, shop, do the housework. It's with me all the time." Similarly, it was with Leopold all the time, and he said to her once with satisfaction, "You hear as I hear."[25]

That year at Eastman started Evelyn's performing career. After the Maeterlinck in January there followed the Graham concert in New York, with the Trio in seven of the eighteen dances. Though Graham later would say of these early works that they were "childish things, dreadful," one of her biographers, Don McDonagh, claimed that the concert "changed the course of dance in the twentieth century." At the very least, a sizable audience paid to see it, was impressed and carried away a sense of something new in dance; something later called simply Martha Graham.[26]

For Evelyn and the two girls, the trip to New York was an adventure. They came down by overnight train a week in advance, missed Graham and her accompanist, Louis Horst, at the station, went down to her studio on Tenth Street and, still unable to find her, went out to breakfast. It was about as much as they would see of New York, for on their return to her studio she was there, and after settling them in a nearby hotel she summoned them for a rehearsal that continued almost unbroken throughout the week.[27]

The program, as Evelyn recalled it, went well. As a performer, she never was bothered by nerves; in fact, she felt more at ease onstage than off. Once the music began, her nerves would disappear, and she knew they would. Thereafter, it was just "myself onstage and what I could do." Later, married to Leopold, she discovered that he did not share that feeling, and sometimes listening to him perform publicly she would grow nervous with him as what had gone brilliantly in rehearsal began to blur.

Back in Rochester after the New York performance, Graham repeated the concert with a few changes in the program. She also mounted a production of her ballet *The Flute of Krishna,* an East Indian idyll, in which she gave the leading roles to Robert Ross and Evelyn. It was put on for a week, with three performances a day, as a prelude, with symphony orchestra, to silent movies. The production, with its choreography by Graham, has a historical interest, for just before the week's run about four minutes of the ballet was filmed at the Research Studios of Eastman Kodak as an experiment in color with a film called Two Color Kodachrome, consisting of a blue-green-dyed image on one side of the film base and orange-red on the other. It is not much to look at, but it is probably the earliest film of any ballet in color; it is also the earliest film of a Martha Graham ballet; and it is remarkable in that the ballerina later met and married one of the inventors of three-color Kodachrome.[28]

That summer there was a Graham concert in New Hampshire; then another in the fall in New York, with new dances for the Trio as well as several duets for Sabin and MacDonald; then more concerts, until in the spring of 1930 Evelyn left the company, which was expanding, and returned home to recuperate from anemia. Soon after, the Eastman School offered her the use of a studio in which to work and teach in return for occasional coaching in the opera department and for appearing as guest soloist in the annual week-long Festival of American Music, of which one evening always was devoted to ballet. By then Evelyn was a well-known figure in Rochester's music circles.

One night in 1934 a friend invited her to accompany him to the Godowskys' house for some music. Leo that evening had gathered three other string players and Leopold at the piano. It was the first time that Evelyn had met either man, and though she was impressed by Leopold's playing, it was the general joy in music-making that impressed her most.

These evenings as Leo and Frances presented them were not parties. Liquor was never served; at most, Frances would offer tea, toast and perhaps scrambled eggs, sometimes made with matzos. The gathering, even including players, seldom numbered more than twenty, and the emphasis throughout was on the music. Evelyn liked the evening's style, was invited again and became a friend of the Godowskys. In time, after meeting Evelyn on several occasions at the house, Leopold invited her out to dinner, and gradually their love for each other developed.

Meanwhile, with the problems of Kodachrome solved and perhaps, too, because of love, Leopold's desire to return to music full time increased, and in November 1938 he wrote to Randall:

. . . Just now I seem to be working at the usual pace, Kodak being in a very active phase and taking long well-filled hours, every day. In addition, I just gave a piano recital here and am playing in New York with the W.P.A. orchestra twice in the next three weeks — with more concert dates later on. This means practicing at night under the fear of God. Nevertheless . . . the sounds that emerge from the piano are encouraging for about the first time that I can recall.[29]

Like his Uncle Walter, Leopold seemed to have inexhaustible reserves
of energy. For him a career in a research laboratory, another in concert
halls, another partial one assisting his parents with their school, an active
social life and falling in love were not too much. Saying "I would rather
burn out than rust out," he was always ready to take on another commitment. Yet, despite all his activities, one pursuit, the most demanding,
was conspicuously absent: his composing. And Randall, who always
mourned its absence, wrote,

> I wish I saw signs in the sky that your frenzied existence were to be
> tranquillized. Greatness plus popularity plus consideration of others and
> being generally well-bred is a combination that does not lead to a simple
> life. Couldn't you give up one of these characteristics and enjoy some
> freedom. I couldn't. Not possibly; but I thought perhaps *you* could.[30]

What Leopold chose to give up was science, the work in which thus
far he had made his greatest mark. Even though Mees, in a serious conversation, prophesied a limitless future for him at Kodak, on December
31, 1939, Leopold ended his active connection with the company and
became a consultant. But for as much as two years before then his focus
had shifted back to New York.

Not everyone was enthusiastic about his return to music. Godowsky,
like Mees, wished the partnership in science could continue; and many
of Leopold's relatives felt that he had proved himself in science, and
asked — for this was the articulate Damrosch family — what similar position, starting at age forty, could he win for himself in music, being
neither a virtuoso performer nor a proven composer?

What most of them could not appreciate was the intensity of his feeling about music. He remarked to a friend in the research laboratory,
Arnold Weissberger, "Life is too short and too precious to spend it inside
a factory." Considering the intellectual excitement of his work at Kodak,
the remark is unfair and must be taken as the anguished cry of a man
who wants to do something else even more. As he explained to Evelyn,
"I would rather be a second-class musician than a first-class scientist."[31]

His parents understood his feelings, but they were not impartial and
perhaps, in the long run, not even helpful. Clara, during his Rochester
years, wrote to him constantly about the school's problems, always insisting that he should not think of them, even as she tangled them into
his life: "I know you want to hear of the meeting on School matters
. . . Our offers of possible help towards meeting deficit are listed on
enclosed sheet — Please return."[32]

The school, lacking a foundation, Carnegie or Flagler to support it,
almost closed during the depression, and it doubtless was natural for
parents to look to a talented son for help, particularly after 1935, when
his photography patents began to earn royalties. Leopold never failed

them either with advice or money, but his care for their problems ensured that on his return to New York and a full life in music he would also return to the school, as associate director. For his career as a performer and composer, however, he might have been wiser not to split his time and attention.

Nevertheless, the move back to New York began happily. In his first two months he completed the *Suite for Two Pianos,* his first original composition in ten years. He began to make plans for a New York recital with a cellist, Luigi Silva, and accepted an invitation from Carnegie Hall to deliver a lecture, "The Evolution of the Piano and Its Literature," one of a series offered by the hall to celebrate its golden anniversary season, 1940–41. The program stated joyfully, "After ten years of service [to Eastman Kodak] . . . his plans for the present are to concentrate his efforts upon composition and the administration of many affairs at the Mannes Music School."

Before then, however, on July 16, 1940, he married Evelyn Sabin in a simple Presbyterian ceremony in John and Helen Tee Van's apartment. Beside the Tee Vans and Helen's old nurse, Annie, the only persons present were Betty MacDonald and her husband. Almost immediately after the minister's final words, the couple left for Martha's Vineyard to see his parents and then on to Rochester to see hers. On the way Leopold played a recital in Woodstock, New York, and another in Cooperstown.[33]

His marriage took many of his family and friends by surprise, for he had talked very little of Evelyn. Even Randall, on being told of it, wrote that he was struck dumb,

> — not so much with surprise as with emotion. I know from our rather shy and reticent conversations on the subject that you wanted to be married, and I know how soberly and deeply you have contemplated it . . .
>
> I can't (quite obviously) break into backslapping style. Send you telegrams saying things like "How about hush money?" Or tease you about birth control. Perhaps you have worked through to that mood. If so, give me a little time. At present I find your getting married a terribly serious and important event. I approve of it thoroughly, if that's of any consequence — which it isn't. I also consider it indispensable to your contentment and thus to your realizing and achieving anything like what you are capable of. You've got a lot of friends, but not many care *more* than I do what happens to you or what you make of a potentially incomparable life.[34]

But others close to Leopold, including some in his family, wondered whether, given his age and problems, marriage was a sensible way to proceed if he hoped to make the most of his many talents. Marya soon was saying loudly that he should have remained single.

CHAPTER 32

John Tee Van and the giant pandas. Leopold, Evelyn and Martha Graham. Marya and Gretchen Finletter. Clara dies. Leopold and the Mannes Trio.

IN SEPTEMBER 1941 John Tee Van, who was then general associate at the New York Zoological Society's Bronx Zoo, suddenly became a news story followed with interest by thousands of animal lovers as he departed on a 34,868-mile trip to western China to bring back a baby giant panda. For two summers in 1939 and 1940 a young female giant panda, Pandora, had been the star attraction of the society's exhibit at the New York World's Fair, and when, in May 1941, she died of indeterminable cause, millions who had seen and photographed her antics felt a loss. She had imprinted deeply in the national mind the image of a panda as a particularly charming, cuddly bear.[1]

In Pandora's death Mme. Chiang Kai-shek, then the most important woman in China, saw an opportunity for a political gesture, and she planned to give the American people, in gratitude for their support of the United China Relief Fund, another baby giant panda. Someone, however, would have to go to western China to collect it, and the Zoological Society designated John. His trip out was uneventful, though as he neared Chengtu, the capital of Szechwan province, where he expected to find one panda, size and sex unknown, he began to hear rumors of two. Both were said to be young, only sixty pounds, and they were thought, as far as anyone could determine, to be male and female. The possibility of two pandas, young enough to adjust to captivity and possibly even to mate, overturned John's zoological soul, and he began to covet.

Giant pandas, even in their habitat, a very small area of western China, are extremely rare, and zoologists today estimate that there are only about three hundred in the world, including some fifty in zoos. The number seems unlikely to increase greatly, for adult pandas, whether wild or in zoos, tend to dislike each other, and thus far only the Chinese and the Mexicans, and the latter only in the last few years, have succeeded in raising one in captivity. Until recently, no panda surviving more than ten days had been born outside of China, and in 1941 it was still true that any panda anywhere had been born wild on the precipitous mountain slopes directly north of Yunnan.

Besides their general dislike of captivity and a tendency to die early, pandas offer a number of problems to zoos. They are big, the male growing to 350 pounds and the female, to 300 pounds, and though vegetarians, they have sharp teeth and nails. Their sex does not become apparent until maturity, about six years, and sometimes not even then; in addition, they are clumsy in coupling, generally not interested, and careless of babies, which are born small, about four inches long and three and a half ounces in weight. Finally, despite their charming playfulness as adolescents, with age, regardless of sex, they often grow lethargic and sometimes savage, so they sometimes must be cared for through remote controls. All in all, they are not exactly as the public perceives them.

Nevertheless, through intermediaries John asked for both pandas, and Mme. Chiang soon purred in a broadcast to the United States, "We would like to present to America, through you Mr. Tee Van, this pair of comical, black-and-white furry pandas. We hope that their cute antics will bring as much joy to the American children as American friendship has brought to our Chinese people." A few days later John started for home, and then, when he and the pandas were aboard the *President Coolidge,* in a convoy out of the Philippines, the Japanese attacked Pearl Harbor.

Zoologically speaking, the chief problems of the trip were heat and food. For the pandas, living normally in mountains of seven thousand to ten thousand feet, Hong Kong was about the limit of physical comfort. In the three weeks that followed, at sea level in and near the Philippines, though John rushed them into the mountains while waiting for the ship to sail, they became dehydrated and nearly died. They also developed a slight indigestion in the shift from Chinese to Philippine bamboo shoots. Since each ate about twenty pounds a day, much of John's time was taken in arranging for a continuous supply. He also fed them a porridge of boiled corn meal, Pablum, evaporated milk, honey and water.

His one disciplinary incident occurred when he and the pandas were only ten minutes from home, in a boxcar crossing the New Jersey flats. He had been exercising the pandas for an hour, and the larger refused to re-enter its cage. In the tussle that followed, the panda almost had the best of it, and only minutes before John expected to greet his colleagues with a report that everything had gone well, he was left bloodied, dirty and exhausted.

The zoo was ready with an enclosure built to resemble a Chinese land-scape, and the animals soon were on exhibit and as popular with visitors as Pandora had been. By means of a public contest they were named Pandee and Pandah, though later to everyone's disappointment Pandee, the supposed male, turned out to be female and died early, in 1945; Pandah survived until 1951. The following year John, still holding only a high school degree, was appointed director of the Bronx Zoo, and most of the news stories stressed his work with the pandas. In the public's mind he always was associated with them.

In his zoological career, his work with pandas was far less important than his studies of tropical fish and insects, yet to many of the Damrosches he did not become a subject of pride until the trip to China. For these family members the pandas were his equivalent of the discovery of Kodachrome. Though the analogy was false, in this family of musicians, with their long tradition of public performance, success or even the rec-ognition of quality often was tied to public acclaim.

In the autumn of 1940, following their marriage, Leopold and Evelyn started their life together in New York in a tiny two-story house at 11 East Eleventh Street. To Clara it seemed unnecessarily far from the fam-ily home and school, in the mid-seventies, and she also was distressed that Evelyn returned to Rochester on weekends in order to continue with several of her pupils. To Clara, this was not the way to make a home for Leopold. When she began to murmur her thoughts, Leopold spoke to her firmly, explaining that he and Evelyn, aged forty-one and thirty-three, were of a different generation with a different style of living. Clara took the rebuff kindly, but her attitude toward Evelyn, though always correct, continued cautious. Leopold, after all, had married once, been divorced and had conducted many romances. She would wait and see whether this marriage lasted before committing her emotions to it.

Her attitude influenced David and others in the family. Uncle Walter and Aunt Margaret gave a dinner party half in honor of Leopold and Evelyn, the balance for Ezio Pinza and his new wife, a dancer. Among the younger generation, Leopold's first cousins, everyone was pleasant but self-absorbed. With the exception of Clair Seymour, their interest was entirely in Leopold, the family genius, so charming, so successful, and they tended to treat Evelyn as a cipher who in marriage had made an extremely lucky catch; but, then, as Evelyn observed later, "They were, for the most part, not interested in dance; it meant little or nothing to them, and so they had little or no interest in me." She soon discovered that within the family three of her warmest friends had married into it, Aunt Hetty, Aunt Margaret and, above all, John Tee Van.[2]

But in the first year of marriage she hardly thought of her relations with the family. Leopold's energy and humor made life a delight, his excitement at resuming his work in music full time was contagious, and she found herself entranced by the family's ritual of Christmas. Not only was there a large family gathering on Christmas Eve at the Mannes apartment, where there was a full Christmas tree with real candles, German ornaments and carols, with almost everyone singing in German, especially "*Stille nacht, heilige nacht . . .*" but even in their own apartment Leopold insisted that the two of them have a tree, decorated exactly according to custom. They went out to buy it together, and after setting it up, he showed her how to make the candle holders out of twisted wire that ended, below the branch, in a lead weight to hold the candle upright, and how to gild the walnuts with a string attached by sealing wax — just as his grandmother had taught his mother and aunts. The intensity with which he approached Christmas and the emotion he put into it impressed her, and she felt she never before had experienced Christmas so richly. In addition, she was pregnant, and that was a great joy.

During that winter Leopold had his teaching and administrative work at the school, and he also prepared a recital with the cellist Luigi Silva for the spring, which came to performance in Town Hall on Saturday afternoon, April 6, 1941. For Leopold it was his first New York recital in ten years, and for Silva, his United States debut. The chief works on the program were three sonatas, Boccherini's in C, Brahms's in F and Beethoven's in A, an austere but interesting selection of works not often heard. The critics for the *Times* and *Herald Tribune* each made the same point. After some complimentary remarks, the *Times* critic wrote, "Mr. Mannes was self-effacing . . . he failed to realize many of the potentialities of the piano parts." The critic for the *Herald Tribune* complained of "a certain aristocratic reserve about the romantic possibilities of the Brahms sonata, as if Mr. Silva were gauging the performance for relatively intimate surroundings rather than a large auditorium."[3]

No matter whose the fault, this apparent inability to project nuances in a large hall was the failing to which both men tended when not performing effectively. The criticism periodically would recur. In rehearsal, in a small hall the nuances would project; in a large hall, sometimes not. The problem, though, was one of projection; the underlying musical ideas always were there.[4]

Evelyn carried her baby easily to full term, but it was stillborn, a perfectly formed girl, which in the last hours, apparently, had strangled on the umbilical cord. Although no one liked to say so, the obstetrician seemed at fault. For both parents it was a shattering experience; for Leopold, now in his forties, it was the second child lost; for Evelyn, the start of months of severe ill health. After she was sent home by the doctor,

she began to hemorrhage and was raced back to the hospital in an am-
bulance. For a time it was thought that her blood type and Leopold's
were incompatible, but that proved not so. Yet recovery was very slow.
It was a discouraging time.[5]

One day when Evelyn was convalescing at Eleventh Street, Martha
Graham came to call. Evelyn had not seen her for some time, and they
chatted happily for several hours. Graham soon admitted to an ulterior
purpose: she had come to ask Evelyn to rejoin the company. The idea
was not impossible, she said. Leopold was leading a professional performer's life, and Evelyn's return to dance might fit in well with it. Indeed, she wondered whether dance perhaps was not essential to Evelyn
for spiritual and physical health. For Evelyn, face to face with Graham
and yet with Leopold's presence in the room around her, it was a startling moment.[6]

Years later, when orally prodded one day, she said with fire, "I have
had two inspirations in my life, Martha Graham and Leopold Mannes."
By then, however, it was clear that part of her strength in life had been
that she always had understood her relation to both. There was no confusion; not even in that moment on East Eleventh Street, when every
muscle ached with the remembered joy of dance. Her adventure now
was with Leopold. She intended to have another child, if possible.

Yet she knew what she was giving up, if only because no medicine in
that long, dreary spring did as much to restore her health as Graham's
continued belief in her artistry. Sadly she told Graham how she already
had tried to thank her: the lost child, if it had lived, would have been
named Martha.

Like Helene von Heimburg, who had given up singing under Liszt to
marry Leopold's grandfather, Evelyn gave up as much for the grandson,
and, like Helene, she never looked back. Later, in assessing her decision
that day, she emphasized other reasons: she was older, the life was demanding, she had danced professionally for sixteen years. Though all
these were true, they were subsidiary to a life with Leopold that included, she hoped, children. That was her commitment.

Life that year, however, seemed to have a store of cruelties. As early
as June 1941, six months before Pearl Harbor, Leopold received a letter
from the U.S. Department of Commerce suggesting that "you, as one
of the nation's well-known inventors, can be of material help . . . toward aiding the national defense program." It was a call that Leopold
did not want to hear. Nevertheless, that summer he again began to put
science first. His work during the war was done not in Washington but
in the research laboratory at Eastman Kodak in Rochester, and at Wright
Field, an air force base near Dayton, Ohio, where he and others worked
chiefly on problems of haze in aerial color photography.[7]

The immediate casualty in his musical life was his composing, which he never again attempted. Except for the short interim in 1940, when he had composed the *Suite for Two Pianos,* he had completed nothing original since 1930. By the war's end, in 1945, he evidently felt the gap of fifteen years was too great to be bridged. He could not pretend, even to himself, that he could begin at forty-five. And he never again tried, not anything original, but the renunciation left him with a deep wound.

In anyone's life there are many "ifs," but in Leopold's they seem particularly poignant. What if he and Godowsky had discovered Kodachrome promptly, and he had spent only three years in Rochester instead of nine? Or if the war had not begun until 1945, allowing him six years in New York to establish his musical career? Or if he had been only a musician, nothing more, and someone else had discovered Kodachrome with Godowsky? The boy at Riverdale school who joined his friend Leo in a search to improve color photography paid a high price for his scientific skill.

Though the war was a disaster for Leopold and his return to music, for Marya it resolved one personal problem. The husband she did not want was eager to join the naval air force and anxious to fly away a free man. So the divorce was easy. Meanwhile Marya had taken a job with a group called the International Coordination Council, which "consisted of several distinguished prewar refugees, now U.S. citizens, and Americans who hoped to channel their knowledge and talents into constructive use against the Axis enemies." By October 1941 Marya's part in this self-appointed, civilian effort had turned into the Short Wave Research, Incorporated, a tiny organization associated with and paid by the Office of War Information. Marya was its president and continued so until May 1943. Despite the corporate name and title, her job and that of her one or two assistants consisted mainly of interviewing hundreds of refugees from Europe with an eye to their use by the OWI as broadcast writers, speakers or researchers. She also listened to German-language short-wave broadcasts and read the German-language press in a search for possible espionage. Just as in the previous war, there were constant rumors of German submarines landing men with radios or local German-Americans disclosing troop and convoy movements.[8]

But then she was recruited by the Office of Strategic Services to go to Lisbon and Madrid as a counterintelligence agent. Though she would be paid by the OSS, her cover was *The New Yorker,* for which she was to write "Letters" from the two capitals, and presumably other works.[9]

For her counterintelligence work in Madrid, for example, she lived at the Ritz Hotel, associated with rich industrialists, wined, dined and bedded with a variety of men, was hated and despised by their wives and, as she admitted in her autobiography, accomplished "very little." The chief lesson to be derived from her experience, she concluded, was "that henceforth no female as conspicuous as myself should be sent abroad as an agent, especially in Latin countries."[10]

Unlike most people involved in the war, because of her cover position as a writer she was able to turn her assignment to great personal advantage. Any time she spent in research or at her typewriter was time well spent to establish her cover, so she was able to write and sell a number of articles, such as one for *Vogue* on fashion in Lisbon. But most important, of course, was the cover itself, *The New Yorker*. During the years 1943 and 1944 it published not only "Letters" from Lisbon, Madrid and Barcelona, all major pieces, but six other works by Marya. Such a large presence in one of the country's most important magazines added greatly to her reputation as a writer.

To go abroad, however, she left her four-year-old son with Clara and David, and on her return she found a child "who looked at me as if I were a stranger. No greater reminder of what I had done to him was needed." Nevertheless, she had no intention of changing the pattern of her life, and she set about building her career as a journalist and freelance writer "at a child's expense."[11]

She invited Clair to live with her and play Tante's role of summer mother while she accepted assignments that took her away for long periods. For *Vogue* she went to Milan and Rome with a photographer to do a series of articles on writers and artists in post-Fascist Italy, and for *The New Yorker* she went to Palestine to write a "Letter from Jerusalem." But even when home, she constantly was calling relatives to take the boy for a holiday, a weekend or a fortnight. His June 1947, for example, consisted of two weeks with Ruth Reed and her family, a weekend with his father, the rest at camp; and in September, though only nine, he was sent off to boarding school. Given his parents' inability to make a home for him, their decision perhaps was wise, but Marya's protestation to her disapproving parents — "my own personal desire is of course to have him around" — was doubted by others. As the number of outlets for her writing increased, so did her excitement for her life as she was leading it. When in 1946 Condé Nast, the publisher, offered her a position as feature editor on its new magazine, *Glamour,* she accepted, but only for a year. She would not be tied down, and she had begun a novel.[12]

In a quite different fashion her cousin Gretchen Finletter also began to find success as a writer during the war years. Like many of her generation, those born in the 1890s, she worshiped Chekhov, and having failed in the early 1930s with plays, she turned in the next decade to short stories, small scenes in which the underlying social values emerged in the relationships of the people and the manner in which they addressed each other. In 1942 and 1943 she published stories in *The New Yorker, Town & Country* and *Harper's Bazaar*, but more important was an autobiographical series that appeared in the *Atlantic Monthly*, at a rate of about six a year, from October 1943 through May 1946. They established for Gretchen a steady following, and when collected and presented as a book, *From the Top of the Stairs* (1946), they had a substantial sale, which still continues through secondhand bookstores.

Perhaps a cause of their success was World War II, which seemed to upset so many values that people had thought unchanging. Gretchen's account of life in her family before World War I had the charm of nostalgia for a more innocent world that was lost; yet at the same time, it was reassuring. The values that Walter and Margaret had put into their family life seemed not only attractive but, perhaps, even eternal.

> In the middle of this [Gretchen's birthday party] my father entered the room, and at the same moment the waitress announced supper. My father then did a horrifying thing. He went to the piano and started to play a march. I was so appalled at this break with custom that I could not speak. Then I signaled him to stop.
>
> "Louder?" said my father and played on.
>
> "Supper is served," repeated the waitress.
>
> I reached the piano. "Don't play!" I begged. "None of the fathers play piano!"
>
> "More fools they," replied my father, continuing. "Now all of you march around the room twice." We marched around the room twice and I did not dare lift my eyes.[13]

But of course it turned out that the children enjoyed the music, and the little parade snapped everyone to attention, gave the afternoon a fresh start, and the supper went better because of it.

Then there was the relationship of the parents:

> The question of religion was a curving line between my parents. My father usually had a concert on Sundays and did not go to church. He did not think much of the music that was played there — I think it made him nervous — and anyhow, Sunday was his busy day. He did not, however, feel any the less religious or any less an authority with my mother in understanding the workings of the Deity. He always referred to God as The Almighty, and this practice annoyed my mother. I think she felt that if my father did not work enough at religion to go to church, as she did, and did not read the religious books, as she did, he should not be so know-it-all about what The Almighty was up to. She would tell him he didn't know what he was talking about.[14]

On the other hand, when Margaret, who was a suffragist, announced that she was going to march in the first big suffrage parade, Walter took all the children to see her. Suffragism in those days invited ridicule and sometimes violence, and Gretchen worried that someone might throw an egg at her mother. There was, in fact, considerable jeering, not all of it good-natured, and then one of her sisters screamed, "Look — in the second line — at the end!"

Walter said, "Now when I give the signal."

The line drew nearer. "One, two, three," cried Walter, and he and the girls cheered. "My father was very proud of my mother. I think he would have paraded too if he had been invited, and he wanted her to get her due." [15]

Marya's first novel, *Message from a Stranger* (1948), published two years after Gretchen's book, presented a very different world, one in which there was no place for such a simple statement as "My father was very proud of my mother." Though fiction, the book was full of autobiographical touches; in the remote background, Clara and David's world, in the forefront, Marya's. Despite a broad range of characters, there is no happy marriage, no lasting relationship, no extended family, no young children. It is a book about adults, some old, some young, but all isolated individuals in a big-city culture. Whereas the relationships that Gretchen portrayed could have existed in a hundred cities across the country, those depicted by Marya were possible only in New York.

Technically the novel is interesting. The heroine, Olivia Baird, "one of the best-known women writers in the country" — she is Marya as Marya wished to be seen — dies in the opening sentence, and the story is told as she is called back during the next twelve months in the thoughts of the survivors, principally her first and second husbands, her lover and her two children. She is a good wife, a superb mistress and a loving, sympathetic mother. [16]

The book's defects and virtues are not unrelated. The plot is rather contrived and the characters somewhat unreal, chiefly because they are ideas about people rather than the individuals themselves. Marya's talent, apparently, was less for creating characters than for discussing them. On the other hand the book is filled with observations, even wisdom, beautifully expressed. On gaining maturity: "All growth is slow — except malignant growth." On a writer who went to Hollywood and stayed: "He's forgotten that making a thousand people think is possibly more satisfying than making eighty million stop thinking." Or on how easy was the formula for professional liberalism: "All you had to do was to sit at a desk, disagree with the government, and talk about the man in the street. For facts you could substitute indignation, for information a self-righteous dogmatism just as inflexible as its reactionary equivalent."[17]

There was also a great deal about the experience of death for the deceased and the living, a spirited defense of what many would call sexual promiscuity and, throughout, a discussion of family roots and values. She professed to admire her parents' ways, and she believed in continuity. Roots can grow only "in the rich loam of human experience. And part of that loam was physical: the clock, the chair . . . the fading portrait . . . they evoked an atmosphere which could be a benediction as well as a curse." Homes should have warmth, serenity and a quality of taste, "the kind of warmth and serenity which existed in the home of my parents."[18]

For those who knew her best there was a contradiction between what she wrote and how she lived. In these years in conversation she was very scornful of so-called bourgeois values, just those which Gretchen, Leopold and others in the family thought contributed to a happy, serene home. Yet when challenged, she could not define "bourgeois" without denigrating the values she had extolled in her novel, and the suspicion always hung heavy that, as she used the term, it was merely a rhetorical screen thrown up to cover a selfish act.[19]

She herself, evidently, was aware of the contradiction, for, asked to send in advance some details of her personal life for an introduction at a Famous Authors Luncheon, she balked. "You had better not go into it," she wrote, and provided only a short paragraph that mentioned neither of her two husbands nor her child.[20]

The book's sales, to her exasperation, were merely average. Perhaps the theme of death was against it, but at the end of its first three months it had sold only 11,596 copies and still had $1,689.40 to earn to repay the advance against royalties. In later paperback editions, however, it gradually built an audience of about 200,000, which was very loyal to her. Even fifteen years later she still received an occasional letter of appreciation. But unlike her heroine, she was not content to make a thousand people think; she wanted big-time celebrity, to be cheered by millions.[21]

Early in 1942 Leopold and Evelyn moved from their house on Eleventh Street — "Elevelyn Street," as Leopold called it — and moved into 120 East 75th Street, where his parents, Aunt Hetty and the Tee Vans had apartments. The family enclave had not been their first choice; in fact, they had been about to move into an apartment in another building when the owner took it off the market. There were advantages to the family building, however. Evelyn was still not well, and with Leopold much of the time in Rochester or at Wright Field, it was comforting to be near family. And these advantages multiplied when Evelyn again became pregnant. The first three months were unusually difficult, but on December 3, 1943, she was delivered of a healthy girl, whom they called Elena, a variant of Helen, which was common in both families.

The disadvantages of such close family living were only too obvious. Leopold inevitably became more and more embroiled in his parents' affairs, both personal and at the school, and by the war's end any chance of his not returning to the school had vanished. Their reliance on him was too great.

In these years, as family finances went, Leopold was remarkably rich. His patents had begun to bear royalties in 1938 and would continue until 1952, paying him in all perhaps about a million dollars. There were two problems in connection with the money. Everyone, seeing the incredible expansion in color photography and knowing little or nothing of patents or of Leopold's agreements with Godowsky, Eastman Kodak and Kuhn, Loeb & Company, assumed that he was much, much richer than he was, and his generosity confirmed the misbelief. It always had been a Damrosch tradition to use money rather than accumulate it, but Leopold gave it away, both to individuals and the school, at a rate that, as a friend observed, was "a form of economic suicide." Indeed, some friends began to wonder if there was not some psychological quirk at the base of his generosity.[22]

His aid to his parents was easy to understand. As they approached the end of their lives, to musicians and nonmusicians alike they were admirable. On April 13, 1947, his father for the last time conducted one of the David Mannes Free Concerts at the Metropolitan Museum of Art. He was eighty-one, had conducted the concerts, generally four or five a year, for thirty years, and had played to nearly two million people. Some of these, brought as children, went on to become professional musicians, such as Myor Rosen, first harpist of the New York Philharmonic from 1960 to the present. Most, of course, were amateurs who came simply to enjoy music they otherwise would not have heard. And they were grateful to David, for they knew, as the *Times* editorialized, that "the concerts would not have exerted such an influence if it had not been for the effort and idealism of the artist who founded them."[23]

Taken as a whole David's life in music was extraordinary, although, as Henderson had said of Walter, he did not achieve "celebrity in any one department of his art." David had been a good concertmaster but not a great violinist. As a conductor he put together good programs, but was not a great interpreter. He and Clara had been, for nearly fifteen years, the country's outstanding violin-piano duo, but they had given it up to found a school, and it was as a teacher that David perhaps had the greatest influence. In addition to the millions he had reached with his museum concerts, he had touched thousands deeply with his work at the Third Street Music School Settlement, the Music School Settlement for Colored People and, finally, the David Mannes Music School. It was a life well spent, and the son was proud of the father.

But aside from the quality of his parents, there was the fun of them. In the summer of 1947 for a vacation they went to Canada and among other trips took an overnight boat up the Saguenay River. In the evening, as Clara wrote to Leopold, an orchestra played, and his father, eighty-one, and his mother, just short of seventy-eight, "actually danced a bit — and believe it or not were applauded!! And compliments kept coming to us from strangers! A joke isn't it? We will probably go in for some lessons again!! your ever frivolous & extravagant, Mother."[24]

Though Clara and David were seldom, if ever, extravagant, without Leopold's aid his parents would have been in serious difficulties, for except for their salaries from the school, they had very little on which to live, and increasingly he was paying their expenses. The fact bothered them, and on October 30, 1947, Clara wrote him an ultimatum:

Last night, when father and I came home, we definitely decided on certain matters troubling us both! . . . Neither of us can any longer stand the great sacrifice of time, money and thought you are giving to the school. In addition to this, your ever-generous spirit and sympathy is also draining not only your financial resources, but your strength as well. Before coming down to our definite material considerations, I want to say that father fully realizes that at nearly 82 he cannot do what for so many years he was able to do with my co-operation — not only build up a fine school, with eminent faculty, but attract the interest of wealthy friends to help its growth financially. And now, besides all the burdens personal and financial, you have taken over my own health condition and it has become another drain. This is *not* necessary and I am enclosing a check for $1,000 to at least nearly repay this expense. [He had installed air filters in her apartment to help her with her asthma.] . . . In addition, father and I want you to know that, should [Louis] Graveure *not* make up his salary in lessons, *we* insist on taking over the deficit. Unfortunately we cannot reduce our salary. We can only hope that somehow the Mannes Music School can be advantageously sold either as building or as school and before we depart this chaotic world we will know that you are free to lead your own precious life.

All this is *final*
Hugs from us both
Mother[25]

But of course Leopold paid no attention. Closing the school, selling its buildings, obliterating its name while Clara and David were alive was out of the question. They were extraordinary, but not so extraordinary that he could dismantle their life's work before their eyes. Between the lines so bravely stated was a cry for help to which Leopold, as always, responded.

The following March, one evening as Clara, David and Helen Tee Van were walking the block on Lexington Avenue to the school to hear Leopold in a piano-violin recital, Clara suddenly staggered, and except that David and Helen caught her, she would have fallen. Within seconds she was dead in the street, of a heart attack, and they carried her body home.[26]

At the school Evelyn, waiting for them to join her, was beckoned from her seat and told what had happened. She decided against an announcement; the recital was to go forward. She would tell Leopold after he had played.

Later, when he went to the funeral home to collect Clara's ashes, the assistant handed him the urn with the remark "Here's Mom." In that moment Leopold, the gentlest of men, knew the homicidal urge, and if the man had been so unfortunate as to touch him, Leopold would have killed him. Such vulgarity, such familiarity toward a woman whose life had been the pursuit of an ideal! Marya, who was with Leopold, hurried him out to the street.[27]

Leopold's work at the school now became, if possible, more important. Though he did not assume the title of president until 1950–51, he was already the school's chief executive, and the staff and students alike looked to him as their leader. His life, however, was not entirely administrative, and in these years he started a friendship and a piano trio, both of great importance to him.

The friendship was with the conductor George Szell, who had left Europe at the start of World War II and come to New York, where Leopold promptly hired him for the school. For five years, from 1940 to 1945, Szell taught instrumentation and composition at Mannes while establishing himself by guest appearances as an outstanding conductor of opera and symphony. In 1946, he accepted the post of musical director of the Cleveland Orchestra, which in his tenure, from 1946 to 1970, he developed into one of the world's best. His friendship with Leopold, however, was not weakened by distance but grew steadily deeper, embracing not only their common love of music, particularly the works of Schumann, but all aspects of life. For both it was a friendship in which each stimulated the other to new thought and better work.

The trio, usually called simply the Mannes Trio, was formed in the fall of 1948 and played its first recital on January 12, 1949, at Town Hall. The cellist again was Luigi Silva, the violinist, Vittorio Brero. In a pre-recital interview with the *Times,* Leopold explained why he had formed a trio and talked of the difference between a piano trio and a string trio or string quartet.

There is, of course, an incomparably larger and more rewarding quartet literature . . . The trio, however, attracts both the pianist and the string player because here, although good ensemble is imperative, the opportunity for a more individual style of playing is vastly greater than it is in the quartet. A trio is more like three soloists playing together.

Quartets by their very nature must stress the quality of ensemble. The so-called "solo quality," unless judiciously handled, can be dangerous and disruptive. The trio is essentially an attempt to blend two entirely different kinds of instruments; with the two strings playing for the most part in widely different registers, each one retains its own particular character.

What is particularly interesting in the piano trio, compared to the violin-viola-cello trio, is that it is not so much a genuine trio as a duet between piano and a double-voiced stringed instrument reminiscent of the mythical, multi-headed Hydra. The pianist is really playing a sonata with a stronger instrument than either the violin or cello alone and the combination is a better match for his sonority. This gives him a feeling of greater scope and freedom.

Note how freely and readily the piano parts of most trios are written. In some cases they almost approach the complexity of a piano concerto. The strings form a unit in which each one shares a varying degree of responsibility, with much more opportunity for an individualistic performance than could ever be tolerated in the course of string-quartet playing.

I would say that the conspicuous difference between the string quartet and the trio is that one is an ensemble combination which attempts to fuse itself into a single entity, while the other is an ensemble of three soloists who are making music together, but who never lose their individual identities.[28]

And he went on to say that in addition to playing the literature for piano trios, they planned to vary the programs by occasionally adding or subtracting an instrument to allow duets and quartets.

The recital went extremely well, the program consisting of Schumann's *Trio in D Minor,* Opus 63, Beethoven's *Trio in B-flat Major,* Opus 97, Casella's *Siciliano e Burlesca,* Opus 23bis, and Martinů's *Quartet* (1947) for oboe, violin, cello and piano. Brero, at the time, was making his New York debut, but the critic for the *Herald Tribune,* Francis D. Perkins, recalled that the other two had played in Town Hall before.

His judgment of the performance was the sort to make a performer's heart glad: "This new group can be regarded as a valuable asset in the chamber music field." Howard Taubman for the *Times* wrote: "The new Mannes Trio made an auspicious debut . . . The program was nicely balanced." With such reviews there was no question that the men could continue to play together, find an audience, explore new music and have a good time doing so.[29]

From Cambridge, Massachusetts, Randall wrote, "How happy it would make your mother to know that you were playing, and playing chamber music, in public." It was a continuity that pleased all who knew the family; before his father and mother, after all, there had been his grandfather playing chamber recitals with Hans von Bülow in Chickering Hall. For Leopold it was a tremendous lift, and the following winter he and his colleagues played three recitals in Town Hall to near-capacity audiences and good reviews. At last, as he was turning fifty, his musical career as a performer was started and apparently with no limits in sight.[30]

CHAPTER 33

Walter and Margaret die. Leopold and the Prades Festival. His marriage. Ellie alone in Europe. Leopold and the Mannes College of Music. His philosophy.

AFTER 1942 Walter, the dean of American conductors, gradually retired, and by 1947 both he and Margaret were showing signs of senility. In that year, too, they suffered a terrible loss, spiritual as much as financial, when in October a forest fire swept through Bar Harbor, destroying many of the houses, the Jackson Memorial Laboratory and a part of Acadia National Park. At Blaine Cottage the destruction was total, not only of the house with its contents, including many mementos of Blaine's long career in American history, but also of the landscaping, Walter's joy of many summers. He had made miniature gardens of different plants, built terraces, installed a fountain and a pool and created vistas that offered a sharpened sense of perspective through the careful positioning of taller and shorter trees. But of house and grounds all that remained after the fire was a charred desert with only the foundation and a few tree trunks upright.

Walter and Margaret were too old to begin again, and when they went to Maine thereafter they were guests of their daughter Gretchen. As their powers declined — Margaret's were the swifter to fail — each became senile in character. Margaret, for instance, became steadily quieter and more introspective. In their New York house, at 168 East 71st Street, where Alice and Herman Kiaer had an apartment on the upper floors, Margaret would sit by the window, apparently reliving the days of her girlhood in Washington, and ask, "When are we going to New York?"

In July 1949, while at Gretchen's house in Bar Harbor, she died, and in a brief note to his secretary in New York Walter wrote in a shaking script, "I know I will have your sympathy. Yesterday my darling Margaret died and in consequence I am in a kind of despair. I know I will have your sympathy!" [1]

He, on the other hand, with senility became more ebullient and difficult to control. In the manner of the old he hated the nurse-companion his daughters hired for him and always was brushing the woman aside. One night late, about two in the morning, he took it in his head to put on his white tie and tails. Over her protests he rushed into the street, with her in pursuit, and at Park Avenue hailed a cab. She followed in another, pulling up behind his in front of the old Metropolitan Opera House at Broadway and Fortieth Street. As she got out, he was banging on the locked door: "I'm Walter Damrosch. I'm conducting tonight. Let me in." [2]

Later, to a former member of his orchestra who called on him, he described a tour to the Orient. "Just back from Japan. They loved us in Tokyo. Rave reviews everywhere. Marvelous! Marvelous!" To some of those who loved him it seemed a wonderful way to go: no bitterness, no regret, only pleasure, and enthusiasm for the music still running through his head. In his final hours, as he lay on his bed dying, age seemed to withdraw. His cheeks became pink again, his eyes sparkled and he smiled. [3]

Walter died on a Friday, December 22, 1950, and the following night the Philharmonic-Symphony under George Szell offered him a musical tribute in the hall that Walter had inaugurated with a festival and that existed only because he had excited Carnegie to build it. Before the scheduled program Szell led the orchestra in *Nimrod* from Elgar's *Enigma Variations,* a series of portraits of Elgar's friends. On the score, at the start of *Nimrod,* Elgar had written: "It is the record of a long summer evening talk, when my friend Jaeger grew nobly eloquent — as only he could — on the grandeur of Beethoven and especially of his slow movements." Perhaps Leopold had told Szell of those long evenings in Scotland when Walter, as a very young man, fresh from his studies with von Bülow, had expounded the glories of Beethoven to the Carnegies and their guests, or perhaps Szell had in mind Walter's educational concerts and "Music Appreciation Hour," but however he arrived at the choice, it hardly could have been more appropriate. For not only had Walter been for many years a champion of Elgar, but even more than Wagner or Brahms, Beethoven had been the greatest joy of his musical life and the touchstone by which he judged all music. [4]

Two days later the family held a funeral service for him in St. James Episcopal Church at Seventy-first Street and Madison Avenue, with his nephew Frank Jr. assisting the local minister. The service was more musical than prayerful, with Bach, Wagner and Brahms performed before it, Luther's hymn sung during it and Chopin's *Funeral March* played as a recessional. In addition, as an interlude the violinist Albert Spalding played the second movement of Bach's Concerto in E Major, which he and Walter often had performed together. Later Walter was buried beside Margaret in the cemetery at Bar Harbor.[5]

The following Sunday Olin Downes, writing in the *Times,* summed up Walter's career. "It is a striking circumstance," he noted, that Walter should have died so close to the end of the first half of the twentieth century, "for that is the period of America's musical coming of age, in which especially in the field of symphonic music, she has outdistanced every other modern nation, and no other single musician has contributed as much that was fundamental and far-reaching in that development as Walter Damrosch."[6]

Leopold's trio survived its first crisis when, at the end of its second season, the violinist, Vittorio Brero, withdrew. He was older than the other two and offered as a reason, somewhat apologetically, that he wished to return to Europe. An unstated reason, perhaps, was his wife's inability to speak English and consequent sense of isolation in the United States. Leopold and Luigi Silva, however, were able to capitalize on the loss by recruiting Bronislav Gimpel, a more expert, individual player, and the trio officially changed its name to the Mannes-Gimpel-Silva Trio, though many continued to call it the Mannes Trio. Either way, the name was not something about which Leopold cared.

The reviews continued excellent and, after the first recital with Gimpel, Harold Schonberg of the *Times* began, "A trio of first-rate musicians . . . gave a concert last night." He went on to scold each player for some fault, but overall offered remarkable praise. The trio's bookings increased and Decca Records began negotiations to make several recordings.[7]

Leopold, meanwhile, was active in the Prades Festival, which brought him into contact again, both personally and artistically, with his parents' friend the cellist Pablo Casals. In 1947 Casals, as a gesture of disapproval of the Franco regime in Spain, had announced he would give no more concerts in countries recognizing that government and also would not return to Spain while Franco ruled. He took up residence in Prades, a small Catalan village in France, close to the Spanish border, and kept to his word, refusing all engagements. "My physique is more that of Sancho Panza," he admitted to a friend, "but my viewpoint is Quixote's." He was only seventy, still at the height of his powers, and his withdrawal, though without immediate effect politically, left a loud silence in the world of music.

Impresarios besieged him with contracts to play, all of which he refused, and then in 1949 he was visited by the American violinist Alexander Schneider, who had been authorized to offer him a series of performances in the United States at high fees. "It is not a matter of money," Casals said; "it is a question of morality," and refused. But he listened when Schneider proposed a festival of performances in Prades, in June 1950, to commemorate the bicentenary of Bach's death. Apparently one of Schneider's most persuasive arguments was that Casals, by his silence, was depriving a younger generation of musicians of hearing Bach sound as he might if performed by Casals and other of the world's great musicians. He suggested that the program include all the Brandenburg Concertos and the six solo cello suites, which Casals had rescued from oblivion, and whatever else of Bach Casals might wish. It would be not a matter of money but of education for the young and of honor to Bach. Casals agreed.

Executive committees were formed in France and the United States to organize the festival, to raise money and to select young artists to form the festival orchestra. These gathered in Prades, a village of about forty-five hundred, with a single hotel (twenty-seven rooms, one bath) about eight weeks in advance in order to rehearse daily with Casals and develop an ensemble. This was, in the planning, an important part of the festival's educational function. Later, soloists came, and the rehearsals went on every day and many evenings. Finally, shortly after 8:30 P.M. on June 2, in the Church of St. Peter, in the center of town, the Bishop of St. Fleur delivered an interminable address, ending with the admonition that applause in a church would be inappropriate. So, in silence, Casals came out; everyone stood. He bowed, sat and, indicating with his bow that they, too, should sit, with the opening low G of the first suite for solo cello he began the celebration of Bach.[8]

Leopold, who had been an active, generous member of the United States executive committee, also performed in the festival. In all there were twelve programs, six "orchestral" and six "chamber music" evenings, all devoted to Bach, and Leopold played twice, excerpts with others from *The Musical Offering* and a *Sonata for Flute and Piano* with John Wummer. Both were recorded by Columbia Records, which had contributed $20,000 to the festival's expenses in return for the exclusive right to record its programs.[9]

Like most musicians who played, Leopold found the Prades experience extraordinary. Casals infused everyone with his own dedication, and the following year a repetition was held, this time with the repertory enlarged to include Mozart and Beethoven and with the concerts performed at nearby Perpignan, a much larger town. The organizing spirit again was Alexander Schneider, but Leopold this year, though continuing to work on the American executive committee, was unable to attend. As a gift to his eighty-five-year-old father, however, he sent David over with Clair Seymour as a companion.

For David, who had not seen Casals since before the war, the anticipation of renewed friendship was agitating, and after he had settled in his hotel room, he and Clair, led by a member of the festival staff, hurried to the hall where Casals was about to conduct a rehearsal. "It was a mistake all around," Clair said later. The two old men caught sight of each other, rushed eagerly to embrace and, while others waited, exclaimed, chattered and re-embraced several times. "Uncle David was very excited, and so was Casals, who hurried to the podium, flushed and with his lips still moving. More than six times," Clair recalled, "Casals raised his arms to begin, but then lowered them, unable to gather his concentration. Thereafter, by design, we met only after the music."

Not long after leaving Casals for the last time and hearing, apparently, a little private music-making, David wrote to Leopold, in a hand made almost undecipherable by age and emotion: "What has been one of the greatest experiences of my life came to a climax in the little town of Prades. I heard Pablo at his best which [left me?] at the close of the programs in a trance of wonder. And you, Leopold, made this possible — What can I say to you for this priceless gift?" [10]

For the first few years the magic of the festivals held, and Leopold, who had returned the third year, when for acoustical reasons the programs were again given in Prades rather than Perpignan, attempted later in *Musical America* to explain it.

> In many ways the two experiences [the 1950 and 1952 festivals] had much in common. Each time one had the sense of being in a place where practically everyone was motivated and inspired by the desire that music be made in a way expressive of its deepest meanings — not just an abstract art form, but as the fullest expression of humanity . . . [the feeling] comes directly from the extraordinary man who is, of course, the very reason for the whole effort . . . With Casals it is difficult to separate the man and the artist. Indeed, it is just this fact which explains his greatness as an artist. Those who heard Casals play were conscious of a power of communication which he seems to possess to a degree rarely attained by others. This power of communication, which he has developed throughout his entire life, has now reached a point where freedom of expression has become almost absolute. To hear Casals now is to hear the achievement of what any artist inevitably must strive for — a complete transcendence of the instrument in eloquent communication of the inner meanings of the music. [11]

Although Casals' instrument was not Leopold's, nevertheless it was Casals' playing that had brought Leopold as a youth, interested in mountain-climbing and color photography, back to music as his major occupation, and it was Casals' career and character — artist and man — that informed Leopold's educational ideals at the Mannes School. He always was telling students in many different ways that technical proficiency was not enough. The musician must be a man of the widest possible education, interests and, above all, integrity.

More specifically relating his experience at Prades to music-making, he said of Casals:

> No smallest element of a musical composition is without meaning in relation to the human being. This means that no rhythmic pattern is merely a mathematical sequence in time; nor is any phrase or passage the mere rise and fall of notes in the abstract sense. All phrases are inflected to a greater or smaller degree, both rhythmically and dynamically, in such a way that they become related instinctively to the most fundamental pulses and respirations which govern our existence.[12]

He meant such pulses and patterns as the heartbeat, breathing and walking. A phrase will seem fast or slow, long or short, in part because of what every person instinctively recognizes as normal pulse or breathing. The traditional Italian musical directions reflect this humanistic background in such phrases as andante, "going," that is, in an average walking pace; allegro, "merry"; and cantabile, "singing." It is a theory that well describes music from Bach through early Stravinsky, but not late Stravinsky, twelve-tone or serial music. Or, presenting the theory in another guise, when composers in adopting twelve-tone and serial styles of music abandoned these relations to basic human pulses, for that very reason they lost most of their audience. For to the average listener, whether he can articulate the thought or not, such relationships seem basic to music.

In holding such a theory, and in talking about music "as the fullest expression of humanity," Leopold proclaimed himself out of step with contemporary music of the 1950s. Otto Luening, who in that decade began to work with electronic music and served on many committees with Leopold, considered him a fine, "conservative" musician "with no interest in the coming generations." He felt that Leopold with his photographic experiments had taken a long step into the twentieth century in a way that he did not do with his music; hence, to Luening, Leopold was a greater scientist than musician. That view presupposes, of course, that the steps taken into electronic and serial music were an advance.[13]

It was a surprise to those close to Leopold and Evelyn that she never accompanied him to Prades. There were always reasons: one year Elena was sick; another, Evelyn; yet to some observers the reasons seemed only pretext, and they wondered whether the marriage was failing. Marya, after all, was announcing to anyone who would listen that it was "a disaster," but others, with a different view of Leopold, thought it surprisingly successful.

The confusion arose, as Evelyn once observed, because no one, not even she, ever grasped the whole of Leopold's personality: it was too vast, too talented, too free, too guilt-ridden, too energetic and, above all, too contradictory, for any one person to comprehend it all. Even Leopold, at times, seemed unable to understand himself or what he was doing or why. As one friend observed: when he pulled it all together, Kodachrome; when he lost control, chaos.[14]

Evelyn's personality, not surprisingly, changed under the impact of Leopold's and of her various roles as mother, sister-in-law and member of the Damrosch family; and she, too, became something of a puzzle to those who knew her. Having lost one child and having been warned by her doctor against bearing another, she became extremely protective of Elena, too much so, in the opinion of some. She hovered near her, frequently answered for her, and Elena, not having to speak, often did not. Leopold grew worried. "I know she's intelligent," he told a neighbor at Martha's Vineyard, "for when I say, 'Bring me the red book on the tray,' she can do it." Except to her parents, however, Elena spoke little till she was past three, and even at thirteen, at least in public, was remarkably silent.[15]

One reason, according to some, was the volubility of the family. At any gathering, Christmas Eve or a birthday party, the talk would be loud, free and often derogatory, and Elena's response to it was retreat; she would nod or shake her head politely, but she would not speak to an aunt, uncle or cousin who addressed her in a strident, domineering voice. Marya's son, David, five years older, also was apt to be rather silent at family events and, feeling a bond with Elena, would try to talk quietly with her. "But she never would say more than yes or no."

Evelyn herself in these years became more "mousy," a description frequently applied to her, and often was sick. "Hypochondria," snorted Marya and most of the family. On the whole they all had health, and they wished, not unkindly, for Leopold's wife to be as outstanding as he, a beautiful, brilliant artist. In fact, though Evelyn never asserted it, she was a good facsimile, but knowing she failed their expectations, on family occasions she, too, retreated. "Remember," Leopold would say to encourage her, "you are an artist!" But with the exceptions chiefly of the Tee Vans and Clair Seymour, to most of the family she was Leopold's inexplicable choice for wife.

With Marya she had, as most recognized, a special problem. Marya and Leopold always had been close — too close, many said — and Clair, who was not given ordinarily to psychiatric reasoning, wondered whether the intensity had not developed out of teasing. Leopold as an older brother at times had been very hard on Marya. "Sadistic," said Clair, but Clair was a gentle person. For whatever reason, Marya did not want any woman closer to Leopold, in confidence, than herself, and a successful marriage meant, for Marya, exclusion.

She fought for Leopold by denigrating Evelyn, unconsciously perhaps trying to push him toward divorce. She seldom dared to say much in front of him, but she freely told others that he never should have married Evelyn, that he should have remained single, that the best way of life for both Leopold and herself, brother and sister, would be adjoining apartments, where each could have lovers, free and independent. He had told her, or so she quoted him, "If I marry, it should be to someone very passive and undemanding, for I often don't want anyone else around." Then Marya would add sarcastically, "And that is just what he got."[16]

An answer to Marya would have been for Leopold, who was less involved with her than she with him, to exclude her from his life. But he could not do it, and the situation festered: Marya, loud and disapproving; Evelyn, in her presence, or in any large family gathering, ever quieter. Finally, for the third time, in 1948 Marya married. The man, Christopher Clarkson, was a civil air attaché for the United Kingdom, and Marya went to live with him in Washington. For Evelyn the change partially solved one problem.

A greater one, however, remained: Leopold's philandering. It had started again not long after marriage, and the fact, which was soon plain to those close to him, was a reason that many assumed the marriage to be a failure. They waited for the separation and divorce.

Leopold, meanwhile, among the many mistresses had formed a liaison with one, Miss X, that continued for three years. The woman, who had been born and partially raised in Germany, was eager to marry him and, perhaps because she spoke German and was attuned to German culture, thought she had a better chance than most. She expected Leopold to divorce, but as an acquaintance of all the parties observed, "Anyone with half an eye could see that was never going to happen." Leopold loved Evelyn and Elena. Still, Miss X waited, until finally actions not taken spoke louder than any words Leopold had uttered, and, faced with a marriage that did not break, Miss X had a nervous collapse. Leopold's sense of guilt was doubled.[17]

It was some time later that David Mannes one day said with feeling to Evelyn, "You do love him, don't you!" and she felt his tone conveyed an acceptance, an appreciation of her that had not been there before. Clara, too, in her last years grew warmer. Apparently, consciously or not, the parents had withheld a full emotional commitment to Evelyn, because they had expected the marriage to end in divorce. Another person, too, made a gesture that touched her. At Christmas she received a plant, not for herself and Leopold but for herself alone, from Aunt Margaret, and something in the older woman's wording of the card suggested a deep sympathy.

There were so many divisions in Leopold's life — science and music, performance and administration — that perhaps it was in some way possible for him to be both a faithful husband and a philanderer. In any event he continued both his marriage and infidelities and soon had started, among many short-term affairs, a liaison with Miss Y that would continue for nine years.

Perhaps Leopold's most unattractive trait was his habit of talking down his wife to his mistresses. His technique was the classic one of presenting himself as misunderstood at home and bound to an ailing wife whom he could not abandon. With his dark eyes, elegance, extraordinary mind and humor, he was very persuasive, and, of course, the mistresses yearned to believe. Further, because he appeared to them as a man of wealth, most of them saw no reason not to hope for marriage: he could afford a settlement for his wife and child. After he died, many of the women called on either Marya or on Jeannette Haien, a concert pianist who lived in Leopold's building and who, they knew, was close to him. Only one asked for money. The others wanted to be reassured that "he spoke of me sometimes, didn't he?" And each, when she learned that she was just another in a tawdry succession, wept.[18]

Evelyn had not married Leopold in ignorance of his problems, but she had felt that what counted was the relationship he had with her; what he had with others was not her concern. There were, of course, ups and downs in the marriage, occasional harsh words and scenes, but one day while reading Henry James's *The Golden Bowl* she came across a passage that clarified her feelings to herself. Remarkably, almost forty years later, she was able to recite it with hardly a word misplaced.

> When you only love a little you're naturally not jealous — or are only jealous also a little, so that it doesn't matter. But when you love in a deeper and intenser way, then you're in the very same proportion jealous; your jealousy has intensity and, no doubt, ferocity. When however you love in the most abysmal and unutterable way of all — why then you're beyond everything, and nothing can pull you down.[19]

Like James's Maggie Verver, Evelyn through the depth of her love gained a tremendous strength, and the mistresses constantly were astonished, even infuriated by her decency. Though Evelyn seldom was the only woman in Leopold's life, after their marriage there was never a time that she was not the most important. And at the end, in his sickness and death, she was with him, as the more powerful part of his personality wished her to be.

★

In the spring of 1951 Ellie, at the age of seventy-nine, decided to go abroad with a friend, but the friend dropped out, and Ellie, over her children's protest, went alone.

She stayed in Paris for two and a half weeks, started a journal about her thoughts and impressions and received a steady stream of mail from her anxious daughters in the United States. Then, because it rained continually, she moved south, to Aix-en-Provence, where she put up at the Hôtel Roi-René, which she liked very much. She later wrote in her journal:

> On one of my first days there I was walking to the Cours Mirabeau — the beautiful avenue with its three rows of huge old sycamore trees — when I came to the bus terminal — there I saw a Carousel for small children which was going around to the sound of a man's voice singing the usual French popular songs of "l'amour," "Auprès de ma blonde," etc.
>
> The children sat in little box-like cars with small wheels in front of them. Amongst all the dark-haired children there was one big chubby boy with a head of blonde curls, and he was holding out his arms pleadingly, tears streaming from his blue eyes, cheeks flushed with agony! I could hardly bear it as each time he came whirling by, the woman who must have been his grandmother stood there perfectly calm and immobile. I, too, stood rooted to the spot, my own eyes brimming, as this two-and-a-half-year-old was spun round and round — once — twice — three times — four times, and then — the fifth time I saw him contentedly twirling the little wheel in front of him.
>
> It came to me that I, too, was being spun around irrevocably on this whirling planet, far away from home (but by my own volition) and that I, too, must twirl my little wheel of Destiny.[20]

The great change in the Mannes School accomplished during Leopold's tenure as president was a shift toward professionalism, symbolized by the school's becoming a college accredited by the State of New York and thereby permitted to confer a college degree on students satisfying the requirements. More was involved in the change than might be expected. The state had financial and educational standards that had to be met, and more and more students were young aspiring professionals rather than amateurs — although an extension division continued to offer courses to people of any age who wanted to study some aspect of music merely for the love of it. A benefit that Leopold constantly stressed, however, was that students with degrees would be eligible to enter graduate schools at universities; as a college, Mannes would fit into the country's educational system, and in an era in which credentials were of increasing importance, that much was owed the students.[21]

The shift made many people unhappy, for it seemed to betray the ideals of the founders, who had wanted to avoid just this kind of professionalism. Frank Damrosch had created the Institute of Musical Art to train potential performers, but Clara and David with their school had aimed at something different, a school without examinations or diplomas in which the ultimate goal was not a job in music but a spiritual gain through better understanding. Leopold, though, saw the change as building upon rather than sacrificing his parents' ideals, which, in any case, they had modified over the years, particularly in 1934, when, by incorporating the school, they had taken a large step toward making it a more typical educational institution.

The opposing views appear in a letter from one school trustee, Marya, loyally supporting Leopold, to another, Gerald Warburg, who opposed him. She wrote bluntly:

> You want to keep the school as it is (or was) and obstruct either by disagreement or passivity the goal toward which the majority of trustees and directors are striving — and which, indeed, economic necessity demands.
>
> None of us welcome this necessity. All of us feel nostalgic for the *gemütlichkeit* of the past where the personality and ideals of my parents gave the school its unique and special value. And it certainly would be easier for most of us to leave things as they are, with mounting deficits only partially — and with increasing difficulty — met by Leopold's largesses and small individual donations, allowing the school to die a quiet death. But as far as I am concerned there is overwhelming proof that a change of status is now essential. Without a huge endowment, the small private school acting as a sort of musical governess to the rich cannot possibly live.
>
> I do not see why this change of status should lead to loss of ideals or to commercialization, both of which you seem to fear. Perhaps here again I have more faith in its direction than you. But the fact remains that only a major united effort on the part of us all can pull the School through its current crisis. There are really only two alternatives left for it: the enlargement of its scope, or its dissolution in due course.[22]

What emerged in April 1953 was the Mannes College of Music, with a student body that in the next five years, from 1953–54 through 1958–59, expanded its college enrollment from fifty-two to 140 and, in addition, by the spring of 1959 had a college preparatory department of 267 and an extension division of 180. The balance between professionals and amateurs had shifted, and so, too, had the viewpoint: there was much more talk now about training "the career-minded music student" and less about the role in music of amateurs. But to Leopold and a majority of the trustees, there not only had been no choice, but the change was for the better.[23]

Under his leadership, however, it did not become just another music school. It was at the time, and for many years to be, the only school to offer a curriculum based on theories of musical analysis developed by Heinrich Schenker and one of his outstanding pupils, Felix Salzer. The latter, whom Leopold had brought to the school's faculty in 1940, by 1948 had become its executive director. Schenker (1868–1935), a Viennese who had worked principally as a private piano teacher, was an extraordinary scholar, and in his analyses of the works of the great tonal composers — Bach, Chopin, Brahms and, above all, Beethoven — he had developed theories about musical structure, turning chiefly on harmony and counterpoint, so potent that he seemed almost to have discovered new facts about music.

In brief, his ideas presuppose three essential levels of structure. As summarized by Christopher Wintle, "In the background stood the large-scale cadential motion of the piece of music. In the middle ground, a dozen or so techniques were available to transform and prolong this motion. In the foreground these (and other) techniques could in themselves be reapplied to the middle ground elements, with further reapplications until every feature of the piece had been generated." Thus all three levels, with their phrasing, harmony and counterpoint, were related, and a violin student who analyzed a Beethoven symphony in the light of Schenker's theories would understand far more about the significance of his violin part, and how to play it, than one who merely took the usual conservatory courses in violin and theory. He or she would emerge, ideally, a fully rounded musician, not merely an instrumentalist. Thus the Mannes College, like the school, continued to offer a unique kind of musical education.[24]

There were musicians, of course, who did not favor Schenker, particularly those interested in contemporary music, for Schenker's emphasis on tonal music was a repudiation of Arnold Schoenberg and the atonal and serial styles of composing. But the college was not the only conservatory in New York, and those who wanted something different easily could find it elsewhere. Leopold and Salzer did not aim to please everyone but to create a school with a strong profile.[25]

Not all the college's problems were solved, however, and the most stubborn was its finances. Clara and David had never managed to find a truly rich patron, and neither did Leopold. He was not by nature a good fund raiser: he was too proud. Some foundations and individuals enjoy humiliating those who ask for money. Appointments are made, and the applicant kept waiting. The request, though reasonably stated, must be recast on the foundation's forms; suggestions are made about how the applicant's business should be run, and sometimes turned into conditions: accounting methods must be changed, or the grant "matched" with "new" money. Beggars can't be choosers, but Leopold hated begging, perhaps because as a boy he had seen his parents do so much of it.

Also, in all his relations he was personal. Just as in his own acts of charity he shaped the gift precisely to the recipient, often accompanying it with generous portions of his time, so in his fund-raising he could not be objective. He took a rejection as a personal repudiation and would grow depressed. To avoid the unpleasantness of the job he preferred to use his own money.

He would have been wiser to turn more often for help to his trustees, several of whom were well connected financially. But he preferred to use them as little as possible; that way they could not interfere, and throughout the 1950s he ran the college as his private fief. He was, when it came to money — acts of charity, the college's finances — a nineteenth-century patron ill at ease in the mid-twentieth century.[26]

The full extent of his charity cannot be known. After his death, for example, his successor as head of the school discovered that Leopold had a roll of private pensioners, some of them musicians, to whom he sent money regularly. But his tax returns give some information: the returns for the years 1938 through 1963, the year before his death, record gifts to the college of $465,202. Of these, the largest, $241,131, was made in 1953 so that the school could qualify as a college under a state law that required any college to have $500,000 in assets, exclusive of real estate subject to mortgage. In addition, he served as president without salary at a time when others in similar jobs were receiving annually $30,000 to $40,000, and in many smaller ways, such as playing recitals for which he received no pay, he provided services to the college. His hope, of course, was always that "next year" he would uncover the person or foundation that would put the college on a sound basis.

The drag on his financial resources was very great, for in the same period he made gifts of $65,568 to other charities, often no doubt to induce gifts to the college, and he supported not only his family but contributed to the support of his own and Evelyn's parents, as well as others. He was doing what he wished, and it had meaning to a great many people, but from a purely financial point of view he was wasting his assets.[27]

But he did not consider that, and in these years with the trio succeeding, the college expanding, the George Eastman House in Rochester (a museum of photography) adding a Mannes-Godowsky wing, which he inaugurated with a gift and a speech, he seemed as always able to sustain two, even three careers, while at the same time thinking deeply on religious and philosophical subjects. As a scientist, for example, he was stirred by the controversy over the development of the hydrogen bomb, deplored the treatment of J. Robert Oppenheimer by the Atomic Energy Commission, of which Lewis Strauss of Kuhn, Loeb & Company was now chairman, and approved the unanimous re-election of Oppen-heimer, in October 1954, as a director of the Institute of Advanced Study at Princeton.

For a time he kept in his desk at the college an excerpt from Oppen-heimer's *The Open Mind:*

> Both the man of science and the man of art live always at the edge of mystery, surrounded by it; both always, as the measure of their creation, have had to do with the harmonization of what is new with what is fa-miliar, with the balance between novelty and synthesis, with the struggle to make partial order in total chaos. They can, in their work and in their lives, help themselves, help one another, and help all men. They can make the paths that connect the villages of arts and sciences with each other and with the world at large multiple, varied, precious bonds of a true and world-wide community.[28]

It echoed what he had frequently said in exasperation to Marya: "Stop making such a difference between science and art. It's the same in both: pattern and continuity. Search for the pattern and continuity, in physics, in music." It echoed much in his own life, in his own personality: "the harmonization of what is new with what is familiar, with the balance between novelty and synthesis, with the struggle to make partial order in total chaos." And it also echoed his basic philosophy, at which he had arrived both by nature and reasoning:

> I have said that Christ had only one commandment, and that it covered the whole of life. It was "Love thy neighbor as thyself." Or, as expressed in other words, "Do unto others as you would that they should do unto you." St. Mark has said, "There is no other commandment." And, truly, there is not. As the law of conservation is to science, so should this great Law of justness be to ethics. It expresses most perfectly the spirit of the true scientific mind, the taking into account of everything and everybody, absolute honesty and fairness of judgment. The morality as developed by the church today does not approach the lofty plane of this one great teach-ing of Christ. "Love thy neighbor as thyself" is a perfect statement of morality in relation to the welfare of the rest of the world, "thy neigh-bor." That very point causes it to fill the space left by the empirical laws of the Ten Commandments. It affords a basis of judgment that leads to an attitude of right and wrong, much more just than that of the rigid precepts of Moses.[29]

He was neither a practicing Christian nor a practicing Jew, and by the tenets of both religions he was in some respects a thoroughly immoral man. Yet by how far he exceeded the practices of most who profess in his acts of charity, his search for a meaning in life and his idealism.

CHAPTER 34

End of the Mannes Trio. Deaths in the family. College finances. Marya and The Reporter. Ellie dies; Damrosch Park. Leopold at the Van Cliburn piano competition. Marya and McCall's. Leopold's decline and death.

IN JANUARY 1955 the Mannes-Gimpel-Silva Trio played Beethoven's Triple Concerto in Town Hall with Thomas Scherman and the Little Orchestra Society. The work, the only one of its kind in the classical repertory, is seldom performed, perhaps because its themes, being neither very beautiful nor emotional, have small appeal for the general public. On the other hand, the structure of the piece is fascinating. As Beethoven demonstrated, to compose a concerto in which each main theme must be stated four times — once by the orchestra and once each by the solo instruments — one must perforce make the themes simple, short and unexpansive if the piece is not to be overlong. Similarly, with three solo instruments there is a problem of balance, the chief danger being that the low-voiced cello will be overwhelmed. Beethoven consequently kept its part mostly at the top of its range, where its sound is penetrating but also, unfortunately, apt to be "edgy," and in addition, to enhance its importance, he frequently gave it the lead in introducing themes. The result is a work intriguing to those aware of the technical problems but "dry" or even boring to others. What it needs in performance to sweep the audience along is the grand manner, and according to the *Times,* the three soloists achieved it.[1]

Their work was steadily successful; they were good, even very good, but by now it was clear that they were not destined to be the world's best, and Gimpel, just before a concert in the spring, announced to his colleagues that he would return soon to Europe to pursue his career as a soloist. The other two had known he was upset by a divorce from his wife but had no reason to expect anything so drastic, and the recital that evening went poorly. From the first notes Evelyn, in the audience, knew something had happened.

Gimpel's withdrawal ended the trio. Though Leopold and Silva searched for another violinist, they never found one to their liking, and the difficulty may have been psychological. Both were over fifty, with commitments to teaching and administration, and the disappointment, survived once, on Brero's departure, was very great. In addition, Leopold, whose judgment in musical matters was faultless, recognized their limitations but lacked the usual performer's ego that could overlook them. Felix Salzer remarked once that Leopold was "too aristocratic" for large halls and a public career. He could not exhibit his most delicate feelings before a crowd, as the greatest performers do; yet anything less than the greatest communication, such as Casals achieved, was disappointing to him. In any event, with the end of the trio, except for recitals at the college, where he often played magnificently, and an occasional benefit at Chilmark, on Martha's Vineyard, where he spent the summers, after 1955 he gave up public performance and devoted himself entirely to the college. Or rather, to the students, for in his personal manner he always was more interested in the students than the institution.[2]

David Mannes, meanwhile, passed his ninetieth birthday, celebrated in the college auditorium with a recital by Myra Hess and Isaac Stern, and soon afterward began to weaken. By the winter of 1958–59, when he became ninety-two, his end seemed near, and yet he lingered on, as Marya later wrote, "bereft of joy, of will, of consciousness most of the time, and of the music which, along with a wife now ten years dead, were his imperative supports."[3]

He was kept alive largely by artificial sustenance and chemical injections, and one day when Marya was at his bedside, he refused the food the nurse tried to force into his mouth. "Why must I go on?" he asked Marya. "Why?" And she and Leopold asked the doctor to stop the artificial supports of life. When he did, David died.

Fifteen years later, in Marya's final book, *Last Rights* (1974), she pondered the morality of what she called "one form of passive euthanasia." She concluded that the will to die "is the direct reflection of the quality of life." Those who when helpless, she suggested, wish for life to continue on any terms have never known it at its fullest. Not having lived to their fullest capacities, they still believe any life to be better than none. "Their dread of death supersedes all else." Whereas those who throughout their lives have had a strong sense of purpose, the pattern for the Damrosches generally, would choose to die "soon after they can no longer function in their chosen work. They may have loving mates and children, but their impotence as productive beings is the paramount factor."

For Marya and for Leopold, apparently, their father's wish to die was not only easily understood but admirable. He had said, in effect, "My work is done," and his death was a final act of will.

In the spring of David's death, April 1959, the college entered another financial crisis, and this time Leopold no longer had the capital assets to bail it out. In 1953, the year it became a college, he had contributed almost a quarter of a million dollars to its endowment, but this fund in six years had been all but consumed by operating expenses and now produced an income of only $900 a year. The annual deficit, meanwhile, ran at about $75,000. To keep its state charter the college needed to restore its total resources to $500,000, which meant raising a capital fund of $250,000 within two years; and to obtain accreditation from the Middle States Association of Colleges it was required to enlarge its library at a probable cost of $150,000. It also needed money for the annual deficit.[4]

For both Leopold and the board of trustees the situation seemed worse than it was because of the change in Leopold's financial position. The old pattern of running the school was no longer possible, and as yet a new one had not evolved. Leopold had not the practice of making use of his trustees, so when he finally told them the figures of the situation, their first inclination, embodied in a resolution, was to close the school. Incredibly, Leopold agreed. In his new situation of relative poverty he must have felt disoriented, and perhaps, too, with his father dead he felt the moment had come to end the college. The faculty and students, however, were more resolute than the president and trustees, and insisted, maybe out of financial ignorance, that the college could be saved.

Some of the faculty persuaded their colleague Sidney Gelber to talk as an unofficial representative to both Leopold and the trustees. Gelber, a professor of philosophy, first at Columbia University and then at the State University of New York at Stony Brook, had become associated with Mannes College in 1953, when, in connection with its advance to college status, he had been called in to help set up the liberal arts courses. Since then he had taught both philosophy and world history at Mannes, and, a good amateur pianist, he had followed its affairs with sympathy; he was part of the school and yet, because his chief employment and interest were elsewhere, not part of it. As such, he proved well placed to act as scold and cheerleader to all parties.

To Leopold and the trustees he was mainly a scold, playing on their guilt. How could they vote to close the college? With Leopold the guilt was there, ready to be tweaked. With the trustees, who because of past reliance on Leopold were unused to acting forcefully, the guilt had to be created. How can you men and women with social and financial positions in the city allow the college to close because you cannot raise what is really a small sum of money? What will people think of you? To the faculty and students, he was more the cheerleader, urging them on with their raffles, benefit recitals, solicitations for small donations, petitions and publicity.[5]

By the fall of 1960 it was clear that the college would survive and be stronger than before, chiefly through merger with the smaller Chatham Square Music School, which brought to the college, according to the *New York Times,* a dowry that "included an endowment in excess of $200,000, as well as some pianos, a desk, and a tape recorder in need of repair." It also brought sixty students, all aiming at professional careers and eager to make use of the Mannes library, orchestra, chorus and degree. And the Chatham students, faculty and trustees came without backward glances, for their former building, a converted house on Clinton Street, had been condemned to make way for a hospital. It was a merger by which everyone gained. Mannes College, like the proverbial cat, had yet another life, but this time with a difference: the relationships between Leopold, his trustees and faculty had altered.[6]

Marya in these years was growing to be a power in the land. In 1952 she had moved back to New York with her husband, Christopher, and at a cocktail party met Max Ascoli, a publisher and editor who was starting a new magazine, *The Reporter.* He knew of her, and after a brief conversation she was hired to write a bimonthly column on television.[7]

The magazine prospered, and with it, Marya. Her style and opinions, thoughtful, humanitarian and well expressed, fitted neatly into the magazine Ascoli was creating, and she quickly became a roving social critic, writing on any subject she wished, and providing short satiric verses, often on politics, over the pseudonym SEC.

Many of her essays, including some published elsewhere, were gathered in two books, *More in Anger* (1958) and *But Will It Sell?* (1964), and they give an excellent picture of life in the United States, from 1950 to 1964, as it was lived by the urban, college-educated class of people and their children. Indeed, many persons, while admiring Marya's two novels, think her social criticism is more likely to last, particularly if sociologists and historians begin to make use of it.

In her point of view she was often the voice of the minority, those who were out of step with majority opinion and questioned it. She wrote strongly, for example, against the misuse of television, both by those who produced it and those who watched it. On the producers' materialism, for example: Television is developing "a race which believes that a high standard of living is the final aspiration. I would be inclined to call it the last ditch."[8] On the producers' artistic dishonesty: "I can't talk dialect, any dialect . . . Never mind if people speak like that and all you want to do is to show human beings the way they are. Dialect is out" — because it might offend some potential purchaser of the sponsor's product.[9] And, most important, on the damage to children's ability to fantasize:

> Until a child can meet reality, he must live in fantasy. But he must create his own fantasy. And it is television's primary damage that it provides ten million children with the same fantasy, ready-made and on a platter. Nor is this, with very rare exceptions, the fruitful fantasy of poets or artists but the unreal world of television itself, which bears no relation to that of a child but which envelops him, willy-nilly, in a false adult vision which, in turn, is not even truly adult. And on this infinitely sensitive and apparently unerasable recording-tape of the child's mind is printed a shadow world of blurred values, where the only reality is the product Mom must buy.[10]

Radio in its first twenty years had developed such programs as the NBC "Music Appreciation Hour," the CBS "American School of the Air" and the Texaco broadcasts of the Metropolitan Opera. There was nothing comparable on television. Marya, in making her protests, became the country's outstanding critic of television, and though she was ineffectual, it was good that the protests were made: they are, for these years, the bright spot in an otherwise dreary record of commercial greed.

She also wrote on the prejudices to which newspapers pander and was invited to speak at forums on the responsibility of the press. She was a good speaker; she had the showmanship to dress for the part and to act it. She wrote on the selling to a gulled public of abstract art, "primarily design without context";[11] and on contemporary music, "wanderings, interminable wanderings in sound, interrupted now and then by excursions into noise."[12] She wrote at times on political subjects, often with courage, because she was against the stream of opinion, and she questioned sharply the country's increasing worship of youth and the young. "There is no 'trick' in being young: it happens to you. But the process of maturing is an art to be learned, an effort to be sustained. By the age of fifty you have made yourself what you are, and it is good, it is better than your youth. If it is bad, it is not because you are older but because you have not grown."[13]

By 1960 she was well known among persons who read, and generally admired. When, in June 1960, she wrote a letter to Adlai Stevenson about the presidency, urging him "to want it more," he wrote a thoughtful, though evasive, reply. In *The Reporter* she had found a pulpit for her opinions that exactly suited her.[14]

★

In October 1962 Leopold went to Fort Worth, Texas, to serve as chairman of the jury in the First Van Cliburn International Piano Competition. Cliburn, who had been an excellent pianist from childhood and won most of the leading piano competitions in the United States in the early 1950s, had catapulted to fame in April 1958 by winning the International Tchaikovsky Competition in Moscow. Six months earlier, with Sputnik I and II, Russia had beaten the United States in launching artificial satellites into orbit around the world, and the United States was eager for any victory over the Russians, even one in music. Not since Jenny Lind was any musician received in New York with as much excitement as Cliburn on his return from Moscow, and he was given a tickertape parade up Broadway. His career later dwindled, but in 1962 he was still at the top of his fame, and the competition, in which he had a hand, though its driving force was its general chairman, Grace Ward Lankford, was publicized and presented with great flair and a Texan abundance of money. First prize was $10,000 and an even greater value in publicity.[15]

The contest, with attendant festivities, continued for a week, and the musical portions were held in the thirteen-hundred-seat Ed Landreth Hall at Texas Christian University, where, despite a conflicting football weekend, the hall frequently sold out at $5.00 a seat. The jurors came from the United States, Mexico, Brazil, England, Russia and Japan, and among the famous pianists were Lili Kraus, Lev Oborin, Leonard Pennario and Jorge Bolet. The roster of contestants was equally international and included for the first time in an American competition several Russians. Leopold enjoyed it all.

The contestants quickly were reduced to nine finalists, who were to play with the Fort Worth Symphony — a community group that included many professionals — either Prokofiev's Concerto No. 3 or Rachmaninoff's *Rhapsody on a Theme of Paganini* and the first movement of either Beethoven's Concerto No. 3 or his Concerto No. 4. The winner, twenty-three-year-old Ralph Votapek, of Milwaukee, performed the Prokofiev and the Beethoven No. 4; Nikolai Petrov, a Russian, awarded second prize, played the same, but Mikhail Voskresenky, another Russian, who placed third, chose the Rachmaninoff and the Beethoven No. 3. Curiously, though all the contestants played the same piano, they made it sound quite different: the Russians, strong and brilliant; the Americans, warm and lucid; and the French, elegant and pearly. Presumably the difference was a reflection more of their teachers' piano characteristics than their own.

In December the competition's winner, Votapek, as part of his prize gave a recital at Carnegie Hall. Unfortunately it was greeted by a review in the *Times* that, despite some complimentary remarks, was harsh in tone and flecked with sarcasm.[16] It was a defeat from which his career never fully recovered, though he played for some years with success in South America. But, a very young man, he may have lost more than he won in Fort Worth.

The value of such competitions or awards has always been questionable. Music, whether in composition or performance, does not lend itself easily to contests, and yet, beginning with ancient Greece, almost every nation has brought together its singers, and often dancers, in religious or secular festivals and offered prizes of one kind or another. But often, as the German choral groups with their *Sängerfeste* had demonstrated, the prize mattered less that the spirit of the assembly, the buzz of ideas as musicians for days at a time thought and talked of nothing but music.

For that spirit Leopold, though as skeptical as most about competitions, always was willing to serve on juries or audition committees, and part of the respect he was accorded by colleagues like Szell or Casals was their recognition that he, a musician of first-class capability and taste, was willing to work hard to foster such qualities in others. Many a student who had failed an audition or lost a contest received a prize in the form of a conversation with Leopold about the problems of his or her technique or interpretation and how these could be solved. In such matters he had not only extraordinary judgment but enthusiasm, and musicians revered him for both.

Two months after Leopold returned from Fort Worth, full of stories, the last survivor of his parents' generation died, Tante Ellie, the youngest and first of the family to be born in the United States. With characteristic vigor, in her eighty-eighth year she had announced one day to her son and daughter-in-law that she had lived long enough with them and for her last years she would go to a nursing home, and so she died in Westerly, Rhode Island, aged ninety.

Her obituary in the *Times* made friends smile: it was so Damrosch. Not a word about the cause of death or of any religious or memorial service, but a complete list of her Damrosch relatives (except for Marie Wiechmann), with a sentence or two about each: daughter of Leopold, who had founded the New York Symphony, and Helene von Heimburg, a lieder singer; and sister of Frank and of Walter and of Clara; and then a statement that was news to most who read it: "The family will be honored here with the creation of Damrosch Park within the Lincoln Square project at West 62nd Street." The notice in the *Herald Tribune* quoted the announcement of the Parks Department: "Since 1871 the Damrosch family has exerted an influence on the musical life of New York City and of the nation in general which is probably unequalled by any other family in the country."[17]

The Lincoln Square project, which ultimately, as Lincoln Center, housed the New York Philharmonic-Symphony, the Metropolitan Opera, the Juilliard School and several other constituents, did indeed include an outdoor bandshell and park that in time would be named for the family in recognition of their achievements. Among family members credit for the idea was given to Walter's eldest daughter, Alice, who supposedly suggested it, with reasons marshaled, to Robert Moses, who in his various city and state positions was the force oehind the project. But no one ever persuaded Moses to do something he did not want to do, and he seems from the start to have conceived of an open space that could be used for outdoor concerts and occasions. Though the park first had been announced in October 1959, Ellie, no doubt, would have been delighted that her obituary offered an opportunity to remind everyone that no family in the city — in the country — had done more for music than the Damrosches.[18]

In the early 1960s Marya's career began to achieve the kind of celebrity for which she always had longed. Even before she left *The Reporter* in 1963, she had begun to appear as a guest on various television shows and even to have a show of her own for a season, generally some kind of talk show, interviewing guests or reporting news with commentary. She was good on television, attractive, articulate and courageous enough to speak her mind even if it meant criticizing the behavior or ideas of others. At the same time she continued her writing, principally with a monthly article in *McCall's*, the publication of *But Will It Sell?* and articles for the *Herald Tribune*, the *Times* and *Newsfront*, and she also developed an extremely successful career as a lecturer, traveling all over the country and speaking on almost every conceivable subject. With fame, and the money it brought, she moved her family to the Dakota apartment house, where many celebrities lived, and on June 12, 1964, in a climax of success she was the subject of a *Life* "Close Up," an article with pictures of her summer life at Sagaponack, Long Island.

Yet as those close to her knew, her success had not brought her happiness. Her husband was leaving her for another woman, and whatever the rights and wrongs of it, the fact was that Marya at sixty, for all her experience, still had not managed to form a lasting relationship with any man. In this period it was said of her in New York that no man receives his final decree of divorce but within the week he is invited to dine by Marya Mannes. It was not a reputation that improved with age, and some people, besides regretting her behavior, pitied it.

Worst of all, occasionally now in her writing she began to be dishonest, perhaps more from confusion than intent. For *McCall's* she wrote an article, "A Sharp Look at the Men's Magazines," in which she tackled the subject of pornography and the degradation of women as sex objects:

> These roguish publications share one major element. This is the implicit premise that Woman is an Object, and that this Object is her body. She has no other function than to be lusted after and lurched at. The Measurements are All. Aside from her own joyful cooperation, nothing else really matters: things like mind or spirit — you know, those things.[19]

To those who knew her best: Was this not, at least in part, the game that Marya always had played? So who was she to complain?

Even those who did not know her background and personal life sometimes called her bluff. In response to another *McCall's* article, "Letter to the Young," a reader wrote:

> For eight years I (and those who are behind me in writing this) have worked with over 400 teenagers. I suggest Miss Mannes do the same before bubbling over with her empty-headed advice to the kids.
>
> It is her kind of advice kids parrot about sexual freedom and then wonder why they've gotten into trouble and begin to express a few big regrets . . . [She states], "As to this vastly greater sexual freedom you possess, we should count it more a gain than a loss." Brilliant. Ask the thousands of kids who tried it. Ask the unwed mothers. Look at the divorce records, the illegitimate births, the abortions and the broken lives. TALK to those kids. Ask them if it's more a gain! . . .
>
> She extols the kids' "frank recognition that romance and sexual pleasure do not necessarily go together. You thereby put sex in its place instead of surrounding it with a sentimental nimbus." Great. So let's all have sexual pleasure where, when and how we may and hope romance peeks in along the way somewhere. This, of course, will improve society. We'll all be giants of emotional stability and perfect examples of family life. It could be possible, Miss Mannes, that sexual freedom isn't sexual freedom at all. It becomes sexual slavery. Work with a few kids for a while. Kids become slaves to it. Do they know where excess begins? Do you?[20]

What could Marya, who knew nothing of children, not even of her own child, respond? That at sixty-two, though her aunts, uncles, parents all were dead, she still was competing with them for public acclaim? Still in revolt against their standards of family life? In revolt, in particular, against her parents' romance, by light of which her couplings with shifting partners seemed — slavery?

She could claim, if challenged, to practice what she preached, and so seem honest. But she did not tell the college students, with whom she was popular, that her commandments had brought her in middle age to profound, lonely unhappiness. She told them what most of them seemed to want to hear. And that was less honest than Uncle Walter, years earlier, trying to tell her something she did not want to hear.

★

For Leopold the trip to Fort Worth and the Van Cliburn competition proved a last pleasant interlude in what was an accelerating slide into deep depression and, ultimately, death. By 1962–63 his financial position had worsened to a point where he had to humble himself to the college trustees and request a salary. Used to thinking of him as rich, they were not sympathetic and voted him $10,000 a year, about a third of what the presidents of similar schools were paid.

But soon more was needed. Leopold never had been interested in money or clever with it, and in his efforts to recoup the expenses of his father's final illness, he had made some risky real estate investments. One by one they turned bad. So for 1963–64 he asked the trustees for an increase — and was turned down.

He returned to his apartment from the meeting deeply shaken. "You see," he said to Evelyn, "they think nothing of me. I am expendable, unnecessary." That night he and Evelyn went upstairs in their apartment house to have dinner with the Ballards. Mrs. Ballard, Jeannette Haien, soon to join the college faculty, opened the door to greet them and, when she saw Leopold's face, burst into tears.

To several persons close to the situation the trustees' actions in this year seemed inexplicable, requiring something more for a basis than mis-understanding. Though it is true that the world often is slow to believe that a rich man has become poor — surely some secret pockets of wealth remain — the trustees' actions at times appeared cold to the point of being punitive. Consciously or not they seemed to want to humiliate this man who was both musician and scientist and had played the role of grand seigneur.[21]

It is only speculation, but many businessmen who serve on boards of artistic enterprises seem to have a love-hate relationship with the artists whose purposes they are supposed to serve. They are sensitive enough to appreciate that the artist has something they do not, or have in less degree, and they resent the superiority. Let the artist then get in financial trouble, and the businessmen, or some of them, will be quick not to offer sympathy or help but to assert a superiority of practical judgment accompanied often by disciplinary remarks and actions, as if the artist of fifty-five or sixty was a little boy of twelve. This seems to have been the attitude of the leaders of the trustees. They had in Leopold, though they do not seem to have realized it, the country's outstanding conservatory president. It does not denigrate the others to say that he was the equal of the best as a musician and the superior of all, by reason of his science, languages and general background, as an educator. Yet the trustees seemed often, instead of working to preserve him for the college, to wish to hasten him with coldness and small indignities into retirement.

To a much smaller extent his relationship with the faculty also became more difficult, paradoxically, in part because of his own policies. By expanding the school into the college and increasing its enrollment, he had made it more of an institution that of necessity would function through department heads and faculty committees. Yet the trend countered his preference for personal relationships, even as the dwindling of his resources made it impossible for him to continue as grand seigneur. He hated to be asked as president to attend a faculty committee meeting: it was too close to a summons. His door always was open. Why could they not, as they had done in the 1940s and early 1950s, come to him? Though the faculty loved him for his imagination, such as persuading Gérard Souzay to teach a master class in French song, he was aware that in the new environment he functioned less well.

To aid him, in October 1962 the trustees hired Richard French to serve as an administrative vice-president, a new post. French, apparently, thought he saw in Leopold an aging lion who could be driven from the scene, and was indiscreet enough to say so. Leopold, uncovering the start of an intrigue, had the man fired. It was still his school.[22]

Yet his sense of failure steadily grew stronger and was intensified when his mistress of nine years, Miss Y, broke off the relationship. They had lunched together regularly and sometimes gone to concerts in the evening, and like other of his mistresses, she, too, at one time had hoped that he would marry her. The break was occasioned in part by her realization that, though she had given herself to him without reservation, he had never returned her love in the same degree. There were not only his wife and child, whom he would not leave, but the many other mistresses. She would remain his friend, but the intimacy was finished.[23]

For Leopold the break was a severe blow. The steady relationship, like his marriage, had been a ballast in his life, and on its sudden removal he began a feverish, floundering round of infidelities. What worried him most, he told Jeannette Haien, was that Miss Y must think ill of him. He had failed her, too. In the end, as a man with a woman, he always proved unsatisfactory. One day in conversation with Jeannette, as he was complaining in his manner about his wife, Jeannette suggested that if it would solve any problems, he should divorce Evelyn, but Leopold, suddenly serious, replied, "She is the only person I have ever truly loved, and I still do."[24]

His father had suffered depressions, sometimes for weeks, but Leopold's continued steadily through the winter of 1964 into the spring. His doctor prescribed certain drugs, but they seemed to combine poorly with Leopold's increased drinking. He, who had been so handsome, became heavy, even bloated, and Randall Thompson, who dropped into Leopold's office for a visit, was aghast at the change. Evelyn arranged for him to see a psychiatrist, and later, so did Miss Y and Jeannette, but in neither instance was Leopold prepared either to talk or to listen. He left the second doctor's office insisting the man was a fool because he had mispronounced "Edvard Munch."

At home Evelyn, who was far less perturbed than he about the money, tried every way she could to break the depression, but without success. His chant became: "Martha's Vineyard! If only I can hang on till summer and the Vineyard."

Once there, the depression apparently began to lift. He started discussing with Evelyn what he still could do in music, surprised her constantly by playing on the piano or phonograph works that had a special meaning for them and agreed to enter the local hospital in August for a series of tests. The days immediately preceding were idyllic, and she became convinced his mood truly had changed. When she drove him to the hospital, they talked little; nothing seemed to need saying. In the hospital room, after kissing him good night, she left with a lighter heart than she had known for months. And that night he died.[25]

The medical reason was a cerebral hemorrhage, and Evelyn wondered whether he had not suffered a series of small strokes throughout the preceding months.

Possibly there can be also artistic or psychological reasons for death. In his musical life Leopold had seen the doors of opportunity close, one after another. First, on his composing, a casualty perhaps of his work on color photography or perhaps, more fundamentally, of his inability to separate himself for any length of time from persons toward whom he felt a sense of duty — or guilt — however slight.

Then, with the breakup of his trio, on his career as a performer. The obvious reason, Gimpel's withdrawal, was mere chance or misfortune. But again, perhaps, there was another, more basic reason: his musical taste and intelligence, which kept him dissatisfied with anything less than the very best.

Finally, at the college he perhaps thought he saw a door closing once again, this time on his career as an educator. The job had changed, and he had not. Where at sixty-four could he go, what could he do in music and still have a productive life? He began to feel that nothing he had attempted in music had prospered. He was wrong. The college endured and was a rare achievement. So, too, was his role in photography, but he was too close to both to see either. When he received word that he and Leo Godowsky had both been given the Progress Award of the Royal Photographic Society of London, he said to his secretary, "I wish I had written the *Jupiter* Symphony."[26]

It was a cry of despair.

Two days after his death on August 11, 1964, the *New York Times* gave him an editorial tribute that well summarized the feelings of the musical world. "Musicians here and abroad admired him as educator, pianist, philosopher, scientist and a strong force in raising standards of music." Like his uncles and parents, he had not achieved the absolute top rank in any phase of his career, yet like them, he had made himself a "force" in music.[27]

Marya, on Evelyn's invitation, at the graveside spoke of him more personally.

> Here rests — at last — a man who knew little peace except in music, on his boat alone, or in the company of those who loved and understood him.
>
> Leopold was a universal man — as much at home with the structure of the atom as with the form of a fugue; a man of limitless intelligence, a playful wit, and a deeply generous spirit. He gave far more to the world than he received from it.
>
> Yet this man with such great resources was not only totally free of the competitive spirit which this brutal time seems to demand for survival — he was almost painfully modest. Although we who loved him knew him to be so much better than most of us, he himself thought he was never good enough.
>
> So, naked and vulnerable to the end, this gentle and brilliant man is now clothed by his mother earth and shielded by our profound and compassionate love.[28]

EPILOGUE

Dedication of Damrosch Park. Speculation.

On May 22, 1969, New York City's parks commissioner and others officially dedicated Damrosch Park at Lincoln Center, 2.34 acres of open space with trees, benches and a bandshell at one end for outdoor concerts. Among the speakers and representing the family was Marya. As always on such occasions she played her part well, with a short speech, neatly phrased and touching lightly on some serious ideas.

"This family and this city," she said, "are inseparable." It was a fact, at least for the family's work in music. Though Leopold, with Godowsky, had discovered Kodachrome in Rochester, and Alice had founded the U.S. Women's Olympic Ski Team in the Alps, in music, despite all the tours, radio programs and schools with national, even international enrollment, the family had remained based in New York.

She recalled its immigrant background, to which she felt much of its burst of activity and talent could be ascribed. In response to the welcome and freedom its members enjoyed in the United States, she said, "They felt that they owed this city and this nation something for accepting them." It was a feeling shared by many immigrants, who had found themselves stimulated by the release of talent through opportunity, the cross-fertilization of cultures and the interplay of generations, and nowhere in the United States were these greater than in New York City.

She talked briefly of the family's values and of their belief in self-discipline if freedom was to bear fruit. From Edmund Burke she quoted, "Society cannot exist unless a controlling power upon will and appetite are placed somewhere — and the less of it there is within, the more there must be without," adding of her family, "These self-imposed disciplines that so characterized the first two generations of the Damrosch and Mannes families did not, however, lock them into the traditions which molded them. They owed their music to the past, but they blazed new paths into the future. If they were not precisely revolutionaries, they were most certainly innovators."

She did not enlarge on the thought, but a characteristic of the German immigrants of her grandparents' generation was their willingness to innovate in matters of art, education and government while continuing staunchly conservative in their personal lives. The trait is evident in Wisconsin, where German immigrants, the dominant group, created a state with advanced social legislation yet conservative social mores, and it seems to have originated in the middle-class German Socialist, agnostic and artistic spirit of the mid-nineteenth century in which Leopold and Helene Damrosch shared. It was a tradition that the family in the United States attempted consciously to pass down, and that Marya, in revolt, reversed, innovating in her personal style of living while remaining relatively conservative in her ideas about art and politics. But her cousins, for the most part, cleaved to their German heritage.

There were two quirks in her speech that may have amused or irritated those who knew the family well. In describing the family's musical background she did not mention her grandmother Helene, which her Uncle Frank surely would have done, and in her list of those commemorated by the park — her grandfather Leopold, her uncles Walter and Frank, her parents and her brother — she placed Walter before Frank, which undoubtedly angered Helen Tee Van. Probably today, however, the only family member of whom the general public is aware is Walter. Nevertheless, the park, quite properly, was dedicated to the family.[1]

By report of Walter's mother-in-law, Mrs. James G. Blaine, Andrew Carnegie's favorite maxim was "From shirt sleeves to shirt sleeves, three generations," and though the fourth generation of Damrosches did well in other fields, in music, at least, it reverted to shirt sleeves. And even in the third generation there was only one, Leopold, able to pursue a career in music, and even he at times seemed almost overwhelmed by the burden of the family tradition. Beyond the mysteries of talent — the Bach family, for example, continued several generations longer and with far greater numerical strength — what happened and why?

The answers, I think, can best be found in the lives and careers of Leopold and Marya, the two who of all the third generation achieved the most in the way of public recognition, adding to the family's glory, and also suffered the most, because of the family. Their experience to some extent is that of all the third generation, except writ larger, and perhaps provided the example from which the fourth instinctively turned away.

Marya's old age was extremely unhappy. Despite her constant talk of values, she seemed to have none that could sustain her. Aging, for her, was a disaster, a cause of prolonged, daily anguish. Sexual attraction was basic to her way of life, and even when she no longer could dance the minuet to its conclusion, she would begin the introductory to-and-fro. What is probably her last work, published in 1978, when she was seventy-four, describes how she smiled daily from her apartment window at a doorman across the street until finally he was led to ask if he could "come up some time and visit," which she refused.[2]

Not even the memory of intercourse assuaged her unhappiness. The need for it, to feel herself physically attractive and attracted to a man, had become an addiction. She had been modern, disbelieved in an angry god, and yet for her the Delphic rule, the Mosaic commandment had proved in the end to be self-executing. Adultery or fornication, on the scale she had committed them, had led to misery.

Combined with the loss of youth and beauty was the loss of celebrity. She despaired over parties to which she was not invited, lamented the gradual loss of her position on television and in magazines and in any gathering, however small, yearned for the spotlight. She found no recompense or serenity in literature, music or anything of the spirit. Even her own accomplishments, her shelf of published works, gave her no satisfaction; the latest rejection was always uppermost in her mind. She became full of self-pity. The emotion marred her autobiography, *Out of My Time* (1971), and it grew steadily greater. She drank too much, and she became in conversation what she never had been: boring.

After Leopold's death in 1964 she had written to Mary Bancroft, "It was an inevitable but unnecessary death. Call it suicide, really."[3] Perhaps she already had in mind her concept of the need to feel "a productive being" as "the paramount factor" in wishing to live. In her own case, she was advised by her doctor that senility, which had shown its first signs, could be slowed greatly if she would give up drinking. Instead she drank even more, until finally oblivion erased mind, memory and unhappiness. She was a spiritual suicide. Her life, a passionate pursuit of self-interest, had led to self-destruction.

It may be that Marya's personality was a sport in the Damrosch-Mannes family, but some friends and relatives considered it, at least in part, caused by the family and saw in it a revolt against her parents and their values that never matured. She remained, as many children sometimes appear, two personalities: one who admired her parents' values, and another who, unable to live by them, or up to them, took refuge in decrying them. Feeling instinctively that she could not match their romance, or those of her grandparents or aunts and uncles, she advocated a new, "liberated" way of life, and from the moment she tore apart her first marriage, she was committed to her new way if she was not going to admit a mistake.

Leopold, on the other hand, was committed intellectually to the ideal that he saw in his parents and knew had operated for his grandparents. As Mary Bancroft once observed of the two: "Marya thinks with her emotions; Leopold, with his mind." Marya called her failings virtues and made of them a crusade; Leopold, though he indulged them excessively, never doubted that they were failings and, in excess, dangerous to the best possible life.[4]

Marya, asked once why she and Leopold should have had such extraordinary sexual energy, had no explanation. Mary Bancroft thought it the result of "a cold mother" who was yet an emotionally dominating parent; others, pointing to Walter, thought it was often a concomitant to extraordinary energy in other fields. Most persons considered it a curse. However Don Giovanni may be portrayed in books or on the stage, in real life he, or she, is a tragic figure.

It may be that the need, apparently felt by both Marya and Leopold, for constant reassurance that they were loved, or were attractive to others, was connected in some way to the strong competition in the family, in which their mother, in particular, indulged. Because of the changes in urban life and the great increase in methods of publicity, the Damrosch far more than the Bach family lived in the center of the public eye. Frank had disliked it enough to leave New York for Denver, and many have wondered whether he might not have been happier if he could have remained there. Would Walter have done better, for music and himself, if, instead of following so directly in his father's steps, he had founded an orchestra in Chicago, where he always was popular? Or would Clara and David have done better, for all concerned, to have founded their school, not in New York in competition with Frank's Institute of Musical Art, but in some other city? When the Damrosches of the second generation, like some of the medieval Italian families, chose to concentrate their lives and activities in a single city, they undoubtedly compounded their influence, but they also increased dangerously the sense of competition among them.

Frank, on his return to New York, continued to dislike the publicity and for all his forbearance cannot have enjoyed the constant comparison to Walter, and by the fourth generation, when family pressures had built still higher, family members, perhaps wisely, followed the pattern set by Alice, scattered into other professions and lived and worked in such cities as Boston, Philadelphia, Montreal, San Francisco and Manila.

But for the children of the third generation and elder members of the fourth, the publicity and competition were always there. They grew up in a city where their parents' and grandparents' names and photographs were constantly in the newspapers and journals, making it very easy to confuse achievement with public acclaim. Certainly Marya confused the two. Leopold did not, but, then, he was put under his own special sentence of execution when Ysaÿe told Clara that her son was "the reincarnation of Mozart."

By all reports and evidence, Clara of all the family was the most concerned with its image, the most pretentious about its achievements, the most censorious of any failings, the most anxious for her children, particularly her son, to be successful in the world's eyes. It was she, after all, who had taken the portrait of her father and kept its frame trimmed always with fresh greens. Unquestionably the pressure on her children was great, and because no brothers or sisters of their Damrosch grandparents, except for the unmarried Tante, had come to the United States, there were no shelters away from home where nonmusical aunts and uncles laughed about the family, even insisting, perhaps, that Tante Marie Wiechmann was not so bad. Within the family the focus on success was sharp, and in the Mannes branch, where both parents were musicians, doubly intense. That the two children accomplished as much as they did is perhaps a miracle.

Leopold seems to have been saved from Marya's fate by his adherence to the family's tradition of service. Music, and any achievements with it, were not for personal glory but for others, perhaps for the composers, perhaps for students, perhaps just for the ennoblement, even if temporary, of an audience. He also was saved by his ability to love, which he may have underestimated, for he was able to stir responses of lasting affection in many men and women. Fifteen years after his death, so vivid was his personality, many persons still spoke of him as if alive. The past, even years in the past, was only yesterday. And finally, of course, he was saved by the love of a woman. Through Evelyn he knew what Victor Hugo called "the supreme happiness of life: the conviction that we are loved, loved for ourselves, or in spite of ourselves."[5]

And in the way of love, Evelyn received something, too. After Leopold's funeral Marya one day said to her, "You can't have been very happy with him." Evelyn started to protest, and then faltered. How could she explain the happiness she had known? Leopold had loved Richard Strauss's *Four Last Songs,* and many, many times the two of them had listened to the Elizabeth Schwarzkopf recording of the fourth, *Im Abendrot,* which begins:

> *Wir sind durch Not und Freude*   Through our lives' joys and sorrows
> *Gegangen Hand in Hand;*   We have journeyed hand in hand;
> *Vom Wandern ruhn wir beide*   From our travels let us rest now
> *Nun überm stillen Land.*   In this strange and silent land.[6]

It is so much easier to explain unhappiness.

Notes
Bibliography
Index

NOTES

To avoid continual repetition of library names and collections, as well as of certain documentary sources frequently cited, abbreviations formed of initials have been used throughout. These are listed, with brief descriptions of the material represented, in sections I (a) and (b), which includes an important Note, of the Bibliography.

Some books and articles are cited by shortened titles. Full titles are given in the Bibliography.

In addition to the abbreviations referred to above, the following are used for members of the family whose names frequently occur.

FIRST GENERATION

LD	Leopold Damrosch
HD	Helene Damrosch, Leopold's wife
Tante	Marie von Heimburg, Helene's younger sister

SECOND GENERATION

FD	Frank Damrosch
HMD	Hetty Mosenthal Damrosch, Frank's wife
WD	Walter Damrosch
MBD	Margaret Blaine Damrosch, Walter's wife
CDM	Clara Damrosch Mannes
DM	David Mannes, Clara's husband
EDS	Elizabeth (Ellie) Damrosch Seymour
HTS	Henry T. Seymour, Ellie's husband

THIRD GENERATION

FD, Jr.	Frank Damrosch, Jr., son of FD and HMD
HTV	Helen Tee Van, daughter of FD and HMD
ADK	Alice Damrosch Kiaer, daughter of WD and MBD
GDF	Gretchen Damrosch Finletter, daughter of WD and MBD
LDM	Leopold Damrosch Mannes, son of CDM and DM
ESM	Evelyn Sabin Mannes, second wife and widow of LDM

MM   Marya Mannes, daughter of CDM and DM
LDS   Lawrence Damrosch Seymour ⎫
CS   Clair Seymour   ⎪
ESR   Elizabeth Seymour Ransom   ⎬ children of EDS and HTS
RSR   Ruth Seymour Reed   ⎭

Also, for these persons other than family:

AC   Andrew Carnegie
HHF   Harry Harkness Flagler
LG, Jr.   Leopold Godowsky, Jr.
GM   the author
RT   Randall Thompson

And for these organizations:

OS of NY   Oratorio Society of New York
SS of NY   Symphony Society of New York
NYSO   New York Symphony Orchestra
MAS of NY   Musical Art Society of New York
IMA   Institute of Musical Art

Chapter 1

(*pages 9–18*)
1. *Tante's Story,* 19 (For location, see Bibliography, Note on certain abbreviations, under Marie von Heimburg).
2. Crowthers, "FD, His Life." Stebbins, *FD,* 33. WD, *My Musical Life,* 10, 170.
3. *History of the Liederkranz of the City of New York, 1847 to 1947, and of the Arion, New York.* Also, *Arion New York von 1854 bis 1904.* In Apr. 1920, after sixty-six years of separate existence, the Arion rejoined the Liederkranz. The association continues.
4. Information about the family's migration to New York appears chiefly in *Tante's Story,* 17–19; FD, *Biographical Material on LD.* WD, *My Musical Life,* 10; and Stebbins, *FD,* 31, 39.
5. The statement is made by Rice, *Musical Reminiscences,* 33. Gertrude Schirmer Fay, interview GM, was told as a child, circa 1900, of this greeting to LD and this reason for it. She supposed that her paternal grandfather, Gustav Schirmer, was aboard the tender with others from his store and publishing house. Stebbins, *FD,* 34.
6. Strong, *Diary,* vol. 4, 354. Strong's opinions are always interesting: "The performer introduced 'a cadenza' of his own, creditable to his manipulation, disgraceful to him as an artist. Who is worthy to append a bit of his own writing to a composition of Beethoven's?"
   The statement, sometimes made, that LD also conducted the concert and thus appeared in his Philharmonic debut as conductor, composer and soloist, is false. See Shanet, *Philharmonic,* 438, note 93.
   On LD's appearance: Rice, *Musical Reminiscences,* 42; Lawrence F. Abbott, letter to WD, 6/4/1931, NYPL, WD Coll., Cat. 1, Box 2; and U.S. passport issued to LD, 8/12/84: 52 years, 5 feet 11 inches; forehead, broad; eyes, gray;

nose, straight; mouth, firm; chin, round; hair, gray; complexion, fair; face, full; NYPL, WD Coll., Cat. 16, Box 39.

On LD's behavior in rehearsal: Franko, *Chords and Discords,* 62–63; Frank H. Cook, letter to WD, 4/10/35, NYPL, WD Coll., Cat. 1, Box 2.

7. There is disagreement among sources whether the number of the house on 35 Street was 220, 222, or 331, and also about the number of floors, which probably was four if the basement-kitchen is included. *Tante's Story,* 19; FD, *Biographical Material on LD,* 7; EDS, *Reminiscences as told to HTV;* and Stebbins, *FD,* 39.

8. *Tante's Story,* 19–20; WD, *My Musical Life,* 10; Stebbins, *FD,* 39; EDS, *O'mama's Story,* 1; and for an American musician's view of German houses, see Fay, *Music-Study in Germany,* 15, 95.

9. Stern, *Gold and Iron,* 40.

10. Shanet, *Philharmonic,* 46, points out that a similarly named predecessor of the Philharmonic, 1799–1816, was more active; and Fay, *Music-Study in Germany,* 42, that the best European orchestras in 1870 still were better than the Philharmonic.

11. FD, *Biographical Material on LD,* 6. *Tante's Story,* 23.

12. EDS, *O'mama's Story,* 3.

13. *Tante's Story,* 20, 21, 22.

14. Stebbins, *FD,* 39.

15. Luening, *Odyssey of an American Composer,* 359. Luening, born in Wisconsin in 1900 to parents of German background, had a repertory of fifty songs in German and English by the time he was three and a half, pp. 19, 25–26. For an American mother who sang, see Welling, *As the Twig Is Bent,* 228.

16. Stebbins, *FD,* 40; WD, *My Musical Life,* 11; CDM, *Born on a Sunday,* 7. EDS, *Reminiscences as told to HTV,* 1. EDS, *O'mama's Story,* 3.

17. Crowthers, "FD, His Life," and *Otto Eidlitz.*

18. *Tante's Story,* 9–10, 14. Three songs in LD's Opus 6 are dedicated to Frau M. Kaufmann and three in Opus 7 to Frau Mathilde Eppenstein. *Collected Songs of Leopold Damrosch* (New York: Schirmer, 1903).

19. LD, letter to unnamed friend in Breslau, 5/19/1872. A typescript in German, CS Coll.; a translation in typescript by HMD, LOC, D-TV Coll., Box 1.

Chapter 2

(pages 19–28)

1. WD on *Heimweh,* in an address on the General Electric Radio Program, 2/17/1935, NYPL, WD Coll., Cat. 17, Box 40.

2. LD, letter to Tante, 8/7/1874, CS Coll. He became a citizen on 5/13/1880, NYPL, WD Coll., Cat. 16, Box 39. At the time, residence for five years was required before an immigrant could apply for citizenship.

3. EDS, *Reminiscences as told to HTV,* 4.

4. HD, letter to Tante, 7/9/1874, CS Coll.

5. CDM, *Born on a Sunday,* 3, 13.

6. LD, *Student Autobiography;* the next five, short quotations are from this autobiography. See also FD, *Biographical Material on LD;* Poem for Dorothea Damrosch (LD's stepmother) on her hundredth birthday, LOC, D-TV Coll., Box 1; Stebbins, *FD,* 256; and Katherine A. Bischoff letter to WD, 3/17/1933, NYPL, WD Coll., Cat. 16, Box 39.

7. WD, letter, 12/26/1929, to Eleanor Dobson, assistant editor of the *Dictionary of American Biography.* LD's marriage certificate, dated at Oldenburg 8/20/1858,

states that his father is Heinrich Damrosch. For both, NYPL, WD Coll., Cat. 16, Box 39.

8. LD, letter to Tante, 6/6/1883, typescript in German, CS Coll.; a translation, typescript, HMD, LOC, D-TV Coll., Box 1. The letter is from a group of letters written by LD to Tante in German. The originals are lost. The letters exist in typescript transcriptions, CS Coll., and typescript translations by HDM, LOC. The LOC also has eight of the letters transcribed but still in German. Between the two collections there are a few, very slight differences. The translations used in this book, largely the work of Bruni Mayor, are new.

9. FD, *Biographical Material on LD*, 4. WD, *My Musical Life*, 5.

10. *Tante's Story*, 23.

11. CDM, *Born on a Sunday*, 2.

12. WD, *My Musical Life*, 4. Stebbins, *FD*, 23.

13. CDM, *Born on a Sunday*, 1.

14. Stebbins, *FD*, 24.

15. Stebbins, *FD*, 23.

16. CDM, *Born on a Sunday*, 11; WD, letter to Joe Emerson, 4/20/1935, NYPL, WD Coll., Cat. 13, Box 31.

17. *Tante's Story*, 1–3.

18. WD, *My Musical Life*, 16–18; CDM, *Born on a Sunday*, 8; EDS, "Our Christmas," an account written in a journal, RSR Coll. Clara's G minor *Gavotte* is almost certainly the one in Bach's *English Suite No. 3*, in G Minor, a piece often learned by children. The left-hand trill on *g* continues for three and a half bars, whereas in the right hand the longest trill is only a single bar.

19. Thomas, *A Musical Autobiography*, 22. The surrounding editorial comment by George P. Upton and Leon Stein (in the Da Capo Press reprint) is important. Also Russell, *The American Orchestra and Theodore Thomas*.

20. Strong, *Diary*, vol. 4, 249–250; and 484, on 6/16/1873: "His garden concerts are growing in brilliancy and in public favor . . . Thomas's people rehearse daily. If our society would consent to do likewise, it could beat them out of sight, being numerically so much stronger than they." See also Rice, *Musical Reminiscences*, 19–31. He gives programs for a typical Beethoven, Mozart or Wagner "night"; also Thomas, *Autobiography*, 55; and on size of the orchestra, 57, 132.

21. Thomas, Rose Fay, *Memoirs of Theodore Thomas*, 63–64.

22. For the figures see Rice, *Musical Reminiscences*, 20–21, 27. Fay, *Music-Study in Germany*, 258.

23. WD, *My Musical Life*, 22; also WD, "Listening Backward," *Century* magazine, Nov. 1927, 3, of which a copy is in NYPL, WD Coll., Cat. 17, Box 40; Stebbins, *FD*, 43. See also *Tante's Story*, 25. For descriptions of Thomas' personality and physique, Thomas, *A Musical Autobiography*, 243–244; Franko, *Chords and Discords*, 59–64; Russell, *The American Orchestra and Theodore Thomas*, 114; Mason, *Memories*, 197–202; Finck, *My Adventures*, 173–180.

Chapter 3

(pages 29–37)

1. Thomas, *A Musical Autobiography*, 335. Mason, *Memories*, 149.

2. Ware and Lockard, *P. T. Barnum Presents Jenny Lind*.

3. Bowen, *Free Artist*, 245; also 227, 242–243. Strong, *Diary*, vol. 4, 436; also 438, 456–457, 474, 477. On the serenade and first concern, *NY Times*,

9/13/1872, 5:5, and 9/24/1872, 4:7. Rice, *Musical Reminiscences*, 16–17. Schonberg, *The Great Pianists*, 253–263. Rubinstein was signed in Vienna by Jacob Grau with money advanced by William Steinway. The tour was managed by Jacob's twenty-one-year-old nephew Maurice Grau, later an opera impresario and manager at the Metropolitan Opera, 1891–1903. For difficulty in persuading audiences to accept piano recitals, see Mason, *Memories*, 186.

4. WD, from a talk at the Metropolitan Museum of Art, Dec. 1943, NYPL, WD Coll., Cat. 10, Box 27. Also WD, letter to Edith Behrens, 11/1/1939, WD Coll., Cat. 1, Box 1.

5. For Arion's activities, see *History of the Liederkranz; Arion New York von 1854 bis 1904;* and *NY Times*, 9/4/1875, 4:6; 2/6/1876, 7:2; 12/14/1879, 7:2; 12/11/1880, 4:7; 12/18/1881, 8:7; and 4/23/1883, 4:7. For similar activities among German immigrants in Wisconsin, see Luening, *Odyssey*, 44. Helene's activities as a soloist are hard to trace, but Odell, *Annals*, vol. 9, pp. 182 and 312, reports her performing with the Arion on 10/15/1871 and 4/5/1873; and vol. 10, p. 748, in Rossini's *Stabat Mater*, St. Stephen's Church, Brooklyn, on 4/6/1879. There were also lieder recitals at Miss Porter's School, Farmington; *Tante's Story*, 21.

6. WD, *My Musical Life*, 23; Stebbins, *FD*, 43–44; Krehbiel, *Notes on the Cultivation of Choral Music and the Oratorio Society of New York*, 55–59.

7. From an unpublished memoir of Walter Naumburg about his father, Elkan, in possession of Elkan's great-nephew Edward Naumburg, Jr.

There is a story that Mrs. Morris Reno was the first to suggest the idea of an oratorio society, see *NY World*, 5/7/1891, 3:2. But in Damrosch sources the credit consistently is given to Rubinstein.

8. See notes 6 and 7 above; also *Tante's Story*, 21. Strong, *Diary*, vol. 4, 491, noted on 8/26/1873 that a new oratorio society was being organized by LD to replace the defunct Harmonic Society and Mendelssohn Union, and, at 521, that he was offered the presidency on 4/7/1874, but declined. Barnard's successor was Spencer W. Coe, not Strong.

9. The history of the Oratorio Society of New York (hereafter OS of NY) has been summarized in various forms. Chief among these are: *OS of NY, Record of the Concerts of the OS, 1873–1904;* OS of NY, 1873–1898, *Book of the Festival* (25th-anniversary essays on LD, founding, musical history, etc.); both in NYPL; *An Historical Sketch of Thirty-seven Seasons of the OS of NY, 1873–1874 through 1908–1909*, prepared by William Burnet Tuthill, secretary, Archives, OS of NY; and *Festival of Music, OS of NY, 1920*, with a history of the OS and analysis of its repertory by H. E. Krehbiel, and facsimile of the "First Soirée — First Season," NYPL. Also Krehbiel, *Notes on the Cultivation of Choral Music and the OS of NY;* and Rice, *Musical Reminiscences*, 34. Family sources include: *Tante's Story*, 21, 26; FD, *Biographical Material on LD*, 9–10; WD, *My Musical Life*, 23, 174–175; Stebbins, *FD*, 44, 168.

10. *NY Tribune*, quoted in Krehbiel, *Notes on the Cultivation*, 58–59. The reviewer, often in those days not identified, was J. R. G. Hassard.

11. From an unpublished memoir of Walter Naumburg about his father Elkan, in possession of Elkan's great-nephew Edward Naumburg, Jr. According to Walter Naumburg, LD played violin regularly in a quartet that gathered at Elkan's house. There was friendship between the families, and HD used to bring over her daughters. The Reno family also were frequent visitors. Then came the break, and along with the Damrosches, the Renos apparently were dropped.

Elkan Naumburg was born in Bavaria in 1835 and came to the United

States at fifteen, settling in Baltimore. In 1864 he moved to New York, where he lived until his death, in 1924. In 1905 he founded the Naumburg free symphony concerts in Central Park, which still continue. They were financed first by Elkan, then by his sons Walter and George and today by a fund created by Walter's will.

12. *NY Times,* 12/26/1874, 4:6.
13. Tolstoy, *What Is Art?*

Chapter 4

(pages 38–48)

1. HD, letter to Tante, 6/14/1874, CS Coll.
2. *Tante's Story,* 21; FD, *Biographical Material on LD,* 8; GM correspondence with the school; Thomas, *A Musical Autobiography,* A12 (meets wife at the school), 43 (on Karl Klauser). Also on Klauser, Mason, *Memories,* 202–205.
3. LD, letter to Tante, 6/21/1874, CS Coll.
4. EDS, *O'mama's Story,* 5. CDM, *Born on a Sunday,* 9–10. LD, letters to Tante, 6/21/1874, 8/7/1874; HD, letter to Tante, 7/9/1874; all three in CS Coll.
5. HD, letter to Tante, 7/9/1874, CS Coll.
6. LD, letter to Tante, 6/21/1874, CS Coll.
7. *Tante's Story,* 23; Elizabeth Long, "WD talks on how Church music can be improved," NYPL, WD Coll., Cat. 17, Box 40.
8. For more on LD's compositions, see Chap. 6.
9. Rice, *Musical Reminiscences,* 17; on Chickering Hall, "better suited to recitals and to chamber music than to the modern orchestra," 14–15. Schonberg, *The Great Pianists,* 232–238. The piano in these years was improving constantly in tone and power, and the competition between piano firms was keen. The Steinway company would not allow any piano but its own in Steinway Hall, regardless of the artist's choice; see Shanet, *Philharmonic,* 129n.
10. Bergmann has been neglected by writers. The most available account of him appears in Shanet, *Philharmonic,* 137, 149, 154–155, 157n., and 438, note 89, with citations to newspaper obituaries and memorials. The *NY Tribune* obituary, 8/14/1876, was reprinted in *Dwight's Journal of Music,* 8/19/1876, 287; also a *Tribute* by Dr. R. Ogden Doremus, a former president of the NY Philharmonic Society, in 12/9/1876, 345.
11. Shanet, *Philharmonic,* 109–110, 142, 228–229, 293.
12. *Tante's Story,* 27; WD, *My Musical Life,* 13–14; Stebbins, *FD,* 47.
13. *Tante's Story,* 13; WD, letter to Franz W. Beidler, Wagner's grandson, 12/14/1936, NYPL, WD Coll., Cat. 3, Box 8. Stebbins, *FD,* 19. The exact date on which LD learned that he, and not Thomas, would replace Bergmann at the Philharmonic is not known. But from an analysis of the news reports in *Dwight's Journal* about Thomas' activities, it seems clear that by late July, or before LD left for Bayreuth, Thomas had taken himself out of the running.
14. The first cyclic performance of *The Ring* (8/13, 14, 16, 17/1876), which included the world premières of *Siegfried* (8/16) and *Götterdämmerung* (8/17), took place at the Festspielhaus, Bayreuth, with Hans Richter, conductor, and under Wagner's personal supervision. LD arrived on 8/1, in time to hear the rehearsal of *Götterdämmerung* on 8/5; on the following four days were dress rehearsals of the four operas, all of which he attended, so that he saw and heard two cycles complete and, in addition, at least one opera in partial re-

hearsal, and probably more. His articles appeared, as noted in the text, in the *NY Sun*. Copies of the 8/23, 8/26 and 9/3 articles are in LOC, D–TV, Box 7.

15. WD, *My Musical Life,* 14–16; GM interview with Gertrude Schirmer Fay, Gustave's daughter.

16. *Dwight's Journal,* 1/20/1877, both on 375.

17. Thomas, *A Musical Autobiography,* 74 (an artful account); Shanet, *Philharmonic,* 158–161; Russell, *The American Orchestra,* 116.

18. WD, *My Musical Life,* 25–26; Stebbins, *FD,* 49–50; FD, *Biographical Material on LD,* unnumbered page; Rice, *Musical Reminiscences,* 35.

19. The histories of both the SS of NY and the NYSO exist in a variety of documents, chief of which are: *SS of NY, Minutes of Proceedings of the Board of Directors, 1878–1893,* NYPL; *SS of NY, An Historical and Bibliographical Review,* by Clarence Edward Le Massena, a typescript of 31 pp., for public distribution, NYPL; The Constitution of the SS of NY, NYPL, WD Coll., Cat. 11, Box 28; a list of conductors, dates and number of concerts, 1878–1928, NYPL, WD Coll., Cat. 11, Box 29; WD, *My Musical Life,* 23; Stebbins, *FD,* 50–51. The quotation "The general desire . . ." *SS of NY, Minutes,* 10/22/1878.

   LD's letter to S. M. Knevals, 10/21/1878, formally accepting the post of conductor, is in the PML. It is only two sentences, without mention of number of concerts, dates or pay: "I accept with pleasure the position as conductor . . ."

20. *SS of NY, Minutes,* 10/22/1878.

21. WD, "Looking Backward," states: "There was great indignation among a certain group of music lovers over the ousting of my father, and they called a meeting . . ." But he does not name them. A reprint of the article is in NYPL, Cat. 17, Box 40. See Russell, *The American Orchestra and Theodore Thomas,* 116, where he states, though without citation, that LD was a man

   > of the happiest and most attractive address. He had many friends in New York, some of power and influence. These felt he had been unfairly treated by the Philharmonic. The catastrophic failure of his year of leadership they attributed to causes beyond his control; a strong Damrosch faction grew up in New York. The more it waxed the more bitter it became against the man that, according to its assertion, had ousted the good Doctor by rivalry.

22. *NY Times,* 4/6/1879, 6:6.

Chapter 5

(*pages 49–59*)

1. Franko, *Chords and Discords,* 62–63.

2. GM interview with Gertrude Schirmer Fay. For a member of the older generation, see William Mason (1829–1908), *Memories of a Musical Life,* 246: "In modern times there is also a tendency to excessive use of tempo rubato."

3. Rice, *Musical Reminiscences,* 36: "It was my first hearing of the work, and probably its first adequate performance in New York." *NY Times,* 3/19/1880, 5:2. The identity of the disapproving newspaper, which Johnson, *First Performances,* quotes at greater length and mistakenly ascribes to the *NY Evening Post,* has been lost and, despite a search by both of us, not yet rediscovered. I have used the review here because it so neatly names LD's usual virtues as his failings. *Dwight's Journal,* 3/27/1880, 56:3, refers, without specifying, to negative reviews.

4. Statement made in Stebbins, *FD,* 51, without citation. I could not find the reference, but the biography was written carefully, and some of the family's documentary sources, available forty years ago, have disappeared.

5. WD, *My Musical Life,* 76. For contemporary descriptions of von Bülow's style, see Fay, *Music-Study in Germany,* 176–177, and Rice, *Musical Reminiscences,* 17: "His playing seemed to lack the vivid color of Rubinstein." Schonberg, *The Great Pianists,* 232–238. Stebbins, *FD,* 46. LD and von Bülow had played together often in Germany, WD, *My Musical Life,* 74, and WD, letter to Franz W. Beidler, 12/14/1936, NYPL, WD Coll., Cat. 3, Box 8.

   In an interview given by FD, "FD, A Biographical Sketch," *Musical Times,* 12/1/1904, 782–787, he claimed to have attended 139 of von Bülow's appearances.

6. Crowthers, "FD, His Life." *Otto Eidlitz,* 5. Stebbins, FD, 45–46.

7. The cause of Richard's death is unknown; Ernst died during a cholera epidemic when his mother became ill and could not feed him; Hans died of whooping cough; *Tante's Story,* 16. WD, *My Musical Life,* 1, states that Richard was the eldest child and gives him Frank's year of birth, 1859. Stebbins, *FD,* 17, corrected this, putting Richard's birth in 1861.

8. *Tante's Story,* 22; EDS, *Reminiscences as told to HTV,* 7. On LD's income, my estimate, very speculative. CDM, *Born on a Sunday,* 9. Thomas and Steinway, Franko, *Chords and Discords,* 60.

9. EDS, *O'mama's Story,* 4. *Tante's Story,* 9.

10. EDS, *Reminiscences as told to HTV,* 11.

11. Records of City College show that he completed his sophomore year, June 1877, ranking 29 in a class of 68.

12. FD, *Biographical Material on LD,* 5. Stebbins, *FD,* 52–53.

13. On Joseph Mosenthal, see Mason, *Memories,* 197, and Thompson's *International Cyclopedia,* 9th ed. On Hetty, Stebbins, *FD,* 45, 55.

   FD loved to dance, and HMD, handwritten note to her grandchildren, claimed that Mrs. Gustav Mahler (c. 1910) "said Grandpapa was the only good dancer in America"; LOC, D-TV, Box 1. For a description of an extremely sentimental birthday party given him by the von Heimburgs in Germany, see HDM, typescript notes on FD, LOC, D-TV, Box 1; for one given him by WD, in Berlin, see Stebbins, *FD,* 124.

14. Stebbins, *FD,* 55. CDM, *Born on a Sunday,* 12.

15. The success is reflected in the number of stories on it in the *NY Times,* 1880: 2/9, 5:5; 2/15, 7:3; 2/19, 5:6; 2/26, 4:6; 4/4, 7:3; 4/19, 5:6; 4/27, 4:6. Rice, *Musical Reminiscences,* 36. WD, *My Musical Life,* 27; WD, letter to Louis Miller, 2/16/1935 on LD's translation: "He felt this was a necessity for a complete understanding," NYPL, WD Coll., Cat. 1, Box 2. *OS of NY, Record of the Concerts of the OS, 1873–1904,* NYPL.

16. WD, *My Musical Life,* 11–12.

17. WD, ibid., 28–30; Crowthers, "WD, Dean of American Conductors."

18. WD, *My Musical Life,* 31–32.

19. Krehbiel, *Notes on the Cultivation,* 74–75; *OS of NY, Record of the Concerts of the OS, 1873–1904,* NYPL. The *Programme, Music Festival, 1881* (107 pp.) gives information about the choral sections, works, subscribers to the Festival Fund, etc., Archives, OS of NY.

20. WD, *My Musical Life,* 33.

21. Rice, *Musical Reminiscences,* 37–38.

22. The *Times's* reports are too many to list. They begin on Feb. 13, 1881, and continue steadily through March and Apr. Those on the performance are:

5/4, 5:1; 5/5, 5:11; 5/6, 5:1; 5/7, 5:4; 5/8, 7:3; 5/9, 5:5. The tone is generally admiring: the headline on May 5, DR. DAMROSCH'S TRIUMPH; and on May 7, of *Messiah*, THE CROWNING TRIUMPH OF DR. DAMROSCH.

23. Family sources other than WD, *My Musical Life*, are CDM, *Born on a Sunday*, 12; EDS, *O'mama's Story*, 4.

24. *Dwight's Journal*, 6/18/1881, 95–97; more reviews of the concerts, 5/21/1881, 86; 7/2/1881, 105.

25. Ibid., 6/18/1881, 96. The announcement was made just before the start of the Damrosch festival. Also, *NY Times*, 11/13/1882, 5:3, quoting a speech about events in 1880.

Chapter 6

(pages 60–72)

1. Possibly the artist most frequently at these occasions was Max Pinner, a pianist, with whom LD also played professionally. Together they gave four violin-piano recitals in the Union Square Theater, in New York, in Feb. and March 1879, and also played regularly in a trio with Frederick Bergner, cellist, at Miss Porter's School. EDS, *Reminiscences as told to HTV*, 6. WD, letter to Ferenc Molnar, 10/12/1943, NYPL, WD Coll., Cat. 1, Box 3.

2. Franko, *Chords and Discords*, 64. WD, *My Musical Life*, 149; WD, Eulogy on Loeffler, NYPL, WD Coll., Cat. 3, Box 7.

3. CDM, *Born on a Sunday*, unnumbered page starting, "Insert where I write . . ."

4. Ibid., unnumbered page headed, "David and I."

5. *Sidney Lanier, Poems and Letters*, 151, letter dated 10/29/1874. See also, 147, letter 9/13/1874: "Last night I won great favor in the eyes of Mr. Cortada . . . He declareth that I can do great things with a little study: and volunteereth to introduce me to Dr. Damrosch (under whom he saith I must study)." August Cortada was LD's accompanist at the OS of NY.

6. LD, letter to Geraldine Morgan, 1/6/1882, NYPL, WD Coll., Cat. 16, Box 39. The best description of Morgan's career is in Ammer, *Unsung: A History of Women in American Music*, 35. She is mentioned in DM, *Music Is My Faith*, 122; in Stebbins, *FD*, 120–121, 146; and in CDM, *Born on a Sunday*, unnumbered pages headed, "Pleasant and unpleasant incidents."

7. Crowthers, "FD, His Life."

8. FD, letter to Ed Wiener, 8/25/1879, LOC, D–TV Coll., Box 2.

9. See note 7 above. Also Wyer, ed., *Music in Denver and Colorado*, of which 65–67 are FD's essay, "Years in Denver."

10. See *NY Times* 1882: 11/13, 5:3; 11/15, 5:2; 12/3, 9:1.

11. FD, Response at Testimonial Dinner, 1/16/1926, LOC, D–TV Coll., Box 4.

12. *NY Times*, 12/3/1882, 9:1.

13. *Arion New York von 1854 bis 1904*, 76. *NY Times*, 4/1/1883, 9:2. His successor was Frank Van der Stucken, who took the Male Chorus on a tour of Germany in 1892 and from 1895 to 1907 was conductor of the Cincinnati Symphony Orchestra.

14. EDS, *Reminiscences as told to HTV*, 7.

15. Most of the information about the tour of 1883 is based on letters LD wrote in German to Tante. The originals are lost. The letters exist in typescript transcriptions, CS Coll., and typescript translations by HDM, LOC. The LOC also has eight of the letters transcribed but still in German. Between the two collections there are a few, very slight differences. The translations

used in this book, largely the work of Bruni Mayor, are new. LD, letter to Tante, 5/26/1883, CS Coll.

16. See note 15 above. Also LD, letter to Tante, 5/17/1883, CS Coll.
17. LD, letter to Tante, 5/9/1883 and 5/22/1883, CS Coll. Also Milinowski, *Teresa Carreño*, 137–140.
18. LD, letter to Tante, 5/22/1883, CS Coll.
19. LD, letter to Tante, 5/29/1883, CS Coll. On Tante's personality, DM, *Music Is My Faith*, 202; CDM, *Born on a Sunday*, 4–6; Stebbins, *FD*, 106.
20. LD, letter to Tante, 5/30/1883, CS Coll. *Tante's Story*, 18, 31, 41, 43–44.
21. *St. Joseph Gazette*, 5/26/1883.
22. LD, letter to Tante, 5/30/1883, CS Coll. For the dishonest manager of the Academy of Music, Denver, see Stebbins, *FD*, 74.
23. LD, letter to Tante, 6/6/1883, CS Coll.
24. The program, NYPL, WD Coll., Cat. 16, Box 39. Also CDM, *Born on a Sunday*, 15.
25. Dec. 1, 1907: See (New York) *Symphony Society Bulletin*, vol. 1, no. 2. The program was entitled "The Family" and included Wagner's *Siegfried Idyll* and R. Strauss's *Sinfonia Domestica*. H. E. Krehbiel, in the *NY Tribune*, 12/2/1907, 7:4, thought LD's *Vorspiel* "was not impressive"; also *NY Evening Post*, 12/2/1907, 7:2, though the unnamed critic thought the idea of the program was ingenious and the Strauss work a great bore.
26. CDM, *Born on a Sunday*, 2.
27. EDS, *Reminiscences as told to HTV*, 6. NYPL has a large collection of LD's autograph scores. FD edited a collection of 57 songs with English translations by Mary L. Webster. *Collected Songs of Leopold Damrosch*.
28. The cantata *Sulamith* had the longest life. See opening of Chap. 15 and its note 2. The most accessible list of his compositions appears in *Grove's Dictionary of Music and Musicians*, 2nd ed., 1900.
29. Pratt, Waldo, ed., *St. Nicholas Songs* (New York: Century, 1885). San Antonio, see NYPL, WD Coll., Cat. 16, Box 39.
30. EDS, *Reminiscences as told to HTV*, 6.
31. Medina, *History of the Westhampton Yacht Squadron, 1890–1965*, 5, 19, 39, 102.
32. EDS, *O'mama's Story*, 6.
33. CDM, *Born on a Sunday*, 12.

Chapter 7

(*pages 73–79*)

1. For background, see Krehbiel, *Chapters of Opera*, 107–110, 115–117; WD, *My Musical Life*, 51–55; Finck, *My Adventures*, 194–197; Kolodin, *The Metropolitan Opera, 1883–1966*, 6–7; Rosenthal, ed., *The Mapleson Memoirs*, 238 (on Patti and rehearsals), 251 (on finish of Italian opera); Klein, *The Reign of Patti*, 211, 215.
2. Krehbiel, *Chapters of Opera*, 114–115.
3. LD, Notebook, NYPL, WD Coll., Cat. 16, Box 39. According to Kolodin, *Metropolitan Opera*, 90, LD kept the weekly average cost to $3400; "the loss for the year was about $40,000, hardly imposing when spread among seventy stockholders."
4. *NY Times*, 10/11/1884, 5:1.
5. *NY Times*, 11/11/1884, 2:5.
6. The artistic season: Krehbiel, *Chapters of Opera*, 127–133; Kolodin, *Metropolitan Opera*, 88–90. A publication of the Metropolitan Opera Association, *Sou-*

venir, reprints reviews of the season's operas from ten of the city's newspapers, NYPL. The newspapers are *Herald, Times, Tribune, World, Sun, Staats-Zeitung, Evening Post, Commercial Advertiser, Mail and Express* and *Evening Telegram.*

7. *Tante's Story,* 27; WD, *My Musical Life,* 56.
8. Brandt, letter to Marie von Heimburg (Tante), 2/14/1921; original in German, LOC, M-D Coll., Box 3; typescript in German, CS Coll.
9. *Tante's Story,* 27–28; CDM, *Born on a Sunday,* 12–13; EDS, *O'mama's Story,* 8.
10. Krehbiel, *Chapters of Opera,* 134; *NY Times,* 1885: 1/10, 4:7, and 1/11, 7:2.
11. Seltsam, *Metropolitan Opera Annals,* 12, quotes at length from the reviews by Krehbiel, *NY Tribune,* and W. J. Henderson, *NY Times. Souvenir;* see note 6 above. WD, *My Musical Life,* 55–56.
12. *NY Times,* 11/16/1884, 6:5, and 1/11/1885, 7:2.

Chapter 8

(pages 83–97)

1. *NY Herald,* 2/19/1885, 5:4. Also, e.g., Krehbiel, *Chapters of Opera,* 134–136 (probably the most accurate account of LD's illness and death); *Keynote,* 2/21 and 2/28/1885. See *Souvenir,* which reprinted many accounts of the life, death and funeral of LD, NYPL. For an example of the poems, one by Helen Chase, who later became a music critic for the *Brooklyn Eagle,* NYPL, WD Coll., Cat. 16, Box 39:

> Down from the space of reed and brass
> Rich-voiced viol and sweet toned flute
> Faltered the Leader that sorrowful night;
> The "harp of a thousand strings" was mute.

2. CDM, *Born on a Sunday,* 13.
3. EDS, *O'mama's Story,* 8.
4. *NY Times,* 2/16/1885, 1:7.
5. From an unpublished autobiography of Ida May Hill, 1859–1937, who married William J. Starr in 1886. She had been a student of piano and drama at the Cincinnati College of Music, under Theodore Thomas, and had studied piano in Germany with Clara Schumann. The manuscript is in the possession of her granddaughter Lisa Rudd.
6. In addition to the accounts listed in note 1, there are family sources: *Tante's Story,* 28–29; WD, *My Musical Life,* 57–58; CDM, *Born on a Sunday,* 13; EDS, *O'mama's Story,* 8. Also Stebbins, *FD,* 79–80, 85–87.
7. WD, letter to the editor, *NY Herald,* 2/20/1885, 5:5. For Morris Reno's stating that without question WD will succeed at LD's posts in OS of NY and SS of NY, see *Mail and Express,* 2/18/1885, 3:3, also *Souvenir.*
8. Reviews, 2/14/1885, in *Chicago Evening Journal* and *Inter-Ocean,* copies in NYPL, WD Coll., Cat. 9, Box 25. Eaton, *Opera Caravan,* 21–27. Stebbins, *FD,* 81–84. WD, *My Musical Life,* 58–60.
9. WD, *My Musical Life,* 60–61.
10. Stebbins, *FD,* 84–85. On the comparative salaries: The contracts, if written, have disappeared. These figures are taken from the Metropolitan's *Journal, Opera Accounts, 1884–91,* and checked against another journal recording cash disbursements. Both are in the Metropolitan's Archives. The figure of $10,000 for LD's salary, given earlier in the text, is taken from Stebbins, *FD,* 78.

Writing forty years ago, the authors may have had additional sources. It seems possible that the original agreement contemplated $10,000 for LD and a much smaller amount for an assistant conductor, whose post and salary, with WD as his assistant, he absorbed. Anton Seidl in 1888–89, for example, received only $7500 but his assistant, WD, received $2500. In LD's season, 1884–85, two singers received more than he: Materna, $19,875, and Schott, $15,400.

11. EDS, *O'mama's Story*, 8–9.
12. GM interview with Gertrude Schirmer Fay, the Reconciliation Baby.
13. *Tante's Story*, 30; Stebbins, *FD*, 84, published in 1945, while WD was still alive, puts it this way: "In a long talk Tuesday morning [the brothers in Chicago] planned the Damrosch future. Marie was twenty-one, and would be married at once to a young chemist; the father had sanctioned the engagement." But note that he had sanctioned only the engagement, not the marriage, and even the engagement was not announced publicly.
14. GM interview with Ida J. Wiechmann, the daughter-in-law. *Maid of Montauk* by Forest Monroe. Of Wiechmann's scientific works, his book *Sugar Analysis*, 1890, had at least three editions and for several decades was the leading treatise on the subject. See Bibliography for his other books. He worked as chief chemist for several sugar companies, staying longest (1887–1909) with Havemeyer and Elder, which later became the American Sugar Refining Company.
15. Marie Wiechmann, letter to DM, 12/19/1899, LOC, M-D Coll., Box 1.
16. GM interview with RSR; also with CS and Ida J. Wiechmann.
17. GM interview with Ida J. Wiechmann. Her son Richard had heard the story from his mother many years earlier.
18. Finck, *My Adventures*, 256.
19. WD, *My Musical Life*, 189–191. There is correspondence about the seasons 1906 and 1909 in NYPL, WD Coll., Cat. 20, Boxes 50 and 53.
20. EDS, *Reminiscences as told to HTV*, 4; EDS, *O'mama's Story*, 7, 9.
21. Stebbins, *FD*, 91.
22. Ibid., 21.
23. The program appears in Seltsam, *Metropolitan Annals*, 16, and Frank appears as Franz Damrosch. Seltsam lists FD as a conductor only for the season 1885–86, but the programs in the Metropolitan's Archives show that in 1889–90 he conducted five performances of the ballet *Puppenfee*, which followed the opera *Der Barbier von Bagdad*, and in 1890–91, after the same opera, four performances of the ballet *Dresden China*.
24. Wagner's gift to LD: WD, *My Musical Life*, 172, and WD, letter to Franz W. Beidler, 12/14/1936, NYPL, Cat. 3, Box 8; Rice, *Musical Reminiscences*, 39. On the concert performances: WD, *My Musical Life*, 171–174; *NY Times*, 3/5/1886, 5:2: WD, who conducted with "vigor and skill," deserved "the thanks of all lovers and students of music" for presenting the opera complete. WD, *My Musical Life*, 174, quotes in full Cosima Wagner's letter to him, 7/6/1903, setting out the excerpts that may be staged. The original, in English, is in LOC, D-B Coll., Box 10.
    For an example of Seidl's antipathy, see Welling, *As the Twig Is Bent*, 231, in which Seidl refuses to make a presentation to WD: "Me! You do not know what you ask. I could not possibly do this."
25. Stebbins, *FD*, 96–97: at the reception FD was seated next to R. Strauss. For a description of Liszt at the 1873 Sonderhausen Festival, see Fay, *Music-Study in Germany*, 253–262.
26. Stebbins, *FD*, 94, 103. For FD's small part in Herbert's victory celebration following the famous libel suit, see Waters, *Victor Herbert*, 226.

27. WD, *My Musical Life*, 74, 77. Von Bülow, letter to WD, 2/13/1887, a type-script in English of what presumably was handwritten in German, now lost, LOC, D-B Coll., Box 7.
28. WD, *My Musical Life*, 77: ". . . and was completely wrapped up in himself, and besides, he had, to my thinking, only one specialty, the Wagner music-dramas."
29. Ibid., 90, probably makes too much of AC's personal acquaintance with LD, for AC regretted that he had not known LD personally at the unveiling of the latter's memorial monument. See booklet, *A Record of the Sixteenth Season, 1888–89, of OS of NY*, Archives, OS of NY.
30. WD, *My Musical Life*, 81.
31. WD, letter to FD, 5/13/1887, LOC, D-B Coll., Box 1.
32. WD, letter to FD, 7/1/1887, LOC, D-B Coll., Box 1.
33. WD, *My Musical Life*, 79. See also WD letter to Frau M. von Bülow, 2/5/1926, NYPL, WD Coll., Cat. 17, Box 40: ". . . who during the three months I spent with him, influenced my entire musical life . . ."
34. WD, "Extracts from an Address on Beethoven and the Ninth Symphony"; delivered by WD, with illustrations at the piano, on 2/24/1914, NYPL, Cat. 17, Box 40.
35. WD, letter to FD, 8/5/1887, LOC, D-B Coll., Box 1.
36. Ibid.
37. WD, letter to FD, 8/9/1887, LOC, D-B Coll., Box 1.
38. A phrase constantly used by family members whether talking of artistic, financial or merely social events.
39. *NY Herald*, 3/6/1886, 5:3.
40. *NY Times*, 11/5/1887, 4:6.

Chapter 9

(*pages 98–107*)

1. On Mme. Mears, see EDS, *O'mama's Story*, 6–7; CDM, *Born on a Sunday*, 14–15. CDM, *History of Venice*, LOC, M-D Coll., Box 4.
2. *Tante's Story*, 28.
3. EDS, *Reminiscences as told to HTV*, 7.
4. EDS, *O'mama's Story*, 3.
5. Program in Damrosch Coll., Museum of the City of New York; Report of the chairman of the committee, 3/22/1889, NYPL, WD Coll., Cat. 16, Box 39; a booklet, *A Record of the Sixteenth Season, 1888–1889, of the OS of NY*, has an account of the ceremony, Archives, OS of NY; *NY Times*, 5/16/1888, 2:5.
6. *NY Times*, 7/17/1887, 9:1; 7/20/1887, 8:2; CDM, *Born on a Sunday*, 12; Stebbins, *FD*, 89; WD, letter to Franz W. Beidler, 5/28/1937, NYPL, WD Coll., Cat. 3, Box 8. Reportedly there were at least twelve autograph letters from Wagner, and as many each, or more, from Liszt, Carl Tausig, Peter Cornelius, von Bülow and others.
7. Starke, *Sidney Lanier*, 183, note 14.
8. Stebbins, *FD*, 99.
9. Song, *Her Answer*, dated "June, 1887," LOC, D-TV Coll., Box 2.
10. FD, letter to HMD, 5/22/1887, LOC, D-TV Coll., Box 2.
11. *NY Times*, 1/11/1888, 5:3.
12. Stebbins, *FD*, 99–103.
13. WD, *My Musical Life*, 95–96.
14. WD, letter to FD, 6/21/1888; in another letter to FD, same date, he expresses

astonishment that the orchestra had no idea of "unanimous bowing." Both letters, LOC, D-B Coll., Box 1. Bauer, *Harold Bauer, His Book,* 43.

15. WD, letter to FD, 7/4/1888, LOC, D-B Coll., Box 1.
16. WD, letter to FD, 8/4/1888, ibid. *SS of NY, Minutes of Proceedings of the Board,* 1/9/1884, NYPL.
17. Beale, ed., *Letters of Mrs. James G. Blaine,* vol. 2, 210, letter to son Walker, 7/10/1888.
18. EDS, *O'mama's Story,* 7.
19. CDM, *Born on a Sunday,* 17, 20; EDS, *O'mama's Story,* 9. On Prussian militarism, see Fay, *Music-Study in Germany,* 57, 81; on social customs, ibid., 81, 196.
20. CDM, *Born on a Sunday,* 17–22; see also Fay, *Music-Study in Germany,* 22.
21. EDS, *O'mama's Story,* 9–11.
22. Ibid., 10–11; *Tante's Story,* 30–32.
23. CDM, *Born on a Sunday,* 22; *Tante's Story,* 32: "The two girls received the news with tears in their eyes."
24. M. R. Werner, interview GM.
25. The story is told by many members of the family. MBD, letter to daughter Anita, 4/25/1927: "I have always thought I ought to look better all my life and have never quite forgiven God that I didn't." LOC, D-B Coll., Box 2.
26. Stebbins, *FD,* 112.
27. WD, *My Musical Life,* 101; also WD, letter to AC, 4/21/1909, NYPL, WD Coll., Cat. 2, Box 1. Harrison, *A Timeless Affair,* 62.
28. Beale, ed., *Letters of Mrs. James G. Blaine,* vol. 2, 284, letter to daughter Harriet, 11/16/1889.
29. *Tante's Story,* 34; WD, letter to S. T. Williamson, 4/15/1935, NYPL, WD Coll., Cat. 2, Box 4; *NY Times,* 5/18/1890, 1:3.

Chapter 10

(pages 108–120)

1. *Tante's Story,* 33.
2. GM interviews with Seymour family; also Tante's letter to MBD and "H" (Margaret's sister Harriet), 5/20/1928, LOC, D-B Coll., Box 2.
3. *Musical Courier,* 2/25/1891, 179.
4. *NY Tribune,* 2/21/1891, 7:2; agreeing with Krehbiel, *NY Times,* 2/21/1891, 4:6. Hauk, *Memories of a Singer,* 250–254, after protesting her innocence in a long, improbable story, lays the blame on WD, "a nonchalant conductor."
5. WD thought "the German opera crumbled to dust as a natural result of his [Stanton's] curious ignorance and incompetency in matters operatic"; WD, *My Musical Life,* 62. For an interesting fictional account, based on factual research, of Stanton and the crumbling to dust, see Louis Auchincloss' short story "The Wagnerians," in *Tales of Manhattan* (Boston: Houghton Mifflin, 1967).
6. *Musical Courier,* 2/11/1891, 124.
7. In PML. The meeting the next day, 3/23/1889, was a joint meeting of the boards of the OS of NY and the SS of NY at AC's house, 5 West 51st Street. Its chief purpose was to hear a report on the progress of the new music hall.
8. A hall "suitable for uses of the Society" was discussed at a meeting of the board of directors of the Symphony Society, 1/9/1884. Besides Leopold Damrosch, those present were Morris Reno, Stephen M. Knevals, E. Francis Hyde, Hilborne L. Roosevelt, C. C. Beaman and John Crosby Brown, *SS of NY, Minutes of Proceedings,* NYPL.

9. Rice, *Musical Reminiscences,* 115. In Tuthill's pamphlet, *Practical Acoustics,* on p. 23, with three diagrams of Carnegie Hall, he stresses this point: "Particular reference is to be made in the figure to the curved shapes of the ceiling over the stage end of the hall and hence to its purpose and value as a reflecting and acoustic device . . . The value of the ceiling profiles will be appreciated on very little study . . . The importance of the outer ceiling in front of the stage is most apparent."

10. *Musical Courier,* 2/25/1891, 180.

11. Ibid., 3/4/1891, 204, quoting *NY World,* 2/28/1891, 2:5.

12. *NY World,* 5/7/1891, 4:2.

13. *NY Times,* 5/10/1891, 5:3. See also *NY Tribune,* 5/6/1891, 1:4.

14. For an account of the Blumenberg libel suit, see Waters, *Victor Herbert,* 216–226. At Herbert's celebration party following the court's decision WD was toastmaster and FD spoke. For Finck's attitude toward criticism, see his *My Adventures,* 181–182, 188, 252–256; Shanet, *Philharmonic,* 230, 447 note 152; also this book, Chap. 22, note 34.

15. Finck, *My Adventures,* 256.

16. Mueller, *The American Symphony Orchestra,* 72.

17. E. Francis Hyde was president of the N.Y. Philharmonic Society from 1888 to 1901. But probably he was included here by Reno for his work throughout the 1880s for the Symphony Society of NY. For much of that decade he served on its executive committee and even when president of the Philharmonic he continued to work for the NY Symphony. At this time he was still on its board of directors. In addition, he was also a strong support of the London Philharmonic Society!

18. *The Diaries of Tchaikovsky,* ed. and trans. by Lakond, 229. See note 19.

19. Newmarch, *The Life and Letters of . . . Tchaikovsky,* 635. All of the Tchaikovsky quotations that follow are from Newmarch. As the chronology of his entries is clear in her editing, I have omitted the citations here.

20. WD, letter to AC, 4/21/1909, NYPL, WD Coll., Cat. 2, Box 5: "You who twenty years ago helped me to bear the burden of supporting my father's family . . ."

21. AC, *Autobiography,* 52.

22. WD, *My Musical Life,* 143.

23. Ibid.

24. *NY World,* 5/7/1891, 4:2; *NY Times,* 5/7/1891, 4:2.

25. WD, *My Musical Life,* 94.

26. The back cover of the program for the inaugural Music Festival announces: "Besides the principal Auditorium, 'Music Hall' comprises Recital Hall, Chamber Music Hall, Large and Small Banquet Halls and Meeting Rooms with Parlours, suitable for Lectures, Readings and Receptions, as well as Chapter and Lodge Rooms, for Secret Organizations"; Newark Public Library, Art and Music Department. The best description of the hall with many architectural drawings is a book, *Music Hall, 57th Street and 7th Avenue,* apparently prepared with Tuthill's help for the opening. But only one copy was found, in the Archives, OS of NY.

Chapter 11

(pages 121–135)

1. Stebbins, *FD,* 116–132.

2. FD, letter to HMD, 7/23/91, Coll. of Douglas S. Damrosch. This collection

includes three long letters on Bayreuth 1891: 7/20 on *Parsifal*, 7/21 on *Tristan* and FD's visit to Wahnfried, and 7/23 on *Tannhäuser*.

3. Ibid.

4. Ibid.

5. Rice, *Musical Reminiscences*, 117–118. Anna (Mrs. Adolph) Brodsky, *Recollections of a Russian Home*, 178–202; see note 19 below.

6. WD, *My Musical Life*, 146–149. HMD, handwritten note to her grandchildren, LOC, D-TV, Box 1, tells of a dinner for Paderewski, after which everyone danced to Strauss waltzes played four-hand by Paderewski and Marcella Sembrich. Erskine, *My Life in Music*, 104. Schonberg, *The Great Pianists*, 284–291.

7. WD, letter to MBD, 5/22/1892, LOC, D-B Coll., Box 1.

8. WD, poem "To Margaret," 8/15/1892, ibid.

9. WD, letter to MBD, 5/18/1892, ibid.

10. WD, letter to MBD, Friday (summer 1892), ibid.

11. FD, *An Autobiographical Sketch*, typescript, LOC, D-TV Coll., Box 1.

12. A copy is in NYPL; also, Stebbins, *FD*, 140. A summary, "How We Began," *Harmony*, vol. 5, no. 5, Sept. 1899. "FD, A Biographical Sketch," *Musical Times*, 12/1/1904, 782–787.

13. Accounts of this first session appear in *Harper's Weekly*, "People's Singing Classes," 11/5/1892, 1074–1075, by a reporter who was present, John Gilmer Speed; in Crowthers, "FD, His Life," as FD in that year remembered it; and in Stebbins, *FD*, 142–143. The authors talked to people who had been there.

14. AC, letter to FD, 11/25/1892, LOC, D-TV Coll., Box 3. Cooper Union was delighted to house the classes, see two letters of Abram S. Hewitt, its secretary, to FD, 12/5/1894 and 2/10/1900, LOC, D-TV Coll., Box 3. In the earlier letter Hewitt stated: "I do not see how it would be possible to do anything better for the public . . . [which] I congratulate . . . upon your spirit of self-sacrifice."

15. Stebbins, *FD*, 146–147.

16. *Tante's Story*, 34.

17. EDS, *O'mama's Story*, 11–12; *Tante's Story*, 34, and *NY Times*, 11/2/1893, 4:6. Also, GM interviews with Seymour children.

18. CDM, *Born on a Sunday*, 28.

19. WD, *My Musical Life*, does not recount the incident. DM, *Music Is My Faith*, 117–119. It may be followed in the *NY Times* 1893: 12/15, 3:4; 12/17, 9:7; 12/18, 4:7; 12/19, 8:1; 12/23, 12:1. Unless otherwise stated quotations are from the *Times*.

20. Brodsky, *Recollections of a Russian Home*, 197–202, argues that WD won, that he forced the confrontation in order to be able to renegotiate contracts with the orchestra. It seems unlikely.

Brodsky perhaps was typical of many excellent musicians who did not find the United States to their liking. To judge from his wife's account, he enjoyed only those aspects that were most European; the rough and tumble of musical life here was dismaying. He refused, for example, to play in the orchestra's summer concerts at Madison Square Garden because he felt the popular repertory was beneath him. The orchestra's need to sustain itself, to make money, was not his concern. Conversely, David Mannes, a violinist in the orchestra of American birth and training, saw the refusal not as a blow struck for good music, but against it. (DM, *Music Is My Faith*, 107.) There was a kind of musical temperament that found the American scene appalling.

21. See Mueller, *The American Symphony Orchestra*, 341; Bauer, *Harold Bauer, His*

Book, 258, on the cancellation of Ravel's Piano Concerto in G because the local union in Washington, D.C., would not allow a sufficiently skilled harpist to be imported from New York.

22. *NY Times,* 12/19/1893, 8:1.

23. *MAS of NY, Minutes of Meetings, 1893–1917,* NYPL. Stebbins, *FD,* 151, 158–159.

24. *MAS of NY, Programs,* NYPL.

25. FD, letter to HMD, 7/23/1891, Coll. of Douglas S. Damrosch.

26. This is a truth so pervasive that it is difficult to demonstrate by pointing to single facts or opinions. But see Shanet, *Philharmonic,* 108, 294, for a summary of the importance of women in the orchestra's history, and 215 for an example of their power. Kolodin, *Metropolitan Opera,* 386, 523–524, underestimates the role of Mrs. August Belmont and her colleagues in preserving the company, 1935–55, and for a slight corrective see Erskine, *My Life in Music,* 232, 237, where he grows angry over the power, energy and initiative of the women. For the opinion of two artists active in the period 1880–1940, see Bispham, *A Quaker Singer's Recollections,* 315, and Bauer, *Harold Bauer, His Book,* 168. And for praise of a musician's wife, Mrs. Wilhelm Gericke, see Stokowski, *An American Musician's Story,* 88; on Mrs. Gustav Mahler, see Shanet, *Philharmonic,* 217; or consider the support given the three Damrosch men by their wives. Women also had an important role through the music schools they founded. Among the better known were the Hershey School of Musical Art in Chicago and the National Conservatory of Music in New York. Still existing are the Cincinnati Conservatory of Music (today, the College-Conservatory of Music, University of Cincinnati), the Manhattan School of Music and the Diller-Quaile School of Music. See Ammer, *Unsung,* 224–228. And Clara Damrosch Mannes, with her husband, founded the Mannes College of Music, New York.

27. *MAS of NY, Programs,* NYPL.

Chapter 12

(pages 136–143)

1. *Tante's Story,* 36. CDM, *Born on a Sunday,* unnumbered page headed "David and I."

2. CDM, *Born on a Sunday,* 23, and third page of unnumbered insert "David and I."

3. For some evidence of the difficulties of a career in chamber music even for women violinists, see Ammer, *Unsung,* 27–40.

4. DM, *Music Is My Faith,* 121.

5. Material on the Mannes family is chiefly from DM, *Music Is My Faith,* and interviews with DM's daughter Marya Mannes and with Clair Seymour, who for several years in his widowhood ran his house for him. DM's only known surviving Mannes relative, a daughter of his brother Owen, refused to talk about the family.

6. DM, letter to CDM, 9/26/1919, LOC, M-D Coll., Box 1.

7. DM, *Music Is My Faith,* 22.

8. Ibid., 268.

9. Ibid., 29–30.

10. Ibid., 37. There is conflict over Douglas' first name, John or Charles. I have followed DM's autobiography.

11. Ibid., 49. According to MM, who helped her father with his autobiography,

this event was omitted as too rough for the time, 1938, and this line was transferred to the stabbing story.

12. EDS, *Reminiscences as told to HTV*, 5: LD became depressed "especially when one of his compositions was not well received." WD, "Listening Backward," states that his father's black moods "often lasted several days."
13. DM, *Music Is My Faith*, 88.
14. Ibid., 93–95.
15. Ibid., 102–103.
16. Ibid., 120–123.

Chapter 13

(pages 144–151)

1. *NY Times*, 2/18/1894, 16:1, unfavorable but acknowledges that the audience was pleased; also Krehbiel, *Chapters of Opera*, 274. *NY Times*, 3/28/1894, 4:7, highly favorable.
2. WD, *My Musical Life*, 107–108; Krehbiel, *Chapters of Opera*, 254–255.
3. WD, *My Musical Life*, 113.
4. WD, draft of letter to *NY Herald Tribune*, 11/17/1941, NYPL, WD Coll., Cat. 9, Box 25.
5. Krehbiel, *Chapters of Opera*, 256; WD, *My Musical Life*, 365. WD described his purpose in "New York's German Opera Season."
6. Krehbiel, *Chapters of Opera*, 256.
7. WD, *My Musical Life*, 111.
8. *NY Times*, 3/21/1895, 4:7.
9. WD, *My Musical Life*, 113.
10. *NY Times*, 2/16/1896, 12:1. This Sunday issue of the *Times* carried four stories on the Metropolitan and Damrosch companies, all to the latter's favor: 4:7, 11:1, and 11:2. Krehbiel, *Chapters of Opera*, 258.
11. E. Irenaeus Stevenson, "Mr. Damrosch's Latest Opera Season." See also Huneker, *Steeplejack*, 36.
12. WD, *My Musical Life*, 118–121.
13. WD, letter to MBD, 8/11/1892, LOC, D-B Coll., Box 1.
14. HD, letter to MBD, 2/12/1896, ibid. Krehbiel, *Chapters of Opera*, 261–263.
15. There are two accounts of this incident: WD, *My Musical Life*, 115; and Bispham, *A Quaker Singer's Recollections*, 222–223. WD says the letter **A** was sent by Mrs. John L. Gardner, a patron of Boston society. I have followed Bispham, for such ignorance or malice on the part of Mrs. Gardner, an intelligent, gracious woman and founder of the Gardner Museum, Boston, seems absolutely incredible, but either quality seems entirely possible in an opera crew. Further, Bispham's account, published 1920, is the earlier and cites WD as its source.
16. WD, *My Musical Life*, 121–122; Krehbiel, *Chapters of Opera*, 259.
17. WD, *My Musical Life*, 121.
18. Bispham, *A Quaker Singer's Recollections*, 220.
19. *NY Times*, 4/9/1898, 7:2.
20. WD, *My Musical Life*, 124–127; see also Rosenthal, ed., *The Mapleson Memoirs*, almost any page.
21. WD, *My Musical Life*, 128.

Chapter 14

(*pages 152–163*)

1. The bulletin was published in the first issue of *Harmony*, vol. 1, no. 1, 10/20/1894. All issues of *Harmony* cited in this chapter are in NYPL.
2. *Harmony*, vol. 1, no. 2, February 1895.
3. Stebbins, *FD*, 173.
4. Ibid., 73, 150, 191.
5. *Harmony*, vol. 1, no. 7, July 1895.
6. Ibid., vol. 1, no. 8, August 1895.
7. Ibid., vol. 2, nos. 5 and 7, June and September 1896.
8. Also often sung in *Judas Maccabeus*.
9. *Harmony*, vol. 4, no. 4, June 1898, editorial. The journal quotes at length critics' reviews of the various concerts.
10. Ibid., vol. 2, no. 12, Feb. 1897; vol. 3, no. 1, March 1897; vol. 3, no. 3, May 1897.
11. Stebbins, *FD*, 147, 243; Joseph Mosenthal's death, 1/6/1896, was reported sympathetically in *Harmony*, vol. 1, no. 12, January 1896; the activities of Herman Mosenthal, in the same issue and also in vol. 1, no. 4, 1895; and in almost every issue there would be an affectionate anecdote about FD.
12. *Harmony*, vol. 3, no. 4, June 1897.
13. The concert was September 20; besides the PCU chorus, the Seventh Regiment Band played. See *Harmony*, vol. 2, no. 8, October 1896, with quotations from reviews in the *NY Tribune, Herald* and *Times*.
14. Barnhart's obituary, *NY Times*, 9/5/1948, 41:1. For the end of the PCU, see Chap. 22, note 2.
15. Letter of Vivian Holcombe, Marjorie's daughter, to GM. A letter of Marjorie's mother to DM, 12/19/1899, shows that by then Marjorie, born 9/29/1886, had accomplished the change, LOC, M-D Coll., Box 1.
16. DM, *Music Is My Faith,* 131. The portrait was inherited by CDM, but on the breakup of the Mannes apartment, following the death of DM, 4/24/1959, it seems to have disappeared. It presumably is the one described by CDM, *Born on a Sunday,* 7, and painted by a Mr. Gross of Brooklyn, father of one of LD's piano pupils.
17. The first volume of the New York Social Register appeared in 1888 and listed about 2000 families.
18. FD, Response at Testimonial Dinner, 1/16/1926, LOC, D-TV Coll., Box 4; Stebbins, *FD*, 195.
19. CDM, *Born on a Sunday,* 3.
20. Tante taught German at Spence from 1897 to 1906. FD also taught music there from an uncertain date until 1904, the year he became supervisor of music in the New York public schools. GM correspondence with the Spence School. WD and MBD sent all four daughters to the school.
21. CDM, *Born on a Sunday,* 6.
22. GM interview with Gertrude Schirmer Fay.
23. *Tante's Story,* 36; CDM, *Born on a Sunday,* unnumbered page in section entitled ". . . absorption of music"; DM, *Music Is My Faith,* 133–134.
24. CDM, *Born on a Sunday,* unpaginated section, "Pleasant and unpleasant incidents abroad."
25. Ibid., unpaginated section, "David and I."
26. DM, *Music Is My Faith,* 142–143.
27. CDM, *Born on a Sunday,* see note 24 above.

28. DM, *Music Is My Faith*, 146; *Tante's Story*, 37.
29. DM, *Music Is My Faith*, 147–148; *Tante's Story*, 37–38.

Chapter 15

(*pages 164–172*)

1. OS of NY, *Book of the Festival*, Apr. *12–16, 1898*. The booklet, besides containing many facts and figures, has articles on LD, on the OS of NY and on LD's *Sulamith* (by H. E. Krehbiel). NYPL.
2. *NY Times*, 4/13/1898, 7:3. In reviewing the performance at Carnegie Hall's inaugural festival, a *Times* critic wrote, 5/9/1891, 4:6, "The cantata is written in a mellifluous, sentimental style, which is quite appropriate to the words." For discussion of LD's compositions, see Chap. 6.
3. On Helene's retirement: She is listed in the festival booklet as an active member of the society, and on her death her family issued an "In Memoriam" card, stating that she had taken "an active part" in the society "until 1898," i.e., the start of the 1898–99 season. The card is in the FD Scrapbooks, vol. 3, on microfilm at NYPL, Reel 8; originals in LOC.
4. *NY Times*, 4/14/1898, 9:2.
5. *NY Times*, 12/4/1898, 6:2. A program for the concert on 2/6/1900 is in the Archives, OS of NY.
6. *Musical Courier*, 12/7/1898, an unpaginated edition, toward the rear of the second section.
7. Bispham, in *A Quaker Singer's Recollections*, tells many anecdotes about the song: singing it before Kipling, before Teddy Roosevelt in the Executive Mansion in Albany and in the White House in Washington. His recording of it, made about 1906, was included in a collection of American art songs, 1900–40, selected and annotated by Philip L. Miller: *When I Have Sung My Songs*, New World Records #247. Leonard Warren made a recording of it in 1958, *Rolling Down to Rio*, RCA Victor LM 2206.
8. *Musical Courier*, 4/26/1899, 18. *NY Times*, 4/22/1899, 8:7.
9. *NY Sun*, 1/21/1900 (second section), 3:6, under the headline WAGNER FOR YOUNG WOMEN. For one young man who never "enjoyed anything of the kind as much," see *J. P. Morgan, Jr., 1867–1943* (Charlottesville: University of Virginia Press, 1981), 25.
10. GM interview with Gertrude Schirmer Fay. The opera's American première, at Oscar Hammerstein's Manhattan Opera House, was 2/19/1908. Since Gustave Schirmer died on 7/15/1907, the lecture-recital probably was in the 1906–07 season. A program for a *Pelléas* lecture-recital, 12/10/1907, at the Lyceum Theatre, New York, is in the Museum of the City of New York, Damrosch Coll.
11. WD, letter to MBD, 10/27/1901, LOC, D-B Coll., Box 1:

> We had a tragedy at the matinee. That poor dilapidated little butterfly Mme. Sanderson drank a glass of champagne before singing Manon and during the first act was so drunk that she did not sing a note but tottered about aimlessly, smiling inanely. At the conclusion of the Act, Flon [the conductor] told her she would not continue — hysterics, etc. etc., and Seygard finished the opera bravely. Of course everybody in an uproar and Eames bravely standing by Sanderson and insisting that it was an illness and not drunkness. Eames is very nice . . .

12. The facts about the Philharmonic in this and following paragraphs are taken chiefly from Shanet, *Philharmonic*. The orchestra's problems at the time ap-

parently were not widely known and seldom as well reported as in *Theatre*, July 1902, "Walter Damrosch and the Philharmonic," by Emily Grant von Tetzel. This article also in NYPL-Theater Division, Robinson Locke Collection Scrapbook, vol. 144, *WD*.

13. WD, *My Musical Life*, 206.
14. Finck, *My Adventures*, 319, 322. Finck, careless of fact, states that Grau died in office at the Metropolitan. But he retired and did not die until 3/14/1907, in Paris.
15. Kolodin, *Metropolitan Opera*, 10, 156, 159, 164; Morgenthau, *All in a Life-Time*, 99–105; Birmingham, *Our Crowd*, 306–307, quoting articles in the *NY Herald*.
16. *NY Times*, 3/1/1903, 7:5.
17. *NY Times*, 4/12/1903, 25:6.
18. AC, letter to WD, 6/19/1902, LOC, D-B Coll., Box 7.

Chapter 16

(pages 173–182)

1. GM interviews with the four Seymour children.
2. GM interview with LDS.
3. Stebbins, *FD*, 179; "FD, A Biographical Sketch."
4. *NY Times*, 10/16/1898, 16:2: *Notes of Conversation with Mr. FD on Monday, Oct. 4, 1915*, NYPL, WD Coll., Cat. 5, Box 14; Stebbins, *FD*, 181, 196–197; "FD, A Biographical Sketch."
5. WD, *My Musical Life*, 327–328, claims that he created the concept in 1891; makes the same claim in a letter to the *NY Times*, 3/16/1928, NYPL, WD Coll., Cat. 17, Box 40; and either he or an admirer repeats the claim in *Symphony Society Bulletin*, 10/23/1922. For the original advertisement of WD's series, see *NY Times*, 12/6/1891, 7:6. In later life WD became rather expansive about his accomplishments, tending· to add to his own those of others: e.g., that he was responsible for bringing Victor Herbert to the United States; see LOC, Recorded Sound Section, Reel 61, Side A, from a radio broadcast on his eightieth birthday.
6. GM interview with Robert D. Brewster. Margaret Davies, "Sir Robert Mayer at 100," *Illustrated London News*, June 1979.
7. The history of this project is most easily followed in *Harmony*, 2/1896, 12/1899, 1/1900, 4/1900, 5/1903, 5/1904; and Stebbins, *FD*, 187–189.
8. *NY Tribune*, 4/21/1900, 6:6.
9. *Musical Courier*, 4/25/1900, 18.
10. Ibid., 5/9/1900, 18; and again, 5/30/1900, 18; and 6/6/1900, 20.
11. DM, *Music Is My Faith*, 19–20, 108, 124, 147, 151, 153.
12. Ibid., 125–126.
13. CDM, *Born on a Sunday*, unpaginated section titled "David and I."
14. GM interviews with CS and Barbara Levy.
15. CDM, *Born on a Sunday*, unpaginated section on Leopold; Stebbins, *FD*, 195; DM, *Music Is My Faith*, 173.
16. DM, *Music Is My Faith*, 147.
17. CDM, *Born on a Sunday*, unpaginated section on Leopold.
18. GM interview with Mary Bancroft, to whom CDM repeated the remark, ascribing it to Ysaÿe.
19. *Tante's Story*, 38.

20. *NY Times,* 10/20/1904, 7:5 (news item) and 7:7 (death notice); *Musical Courier,*
    11/23/1904, 28.
21. *NY Times,* 3/16/1877, 5:2; and 12/2/1904, 6:1; the latter also in Aldrich, *Concert
    Life,* 83.
22. MM, *Message from a Stranger,* 245–246.
23. Typical of families! Someone clipped the story without noting the date and
    paper. Clipping is in the Museum of the City of New York, Damrosch Col-
    lection. It is quoted in Stebbins, *FD,* 211. Because it appears in Stebbins and
    because the museum's collection was the gift of HTV, it almost certainly was
    cut by FD or HMD.

Chapter 17

(pages 185–200)

1. WD, *My Musical Life,* 210–211. See also WD, letter to HHF, 12/23/1902,
   welcoming him to Philharmonic affairs: polite, perfunctory, between strangers;
   in PML.
2. See *Musical America,* 1/4/1908, 3, "New York's Permanent Orchestra and the
   Men Who Made It Possible"; WD, *My Musical Life,* 210–212, 215. On Seligman family, see Chap. 10, note 7; also WD, letter to Henry Seligman,
   4/10/1918, on financial problems of OS of NY, NYPL, WD Coll., Cat. 13,
   Box 34.
3. AC, letter to MBD, 1/12/1910, LOC, D-B Coll., Box 7, in which he sends
   $5000 as a birthday present on occasion of WD's 25th anniversary as a con-
   ductor. Although this sounds like a gift for a special occasion — and WD at
   the anniversary dinner donated the check to the Symphony's pension fund —
   other references in WD's letters to AC's generosity over the years suggest
   that there were many such gifts, though perhaps first of smaller amounts.
   See WD, letter to AC, 4/12/1909, NYPL, WD Coll., Cat. 2, Box 5. Donation
   of gift, ibid., Cat. 1, Box 1.
       WD's son-in-law Thomas Finletter once estimated to a family friend, M. R.
   Werner, that AC, in gifts to WD personally and to WD's organizations, had
   contributed to WD's life and career about $1 million; M. R. Werner, inter-
   view GM.
       To give some perspective to a gift of $5000 a year: WD's salary as conduc-
   tor of the Symphony for the season 1914–15, Oct. 1 through May 15, was
   $25,000 for all concerts, with travel expenses extra. See HHF, letter to WD,
   5/15/1914, NYPL, WD Coll., Cat. 11, Box 28.
       According to Gilbert Harrison, biographer of Anita McCormick Blaine,
   she set up a trust fund for her sister-in-law MBD. Harrison, telephone interview GM. The fund was well managed by MBD, who increased it, according to Felicia Geffen, WD's secretary in his later years. Interview GM. Perhaps the original capital gift was $100,000, the amount of a trust Anita set up
   for MBD's sister Harriet; see Harrison, *A Timeless Affair,* 135–136, where he
   also gives an example of how Anita give MBD a gift of $875. Anita, widow
   of Emmons Blaine, never remarried and had a lifelong affection for her sis-
   ters-in-law and for WD. The fourth daughter of WD and MBD was named
   after her Aunt Anita.
       HHF, letters to WD, in PML, show that he, too, made large cash gifts of
   unspecified amounts to WD personally. These began as early as 1937 and
   seem to have continued regularly, twice a year, until WD's death, in 1950.
   Apparently the average annual amount was $15,000. See letter of Felicia Gef-

fen to WD, 6/14/1944, LOC, D-B Coll., Box 6: "Later in July you receive the Carnegie check of $2500, and Mr. Flagler's check of $7500."

HHF probably gave the New York Symphony in the years 1903–1928 roughly $2.5 million. In Boston H. L. Higginson, from 1881 to 1917, probably gave the Boston Symphony roughly $2.3 million.

4. *NY Times*, 8/6/1903, 7:3.

5. *NY Times*, 11/7/1904, 9:3. Though unsigned, the review presumably is by Richard Aldrich. He succeeded William J. Henderson, who on 9/21/1902 had shifted to the *NY Sun*.

6. *Symphony Society Bulletin*, vol. 1, no. 4 (1907), "The Sunday Concert Matter"; *Musical America*, 12/21/1907. Welling, letter to WD, 6/15/1911, returned with WD's comment, NYPL, WD Coll., Cat. 5, Box 14. See also *NY Times*, 11/23/1903, 7:1, reviewing first Sunday afternoon concert; WD, *My Musical Life*, 187–188.

7. WD, letter to Walter Neumann, 3/29/1907, NYPL, WD Coll., Cat. 20, Box 53. *Musical America*, 10/12/1907. WD, letter to HHF, 3/26/1916, PML. See also WD, letters to HHF, 3/10/1908 and 4/27/1912, PML. He played at Ravinia from 1905 through 1910, see NYPL, WD Coll., Cat. 20, Box 50; at Willow Grove, 1897 through 1907, ibid., Cat. 5, Box 13, and 1897 program in Damrosch Coll., Museum of the City of New York; and for some correspondence on Louisville, NYPL, WD Coll., Cat. 20, Box 53.

8. WD, letter to Caesar Addimando, 5/14/1906, and other examples, NYPL, WD Coll., Cat. 3, Box 8.

9. *NY Times*, 11/23/1903, 7:1, in which the critic reported of the orchestra, reviewing its first concert, "[The] strings have muscularity but little sensuous charm; the brasses are sometimes rude, and the woodwinds — alas the woodwinds showed the inevitable tendency to play out of tune."

10. WD, *Eulogy for Barrère*, 12/4/1944, NYPL, WD Coll., Cat. 3, Box 6. Other material on Barrère and the union, ibid., Cat. 13, Box 33.

11. *NY Times*, 5/21/1905, 2:2 and 6/1/1905, 20:3. WD, *My Musical Life*, 212–214. The wrangle continues: for other cases and angry correspondence between WD and Joseph N. Weber, president of American Federation of Musicians, see NYPL, WD Coll., Cat. 13, Box 33.

12. Poughkeepsie: NYPL, WD Coll., Cat. 20, Boxes 51 and 52.

13. Hartford: Ibid., Box 52; Montclair, ibid., Boxes 51 and 52.

14. Engles: Ibid., Cat. 3, Box 7, also Cat. 18, Box 46.

15. *Chicago Examiner*, 1/7/1906, by Millar Ular, in NYPL-Theater Division, Robinson Locke Collection Scrapbook, vol. 144, *WD*.

16. *NY Times*, 11/1/1908, Part 6, 7:1–7. On Beethoven cycles, see notes 17 and 18 below.

Eugene Onegin: WD admired the opera greatly and tried hard to make it available and known throughout the country. He gave the American première on 2/1/1908, in concert in Carnegie Hall, in English; took excerpts on tour, and urged Schirmer to publish a vocal score or at least the choruses in translation. But he failed to stir interest, though his efforts may have influenced the Metropolitan to present the opera on 3/24/1920, in Italian, with Claudia Muzio and Giovanni Martinelli, conducted by Artur Bodanzky. After seven performances the production was dropped. In the 1960s and 1970s at the Metropolitan, however, the opera became popular. NYPL, WD Coll., Cat. 5, Box 14 (correspondence with Moscow publisher); Cat. 13, Box 31 (letter to Schirmer); Cat. 15, Box 38 (letter of H. E. Krehbiel to WD declining to do translation). Review of première, *NY Times*, 2/2/1908, 9:3; also in

Aldrich, *Concert Life*, 210.

Mahler concerts: They were on 11/29, 12/8 and 12/13/1908. At the second, Mahler conducted the American première of his Symphony No. 2. *Symphony Society Bulletin*, vol. 2, no. 3, Special Mahler Number.

While in New York, Mahler and his wife, Alma, apparently became friends with Frank and Hetty Damrosch. According to Hetty, writing for her grandchildren, "Gustav Mahler was very fond of Grandpapa and came to our house frequently. He was a very strange sort of genius, but with Grandpapa he was always simple and charming." Frau Mahler thought "Grandpapa was the only good dancer in America." LOC, D-TV Coll., Box 1.

There is also, ibid., Box 3, an undated letter from Mahler, in New York, to his "friend" (presumably FD) in which he states that he pays no attention to critics, does not gossip, has no misunderstanding with the excellent orchestra, is uncertain whether he can attend the recipient's concert, but would like to go to the choir rehearsal and would be grateful if he could be picked up at his hotel so that they can arrive together.

For WD and Mahler, see WD, *My Musical Life*, 354–355; also correspondence, NYPL, WD Coll., Cat. 6, Box 18, and contract, ibid., Cat. 7, Box 20. On touring with Mahler, Olga Samaroff Stokowski, *An American Musician's Story*, 158–163.

17. *Musical Courier*, 4/8/1908. *NY Times*, 4/6/1908, 7:4; and also favorable, e.g., *NY Telegraph*, 4/6/1908 and *Musical America*, 4/11/1908.

18. For von Bülow, see WD, *My Musical Life*, 216–217 (he forgets the 1908 cycle). Pause between slow movement and finale: according to *NY Tribune*, 3/17/1909, Weingartner had done this with the Philharmonic some five years earlier. Aldrich in *NY Times*, 3/17/1909, 18:2, and also in *Concert Life*, 254, thought the program interesting and well performed. The *NY Telegraph*, 3/17/1909, was enthusiastic and wanted the cycle repeated. The next year Mahler, in his first season with the Philharmonic, 1909–10, gave a Beethoven cycle and was criticized severely for tampering with Beethoven's orchestration; see Shanet, *Philharmonic*, 213.

On the multiple singers for the vocal quartet: Taylor, *Music to My Ears*, 170, states: "I must say that the florid counterpoint of that passage emerged with more clarity and distinctness than I've ever heard before or since."

19. *NY Times*, 11/1/1908, Part 6, 7:1–7.

20. Shanet, *Philharmonic*, 192–195, 202–204, 207–220; Aldrich, *Concert Life*, 6, 24, 245.

21. *Boston Evening Transcript*, 11/17/1915, 22:1 and 2, signed H.T.P., and in length and detail a major appraisal.

With critics, of course, it depends a bit on whom you read. It is always possible to find someone to make a point. A better test of an orchestra, perhaps, than reviews of its performances is the caliber of artists who continually play with it, for the best artists, after a while, will cut out the inferior orchestras. By this test, too, the New York Symphony in the years 1905–25 was one of the best. Rather than a list of names, here are four examples of how artists felt about WD and the orchestra. The flutist Barrère, who could have had the first desk in any orchestra he chose, remained with the New York Symphony from 1905 to 1928. The pianist Josef Hofmann, who had played with it often in New York and on tour, asked Damrosch to make the opening remarks at a concert celebrating the fiftieth anniversary of his American debut, 11/29/1887. (For excerpts of WD's remarks, see NYPL, WD Coll., Cat. 3, Box 7.) The violinist Mischa Elman, on completing a tour, wrote a long letter about "the beautiful playing of the orchestra, which is due so much to the conductor . . . Wonderful, wonderful." LOC, D-B Coll., Box 7. And the pianist Harold Bauer, touching on an attribute of greatness in a conductor, his ability to "bring along" artists, wrote in a letter to WD, 12/25/1926:

> I want you to know that I, for one, look back upon my associations with you and your orchestra as among the most fortunate and the most important events of my life. Long ago, when I came only every other year to tour in this country, I used to wait with anxiety and impatience to learn from my manager whether or not I was to play under your direction, and when the news finally arrived, as it did without a single exception, that you had once again invited me, it gave me a feeling of confidence and encouragement that nothing either before or since has ever equalled. You have seemed to represent a kind of constant factor in my career and to play at your concerts has been something which included my highest aspirations, a measure of such worth as I might possess and a periodical stamp of approval — *all three* of these! I can never forget this and I shall be deeply and *most selfishly* grateful to you for all you have done for me, as long as I live.

NYPL, WD Coll., Cat. 3, Box 6. On this point see also Spalding, *Rise to Follow*, 92–98.

For a conductor's thanks to WD, Albert Coates, letter to WD, 1/2/1921, ibid., Cat. 6, Box 18; and for WD's care in Bruno Walter's programs in the latter's first season in New York, see WD, letter to Bruno Walter, 10/7/1922, ibid., Cat. 6, Box 19.

22. MBD, letter to ADK, 1/26/1918, LOC, D-B Coll., Box 2.
23. Welling, *As the Twig Is Bent*, 106; Erskine, *My Life in Music*, 67–69.
24. GM interview with M. R. Werner, journalist and free-lance writer.
25. Welling, *As the Twig Is Bent*, 230.
26. WD, letter to MBD, undated but clearly between 4/17 and 4/23/1909, LOC, D-B Coll., Box 1. Also WD, letters to MBD, 4/17 and 4/23/1909, ibid. Shanet, *Philharmonic*, 211.
27. WD, letter to AC, 4/21/1909, NYPL, WD Coll., Cat. 2, Box 5. Also, AC, letter to WD, 3/5 (1909?) and 4/16/1909, ibid.
28. WD, letter to MBD, 4/23/1909, LOC, D-B Coll., Box 1.
29. GM interview with MM. ESR, letter to GM.
30. WD, letter to MBD, 4/30/1909, LOC, D-B Coll., Box 1.
31. WD, letter to MBD, 12/20/1907, ibid.
32. WD, letter to MBD, "Tuesday" ?/?/1908, ibid.
33. WD, letter to MBD, 6/24/1908, ibid.
34. WD, letter to MBD, 5/18/1909, ibid.
35. GM interview with MM. GDF, *From the Top of the Stairs*, 144–145.

Chapter 18

(pages 201–216)

1. DM, *Music Is My Faith*, 196. Possibly the earliest review of a public performance, in Mendelssohn Hall, New York City, playing Bach, Beethoven, Brahms, is *NY Times*, 3/23/1905, 9:1.
2. CDM, *Born on a Sunday*, unpaginated section headed "subconscious absorption of music." DM, *Music Is My Faith*, 196–198, says less. *Musical America*, 4/20/1912, 31. Other reviews to the same effect: *NY Times*, 3/23/1905, 9:1; 3/9/1908, 7:2, reprinted in Aldrich, *Concert Life*, 221; and 11/19/1912, 9:4; *NY Tribune*, 12/16/1912; *Musical America*, 4/27/1912; *Detroit Free Press*, 3/7/1913;

Chicago Inter-Ocean, 3/23/1913; (London) *Times,* 6/18/1913; (London) *Standard,* 6/25/1913.

3. MM, *Out of My Time,* 10; GM interviews with family; on Westover, GM interview with CS.

4. CDM, *Born on a Sunday,* 37. The recital was 3/8/1904; reviewed *NY Times,* 3/9/1904, 9:2. According to DM, *Music Is My Faith,* 241, 262–263, it was the beginning of their long friendship with Casals.

5. GM interview with MM. DM, *Music Is My Faith,* 223–224, has the prisoner a childhood neighbor, not his brother. According to MM, who helped with her father's book, the change was made to preserve everyone's privacy. DM gives no date but the year was probably 1915 or 1916. See article and editorial on music at Sing Sing, *Musical America,* 4/10/1915, 41, and 4/17/1915, 22.

6. *Musical America,* 5/8/1915, 41.

7. Ibid.

8. DM, speech at the Annual Meeting of the Federation for Child Study, 11/3/1915, LOC, M-D Coll., Box 4.

9. DM, "Technique, Not the Golden Stair to Attainment, but the Spirit of Adoration, the First Requisite of Finding the Means of Expression."

10. The Music School Settlement, Annual Reports, 1901, 1906–07—1915, NYPL. The reports of the president, of the director, et al. give the school's history. In the First Annual Report, 1901, "especial thanks are due to Mr. David Mannes."

11. *Tante's Story,* 39.

12. The concluding sentences of *Tante's Story,* 43–44.

13. The following section, unless otherwise noted, is based on interviews with MM and the four Seymour children, and on documents, letters and pictures they produced; also, from the next generation, on letters and on interviews with Leopold and Douglas Damrosch. Of special importance for stirring memories were two series of short stories (unpublished) that Ruth Seymour Reed wrote in middle age, *Dear Family* and *The Somersets.* In these the only fiction is an occasional change of name.

14. Stebbins, *FD,* 199–200, 219; and note 13 above. The "cottage" had five bedrooms on the second floor and three, for staff, on the attic floor. It sat on about an acre of land and had a good view of the harbor and ocean. A picture of it appears in "FD, A Biographical Sketch."

15. GDF, *From the Top of the Stairs,* 22–24, 50, 146–148; and note 13 above.

16. DM, *Music Is My Faith,* 239, 241, 262–263.

17. Quoted by Elbridge L. Adams, "The Negro Music School Settlement."

18. Ibid. Also DM, *Music Is My Faith,* 213–220; *NY Times,* 3/20/1912, 9:3.

19. *NY Evening Journal,* 5/1/1912, 24:6; and quoted in Adams, "The Negro Music School Settlement." The fact that Adams' quotation varies slightly from the published editorial suggests that he perhaps was working from a typescript of what he or the board had sent to the *Evening Journal* and had been rewritten there.

20. Adams, "The Negro Music School Settlement"; *Musical America,* 4/27/1912, 28, and 5/11/1912, 19.

21. DM, *Music Is My Faith,* 218–219.

22. CDM, *Born on a Sunday,* unnumbered pages; DM, *Music Is My Faith,* 230. London reviews: *Times,* 6/18/1913; *Daily Telegraph,* 6/18/1913 and 7/3/1913; *Standard,* 6/25/1913; *Referee,* 7/6/1913.

23. DM, *Music Is My Faith,* 232. He has mistaken the year. The letter accepting his resignation is dated 4/27/1915; LOC, M-D Coll., Box 4. And he was to

serve only until June 1, 1915; Music School Settlement, Annual Report, 1915. For some public comment, *Musical America*, 5/8/1915, 4:1, and 5/15/1915, 8.

24. DM, *Music Is My Faith*, 219.
25. *Musical America*, 3/21/1914, 37; *NY Times*, 3/12/1914, 3:8.
26. *Musical America*, 4/17/1915, 41; *NY Times*, 4/13/1915, 11:2.
27. GM interview with MM.
28. GM interview with MM; and MM, *Out of My Time*, 23. DM, *Music Is My Faith*, does not mention the Chatham depression, but talks of others, 29, 36, 69, 77, 88–90, 97, 145. In her autobiography MM remembers the Chatham depression extending into several months; in the interviews she put it shorter. And, in fact, CDM and DM were able to give a recital in Bar Harbor in August, *Musical America*, 8/21/1915, 29.

Chapter 19

(pages 217–231)

1. GM interviews with the Seymour children, chiefly CS, and with Dora Duncan (Barker) and Anita Zahn. The latter were Duncan dancers who attended the school and also were in Switzerland in 1920 with CS and Elizabeth Duncan. According to Irma Duncan, *Duncan Dancer*, 6, "only children aged six to ten" were accepted at the school. In Munich, though CS was ten, Duncan would have taken her. Two schools in which CS taught dance are the School of Three Arts (Nellie Cornish), Seattle, 1920–21, and Town and Country School, Washington, D.C., 1930–32.
2. Description taken from *NY Times*, 2/16/1911, 11:3, review by Carl Van Vechten of a performance in Carnegie Hall with WD and the NY Symphony.
3. Bauer, *Harold Bauer, His Book*, 71.
4. Duncan, *My Life*, 222–223. The contract in WD's handwriting is very brief, on NY Symphony paper, and dated 10/10/1908. It proposes "at least two performances in New York," with all expenses to be jointly borne and all profits to be divided equally. NYPL, WD Coll., Cat. 3, Box 6.
5. On the inartistic German pit orchestras, see Martin Shaw, *Up to Now* (London: Oxford University Press, 1929), 67. Shaw conducted for Duncan. The publicity releases, NYPL, WD Coll., Cat. 9, Box 25 (in folder 1885–1920). Duncan, *My Life*, 223–224.
6. Luening, *Odyssey*, 73.
7. GDF, *From the Top of the Stairs*, 213–217. GM interview with CS.
8. WD, copy of letter to "Dear Osborn," 7/17/1909, NYPL, WD Coll., Cat. 3, Box 6.
9. Managers: F. W. Haensel, of Haensel and Jones, letter to WD, 6/23/1911: "While I am convinced there is no great demand for Duncan here in the East, I do believe that the South and the far West will turn out to see her, at least enough to make a very handsome profit if not an enormous one." NYPL, WD Coll., Cat. 20, Box 54. See also two letters WD to MBD, 10/13/1909 and "Friday, 9 A.M." (probably 10/15/1909), LOC, D-B Coll., Box 1.
    NY Times, 2/16/1911, 11:3. Before the *Liebestod* WD said to the audience:

    > It had been my intention simply to play this music from *Tristan*. Yesterday, however, Miss Duncan modestly asked me if I would go through the Liebestod with her. She has, as is well known, a desire to unite dancing to music in a perfect whole, as an art which existed in the time of the early Greeks. Whatever she does now, of course, must be largely experimental. However, the results which she has already

achieved with the Liebestod are so interesting that I think it only fair to set them before the public. As there are probably a great many people here to whom the idea of giving pantomimic expression to the Liebestod would be horrifying, I am putting it last on the program, so that those who do not wish to see it may leave.

Von Vechten's reviews of four Duncan-Damrosch concerts from the *Times*, 11/10/1909, 11/17/1909, 2/16/1911 and 2/21/1911, have been republished in *Isadora Duncan*, ed. by Paul Magriel.

10. GDF, *From the Top of the Stairs*, 215–216.
11. DM, *Music Is My Faith*, 204–205.
12. GM interview with Anita Zahn, who was told this by Max Merz, musical director of the Duncan School; confirmed in general by CS. For an angry attack on Duncan for using the classics for dance, see Terry, *Isadora Duncan*, 110–111, quoting Gilson MacCormack, writing for the August 1927 issue of *Dancing Times* of London.
13. GM interviews with family, chiefly RSR.
14. Irma Duncan, *Duncan Dancer*, 339–341. According to Irma Duncan, the idea of the pageant was Walter's and he told her: "Isadora Duncan's delineation of Beethoven's Seventh Symphony, twenty-five years ago helped to open my eyes and mind to the significant connection between the art of music and dance. When I started work on the scenario of the dramatization of the Ninth, it was as if Beethoven's music controlled me, and prevented me from introducing any element which smacked of the rhetorical or artificial."
    Note: WD in his autobiography, *My Musical Life*, does not mention Duncan, an extraordinary omission. The likely reason seems that the book was published in 1923, when Duncan was still alive. Gossip once had declared the two to be lovers, and it probably seemed better to avoid any reference to her. Anything he might have said would have started the gossip again.
15. *Musical Courier*, 2/4/1933, 10; *Musical America*, 2/10/1933, 62.
16. This account and the three quotations are taken from FD, *Some Essentials in the Teaching of Music*, 79, 82. FD, *Institute of Musical Art, 1905–1926*, 2–3, 7–10, 218–219, also presents his educational beliefs and theories.
17. Most of these ideas are set out in "Making a Modern Conservatory of Music" by J. F. Cooke, who interviewed FD, *Etude*, vol. 24, no. 3, March 1906. See also *Etude*, vol. 24, no. 2, for "The Advent of Endowed Institutions in American Musical Education" by J. F. Cooke with much on FD.
18. FD, letter to HMD, 7/9/1901, LOC, D-TV Coll., Box 2.
19. FD, letter to HMD (letter lacks opening page, but clearly July 1901), ibid.
20. *NY Times*, 12/10/1901, 6:4, "Mr. Carnegie's Oratorio Party"; Stebbins, *FD*, 201.
21. AC, letter to HMD, "July 16" [surely 1902] "on the train," LOC, D-TV Coll., Box 3. Hetty as sometimes "pushy," GM interview, Gertrude Schirmer Fay, and see AC, letter to HMD, 4/20/1903, LOC, ibid., in which he scolds her for imposing a friend on Mrs. Carnegie: "Beware. Beware, don't let feelings run away with the Head," and closes, "Your friend always, A.C." Another friendly letter disapproving of the school, AC, letter to FD, 3/27/1905, ibid.
22. FD, "The Fulfillment of an Ideal, How the Institute Came into Being." FD, Response at Testimonial Dinner, 1/16/1926, LOC, D-TV Coll., Box 4. Stebbins, *FD*, 201–204. On the Schirmer Library, *Musician*, January 1907, 26. See also FD, *Institute*, 4–5.
23. Birmingham, *Our Crowd*, 163, 254–255, 367.
24. John L. Wilkie, Speech at Dinner Meeting, 25th anniversary of IMA, at Hotel Commodore, 4/2/1930, LOC, D-TV Coll., Box 4.

25. *Musical America,* 11/18/1905, 2, and 4/2/1910, 1. FD, "The Fulfillment of an Ideal." FD, *Institute,* 49, gives statistics on the enrollment for the first year.
26. See IMA Catalog, 1913–1914, NYPL; and 1906–1907 and 1927–1928, LOC, D-TV Coll., Box 4. *Baton,* vol. 1, no. 1, January 1922, articles by FD, "A Welcome" and "Atmosphere," and vol. 1, no. 3, March 1922, "Good Reading." For FD's opening-day address see FD, *Institute,* 55.
27. Yurka, *Bohemian Girl,* 32–33.
28. GM correspondence and interviews with LDS and Leopold and Douglas Damrosch, sons of FD, Jr. Stebbins, *FD,* 222, glosses over the elopement. Gertrude Schirmer Fay recalled, in GM interview, that FD, Jr.'s, Anglo-Catholicism "took everyone by surprise."
29. RT, letter to Lucy Poate Stebbins, 11/15/1942, LOC, D-TV Coll., Box 4.
30. GM interview with Gertrude Schirmer Fay.
31. RT, letter to Lucy Poate Stebbins, 11/15/1942, LOC, D-TV Coll. Box 4.

Chapter 20

(*pages 232–236*)
1. GM interview with MM and four Seymour children. WD, *My Musical Life,* 18–19.

Chapter 21

(*pages 237–252*)
1. DM, *Music Is My Faith,* 234.
2. Ibid.
3. *Musical America,* 11/4/1916, 27. Also "David Mannes and the David Mannes School," *Clef,* July 1916, 3.
4. An example, not of arrogance, but of a piano virtuoso's misunderstanding of *Hausmusik* occurs in Stokowski's *An American Musician's Story,* 260–262. Subjected to an evening of it, in which the playing was bad, she wondered, "What would these cultivated Germans [do] if somebody passed an evening reading their Goethe and Schiller aloud in the same manner?" Surely they would approve, on a theory of learning by doing.
5. Memorandum: LOC, M-D Coll., Box 4.
6. DM, *Music Is My Faith,* 241–242.
7. Ibid. GM interview with MM.
8. For an example of HTS's humor and MBD's generosity to his family, see a resolution he prepared for their joint signatures, 4/26/1910, requiring her to cease and desist from paying public transportation fares for the Seymour family because he discerned "an approaching improvement in his temporal affairs," and her generosity had led to "unbecoming strife" and even "physical contests in the public streets." LOC, D-B Coll., Box 5.
9. GM interviews with the Seymour children and RSR's story *Strange Summer.* See Chap. 18, note 13. The poem, untitled and undated, but plainly before the U.S. entry in the war, is in the TAR Coll.
10. *Tante's Story,* 22.
11. Citizenship: NYPL, WD Coll., Cat. 16, Box 39; also, WD, letter to Franklin S. Edmonds, 9/25/1939, Cat. 1, Box 3; MBD, letter to daughter Alice, 5/2/1918, LOC, D-B Coll., Box 1.
12. CDM, *Born on a Sunday,* 6.
13. GM interview with LDS. *Musical America,* 1917, 3/3, 22; 9/15, 31; 10/13, 36;

and 12/8, 29. *NY Times*, 11/16/1917, 9:2; and 12/2/1917, I, 18:1. Herbert R. Axelrod, ed., *Heifetz*, 138, 152, 229 (Neptune City, N.J.: Paganiniana, 1976).

14. Mustache: WD, *My Musical Life*, 196. *Lusitania:* WD, letter to MBD, "Sunday" (5/?/1915), LOC, D-B Coll., Box 2.

15. WD, letter to MBD, "Wednesday," ibid.

16. WD, letter to MBD, "Friday morning," ibid.

17. WD, *My Musical Life*, 196.

18. *Musical America*, 2/10/1917, 48.

19. WD, letter to MBD, "Friday 4 PM" (2/9/1917), LOC, D-B Coll., Box 2.

20. Harrison, *A Timeless Affair*, 179.

21. William Henry Harbaugh, *The Life and Times of Theodore Roosevelt* (New York: Collier, 1963), 474–479.

22. Philip C. Jessup, *Elihu Root* (New York: Dodd, Mead, 1938), vol. 2, 311–329.

23. In general, the effects of the war on music and musicians are followed most easily in the issues of *Musical America*, 1917–18. Also, for these years the *NY Times* Index has an entry, "German Music," that refers to most of the pertinent stories, and for a monthly journal that concentrated on the subject and published many of the basic documents pro and con, see *The Chronicle*. Summaries appear, sometimes with interesting details, in Kolodin, *Metropolitan Opera*, 269–270, 282, 294; Shanet, *Philharmonic*, 227–230; Howe and Burk, *The Boston Symphony*, 131–141; and Otis, *The Chicago Symphony*, 305–321. Stokowski, *An American Musician's Story*, has a report on the Karl Muck incident. See also WD, *My Musical Life*, 195–197, 260, 337–343; Aldrich, *Concert Life*, 546, on WD, Theodore Roosevelt and Muck; and Luening, *Odyssey*, 236, for the organist fired in Chicago.

24. *NY Times*, 11/1/1917, 10:2.

25. WD, letter to *NY Herald* on Muck, 11/3/1917, clipping in NYPL, WD Coll., Cat. 6, Box 18. The letter was printed, with strong impact, in a "box" set at the top of the page. It also appeared in the *NY Times*, 11/3/1917, 22:1–3, as part of a long story on the Muck incident and on H. L. Higginson's speech about it at a subsequent concert. Immediately following was a story on Theodore Roosevelt: "Any man who refuses to play the *Star Spangled Banner* should be forced to pack up and return to the country he came from." Aldrich in *NY Times*, 11/4/1917, I, 5:7; and in *Concert Life*, 546. The incident can be followed also in *Musical America*, 11/10/1917, 1; 11/17/1917, 4; 12/1/1917, 7–8, 49, and following. But much that was inaccurate was reported as truth. For some later summaries, probably more accurate, see Howe and Burk, *Boston Symphony Orchestra*, 131–141, and Stokowski, *An American Musician's Story*, 144–147.

26. *Musical America*, 11/24/1917, 7, in the weekly column "Mephisto's Musings."

27. Some reports of WD's many speeches and impromptu remarks appear in *NY Times*, 10/26/1917, 13:1; 2/17/1918, I, 5:5; in *Musical America*, 11/3/1917, 20, 30; 12/22/1917, 7.

28. *Musical America*, 12/1/1917, 7–8; *Chronicle*, Nov. 1918, in "Commentaries" by the editor.

29. Correspondence between WD and YMCA, July 1918, NYPL-MD, WD Coll., Cat. 13, Box 31. WD, *My Musical Life*, 221–224, 234–243. "Profile" of WD, "Godfather to Polyhymnia," by Deems Taylor.

30. Second assistant secretary, Department of State, letter to FD, 12/28/1917, LOC, D-TV Coll., Box 4. The letter suggests indirectly that complaints about FD's loyalty had been made, and he knew of them.

31. Stebbins, *FD*, 220–225. Mrs. Jay's article, "Intern All German Music!!!" appeared in *Chronicle*, Aug. 1918. In Oct. the editor published endorsements of it from Joe N. Weber, president of the American Federation of Musicians, AFL, Frances Alda, John Philip Sousa and Margaret Matzenauer. The only letter published in opposition, and put under a headline of German Gothic type, was from Artur Bodanzky, conductor at the Metropolitan Opera.

32. Kupferberg, *Those Fabulous Philadelphians*, 105; Shanet, *Philharmonic*, 230.

33. WD, letter to the Rev. William Norman Guthrie, 3/11/1919, NYPL, WD Coll., Cat. 1, Box 1.

34. Repertory figures: Shanet, *Philharmonic*, 227–228. WD, *My Musical Life*, 1, and on Muck 339–343. Le Massena, *SS of NY*, 15, a typewritten history, 31 pp., "for distribution."

35. Among the admirers was Mary Ellis Peltz, a personal friend of WD and a radio commentator and author of several books on opera; also from 1957 to 1981 archivist at the Metropolitan Opera. She had the interesting idea, with which CS and RSR were inclined to agree, that WD, in "denying" his German heritage, cost himself some modicum of artistic achievement. As I do not agree, or perhaps do not understand, I have not taken it up, but the idea should be recorded. WD, interview with *NY Times*, 1/31/1932, VIII, 7:7; typescript of the complete interview in NYPL, WD Coll., Cat. 10, Box 26.

Chapter 22

(pages 255–269)

1. Transcript of a conversation in 1937 between FD and RT, LOC, D-TV Coll., Box 4. See also RT, letter to Stebbins, 11/5/1942, ibid. Delano obituary, *NY Times* 4/3/1920, 13:5. He had solicited gifts on the understanding that if not used for the MAS of NY, they could be transferred to the IMA; see Stebbins, *FD*, 228. In the event, the endowment fund of the MAS of NY, $60,000 including the current gifts, was transferred to the IMA and used to establish a department for choral singing. See FD, *Institute*, 187.

2. It is difficult to fix a date on which the People's Choral Union and Singing Classes came to an end. The latest issue of *Harmony* I have seen is May 1904, but the classes continued long after that. Stebbins, *FD*, 229, states that FD returned for the 25th-anniversary concert and that the occasion was marked by the publication of a booklet, but I have not seen a copy. There is a program of the concert, with suitable silver border, in Archives, OS of NY; and *Musical America*, 3/13/1917, 23, reports of the event: "For the past four years Dr. Damrosch has not regularly conducted the chorus, but the twenty-fifth anniversary concert . . . was conducted by him in conjunction with Edward Marquard, the present conductor." Plainly, Marquard replaced Harry Barnhart, either directly or in succession.

   I suspect the following: Barnhart, who had succeeded FD in 1912, soon proved more interested in his own Community Chorus movement, which was less musical in its aims, putting numbers of singers ahead of quality. With the advent of World War I and its stress on patriotism, this movement became popular. (See Barnhart obituary, *NY Times*, 9/5/1948, 41:1.) At some point before 1917, Marquard, who had started under FD in 1895 (see Stebbins, *FD*, 176), replaced Barnhart. But with the U.S. declaration of war on Germany, 4/2/1917, and the Selective Service Act of 5/18/1917, the classes began to lose their men. After the war, though the choruses did not revive, former members occasionally held reunions, which Frank and Hetty attended as guests of honor, e.g., 1928 and 1929; see Stebbins, *FD,* 241–242. The poem to FD, read at the dinner on 11/16/1929, is in LOC, D-TV Coll., Box 5; a photograph of that dinner is in the Damrosch Coll., Museum of the City of New York.

3. See Rice, "A Tribute to F.D."

4. DM, *Music Is My Faith,* 254–257.

5. GM interviews with CS, RT and Katharine Foy. David and Clara Mannes continued to play together occasionally at the school, and *Musical America,* 11/27/1926, 38, announces a series of Beethoven piano-violin recitals for faculty, students and guests on four Sunday afternoons.

6. DM, *Music Is My Faith,* 258–259. DM incorrectly states Scalero's years at the school as six, but they were nine, 1919–20 to 1927–28. GM interview with RT, who was director of the Curtis Institute from 1938 to 1940.

7. DM, *Music Is My Faith,* 244–253. His obituary, *NY Times,* 4/25/1959, 21:4, estimates his total audience over thirty years at two million. See also articles on his retirement, *NY Times* 1947, 4/13, 62:2; 4/14, 25:1; and editorial, 4/14, 26:1. The *NY Sun,* 1/4/1937, 32:2, gives history and attendance figures for the years 1918 through 1936. See also *NY Times,* 1/10/1937, I, 1:3, on twentieth anniversary.

8. Welling, *As the Twig Is Bent,* 232.

9. GM interviews with LDS and Symphorosa Livermore, who attended the weddings of all four of Walter's daughters.

10. WD, *My Musical Life,* 18–21; MBD, letters to daughter Alice, 11/9/1918 and 11/20/1918, LOC, D-B Coll., Box 2. See also GDF, letter to Alice, 11/17/1917, ibid., Box 4.

11. Deems Taylor, "Profile" of WD, "Godfather to Polymnia."

12. GM interview with ESR; MM, *Out of My Time,* 98.

13. MBD, letter to daughter Alice, 11/20/1918, LOC, D–B Coll., Box 2.

14. Wiechmann was born on Nov. 14, 1890, graduated from Harvard College in 1912 and from Columbia University Law School in 1915; worked for Sullivan & Cromwell from 1915 to 1917 and from 1919 to 1957; and died in 1964. He worked chiefly on corporate finance and reorganization law and on copyright and estate law.

15. GM correspondence with Marjorie's daughter, Vivian Holcombe.

16. Much of the background here can be found in the entry "Jews," by Arthur A. Goren, in *Harvard Encyclopedia of American Ethnic Groups;* also in other entries, such as "Immigration" and "Prejudice." See also Steinberg, *The Ethnic Myth,* 95–103, 112–116 and 224–228; and Birmingham, *Our Crowd,* 289–297.

17. A literal translation of the Hebrew word *dam* is blood, and of *rosh,* head; so "redhead" seems a reasonable translation of Damrosch. When Jews began acquiring surnames in the late Middle Ages, they often were derived from occupations, places of family origin or personal characteristics, or were bestowed by community officials. But when the name, which is not common among Hebrews, first attached to the Damrosch family, and why, is not known. GM correspondence with the Leo Baeck Institute, New York, and the Hebrew Union College, Cincinnati.

The belief, which occasionally surfaces, that Leopold Damrosch on coming to the United States changed the family name (some say from the German Blutkopf) is unfounded. The earliest family and official documents to survive, from the mid-nineteenth century, in Germany, all use Damrosch.

18. GM interview with Edith Simonds Moore, first wife of LDM.

19. Ibid. The remark was made by Warburg to Edith Simonds Moore.
20. GM interview with Christopher Clarkson, MM's third husband, who often heard DM make the remark. WD refused equally strongly to be typed a "German-American"; see WD, letter to Frau von Bülow, 2/5/1926, NYPL, WD Coll., Cat. 17, Box 40.
21. WD, *My Musical Life*, "The European Tour," 272–322. Orchestra personnel: the concertmaster was Gustave Tinlot; first viola, René Pollain; first flute, Georges Barrère; first oboe, Pierre Mathieu; and first bassoon, Louis Letellier. Repertory: among recent premières of French works offered by WD and the orchestra were the U.S. première of Ravel's *Daphnis and Chloe Suite No. 2*, 11/19/1914, and the world première of Ravel's *Introduction and Allegro for Orchestra*, 12/3/1916. On 11/3/1906, he and the orchestra had presented Saint-Saëns in the composer-pianist's American debut; see NYPL–MD, WD Coll., Cat. 3, Box 8; also WD, letter to Bernhard Ulrich, who was Saint-Saëns's agent, 11/24/1906, ibid., Cat. 5, Box 13.
    For direct thanks to WD of the French musicians for aid given, see the red leather box in book form entitled *A Walter Damrosch — 14 Juillet 1918*, compiled by Nadia Boulanger, NYPL, WD Coll., Cat. 3, Box 9. See also Rosenstiel, *Nadia Boulanger*, 136–138.
22. Bandmasters' School: WD, *My Musical Life*, 243–265. WD, copy of letter to General Pershing, Paris, 8/24/1918, NYPL, WD Coll., Cat. 12, Box 30. This box contains many letters and documents on the American Friends of Musicians in France and on the Bandmasters' School. See also ibid., Cat. 14, Box 35, for more correspondence and a history of the Bandmasters' School. There are also numerous references to it in documents and letters in LOC, D-B Coll., "Fontainebleau Material."
    The American School at Fontainebleau: Virgil Thomson has claimed to be and been quoted as being one of the three Americans who "discovered" Nadia Boulanger "for America," in 1921. The other two he cites as Aaron Copland and Melville Smith; Thomson, *A Virgil Thomson Reader*, 389. But if any American musician discovered Boulanger for America, it was WD, who, among other gifts to the younger generation of American musicians, helped to create the American School at Fontainebleau, to put Boulanger on its faculty and, through the school's American friends and publicity, to advertise her to American music students. He also gave the American première of her sister Lili's *Faust et Hélène* on 12/26/1918. See also Rosenstiel, *Nadia Boulanger*, 137, 142, 143, 146–147, 152–154.
23. Flagler: WD, *My Musical Life*, 274. On tour arrangements, see WD, speech to orchestra, NYPL, WD Coll., Cat. 20, Box 54.
24. Spalding had made his American debut with WD and the NY Symphony, 11/8/1908, playing Saint-Saëns's Violin Concerto No. 3 in B Minor, and two days later Tchaikovsky's Violin Concerto; see *NY Times*, 11/9/1908, 7:3, 11/11/1908, 9:3 and Aldrich, *Concert Life*, 232; also NYPL, WD Coll., Cat. 5, Box 14. In his autobiography, *Rise to Follow*, he has an account of the debut, of WD's kindness to him in the face of a savage review by H. E. Krehbiel and of Damrosch family life at Bar Harbor. For an account of an amusing contretemps in his relations with WD and MBD, see NYPL, WD Coll., Cat. 3, Box 8.
25. The programs for the first three concerts are given in WD, *My Musical Life*, 278–281, and also in the tour's commemorative pamphlet, *Symphony Pilgrims Abroad*, LDS Coll. Spalding, *Rise to Follow*, 270–278, has an account of the tour.

26. WD, *My Musical Life,* 316. David and Clara Mannes frequently had played Lekeu's *Sonata for Violin and Piano,* perhaps his most celebrated work.
27. WD, ibid., 280. Also reprinted in the pamphlet *Symphony Pilgrims Abroad.*
28. WD, letter to FD, Bellingham 6/21/1888, LOC, D-B Coll., Box 1; WD, *My Musical Life,* 320.
29. WD, *My Musical Life,* 287.
30. Ernest Newman, *Sunday Times,* 6/20/1920, 6:6, in his regular column, "World of Music." To modern ears his points seem fairly taken on the basis of WD's recording of Brahms's Symphony No. 2, Past Masters Records No. 19, reissuing, in January 1979, a Columbia recording, No. 67389/93D, made in 1926. The reissue's Notes state:

> "There are moments of great repose and autumnal beauty countered by heavy-handedness and lack of grace. Its chief deficiency is a clear musical pulse. The music wanders aimlessly with no consistent idea of musical direction . . . It leaves one strangely satisfied in spite of its shortcomings. One senses the strong personality of Damrosch at work which transcends all other considerations . . . Better this flawed, but vital, performance than the deadly dull ones that are distressingly common today. [Betty and Leo Mack]

31. On Elgar, WD, *My Musical Life,* 319, "the greatest symphonic composer since Brahms"; and a two-page typescript, *Sir Edward Elgar,* apparently a copy of an address to the American Academy of Arts and Letters, 11/14/1935, NYPL-MD, WD Coll., Cat. 3, Box 7.
32. Michael Kennedy, *Portrait of Elgar* (New York: Oxford University Press, 1968), 242.
33. Ernest Newman, *Sunday Times,* 6/20/1920, 15:5.
34. Finck, *My Adventures,* 254 — except that the review Finck quotes, without citation, is not the one published in *Sunday Times,* 6/20/1920. Finck's quotation starts: "His performance of Elgar's First Symphony on Saturday was unspeakably, irredeemably bad — coarse, clumsy, tasteless, soulless . . . I am irresistibly reminded of the boy who became a butcher because he was so fond of animals." Did Newman perhaps publish another review elsewhere? Did Finck, knowing Newman had been hostile, perhaps make it up?

   "Never again" is a strong statement, and someday someone may have the pleasure of proving me wrong. Nevertheless, a single performance or even two, if discovered, won't change the basic truth of the remark. The "drop-off," whether to zero or one, is remarkable.
35. Bauer, *Harold Bauer, His Book,* 82.
36. WD, *My Musical Life,* 154–156.

Chapter 23

(pages 270–283)
1. The college lists him officially as a member of the Class of 1921.
2. The coincidence of ideas evidently impressed LDM, for he told many persons of it. A report of it appears in CDM, *Born on a Sunday,* unpaginated section, "The early story of an invention in the Mannes family"; and in most published accounts of the discovery of the Kodachrome Process, e.g., Max Eastman, "How They Captured the Rainbow"; also in Allen Hackett, *Quickened Spirit: A Biography of Frank Hackett,* 109–110, where the boys on their walk "sat down on opposite sides of the road," wrote out their ideas and "agreed on an approach through lenses." But most, including Godowsky, think the actual writing-down of ideas was done either back at school or in the Mannes apartment.

There is considerable material on LDM in Riverdale's Archives, including pictures, in many of which LDM is standing to one side or in the back. In one, entitled "Everybody plays soccer, 1914," he is in the picture but, unlike the others, not dressed for soccer. In *Yearbook, 1915,* apparently a unique publication, he was voted the school's "grind," as well as winning votes as its "brightest" and "most modest." In a list of characteristics, his best girl is "any piano," and his future occupation, "organ grinder." A copy of the *Riverdale Review,* March 21, 1917, reports a recital at the school by his parents. According to Allen Hackett, the headmaster's son, they came often to play, and "Mr. Mannes was always very princely and deferred to her in a most attractive way."

3. CDM, *Born on a Sunday,* "The early story of an invention in the Mannes family."
4. GM interview with LG, Jr.
5. CDM, *Born on a Sunday,* "The early story of an invention in the Mannes family." The camera apparently improved the focus of the three colored exposures so that on projection of the three films in superimposition, there was less color-blurring, "fringing," at the edges of the image.
6. The postcards, disintegrating and mostly illegible, were discovered, after CDM's death, in a trunk. The transcript, with a record of the petitions, are in the Office of the Registrar, Harvard College.
7. GM interviews and correspondence with RT. A copy of the manuscript of *Indianola Variations,* dated 6/11/1918, is in the library of the Mannes College of Music. The college has a large collection of LDM's compositions, published and unpublished.
8. On Scalero, GM interviews, etc. with RT.
9. *NY Times,* 11/5/1922, VIII, 4:1, "Some Animals in Music."
10. CDM, *Born on a Sunday,* "The early story of an invention in the Mannes family."
11. U.S. Patent, 1,516,824, granted 11/25/1924. Patents, however, run from the date of application, not from the date of granting.
12. LDM recalls this event in a letter to LG, Jr., 9/6/1949; ESM Coll.
13. Wall, *History of Three-Color Photography,* 158.
14. The figure of $800 lent by the parents is taken from Time-Life, *Color,* 62, the research for which was done in the 1960s. There is no reason to doubt it, though LG, Jr., interviewed by GM in 1979, hesitated to set a figure.
15. This story, which appears in most accounts, confirmed by LG, Jr., GM interview. LG, Jr., with his mother and father, sailed on *The Southern Cross* in the first week of June; *Musical America,* 6/10/1922, 2.
16. Strauss, *Men and Decisions,* 98.
17. Staubach, ibid. GM interviews with LG, Jr., and MM.
18. From "Kodachrome, It Was Music for Our Eyes," probably the best account of the discovery of the Kodachrome process. It was based on extensive interviews with LG, Jr.
19. The sense of moral obligation: Wechsberg, "Profile" of LG, Jr., *New Yorker,* 11/10/1956, 86. Written in 1956, this was one of the first popular accounts to appear and is still one of the best.
20. GM interviews with relatives and Gertrude Schirmer Fay. The limp must have been slight, for not all agree on it, and it seems to have disappeared with age.
21. Notes for an article on HTV by Jocelyn Crane Griffin, Douglas S. Damrosch Coll. Also see Iglauer, "The Wonderful Zoo in the Bronx."
22. Iglauer, "The Wonderful Zoo in the Bronx."

23. Ibid. On his being appointed director of the zoo: "Talk of the Town," *New Yorker*, 9/6/1952, 29–30. GM interviews and correspondence with Douglas S. Damrosch.
24. GM interview and correspondence with Leopold Damrosch. Stebbins, *FD*, 232–233.
25. CDM, *Born on a Sunday*, in an unpaginated section entitled "to be inserted in the part telling about our years at Lake Champlain."
26. Ibid. GM interview with Edith Simonds Moore, LDM's first wife.
27. GM interview with Edith Simonds Moore.
28. MM, *Out of My Times*, 85, and Commencement Address, Mannes College, 6/4/1979.
29. GM, many interviews, and with CS.
30. MM, *Out of My Time*, 30. There is material from MM's days at the Veltin School in BUL, MM Coll., Boxes 9 and 10.
31. GM interview with MM.
32. The older man, Robert W. Wood, MM, *Out of My Time*, 61; the younger (unidentified), 59; "release from a society," 60; "freedom," 65.
33. Ibid., 87; on Colin MacKenzie, 91–92. Letters to her parents describing the year in London are in BUL, MM Coll., Box 11.
34. MM, *Out of My Time*, 82. MM, letter to parents, 11/2/1923: "My English nickname is 'Dammie.' They call me that because: before Mother had ever written them, they thought my name was Damrosch, and referred to me always as such." BUL, MM Coll., Box 11.
35. MM, *Out of My Time*, 104.
36. Ibid., 98–99.
37. Ibid., 108.
38. *NY Times*, 4/1/1926, 30:1; the engagement was announced, *NY Times*, 11/11/1925, 23:3, in which he is a stage designer and she is a playwright.

Chapter 24

(pages 284–295)

1. Taylor, "A Missionary Retires"; also W. J. Henderson, "W.D." See note 11 below. Mason, *The Dilemma of American Music*, 62–80, discusses its problems, praises WD and offers a list of American works played most frequently by the country's thirteen leading orchestras, 1919–20 to 1925–26.
2. WD, letter to Frederick E. Pratt, 4/11/1931, NYPL, WD Coll., Cat. 18, Box 43.
3. Sive, *Music's Connecticut Yankee*, 98–99; also Cowell, *Charles Ives and His Music*, 67–68.
4. Ibid. (both).
5. Perlis, *Charles Ives Remembered*, 156, quoting an oral history by Bernard Herrmann.
6. Ibid., 156n. Cowell, *Charles Ives*, 131n.
7. WD, letter to Lawrence Gilman, 5/15/1937, NYPL, WD Coll., Cat. 4, Box 12, folder E; see also WD, letter to Olin Downes, 3/9/1928, ibid., Cat. 17, Box 40; WD, letter to Marion Bauer, 4/24/1931, ibid., Cat. 10, Box 26.
8. WD, "Threescore and Ten," *NY Times*, 1/31/1932, VIII, 7:6; typescript in NYPL, WD Coll., Cat. 10, Box 26.
9. The typescript of his remarks at the first concert, 11/29/1925, is in NYPL, WD Coll., Cat. 17, Box 40: "The present outbreak of music of a sort which

seems incomprehensible need not worry anybody. If it is a sincere expression of what this age actually feels, all our opposition won't hurt it a bit. If it is not, it will die of itself." The works played were: Loeffler's *Memories of My Childhood;* Honegger's *Pacific 231;* Schoenberg's *Presentments, The Changing Chord,* and *The Past* from *Five Orchestral Pieces;* first movement of Poulenc's *Sonata for Two Clarinets;* Prokofiev's Violin Concerto No. 2; Stravinsky's *Ragtime;* and Hindemith's *Nusch-Nuschi Tänze;* also *The Ride of the Valkyries* (presented after Honegger's locomotive tone-poem *Pacific 231* as a study of "motion through the air") and the *Blue Danube Waltz.* The subscription concert immediately preceding this one of modern music also had offered two contemporary American works: Besides Brahms's Symphony No. 2, Daniel Gregory Mason's *Three Country Pictures* and Deems Taylor's *Through the Looking Glass.*

10. GM interviews with Samuel Orlinick and RSR.
11. Schoenberg, letter to WD, 2/22/1934, following a speech by WD in Chicago, apparently at the Arts Club, LOC, D-B Coll., Box 10. WD met Schoenberg in Vienna in June 1922 and "had a long interesting talk"; WD, letter to HHF, 6/6/1912, and letter to MBD, 6/2/1922, both LOC, D-B Coll., Box 2. For Ernest Bloch's thanks to WD, see (an extremely emotional) letter, 1/12/1929, also "Sunday" (a continuation), originals in LOC, D-B Coll., Box 7, copies in NYPL, WD Coll., Cat. 18, Box 42; Loeffler, letter to WD, 12/30/1923, NYPL, WD Coll., Cat. 3, Box 7; Daniel Gregory Mason, letter to WD, 12/15/1926, ibid., Cat. 3, Box 7; and see correspondence between WD and Deems Taylor, ibid., Cat. 8, Box 22.
12. WD, letter to Mary Agnes Magie, 5/19/1932, NYPL, WD Coll., Cat. 18, Box 43; see also WD, letter to Olin Downes, 2/24/1938, ibid., Cat. 5, Box 16, and WD, letter to Barry Faulkner, 5/28/1942, ibid., Cat. 8, Box 22.
13. *NY Times,* 12/3/1905, 7:1; "Hector Berlioz Intrudes on American Compositions," *Musical Courier,* 12/6/1905, 19, and "Looking for a Distinguished Composer — What the Dailies Think" (excerpting eleven newspapers at length), ibid., 26. Plainly Blumenberg hoped to discredit WD, who recently had testified against him in the Victor Herbert *vs.* Blumenberg libel suit and, at the suit's conclusion, had served as toastmaster at Herbert's victory dinner; see Waters, *Victor Herbert,* 192–226.
14. WD, letter to Paul D. Cravath, 4/14/1911, NYPL, WD Coll., Cat. 9, Box 25; WD, letter to Loeffler, 4/14/1911, ibid.; official notice setting the terms of the contest, together with considerable correspondence about it, ibid.
15. *NY Times,* 8/5/1909, 7:3. WD performed an excerpt with the NYSO on 2/20/1910; review *NY Times,* 2/21/1910, 9:2. For "Part II" of the pageant, NYPL, WD Coll., Cat. 18, Box 41.
16. *Variety,* 10/18/1912, 13; *Musical Courier,* 11/6/1912, 28; *NY Times,* 11/15/1912, 13:4.
17. Loeffler, letter to WD, 3/26/1913, published complete in WD, *My Musical Life,* 150–152; some correspondence on *Cyrano,* NYPL, WD Coll., Cat. 4, Box 10.
18. WD address, "Music and the Americans," 12/8/1910, LOC, D-B Coll., Box 2.
19. WD, *My Musical Life,* 268; WD, letter to Lawrence Abbott, 6/16/1941, in Abbott's possession.
20. GM interviews with CS and RSR; obituary of ADK, *NY Times,* 4/24/1967, 33:2; GDF, *From the Top of the Stairs,* 91; Rice, *Musical Reminiscences,* 120.
21. Kimball and Simon, *The Gershwins,* xxxi, 35–36.

22. Ibid., xxxiii, 50–52. Cron et al., *Portrait of Carnegie Hall*, 38, assert without documentation that "at Whiteman's suggestion" WD commissioned the concerto. Whiteman may have suggested it, but if so, I think his influence, because less immediate and continuous, to have been far less potent than that of Alice and the family.

23. Abbott, "A Jazz Concerto," *Outlook*, 12/16/1925, 582; GM interview with Abbott. *Symphony Society Bulletin*, 12/2/1925.

24. *NY Herald Tribune*, 12/4/1925, 19:2. Samuel Chotzinoff, *NY World*, 12/4/1925, 16:3, thought it a masterwork: "He alone actually expresses us. He is the present, with all its audacity, impertinence, its feverish delight in motion, its lapses into rhythmically exotic melancholy." Olin Downes, *NY Times*, 12/4/1925, 26:3, liked the second movement best, but thought "the themes of the concerto are denatured. They lack inherent energy and physiognomy, and are tinctured with a kind of harmony that frequently sounds forced and dry, in place of the richness and occasional chromaticism of the rhapsody." According to the *Symphony Society Bulletin*, 12/15/1925, the third performance in New York, 1/3/1926, was "by popular request." The fourth performance in New York was 12/26/1926. The success has continued steadily, its latest manifestation being a ballet by Jerome Robbins entitled *Gershwin Concerto*, given its première by the New York City Ballet on 2/4/1982.

25. *George Gershwin's Song Book*, from the Introduction by Gershwin. It is remarkable how much more exciting — on just these points — are Gershwin's recordings of his works when compared with those of more "serious" pianists. See also Gershwin's pleasure in playing for radio, which he felt demanded a crisp, clear style with little pedal: "Selected Broadcasts" by David Sandow, *Musical America*, 12/29/1928, 26.

26. For WD's pursuit of the première, Kimball and Simon, *The Gershwins*, 107–108; other correspondence, LOC, D-B Coll., Box 9; for Damrosch party "to meet George Gershwin," 12/14/1928, NYPL, WD Coll., Cat. 21, Box 55. For two letters of Gershwin to WD, 11/30/1927 and 11/6/1928, and WD, letter to Arthur Judson about the première of *American in Paris*, 12/28/1928, see LOC, D-B Coll., Box 9.

27. Irving Weil, "Jazzbo on Montparnasse," *Musical America*, 12/22/1928, 7. On Gershwin's death, WD was one of the honorary pallbearers.

28. WD, "More Composers Commissioned by New York Orchestra," *NY Review*, 2/13/1926, also in LOC, WD Scrapbooks, No. 3 of the Symphony Society of New York; see also WD, in "Gershwin Concerto to Have December Hearing," *Musical America*, 10/17/1925, 30.

29. Pulitzer scholarship: *NY Times*, 4/27/1925, 19:1: "In view of the great merit of the works presented," the committee awarded two scholarships, the other to Douglas Moore. A copy of the *Petite Suite* is in the Mannes College Library, also in RT Coll.

30. GM interviews with MM, CS, RSR and Edith Simonds Moore.

31. WD Fellowship: *NY Times*, 2/28/1922, 17:1, reporting on the benefit concert at which three orchestras (212 members), the NYSO, NY Philharmonic and Philadelphia Orchestra, combined to play under conductors Bodanzky, Coates, Mengelberg, Stokowski and Stransky. The concert netted $18,000, and a bronze plaque was presented to WD to commemorate the 50th anniversary of his arrival in the country. For a description of RT and his works on winning the fellowship, see *Musical America*, 6/10/1922, 2.

32. Manuscript of *Etude in 4 Notes* in Mannes College Library. Manuscript of the *Suite*, with dedication "To Leopold Damrosch Mannes, because he wrote 2/3 of the subject . . ." in RT Coll.

33. GM interview with RT.
34. RT on LDM as a composer, letter to GM, 10/3/1979.
35. On LDM as a performer: Unanimous opinion of persons interviewed; see also *NY Times,* 4/6/1941, I, 46:3, in which he is described in a recital with a cellist as "self-effacing."
36. GM interview with Edith Simonds Moore.
37. GM interviews with RSR and Edith Simonds Moore; also *East Hampton Star,* 8/14/1925.
38. LDM engagement, marriage announcement and marriage, *NY Times,* 5/1/1925, 19:1; 4/16/1926, 19:7; and 5/14/1926, 30:1. Organ characterized by RT.

Chapter 25

(pages 296–303)

1. Betty Loeb's four children were Morris (who married Eda Kuhn), Guta (Mrs. Isaac N. Seligman), James and Nina (Mrs. Paul F. Warburg). A stepdaughter, Therese (Mrs. Jacob H. Schiff), was also an important contributor. There were many other supporters, of course, but none so consistent or generous.
2. Accounts of the dinner, with lists of guests and transcripts of the speeches, are in *Baton,* Jan. 1926, 2, and Feb. 1926, 2. Typescript of the dinner proceedings, 36 pp., LOC, D-TV Coll., Box 4.
3. The clearest reports of the foundation, its Juilliard Graduate School and later merger with the IMA, on which the following account chiefly is based, occur in Erskine, *My Life in Music,* 52–58, 70–78, 116–117, 121, 134–135, 148–149, 263; Erskine, *Memory of Certain Persons,* 369–374, 388–391; FD, *Institute of Musical Art, 1905–1926,* Chaps. 12 and 14; Olga Samaroff Stokowski, *An American Musician's Story,* 174–175, 180–189; and Crowthers, "To the Glory of Music, A Fund for the Art," *Baton,* Nov.–Dec. 1931, 3.
4. The Juilliard Foundation and the Metropolitan Opera: Kolodin, *Metropolitan Opera,* 17, 28, 29, 32, 37, 326–327, 379, 385, 389, 397, 403. Erskine, *Memory,* 389.
5. Erskine, *My Life in Music,* 74, 77.
6. Ibid., 53; FD, *Institute,* 199, quoting the Directors' Report for 1924: "We still hope that the Trustees of the Juilliard Foundation may some day see their way to cooperate more closely with us without changing their plans in principle. Such cooperation would unquestionably lead to a very large pecuniary saving and would add to the efficiency of both institutions." FD, ibid., 203, reports that at a meeting of the institute's executive committee on 10/22/1925 Noble presented the plan for merger. Preparatory meetings had been held; agreement was swift.
7. FD, *Institute,* 204.
8. For some of the criticism, see *NY Times,* 10/26/1925, 25:1, *Musical America,* 12/11/1926, 1, and *NY Times,* 1/26/1926, 24:4.
9. Announcement: *NY Times,* 1/25/1926, 1:5, and editorial 1/26/1926, 24:4. Details: *NY Times,* 11/26/1926, 21:8, and *Musical America,* 11/27/1926, 2, and 12/4/1926, 2. FD, *Institute,* 205, sets out the agreement of merger. The first board meeting of the new Juilliard School of Music's board of directors was 11/23/1926; see Erskine, *My Life in Music,* 54.
10. Stebbins, FD, 238.
11. FD, *Institute,* 220.
12. Erskine, *My Life in Music,* 175, 25; Shanet, *Philharmonic,* 268.
13. Crowthers, "To the Glory of Music, A Fund for the Art," and Erskine, "The Juilliard Policy, in Operation Throughout the Country," both in the joint

Nov.–Dec. 1931 issue of *Baton*. The same issue contains articles by FD and
Ernest Hutcheson on the roles of the institute and the graduate school; descriptions of the dedication ceremonies, of the new building and of the faculty of the graduate school; and a long article by the editor, Crowthers, "John
Erskine, A Portrait of Our President."

Typescript of the commencement address of William Schuman, president
of the Juilliard School, 1945–63, to the last class to receive diplomas from the
IMA, with a tribute to FD, LOC, D-TV Coll., Box 4. According to Erskine,
My Life in Music, 263, attendance at the school on 1/7/1947 was 2106.

14. The previous edition of *Grove*, 1954, was not so direct; nor is *The International Cyclopedia of Music and Musicians*, 1964 or 1975.

Chapter 26

(pages 304–314)

1. *NY Times*, 12/15/1926, 1:2; *NY World*, 12/19/1926, Metropolitan Section, 5:1;
   and *NY Evening Post*, 12/15/1926, 1:7. Material on resignation, NYPL, WD
   Coll., Cat. 1, Box 2. The original of his letter of resignation to HHF,
   11/21/1926, is in PML.
2. Letters of regret and praise, NYPL, WD Coll., Cat. 1, Box 2; *NY Times*,
   12/15/1926, 1:2; *NY Herald Tribune*, 12/17/1926, 28:6. The Goldman letter and
   a similar one from Daniel Gregory Mason to WD, 12/15/1926, are in NYPL,
   WD Coll., Cat. 3, Box 7. See also Chap. 24, note 1.
3. What seems to be the first mention of retirement appears in a proposal for
   merger between the NYSO and "the Bodanzky orchestra" (National Symphony Orchestra), circa 1920–21, which states that WD "has expressed his
   intention after thirty-seven years to retire." NYPL, WD Coll., Cat. 11, Box
   29. See also WD, letter to MBD, 6/14/1922, LOC, D-B Coll., Box 2.
4. WD, "Threescore and Ten," *NY Times*, 1/31/1932, VIII, 7:6; typescript in
   NYPL, WD Coll., Cat. 10, Box 26.
5. WD, "Looking Backward."
6. Ibid.
7. Sargeant, *Geniuses, Goddesses and People*, 42, 65; "Arthur Pinworth" (Sargeant), "In the Firing Line of an Orchestra."

   Another of the orchestra's violinists and on occasion its concertmaster, Jack
   Danziger, in an interview with GM stated: "Damrosch was a good, solid
   conductor, very easy to follow. He was scouted unfairly in later years because he was without the flamboyant arm gestures that the public liked and
   came to expect in its star conductors — Stokowski's accent, hands and hair,
   and Toscanini's tantrums." Deems Taylor, *Of Men and Music*, 151, agrees
   with Danziger. See also Henderson, "Walter Damrosch"; and Sinclair, "Six
   Orchestral Conductors."
8. President's Report, 5/18/1925, NYPL, WD Coll., Cat. 11, Box 29.

   WD had a long and pleasant acquaintance with Bruno Walter, based in part
   on their common German heritage. See NYPL, WD Coll., Cat. 16, Box 19.

   Apparently, Ossip Gabrilowitsch brought BW to WD's attention with a
   letter, 3/8/1922, recommending BW as "*the* leading man among European
   conductors at the present time" and one who "wants some engagements in
   America"; NYPL, WD Coll., Cat. 6, Box 18. Then WD and BW met in
   Munich; see WD, letter to HHF, 6/6/1922, LOC, D-B Coll., Box 2, and
   WD, *My Musical Life*, 178. And the relationship thereafter continued happily.
   In 1944 WD had a part in the celebration of BW's 50th anniversary as a

conductor; see NYPL, WD Coll., Cat. 6, Box 19; also BW's *Theme and Variations,* 268, 275, 284–285.

9. President's Report, 5/18/1925, NYPL, WD Coll., Cat. 11, Box 29. See also memorandum to HHF dated 2/24/1923, unsigned but apparently by WD (NYPL, WD Coll., Cat. 11, Box 29), on pressures from the union and how to meet them, including the possibility of merger with the Philharmonic. Also correspondence on this point between WD and HHF. Edwin T. Rice, who was treasurer of the SS of NY at the time of the merger, states that by then HHF's annual contribution was exceeding $200,000; Rice, *Musical Reminiscences,* 119.

10. Shanet, *Philharmonic,* 232–233. Typescript of a proposal of merger between the SS of NY and "the Bodanzky orchestra"; see note 3 above.

11. Shanet, *Philharmonic,* 244, 247. For WD's public protest at the introduction of a claque into symphonic concerts, made at a dinner to honor Mengelberg, 4/5/1922, and the controversy the speech aroused, NYPL, WD Coll., Cat. 10, Box 26, and Cat. 17, Box 40.

12. Memorandum, "Tentative Suggestions for Consolidation . . .": "revised after conference at Harbor Hill [Mackay's house, Roslyn, N.Y.], July 7, 1926," and "rerevised after conference with H.H.F. at Millbrook, July 13." LOC, D-B Coll., Box 9.

13. Ibid.

14. The full terms of the consolidation were published in *NY Times,* 3/27/1928, 1:3, and *Herald Tribune,* 3/27/1928, 1:3.

15. Ibid.

16. *NY Times,* 3/16/1927, 29:1; *Musical America,* 3/19/1927, 4.

17. EDS, letter to WD, 3/16/1927, and WD reply, 3/17/1927, NYPL, WD Coll., Cat. 5, Box 15.

18. *NY Times,* 2/11/1928, 11:1; program for concert, NYPL, WD Coll., Cat. 11, Box 29, also in SS of NY *Bulletin,* bound copies, for season 1927–28, NYPL.

19. Sargeant, *Geniuses,* 74, states that the players learned of the merger from the newspapers; the feudal relationship, 67.

20. GM interview with Danziger; for Danziger on WD as a conductor, see note 7 above. "Arthur Pinworth" (Sargeant), "In the Firing Line of an Orchestra."

21. Sargeant, *Geniuses,* 74, 76.

22. Ibid., 76.

23. Ibid., 78.

24. WD, letter to Toscanini, 3/28/1928, and Toscanini's reply, 3 (but should be 4)/1/1928, LOC, D-B Coll., Box 9.

25. WD, letter to HHF, 4/2/1928, LOC, D-B Coll., Box 9.

26. Ibid.

27. Shanet, *Philharmonic,* 267, quoting *Musical America,* 1915; on the assault, Sachs, *Toscanini,* 139.

28. Sargeant, *Geniuses,* 82.

29. Rice, *Musical Reminiscences,* 119.

30. Shanet, *Philharmonic,* 256, 255, 272. Shanet's discussion of Toscanini's leadership of the Philharmonic is far better focused and balanced than most. See also Mueller, *American Symphony Orchestra,* 56–58, on the gains and losses resulting from the consolidation.

31. For correspondence over WD's dates with the orchestra, LOC, D-B Coll., Box 9.

The Bloch rhapsody, *America,* had won a composition prize offered by *Mu-*

sical America for a symphonic work. The judges were Stokowski, Kousse-vitzky, Damrosch, Stock and Hertz. In the same week as Damrosch in New York the other four conductors led local premières of the work in Philadelphia, Boston, Chicago and San Francisco.

For text and notes on WD and Gershwin's works, see Chap. 24.

32. WD, letter to HHF, 3/31/1929, LOC, D-B Coll., Box 8.
33. WD, letter to Paul Cravath, 4/11/1929, LOC, D-B Coll., Box 9. WD's and Mackay's exchange, 4/12 and 4/16/1929, LOC, ibid.
34. MBD, letter to ADK, 5/6/1929, LOC, D-B Coll., Box 2. See also letters of 3/24 and 4/14/1929, ibid.

Chapter 27

(pages 315–328)

1. MM, letter to LDM and Edie, 3/9/1927, LOC, M-D Coll., Box 2.
2. GM interview with Edith Simonds Moore.
3. RT, letter to LDM, 12/26/1928, RT Coll.
4. *New Songs for New Voices,* ed. by Louis Untermeyer and Clara and David Mannes (New York: Harcourt, 1928). As the Foreword states, Leopold D. Mannes also worked on the book's manuscript. Besides Wylie, Milne and Belloc, other contemporary poets providing texts were Robert Graves, Edna St. Vincent Millay, Walter de la Mare and Carl Sandburg.

The book was launched on 10/17/1928 with a press party at the Mannes School, at which LDM at the piano and Greta Torpadie, soprano, presented 25 of the new songs. *Musical America,* 10/27/1928, 12.
5. GM interview with Edith Simonds Moore.
6. MM, letter (to parents) (6/30/1927), LOC, M-D Coll., Box 2.
7. GM interview with Christopher Clarkson, MM's third husband. The Wiechmann house was Wompenanit, and after Ferdi's death in 1919 it was taken over by his daughter, Marjorie, then Mrs. Robert T. Swaine. MM and her second husband, Richard Blow, left their home in Italy before World War II in part to avoid for her the impact of the racial laws; see MM, *Out of My Time,* 168.
8. MM, *Message from a Stranger,* 118–119, also 193–197. The Manneses' attitude toward their American identity is very different from many of those with a similar heritage today. For example, Joseph Papp, the theatrical producer, in an interview with the *NY Times,* 12/13/1981: "My father was a Polish Jew. I'm an American Jew, or I'm Jewish American, whichever way you put it. Sometimes I am just a Jew. But I'm never just an American. It's impossible because there's always a sense that you're an alien."
9. MM, *Out of My Time,* 6; also *More in Anger,* 152.
10. *Baton,* March 1928, 5, reprinted excerpts from the book, including the statement about LD quoted in the text.
11. Saleski, *Famous Musicians,* vii–viii.
12. GM interview with Mary Ellis Peltz; see Chap. 21, note 35.
13. *Partisan Review,* 1980, no. 4, "An Interview with Virgil Thomson," by Diana Trilling, 544, 552–553. The interview is reprinted in *A Virgil Thomson Reader.*
14. MM, *Message from a Stranger,* 119.
15. GM interview with Gertrude Schirmer Fay.
16. Baptism: GM interview with ESR. See MM, *More in Anger,* 172.
17. MM, letter to Leopold and Edie, 3/9/1927, LOC, M-D Coll., Box 2.
18. GM correspondence with Margot Finletter Mitchell.

19. WD, letter to Mrs. Fritz Busch, 10/2/1929, NYPL, WD Coll., Cat. 6, Box 18, in which he states MBD was abroad for "a few weeks in August." In fact she was away until the end of Sept. See WD, letters to MBD, 8/26, 9/1, 9/9 and 9/16, 1929, LOC, D-B Coll., Box 2.

    WD, letter to HHF, 8/23/1929, PML, explaining that Margaret has gone to Europe alone: "Over a year of continuous family and housekeeping has been a little too much, and she certainly needed a rest from us all, including her devoted husband."

20. The brochure and an EDS letter to HTS from Salzburg, 8/19/1927, where she heard Lotte Lehmann in *Fidelio,* TAR Coll. GM interviews with Seymour children and Seymour grandchild, Barry Seymour Boyd.

21. GM interviews with CS, RSR and Barry Seymour Boyd. The book was *Siamese Cat* by Elizabeth Morse, illustrated by Ruth Seymour (New York: Dutton, 1929).

22. GM interviews with Elizabeth D. Woolsey, who heard directly from Alice the advice given to Polly to go to Vienna, with M. R. Werner, the friend who advised Polly to return to New York, and with Langdon Van Norden, who heard the family discuss Polly's choice of color. A photograph, *NY Herald Tribune,* 1/11/1931.

23. GM interview with Edith Simonds Moore.

24. For further details, see Chap. 17, note 3. Felicia Geffen, WD's secretary, letter to WD, 6/14/1944, LOC, D-B Coll., Box 6: "Later in July you receive the Carnegie check of $2500, and Mr. Flagler's check of $7500."

25. Tante: WD, letter to HTS, 10/20/1928, revealing that he has paid all of Tante's unusual expenses for several years; TAR Coll.

    GM interviews with Leopold and Douglas S. Damrosch, and letter from FD, Jr., to HTS, 10/28/1928, thanking him for the cancellation of a debt ($150); TAR Coll.

    GM interview with Leopold Damrosch, "young Leopold." WD, letter to MBD, 12/9/1929, LOC, D-B Coll., Box 2. In this letter he states that he has enclosed a letter from Frank Jr., 9/3/1929, that gives the background. It is in D-B Coll., Box 5, in a folder "Damrosch family unidentified."

26. WD, letter to FD Jr., 9/9/1929, LOC, D-B Coll., Box 2.

27. GM interview with Douglas S. Damrosch.

28. GM interview with Eleanor (Mrs. Douglas S.) Damrosch.

29. GM interviews with MM, CS and RSR. CDM, *Born on a Sunday,* in an unpaginated section, "David and I." See CDM, letter to LDM, 9/7/?, while aboard the *Rex:* "We have been repeatedly approached by charming women and men about our dancing — about which they seem to be enthusiastic"; and CDM, letter to Leopold, 9/4/1947; both LOC, M-D Coll., Box 1.

Chapter 28

(*pages 331–343*)

1. GM interview with Symphorosa Livermore.

2. Ibid.

3. GM interview with M. R. Werner.

4. WD, letter to MBD, 8/26/1929, LOC, D-B Coll., Box 2.

5. The claim made in her obituary, *NY Times,* 4/24/1967, 33:2, that she was the first American woman to climb the Matterhorn's *north face* is false. That was not achieved by any woman until July 13–14, 1965, and then by a Swiss, Yvette Vaucher.

6. ADK, letter to MBD, 11/3/1931, LOC, D-B Coll., Box 3.
7. Bess Ransom: Feature article in the *Hartford Daily Times,* 2/7/1936, following her selection by *American* magazine, Feb. 1936, 55, as one of "America's Interesting People." Poem in TAR Coll.
8. GM interview with Edith Simonds Moore.
9. MM, letter to DM, "Darling Fippy" (no date), LOC, M-D Coll., Box 2.
10. Examples: MM, letter to DM, "Dear Old Fip," "Friday," ibid. See MM, *Out of My Time,* 25: "My mother hated to speak of 'the facts of life' or, for that matter, bodily functions of any kind."
11. MM, letter to LDM, "Itzie" 7/21/[1929], LOC, M-D Coll., Box 2.
12. MM, *Out of My Time,* 144.
13. Ibid.
14. GM interview with MM.
15. GM interviews with CS and RSR.
16. GM interview with RT.
17. GM interview with Mary Bancroft.
18. MM, *Out of My Time,* 144.
19. GM interview with MM. Except for a few slight changes, chiefly for punctuation, this is how she remembered the conversation.
20. GM interviews with CS and RSR.
21. GM interview with ESM.
22. Quoted in Staubach, "Kodachrome."
23. Ibid.; also GM interview with LG, Jr.
24. MM, letter to LDM, "Leppy sweetness," 8/11/1925, states: "God knows you kept your wimmen friends dark long enough." LOC, M-D Coll., Box 2. GM interviews with LG, Jr., and RT. RT, letter to LDM, 8/4/1927, RT Coll.
25. RT, letter to LDM, 11/10/1929, RT Coll.
26. From typescript draft of Bancroft's *Autobiography of a Spy,* 112, to be published by Morrow, probably in 1983.
27. GM interview with Mary Bancroft.
28. See Mary Bancroft's autobiography, soon to be published. See also Leonard Mosley, *Dulles* (New York: Dial Press / James Wade, 1978), and W. A. Swanberg, *Luce and His Empire* (New York: Scribner, 1973).
29. GM interview with Mary Bancroft.
30. RT, letter to LDM, 7/29/1931, RT Coll. GM interviews with RT and Edith Simonds Moore.
31. GM interview with Mary Bancroft.
32. Ibid. Also her autobiography; see note 26 above.
33. Bancroft, autobiography, 128–129.
34. Ibid., 129–130.
35. GM interview with Mary Bancroft.

Chapter 29

(*pages 344–357*)
1. Edith Iglauer, "The Wonderful Zoo in the Bronx."
2. HTV, "The Voyage of the Arcturus."
3. Joyce (Mrs. Donald R.) Griffen, in an account of HTV written for New York Zoological Society files and sent to Eleanor Damrosch, 6/8/1977. Griffen states that the underwater painting began as early as 1927 on an expedition to Haiti, but the subject matter, coral reefs, suggests Bermuda. Off Haiti

she apparently made underwater sketches with a lead pencil on zinc plates. Much of her work has been preserved in the Helen Damrosch Tee Van Collection, University of Oregon Library, Eugene, Oregon.

4. From Appendix E, "Bathysphere Dive Thirty-Five," by John Tee Van, to William Beebe, *Half Mile Down.*

5. GM interviews with Dorothy Seymour, CS, ESR and RSR.

6. ADK (A. D. Wolfe), "Ten Years of Ski Racing for Women."
   Note: Alice, married three times, wrote under three names, A. D. Pennington, A. D. Wolfe and A. D. Kiaer, in addition to her maiden name before marriage. Perhaps her first published work was a poem, "The Early Dive" (*Scribner's* magazine, Sept. 1912), celebrating a plunge into a lake and the exhilaration felt on rising to the surface. Another poem, "Swimming by Night," also celebrates a mystical joy in physical exertion; TAR Coll. "Perugino to His Pupils" is in LOC, D-B Coll., Box 3. She published many more reports on women's skiing than the few cited here.

7. ADK, "Ten Years of Ski Racing for Women." For a recent summary of Alice's role, see Dinah B. Witchel, "Alice in Skiland."

8. Ibid.

9. GM interviews with Elizabeth D. Woolsey and Theodora Taggert. The acquaintance, M. R. Werner. Gertrude Schirmer Fay on Alice: "She picked people up and put them down very hard."

10. ADK (Wolfe), "American Skiers at the Olympics, Women." Also in *American Ski Annual, 1937–38,* a letter to the editor by Arnold Lunn, and "The 1937 Women's Team" by Elizabeth D. Woolsey. In the latter Woolsey states: "That we are at last beginning to earn international recognition is due entirely to the efficient managership of Alice Damrosch Wolfe, whose idea it was, and who has devoted every winter to carrying it out." See also, in same issue, "U.S. Teams in International Competition" by Roland Palmedo.

11. ADK (Wolfe), "American Skiers at the Olympics, Women."

12. GM interviews with Herman S. Kiaer and Elizabeth D. Woolsey. On the Austrian Nazis, see ADK, letters to her parents, 3/20 and 12/27/1938, LOC, D-B Coll., Box 3.

13. Elizabeth D. Woolsey, "Women's Racing, 1940," in *American Ski Annual, 1940–41.* GM interview with Herman S. Kiaer.

14. Von Karajan, on his first visit to the United States, in 1955, touring with the Berlin Philharmonic, was greeted by pickets protesting his membership in the Nazi party, and was upset by the incidents and name-calling. Alice tried hard to make him feel at home with a series of small, comfortable dinner parties. GM interview with Herman S. Kiaer.

15. GM interview with Herman S. Kiaer.

16. For the following account of LDM in Rochester I am particularly indebted to the following: Leopold Godowsky, Jr., Walter Clark, Wesley T. Hanson, Jr., and Arnold Weissberger, all of whom worked in the research laboratory; also to Margaret Baum, Guy F. Harrison, James Sibley Watson and Evelyn Sabin (later Mrs. LDM), who also knew him in the Rochester years; to Philip L. Condax, director, Department of Technology, International Museum of Photography, George Eastman House, Rochester; and to Richard Platt, an English photographer who has done research on the history of the Kodachrome process, including interviews with Clark, Weissberger, Condax and Godowsky.

Many articles have been published on the Kodachrome process of which the following are a selection: LDM and LG, Jr., "The Kodachrome Process

for Amateur Cinematography in Natural Colors"; E. R. Davies, "The Ko-
dachrome Process of 16 mm. Colour Kinematography"; Max Eastman, "How
They Captured the Rainbow"; D. A. Spencer, "The First Hundred Years of
Colour"; Arnold Weissberger, "A Chemist's View of Color Photography";
Horst Staubach, "Kodachrome"; and "The Musicians Who Found the Key
to Color Film."

    C. E. Kenneth Mees describes the creation, direction and a few of the
accomplishments of the Eastman Kodak Research Department in his address,
11/9/1955, "Myself and My Journey Down the River of Time." At that point,
Mees, born 1882, had spent 44 years with Eastman Kodak, 54 in the study
of photography, and was retiring.

17. This use of music is not uncommon among musicians. Harold Bauer and
Pablo Casals, for example, developed to perfection a parlor trick, "mental
telepathy," in which one would correctly identify a playing card shown only
to the other. The suit was indicated by four slightly different foot positions,
and the number by silently counting the beats of an agreed-on composition
and stopping on a prearranged signal. H. L. Kirk, *Pablo Casals*, 171.

18. LDM, from an Address in the Dryden Theatre of George Eastman House,
5/26/1952, on the opening of the Mannes-Godowsky wing, Coll. of ESM.

19. Ibid.

20. The expression "two wandering musicians" — *"hergelaufene Musikanten"* —
was used by an Austrian scientist; GM interview with Arnold Weissberger.

21. GM interviews with LG, Jr., and Mary Bancroft.

22. GM interviews with LG, Jr., Margaret Baum and Mary Bancroft.

23. Quoted in Staubach, "Kodachrome."

24. Ibid.

25. Hints: For an example, see *NY Times*, 4/13/1935, 17:7.

26. For a good summary appraisal, see Davies, "The Kodachrome Process."

27. R. W. Wood, letter to LDM, 12/3/1935, LOC, M-D Coll., Box 3.

28. LDM, Address; see note 18 above.

29. See *NY Times*, 8/19/1941, 23:6; 8/24/1941, X, 7:5; 12/18/1941, 29:8; also Spencer, "The First Hundred Years," and *Color*.

30. LDM, Address; see note 18 above. Arnold Weissberger, "The Innovators, a
Climate for Innovation," *Chemtech*, June 1980, touches on this point with
interesting examples: "Invention costs less than innovation. That holds true
even when several people do research for years. It's when you reduce invention to practice that you really have to spend money. One of the important
management responsibilities is to decide when a product has been advanced
enough in the research lab to justify a scale-up."

Chapter 30

(pages 358–374)

For this chapter on radio and the "Music Appreciation Hour" I have made exceptional use of Erik Barnouw's *A Tower in Babel*, vol. 1 of his 3-vol. *A History
of Broadcasting in the United States*, and of M. Elaine Goodell's doctoral thesis,
Walter Damrosch and His Contributions to Music Education. The latter, dated 1973
and 569 pp. long, gathers into a single, coherent volume an extraordinary amount
of material, much of it quoted in full. Citations of the thesis will be Goodell,
WD, with page number.

    1. On 11/20/1927 *Musical America*, with Deems Taylor as editor, started a listing
of radio programs featuring music, "Turn the Dial," and on 12/17/1927, a

review page of such programs, "Broadcasting Across the Country" by David Sandow. These were in addition to feature articles and continued under changing titles — "Selected Broadcasts" and "Radio" — until in August 1929 A. Walter Kramer succeeded Taylor, after which there was less on radio programs.

Barnouw, *Tower*, 27; also La Prade, *Broadcasting Music*, 4–5. The program was engineered by Lee de Forest, an important figure in radio. It was a true "wireless" broadcast; *Walküre* previously had been heard outside the house by telephone.

For some private reason historians of the Metropolitan Opera steadily have ignored this broadcast, though it is well documented. Usually they follow Kolodin, *Metropolitan*, 361, 366, giving the date of the first broadcast from the stage as 4/21/1931 and of the first broadcast from the stage by the company, 12/25/1931, a matinee performance of *Hänsel und Gretel*. Seltsam, *Metropolitan Opera Annals*, 540, states incorrectly that the latter was "the first broadcast of a complete opera from the Metropolitan.

2. *NY Times*, 1/14/1910, 2:2.
3. Barnouw, *Tower*, 43 and 77, 69–70, 84–87, 88.
4. Ibid., 88.
5. "The Wireless Transmission of Music," by H. R. Rivers Moore, *Music and Letters*, 1923, 158–161. Also, WD speech in Chicago, 10/9[1935], to the National Advisory Council on Radio in Education, NYPL, WD Coll., Cat. 10, Box 27. CDM's disapproval was expressed within the family.
6. Finck, *My Adventures*, xvi.
7. WD, "Music Over the Radio," speech to Canadian Club of Montreal, 4/20/1931, NYPL, WD Coll., Cat. 10, Box 26. Also, WD, draft for a publicity release, April 1928, ibid., Cat. 18, Box 41, and WD quoted by David Sandow, "Selected Broadcasts," *Musical America*, 11/13/1928, 13.
8. The dates for the lecture-recitals: 10/29, 11/19/23 and 1/7/1924; for the concerts: 1/4, 1/11 and 2/1/1924.
9. NYPL, WD Scrapbooks, Clippings, vol. II(a), Nov. 1923–Aug. 1924, Reel 10; also Goodell, *WD*, 281.
10. *NY Times*, 1/24/1926, VIII, 17:3, and 1/24/1926, 18:1. Clipping from the *Fall River* (Mass.) *Herald*, 1/25/1926, NYPL, WD Scrapbooks, Clippings, vol. VII, 1925–26, Reel 11, also Goodell, *WD*, 283. On Reel 11 also other clippings on WD as an announcer: *Youngstown* (Ohio) *Telegram*, *Minneapolis Star* and *Minneapolis Tribune*.

WD, *My Musical Life* (3rd ed.), 368–369, seems to refer to this concert, though dating it 1925.
11. The letter of agreement between the SS of NY and AT&T, NYPL, WD Coll., Cat. 18, Box 41. *NY World Telegram*, 4/11/1927, DAMROSCH FORESEES RADIO AS GREAT CULTURAL AGENT, also in NYPL, WD Scrapbooks, Clippings, vol. IX, 1926–28, Reel 11.

NBC at the start had two networks, "red," based on WEAF, and "blue," on WJZ. The colors originated in the colored lines on a map to show the network of subscribing stations across the country. Barnouw, *Tower*, 191, 272.
12. Typescripts of the programs are in LOC, D–B Coll., Box 6. Goodell, *WD*, Appendix G, 474–477, quotes the broadcast on 11/20/1926 complete.
13. D. Thompson, letter to WD, 12/20/1927, NYPL, WD Coll., Cat. 18, Box 41. According to the typescript of the broadcast, see note 12 above, WD omitted the first and third sentences. See Goodell, *WD*, 287–288.
14. WD, letter to ADK, 2/10/1929, relates some of the behind-the-scenes nego-

tiations over the program. LOC, D-B Coll., Box 2. For the Advisory Council, see Barnouw, *Tower,* 204–206. On GE's aggressive advertising, see correspondence in spring of 1929, NYPL, WD Coll., Cat. 18, Box 42, and see Goodell, *WD,* 290–292.

15. Barnouw, *Tower,* 190–192 on WD's appointment as music counsel. NBC began operations on 11/15/1926 with a party in the Grand Ballroom of the Waldorf-Astoria. The broadcast of it began 8:05 P.M. There were local and remote features: locally, WD with the NY Symphony, also the OS of NY; from Chicago Mary Garden sang *Annie Laurie;* from Kansas City, Mo., Will Rogers philosophized, etc. WD, in effect, was NBC's music counsel even before the corporation was born. See also Merlin H. Aylesworth, "Men, Mikes and Money, Part 1," *Collier's,* 4/17/1948, 14–15.

16. *NY Herald Tribune,* 5/13/1927, 16:1. *NY World,* 5/13/1927, 1:2. *NY Times,* 5/13/1927, 27:2. The press conference was picked up by papers around the country; NYPL, WD Scrapbooks, Clippings, vol. 9, 1924–28, Reel 11.

17. WD press release on Address to the School Principals, 2/24/1927, NYPL, WD Coll., Cat. 18, Box 41.

18. Stokowski: Goodell, *WD,* 297, citing *Philadelphia Public Ledger,* 4/3/1927, 14. See WD correspondence, NYPL, WD Coll., Cat. 18, Box 41, e.g., WD, letter to Merlin H. Aylesworth, 3/19/1927: "Here is another letter from a school orchestra . . ."

19. WD, undated memorandum to Merlin H. Aylesworth, NYPL, WD Coll., Cat. 18, Box 41. Walter's awareness of the budget: S. J. Woolf, "Damrosch Waves a Baton Over America," *NY Times* magazine, 3/2/1930, 1.

20. WD, letter to MBD, 9/29/1927, LOC, D-B Coll., Box 2.

21. A verbatim report of the broadcast, including remarks before and after, NYPL, WD Coll., Cat. 18, Box 41. Goodell, *WD,* Appendix H, 478–493, quotes it complete. See also "Damrosch Enlists Radio to Reach Children," by Frances Q. Eaton.

22. GM interviews with Lawrence Abbott, WD's assistant for the program 1936–41 and with Howard W. Keresey who as librarian at NBC, 1931–44, sat beside WD at the piano for the broadcasts. Keresey, who was librarian with the NY Philharmonic, 1944–71, felt that WD "was a perfectly satisfactory conductor although not great. From a point of view of background, training and understanding he was exceptional." See Chap. 26, note 7.

23. The verbatim report, see note 21 above. The battle to put music into the curriculum, for credit, was a long one, with many heroes. For an account of others, see Browning, *Joe Maddy of Interlochen,* 137, 144, 186.

24. The easiest place to follow the national response is the WD scrapbooks in LOC and on microfilm at NYPL, Reel 12; also in Goodell, *WD,* 304–319. See also 500,000 CHILDREN ATTEND BROADCAST, and "The Vision of Educational Radio" by David Sandow, *Musical America,* 2/18/1928, 1 and 3.

25. WD, letter to HHF, 5/13/1929, PML: "RCA found their hands so full with the purchases of the Keith Vaudeville, the Victor Company and the Photophone, not to mention national and international wireless telegraphy, that they wanted to disembarrass themselves of all things not directly connected with these purely business enterprises. Thank Heaven the NBC eagerly stepped forward and will take over the Children's Concerts."

26. Alice Keith's work can be followed in NYPL, WD Coll., Cat. 18, Box 41, 42; also in Goodell, *WD,* 323–331. She seems to have been the victim of an economy measure. A memorandum of estimated expenses for 24 educational concerts, 1929–30, suggests that her position be combined with another at a

saving of $3500 on a budget of $109,000; NYPL, WD Coll., Cat. 18, Box 42. Also presented in full, Goodell, *WD,* 357. See also "Education by Radio to be Nation-Wide" (unsigned), *Musical America,* 4/21/1928, 6.

27. John W. Elwood, letter to WD, 8/8/1928, and other correspondence on this subject, NYPL, WD Coll., Cat. 18, Box 41.

28. "Selected Broadcasts" by David Sandow, *Musical America,* 11/3/1928, 13; also, ibid., 12/8/1928, 18.

29. La Prade (1889–1969) wrote many books and articles on music education. Among the books were *Alice in Orchestralia* (1927); *Marching Notes* (1929), reissued as *Alice in Music Land* (1953); and *Broadcasting Music* (1947). He stayed with NBC until his retirement in 1954, acquiring some fame as conductor of a program called the "NBC Home Symphony" and serving an NBC's director of music research. For many summers he taught conducting at Chautauqua. For a description of him, see "Selected Broadcasts," by David Sandow, *Musical America,* 10/13/1928, 14.

30. The falling-out distressed many, for Walter and La Prade seemed ideally suited. But neither man ever spoke of the cause, not even to La Prade's successor, Abbott, who often talked with each.

Mrs. La Prade, however, offered a clue in an interview with GM, 1979. Much of the preparatory work of the program was done each summer at Blaine Cottage, Bar Harbor, where La Prade would be Walter's house guest for as long as four or five weeks. For the last two or three of these Mrs. La Prade would join them. Summer life at Bar Harbor was very social, and though the men worked hard during the day, the evenings and some afternoons were given over to outings and card or dinner parties. La Prade disliked being drafted to play cards and to talk to society women; his wife also disliked it. She was thirteen years his junior, young and pretty, and she found Walter and his ways unattractive. In New York if he received flowers after a performance, he would send them all to her apartment. At Bar Harbor, according to her, he paid her excessive attention, often making suggestive remarks, and on occasion, definite sexual advances. She was revolted.

With a single exception, all other ladies interviewed on this point felt that such advances — now that Walter was turning seventy, a grandfather and in his own home — were quite uncharacteristic. Walter's style with ladies was very gallant, often spiced with winks and even, perhaps, suggestive remarks, but all these led nowhere. And he delighted in a response in kind.

Entirely typical, however, would be the desire to put a pretty woman, considerably younger than everyone else in the group, at ease, and his method would be gallantry. To someone not used to the style, it may have seemed to convey more than intended. Thus a misunderstanding might have developed that only could grow greater even as Walter tried to make it grow less.

Or perhaps he simply lost his head and manners, and La Prade broke with him.

31. A complete set of transcripts of the broadcasts, all series, in the first year, 1928–29, are in NYPL, WD Coll., Cat. 18, Box 41; see also Box 42. A set of programs for the second year, all series, are in NYPL, WD Scrapbooks, Programs 1929–30, Reel 10. Recordings of many of the concerts, 1936–37 through 1940–41, are on tape at LOC, Music Division, Recorded Sound Section. Goodell, *WD,* 569, reports recordings 1935–41, not complete, at NBC Central Files. She also, in Appendix J, 497–513, prints complete a sample Series A, B, C and D program from the 1928–29 season, together with a page for each of the questions and answers in the appropriate teacher's man-

ual. Copies of the teachers' and students' manuals are in many of the collections.

32. Conclusions taken from the analyses in Goodell, *WD*, 360, 361.

33. WD, complete press release on Stokowski, 10/20/1932, Oliver Daniel Collection, and *NY Times*, 10/20/1932, 24:2, editorial, 10/21/1932, 20:5, *NY Herald Tribune*, 10/20/1932, 23:7.

34. WD, letter to Pitchfork Smith, 4/17/1932, and Smith's reply, 4/21/1932; also Frank Willard Kimball, letter to WD, 1/18/1932; NYPL, WD Coll., Cat. 18, Box 43.

35. For the third edition of *My Musical Life* (1935) WD added a chapter, 367–379, titled "Music and Modern Magic," in which he gave samples of his teaching methods, including these on Symphony No. 5. A typescript of the chapter, possibly a draft, is in NYPL, WD Coll., Cat. 1, Box 1.

36. Broadcast, 2/17/1939, Series C, tape recording LWO 5375, tape no. 18, Part A, LOC, Music Division, Recorded Sound Section.

37. Slightly varied form of jingle: In his lecture recital, 3/19/1927, he reversed the first two lines, LOC, D-B Coll., Box 6. Schonberg, *The Great Conductors*, 345. In his disgust Schonberg sees little else than this in WD's career. See also "Broadcasting Across the Country" by David Sandow, *Musical America*, 4/7/1928, 8, questioning whether the Andante of Beethoven's Symphony No. 1 can be described as a domestic spat.

38. WD, *My Musical Life* (3rd ed., 1935), 367–379, states his theories of teaching. Also, in an interview with S. J. Woolf, "Damrosch Waves a Baton over America," *NY Times* magazine 3/2/1930, 1: "I know that many [listeners] . . . are not acquainted with musical forms, and often I try to give a concise outline of the particular type of composition that I play as well as the idea that is expressed. All of these things contribute to a greater appreciation of music, but this does not imply that they are necessary for the enjoyment of any piece of good music. Nothing is essential for that but its performance in a proper way."

39. One of the most savage attacks on WD personally and as an artist ends: ". . . some day the American people will have to pay dearly for the musical vulgarity he has spread over the land"; Martin L. Goodale, "Walter Damrosch," *American Mercury*, March 1935, 352–359. With the movie *Fantasia* Walt Disney and Stokowski were far more pictorial and, perhaps, more vulgar.

40. Gunther Schuller, composer, conductor and for ten years president of the New England Conservatory, in 1982 estimated the country's musical population at "somewhere around 3 to 5 percent." He went on to say: "The real trouble with our situation is that these [other] 95 percent are totally unreachable by us. They live in another world, totally unrelated to anything I am talking about in this article . . . the primary and secondary public schools, a virtual musical wasteland . . . We have here an essentially victimized American population whose freedom of choice in matters musical is virtually denied them by, on the one hand, the failure of education and, on the other, the omnipresence of the commercial/popular-music establishment, voracious in its appetite and greed." Schuller, "A Stranglehold on the Arts," *Keynote*, May 1982.

One percent of the population; WD, letter to W. J. Henderson, 12/27/1933, NYPL, WD Coll., Cat. 1, Box 3.

WD himself used the term "democratizing of music" to describe the effect of radio in expanding the musical audience. See speech, "Democracy Turns to Music," University of the State of New York, 10/18/1934, NYPL, WD Coll., Cat. 19, Box 48.

41. A typed *Report on the Music Appreciation Hour, 1930,* dated 1/6/1931 and directed to Mr. Elwood, NYPL, WD Coll., Cat. 18, Box 42. It also notes a steady increase in the number of letters received and distribution of the teachers' manual.

42. Cited in "Music on the Radio," *School and Society,* 10/20/1934, 517.

43. *An Account of Music Broadcasting by NBC,* 8. This was a brochure published by NBC, 1938, and did not identify the source of the survey.

44. Adults: the folders marked "fans" in NYPL, WD Coll., Cat. 18, Boxes 41–47, have a large number of letters from adults, many of whom were elderly. See "Radio" by David Sandow, *Musical America,* 5/10/1929, and on a possible adult educational program, "Selected Broadcasts," ibid., 10/20/1928, 14.

On the importance of the manuals for teachers and students, Gordon, *All Children Listen,* 21.

For some opinions of educators on the programs, see *Education on the Air, Third Yearbook,* 137, 203–204, 245–258. The last is a study, "Measures of the Effects of Radio Programs in Rural Schools," by Margaret Harrison, on which Goodell, *WD,* 426–435, 514–519, comments.

Not all teachers were pleased with the programs, and some unfavorable comment appears in *Education on the Air, Ninth Yearbook,* 116–120, 152, 155–156. The greatest problem seems always to have been with the youngest children, grades 3 and 4, whose attention in a half-hour, without an orchestra to watch, would began to wander. With these, apparently, the home-room teacher's enthusiasm was vital to the program's success.

45. Salary cut: WD, letters to Merlin H. Aylesworth, 10/3 and 10/21/1932; letter from Aylesworth to WD, 10/24/1932; NYPL, WD Coll., Cat. 18, Box 43. On the reductions in salary for the "Symphony Hour": WD, letter to George S. McClelland, 9/9/32, ibid., and 8/12/1929, ibid., Cat. 18, Box 42 (but folder 1930-B).

46. Fund drive: Correspondence, NYPL, WD Coll., Cat. 18, Box 44.

47. WD, letter to Margaret G. Ruggles, 3/9/1943: "But as the war news had cut so much into the 'commercial hours' of the Blue Network it seems to have been a financial necessity for them to ask me to reduce my concerts by half-an-hour and to give them only for the little children. I felt that unless I could continue the educational series for the four school years, they would profit the listeners but little." NYPL, WD Coll., Cat. 18, Box 47 (but in folder 1940); GM interviews with Lawrence Abbott and Julian Street, who handled the publicity at NBC for the program. Though the Blue Network stressed WD's resignation and its war broadcasts, *Newsweek* reported, 6/8/1942, 72, that the real reason was the network's desire to replace a sustaining program with one sponsored. On the whole the press stories were not clear; everyone's attention was elsewhere.

48. WD's resignation was discussed as early as 1935, but nothing was done. John F. Royal, letter to WD, 2/16/1935: "It is true — no one could really succeed you." NYPL, WD Coll., Cat. 18, Box 45, Letters of regret, ibid., Box 47.

49. W. J. Henderson, "Walter Damrosch." MBD disliked Henderson's emphasis on WD's smile as the source of people's love for him and drafted a letter to Henderson, which she did not mail. In it she stressed WD's character, his speaking ability, his educational programs and his readiness to pioneer; LOC, D-B Coll., Box 2. WD mailed Henderson a polite response, 1/18/1932, in which he said of his smile, "I am so glad that I do not let the outside world in on those inevitable tragic moments and moods that come to every man . . ." NYPL, WD Coll., Cat. 1, Box 3.

50. Toni A. Hecker, letter to WD, undated, NYPL, WD Coll., Cat. 18, Box 45 (folder 1934-Fans). WD had suggested that his listeners write a poem, and Hecker's letter starts with one, but the constraints of verse somewhat shackled his spirit, and his true self comes through plainer in prose.

51. This story, known by most Damrosch relatives, apparently was reported publicly by WD for the first time in a speech, "Music Over the Radio," to the Canadian Club of Montreal on 4/20/1931; NYPL, WD Coll., Cat. 10, Box 26. See also Elizabeth Garrison O'Brien, letter to WD, 11/23/1935, with a clipping from the *Philadelphia Inquirer* that tells the story; ibid., Cat. 18, Box 45; and Gordon, *All Children Listen*, 22.

Chapter 31

(pages 375–388)

1. GDF's plays: 1926–27, in Chicago, *The Runaway Road;* 1929–30, *Garrick Gaieties;* 1930–31, *The Life Line* (17 perf.), for WD and MBD correspondence about, see NYPL, WD Coll., Cat. 17, Box 40; 1931–32, *The Passing Present* (16 perf.); 1933–34, *Picnic* (2 perf.). See clippings, etc., LOC, D-B Coll., Box 5.

    MM's plays: Summer 1925, at Woodstock, N.Y., *Foul Is Fair*, clippings from three local papers, BUL, MM Coll., Box 16, and MM letter about production, Box 11; 1930–31, *Café* (4 perf.), for MM and LDM letters about, ibid. At the final performance of *Café*, of 567 seats in the orchestra only 48 were sold.

2. MM, *Out of My Time*, 208.

3. MM, letter to LDM, 1/17/1933, LOC, M-D Coll., Box 2.

4. MM, *Out of My Time*, 156. Much of her work on *Vogue* is collected in BUL, MM Coll., Box 14, and her correspondence with potential contributors, Box 11.

5. MM, letter to LDM, 11/13/1934, LOC, M-D Coll., Box 2.

6. MM, *Out of My Time*, 156.

7. MM, letter to LDM, "Sunday" (spring 1936), LOC, M-D Coll., Box 2.

8. Ibid.

9. MM, letter to CDM & DM, "Hotel Ambasciatori, Rome" (summer 1936), LOC, M-D Coll., Box 2.

10. See MM, *Out of My Time*, 168, 116. GM interviews with Christopher Clarkson and David J. Blow.

11. MM, *Out of My Time*, 168.

12. Stebbins, *FD*, 246–255. Erskine, letter to WD, 5/26/1933, on occupying FD, NYPL, WD Coll., Cat. 19, Box 48.

13. Stebbins, *FD*, 253.

14. HMD, on *FD*, 1, LOC, D-TV Coll., Box 1. *NY Times*, 10/26/1937, 22:2. Also *NY Times*, 10/23/1937, 17:1, *NY Herald Tribune*, 10/25/1937 news story and editorial; *Musical Quarterly*, April 1939, "A Tribute to Frank Damrosch," by Edwin T. Rice.

15. HMD, on *FD*, 11, LOC, D-TV Coll., Box 1.

16. CDM, letter to LDM, 12/29 [1937], LOC, M-D Coll., Box 1. Marie Wiechmann, *NY Times* obituary, 12/29/1937, 21:4.

17. GM interviews with four Seymour children and Dorothy Seymour. *NY Times* obituary, 3/23/1938, 23:4.

18. GM interview with M. R. Werner.

19. On the finale to Beethoven's Symphony No. 9, see Chap. 19. References

that follow are to NYPL, WD Coll. The Golden Jubilee at Metropolitan and opera in English, Cat. 1, Box 2 and Cat. 9, Box 25. *A Man Without a Country*, Cat. 4, Boxes 11 and 12. The union fight, Cat. 5, Box 17, Cat. 13, Box 33. The Federal Bureau of Fine Arts, Cat. 14, Box 36. The movies were *The Star Maker* and *Carnegie Hall*, Cat. 2, Box 5. On the honorary degrees, Brown (1932), Cat. 19, Box 48; Maine (1938), ibid. On the World's Fair, Cat. 5, Box 16.

20. "WD goes to a funeral," a typed note, 10/17/1937, LOC, D-B Coll., Box 6.
21. *NY Times*, 8/24/1939, 1:2; *NY Herald Tribune*, 8/24/1939, 1:2.
22. GM interview with Symphorosa Livermore.
23. GM interviews with Symphorosa Livermore, M. R. Werner, Sidney Howard Urquhart. *NY Times* obituary, 12/2/1964, 47:1. Margaret Howard, letter to Felicia Geffen, "Sunday," Felicia Geffen Collection.
24. GM interview with Otto Luening.
25. GM interviews with Otto Luening and ESM.
26. McDonagh, *Martha Graham*, 50.
27. According to ESM, some of McDonagh's more extravagant statements are fiction. For example, "MacDonald and Sabin would gather and save the ravelings from Graham's teaching costume."
28. There is a print of the film in the NYPL–Dance Division.
29. LDM, letter to RT, 11/16/1938, RT Coll. According to Guy F. Harrison, in those years conductor of the Rochester Civic Orchestra and associate conductor of the Rochester Philharmonic, LDM never performed with an orchestra in Rochester; he was, however, "quickly accepted in musical circles." Harrison, letter to GM, 7/26/1982.
30. RT, letter to LDM, 3/7/1939, RT Coll.
31. GM interviews with LG, Jr., Arnold Weissberger and ESM.
32. CDM, letter to LDM, "Wednesday" (early 1930s), LOC, M-D Coll., Box 1.
33. LDM, letter to RT, 8/1/1940, RT Coll.
34. RT, letter to LDM, 7/16/1940, RT Coll.

Chapter 32

(pages 389–403)

1. The sources for this section on John Tee Van and the pandas, beside interviews with surviving family members, are: JTV, "Two Pandas — China's Gift to America," *Animal Kingdom, Bulletin of the New York Zoological Society*, 3/10/1942, 1–18; David Crockett Graham, "How the Baby Pandas Were Captured," ibid., 19; "Talk of the Town," *The New Yorker;* Edith Iglauer, "The Wonderful Zoo in the Bronx"; Lee S. Crandall, *Management of Wild Mammals in Captivity*, 1964, 318–323; GM, correspondence with Danny C. Wharton, New York Zoological Society, 1979; "With a little help from Science, panda has a blessed event," *Smithsonian*, September 1979, 44–47; *NY Times*, 8/13, 14 and 19/1980, stories on panda born in Mexico City, which survived eight days.
2. GM interviews with ESM and CS.
3. *NY Times*, 3/30/1941, IX, 7:6 and 4/6/1941, I, 46:3; the critic was "R.P.," *NY Herald Tribune*, 4/6/1941; the critic was Francis D. Perkins.
4. GM interviews with Felix Salzer, Julia Lee, Katharine Foy; and also critics in note 3 above.
5. GM interviews with ESM and RSR.
6. GM interviews with ESM.

7. Thomas R. Taylor, letter to LDM, 6/9/1941, LOC, M-D Coll., Box 3. GM correspondence with Walter Clark, who referred to Brigadier General George W. Goddard, *Overview, A Life-Long Adventure in Aerial Photography* (New York: Doubleday, 1969), 238–240. LDM also worked on and wrote "A Method of Continuous Tape Recording with Reference to Magnetic Compass Points for an Acoustical or Radio Locator Scanning System"; see report dated 9/23/1942 made to Eastman Kodak Company, Research Laboratory, ESM Coll.

8. MM, *Out of My Time*, 173–179. There is correspondence about these activities in BUL, MM Coll., Boxes 10 and 11.

9. MM, *Out of My Time*, 179–185.

10. Ibid., 184–185. MM, letters to family from Lisbon and Madrid, 6/14, 7/23 and 31/1944, LOC, M-D Coll., Box 2; and financial records and OSS reports from Portugal and Spain, BUL, MM Coll., Box 11.

11. MM, *Out of My Time*, 197.

12. MM, letters to parents, 6/27, 7/28, and 8/22/1947, LOC, M-D Coll., Box 3. MM, *Out of My Time*, 200.

13. GDF, *From the Top of the Stairs*, 20–21.

14. Ibid., 23.

15. Ibid., 28, 33.

16. MM, *Message from a Stranger*, 86, 20, 164.

17. Ibid., 58, 115, 137.

18. Ibid., 201–202.

19. GM interview with ESM.

20. MM, letter to Charles Lee, 2/3/1948, BUL, MM Coll., Box 12.

21. The royalty report and other correspondence about the novel; ibid.

22. The estimate of a million dollars is based on a conversation with LDM's lawyer, James E. Hughes, Sr., who for my benefit re-examined LDM's tax returns for the years 1938–64, when LDM died. "Economic suicide," GM interview with Jeannette Haien (Mrs. Ernest S. Ballard, Jr.). Almost everyone interviewed had an individual story of LDM's generosity. Let one suffice: Teaching violin at the Mannes School in the early 1950s was Vera Fonaroff, a close personal and artistic friend of Pablo Casals, but without any money. LDM sent her as his guest and representative to one of the Casals festivals at Prades.

23. *NY Times* editorial, 4/14/1947, 26:1; see ibid., 25:1, and 4/13/1947, 62:2.

24. CDM, letter to LDM, 9/4[1947], LOC, M-D Coll., Box 1.

25. CDM, letter to LDM, 10/30/1947, ibid. See also CDM, letter to LDM, 2/4/1948, ibid. Graveure taught singing.

26. *NY Times* obituary, 3/18/1948, 27:1. The obituary's statement that she died at home was an effort to avoid sensationalism. GM interview with ESM, Jeannette Haien and MM, all together.

27. GM interviews with Jeannette Haien and MM.

28. *NY Times*, 1/9/1949, II, 7:2.

29. *NY Herald Tribune*, 1/13/1949, 17:3; *NY Times*, 1/13/1949, 27:3.

30. RT, letter to LDM, 2/6/1949, RT Coll.

Chapter 33

(*pages 404–417*)

1. On WD's landscaping at Bar Harbor, see WD letter to HHF, 6/22/1925, PML. On senility: GM interview with Felicia Geffen. WD, letter to Felicia Geffen,

n.d., LOC, D-B Coll., Box 6. For a similar letter to HHF, PML. MBD obituary, *NY Times,* 7/29/1949, 21:3.

2. GM interview with Felicia Geffen. According to WD's granddaughter Sidney Howard Urquhart, "That is just the kind of incident my mother never would tell me, for fear it would discredit the family."

3. GM interviews with Douglas S. Damrosch and Felicia Geffen.

4. *NY Times,* 12/24/1950, I, 36:2. On Beethoven as the standard by which he judged all music, see Chap. 8, note 34.

5. *NY Times,* 12/27/1950, 28:2.

6. *NY Times,* 12/31/1950, II, 7:1. There were, of course, many other summation-of-career articles in newspapers and journals, e.g., *NY Herald Tribune,* 1/22/1950, I, 4; *Musical America,* 1/15/1951, 14; *Fontainebleau Alumni Bulletin,* April 1951.

7. *NY Times,* 1/18/1951, 30:7. Recordings: Decca Gold Label DL 9555, Clara Schumann, *Trio,* Op. 17, and Beethoven, *Trio No. 8,* Op. post.; and DL 9604, Schumann, *Trio No. 1,* Op. 63 and Schubert, *Nocturne,* Op. 148.

8. Background on Prades Festival: Kirk, *Pablo Casals,* 439–470; the quotations, 440, 450. LDM, "Spirit of Casals Vivifies Prades Festivals."

9. Recordings: Prades Festival 1950, Columbia ML 4347, Bach, *The Musical Offering* (excerpts) and Col. ML 4354, Bach, *Sonata for Flute and Piano.* Festival 1952, Col. ML 4717, Schubert, Variations on *Trock'ne Blumen* from *Die Schöne Müllerin,* and Col. ML 4718, Schumann, *Funf Stücke im Volkston,* with Casals.

10. GM interview with CS; DM, letter to LDM, n.d., LOC, M-D Coll., Box 1. Eleven other letters on this festival are filed under Clair Seymour, ibid.

11. LDM, "Spirit of Casals Vivifies Prades Festival."

12. Ibid. LDM gave a speech on this subject, "Music and the Human Body," at the Rockefeller Institute, 2/24/59, where his audience consisted mostly of scientists and medical doctors. "I have come to believe that the time or pulse values in music would never have the impact on us which they have, were it not for certain so-called 'built-in clocks,' which we all possess and with which we spend all of our lives. I am referring to the heart beat, the respiratory rate, and the rhythmic movements of the limbs in normal propulsion: that is, the walk, the run and the dance . . . And just as these clocks operate at different rates under different conditions, so do different musical pulses affect us differently in our emotional response. What I shall try to show . . . is that in listening to music we cannot help but use these basic clocks as subconscious references, which, in turn, profoundly affect our responses." A copy of the speech, which includes references to the musical examples used, is in the Mannes College Library.

13. GM interview with Otto Leuning.

14. This section is based on many interviews with ESM, MM and other members of the family; also with Ernest Ballard, Jr., Carl Bamberger, Lotte Bamberger, Mary Bancroft, Elizabeth Berdell, Sidney Gelber, Leopold Godowsky, Jr., Jeannette Haien, Julia Lee, Genia Nemenoff, Randall Thompson, Mary Weaver and Miss Y. Kodachrome, chaos: Jeannette Haien.

15. GM interview with Elizabeth Berdell.

16. GM interview with MM. Others interviewed by GM reported almost identical phraseology.

17. GM interview with Elizabeth Berdell, who had entered the Mannes School as a student of singing, later worked there as a telephone operator, and in the summers on Martha's Vineyard rented a cottage from LDM, where she often saw the family.

18. GM interviews with MM and Jeannette Haien.

19. Henry James, *The Golden Bowl* (New York: Scribner, 1909), vol. 2, 262.
20. EDS, *Journal of Summer Trip,* RSR Coll.
21. This section is based chiefly on newspaper articles about the school and interviews with ESM, MM, Ernest Ballard, Jr., Sidney Gelber, Jeannette Haien, James E. Hughes, Sr., Julia Lee and Felix Salzer. A man who was chairman of the board of trustees in these years declined to be interviewed.
22. MM, letter to Gerald Warburg, 11/6/1951, LOC, M-D Coll., Box 2.
23. Figures on enrollment from "In the Balance, Loss of Mannes College Would Be a Disaster to the Community," by Howard Taubman, *NY Times,* 4/19/1959, II, 9:1. The "career-minded music student," from speech by William Schuman at party to announce the change; *NY Times,* 4/28/1953, 31:2.
24. Schenker's theories are avilable in English in *Free Composition [Der Freie Satz]* trans. by Ernst Oster, 2 vols. (London: Longman, 1979); and in *Five Graphic Music Analyses [Fünf Urlinie-Tafeln]* trans. by Felix Salzer (New York: Dover, 1969).

    Salzer's chief works available in English are: *Structural Hearing: Tonal Coherence in Music* (New York: Boni, 1952), 2nd ed. 1962; and with Carl Schacter, *Counterpoint in Composition* (New York: McGraw-Hill, 1969). Hans Weisse, another disciple of Schenker's, also taught at the Mannes School.

    The quotation from Christopher Wintle appears in his review of *Free Composition,* above, in the *Times Literary Supplement,* 9/19/1980. Among the followers of Schenker there are as many factions, and as bitterly opposed, as among the followers of Freud.
25. Otto Leuning, for example, thought that under LDM the school "was stuck in the nineteenth century"; GM interview.
26. GM interviews with Margaret Baum, with whom LDM had several discussions about his difficulties with fund-raising, and with Sidney Gelber.
27. GM interviews with James E. Hughes, Sr., LDM's attorney, and Sidney Gelber.
28. J. Robert Oppenheimer, "Prospects in the Arts and Sciences," *The Open Mind* (New York: Simon & Schuster, 1955), 145–146; GM interview with Julia Lee.
29. From an article or speech, "Does Science Lead Us to a True Christianity," which may not have been published or delivered. A typescript, lacking the final page(s) and with several corrections and additions in LDM's hand, is in LOC, M-D Coll., Box 4.

Chapter 34

(pages 418–430)
1. *NY Times,* 1/18/1955, 32:2.
2. GM interviews with ESM, Felix Salzer, Julia Lee and Jeannette Haien.
3. This and the quotations that follow in this section from MM, *Last Rights,* 69–72.
4. Howard Taubman, "In the Balance, Loss of Mannes College of Music Would Be a Disaster to the Community," *NY Times,* 4/19/1959, II, 9:1.
5. GM interviews with Sidney Gelber and James E. Hughes, Sr.
6. Allen Hughes, "Benefits of Recent Merger with Chatham Square Music School Discussed," *NY Times,* 10/16/1960, II, 11:5.
7. MM, *Out of My Time,* 207.
8. MM, *More in Anger,* 112.
9. Ibid., 118.

10. Ibid., 108.
11. Ibid., 127.
12. Ibid., 134.
13. Ibid., 34.
14. MM, letter to Adlai Stevenson, 6/22/1960, and his reply, BUL, MM Coll., Box 12.
15. The context can be followed in *NY Times,* 10/1962, 4, 45:5; 5, 27:1; 6, 12:1; 7, 77:3; 8, 18:1.
16. *NY Times,* 12/6/1962, 56:1, by H. C. Schonberg.
17. EDS obituary, *NY Times,* 11/2/1962, 31:1; *NY Herald Tribune,* 11/2/62, 22:2.
18. *NY Times,* 10/13/1959, 1:8; *Musical America,* 11/1/1956, 6; *Musical Courier,* Nov. 1959, 6. The original announcement did not include LDM among those of the family to be commemorated — LD, FD, WD, CDM and DM — presumably because he was still alive. The bandshell was to be the gift of the Guggenheim Foundation.
19. MM, "A Sharp Look at the Men's Magazines," *McCall's,* Oct. 1966.
20. MM, "Letter to the Young," *McCall's,* Sept. 1966. Dauna Sandmire, letter to Robert Stein, editor of *McCall's,* 8/20/1966, BUL, MM Coll., Box 12. The magazine published a bland three-sentence summary of Mrs. Sandmire's criticism in its "Letters" section, Dec. 1966.
21. GM interviews with ESM, Sidney Gelber, Jeannette Haien, James E. Hughes, Sr., and Julia Lee.
22. Appointment of Richard French, *NY Times,* 10/1/1962, 38:4; GM interviews with Sidney Gelber and ESM.
23. Miss Y will not allow me to quote her or to mention her name, but she contributed much to my picture of LDM. Her identity was well known to most of LDM's friends.
24. GM interviews with Jeannette Haien.
25. GM interviews with ESM and Jeannette Haien.
26. GM interview with Julia Lee.
27. *NY Times* editorial, 8/13/1964, 28:2; obituary, 8/12/1964, 35:1; other obituaries, *NY Herald Tribune,* 8/12/1964, 22:2; *NY World Telegram,* 8/12/1964, 29:1; *Vineyard Gazette,* 8/14/1964. See also *NY Times,* 8/31/1964, 21:3, on Prof. Sidney Gelber's being granted leave from State University of New York at Stony Brook to be president pro tem for one year at Mannes College of Music.

The winter following LDM's death, Szell dedicated to his memory a Cleveland Orchestra concert in New York with two of LDM's favorite works: Prokofiev, Symphony No. 5 and Bartók, Concerto for Orchestra. Reviews, with comments on LDM, *NY World Telegram,* 2/22/1965, 9:5, and *NY Times,* 2/22/1965, 14/3.
28. RT Coll.

Epilogue

(pages 431–435)
1. MM, speech at dedication of Damrosch Park, 5/22/1969, LOC, M-D Coll., Box 3.
2. The opinions in this concluding section are my own but were tested in interviews with MM's surviving relatives of her generation, several of the fourth generation and a number of her friends.

"Shirt sleeves": *Letters of Mrs. James G. Blaine,* vol. 2, 208.

MM, "The Story of Ben and Louis." About eight months earlier she had published her sonnet sequence, "Canticles to Men," in part a celebration of intercourse remembered.

3. Mary Bancroft Coll.
4. GM interview with Mary Bancroft.
5. Victor Hugo, *Les Misérables*, "Fantine," book 5, chap. 4.
6. The poem is by Joseph von Eichendorff.

SELECTED
BIBLIOGRAPHY

Unpublished Material

The abbreviation used in the notes to specify each collection precedes its description.

1. Collections

(a). Collections in libraries, of which only a very small part has been published, either in autobiographies by family members or in the Stebbinses biography of Frank Damrosch.

Family members in the third generation gave their own and their parents' papers to various libraries, apparently without plan, and my brief descriptions of the collections are very general. There is overlapping among them; several, for example, contain typed copies of Leopold Damrosch's *Student Autobiography*. It is also important to note that in most of the libraries, particularly in the Library of Congress and the New York Public Library, there is Damrosch material outside the collections: letters, musical manuscripts, scrapbooks, clipping files, tape recordings, etc. These often are catalogued separately.

LOC: Library of Congress, Music Division

D-TV Coll.: Damrosch–Tee Van Collection (primarily on Frank Damrosch)

D-B Coll.: Damrosch–Blaine Collection (primarily on Walter and Margaret Damrosch and their children; personal lives)

M-D Coll.: Mannes-Damrosch Collection (primarily on Clara Damrosch Mannes, David Mannes and their daughter Marya's personal life)

All three of the above collections contain, often in typed copies, papers pertaining to the first generation, Leopold and Helene Damrosch and Marie von Heimburg (Tante); also some material on the Seymour family in the second and third generations.

LOC, Frank and Walter Damrosch Scrapbooks of Programs and Clippings (also on microfilm at the NYPL)

LOC, Recorded Sound Section (Tape recordings of Walter Damrosch broadcasts, chiefly of the NBC "Music Appreciation Hour")

NYPL: New York Public Library, Music Division

WD Coll.: Walter Damrosch Collection (a huge collection, primarily his office files)

Scrapbooks of Programs and Clippings, Frank and Walter Damrosch (microfilm of LOC material)

BUL, MM Coll.: Boston University Library–Marya Mannes Collection (primarily on her adult life and public career)

PML: Pierpont Morgan Library (a small collection, chiefly Walter Damrosch's correspondence with Harry Harkness Flagler)

Museum of the City of New York–Damrosch Collection (miscellaneous; chiefly on Frank Damrosch)

Newark Public Library, Art and Music Department (very small; chiefly on Walter Damrosch and the inauguration of Carnegie Hall)

Archives of the Oratorio Society of New York (small, but with some unique material)

University of Oregon–Helen Damrosch Tee Van Collection (chiefly her drawings for scientific expeditions and children's books)

(b). Collections in private hands

ESM Coll.: Evelyn Sabin Mannes Collection (chiefly on Leopold D. Mannes' work on Kodachrome)

RSR Coll.: Ruth Seymour Reed Collection (miscellaneous, including two series of stories — memoirs — about her childhood in the family)

TAR Coll.: Thomas A. Reed Collection (chiefly on Seymour family)

CS Coll.: Clair Seymour Collection (typed copies, in German, of 46 letters, most of them from Leopold Damrosch to Tante about his 1883 tour with the New York Symphony)

RT Coll.: Randall Thompson Collection (chiefly 44 letters between him and Leopold D. Mannes, 1919–1949)

Note on certain abbreviations: the following abbreviations and descriptions are of papers in the library and private collections that are constantly cited.

Leopold Damrosch, *Student Autobiography:* LD, *Student Autobiography,* a translation in typescript (original apparently lost), 14 pp. A handwritten note on the front, probably by FD, states: "Written when he was 18 as a graduation thesis from the high school in Posen." LOC, D-TV Coll., Box 1; second copy, LOC, D-B Coll., Box 1; third copy, LOC, M-D Coll., Box 3; other copies in family collections.

Marie von Heimburg, *Tante's Story: Tante's Story,* typescript, apparently the original, 44 pp., LOC, D-B Coll., Box 1; M-D Coll., Box 3. Many copies in family collections.

Frank Damrosch, *Biographical Material on Leopold Damrosch:* FD, *Biographical Material on LD,* 18 pp., typescript and 8-p. holograph, LOC, D-TV Coll., Box 1.

Clara Damrosch Mannes, *Born on a Sunday:* CDM, *Born on a Sunday,* typescript, with many pages and half-pages unnumbered, but about 100 pp., with autograph corrections, LOC, M-D Coll., Box 3.

Elizabeth Damrosch Seymour, *Reminiscences as told to Helen Tee Van:* EDS, *Reminiscences as told to Helen Tee Van,* typescript, 11 pp., LOC, D-TV Coll., Box 1.

Elizabeth Damrosch Seymour, *O'mama's Story:* EDS, *O'mama's Story,* typescript, 12 pp., an account for her Seymour grandchildren, RSR Coll.

2. Unpublished Studies

Goodell, M. Elaine. *Walter Damrosch and His Contributions to Music Education.* Ph.D. thesis, the Catholic University of America, 1973. (Extensive bibliography.)

Himmelein, Frederick T., III. *Walter Damrosch, A Cultural Biography.* Ph.D. thesis, University of Virginia, 1972.

Mellion, Annette Elsie. *Dr. Walter J. Damrosch: A Treatise on His Contribution to Music Education in the United States.* Master of Science thesis, Juilliard School of Music, 1947. (Mellion was able to interview WD in connection with this. A typescript copy of the thesis is in NYPL.)

Perryman, William Ray. *Walter Damrosch: An Educational Force in American Music.* Ph.D. thesis, Indiana University, 1972. (Extensive bibliography.)

3. Interviews

(a). Interviews by the author with members of the family and in almost every case followed by correspondence. Listed by position on the family tree.

THIRD GENERATION

Herman S. Kiaer
Anita Blaine Damrosch Littell
Ida Jerdone Wiechmann
Edith Simonds Moore
Evelyn Sabin Mannes
Marya Mannes
Christopher Clarkson

Lawrence Damrosch Seymour
Dorothy Ross Seymour
Clair Seymour
Elizabeth Seymour Ransom
Robert B. Ransom
Ruth Seymour Reed

FOURTH GENERATION

Leopold Damrosch
Douglas S. Damrosch
Eleanor Southern Damrosch
Sidney Howard Urquhart
Elena Mannes

David J. Blow
Barry Seymour Boyd
Michael Boyd
Thomas A. Reed

(b). Interviews by the author with others; in almost every case followed by correspondence.

Lawrence J. Abbott
Louis Auchincloss
Ernest Ballard, Jr.
Carl Bamberger
Lotte Bamberger
Mary Bancroft
Dora Duncan Barker
Margaret Baum
Elizabeth Berdell
Robert D. Brewster
Alice Brooks
Walter Clark
Philip L. Condax
Oliver Daniel
Jack Danziger
Alfred Drake
Gertrude Schirmer Fay
Katharine Foy
Felicia Geffen
Sidney Gelber
Leopold Godowsky, Jr.
Jeannette Haien
Wesley T. Hanson, Jr.
James E. Hughes, Sr.
Howard W. Keresey
Virginia La Prade

Richard P. Leach
Julia Lee
Barbara Levy
Symphorosa Livermore
Otto Luening
Ernest McAneny
John G. McCullough
Edward Naumburg, Jr.
Genia Nemenoff
Richard T. Nicodemus
Samuel Orlinick
Mary Ellis Peltz
Richard Platt
Lisa Rudd
Felix Salzer
Ruth Albert Spencer
Tom C. Stix
Theodora Taggart
Randall Thompson
Langdon Van Norden
Mary Weaver
Arnold Weissberger
M. R. Werner
Anthony Whittier
Elizabeth D. Woolsey
Anita Zahn

4. Personal correspondence with the author

Margot Finletter Mitchell (family)
Vivian Swaine Holcombe (family)
Allen Hackett
Gilbert Harrison

Guy F. Harrison
Edward P. Morgan
Edward A. Weeks

5. Oral histories

Clair Seymour: two taped interviews of approximately sixty minutes each; at the Oral History Project, School of Music, Yale University.

Published Material

6. Books by family members (listed by the member's position on the family tree)

Frank Damrosch
Popular Method of Sight-Singing. New York: Schirmer, 1894.
Some Essentials in the Teaching of Music. New York: Schirmer, 1916.
Institute of Musical Art, 1905–1926. New York: Juilliard, 1936.

Walter Damrosch
  My Musical Life. New York: Scribner, 1923; popular edition, 1930; third edi-
    tion, with chapter on radio added, 1935.
Ferdinand Wiechmann
  Sugar Analysis, 1890; 3rd ed., 1914.
  Lecture Notes on Theoretical Chemistry, 1893; 2nd ed., 1895.
  Chemistry — Its Evolution and Achievements, 1899.
  Maid of Montauk (under pen name Forest Monroe), copyrighted by A. F.
    McKay. New York: William R. Jenkins, 1902.
  Notes on Electrochemistry, 1906.
David Mannes
  Music Is My Faith. New York: Norton, 1938.
Helen Tee Van
  Red Howling Monkey. New York: Macmillan, 1926.
  The Trees Around Us. New York: Dial Press, 1960.
  Insects Are Where You Find Them. New York: Knopf, 1963.
  Small Mammals Are Where You Find Them. New York: Knopf, 1966.
Gretchen Damrosch Finletter
  The Passing Present (a play in three acts). New York: S. French, 1932.
  From the Top of the Stairs. Boston: Little, Brown, 1946.
  The Dinner Party: From the Journal of a Lady of Today (a novel). New York:
    Harper, 1955; reissued 1982, Atheneum.
Marya Mannes
  Message from a Stranger (a novel). New York: Viking, 1948.
  More in Anger (essays, about a third of which first appeared in *The Reporter*).
    Philadelphia: Lippincott, 1958.
  Subverse, Rhymes for Our Times (topical verse, most of which first appeared in
    The Reporter over the pseudonym "Sec"). New York: Braziller, 1959.
  The New York I Know (essays on the city, with photographs by Herb Snitzer.
    The essays first appeared in *The Reporter*). Philadelphia: Lippincott, 1961.
  But Will It Sell? (essays and verse, chiefly from *Vogue*, *Glamour* and *The Re-
    porter*). Philadelphia: Lippincott, 1964.
  They (a novel). New York: Doubleday, 1968.
  Out of My Time (autobiography). New York: Doubleday, 1971.
  Uncoupling, The Art of Coming Apart: A Guide to Sane Divorce, by Norman
    Sheresky and MM. New York: Viking Press, 1972.
  Last Rights: A Case for the Good Death. New York: Morrow, 1974.

7. Articles by family members

Leopold Damrosch
  An eyewitness account of the first *Ring* cycle at Bayreuth, *NY Sun*, Aug. 13,
    18, 23, 26 and Sept. 3, 1876.
Frank Damrosch
  "Years in Denver," *Music in Denver and Colorado*, ed. by Malcolm G. Wyer,
    being vol. 1, no. 1 of *The Lookout*, pub. by the Denver Public Library,
    Denver, 1927.
  "Influences of Choral Singing," *Harmony*, vol. 1, no. 2, Feb. 1895.
  "On the Purposes and Aims of the People's Singing Classes," *Harmony*, vol.
    2, no. 7, Sept. 1896.
  "The Fulfillment of an Ideal, How the Institute Came into Being," *The Baton*,
    vol. 9, nos. 4 and 5 (joint), 1930.

"Opening Day Address" at the Institute of Musical Art, 10/31/1905, in FD, *Institute of Musical Art,* 1905–26.
"A Welcome" and "Atmosphere," *The Baton,* vol. 1, no. 1, Jan. 1922.
"Good Reading," *The Baton,* vol. 1, no. 3, March 1922.
"Speech at the Testimonial Dinner, Jan. 16, 1926," *The Baton,* Feb. 1926.
"The Institute of Musical Art, Its Place in the Juilliard School," *The Baton,* Nov.–Dec. 1931.
Walter Damrosch
"New York's German Opera Season," *Harper's Weekly,* 2/9/1895.
"Listening Backward," *The Century* magazine, Nov. 1927.
David Mannes
"Technique, Not the Golden Stair to Attainment, but the Spirit of Adoration, the First Requisite of Finding the Means of Expression," *The Clef,* Nov. 1913.
"The Music School Settlement," *The Clef,* ?, 1914, 14, and repeated Feb. 1917, 5.
Director's Reports, Society of the Music Settlement of the City of New York, Annual Reports, 1910–15.
Alice Damrosch Kiaer
"Ten Years of Ski Racing for Women," *Skiing, The International Sport,* ed. by Roland Palmedo (under name A. D. Wolfe).
"American Skiers at the Olympics, Women," *American Ski Annual, 1937–38* (under name A. D. Wolfe).
"Whither the Amateur" and "American Women's Team, 1938," *American Ski Annual, 1938–39* (under name A. D. Wolfe).
(And many other "reports" on women's skiing.)
Gretchen Damrosch Finletter
Twelve short stories, first published in *The Atlantic Monthly,* October 1943 to May 1946, appeared as chapters in *From the Top of the Stairs.*
"Was This Romance?" *The Atlantic Monthly,* Aug. 1944.
"Exit the Cad," ibid., May 1947.
"All the Other Girls," *The New Yorker,* 3/7/1942.
"The Tutor," ibid., 8/1/1942.
"Grandma, What Big Eyes," ibid., 5/22/1943.
"The Panda's Eyes," *Harper's Bazaar,* Apr. 1942.
"The Red Duchess in Washington," *Town & Country,* Apr. 1943.
Leopold Damrosch Mannes
"The Kodachrome Process for Amateur Cinematography in Natural Colors," (with Leopold Godowsky, Jr.), *SMPE Journal* (Society of Motion Picture Engineers), July 1935.
"Spirit of Casals Vivifies Prades Festivals," *Musical America,* Feb. 1953, 8.
Helen Tee Van
"The Voyage of the Arcturus," *The Baton,* Nov. 1925.
John Tee Van
"Two Pandas — China's Gift to America," *Animal Kingdom, Bulletin of the New York Zoological Society,* March 10, 1942.
"The Bathysphere of 1934," Appendix C in *Half Mile Down,* by William Beebe. New York: Harcourt, 1934.
"Bathysphere Dive Thirty-Five," Appendix E, ibid.
(And some thirty technical articles, mostly on fish and appearing chiefly in the New York Zoological Society *Bulletin.*)
Marya Mannes
Many of her articles were collected in her three books of essays, *More in Anger,*

The New York I Know, and *But Will it Sell?* Those will not be listed here. What follows, therefore, is a small selection of the balance, which runs, probably, well over a hundred, for as a feature editor and writer for such magazines as *Vogue, Glamour, The New Yorker, McCall's* and *The Reporter* she published articles regularly for about forty years.

"Profile of Theresa Helburn," *The New Yorker,* 12/6/1930.

"Letter from Lisbon," ibid., 7/1 and 22/1944.

"Letter from Madrid," ibid., 10/28/1944.

"Letter from Barcelona," ibid., 11/18/1944.

"Letter from Jerusalem," ibid., 8/17/1946.

"The Heroine with the Heart of What?" (a questioning of the new emphasis on sexual enjoyment), *McCall's,* June 1965.

"Letter to the Young" (an argument for sexual freedom), ibid., Sept. 1966.

"A Sharp Look at the Men's Magazines" (on women treated as sex objects), ibid., Oct. 1966.

"Silent Night," *Vogue,* 12/15/1944.

"Who Is Doing Your Part in the War?" *Vogue,* 2/1/1945.

"Who Owns the Air?" (A speech on television, delivered in Milwaukee, 3/23/1959, and issued as a pamphlet by Marquette University, 1960.)

"The Responsibility of the Newspapers to the Arts" (speech in a symposium, *Social Responsibility of the Newspapers,* pub. by Marquette University, 1962).

"The Long Vigil" (on watching the events of the Kennedy assassination on television), *The Reporter,* 12/19/1963.

"Canticles to Men, A Sonnet Sequence," *New Letters, A Continutation of The University Review* (University of Missouri, Kansas City), Winter 1978.

"The Story of Ben and Louis," *New York* magazine, 10/30/1978, 13.

8. Books by others about family members

[Leopold Damrosch.] *Souvenir* (an account of the Damrosch season at the Metropolitan Opera, 1884–85, including reviews of all productions and accounts of Damrosch's life, death and funeral published in the city's ten leading newspapers). New York: F. A. Ringler, 1885.

Frank Damrosch, Let the People Sing, by Lucy Poate Stebbins and Richard Poate Stebbins. Durham, North Carolina: Duke University Press, 1945.

9. Articles by others about family members (listed by member's position on the family tree and thereunder chronologically). Reviews of performances and news stories are not included.

Leopold Damrosch

Archer, Frederic. "Dr. Leopold Damrosch," *The Keynote,* 2/21/1885. (Many other articles on him following his death are collected in *Souvenir,* see Bibliography, Section 8.)

Rice, Edwin T. "Personal Recollections of Leopold Damrosch," *The Musical Quarterly,* July 1942 (reprinted in *Musical Reminiscences*).

Frank Damrosch

Speed, John Gilmer. "People's Singing Classes," *Harper's Weekly,* 11/5/1892, 1074–75.

"How We Began," *Harmony,* vol. 5, no. 5, 1899, 1.

"Frank Damrosch, A Biographical Sketch," *The Musical Times,* 12/1/1904, 782–787.

Cooke, J. F. "The Advent of Endowed Institutions in American Musical Education," *Etude,* Feb. 1906.

———. "Making a Modern Conservatory of Music." *Etude,* March 1906.

Crowthers, Dorothy. "Frank Damrosch, His Life," *The Baton,* vol. 9, nos. 4 and 5 (joint), 1930.

Rice, Edwin T. "A Tribute to Frank Damrosch," *The Musical Quarterly,* Apr. 1939, 129–134 (reprinted in *Musical Reminiscences*).

Walter Damrosch

"Blaine and Music" (libelous editorial about WD and Carnegie Hall), *Musical Courier,* 2/25/1891, 180.

Stevenson, E. Irenaeus. "Mr. Damrosch's Latest Opera Season," *Harper's Weekly,* 3/21/1896, 271.

"Wagner for Young Women," *NY Sun,* 1/21/1900 (second section), 3:6.

von Tetzel, Emily Grant. "Walter Damrosch and the Philharmonic," *Theatre,* July 1902.

"The Sunday Concert Matter," *Symphony Society Bulletin,* vol. 1, no. 4, 1907.

"New York's Permanent Orchestra and the Men Who Made It Possible," *Musical America,* 1/4/1908, 3.

Sinclair, D. W. "Six Orchestral Conductors," *American Mercury,* March 1924, 285 (compares Stransky, Bodansky, Hadley, Damrosch, Monteux and Mengelberg, awarding greatness only to the last).

Taylor, Deems. "A Missionary Retires," *The New Republic,* 1/12/1927.

Eaton, Frances Q. "Damrosch Enlists Radio to Reach Children," *Musical America,* 1/21/1928, 6.

Crowthers, Dorothy. "Walter Damrosch, Dean of American Conductors," *The Baton,* Apr. 1929, 10.

Taylor, Deems. "Godfather to Polymnia," a "Profile," *The New Yorker,* 11/2/1929, 28–31.

Woolf, S. J. "Damrosch Waves a Baton Over America," *NY Times* magazine, 3/2/1930, 1.

Henderson, William J. "Walter Damrosch," *The Musical Quarterly,* Jan. 1932, 1.

"Threescore and Ten," *NY Times,* 1/31/1932, VIII, 7:6.

Sargeant, Winthrop (Arthur Pinworth). "In the Firing Line of an Orchestra," *Saturday Evening Post,* 1/7/1933, 14 (compares four conductors: Toscanini, Stokowski, Mengelberg and Damrosch).

Goodale, Martin L. "Walter Damrosch," *American Mercury,* March 1935, 352–359 (one of the harshest and most personal criticisms of Damrosch).

Woolf, S. J. "Fifty Years of Momentous Change in Music," *Literary Digest,* Apr. 1935, 24.

Downes, Olin. "On Walter Damrosch" (following his death), *NY Times,* 12/31/1950, II, 7:1.

Fontainebleau Alumni Bulletin, Apr. 1951.

Howard, Polly Damrosch. "1918 — An Idea Is Born," *Fontainebleau Alumni Bulletin,* Nov. 1961.

Howard, Polly Damrosch, and Anita Damrosch Littell. "Walter Damrosch and Opera," *Opera News,* 1/27/1962, 9–13.

"Topics — Centennial of an Impresario," *NY Times,* 1/30/1962.

David Mannes

Leuff, Constance D. "David Mannes," *American* magazine, Aug. 1911, 72.

"David Mannes," *Musical America,* 3/16/1912.

Adams, Elbridge L. "The Negro Music School Settlement," *The Clef,* Winter 1915, 4.

"Music Settlement Loses Services of Its Director, David Mannes," *Musical America*, 5/8/1915, 4; and 5/15/1915, 8.

"David Mannes and the David Mannes Music School," *The Clef*, July 1916, 3.

King, William. "Museum Concerts Repay Debt," *NY Sun*, 1/4/1937, 32:2.

"14,000 Pay Tribute to David Mannes," *NY Times*, 1/10/1937, I, 1:3.

"Mannes Ends Role at Museum Today," *NY Times*, 4/13/1947, 62:2, and editorial, ibid., 4/14/1947, 26:1.

John Tee Van
Iglauer, Edith. "The Wonderful Zoo in the Bronx," *Harper's* magazine, Sept. 1958, 46–54.

In "The Talk of the Town," *The New Yorker*, 9/6/1952, 29–30.

Alice Damrosch Kiaer
Witchel, Dinah B. "Alice in Skiland," *Skiing*, Feb. 1980, 28.

Leopold Damrosch Mannes
Eastman, Max. "How They Captured the Rainbow," *Reader's Digest*, Apr. 1951, 81–84 (condensing article in *The Christian Science Monitor*, 3/19/1951).

Wechsberg, Joseph. "Profile of Leopold Godowsky, Jr.," *The New Yorker*, 11/10/1956, 86.

Taubman, Howard. "In the Balance, Loss of Mannes College of Music Would Be a Disaster to the Community," *NY Times*, 4/19/1959, II, 9:1.

Hughes, Allen. "Benefits [for Mannes College] of Recent Merger with Chatham Square Music School Discussed," *NY Times*, 10/16/1960, II, 11:5.

Staubach, Horst. "Kodachrome, It Was Music for Our Eyes," trans. by Rolf Fricke, *Color Photography*, 1976, 5–14.

"The Musicians Who Found the Key to Color Film," in *Color*, a Time-Life Book, 1978, 54–69.

Marya Mannes
"Close Up," *Life*, 6/12/1964.

Kissel, Howard. "Marya Mannes: Softspoken Heresies," *Women's Wear Daily*, 8/25/1972.

10. Other books and articles. (Those used only for one or two specific points are described in the appropriate note.)

Aldrich, Richard. *Concert Life in New York, 1902–1923*, ed. by Harold Johnson. New York: Putnam's, 1941. Reissued, Freeport, N. Y., Books for Libraries Press, 1971. (Aldrich was critic for *NY Times*, 1902–1923.)

Ammer, Christine. *Unsung: A History of Women in American Music*. Westport, Conn., Greenwood Press, 1980.

[Arion Society.] *History of the Liederkranz of the City of New York, 1847 to 1947, and of the Arion, New York*. Compiled by the History Committee of the Liederkranz. New York: Drechsel, 1948.

———. *Arion New York von 1854 bis 1904*. New York, privately printed, 1904.

Barnouw, Erik. *A Tower in Babel: A History of Broadcasting in the United States*, Vol. 1 — *to 1933*. New York: Oxford University Press, 1966.

The Baton (the publication of the Institute of Musical Art, 1922–31).

Bauer, Harold. *Harold Bauer, His Book*. New York: Norton, 1948.

Beale, Harriet S. Blaine, ed. *Letters of Mrs. James G. Blaine*, 2 vols. New York: Duffield, 1908.

Birmingham, Stephen. *Our Crowd: The Great Jewish Families of New York*. New York: Harper, 1967.

Bispham, David. *A Quaker Singer's Recollections*. New York: Macmillan, 1920.

[Blaine, James G.] See Harriet S. B. Beale and David Saville Muzzey.

Bowen, Catherine Drinker. *Free Artist: The Story of Anton and Nicholas Rubinstein.* Boston: Little, Brown, 1939. See Anton Rubinstein.

Brodsky, Anna. *Recollections of a Russian Home: A Musician's Experiences,* 2nd ed. London: Sherratt & Hughes, 1914.

Browning, Norma Lee. *Joe Maddy of Interlochen.* Chicago: Regnery, 1963.

Burr, Wesley R., et al., eds. *Contemporary Theories about the Family,* Vol. 2, *General Theories — Theoretical Orientations.* New York: Free Press, 1979.

Carnegie, Andrew. *Autobiography of Andrew Carnegie.* Boston: Houghton Mifflin, 1920. See J. F. Wall, Burton J. Hendrick.

[Carnegie Hall.] See Theodore O. Cron, Ethel Peyser, Richard Schickel, and William Burnet Tuthill.

———. Program book, *Music Festival, Under the Direction of Walter Damrosch, for the Inauguration of "Music Hall," founded by Andrew Carnegie, May 5th, 6th, 7th, 8th, 9th, 1891.* New York: Cherouny Printing & Publishing Co., 1891.

———. *Music Hall, 57th Street and 7th Avenue* (a book prepared, apparently, for the opening. Contains many architectural drawings, presumably prepared by the architect. The only copy discovered is in the Archives of the Oratorio Society of New York).

[Carreño, Teresa.] See Marta Milinowski.

Cowell, Henry and Sidney. *Charles Ives and His Music.* New York: Oxford University Press, 1969.

Cron, Theodore O., and Burt Goldblatt. *Portrait of Carnegie Hall.* New York: Macmillan, 1966.

Damrosch Opera Company. See Walter Damrosch, Irving Kolodin, Henry E. Krehbiel, David Mannes. (No full, accurate history of the company has yet been published, and the best accounts of it are still to be found in contemporary newspapers.)

Davies, E. R. "The Kodachrome Process of 16 mm. Colour Kinematography," *The Photographic Journal* (of the Royal Photographic Society), April 1936.

Demos, John, and Sarane Spence Boocock, eds. *Turning Points: Historical and Sociological Essays on the Family.* Chicago: University of Chicago Press, 1978.

Duncan, Irma. *Duncan Dancer, An Autobiography.* Middletown, Conn.: Wesleyan Press, 1966.

Duncan, Isadora. *My Life.* New York: Boni and Liveright, 1927. See also Irma Duncan, Paul Magriel, Francis Steegmuller and Walter Terry.

Dwight's Journal of Music: A Paper of Art and Literature. Founded by John Sullivan Dwight. Boston, 1852–81.

Eaton, Quaintance. *Opera Caravan, Adventures of the Metropolitan on Tour, 1833–1956.* New York: Farrar, Straus, 1957.

Education on the Air
  ———. First Yearbook of the Institute for Education by Radio, ed. by Josephine H. McLatchy. Columbus, Ohio: Ohio State University Press, 1930.
  ———. Third Yearbook.
  ———. Ninth Yearbook.

[Eidlitz, Otto.] *Otto Eidlitz.* New York: privately printed, 1929.

Erskine, John. *The Philharmonic-Symphony Society of New York: Its First Hundred Years.* New York: Macmillan, 1943.

———. *The Memory of Certain Persons.* Philadelphia: Lippincott, 1947.

———. *My Life in Music.* New York: Morrow, 1950.

[Ethnic Groups.] See Stephen Birmingham, Otto Luening, Richard Polenberg, Thomas Sowell, Stephen Steinbert and *Harvard Encyclopedia of American Ethnic Groups.*

Ewen, David. *A Journey to Greatness, The Life and Music of George Gershwin.* New York: Holt, 1956.

[Family Life.] See Stephen Birmingham, Wesley R. Burr, John Demos, Jane Howard, Christopher Lasch, Alan MacFarlane, Robert May, Virginia Tufte and *Harvard Encyclopedia of American Ethnic Groups.*

Fay, Amy. *Music-Study in Germany.* Chicago: Jansen, McClurg, 1880. Many subsequent editions, New York: Macmillan, 1896–1913; also in England, France and Germany.

Finck, Henry T. *My Adventures in the Golden Age of Music.* New York: Funk & Wagnalls, 1926. Reissued, New York: Da Capo Press, 1971.

Fontainebleau Alumni Bulletin (the publication of the American School of Music at Fontainebleau).

Franko, Sam. *Chords and Discords, Memories and Musings of an American Musician.* New York: Viking, 1938.

Freund, Gisèle. *Photography & Society.* Boston: Godine, 1980.

George Gershwin's Song Book, ed. by Herman Wasserman. New York: Simon & Schuster, 1941 (rev. ed.). See Robert Kimball.

Gordon, Dorothy. *All Children Listen.* New York: George W. Stewart, 1942.

Harmony (the publication of the People's Choral Union and Singing Classes, 1894–1904?).

Harrison, Gilbert A. *A Timeless Affair, The Life of Anita McCormick Blaine.* Chicago: University of Chicago Press, 1979.

Harvard Encyclopedia of American Ethnic Groups, ed. by Stephen Thernstrom. Cambridge: Harvard University Press, 1980.

Hauk, Minnie. *Memories of a Singer.* London: Philpot, 1925.

Hendrick, Burton J. *The Life of Andrew Carnegie,* 2 vols. New York: Doubleday, 1937.

———. *The Benefactions of Andrew Carnegie.* New York: Carnegie Corporation, 1935.

Holde, Artur. *Jews in Music.* New York: Philosophical Library, 1959.

Howard, Jane. *Families.* New York: Simon & Schuster, 1978.

Howe, M. A. De Wolfe, and John N. Burk. *The Boston Symphony Orchestra, 1881–1931.* Boston: Houghton Mifflin, 1931.

Huneker, James Gibbons. *Steeplejack.* New York: Scribner, 1920.

[Ives, Charles.] See Henry Cowell, Vivian Perlis, Helen R. Sive.

Johnson, H. Earle. *First Performances in America to 1900, Works with Orchestra.* Detroit: Information Coordinators, Inc., 1979. Bibliographies in American Music Number Four, The College Music Society.

Kimball, Robert, and Alfred Simon. *The Gershwins.* New York: Atheneum, 1973.

Kirk, H. L. *Pablo Casals.* New York: Holt, 1974.

Klein, Herman. *The Reign of Patti.* New York: Century, 1902.

Kolodin, Irving. *The Metropolitan Opera, 1883–1966, A Candid History,* 4th ed. New York: Knopf, 1966.

Krehbiel, Henry E. *Notes on the Cultivation of Choral Music and the Oratorio Society of New York.* New York: Edward Schuberth & Co., 1884. Reprinted: AMS Press, 1970.

———. *Chapters of Opera, being Historical and Critical Observations and Records concerning the Lyric Drama in New York from its Earliest Days down to the Present Time.* New York: Holt, 1908.

Kupferberg, Herbert. *Those Fabulous Philadelphians, The Life and Times of a Great Orchestra.* New York: Scribner, 1969.

Lakond, Wladimir. See Tchaikovsky.

[Lanier, Sidney.] *Sidney Lanier, Poems and Letters.* Introduction and notes by Charles R. Anderson. Baltimore: Johns Hopkins, 1969.

La Prade, Ernest. *Broadcasting Music.* New York: Rinehart, 1947.

Lasch, Christopher. *Haven in a Heartless World, The Family Besieged.* New York: Basic Books, 1977.

Le Massena, Clarence Edward. *Symphony Society of New York, An Historical and Bibliographical Review* (typewritten, for distribution, 1924; 31 pp. At NYPL).

[Liederkranz Society.] *History of The Liederkranz of the City of New York, 1847 to 1947, and of The Arion, New York.* New York: Drechsel Printing Co., 1948.

Locke, Robinson. *The Robinson Locke Collection of Dramatic Scrapbooks,* vol. 144, "Walter Damrosch" (NYPL-Theater Division).

Luening, Otto. *The Odyssey of an American Composer, The Autobiography of Otto Luening.* New York: Scribners, 1980. (German ethnic background.)

MacFarlane, Alan. *The Family Life of Ralph Josselin, A Seventeenth-Century Clergyman: An Essay in Historical Anthropology.* Cambridge: Cambridge University Press, 1970.

Magriel, Paul, ed. *Isadora Duncan.* New York: Holt, 1947.

Mapleson, J. H. *The Mapleson Memoirs, the Career of an Operatic Impresario, 1858–1888,* ed. by Harold Rosenthal. New York: Appleton-Century, 1966.

Mason, Daniel Gregory. *The Dilemma of American Music.* New York: Macmillan, 1928.

Mason, William. *Memories of a Musical Life.* New York: 1901. Reprinted, New York: AMS Press, 1970.

Matthews, W. S. B., ed. *A Hundred Years of Music in America.* Chicago: 1889; reissued New York: AMS Press, 1970.

May, Robert. *Sex and Fantasy, Patterns of Male and Female Development.* New York: Norton, 1980.

McDonagh, Don. *Martha Graham, A Biography.* New York: Popular Library, 1975; original ed. Praeger, 1973.

Medina, Standish F. *A History of the Westhampton Yacht Squadron, 1890–1965.* Privately printed, 1965.

Mees, C. E. Kenneth. *Myself and My Journey Down the River of Time.* Rochester: Kodak Research Laboratories, 1956.

[Metropolitan Opera.] See Irving Kolodin, Henry E. Krehbiel, Henry Morgenthau and William H. Seltsam.

———. In Its Archives: *Journal, Opera Accounts, 1884–91.*

Milinowski, Marta. *Teresa Carreño, "by the grace of God."* New Haven: Yale University Press, 1940. Reissued, New York: Da Capo, 1977.

Morgenthau, Henry [Sr.]. *All in a Life-Time.* New York: Doubleday, 1922.

Mueller, John H. *The American Symphony Orchestra: A Social History of Musical Taste.* Bloomington: Indiana University Press, 1951.

Musical America. Founded in 1898 by John C. Freund, continuing with rare interruptions and occasional changes in publishing schedules to the present. At its most voluminous, roughly 1910–40.

[Musical Art Society of New York.] Minutes of Meetings, 1893–1917 (typescript in NYPL).

———. Programs (Collection, with gaps, 1894–1920. NYPL).

Musical Courier. Founded in 1880 by Marc A. Blumenberg and Otto Floersheim. Ceased publication, 1962. Blumenberg was editor from 1880 to 1918.

Muzzey, David Saville. *James G. Blaine, A Political Idol of Other Days*. New York: Dodd, Mead, 1934.

[New York Philharmonic.] See John Erskine, Howard Shanet.

[New York Symphony.] See Symphony Society of New York.

Odell, George C. D. *Annals of the New York Stage, from Beginnings to 1894*, 15 vols. New York: Columbia University Press, 1937.

Oratorio Society of New York. See below, and Henry E. Krehbiel.

————. *Record of the Concerts of the Oratorio Society, 1873–1904* (a manuscript at NYPL).

————. *A Record of the Sixteenth Season, 1888–89, of the Oratorio Society of New York* (only copy discovered is in the Society's Archives).

————. *Book of the Festival, April 12, 13, 15, 16, 1898, In Commemoration of the Twenty-Fifth Anniversary of the Founding*. New York: Burr Printing House, 1898.

————. *An Historical Sketch of Thirty-Seven Seasons of the Oratorio Society of New York, 1873–1874 to 1908–1909*, prepared by William Burnet Tuthill, Secretary. Privately printed (only copy discovered in Archives OS of NY).

————. *Festival of Music, Oratorio Society of New York, 1920* (contains a history of the Society and analysis of its repertory by H. E. Krehbiel and a facsimile of the "First Soirée — First Season).

Otis, Philo Adams. *The Chicago Symphony Orchestra, Its Organization, Growth and Development, 1891–1924*. Chicago: Summy, 1924.

[The People's Singing Classes.] *"Harmony," the Official Publication of the People's Choral Union and Singing Classes* (1894–1904?).

————. "Years of Song, The People's Choral Union and the Musical Art Society" by Albert Kirkpatrick and Elizabeth Stutsman, in *The Baton*, vol. ix, nos. 4 & 5, 1930, p. 30.

Perlis, Vivian. *Charles Ives Remembered, An Oral History*. New Haven: Yale University Press, 1974.

Peyser, Ethel. *The House That Music Built, Carnegie Hall*. New York: McBride, 1936.

Philharmonic. See John Erskine, Howard Shanet.

[Photography.] See E. R. Davies, Max Eastman, Gisèle Freund, C. E. Kenneth Mees, D. A. Spencer, Horst Staubach, Lewis L. Strauss, Time-Life eds., Edward John Wall, Arnold Weissberger and in Bibliography Section 7, Leopold D. Mannes.

Polenberg, Richard. *One Nation Divisible, Class, Race and Ethnicity in the United States since 1938*. New York: Viking, 1980.

Reis, Claire R. *Composers, Conductors, and Critics*. New York: Oxford University Press, 1955. Reissued, Detroit Reprints in Music, 1974.

Rice, Edwin T. *Musical Reminiscences*. New York: privately printed, 1943. (This contains the following articles reprinted from *The Music Quarterly:* "A Tribute to Frank Damrosch," April 1939; "Thomas and Central Park Garden," April 1940; "Personal Recollections of Leopold Damrosch," July 1942. There is also an uncompleted essay, "Walter Damrosch.")

Rosenstiel, Léonie, *Nadia Boulanger: A Life in Music*. New York: Norton, 1982.

Rubinstein, Anton. *Autobiography of Anton Rubinstein, 1829–1889*, trans. by Aline Delano. Boston: Little, Brown, 1892.

Russell, Charles Edward. *The American Orchestra and Theodore Thomas*. New York: Doubleday, 1927.

Sachs, Harvey. *Toscanini*. Philadelphia: Lippincott, 1978.

Saleski, Gdal. *Famous Musicians of a Wandering Race, Biographical Sketches of Outstanding Figures of Jewish Origin in the Musical World.* New York: Bloch Publishing Co., 1927.

Samaroff, Olga. See Olga Samaroff Stokowski.

Sargeant, Winthrop. *Geniuses, Goddesses and People.* New York: Dutton, 1949.

Schickel, Richard. *The World of Carnegie Hall.* New York: Messner, 1960.

Schonberg, Harold C. *The Great Pianists.* New York: Simon & Schuster, 1963.

———. *The Great Conductors.* New York: Simon & Schuster, 1967.

Seltsam, William H. *Metropolitan Opera Annals: A Chronicle of Artists and Performances,* 2nd printing. New York: Wilson, 1949.

Shanet, Howard. *Philharmonic: A History of New York's Orchestra.* New York: Doubleday, 1975.

Sive, Helen R. *Music's Connecticut Yankee: An Introduction to the Life and Music of Charles Ives.* New York: Atheneum, 1977.

[Sociology.] See entries under Family Life.

Spalding, Albert. *Rise to Follow.* New York: Holt, 1943.

Spencer, D. A. "The First Hundred Years of Colour," *The Photographic Journal,* September 1961.

Starke, Aubrey Harrison. *Sidney Lanier: A Biographical and Critical Study.* New York: Russell & Russell, 1964.

Staubach, Horst. "Kodachrome, It Was Music for Our Eyes," trans. by Rolf Fricke, in *Color Photography,* 1976.

Steegmuller, Francis, ed. *"Your Isadora," The Love Story of Isadora Duncan and Gordon Craig.* New York: Random House, 1974.

Steinberg, Stephen. *The Ethnic Myth: Race, Ethnicity and Class in America.* New York: Atheneum, 1981.

Stern, Fritz. *Gold and Iron: Bismarck, Bleichröder, and the Building of the German Empire.* New York: Knopf, 1977.

Stokowski, Olga Samaroff (Lucie Hickenlooper). *An American Musician's Story.* New York: Norton, 1939.

Strauss, Lewis L. *Men and Decisions.* New York: Doubleday, 1962.

Strong, George Templeton. *The Diary of George Templeton Strong,* ed. by Allan Nevins and Milton Halsey Thomas. 4 vols. New York: Macmillan, 1952.

Symphony Concerts for Young People. Programs, vol. 1, 1898–1914 (in NYPL).

Symphony Society of New York. *Minutes of Proceedings of the Board of Directors, 1878–93* (manuscript; includes Charter, Constitution, and By-Laws. At NYPL).

———. *Symphony Society Bulletins,* vols. 1–21, 1907–28.

———. *Symphony Pilgrims Abroad: A Short Sketch of the European Tour, The First Tour of Its Kind by an American Orchestra.*

———. See C. E. Le Massena.

Taylor, Deems. *Of Men and Music.* New York: Simon & Schuster, 1937 (contains his *New Yorker* "Profile" of Walter Damrosch, "Godfather to Polyhymnia").

———. *Music to My Ears.* New York: Simon & Schuster, 1947.

[Tchaikovsky.] *The Life and Letters of Peter Ilich Tchaikovsky.* Modeste Tchaikovsky; ed. and trans. by Rosa Newmarch. 2 vols. London: Bodley Head, 1906. Reissued, New York: Vienna House, 1973.

———. *The Diaries of Tchaikovsky,* trans. and ed. by Wladimir Lakond (Walter Lake). New York: Norton, 1945. Reissued, Westport, Conn.: Greenwood Press, 1973.

Terry, Walter. *Isadora Duncan, Her Life, Her Art, Her Legacy.* New York: Dodd, Mead, 1964.

Thomas, Rose Fay. *Memoirs of Theodore Thomas.* New York: Moffat, Yard, 1911.

Thomas, Theodore. *Theodore Thomas, A Musical Autobiography,* ed. George P. Upton. 2 vols. Chicago: A. C. McClurg, 1905. Reissued, with new introduction by Leon Stein, New York: Da Capo, 1964, 1 vol.

———. See Charles Edward Russell, Edwin T. Rice, Rose Fay Thomas.

Thomson, Virgil. *The Musical Scene.* New York: Knopf, 1947; reprint, Westport, Conn.: Greenwood, 1968.

———. *A Virgil Thomson Reader.* Boston: Houghton Mifflin, 1981.

———. *Partisan Review,* No. 4, 1980. "An Interview with Virgil Thomson by Diana Trilling."

Time-Life, eds. *Color,* in *Life Library of Photography.* Alexandria, Va.: Time-Life Books, 1970.

Tolstoy, Leo N. *What Is Art?,* trans. by Aylmer Maude. New York: Scribner, 1899, vol. XIX in the works of Tolstoy, coupled with *The Kingdom of God Is Within You.*

Traubel, Helen. *St. Louis Woman.* New York: Duell, Sloan and Pietce, 1959.

Tufte, Virginia, and Barbara Myerhoff, eds. *Changing Images of the Family.* New Haven: Yale, 1979.

Tuthill, William Burnet. *Practical Acoustics: A Study of the Diagrammatic Preparation of a Hall of Audience.* New York: privately printed, 1946 (completed in 1928, before Tuthill's death in 1929).

Wall, Edward John. *The History of Three-Color Photography.* Boston: American Photographic Publishing Co., 1925.

Wall, Joseph Frazier. *Andrew Carnegie.* New York: Oxford University Press, 1970.

Walter, Bruno. *Theme and Variations.* London: Hamilton, 1947.

Walters, Edward N. *Victor Herbert: A Life in Music.* New York: Macmillan, 1955.

Ware, W. Porter, and Thaddeus C. Lockard, Jr. *P. T. Barnum Presents Jenny Lind: The American Tour of the Swedish Nightingale.* Baton Rouge: Louisiana State University Press, 1980.

Weissberger, Arnold. "A Chemist's View of Color Photography," *American Scientist,* Nov.–Dec. 1970.

Welling, Richard. *As the Twig Is Bent.* New York: Putnam, 1942.

Yurka, Blanche. *Bohemian Girl, Blanche Yurka's Theatrical Life.* Athens, Ohio: Ohio University Press, 1970.

INDEX